THE SHEPHERD'S GUIDE

THROUGH THE

VALLEY OF DEBT AND
FINANCIAL CHANGE

A Comprehensive Manual for

Financial Management, Counseling and Spiritual Guidance

Flora L. Williams, PhD, MDiv, RFC

authorHOUSE®

AuthorHouse™
1663 Liberty Drive
Bloomington, IN 47403
www.authorhouse.com
Phone: 1-800-839-8640

Florawill@aol.com, floraw@purdue.edu, 765-474-4232
3815 Gate Road, Lafayette, Indiana 47909

First published by AuthorHouse 8/25/2009

ISBN: 978-1-4490-0572-6 (sc)

Comments and suggestions for the author Flora L. Williams would be greatly appreciated. See address above.

Unless otherwise noted, scripture text is from the New International Version, copyright © 1994 by the
Moody Bible Institute. Ryrie Study Bible Expanded Edition. Charles Caldwell Ryrie, Th.D., Ph.D.
....

Order other books by Flora L. Williams:
Hand in Hand with God: Witnessing on the Way. Publish America. 2006.

Renewal: Spiritual Messages through a Collection of Flora's Poetry
Arolf Publisher. 2007.

Available from: Brethren Press, 1451 Dundee Ave., Elgin, Il. 60120,
By phone: 800-441-3712
On-line: brethrenpress_gb@brethren.org

Printed in the United States of America
Bloomington, Indiana

This book is printed on acid-free paper.

ABOUT THE AUTHOR

Rev. Dr. Flora L. Williams is Professor Emerita, Ordained Minister in the Church of the Brethren, Registered Financial Consultant, Church Musician, Wife, Mother of three, and three grandchildren. The faith journey is her most important venture. She credits accomplishments to the leading and energizing of the Holy Spirit. Her motto is to glorify God and serve others. She has served as university professor, accredited financial counselor, investment advisor, money coach, chaplain and interim/intern pastor.

Her educational journey began at Manchester College and continued at Purdue University. After public school teaching for eight years, she taught for 32 years at Purdue University, the University of California at Davis, Jia Tong University in Shanghai, China, and the Viscosa Federal University in Brazil. After university retirement, she attended Bethany Theological Seminary earning the master of divinity.

Flora has written 18 books on family economics, financial counseling and planning, one spiritual autobiography, and a book of her poetry. She has written over 100 research articles and papers on quality of life, family economics, resource management, counseling, crisis intervention, and poverty issues. She started the major in financial counseling and planning at Purdue University and the graduate program at Viscosa Federal University. She founded and directed the financial advising clinic at Purdue, named "Outstanding Financial Counseling Center" in the United States in 2001.

Many awards include the Sagamore of the Wabash, the highest Indiana award, Golden Medallion for scholarship and encouraging women faculty/ students, Purdue University and Manchester College outstanding alumna awards, AFL-CIO Union Counseling Service Award, National Foundation for Credit Counseling contribution award, Who's Who in America, and Outstanding Achievement in Poetry by the International Society of Poets 2007. She has been on the board of directors for In-Charge Institute and the International Society for quality of life studies. She has written materials and tests for the NFCC to certify financial counselors. She is past president and "distinguished fellow" of the Association for Financial Counseling and Planning Education, an international association. She is a speaker in training professionals and has conducted seminars and intensive session. Participants were from around the world. She also trained union counselors so they could assist others. She has worked with Habitat for Humanity as part of her clinic and with New Focus, a church program, as a "financial coach." Flora's firm is Leona Financial Consulting. She speaks to community groups, churches, banquets, student groups, and disability support groups as she lost her right hand in an accident several years ago. She and her husband regularly do the worship services for nursing homes. She is substitute chaplain.

Flora and her husband Leiw live in Lafayette where they enjoy and perform music, gardening, and traveling.

THE SHEPHERD'S GUIDE

THROUGH THE

VALLEY OF DEBT AND
FINANCIAL CHANGE

A Comprehensive Manual for

Financial Management, Counseling and Spiritual Guidance

Flora L. Williams, PhD, MDiv, RFC
Professor Emerita, Purdue University
Family Economist
Registered Financial Consultant
Ordained Minister, Church of the Brethren

◊◊◊ ⌛ ACKNOWLEDGMENTS ⌛ ◊◊◊

Many thanks go to Allen Kahler, District Minister South/Central District, Indiana, Church of the Brethren, for encouragement to complete this book.

I thank reviewers who offered helpful suggestions:
John Armstrong, Pastor Grace Lutheran Church, Columbus, Indiana; Tom August, Chaplain, Lafayette, Indiana; Jean Bauer, Family Economist, Professor University of Minnesota; Bonnie Braun, Extension Family Life Specialist, University of Maryland; Kirk Burnett, MBA, Managing Financial Counselor and Educator, CCCS, Lafayette, Indiana; Linda Davis, Ordained Minister and Executive Director, Bakersfield Pregnancy Center, California; Eleanor Eaton, Church Leader and Editor, Lafayette, Indiana; Kirk Eicher-Miller, Staff Attorney, Indiana Legal Services; Tom Johnson, Director of Compassion Ministries, Evangelical Presbyterian, West Lafayette, Indiana; Ron Hawkins, Compassion Minister, Covenant Presbyterian, West Lafayette, Indiana; Herman Kaufman, District Minister Northern Indiana Church of the Brethren; Marilyn Lerch, Pastor Bedford, Pennsylvania and Coordinator of the Training in Ministry program Church of the Brethren; Melissa Maulding Extension Specialist Purdue University; Mary McKeefer, Worldwide Disciple Association, Purdue and DePauw Universities and Staff Director Kenya and Uganda; Cheryl Nettleman, Financial Adviser, Lafayette, Indiana; Dallas Oswalt, Lay Leader, Plymouth Church of the Brethren, Michigan and former ICRISAT director, India; William Pritchett, Minister, Lafayette, Indiana; Joe Redmon, Financial Counselor Purdue Employees Credit Union; Kristen Roop, Leader Church of the Brethren; Pat Rolfs, Retired English Teacher, Flora, Indiana; Sue Ross, Financial Advisor and MA, Bethany Theological Seminary; Bobbie Shaffett, Associate Extension Professor, Mississippi State University; Rolf Theen, Professor Emeritus Purdue University; Randy Vernon, Certified Financial Planner, Premier Financial, Lafayette, Indiana; John Wenger, Counselor, Anderson Psychiatric Clinic, Indiana; Rev. Myrna Long Wheeler, Chaplain Brethren Hillcrest Homes, LaVerne, California; Catherine Williams, Vice President of Financial Literacy, Money Management International; and LoraLu Williams, Teacher IVTC, Indianaoplis, Indiana.

I thank Sharon Danes, Professor and Family Economist, University of Minnesota for her authorship of Managing Disagreement and Conflict Over Money Within Couples. I thank Syble Solomon, Author, Life-Wise, for tips for communicating about money. Much appreciation is given for the authors and interviewees of case studies at the end of chapters.

Much appreciation is given to my husband Leiw Williams, my right-hand man, who encouraged me through the years and this endeavor.

Most of all, I thank Creator God for directing this work. He gave me the words to write and the energy to type. My study of the *Word* gave new insights for financial management.

THE SHEPHERD'S GUIDE THROUGH THE VALLEY OF DEBT AND FINANCIAL CHANGE

◊◊◊ ⧗ Contents ⧗ ◊◊◊

9. Not Enough Pasture For the Poor With Us

10. Out of the Snares of Spending and Gambling Addictions

11. Caught in the Thickets of Credit and Debt

THE SHEPHERD'S GUIDE THROUGH THE VALLEY OF DEBT AND FINANCIAL CHANGE

◊◊◊ ⧗ INTRODUCTION ⧗ ◊◊◊

Shepherds are pastors, priests, rabbis, compassion ministers, educators, directors of outreach, mentors, financial counselors, helping professionals, money coaches, and others assisting in financial change. This technical and inspirational book is for those interested in personal financial management and spiritual wholeness combined with educating and counseling. Although many are familiar to shepherds, Scripture verses are applied to financial management. Illustrations are presented to sensitize shepherds to the financial predicaments of people. This book has counseling approaches, tools and information to assist individuals and families in crisis and in change. The content is comprehensive and in touch with today's economic issues.

Shepherds and those "anointed to release the captives"[1] are called to be guides through the storms of life, giving direction and strength for the journey of faith up and down the money trail. Barriers on the path to abundant life include down turns in the economy, financial despair, love of possessions more than God, and conflict in use of money. Some do not have enough money to function well. Some are so preoccupied with their perceived inadequacy they do not contribute to the Kingdom of God financially. Many are misdirected by culture's lures and selfish, greedy ambitions.

Increasingly, conflict occurs between
* Living **for** the Kingdom of God

versus

* Living **in** the kingdom of Human Beings.

The two competing kingdoms clash in money matters. Conflicts between these allegiances are evident in financial anxieties, foreclosures, burdensome indebtedness, bankruptcies, spending beyond income, and family dissention.

Because financial affairs are complex, many people are overwhelmed. Many are overcome with the cares of the world. While some people do not care if finances are in chaos, some do not know how to change. People are possessed by possessions and the powers of darkness. Giving is at an all-time low. Indebtedness and credit are at an all-time high. Churches, as well as parishioners, suffer as the hurricanes of financial turmoil blow anxiety and uncertainty. Many families are living at the edge financially and some have already fallen into a pit.

---

1   Luke 4:18, Isaiah 61:1.

Following the Master Teacher

Conflicts and confusion about finances are reflected in Jesus' teachings. There are 2,172 references in the Bible to money and possessions, three times more than love, seven times more than prayer, and eight times more than belief. Of 38 parables, Jesus addressed money and possessions in 17 of them. Uncertainties in the direction to travel financially are addressed in the Scriptures more than other topics. Evidently, the financial route is one of the most critical spiritual dilemmas.

As Jesus was profound, practical and pertinent, shepherds must be also. This book illustrates steps for overcoming barriers on the trail and for walking with people in their predicaments and decisions along the way. Hope and means for survival are presented.

Jesus used such methods as questioning, story-telling, and data-gathering. He addressed the everyday things of life. He presented alternatives, demanded action – "take up your bed and walk" and "go and sin no more." He spoke with authority to drive out the "tormenting spirits." He practiced prayer, spending time alone with the Great Shepherd to receive direction for the journey.

Jesus met people in their financial decisions and suffering. This gave an opportunity for redemption, healing, and guidance. If shepherds and counselors are to continue the work of Jesus, they can do no less. They must be equipped to encourage people in their struggles with financial faithfulness.

Pioneering the Paths

This book is based on pioneering efforts of the author Flora Williams, her students, and colleagues. Her research at Purdue University included quality of life, welfare reform, financial problems, poverty issues, loan consolidation, and housing costs. She wrote materials for certifying financial and credit counselors. She taught family resource management, family economics, consumer economics, retirement planning, insurance, financial counseling and planning for 32 years at Purdue, University of California at Davis, Jia Tong University in Shanghai, China, and Federal University of Vicosa in Brazil. During 24 years of that time, she started and directed a teaching clinic for clients of all socioeconomic levels. She received the award for the outstanding counseling center in the nation by the Association for Financial Counseling and Education in 2001. She earned the Master of Divinity from Bethany Theological Seminary in 2006. Her experiences combine study of theology, pastoral work, and listening to the Spirit for personal financial management.

Readers may see this study as more than they "want" to know. Therefore, the detail, the stories, and the steps are investments in reading time for expanding the professional's think tank. When called even unexpectedly, the shepherd will be ready to provide appropriate guidance. Beyond compassion, the shepherd is ready with useful questions, effective words, needed financial information, and motivating action.

Education and Training

The financial predicaments and possibilities increase the shepherds' skills in helping people as well as **helping themselves** with financial decisions. Shepherds may not readily see predicaments in other people because they have been trained to think money is not important. They think that good Christians should not pay attention to money whereas, in actuality, they think about money all the time. How can the church teach people to ignore troublesome financial issues when Jesus obviously thought they were important? Many shepherds know so little about financial counseling because the church and seminaries encourage them to ignore the issues for themselves and for people under their care. Customarily, people do not seek counseling from shepherds in financial crisis or decision-making. They perceive the shepherd does not know financial principles or practice them. This book provides remedies for overcoming financial mistakes. These issues can no longer be ignored. The most frequent family problem is finances. Many divorces are related to financial problems.

Shepherds feel vulnerable because they have problems themselves. This book can better equip those who have not had adequate training to do counseling in personal financial or money management. Thus, they will be in position to assist people with financial management. Giving to church, getting out of debt, and budget counseling are included as well as other management tasks. How to respond to the call for abundant life in God's love, peace, and provisions is clearly shown.

Seeking the Lost and Healing the Broken

This book illustrates financial suffering, the dark side of money, caused by a culture which says money is everything. Shepherds are called to seek the lost and heal the sick (Luke 19:9-10). Many people are lost in the complexities and pressures of finances. Many are broken in relationship with God because of wrong financial priorities and practices. Some are just plain broke and need help in finding pasture. Scripture tells shepherds to "instruct those who are rich in the present world not to be conceited or to fix their hope on the uncertainty of riches, but on God, who richly supplies us with all things to enjoy. Instruct them to do good, to be rich in good works, to be generous and ready to share" (1 Timothy 6:17-18 NASB).

Precipitating events and being lost in the valley can cause people to want to change. In addition, the nudging of the Spirit creates a want to change. Perhaps they see a brother's or sister's need while thinking they cannot even meet their own needs. If priorities are askew, the Spirit helps put them in balance.

The book also shows paths for righteousness and the light side of money. These are the "why" and "how" to give more to the work of the kingdom. Ways to motivate generosity are shown. A higher calling to those comfortable in financial wealth is given to sensitize them to the financial distress of people. Shepherds are called, as the old cliché says, to "Comfort the afflicted and afflict the comforted." The call is to move from comfort to simple living to generosity to joy of giving.

Shepherds may be hesitant about expanding their service to counseling in financial affairs. Financial consultants may be hesitant about expanding their expertise to the theology of financial faithfulness. Therefore, shepherds and counselors can identify with people who do not want to learn in new areas of life.

Learning to counsel in financial dilemmas makes shepherds stronger and wiser. They will be considered more valuable as a resource. Concepts in this book will help grow the church family.

Shepherds are called to study financial counseling as part of the call to spiritual development. This book equips them for the new calling. Shown are principles and processes of counseling; financial crisis intervention; the nature of financial management and mismanagement; and how to develop the trusted relationship between counselor and individual. Thus, by expanding their talents, shepherds can be ready to answer the call from the Great Shepherd and those in their care. In learning this response, they are counseled by the Great Counselor who will never leave nor forsake them in this challenging work. Shepherds cannot neglect the call because they do not care. They cannot have excuses because they do not know. Shepherds need not fear this new call when they work with the Great Shepherd. God is already in their lives, prompting them to seek knowledge useful to work with people they meet and serve.

Chapters contain ideas for sermons, information for assisting in financial decisions, inspiration referenced by Scripture about financial management, financial terminology for conversations, practical steps, and approaches for financial rebirth with spiritual growth.

Responses to Questions before Becoming Shepherds of Financial Management

1. In the reading of how to help other people in their financial dilemmas and management, shepherds study financial management for themselves. Knowledge, skills, and attitudes can be applied to their own financial behavior and working within their own families.

2. In response to the criticism of managing one's family before leading other people (Titus, 1 Timothy 3), the shepherd's own family financial problems make him or her more understanding of other families. There is the "moral gap" between what the shepherd knows or wants to do and what he or she does as described by Paul in Romans 7:15.

   The shepherd may find difficulty in leading people to levels that he or she has not experienced. The shepherd, for example, can describe the peace and satisfaction resulting from making severe adjustments in financial management. Peace comes from complete surrender to God no matter what changes need to be made.

3. In fearing that the shepherd is accused of practicing law when counseling in financial affairs, these are responses:
   - Saying this may be just an excuse for not handling technical information. Rather than "practicing law," the shepherd "practices love."
   - Useful information is given, not filling out legal forms which would be practicing law.
   - Alternatives are presented from which the person chooses. This is not legal advice.
   - Questions are listed when referring to other professionals such as attorneys.
   - Education is conveyed rather than representing a person at court.
   - Courage is inspired by knowing the legal, bankruptcy, divorce, or eviction processes.
   - Some peace is felt by knowing where one is in the legal process and what options and time are available for next steps. The shepherd may look in a manual or call another professional for these details. Reference persons with unbiased and non-vested interests are part of the team working together on behalf of the person. The shepherd knows the questions and issues. Options and knowledge are increased when the shepherd talks with the team member specialized in a given area.

4. The established definition of **financial peace and freedom** is planning, getting out of debt, having a reserve in savings, having a sound plan for retirement, and receiving income from varied sources that increase with inflation. An expanded peace for individuals and families in distress and crisis is "not as the world understands" (John 14:27). Financial peace of mind and financial freedom promoted by the shepherd are defined here in contrast to those promoted by the financial planning industry:

   • knowing there are options;
   • having ability to make adjustments in lifestyle and financial behavior;
   • gaining courage to take one step, no longer captive to the situation, fear or habit;
   • moving in spite of fears and anxieties;
   • placing financial needs, resources, and practices under God's control;
   • identifying what will not change as well as what will change;
   • listening to the Spirit for day to day financial behavior;
   • being faithful although not always successful;
   • being content in want or plenty; and
   • trusting God to provide love, peace, and provisions for sustenance.

◊◊◊ ⧗ ⧗ ◊◊◊

Chapter 1. **The Shepherd's Guide to Faithfulness**

The development of blending theology and economics for faithfulness is presented in this book. Theology supports study of financial affairs for work in the kingdom of God. The proclamation of God's gifts for his people is the beginning of wisdom. The Master Teacher addressed financial issues. Practical, real life application in financial management for today's financial issues are presented. Steps for the shepherd to guide financial management through the valley of the shadows to the table of blessings are illustrated.

The theology of personal finances under-girding financial counseling is new on the horizon. Victory over captivity and fear comes from recognizing our financial weaknesses, our financial sins, and turning to the Great Shepherd for wisdom and courage (Acts 13:26). New creations in financial management focus on the good news of the resurrection rather than on life consisting of lots of "goodies" in a materialistic culture. Salvation comes through recognizing our moral debt. Salvation includes the change in financial behavior and forgiveness through saving grace. Thus, financial management is an outward reflection of inward transformation.

God touches heart, soul, mind, and strength when we come to him for financial guidance. The greatest commandment is to love God with all our heart, soul, mind, and strength. This is interpreted to love God by using financial resources for the glory of God and our neighbor's good. Loving God is using one's mind in financial management. Loving God in one's heart is controlling the use of money directed by a Godly conscience. Strength is used to resolve problems by implementing new alternatives and acting with energy from the Spirit.

The Great Shepherd, through individual shepherds, picks up those who have fallen into the pit of financial despair, protects those living on the edge financially, rescues those from evil temptation in the world, and heals brokenness. Brokenness can be in financial attitude or behavior. Brokenness can be when there is an imbalance between spending and sharing; between present and future provisions. Brokenness is a separation from God due to preoccupation with work, financial anxieties, and financial mistakes.

The shepherd can help overcome *financial obstacles* to spiritual growth particularly in times of crisis when people may be more receptive to renewal. Information and experience provided in this book equip shepherds to help overcome spiritual, social, mental, and spiritual obstacles. People may not believe obstacles to financial and spiritual renewal can be overcome. The disciples in Mark 10:26 "were even more amazed and said to each other 'Who then can be saved?'" Jesus said, "With man this is impossible, but not with God; all things are possible with God" (10:27, NIV).

The journey leads to the choice of becoming new creations with total commitment to the God of love. An overarching theme is the promise "… seek first God's kingdom and righteousness, and all these things will be given to you as well" (Matthew 6:33). *Living for God's kingdom is allowing God to be King of one's heart and to reign over financial decisions and actions.* When the Kingdom of God is sought first, trust is in needs being supplied. Priorities are established. Trusting God is believing that in counseling and prayer people can receive alternatives for resolving financial issues.

Practices include frugality, giving generously, and investing wisely, both talents and gold. Travelers are blessed so they can share and be a blessing to those in their path.

Spiritual rewards make life worth living. The spiritual life gives the purpose and the courage to walk in obedience – putting Jesus' into practice. The Spirit gives the rewards. The fruit of the Spirit (Galatians 5:22 NKJ) develops as financial expenses are trimmed and plans developed. Responsible financial behavior is harvested in *love* for other people, *joy* in giving, *peace* rather than financial anxieties, *longsuffering* in living with inadequate resources, *kindness* in sharing money and resources, *goodness* rather than worldliness, *faithfulness* in finances, *gentleness* with those who owe and need forgiveness, and *self-control* in spending and saving.

Righteousness

Abundant life in God's purposes is possible when we seek righteousness with finances with family, with neighbors, and with God. If any of these are out of sync with any of the others, communication is hampered or stifled.

"Right with God" seeks the divine will and purpose, not personal preferences. Worship of any other gods before him is not right. Trust and obedience are prerequisites for work in God's kingdom. The Spirit's guidance and grace are available to people as they struggle in the marketplace, in the workplace, in recreation, and in the family. The burden of providing in the complicated market system is cast upon the Lord. He cares for all his creation including people who have strayed from paths of righteousness.

"Right with family members" includes pursuing peace as much as possible on one's part. Honesty must prevail in all financial affairs. Spouses cannot be cheating in any way or in family responsibilities. Family members cannot be secretive or suspicious in financial matters. Right with one's family includes faithfulness. No other person, thing, or addiction comes before one's spouse. Provision for children and other people is based on unselfishness, not greed or envy. When right with family, God forgives us as we forgive them. Money, therefore, cannot be used for revenge, to get even, or to control others in our lives.

"Right with finances with neighbors and businesses" includes honesty, not withholding what has been promised for the work of God's kingdom, giving to the poor, resisting greed and covetousness. It also includes managing well, not ignoring talents/money, saving, and not trying to buy the gift of God with money (Acts 8:18-21). It includes asking forgiveness for our financial mistakes, addictions, and poor stewardship. Right with finances includes allowing the Spirit to direct the distribution of resources to spending, saving, and sharing. Salvation is available for those who fall short of putting into practice the teachings from Scripture. Salvation is healing the brokenness in any of the relationships.

Rewards in financial management come from righteousness in education, counseling, and support groups. "For though a righteous person falls seven times, he or she rises again, but the wicked are brought down by calamity" (Proverbs 24:16). "A righteous person may have many troubles, but the Lord delivers from them all…" (Psalm 34:19).

Faithfulness

Financial faithfulness is the outward reflection of inward spiritual wholeness in response to God's gifts and faithfulness. "The Lord God who made the world and everything in it is the Lord of heaven and earth…he himself gives all men life and breath and everything else. …God did this so that men would seek him and perhaps reach out for him and find him, though he is not far from each one of us" (Acts 17:24-27). We can live, move and have our being in Christ in financial decisions (Acts 17:28).

Paradoxes must be understood in seeking faithfulness in finances. The Old Testament teaching is living under the rule of the tithe. The New Testament teaching is living under the gift of grace, giving as led by the Spirit, with some people giving much more than a tithe and some much less. People are promised by some preachers today that faithfulness brings blessings financially, known as "prosperity theology." On the other hand, followers are to lose their lives for Christ's sake, accept the cost of discipleship, and bear their cross. "If anyone desires to come after me, let him deny himself, and take up his cross, and follow me" (Matthew 16:24). And yet Jesus said, "…do not worry…your heavenly Father knows that you need them…and all these things will be given to you as well" if you seek first God's kingdom and righteousness (Matthew 16: 31-33). Joseph, in the Old Testament, the first "financial planner," advised saving in the plentiful years for the lean years, planning and saving a portion. Jesus cautioned to have no thought for tomorrow although He praised the faithful steward for multiplying returns on investments rather than hiding them or doing nothing. In creation (Genesis 1:31) "God saw all that he had made, and it was very good." In John 3:16, "God so loved the world that he gave his one and only Son, that whoever believes in him shall not perish but have everlasting life" whereas in 1 John 2:15 it says, "Do not love the world or anything in the world. If anyone loves the world, the love of the Father is not in him. For everything in the world – the cravings of sinful man, the lust of his eyes, and the boasting of what he has and does – come not from the Father but from the world. The world and its desires pass away, but the man who does the will of God lives forever."

People are called to be new creations, fully committed to God. Thus, they try de-programming themselves from worldly patterns and being transformed in financial management. The entire personhood is changed and remolded. This includes money use, management, communication, purchasing goods and services, and distributing to sharing and saving. Meditation on Scriptural teaching can change desires and instruct application. Transformation changes one's identification and authority. The new creation depends upon God, not wealth or the world's means to security. The new creation meditates on the Scriptures and praying rather than striving to fit into the world's mold. New creations give control of their finances to God (Luke 14:33) and, thereby, control addictions.

Followers may experience rejection, perhaps even persecution in subtle ways since the world does not understand this transformation, this allegiance to God. As the supreme value of the American culture is personal independence, the idea of dependence on God, following his commandments, and walking in God's authority and security is repulsive and threatening to some people and, therefore, they are vocal against the mention of God for a criteria for change.

When people love God more than their possessions, they become financially faithful. God is loved more than possessions in financial faithfulness. Temptations like greed, arrogance, hard-heartedness, other gods, lust, covetousness, jealousy, and the world's passions are overcome. God calls his followers to confession, to repentance, and to obedience as they learn from making mistakes in financial affairs.

The shepherd in counseling paves the way for individuals and families to choose the options best for them. The assumption in the free-enterprise system is that the individual or the family are the best judge of their own interests, goals, and dreams, given their resources as they see them. Therefore, people will be more efficient if left to their own discernment than if someone tells them what to do. This is assuming the Spirit is speaking to the heart, mind, soul, and strength for their unique situation and purpose.

The shepherd in financial counseling paves the way for the Great Shepherd's power and leading. Alternatives become apparent. In choosing the best for them at the time, given their "expanded spiritual and financial resources," people are empowered. Rather than the shepherd saying "Cut out this or that," each individual decides where to trim expenses which clarifies his or her values. Security through faithfulness is the reward for fulfilling God's purposes unique to the individual. Joy is found in serving God and sharing with other people.

Illustration of the Shepherd's Action. Karen is assumed to be the best judge of her spiritual and material needs compared to a professional counselor. However, in casual conversation she seeks the pastor's guidance. Karen says long distance calls to her mother across the sea are needed and she is willing to cut out some expenses, be more frugal, or increase income to pay for the calls. The pastor suggests alternative Tele-services, alternate days and hours, limits to time talking, writing a letter, additional e-mails, etc. The pastor is sensitive to Karen's loneliness and suggests different ways for fulfilling it. Pastor and Karen pray for defining "need," "ideal," and "viewpoint" of God at this time and place. They discuss lifestyle choices under the auspices of seeking first the kingdom of God and righteousness realizing things and services will be added as needed. They pray for increased trust in God to provide and answer dilemmas.

A Litany - The Good Fight of Faith

One: Too often many embrace the ways of the world, only to deny the gospel.
Too often we buy what media sells – entertainment rather than contentment
Too often we succumb to the advertisements that call us to be gluttons of greed rather granters of grace.
Too often we fail to challenge voices of destructive power, giving silent consent to abusive power in families, churches, nation and world.
Too often the lure of self-interest overwhelms our call to love God, especially when faithfulness calls us to invest time or money.
Too often we follow the consumer-culture call to clamor for wealth and power at the expense of our neighbors near and far.
Too often we forget that we are not made by this world, but born of God.

All: We belong to God!
    We will run from all these things and follow what is right and good.
    We will pursue a Godly life, along with faith, love, perseverance, and gentleness
(1 Timothy 6:11-12 NLT).

One: Let us invest ourselves in kingdom living, that we may "take hold of life that is really life."

The Great Shepherd's Call

In the midst of financial crisis, bewilderment and anxieties, the Great Shepherd calls shepherds to give direction and peace. In Jesus' first sermon, he stated the activities that God had called him to perform. Shepherds can take the same path.

Direction and peace are achieved by helping people prioritize financial decisions, change thought processes, and assist in specific financial actions. As called to bear each other's burdens, comfort is shown by grieving together knowing that God is crying too. As God went before and with the people in the Exodus, God is present in the crisis and leading forward. Comfort is shown by accompanying people to court or being with them during a frightening financial experience. The call is for new directions and actions spiritually, not for a patch of financial help, just increasing income, or simply getting out of debt. The individual has perhaps conquered the crisis emotionally. The financial disaster in the aftermath calls for counseling. The Great Shepherd also moves people out of their comfort zone to take risks, to manage finances under "New Management."

A time of crisis is a call for decisions under new allegiance to the Lordship of the Kingdom. This call is possible with the Great Counselor bestowing courage through prayer. Identifying resources gives hope and a new commitment to God. Strength comes from using and acting on renewed personal resources, family resources, and community resources. Personal resources include recalling the times and events in which one survived and being aware of what one is doing now that is right. Resource for change is possible upon believing the power of the greatest Resource and accepting it through *prayer* at the beginning, the end, and throughout the crisis management process. The Lord knows what people need and wants to give them good gifts. However, he wants to talk with people about them. Praying "Your kingdom come" is opening communication, inviting him to listen and direct financial decisions. Although it may not lead to success financially, it will lead to faithfulness, contentment in circumstances, and peace.

The Great Shepherd calls shepherds to lead people through *financial crises* to become new creations in Christ in the area of finances. Now the whole of life is no longer hidden from the spotlight of the Son. Precipitating events are frequent: People lose their jobs, face house foreclosure, consider bankruptcy, cannot afford their current lifestyle, lose educational opportunities, have astronomical expenses from an accident, experience a medical catastrophe, cannot share, live above their means, are frightened that they have not prepared for retirement, are ill equipped to handle changes forced upon them, harbor blame or guilt over financial mistakes that are ruining relationships and life expectations, have money illness, have a car breakdown or family breakup, get into tax trouble, and are captive to creeping indebtedness. When another crisis occurs and brings despair with its related expenses, it confuses, devastates, and depresses. A crisis occurs with a public exposure. Panic sets in upon seeing the credit score, credit reports, and/or debt load preventing their employment or qualification for a mortgage.

Shepherds, the anointed ones, as called in Isaiah 61, give good news to the poor, heal the brokenhearted, proclaim freedom for the captives and release the prisoners from darkness. One form of captivity today is obsession with possessions, credit and debt enslavement, poisonous addictions, greed and selfishness, anxiety from sudden loss of income, weight of guilt, selfish ambitions, heavy financial burdens, financial fears, and lack of control over culture's temptations (See 2 Timothy 3:6). Captivity includes earthly desires that dominate, covetousness, and conformity to a pattern set by the culture that does not honor God or build character.

Shepherds continue the work of Jesus by instructing in finances. He said, "I have come in order that you might have life – life in all its fullness" (John 10:10). The call is to share the gifts of hope, this joy, and peace which comes from obedience to Scriptural principles. The Spirit leads in everything including financial affairs.

Shepherds are called to the tumult of life's wild restless sea, raging in hearts and minds over finances. They are called to calm the sea and/or are given strength to follow Christ amidst tumultuous decisions and struggles. They are called to invite people to love Christ more than these – money, possessions, the worldly passions, security in wealth, even one's own life (Luke 14:26). They are called to encourage people to serve and glorify God in their finances. Shepherds are called to explain how finances are involved in loving God with heart, soul, mind and strength and accepting God's infinite love. The purpose is to grow in faithfulness although success, as the world defines, is not achieved nor problems solved. The goal is submission to God. The faith journey leads to Faith controlling them not their worldly passions.

Shepherds are called to assist all people whether they are the "Jones," families trying to keep up with the Jones, or those trying to survive. Priorities are reexamined for "seeking first God's kingdom and righteousness, and all these other things will be given to you as well." Jesus taught "How hard it will be for those who have wealth to enter the kingdom of God" (Mark 10:23). The dilemma is how wealth controls one rather than directed to worthwhile endeavors under God's control. Shepherds are called to address the conflict, the neuroses of living in both kingdoms of God and of human beings. "No one can serve two masters; for a slave will either hate the one and love the other, or be devoted to the one and despise the other. You cannot serve God and wealth" (Matthew 6:24). "Instruct those who are rich in the present world not to be conceited or to fix their hope on the uncertainty of riches, but on God, who richly supplies us with all things to enjoy. Instruct them to do good, to be rich in good works, to be generous and ready to share" (I Timothy 6:17-18 NAS).

Urgent Call

Shepherds are called to seek the lost, not just wait until someone walks into our office. They pray for those with financial troubles. They are willing to learn to counsel in financial matters rather than avoid the issue or to be quick to refer someone out to professional (and very secular) financial counseling. The response may be modest. At least, they can give one good idea and not do any harm. Harm is not sharing technical and inspirational ideas. Harm is quick referral without giving at least one idea. Harm is giving insults. Harm is presenting truth without grace.

Financial worries or worldly passions prevent church attendees from hearing messages in sermons or comments in casual opportunities. They may hear but not implement during the week. These obsessions are keeping people from the Son-shine. Therefore, the shepherd paves the way for the Spirit. Time or ignoring the issues does not heal financial illnesses. Yes, people sing praises on Sunday, forgetting their troubles and cares of the world temporarily. During the week they are haunted if we do not address financial concerns in sermons, prayers, and counseling.

Shepherds counteract the persuasions of the media and peer pressures controlling their members by giving the message of the gospel. Rarely do people spend more time reading the Bible, praying, and talking with faithful believers than watching TV, reading catalogues or passing billboards. "So as a person thinks, he or she becomes." It is a sin to not trust God and not receive inspiration from messages and financial counseling to overcome strong and destructive forces. Shepherds help people listen to the voice of God among the many competing voices getting louder and louder in a society with complex and persuasive technology and marketing.

Restoring Pastor, Compassion Minister, Educator, Outreach Director, Financial Counselor, Helping Professional, Mentor, and Money Coach as Shepherd

How can people hear when they are in the pits of financial despair (Psalm 103) or caught in the thickets of bad habits? They need a shepherd who cares for them as Pastor Ann does. She cares enough to apply counseling skills. She examines each individual's make-up, decisions, and patterns of behavior. She knows the processes and questions for counseling. She knows the complexities of the marketplace, credit world, and legal procedures enough to assess options – or at least know someone who does.

Professionals and lay leaders can be on the shepherd's team. Most importantly, the Great Shepherd is leading the team. The team asks, "What next?" or "What will we do?" The team prays for God to send experts including therapists, social service workers, financial educators, consumer credit counselors, and financial planners. Talking with other shepherds about a case is helpful especially for the novice in financial counseling.

Most people "do not care how much their counselor knows until they know if he or she cares." Ezekiel (34:2-8) talks of false shepherds and the scattering of Israel. This happened because there were no shepherds or shepherds who only took care of themselves. The shepherds were criticized for not strengthening the weak, healing the sick, binding the injured, bringing back the strays or searching for the lost. They were careless and neglectful. Sheep were scattered and became food for wild animals. No one searched for them. The Sovereign Lord said he would hold the shepherds accountable and remove them from tending the flock. The Lord would rescue his flock and he himself would search for them, looking after them. He would shepherd the flock with justice. Zechariah (11:17) mentions woe to the worthless shepherd. Matthew (9:36) speaks about compassion, the sheep are harassed and helpless like sheep without a shepherd.

Just as the Great Shepherd walks with the anointed ones, shepherds are called to walk with people in financial uncertainties, difficulties and disasters. They see the pain, despair, the brokenness when parishioners lose a job, have a divorce, or have a financial disorder. Shepherds provide wonderful care when walking with friends and church members when their loved ones die. Now they are called to lift the fallen out of financial despair. Shepherds are called to assist people to fly like eagles, not to grow weary with burdens of debt, financial irresponsibility, or life in retirement. Shepherds are called to turn agendas to God's kingdom, to use wealth for the glory of God and their neighbor's good.

Roles are inferred by John 5:7 "The sick man answered, 'Sir, I have no one to put me in the pool.'" Sometimes it is the shepherd's role to move someone into the waters. Sometimes it is the shepherd's role to stir the waters.[2]

The Great Shepherd Walks with Shepherds in Financial Issues

The Master Teacher would understand difficulties of counseling. His experience was with Judas who valued money more than loyalty. He dealt with greed and power when the disciples asked who is going to sit with Him in the Kingdom. He had to teach the disciples to feed people

---

2   Patricia Marks, *The Upper Room*, June 2, 2004. P.38.

rather than "send them away." The disciples complained about the woman pouring perfume on his feet and wasting money.

The shepherd's guide is to "Work hard and cheerfully at whatever you do, as though you were working for the Lord rather than for people" (Colossians 3:23). Paul's words were: "Devote yourselves to prayer with an alert mind and a thankful heart. Do not forget to pray for us, too, that God will give us many opportunities to preach about his secret plan-that Christ is for the Gentiles. That is why I am here in chains. Pray that I will proclaim this message as clearly as I should. Live wisely among those who are not Christians, and make the most of every opportunity. Let your conversation be gracious and effective so that you will have the right answer for everyone" (Colossians 4:1-6).

Hand in hand with God, shepherds can journey through the land of finances. In any session, present are the counselor, the client, and the Great Counselor. Encouragement is in the words, "God does not call the qualified. He qualifies the called." (source unknown). So read on.

Equipped to Answer the Call

People are outfitted as shepherds when they know: 1) the processes of counseling, 2) personalities and their different attitudes toward money and responses to counseling, 3) financial management steps in handling crises and change, 4) the competing voices being heard, and 5) ability to quickly establish a relationship of trust and rapport.

The heart is ready when the shepherd loves and shows compassion especially when the relationship and subject matter are challenges. "The heart of any counseling process is a relationship characterized by warmth, genuineness, acceptance, caring and trust."[3] The quality of relating is *therapeutic* in psychological language and *redemptive* in religious language.[4]

One of the most important change agent in financial behavior is the relationship with the counselor. Also, knowledge changes behavior. Scary facts change behavior. Crisis changes behavior. It is the trusting relationship more than education that changes behavior.

The shepherd "leads people" close to the heart of God while they change their financial decisions. The mind generates alternatives, which include greater commitment to Christ's way. The shepherd and individual decide one task at a time after considering possibilities for action. Energy for the action comes from new hope.

An illustration conveys counseling principles. Pastor Howard knows from experience that the counseling process should be orderly, and sequential. Failure in this results in a "loose Band-Aid" that seldom solves the problem. Pastor Howard listens sincerely, directs conversation with skill and is firm while kind. In Corinthians 13:1-2 (NKJ) is a reminder: "Though I speak with the tongues of men and angels, but have not love, I have become a sounding brass or a clanging cymbal. And though I have the gift of prophecy, and understand all mysteries and all knowledge, and though I have all faith to remove mountains, but have not love, I am nothing."

Shepherds are ready to address competing voices: different desires, other family members, worldly culture, constant bombardment of the media, tiredness, lack of comprehension or emotional immaturity, lusts of the flesh, and evil powers. James 4:4b (NKJ) asked, "Do you know

---

3 Howard Clinebell. *Understanding and Counseling Persons with Alcohol, Drug, and Behavioral Addictions.* Nashville, Abingdon Press. 1998. P.330.

4 Ibid.

that friendship with the world is enmity with God? Whoever wants to be a friend of the world makes an enemy with God."

In addition to guidance, the shepherd corrects and holds the individual accountable. James says in 5:19-20 (NRSV), "My brothers and sisters, if anyone among you wanders from the truth and is brought back by another, you should know that whoever brings back a sinner from wandering will save the sinner's soul from death and cover a multitude of sins."

Goals for Counseling in Financial Management

The goal is a radical change in financial behavior and attitude for financial faithfulness, seeking first God's kingdom and obedience to the call to love with heart, soul, mind, and strength. The goals are total commitment as new creations to serve God by serving others. Therefore, the goal is not accumulation of wealth in itself, not financial freedom as coined by professional financial planners, not debt-free as in Christian Budget Counseling, and not contributing the tithe alone to soothe their conscience. The goal may be to teach people to "live within their means" if they are irresponsible and reality has not caught up with them. A spiritual conversion may move them to change priorities. A goal may be intentionally not living within their means to intentionally respond to a higher call of faithfulness. It may be redefining living within means. It may mean giving all or working without pay. They are trusting God to provide financial support. Faithfulness includes good stewardship of use of time, material supplies, wealth, talents, money, and care of the environment both near and far. It includes awareness of manipulation. The call is creativity with radical ways in finances, especially in times of distress, uncertainty, and loss of income.

The call is for financial faithfulness not financial success as the world describes it. For example, rather than planning for retirement in the usual way seeking independence, Sister Jane plans to serve in a home where room and board are provided. Ellen and Joe are planning to build a house for two generations utilizing Joe's father's pension.

Spiritual healing and wholeness as well as financial faithfulness are the goals in financial counseling. The shepherd, in contrast to secular financial professionals, facilitates spiritual development to recovery in financial faithfulness. The shepherd waters and fertilizes the soil for receiving seeds of financial changes so that spiritual growth is possible and, conversely, enlivens spiritual growth so that financial changes are seen and accepted. A stronger relationship with God is probably felt when financial anxieties and wealth are surrendered to the Great Shepherd.

The shepherd restores financial faithfulness by changing behavior and attitude. Unless both the material and emotional needs are understood, removing crutches at a wrong time may cause serious disorientation. People move on the faith journey with knowledge, willingness, and ability to change. The irresponsible individual needs assistance in renewing the mind. The misdirected one may need a "heart transplant." Those captive need ways to get out of debt.

The goals in professional financial planning are economic security by repositioning assets for maximum return, funding for college, retirement planning, and accumulation of wealth for various reasons including contributing to the work of the kingdom. Shepherds refer or work with professional financial planners. At least three names should be given. Although a third of the people in the congregation do not have difficulties, they want assistance with decisions, information, or support for their plans or dreams. They want clarification about the confusing mechanics and financial instruments available to them. They are afraid they will be ripped off again. Some are in a stage of transition and fear the unknown so want emotional support in financial decisions. They want to improve their economic security, enhance their wealth, reduce risks, or optimize their resources.

Opportunities for Financial Counseling and Education

Seeking counseling could be translated into seeking righteousness. People seek righteousness with finances since this affects righteousness with God, with family, and businesses. Some people perceive seeking assistance as a weakness. The shepherd helps people perceive it as a sign of strength.

The mentor who calls weekly has many opportunities to answer questions, do counseling, and provide financial education. Technical information and inspiration can be timely and relevant. Programs for all types of support groups can be vital.

Although need for financial counseling is obvious, the opportunity for shepherds may be subtle. Pastor Bill recognizes the teachable moment. He seizes any opportunity for mentioning a few words, preaching or counseling. A true story - One day after the sermon John told him he could not hear the sermon because he was upset with his wife. He was suspicious of her wearing a diamond bracelet on her arm. Where did it come from? Who gave it to her? Is she over-spending again? Now they were not speaking. Pastor Bill suggested to John that he say how lovely it looked on her beautiful arm in order to restore communication. This only took a moment and worked in their communication. However, the deeper issue may still need to be resolved.

Inward spiritual problems are not so obvious. Some are caused by financial mismanagement. Some problems are a result of bad choices and others a result of external events. Obvious results of financial disorders or problems are bankruptcy, suicide, accidents, inability to concentrate, decreased employment prospects, bitterness, despair, and family disagreements.

Counselor Sue talks about deep emotional habits and assumptions and walks with Bob and Nancy through transformation and recovery. Financial surgery is a necessity. Prioritizing financial demands on a realistic income is a necessity. Prioritizing with a reality-based approach is cognitively focused. This is with awareness of all the emotions this engenders. Counselor Sue works through resistance to make adjustments, and grieves with them in accepting changes.

Counselor Sue guides Bob and Nancy in repentance and a new way to look at finances including reevaluation of lifestyle. Bob and Nancy become new creations in Christ. They find ways to reduce expenses in transportation, increase income by changing investments, be more efficient in electricity use, increase giving to church and a missionary, and experience blessings to share financially and spiritually with other people. Bob and Nancy can now make decisions and feel they have the ability to change. Faithfulness to God in finances is their foremost goal.

Giving Hope

Pastor Wayne observes that hope is easily dampened in the consumer culture. His goal in financial counseling is to revive hope by creating alternatives, technical expertise and a caring relationship. He observes many families in his church are doing the best they can. They just do not have enough money to conscientiously fulfill all the responsibilities in the way they feel obliged to do. Some other families in their income level have been denied benefits, loans, or entitlements because income is too high. This makes them bitter because they see families that did not work as hard as they did getting benefits freely. Pastor Wayne counseled Oscar. Oscar was a man who was going to lose his house and was denied a loan to keep it. If he lost the house, his wife said he would lose her, also. He did not have a good portfolio of financial assets. When he came for financial counseling, his head was down. He was embarrassed. By the end of the session Pastor Wayne helped him develop a portfolio of human assets to take to the bank. It included his coming for financial counseling. He had gifts and hobbies that could supplement his regular income from a stable job. He had done extra jobs in photography. Human assets were identified and restored his confidence to communicate with the bank and his wife. He had hope. He saw some Light for his situation. Oscar left with his head lifted higher. (He did get the loan, partly because he told them he had counseling.)

Pastors Wayne and Sue have counseled people who need a slower walk and more patience than would seem. Pastor Wayne demonstrates faith in them for changing behavior. Pastor Wayne says, "Do not assume an individual is disinterested or incapable because of not doing something or not paying bills on time." The cause may be a poor memory, weak ability, poor mathematics or an overwhelming crisis in another area. "One cannot worry about the pot boiling over when the house is on fire." Demands of job may overshadow and weaken the interest to do comparison shopping, for example.

Families frequently have financial trouble because of trouble elsewhere. Pastor Wayne has justified learning to teach or counsel in financial mechanics because he knows it helps families in their jobs or emotional/mental illnesses. By counseling in marriage problems, they are more able to work on their finances or concentrate on their job.

Practice M's of Financial Ministry

The Spirit empowers changes. People have to want changes. Shepherds in financial ministry use elements for suggesting appropriate direction in the paths of financial faithfulness. Mathematics in the choices are not sufficient although helpful. The "Five M's of Ministry" differentiate pastoral counseling or shepherding from financial education, personal finance, consumer economics or financial planning. The Five M's are:

Mathematics,

eMotions,

Management behavior patterns,

Members of their family, and

Movement to wholeness. All five M's are woven together for the unique personality and situation. From a strictly mathematical calculation, a decision would appear appropriate. Ignoring the other M's would mean failure in implementation.

Management behavior is partially analyzed by money use and partially by attitude toward money. Shepherds help change attitudes as well as structure in handling money. Both must change for fuller commitment to the Lord and solving financial problems. What is the use or attitude? Money is possibly used for power, expression of love, status, feeling important, security, way to control, way for acceptance and respect, simply a medium of exchange, or carefully used in appreciation of someone's sweat and labor. It is just one type of income. Money is a tool or torture, blessing or curse, freedom or bondage. It is used as a measure of one's worth in the world. It can be perceived as an instrument to fulfill God's purposes on earth. Shepherds help decide use of money based on faith, unselfishness, and security in the Lord, not fear or fashion.

Prayer needs to pervade financial counseling. Prayer helps shepherd to listen to people and understand their listening blocks. Prayer, unleashing the Spirit's direction in the one-to-one counseling, brings response to God's call. Prayer unleashes creativity and conquers defeat. Prayer keeps the focus on the problem and the need for alternatives and self-control. Prayer recognizes spiritual cures rather culture's cures of more materialism, more spending, more self-indulgences. Prayer taps the resources for climbing out of financial despair or ignorance and up the mountainside. Prayer seeks God's plan and how people can fit into it rather than planning and asking God to bless their plan. Prayer suggests taking the hand of the Almighty Heavenly Father rather than depending on the "almighty dollar."

Family Economics Framework for Guiding Faithfulness

A flow model describes the system of individual and family economic activities on the path to desired outcomes. The model describes the large scope of activities, the terminology in economic terms, and the interrelatedness of activities. The model shows the influences from the external economy. Also, individuals and families influence the external economy by their decisions. Smoother interactions with the larger economy, business world, church traditions, and culture are possible with the shepherd's guidance. The shepherd can assist at points where the flow is broken and expand concepts for desired outcomes. This is crisis intervention through counseling and education.

Outcomes and Results of Financial Activities

The shepherd assists in decisions of resource management to increase faithfulness and the joy of fulfilling God's purposes unique to each. Rather than starting at the beginning of the flow of how to spend money, ultimate purposes of economic activities can be defined first which will guide intentional activities along the way. Ultimate purposes or outcomes from production and consumption, money and non-money incomes can be redefined. The end result in the model is Quality of Life. Quality of life comes from fulfilling God's purpose, seeking first the kingdom, freedom from captivity of any type, satisfaction (contentment) in richness or poorness, joy of sharing more with other people, well-being in the Lord bigger than circumstances, and joy in spiritual wholeness. Expressed in Psalm 62:10, "And if your wealth increases, don't make it the center of your life" (NLT) or "Though your riches increase, do not set your heart on them" (NIV).

Decisions in each segment of the model can be in light of the ultimate purposes. Purposes are expanded. For example, financial freedom is more than absence from credit and debt. Financial management and consumer practices strive to increase resources to fulfill God's purpose unique to the individual at a particular stage of life cycle. The pervasive power to change the flow is under the Invisible Influence of the Spirit.

Economic anxieties, financial distress and uncertainties are in both the external and internal family environments. Therefore, the shepherd is useful in assisting and educating in complex decisions. Financial peace comes from allowing God's control of personal resource use, addictions, worldly passions, and cultural norms. The promise in dealing with complexity and fear is based on Isaiah 43. The Lord did not promise life would be easy. **He promised to be with us each step of the way.**

The shepherd assists people through sermons of inspiration, education in classes, counseling one-to-one, mentoring, support groups, and mobilizing resources. Resources are internal and external to people to redefine their Quality of Life. These are necessary in times of uncertainty, fear, distress, loss of income, conversion, and life changes.

New Purposes and Rewards from Financial Management

The outcomes or the goals can be defined by the individual to encompass:
- Abundant life in God's love, peace, and provisions,
- Assurance, by seeking first God's kingdom and righteousness, trusting needs will be met,
- Joy in fulfilling God's purposes unique to each, glorifying God, doing justice and loving mercy,
- Financial peace of mind from faithfulness,
- Financial freedom and satisfaction in richness (plenty) or poverty (want),
- Spiritual wholeness of freedom from captivity of any kind,
- Building wealth to share and to build God's kingdom.

Flow Model of the "Family Economy"

External Environment>   **External Environment>**

Influences	Family Function>	Internal Environment>	
Economic System	**Allocations of** *Resources*> Human Nonhuman (Controlled and not controlled)	**Production**, Market activities, paid, brings money income and some payment in kind from all production sources and money transfers. Most goes into household production	Some, through saving reallocated to production, affect capital for business and industry.
	Material	to	Some, through taxes, redistributes the wealth
Economic Conditions Business cycle	Spiritual	**Household Production**, for members, unpaid brings real income from management of money, time and energy; And from services of goods and services through decisions, choices, making, doing and purchasing, utilizes human and nonhuman resources and information for work around house, yard, vehicle and children. Employs equipment, community facilities, life skills, and education. Exchange of goods and services with other families. Controlled resources to consumption, not controlled to application. Realization of price of or tax advantages. to	Some allocated to future use
Market Arrangements			Some decisions affect market arrangements
Businesses			Some, through development of human capital to future
Industries			
Institutions Educational Religious			
Government Provisions Policies Programs		**Distribution**, a final activity of production from agreement of resources and financial affairs based on cost/benefit analysis and value clarification, affecting family ecology. for **Full Income** to	Ultimately to the external ecology Dollar rates affect production. Complaints affect business Some to sharing, charity, United Way, etc.
		Consumption, for fulfillment of wants and needs. for **Psychic Income** or satisfaction from perceived utility and expectations (now fulfilled), from satisfaction of past decisions, routine consumption	Demand for justice and mercy
Geographic Conditions Climate			

Technology and Sciences

Cultural Values and Provisions
    Materialism
    Commercialism
    Spiritualism

from resources not controlled, and new consumption from current decisions of resources controlled. Satisfaction from employment, nonmarket work, and leisure. Realization of utility from goods and services provided by friends, family, and government. Satisfaction from quantity and quality of goods and services---durable and nondurable. Customary health and personal care provisions. Protection, security and community provisions. Participation in group activities. Fulfilled expectations and attitudes based on reference group norms.

Outcomes:
Sense of progress and sense of control. Perceived adequacy of income. Glory to God.

Motivates production-market and nonmarket.

Economic well-being
Lifestyle fulfillment
Spiritual Fulfilment

Quality of Life
    Defined and redefined as
      situation, events, life
       stages, and conversion mandate.

Step One is Setting Goals and Outcomes

Nature of Goals. Goals are the specific designs toward which effort is directed versus wants. The ideal process of financial management begins with "setting financial goals." The second step is "planning," then "decision making," next "implementing," on with "controlling," and last "evaluating." The evaluation ideally leads to new ways to implement or control or even to new goals. Successful management is success in achieving goals. Individuals may be successful managers if their goals are met, although they may not be verbalized or judged as worthwhile by other people.

Goals need to change when individuals receive new information or are in a different situation. Through conversion to a larger purpose, goals need to be changed. However, goals change slowly except in a crisis. Goals, when articulated, give direction for reaching larger purposes. Goals direct the use of resources. Otherwise, people aimlessly wander about in overspending, overly using credit, or under-spending. Goals when following the process of goal-setting reduce despair, uncertainty, and feeling useless. Setting goals reduces confusion and gives guidance for saying "yes" and "no" and "not now."

An ideal manager is like a tree with lofty goals while solid rooting in values, getting energy from the sun the "Son," having seasons for bearing fruit and for rest, unselfishness in providing service (shade from the burning sun rays, rest for the weary soul, food for the hungry), flexing with the winds but not breaking, and if trimmed or cut down establishing more roots and greater fullness. (Have individuals draw a tree illustrating these characteristics during a goal-setting session.) Psalm I gives direction for a living tree planted by the water that does not wither and is productive.) In John 4:10 and John 7:38 the spring of living water is the Spirit of Christ.

The Shepherd Assists in Verbalizing Goals. The shepherd assists people to specify goals in dollars, numbers, concrete terms, detailed outcomes, and changes. The shepherd assists in the process by telling stories of people's goal setting, ways to meet the goals, and how they worked for other people. Some people need help in clarifying goals. The initial questions for identifying goals may be:

- what do you want to be,
- have happen,
- change to be happier or
- not to have "someone after you?

The shepherd helps turn wants into specific goals for the time being, at least. Some examples are amount to save, funding for college, reduced debt, increased giving, vacation trip, support to children after divorce, job related expenses, dependable transportation, attorney fees, debt for ambulance service, survival after loss of job, increased house payment to prevent foreclosure, better communication, etc. A goal may be to take two vacations a year. Goals can be any that are worthwhile and are a part of the overall outcomes suggested above. Goals are unique to the individual at the time. Goals are financial, spiritual, relational, recreational, sharing, saving, and aesthetic as well as material or physical.

An illustration of a technique in helping someone learn to set goals is to ask, "What should we do (try)…this year, weekend, or about_____? Should we do _____, _____, _____, or _____?" This technique forces the other person to choose a goal from acceptable alternatives given. Ownership of the goal increases likelihood of working on it. Verbalization increases the commitment toward the goal. However, be sure the person is not just giving an acceptable answer to shorten discussion on consensus and not really committed to the goal.

Some goals are best not verbalized. If verbalized they would receive undue pressure from others. If not met, the goal-setter does not have to lose face. Some are so personal or accompanied by pain, they do not have to be verbalized.

Assuming individuals are the best judge of their own interests, they will be more efficient in allocating resources to achieve goals they desire rather than what others have chosen for them. It is less effective for someone else telling them what and how to set a goal, which may be another's displaced goal.

It takes marketing, convincing, and charming to get other people to do their part in verbalizing and reaching the group's goals. Meeting some goals is contingent on other people's decisions and behavior. Have an alternate person if the initial person does not cooperate.

The shepherd may ask, "Suppose the other person (spouse, your employer, your coworker, the church member) does not change, what will you do? What are your options? Given that he or she drags you down, will not help or share your goal, what are your options? What steps will you take?"

Have a plan B, an alternative goal so one is not so devastated if he or she cannot meet that particular goal. When a setback or great disappointment happens, quickly concentrate on what is next. Pray, "What do I do next?" "What is another goal?"

The Shepherd Assists in Achieving Goals. To prevent an overload so the individual is torn in too many directions, have no more than two professional, house/yard work, and two personal goals. Goals may be for two years, two months, or two days. However, the planning horizon for most individuals or families is about three years. Being specific helps to achieve goals. Specificity means writing: "On such DATE, I WILL _____." Another process for managing goals is writing on paper individual or group goals in the following procedure:

The efforts designed to meet goals are written in columns as follows:

1	2	3	4	5	6
Specific goal	Date due	Information needed	Resources and money	Who else to contact	How to measure progress

Look at each component in the column. Be creative in using each component listed in the column to meet the goal. Ask God for wisdom and strength. If there is a will for a worthwhile goal, there is a way. Efficiency, which is using the least resources to get the most satisfaction or return, is good stewardship. In other words, eliminate unnecessary expenses, combine actions or uses of something (examples: listening to tapes while driving or caring for a child), rearrange the work place, and simplify life. The task is to examine ways in meeting goals with less cost in some cases and more cost in other cases.

Suggesting alternative ways to meet goals is useful. One can remind others that "Wherever there is a will, there is a way." But also "pray, as in the Lord's Prayer, for protection in the time of testing because "wherever there is a will, there is someone who is in the way." (source unknown)

Individuals must believe in their goals and think they are possible. Belief gives hope. Hope gives energy to work toward the goal. When a person sets a realistic goal and experiences progress, there is hope and there is energy.

Another technique is to write short-range goals and long-range goals on separate cards. Commitment is working on both short-range and long-range goals every day. One must be aware that short-range goals (spending) can undermine long-range goals when day to day activities, routines and crises interfere with long-range goals. Short-range goals if selfish passions that destroy undermine total satisfaction. Short-range needs and activities may undermine commitment to Christ as the continuous commitment. However, needs may change in both short-term and long-term. On the other hand, decisions as to money and time every day affect meeting long-range goals.

Due dates for enrollments, conversions, etc. must be met. Assist persons in the counseling office to start on the goal by starting the first step such as setting an appointment, ordering a form, or their stating the steps they will take.

Have the person share goals with someone. A new commitment to Christ's goals will be stronger if shared with someone, like confession or a spiritual experience. Remember the Chinese motto: "If you share your joy, you double it. If you share your sorrow, you halve it."

Discuss barriers to meeting goals. They may be perceived, real, or just excuses. Discuss how to overcome the barriers. People may not know the way for sure. People in faithfulness and duty move onward and upward as did the women who went to the tomb of Jesus' burial not knowing how the stone was going to be removed.

Everyone involved in achieving the goals should be involved in the planning. Help them accept ownership or think goals are theirs. Have each write on a card how to contribute toward the goal.

Some people need information for steps to take in accomplishing the goal. Mothers at all socioeconomic levels probably have the same goals for their children. However, middle and upper class ones may know the steps and the resources to make goals a reality. A Mentor Mother program assists persons on how to get to where they want to go, to know the resources, know who to contact, know loop holes in requirements, know alternative due dates, and be encouraged.

When it is written and one can see everyday to work on it, the continual focus on the goal is clearer. Otherwise, the short-range goals, the routine, or the crises will undermine long-range goals. One should examine how long-range goals are being submersed in day to day activities or routines. On the other hand, the daily, short-range goals and activities achieve the long-range goal. Day to day activities can be structured to meet long-term goals.

Discipline achieves the dream and accomplishes the goal. A verse reminds us, "Our fathers disciplined us for a little while as they thought best; but God disciplines us for our good, that we may share in his holiness. No discipline seems pleasant at the time, but painful. Later on, however, it produces a harvest of righteousness and peace for those who have been trained by it" (Hebrews 12:10-11).

Have the person choose someone trustworthy to be accountable to for changing behavior. Have them be aware of those who would belittle or discourage so they "do not throw pearls to the swine" (Matthew 7:6). Insist on accountability enforced by various means, even with paying dollars, to someone when he or she does not make progress toward the goals. Someone should check on them for progress. In Alcoholic Anonymous steps, the recovery person has to talk with his or her mentor everyday. Leaving a message is not sufficient accountability.

The shepherd reminds people to ask God to help in order to serve the work of God's kingdom or fulfill the plan for their life. If one meets the goal, give God the credit. God gives the spark that lights the fire for getting started, for showing the way, for putting helpful people and resources in the way, for giving the strength to persevere, for giving the power of the mind, a hopeful heart, and a soul (conscience) to meet the goal in God's way without compromising conviction or integrity.

The Shepherd Assists in Evaluating Goals. Realistic goals should stretch the goal setters, not break them! On the other hand, some people need to raise their sights, and err on the side of thinking idealistically. Some people are afraid others will laugh at them if they set high goals. They need encouragement to raise standards and expectations. The shepherd can show them greater possibilities.

Questions are asked to clarify which goals are most important if they conflict: What is the will of God? God will never ask one to do something or have a goal that breaks the commandments. Criteria are based on loving God with all one's heart, soul, mind, and strength; and your neighbor as yourself. Other goals become secondary.

Evaluation of goals may determine if they are too rigid, too high, too low, too remote for encouragement, too harmful, or too unrealistic. What makes goals unrealistic? They cost someone in health, integrity, ethics, and family. They are not worth the cost. "What good will it be for a person if he or she gains the whole world, yet forfeits his soul?" (Matthew 16:26). Calculate what is given up to obtain the goal? Is foregone now, is it achievable in the future? Is it only possible to fulfill the goal at this time? If one prepares now (short-term goal), will he or she be better able to serve others later on (long-range goal). Every *need heard or seen* now is not everyone's *call* in serving God at a given time.

The goal in mind is the criteria for what to buy or do first. Help them stay focused on the goal. When making a decision, ask "Will this spending, use of credit, selling an item, liquidating an asset, etc. contribute to or hinder the goal?"

In evaluating success toward achieving a goal, look for progress not perfection. Expect resistance and be persistent. Use a measure of achievement which evidences something is accomplished toward the goal. "Success breeds success."

Scriptures for persistence are: "Let us not become weary in doing good, for at the proper time we will reap a harvest if we do not give up. Therefore, as we have opportunity, let us do good to all people, especially to those who belong to the family of believers" Galatians 6:9-10). Another verse to continually repeat is "I can do everything through him who gives me strength" (Philippians 4:13). Slogans facilitate change. Examples are "Never give up." Or "Hitch your wagon to a star."

A wise manager of goal attainment is not so rigid that he or she overlooks or passes up an opportunity that would be a better goal. The Spirit's voice may tell one something else is a better goal. This happens when resources change, one gets new information, or has a crisis. In economics, changing a direction uses the term "sunk cost." Something is considered "sunk" because to pursue the initial direction would be more costly in the long run although one has invested time, energy, and money pursuing the initial goal.

One can realize that on the job, with the family, or with goal achievement there are "good days" and "bad days." The goal can be to have more good days than bad days.

Consequences of mistakes still have to be realized. Time in punishment, grieving over mistakes, or changes still have to occur. The shepherd can "walk" with the grieving person when a goal, a dream, a lifestyle, etc. is shattered. The shepherd can help identify new goals. Out of financial ashes, a garden can grow (Isaiah 61). Everyone can shout "Resurrection!" every time an evil or crippling thought comes to roost.

The Shepherd Assists in Prayer. Sincere, earnest prayers include requests for wisdom in choosing the right goals for the person or family at this time. They include requests for direction in the steps to reach goals. Prayers include requests for strength in overcoming the barriers to reach goals.

Guidance warns: "When you ask, you do not receive, because you ask with wrong motives, that you may spend what you get on your pleasures" (James 4:3). Therefore, prayers include requests for knowing how to *benefit others* when you

> Obtain a job, more money, more wealth;
> Gain controlled energy and health;
> Receive blessings of any types; and
> Enjoy *delights* sent from God because he delights in us.

Promises and assurances for faithful financial management are in Zephaniah 3:17 (NLT): "For the Lord your God is living among you. He is a mighty savior. He will *delight* in you with gladness. With his love, he will calm all your fears. He will rejoice over you with joyful songs." Another message is: "Then the Lord your God will make you most prosperous in all the work of your hands and the fruit of your womb, the young of your livestock and the crops of your land. The Lord will again *delight* in you and make you prosperous…, if you obey the Lord your God and keep his commands and decrees that are written in this Book of the Law and turn to the Lord your God with all your heart and with all your soul" (Deuteronomy 30:8-10). Samuel reports, "He brought me out into spacious place; he rescued me because he *delighted* in me" (2 Samuel 22:19-21). A management step is stated by Job: "Surely then you will find *delight* in the Almighty and will lift up your face to God" (Job 22:26). May it be said of those facing change: "He trusts in the Lord; let the Lord rescue him, since he *delights* in him" (Psalm 22:8). The promise for resource management is: "*Delight* yourself in the Lord and he will give you the desires of your heart" (Psalm 37:4). Become a *delight* for others!

◊◊◊ ⧗   ⧗ ◊◊◊

Chapter 2. **The Shepherd Tends to Those in Financial Management Steps and Crisis Intervention**

Counseling may be by appointment in a planned session or it may occur in an unplanned casual conversation any where and at odd times. Counseling may occur during the weekly call by the mentor. The appointment may be a formal one-to-one session, usually one of three, or group sessions.

Both technical and inspirational words are shared. One goal is to solve financial problems so the individual can have spiritual renewal. Another goal is progress toward solving a problem with severe financial implications. Goals include simply getting someone else's opinion, smoother interaction with businesses, rescue from terror or crisis, economic stability, and finding joy in fulfilling God's purpose unique to each. A goal is to gain life abundant in God's love, peace, and provisions. This abundant life can be obtained in spite of economic ills, anxieties, and financial mistakes.

Spiritual renewal is advanced with the shepherd's relationship in providing love, respect and faith. To establish a trusted relationship ask, "What's on your mind?" Or "How is life treating you?" Questions can identify (1) legal, consumption, work, or management problems, (2) estimate of available resources and income now, (3) estimate of expenses for determining if they are the problem, indicate other problems, or can be changed, (4) decisions that need to be made as the individual sees them currently after some counseling and prioritizing, (5) strengths of the individual as well as fears, hopes, and any plans, and (6) steps before the next session when more in-depth information is recorded and plans are made.

The counselor realizes that often the "presenting" issue is just a safe one at the beginning to assess whether the counselor can be trusted. It is just the tip of the iceberg, or just the least painful question that it can be voiced. The counselee may explain his or her crying although it is far from the real underlying pain, fear, or long term sadness or distress.

The structured interview form directs the process of questioning and obtains needed information more efficiently than random, free form discussion where emotions dominate. Write the presenting problem briefly because the real problem is usually more clarified after completing the form. Helping with a surface issue is still useful. Deeper or real problems may come out after the structured interview guides the discussion.

Sessions may have changed from the initial desire of a one-time session. Comprehensive financial management is ideal but any help can give hope and structure. The "Financial Summary and Plan" is as a guide for the process for those limited in time and experience. Each has a copy and serves as a log of counseling sessions. Prayer begins and ends the session receiving strength from the Great Shepherd for the journey.

FINANCIAL SUMMARY AND PLAN

Name:_____Date:_____Referred by:_____

Presenting Problems/Questions: (Real problems are clarified after further discussion.)

_____

Fears: Other agencies or professionals working with:

_____

Household Composition:

_____

Financial Position: (rough estimate)
   Income (net monthly):   Source:
     minus
  Expenses:
  Debts: Type:
     equals
  Decision Income:
   Value of government services:
   Value of employee benefits:
  Assets (financial):
  Assets (personal):

_____

Creditor and legal problems (current and predicted)? *Harassment? Cut in service? Loss of goods? Court Action? Embarrassment? Immobility?*

_____

Consumption and management problem: Need for long-range planning:

_____

Decisions to be made: (Then rank in order for solving)   Goals: (Short-term and long-term)

_____

Information and resources needed to solve problems or make decisions:

_____

Compliment - Person's strengths, assets, experiences, good management:

_____

Spiritual assessment:

_____

Plan for **person** (**steps** to take): (short term – this week):   Plan for **counselor**, educational material to give:

Plan (budget) from chpt. 4 to implement:
_____
Plan for spiritual renewal: Scripture to read every day, hymn to sing, prayer with someone, etc.:

Financial Management

In the "financial management" approach, client and counselor establish financial objectives. Then money use is analyzed and redirected to meet those objectives.

Real life illustrations help explain financial management. A well-prepared pastor, Pastor Ann observes there are people who make things happen, those who watch things happen, and those who do not know anything happened until a wake-up call alarms them that they are in trouble. Something new in the family happens or an accident changes everything. Management is necessary *not* only in a crisis but also when increased demands are greater than the money currently available. It is necessary when there are changes in demands, resources, or knowledge.

Mismanagement continues when people think more money is the answer. More money postpones mismanagement or problem resolution. Alan and Alison over-estimate income while under-estimating expenses. They continue to raise their expectations and standard of living in some areas such as tele-communications or utilities while real income is decreasing. Alan and Alison do not know how to spread income over a period of time. They continually spend more than they make. They expect different results while handling their money and spending in the same old way.

Shepherds debunk myths and reduce erroneous thinking. Common errors just to mention a few are: "I am in control of my finances." "I do not have choices." "I can maintain a desirable life-style." "I can pay the minimum to keep afloat." "I can have everything, now." "Loan consolidation will solve the whole problem." "I can always take bankruptcy." "Since they cannot get blood out of a turnip, I am going to borrow all I can to get what I want." "No one will ever hire me." "My parents or the government will help me if I do not have a job." "If I work hard, I will always have a job." "If I get a divorce, the government and my parents will support me." As well as erasing false concerns or sorting out unimportant ones, the shepherd lifts up necessary steps, right thinking, and what really matters.

Pastor Ann expects resistance to change. However, she is persistent because she has observed that many people do not want to change, fear change, or do not know how to change. Young and old alike want to avoid pain and changes in patterns of living. They want to enhance lifestyle, not diminish it. People still do nothing even when it is clear something must be done to survive, get out of captivity, and reduce pain and anxiety. Therefore, they avoid cutting up credit cards, changing choices of food and drink, stopping certain forms of entertainment, and stopping association with friends or peers who negatively affect their money use. In conversation with Pastor Ann, Alan and Alison face problems, face other people, and face the changes they must make.

Pastor Ann, on the other hand, helps Alan and Alison hold on to good habits that keep them afloat. In emphasizing the need to change, she emphasizes they are not bad people. Rather, they are using a bad system for the current situation. Pastor Ann asks what Alan and Alison have done well, what gimmicks, and what parts of their current system are working well.

Alan and Alison need a crash budget for a designated period of time and then reevaluate. The landing will be smoother if Alan, Alison, and their children who are required to follow-through are involved in the steering. Each one can cut expenses somewhere and somehow. Ideally spouses and children should attend at least one counseling session together. Steps must be accepted by all or the plan may be sabotaged.

Shepherds learn from their clients, which over time they can use with other people who seek counseling. Mike, in long-term survival mode, educates Pastor Ann and his counseling team on how the "system works." Mike is "street smart." Then there is Krista, who could teach other people many ways to survive on nothing.

Steps in Financial Management

Non-crisis financial management applied by the shepherds uses these steps:

1) List objectives and goals. Goals range from "survival" to "giving more than a tithe." The options to meet goals are to increase income, reduce expenses and/or be more efficient. Problems with saying "meet needs only" are: Who is to say for another what his/her needs are? Whose needs should be met? Expenses are required to function physically, socially, psychologically, and spiritually. All these types are needed. If reducing expenses is the goal to stay within income constraints, ask: What is adequate rather than ideal? What would happen if this thing is cut out or limited? What desires are "met," "not yet," and others "never" because of sinfulness, wastefulness, or values?

2) Assess the current situation. Direct those seeking help to keep a daily record of every expenditure for analysis. The record gives a point of discussion with the counselor and reveals habits and lifestyle. List all income, expenses, debts, taxes, savings, and contributions. Determine balance (surplus or deficit): income minus expenses, debt, taxes, savings, and contributions. Most people will report, regardless *when* they report, that expenses are unusual this week. Unexpected expenses always happen. They had not anticipated a car break down, a birthday gift, photos needed, illness, license plates, taxes, quarterly expenses, school expense, etc.

3) Analyze expenditures. Look for patterns. See what costs more than assumed. See surprises. What expense categories such as debt payments, visiting relatives, or medical should be increased to meet goals? What can be decreased? Limited? In cutting out some items, more healthy options occur in their place. How can expenses meet goals? Individuals can ask forgiveness and repent for past mistakes and decisions such as buying a too expensive vehicle, although they still must fulfill the consequences. Pray for Christ's help in controlling addictions and get group or professional help. Assess willingness, readiness, and ability to change, given their anxieties and fears to make changes. The rule: Ultimately, nothing is a fixed expense. Drastic changes must be made as well as small steps, one at a time.

Necessary expenditures are identified and then reduced further by frugality and efficiency, comparison shopping, and discovering how the same satisfactions can be met less expensively. Why? Reduce spending to share more and save more. Give to a Good Cause and then decide the percent needed to care for oneself.

4) Reevaluate and redesign goals and objectives, short-range and long-term. Realign, refocus, redirect use of all God's gifts for the greatest human benefit. The new goal directs everyday decisions. For example, if the goal is education, spending time and energy to support a car may undermine it. Credit may help. If the goal is getting out of debt, no more credit will be used, food/drink costs will be reduced and other changes made. One becomes free, unburdened, ready for emergencies, and released from paying interest. Priorities are established by what meets goals, what can only be done now such as visiting elderly

grandparents versus a later time, what the consequences are of one purchase versus another, and what is healthy.

5) Plan (budget) with an appropriate format designed for personal needs, personality, and reason for the plan. Plan for God's purposes rather than one's preferences. Use money to provide for family and work in the kingdom of God. To achieve goals and have control, develop a workable system for handling finances. Calendars, envelopes, and spreadsheets are tools. Completion of a chosen budget (see chapter 4) implements financial management and guides reorganization, meeting goals, and solving confusion or problems. Obey God's commandments and do not let the ends justify the means.

6) Implement a plan. Cure the deadly disease of procrastination. Pay bills on time. Avoid late fees, service cut-off, etc. Comparison shop to get the most value for the money and reduce impulsive spending to have more to give for work in the kingdom.

7) Monitor progress and readjust accordingly. Shine the spotlight on miscellaneous or "leaks" in expenditures. Leaks can sink a great ship. Plug the leaks. "Grabbers" are irregular and big expenses which can sabotage a good plan. Grab hold and handle them while cutting elsewhere. Mountains are the large commitments dominating the budget. A little faith can remove them or bring them to manageable size. Maximize return on investments by monitoring and adjusting.

8) Communicate with family, employers, businesses and creditors. Getting cooperation may be feared. However, usually other people are more receptive than anticipated. Pray about this as we can pray about everything.

9) Accept responsibility for changing finances. Do something as Jesus said, "Take up your bed and walk," and "Go and sin no more." Financial responsibilities for children must be assumed. Responsibility is in "giving the first fruits of your labor." Responsibility includes identifying and accepting changes. Changes include spending more money in some areas and less in other areas. The counselor listens to these and helps individuals grieve through the changes required to live within a realistic budget. They count the good gifts God has given and share them. This glorifies and declares love to God.

Results of decisions in every area are shown in the last column of Cash Flow Analysis below: Income sources are listed by the date received. Expenditures are listed when due. Current cash flow of income and expenses is listed and then, after changes, is revised. The effect of change shows amount reduced or saved which can be used for debt, charity, or investments.

Cash Flow Analysis

	Date Receipt or Due Date	INCOME Or **EXPENSES** Monthly	$ Current Current	$ Revised Revised	$ Amount Reduced- Saved for Debt Charity Investment
INCOME net					
Employment					
Spouse's Employment					
Real Estate					
Other Fixed Inc.					
Savings Income					
Securities Inc.					
Other Variable Inc.					
EXPENDITURES					
Housing					
Rent/Payment					
Electricity					
Gas					
Water-Sewage					
Phones					
Water Softener					
TV					
Repairs, supplies,					
Furniture					
Taxes/Insurance					
FOOD					
Groceries					
Eaten Out					
TRANSPORTATION					
Payment/Bus					
Gas/Oil					
Repairs					
Insurance					
License					
Other Fees					
CLOTHING					
Laundry/dry					
PERSONAL CARE					
Allowances					
MEDICAL					
Doctor, dentist					
Medicine					
Insurance					
OTHER					
Newspaper					
Education					
Tobacco, alcohol					
Recreation,					
Entertainment					
GIFTS/CONTRIBUTIONS					
LIFE INSURANCE					
OTHER INSURANCE					
Child support					
SAVINGS					
INVESTMENTS					
TOTAL EXPENSES					
DEBT PAYMENTS					
TOTAL DEBTS AND EXP.					
BALANCE (Net Flow)					

Financial Counseling and Education

Financial counseling encourages a client to change resource use to achieve economic security, sense of well-being, quality of life, and have life abundant in God's love, peace and provisions. The counselor generates alternatives from which individuals choose for solving financial problems or troubles. Creativity is required. Maximization of satisfaction is not guaranteed. Neither is success. However, risk of failure and frustration are reduced. Faithfulness to God is the goal. Joy can result.

Kelly and Joe are more than interested in the shepherd helping them with financial issues because they are considering bankruptcy. Should they be ashamed? Can they work it out? They may lose their house. Therefore, three sessions close together and then referral seem better than sessions once a month. Sessions should be no more than one and half-hours. The hope and policy is to give at least one good idea, and do no harm. Shepherds must speak clearly in love to correct, suggest, and nudge. They must be compassionate even though they may feel judgmental.

Complete information is difficult to obtain, especially during the first session. Therefore, the counselor works with what is known. Besides the current income and expenses are the individual's or family's "sacred cow" – the Golden Calf. For many Americans the "sacred cow" is eating out, drinking, expensive food, entertainment, desire for things, entertainment in expensive media or recreation/sports/hobbies and expenses for pleasures or lusts. Passions are hidden in their hearts. They may withhold secrets from the shepherd. They hesitate to be open to inspection or discussion by the shepherd at least in the beginning. They may be afraid for the Spirit to convict.

Counselor Taylor, Kelly and Joe decide on task(s) to complete before the next session. One task may be begun in the office since tasks are more likely to be completed if started. Counselor Taylor dials the number and hands the phone to Kelly to get information or set up an appointment.

Progress may be accomplished by changing the structure and, then, hopefully, changes in feelings or attitude can follow. At the next session, Counselor Taylor asks, "What were the problems encountered in trying to complete the task(s)." This assumes there were problems and promotes communication rather than Kelly and Joe losing face if the tasks were not completed. Asking what problems occurred increases understanding of perceived or real barriers and opens communication about fears and desires, problems and dreams. Counselor Taylor simultaneously works with changing structures, habits and management as well as spiritual growth which is the spring for changing actions. Counselor Taylor gives hope as she shows respect, honors position, praises attempts, and generates alternatives.

Contrast these principles with an ugly scene observed where a "Christian" financial coach met the client for the second time. The first question was, "Mary, did you write down all the expenses like I told you to?" "No," she said staring blankly with the obvious look of I'm only here as required to keep my Habitat House. "You did not!" the counselor said. "I want to wring your neck, and I could since I am from the South." Mary sat in silence. There she sat, with one leg and six children. The counselor's main goal was to get data for the spreadsheet which came with the series of lessons which she had to complete. When Mary had asked earlier in the group meeting what to do if you cannot pay all the bills even if expenses are written down, the speaker said to wait a few weeks when increasing income would be discussed. One can see in this illustration the violation of counseling principles.

Financial Management Counseling Areas

In the "financial counseling" approach, client and counselor refocus use of money with creative alternatives for improving quality of life. Whether requested by the client or not, every area (see below) is examined in counseling sessions as it affects other areas. The irresponsibility of not examining every area can be compared to going to the dentist for tooth repair who neglects to tell the person of an obvious cancer on his face. Also, non-financial solutions are sometimes used to solve a financial problem and improve life in God's love, peace and provisions.

Although an individual presents questions only in one area, changes in other areas may be the "fix." Counselor Taylor goes through the list, examining possibilities in all areas for small or drastic changes with Kelly and Joe. The Recommendation Checklist (shown later) is to check what is desired and then check when completed. Consideration of each prompts other creative actions. The Checklist educates Kelly and Joe in alternatives for other problems they have or for other times.

The content areas included in comprehensive financial counseling are:

1) Increase income from all possible sources based on the premise that income, in the economic sense, is a flow of goods and services, not money alone. Present advice and information to mobilize resources, obtain different employment, expand business, liquidate assets, examine government entitlements, have rentals, use community resources, take early inheritance, and exchange in-kind goods and services with other people. Check on benefits as a veteran, retired teacher, first generation to go to college, handicaps, etc.

2) Reduce some expenses or wants, maximize use of money, and avoid additional financial burdens. This is done after analysis of family needs, recording current spending, and observing patterns of various family members. Reduce or increase some expenses in other areas. Dollar values of small changes can be summed for each area and then totaled to motivate changes. Individuals are asked to check ways to reduce expenses, get more with less, or practice saying "no" to children, to others, and to commercialism.

3) Adjust debts, manage credit and other financial obligations either with a self-administered plan as an assertive consumer or utilizing non-profit credit counseling services. Apply negotiation theories and skills. Analyze debts by how they hurt if not paid, worry, harassment, loss of goods or services, garnishment or court action, and increased costs. Note interest rates and legal consequences. Show the advantages and disadvantages of credit counseling, loan consolidation, bankruptcy, and borrowing from relatives. Provide forms and addresses to check credit reports, since a high percentage contains errors.

4) Clarify and prioritize wants and goals, then plan to meet them sequentially. This step is done after the first three possibilities are explored. Understand the influences and pressures to consume in various ways. Reconcile wants among family members. Reconcile expenses with income. Fulfill wants in less expensive ways. Prioritize by asking 1) what would happen if they did not buy or do such and such, 2) what can only be done now because of age, children, or opportunity, and 3) what is Scripturally based.

5) Make decisions after listing them in order of urgency (chronologically) with time frames for when to implement. Tackle tough decisions when life is in transition by priority, urgency, and

importance, one at a time. Seek sufficient information. However, postponing action may cost since each day of delay may cost money or delay getting a tax refund, etc. Write specific steps with due dates and the individual responsible to fulfill them. Clarify and rephrase what has been said. In subsequent meetings, ask, "What other decisions need to be made?" What problems did you have in implementing decisions?" Provide possible legal and tax consequences of their decisions. Use a referral source, references and reading material.

6) Establish or reorganize a system of household and financial management. Show appropriate techniques for record keeping, bill-paying on time, tax management, controlling impulsive spending, storing evidence of purchases, and communicating effectively with businesses and relatives.

7) Budget or set up a spending plan with appropriate types of categories based on individualized problems, personality constructs, and behavior patterns. (See Chapter 4.) The financial counselor provides telescopic vision of possible changes of income from all sources, expenses, and decisions at different stages of the family life. Use techniques of "time value of money," cash flow analysis, and net worth analysis (See Chapter 12). These tools are used more extensively by financial planners. The written plan shows implementation.

8) Act effectively to realize consumer rights, to know the steps for recourse when these rights have been violated, and to effectively resolve a consumer complaint. Show how consumer responsibilities are fulfilled. Use a model sample letter for writing an effective complaint letter. Motivate people to have sufficient confidence to do the research, gather important documents, and communicate effectively to those in authority with power for policy decisions.

9) Reevaluate sources of happiness or economic security. Increase and diversify sources of income and investments to increase security. Enhance skills for employment and diversify for job security, transferability and promotion. Change costs of past, current, and future needs in housing, transportation, life insurance, health insurance, marital disruption, children's education, investments, and retirement. Prepare for or make drastic changes in housing for resolving a crisis or maximizing income flow. Plan for or change housing for different stages of life. Generations may have to double up in housing.

10) Plan for retirement by reducing current consumption for accumulating and generating income for the future. This acknowledges the value of money decreases over time, when prices increase, and that there is risk in giving up control of current income. The greater the risk, the greater the possibility of income generated. Planning now may include the necessity of employment after retirement. With a fixed income in retirement, people have to plan on how they will reduce expenses or be more efficient. The retirement worksheet to plan can include these categories: Years projected, his income, her income, fixed expenses, flexible expenses, surplus or deficit. Income is from new sources such as Social Security, pension, inheritance, sale of property, and liquidation of assets. Certain expenses increase while others decrease. Be creative in sharing housing arrangements. Social Security pamphlets on vital concerns to people are available. Statements of Earnings are checked for accuracy. The temptation for early retirement must be checked with realities, requirements for benefits, and information about pension plans. Change other aspects of life to facilitate continued employment or different employment.

11) Champion change and handle adjustments or crises in lifestyle or in finances. List what will change and what will not change for a specific time. Build confidence sufficient for creativity in changing resource use. Have mottos to modify behavior. Expect resistance by family members. Sort out ill-grounded fears from those that need handling. Change attitude as to what is adequate versus ideal. Develop one's own criteria for self-worth consistent with how God values people. Develop new sources of security rather than monetary which are founded on God's character. Identify sources of thankfulness, counting these every night. Do volunteer work to lift the heart. Belong to a support group. Develop new criteria for progress rather than financial. Be better rather than bitter.

12) Pray and ask, "What is the next step?" "What does God want me/us to…?" "What does God not want me/us to …?" Direct the heart to God's purpose for finances rather than one's preferences and receive love, joy, peace, longsuffering, kindness, goodness, gentleness, self-control, and faithfulness (Galatians 5:22-23).

FINANCIAL MANAGEMENT RECOMMENDATION CHECKLIST

<u>Desired</u>   <u>Completed</u>

INCREASE INCOME

No.	Desired	Completed	
1.			Think "Income is a flow of goods and services and not money alone" in order to generate alternatives.
2.			Reposition assets to gain greater return. Change from bank to credit union.
3.			Liquidate a note or investment.
4.			Note the rule of 72: 72 divided by interest rate = number of years for savings to double; and 72 divided by inflation rate = number of years purchasing power will have a fixed income.
5.			Sell unneeded goods, vehicles, collection, _____, _____, _____.
6.			Increase net income by reducing job-related expenses (transportation, child care, place of residence, _____, _____.
7.			Share a job. Get a different job. Work a different shift.
8.			Help another family member obtain a job.
9.			Get a second job without jeopardizing the main job.
10.			Work more hours or less in an economic downturn.
11.			Use community resources.
12.			Obtain entitlements by proper procedures (Medicaid, food stamps, SSI, WIC, utility assistance, education, etc.). Check on regular medical expenses, child-care expenses, etc., to qualify
13.			Take early inheritance. Keep records.
14.			Take less tax withholding. Claim additional dependents.
15.			Turn hobby, talent, or craft into a business reducing startup & overhead costs
16.			Rent out a room, garage, barn, or other space.
17.			Consult, tutor, or give lessons.
18.			Use employee benefits, credit union, profit sharing.
19.			Exchange goods and services with other individuals or families.
20.			Collect money owed to you.
21.			Obtain Earned-Income Credit if income is less than $29,201 in 2002 and a child lives at home. Get EIC in advance by filing form W-5 with employer.
22.			Use legal procedures to obtain child support with parent's Social Security.

REDUCE OR CHANGE EXPENSES, WANTS

23. _____ _____ Record expenses for 2 weeks by tracking system and analyze (Use forms).
24. _____ _____ Reevaluate spending. Ask, "If reduced or cut out, what would happen?"
25. _____ _____ Modify spending by steering your own crash budget, for smoother landing.
26. _____ _____ Realize ultimately nothing is fixed except _____.
27. _____ _____ Remember 60-40 rule in housing: Payment is Principal + Interest = 60 percent of total housing costs. Focus on reducing the 40 percent related costs.
28. _____ _____ Scrutinize miscellaneous spending, leaks in the ship, usually larger than estimated. See who is uncontrolled in impulsive spending.
29. _____ _____ Choose target areas to reduce for a specified period of time & then reevaluate.
30. _____ _____ Use techniques for reducing impulsive spending, after determining why.
31. _____ _____ Use the checklist to examine every area to "get more with less".
32. _____ _____ Choose a way to get similar satisfactions in less expensive, more appropriate and positive ways.
33. _____ _____ Be specific on reduction: when, where, how, who. Estimate $'s saved.
34. _____ _____ Have each member write how he/she can reduce spending and costs.
35. _____ _____ Allow some money for each member to have free range to increase morale and cooperation.
36. _____ _____ Move in with relatives, maybe renting out apartment or house meanwhile.
37. _____ _____ Practice frugality, care for purchases, and practice simple living.

CONTROL CREDIT

38. _____ _____ Rethink "credit is debt," not a resource.
39. _____ _____ Remember credit abuse is devastating like fire, sex, and drugs, if abused.
40. _____ _____ Remember credit use is detrimental like any imbalance when not controlled.
41. _____ _____ Take self-control so you are not controlled by credit. Calculate extra work hours required to pay for having item sooner or for the interest. Compare total cost with cash: Monthly payment X number of payments = Total cost.
    Total cost – cash price = Cost of using credit.
42. _____ _____ Examine advantages and disadvantages of using credit.
43. _____ _____ Figure cost of refinancing, loan consolidation compared with lifestyle change.
44. _____ _____ Be sure to pay interest if borrowed on cash value of life insurance so insurance is not cancelled.
45. _____ _____ Recognize danger signals of over-extension.
46. _____ _____ Compare loan sources at credit union, bank, finance co., employer, cooperatives, charitable agencies, relatives, _____.
47. _____ _____ If you have borrowed from friends or relatives, write contract clarifying terms of repayment, interest, and "strings attached."
48. _____ _____ Do not borrow more than exactly needed except for investment or business.
49. _____ _____ Educate self on details (fine print) of credit contracts: penalties, late fees, wage or bank account, attachments, credit reporting, collection procedures, and policies.
50. _____ _____ Compare sources of credit, types of financing, fees, and APRs.
51. _____ _____ Borrow against equity in house or use reverse annuity mortgage after getting information and realizing strict payment schedule required and dangers involved.
52. _____ _____ Pay at least what you charged this month plus some on last month's charge.
53. _____ _____ Calculate and graph interest portion of payments during the months.
54. _____ _____ Obtain credit reports for family members.
55. _____ _____ Protect your credit rating so it can protect you in an emergency.

ADJUST DEBTS AND FINANCIAL OBLIGATIONS

56. _____ _____ Ask "Whose debt is it?" "Who can pay?"
57. _____ _____ Beware divorce decree is only enforceable between couple (debt collection).

58. _____ _____ Ask "What will happen if not paid?" (See chapter on credit.)
59. _____ _____ Find potential vs. absolute consequences of reduced or nonpayment.
60. _____ _____ List debts. Analyze by secured vs. non-secured, interest bearing vs. nonbearing, interest rates, what will happen if not paid by due dates, and whether discharged by bankruptcy or not.
61. _____ _____ Use sample letter to write creditor, copy for records, use proof of delivery.
62. _____ _____ Work with non-profit credit counselor in agency _____.
63. _____ _____ Complete loan consolidation worksheet or computer program.
64. _____ _____ Complete mortgage prepayment worksheet on computer program.
65. _____ _____ Calculate how many months to recoup costs of changing mortgage.
    _____ _____ Cost of changing divided by amount reduced = months to recoup
66. _____ _____ Intervene in process: collection, wage garnishment, court hearing, _____.
67. _____ _____ Arrange for court, creditor, landlord, doctor, etc. to reduce payments, defer payments, or take more each month to make up for skipped payments.
68. _____ _____ Ask for waiver of 20 percent, coinsurance, interest, late fees, etc.
69. _____ _____ Contact creditor, etc., rather than have them chase you. Be definite in communication even if stating you cannot pay specific amount.
70. _____ _____ Negotiate with ex-spouse or harass to get more support or pay less of house payment to him/her.
71. _____ _____ Subtract minimum expenses from minimum guaranteed net income to determine amount for debt payment, credit, or investment.
72. _____ _____ Compare costs (financial and other implications in getting a job or future loans) of loan consolidation, *Chapter* 7 bankruptcy, *Chapter* 13 repayment, and change in lifestyle.
73. _____ _____ Learn policies and rules of creditors, IRS, etc. and adjust debts accordingly.
74. _____ _____ Talk with a higher authority in the company, hospital, etc.; keep copies of everything; and communicate in writing.
75. _____ _____ Set up self-administered debt repayment plan by writing your plan to the credit company with a conservative payment plan and keeping your word.
76. _____ _____ Plead hardship, charity case, or write-off. Contribute to charity funds later.
77. _____ _____ Realize "Bankruptcy is using a canon to kill a fly." Loan consolidation is postponing problems, maybe increasing stress and fixed payments.
78. _____ _____ Learn to handle harassment, rather than going to extremes. Report violations.
79. _____ _____ Realize amount of paycheck that can be garnished; and/or "judgment proof," amount that cannot.
80. _____ _____ Do extra work such as overtime, waitress 1 or 2 nights just to pay the debts.
81. _____ _____ Use creative, clever alternatives for adjusting debts such as working off debts.

CLARIFY PRIORITIES

82. _____ _____ Redefine priorities after considering alternatives and information above.
83. _____ _____ Develop a standard of living unique to your own interests and values.
84. _____ _____ Use techniques to clarify values and handle dilemma of lifestyle changes.
85. _____ _____ List where to keep up with "the Jones" and where not."
86. _____ _____ Redefine what is "adequate."
87. _____ _____ Plan how to be reprogrammed.
88. _____ _____ Redefine what is the "good life" rather than lots of "goodies."
89. _____ _____ Decide what can only be done now.

90. _____ _____ Set goals and plan to meet sequentially.
91. _____ _____ Determine why you do not set goals and then overcome these barriers.
92. _____ _____ To rank priorities, ask of each item, "If not purchased or done, what will happen?" "What can only be done now?" "How does it meet goals?"
93. _____ _____ Choose your own lifestyle or you will be controlled by others or credit.

94. _____ _____ Explain to family members and others: "We choose this for now. If I had a million dollars, I would not buy it. On the other hand, this is important enough to sell some more eggs to buy it or do without something else."
95. _____ _____ Decide necessities vs. luxuries. Cut luxuries or reduce necessities for luxuries.
96. _____ _____ Remember "they" want your money, not your friendship.
97. _____ _____ Choose that which has the least severe consequences: _____.
98. _____ _____ Write the standard of living you want in 5 years with the money, time and actions required to accomplish this.

MAKE DECISIONS

99. _____ _____ Separate decisions into urgent, major, deferred, and unnecessary or erroneous.
100. _____ _____ Prioritize decisions indicating information needed.
101. _____ _____ Realize postponing a decision is a decision, maybe escalating future costs.
102. _____ _____ Get more information versus acting quickly so not to lose opportunity.
103. _____ _____ Compare at least three places, things, or services.
104. _____ _____ Work with decision income, i.e. gross income minus 25 percent.
105. _____ _____ Decide if you can accept the worst that might happen in alternatives.
106. _____ _____ Use techniques in family decision-making.
107. _____ _____ Use your own guide for planning or the rule of 60 – 20 – 10 –10: Spending, taxes, saving, sharing. Of spending, 60 percent for food and shelter, 10 percent for transportation, 10 percent for clothing and personal care, 10 percent for miscellaneous, 10 percent for debt.

108. _____ _____ Follow management – Plan, Control or Implement, and Evaluate).
109. _____ _____ Write specific plans for 2 months, general for 3 years. Quantify objectives.
110. _____ _____ Record expenses for estimating more accurately, proving evidence, analyzing for changing budget, and tax purposes.
111. _____ _____ Ask for performance not promises, explaining the "Way to hell is paved with good intentions" not followed through, not implemented.
112. _____ _____ Practice and persevere to implement.
113. _____ _____ Use a plan: appropriate, realistic, practical, pertinent with due dates.
114. _____ _____ Use computer program or efficient system for tracking cash flow, where to change due dates, avoid late fees, plan for special events, and prorate for yearly expenses.
115. _____ _____ Develop retirement plan by projecting income sources at various ages, calculating total income, expenses, effect of inflation, surplus or deficit, and making decisions accordingly.
116. _____ _____ Be sure plans meet needs of all family members and that all members support the plans or budget.

IMPROVE OPERATIONAL SYSTEMS FOR HOUSEHOLD AND FINANCIAL AFFAIRS

117. _____ _____ Use envelopes (save, spend, share) for estimating, recording, evaluating.
118. _____ _____ Use calendar—projected expenses and recorded.
119. _____ _____ Use an envelope for receipts with checklist of obligations.
120. _____ _____ Keep a notebook with pages by date income received for calculating expenses, keeping receipts, statements, and miscellaneous expenses.
121. _____ _____ Use worksheets for money and debt control. Check off when paid.
122. _____ _____ Use checkbook – tax deductible items and keep current balance. Write item in register first. Reconcile with bank statement.
123. _____ _____ Develop credit using an accounting system.
124. _____ _____ Change time and place for handling personal business.
125. _____ _____ Graph cost of utilities monthly to motivate conservation.

126.	_____	_____	Use a box or notebook for tax deductible items, receipts, and forms.
127.	_____	_____	Switch who pays bills among members for motivating cooperation.
128.	_____	_____	Set a routine time, place, and supply of items to care for financial obligations.
129.	_____	_____	Provide regular personal allowances for realistic planning, for soliciting cooperation to reduce elsewhere, for teaching management, and for preventing resentment.
130.	_____	_____	Organize a "family council" meeting for resource management and communication in ways earners are supported emotionally and with less stress in household responsibilities and tasks.
131.	_____	_____	Change method of communicating with family members about finances.
132.	_____	_____	Change periodically who is the main manager - who pays the bills, keeps tract of expenses, and controls impulse buying.

ACT EFFECTIVELY TO REALIZE CONSUMER RIGHTS AND RESPONSIBILITIES

133.	_____	_____	Obtain information from dispute resolution, consumer affairs office, attorney.
134.	_____	_____	Write effective letter. Speak to authority with power to make policy.
135.	_____	_____	Use legal services or legal aid if eligible.
136.	_____	_____	Read contract carefully. Get assistance from a qualified individual to explain.
137	_____	_____	Keep correspondence, contracts, receipts, records.

EVALUATE MAJOR FINANCIAL AREAS

138. _____ _____ Identify components of current program and by analysis, revise

_____ transportation

_____ housing

_____ insurance

_____ children's education and funding

_____ tax management

_____ investment

_____ estate distribution

_____ home-based business

_____ other:

CHAMPION CHANGE AND HANDLE CRISIS

139.	_____	_____	Identify why you are afraid of change or resent change; barriers to change whether real or erroneous thinking.
140.	_____	_____	Identify whether resistance to change is lack of information, habit, inability, inexperience, or unwillingness.
141.	_____	_____	Overcome barriers, laziness, or fear.
142.	_____	_____	Realize in changing, one changes self assumptions, goals, roles, help, and resource use.
143.	_____	_____	Say, "I am a person who happens to be _____(poor, ill, divorced, etc.)."
144.	_____	_____	Create solutions to your financial problems after changing assumptions about yourself. Change structure, practice new system, and, hopefully, attitudes will change.
145.	_____	_____	Practice, be patient, persevere. Wait for time to heal and help you adjust.
146.	_____	_____	Put crisis on shelf, longer time each day, until you can concentrate on generating alternatives to improve. Change scenery.
147.	_____	_____	"Work, rather than worry." Work on one concrete activity each day or week.
148.	_____	_____	Realize a crisis provides opportunity for reevaluation of resources.
149.	_____	_____	Seek professional assistance: financial advising, psychological counseling, family therapy, legal advice, accountant service, career counseling, _____.
150.	_____	_____	Assure the greatest gift to children is opportunity to develop ability to be resourceful, to improve, make do, and have financial peace of mind without everything given to them without assuming responsibility for self and others.

151. _____ _____ List and write what will change and what will not change, showing to family.
152. _____ _____ Use mottos to motivate. "Be smart. Turn out the lights." "Never give up." Develop phrases to keep your faith.
153. _____ _____ Expect resistance but be persistent. Realize "no pain, no gain."
154. Accept change under control for opportunity for growth   when faced optimistically.
155. _____ _____ Control the changes in your life or you will be controlled.
156. _____ _____ Change and control attitude or effect an event or person has on you since you cannot always control the events or person's behavior.
157. _____ _____ Ask "What have I learned from this experience?"
158. _____ _____ Be thankful for the gifts, knowledge, and experience given you rather than resenting and hating someone who has wronged you.
159. _____ _____ Delegate, while not relinquishing control.
160. _____ _____ Respond rather than react.
161. _____ _____ Use a non-financial solution to solve a financial problem. Enjoy small/free things or events in life.
162. _____ _____ Belong to a support group or have a regular counselor, someone whom you can trust, listen and advise.
163. _____ _____ Communicate with confidence! Communicate more effectively with family members and with creditors.
164. _____ _____ Role play to practice and build confidence.
165. _____ _____ Do not be so overwhelmed in one crisis you do not recognize danger signs of other impending crises.
166. _____ _____ Count and give thanks each day for the financial and personal assets, strengths, and successes, rather than bemoaning what you do not have.

MAINTAIN OR IMPROVE ECONOMIC SECURITY

If you cannot now reach your goals, dreams, stars, you can:
167. _____ _____ Adjust lifestyle, consumption, sense of progress, source of satisfaction, and source of faith.
168. _____ _____ Get more resources (personal, family, community, money, income producing assets, non-financial, professional advice, sleep, education, inner strengths, etc.).
169. _____ _____ Change wants (reducing certain expenses may be more healthy).
170. _____ _____ Be more efficient (organize your system and household, use resources more effectively).
171. _____ _____ No decision means to continue to be frustrated and resentful.
172. _____ _____ Realize you may not get ahead financially while investing in your children.
173. _____ _____ Enjoy goods already obtained rather than worrying about new purchases.
174. _____ _____ Redefine income adequacy. Redefine ideal versus adequate goods/services.
175. _____ _____ Change definition of "standard package," standard of living, the necessary goods and services without which you would feel deprived.
176 _____ _____ Be entertained by free events, community happenings, or nature's gifts.
177. _____ _____ Diversify investments: types, liquid and non-liquid, risky and secure, different characteristics, different companies for reducing risk of loss.
178. _____ _____ Improve job security and diversify skills; "Work smarter, not harder."
179. _____ _____ Check on your Social Security records and credits every two years.
180. _____ _____ Develop a sense of control and security by calculating expenses, developing plans, making changes, and improving management system.
181. _____ _____ Keep important records up-to-date.
182. _____ _____ Check issues, decisions and tasks for current and future stages of family life cycle for implementation.
183. _____ _____ The counselor or counselee could add others:

Counseling Techniques in Financial Management

Questioning and Listening

Seated across from each other, people's eyes meet but ears do not hear because of hardened hearts or preoccupation with something else. The mind does not understand. Why is listening blocked? Understanding how people listen and why they do not is vital if one hopes to express the message and implement change.

The most important principle in listening is perceiving the individual as important. The person with whom one is talking is the most important person in the world at the time. Therefore, respect, listening, learning, awe, love and humility follow.

One technique is to ask open-ended questions. Ask what, not why. Hear the pain and the passions. Hear what is not said. Be aware of mindsets to slowly help people change patterns of thinking. Discuss options in such a way that people accept solutions as their own. First ask them what options they think they have. Sometimes give humorous options so they are jolted into thinking about feasible, acceptable ones. However, be careful they understand that you're joking.

Beyond listening for patterns of thinking, listen for clues of behavior, and of what is important in their lives. Listen for what people fear. Separate real fears from stated fears and grounded fears from erroneous fears. Sort out the immediate fear from those which can be dealt with later. Sometimes people are not fearful enough to take action. Fear is motivation to take action. Fear of the Lord includes following his commandments in financial behavior.

Sometimes people "play games" or manipulate counselors. Sometimes shepherds are "used" rather than sought for their Spiritual guidance. Some people look to shepherds to make a quick fix without changing behavior or resources. Many have a crisis which had danger signals earlier. Signals were ignored until they reached crisis proportions. Sally has emotional problems and unmet basic needs. She meets these by overspending which causes even more problems. Sally also meets emotional and social needs by talking with the counselor. She is interested in many areas of life, not really in financial issues. They are a pretense to talk, not resolve. However, her counselor works on both. He keeps the conversation focused and comes to closure.

Listening puts life pieces together as in a jigsaw puzzle. Daisey[5] said "People's lives are often broken into many pieces. My role is to help people put the pieces together again. However, I quickly discovered that only God has access to 'the picture on the lid,' only God sees the complete picture and knows what is being created in every situation. This insight helped me to understand how essential it is that I rely on the guidance of the Spirit rather than relying on my own insight as I give counsel. When we try to help others, our own ideas of how to "fix" a situation may fall short of God's greater purpose. Only when we allow God to be the final authority for the pathway to wholeness can the creative process be unleashed." She went on to pray for help in loving other people without assuming she knew what is best for them. Then she trusted God for healing.

Listening for the meaning behind the words is a "must-do." Jake frequently says what he thinks is expected of him, what is socially acceptable, and what he believes will please the counselor. Some people have an inability to express themselves verbally. Alicia is not bad or weak. She is just "not with it" or not aware. To clarify meaning, the counselor rephrases what Alicia says until there

---

5   Daisey Townsend, *Upper Room*, June 11, 2004, P.49.

is agreement. Jake's shepherd listens with the heart, "the third ear," as well as the mind, and errs on the side of grace.

To move forward, then, the counselor assumes what is behind the words, watching the eyes and listening for clues. Frequent similar remarks represent a deeper issue. Counselor Amy's experience informs her what is behind the words of the worried in these statements:

- We are not making ends meet; or we're not getting ahead.
- We are living off credit.
- We want to give more to the church but....
- We need a budget.
- I want to retire early.
- I lost my job.
- I want a divorce.
- My family will never go along with this.
- We cannot talk about finances.
- What is a man to do?

Questions to Ask

After listening, the counselor may say, " I sense that you are feeling......or have had......, or there is a deep unresolved..." "Is this close to being accurate?"... "This may not be resolved today, but we can work on some financial steps to prevent additional burdens." "We can decide one or two changes for this week to assist both the technical and emotional.

The counselor balances patient listening with breaking the cycle of purposeless talking. He or she asks questions 90 percent of time and gives advice or the message 10 percent of the time. Questions such as these serve to focus the discussion:

- What do you think you need to make you happy? How do you think you will be happier if....?
- Why do you want to buy...? Continue spending money for......?
- What needs are met by your spending? Comfort? Security? Self-esteem?

- What steps have you thought about taking?
- What has been working well for you? What have you done that seems helpful, useful, effective?
- What problems do you foresee if you keep doing what is going well for you? (This approach is better than analyzing problems and saying or trying to get those stopped.)

- How did creeping indebtedness happen for you?
- What was important to you at the time? Has this changed?
- How do you think you can reverse the trend?

- What did you learn from this or that experience? Mistakes and their associated costs are tuition for "consumer education" if they learned from them.
- What will you not do or buy again?
- How have you learned to not be so gullible? So easily persuaded?

- Why do you think this happened? (Assess level of abstraction by this question.)

- Explain to me how you want different results while doing things the same way, maybe with slight variations?
- Where are you "spending money to impress people you do not like for things you do not need with money you do not have?" (author unknown)

- When are you going to call me about your trying new ...?
- What problems did you have (since the last session)?
- What individual or thing sabotaged your plans since last time?

- What do you mean when you say you cannot communicate?
- What would happen if you complimented your spouse everyday?
- How can you show more respect for.....? What would happen if....?

-What should/could you do if the individual creating the burden threatens to injure self or withdraw from you permanently if you do not assist them? (issue of abuse)

To examine the emotional side of money and counselee's reference group, ask: Who are you needing to please? Impress? How do you want to be admired? Who do you want to admire you? Who do you need to keep up with? What makes you a good parent or spouse?

Questions on the structured interview form reveals resources, types of problems, fears, values, and plans and other professionals/agencies contacted. After the structured interview, the real issue may surface, leading the counselor to start at a different place than initially. The counselor backs up from the initial question to one more basic. Usually there is need to ask a question going back farther, the real basis for decision or generation of alternatives. For example, the initial question may be about choosing a divorce attorney or what the Bible says about divorced people getting remarried, then the counselor backs up to get reasons why they want a divorce. After the counselor listens to their perceived or real barriers to trying alternatives, the financial costs are defined. Another example is in the mother wanting to know how to reduce income so her child can borrow from financial aid. The "back-up" question could be, "How do we finance our child's education?" Another question is, "What is wrong with borrowing to the maximum?"

Some individuals are habitual at telling tough stories again and again. The counselor can say, "Now, I've heard your story. Let's get beyond that. Let us focus on your options, your goals, something else. What steps can you take?" The next time the counselor asks how the client handled the new focus, the new steps.

For some people, telling one's story is part of the healing process. It surfaces negative feelings before reconstruction of life can begin. People need to ventilate feelings of shame and despair, a time of public confession. Therefore, the shepherd must be careful to not prematurely assure them of God's grace and forgiveness.[6]

After listening to the comfortable story, the counselor finds the story the counselee is not so comfortable telling. Listening with prompting is done in a non-threatening, nonjudgmental atmosphere where the client feels safe and assured of confidentiality.

Listening sorts out fact from fiction. An inscription carved in pewter on a credit counselor's desk for all counselees to read at first encounter is: "His side. Her side. The truth." Acknowledging

---

6   Clinebell. P.336.

this helped the truth to come out more quickly. The counseling session is frequently the first opportunity for spouses to really begin to listen to each other. Arguing is allowed. Counselor and couple learn how they feel or have neglected to communicate. "What they think" they spend and "what they do not know" facilitate discussion. Notice if one is being shut down by the other person with even the most subtle ways. Requiring everyone to keep accurate, complete detailed records of spending for a designated time gives basis for discussion and changing.

Attendees at a financial counseling conference discussed for an hour how to discover addictions. Finally this author said, "Reports on spending are not real accurate. If rough estimates do not balance, a serious problem that cannot be mentioned out loud may exist. For sensitive areas, the counselor hands each a problem list to check so the painful truth is not blurted out loud: money for alcohol, gambling, pornography, spending for someone outside the family, secretive financial behavior, judgments, wage attachments, videos, collections, hobbies, 'things to make me feel better,' not getting along with spouse, etc."

The challenge of the counselor is identifying underlying problems. Recommendations too early based on insufficient information may be ineffective. More information is needed on how the individual processes information. The reason for a budget must be known to use an appropriate format. A plan or budget will not work if information is inaccurate. Therefore, the counselor asks at the second session for any information or changes to add since the first session. Of course, people underestimate expenses and may have overlooked a debt in the initial session. (This is why they have problems in the first place.)

The counselor asks, "What do you think we said? Or "What steps (alternatives) have we discussed that sound appealing, workable, possible to you?" rather than "Do you understand?" (which is a yes or no question).

Why People Do Not Listen

People do not listen to other people when they are preoccupied with more pressing, urgent, interesting thoughts and "emotional clutter." Lou like other people is thinking about what to say next rather than listening. Sometimes they turn the speaker off when the tone or way something said is offensive, belittling, or unacceptable. Sometimes the options or truth are painful and counselees want to avoid pain. Sometimes there are too many changes at the same time and they cannot process them fast enough. Anxiety is too great to try something new. Sometimes they are just hungry or have some other problem or someone distracting them.

Then there is the arrogant individual who does not listen, stuck on his/her own goodness and self-righteousness. Dr. Krause cannot stoop to listen to someone, especially if he does not respect the counselor. On the other hand, the counselor may not have demonstrated an appropriate knowledge base, may not have used the counselee's dominant method for processing information or shown compassion. Dr. Krause will not communicate because he is afraid if he listens and talks too much, he will reveal weaknesses. He uses his arrogance to cover up feelings of inadequacy. He perceives coming to counseling, erroneously, as a weakness rather than strength.

For arrogant individuals such as Dr. Krause the counselor asks, "What financial practices have you been doing that work well?" "What advice would you give someone else in this situation?" Dr. Krause was a medical doctor whose wife had brought him in for counseling since she thought he was spending too much, and on credit. Both were highly educated and accustomed to getting information. Dr. Krause had not been willing to listen to his wife so she thought the counselor could convince him to stop overspending. He was indignant and embarrassed. The approach used with him was to show on a graph how much he was paying each month for interest. Then he was asked what else he could do with the money – getting more things, saving it or giving to his church. The visual presentation focused on the use of money not on him.

Bob was a young engineer making an income which seemed to him relatively large compared to that of his friends and relatives. His wife Erin thought he was spending too much on CDs and other things not disclosed. In gathering data and discussion, Bob discovered he was operating from gross income figures whereas the "decision income" after taxes, fees, United Way, and organization dues was about 32 percent less. He thought he could have whatever he wanted, or at least a few expensive hobbies or big toys, since he had worked so hard to get them. He had been clueless about family expenses, day-to-day and miscellaneous, irregular expenses, and the high cost of food. Establishing goals based on reality and considering family member needs besides his own helped relationships as well as financial stability. Yes, he deserved reward for his hard work. He also deserved to be in control, master of his finances as does everyone in a family. Pertinent questions for his self-esteem were "What else would you want to accomplish? What direction do you want to go? What barriers do you see for this? What are you doing for your spiritual security?" "How do you use other members of your family as resources of information as you make financial decisions?" Bob has to shift from a "deserve" mentality as the root problem and a "rights" attitude to a "gratitude" attitude. Bob can gratefully receive God's gracious gifts.

Hardened Hearts. Hardened hearts as described in the Scripture are those who initially hear the Word, the sermon, the message, or counseling words. Yet, after church is over they cannot tell what it was. Their hardened hearts do not make any difference in the way they live during the week. They do not apply the sermon to how they use their finances. A culture's grip, patterns of living, other voices, the media, the almighty dollar's security, and old habits have a hold on them. "Faith" does not hold them in the stronghold of the Lord although they profess a little faith to keep them going. They are not serving the Almighty, first and foremost. As they grow spiritually, beyond faith, "Faith" will have them. God's purposes will capture them. God will soften their hearts to be shaped from rigid to faithful.

Anxious Hearts. The cares of the world, the weeds and thistles crowd out the ability to change. Although they are knowledgeable and willing, clients are not able to change. Those with anxious hearts do not hear, or if they do, their anxiety makes them unable to try new options. For them it is difficult to move out of their comfort zone, to face new or additional realities, and to transfer spiritual developments to new financial management. The counselor can prescribe activities to overcome crippling anxieties such as helping other people less fortunate, walking everyday, belonging to a supportive-loving group, and other means. Scripture reminds us to cast our anxieties upon the Lord for he cares for us. The yoke is easier to carry when we allow the Lord to help us carry it.

Communication. The counselor should address the client frequently by his or her first name or title, even in prayer. Non-verbal communication is important, such as making sure the body posture communicates an interest in helping. (Pastor Everett did the opposite when he sat on the patient's bed facing the opposite way.) While conducting an interview, avoid slouching in chair, looking out the window, at the ceiling or floor. Maintain good eye contact. The counselor's tone of voice should project both confidence and a willingness to help. Do not misjudge one's depth of feeling or concern for the problem. Although this sounds basic, there are many reports of pastors violating this and "brushing off" concerns. Young people erroneously have been told, "Do not worry about it. It will work out." Some shepherds do not identify with their people's problems. Advice for counselors include: Do not argue with people or react negatively to ideas too soon. Do not engage in compulsive advice-giving, i.e., "If I were you," approach.

Paradoxical Communication. Evan stopped going to church after he had confided in the pastor. He could not face him Sunday after Sunday knowing that he knew his terrible sin. The pastor needs to assure communication and respect will continue with confidentiality? June is good at giving excuses for financial insolvency or irresponsibility. She is defensive and rationalizes, finding these things necessary to protect her self-respect. The Cains cover up real feelings such as anxiety, concern and worry. Willingness and ability for change come with time. The counselor's skill facilitates change. In some cases, rather than being dishonest, people are telling the truth as they perceive it. When not getting the whole story or changing the heart, all the counselor can do at the time is offer suggestions, planting seeds, from which people decide the options and path. Pray for revelation of the truth.

"We" Communication. The counselor uses "we" to convey support and that someone is "walking with" them on solving a financial problem. "We" is not used to assume both parties have the same perspective or opinion. "The use of 'we' statements is a method of not appearing in a superior position, on the one hand, and also of inviting active collaboration by people in resolving their own dilemmas, on the other hand," putting "counselors beside them as allies."[7] The "we" approach helps keep people from feeling threatened. The power of "we" supports the mutuality principle in shepherd counseling.

Supporting the Dream

The dilemma for the counselor is encouraging the dream process and support the people's ability to dream versus asking them to face reality. The counselor may feel it necessary to help modify the dream, after knowing the basis of it. Helpful discussion includes giving suggestions to meet the dream and goals with fewer resources or with less expensive resources. As mentioned before, the goal of a counseling session is to give at least one idea without doing harm. Harm is in belittling the dream. The counselor rejoices with Amos that he can still dream rather than allowing disillusionment and bitterness to cripple him. The counselor handles gently the ideas and dreams of Amos even if they appear irrational. If the dream is perceived as harmful, dream shifting is necessary. It is better to err on the side of grace and compassion. The counselor facilitates achievement and builds morale to achieve the seemingly "impossible dream." As the disciples were ordinary people who did extraordinary things with the power of the Spirit, the counselor facilitates this infilling of the Spirit to achieve dreams.

Summary

In summary, financial counseling directs problem-solving by discovering the root causes, clarifying misconceptions and allaying ungrounded fears, communicating relevant information, predicting trouble, isolating the immediate problem, and helping clients embrace change. Alternative solutions are discussed. Resources and their use are evaluated. Structured plans are established.

---

7   Howard Clinebell. *Understanding and Counseling Persons with Alcohol, Drugs, and Behavioral Addictions.* Nashville: Abingdon Press. 1998. P. 335.

Concrete steps are taken toward solving problems. A crisis may become an opportunity for growth and positive change through the counselor's communication.

Counseling, like preaching, is a dialogue between the Spirit of God and the heart of the listener. Shepherds facilitate this dialogue by praying with people, creating a conducive climate, and telling stories that touch the heart. In prayer, the Spirit is asked to guide the *minds* of both counselor and client with facts and thinking, the *souls* through faith, the *heart* with emotions, and the *strength* with energy to act or change. In prayer, the listener is asked to respond with understanding financial behavior in terms of loving God with heart, soul, mind, and strength (Mark 12:30).

Crisis Intervention Management

Who is having a crisis? Does the shepherd notice the one who is limping, who is broken? Does the shepherd catch the "bid" the individual gives which would indicate a deep concern or a grave confusion? Then, the shepherd follows through with a question. A crisis is when something has happened which necessitates outside help. Lost and scared people cannot think straight or see possibilities, thinking "this is the end." The shepherd helps people see hope "when there is an end, there is a beginning" (hymn phrase). One Chapter has ended but not the book. "In the bulb there is a flower.......only God can see."[8]

The shepherd counselor leads the steps by utilizing one or more approaches. Steps in "crisis counseling" involve picking up the pieces, stopping the bleeding, and starting some healing. This includes time to grieve and recover from shock. This includes identifying resources personally and spiritually, naming options, getting help, facing reality, refocusing, relearning, and taking one step. This includes redefining one's identity and source of security. The goal is to get through the day and move through the shock and denial stages to generate alternatives for accepting a new *Chapter* in life.

In this "solution-oriented" counseling, it is unnecessary to search for all the underlying causes. The goal is to mobilize resources to meet the immediate crisis.[9]

Immediately when a crisis occurs, the shepherd can help the person ask, "What next?" rather than just moaning and groaning, scared to death. Rather than focusing on *why* something happened, energy and discussion can focus on "What next?" Three options help people feel they can have hope. The crisis counselor asks, "What now? What can one do?" "What can the Great Shepherd do?" After denial stage, acceptance that something or someone will not change at this time is useful for moving forward. The shepherd can assist people to write on a card what will change and on another card what will not change.

Everything is fuzzy to people when in crisis and their minds wander. Since the attention span is short, the shepherds help to refocus or keep them engaged. Repetition is all right because they may have trouble listening as anxieties may overcome them. Rephrasing is good until reaching an agreement. The counselor stops cyclical thinking and presents alternatives. The counselor encourages those in crisis to think outside their "box," the narrow range of options they see available to them. Together counselor and person lists priorities in order of urgency the steps that need to be taken.

---

8   In the Bulb there is a Flower. Natalie Sleeth. 1985. Copyright 1986 Hope Publishing Co.

9   Clinebell. Ibid. Pp. 366-367.

The shepherd can shorten the time of explanations if messages are presented in the counselee's dominant method of processing information. Cues from words used by the counselee can indicate whether the counselee is visual, auditory, or kinesthetic. Then, if visual, the shepherd uses pictures, drawings, graphs, and the word "seeing." If auditory, the shepherd uses tapes, talking, sermons, Scripture references, and the word "hearing." If kinesthetic, which is feeling, the shepherd touches the heart, expresses emotion, and transfers by stories. Learning time is shortened by determining the dominant method of processing and the receiver will grasp the message more quickly. All three methods are used in group counseling or when the counselor does not know the dominant method.

Pastor Mike is a "crisis intervener" as well as a "change agent." He is an expert in counseling. He separates them from the problem, the work from the worker, and helps them fight the enemy, not each other. He is good at assisting people to rethink goals and expectations. He reminds them how they survived in previous crises and how they learned from them; and, therefore, they can make it again.

In some cases, rather than crisis intervention, the shepherd's role is assisting individuals to *manage a financial crisis* or to manage crises as a way of life. Change in outlook as well as income and outlays are required. Simple steps are implemented, such as spending a certain number of hours each day on the crisis or crises (rather than all the time) and, in addition, time on God-infilling perhaps by being "in the Word."

The crisis from being lost in the valley of financial despair can open the minds and hearts of people to seek God's wisdom through Biblical teachings. They may be open to talk with shepherds who can guide them in paths with stronger shoes or out of captivity, confusion, and fear. The crisis opens possibilities to change priorities, procedures, or expectations. Perhaps a crisis has been thrust upon them. Perhaps mistakes have caught up with them. Perhaps underestimating expenses and overestimating income have brought crushing reality to their increased standard of living, while real income and purchasing power have been decreasing. Perhaps they are in legal, consumption, or management trouble. The old goals did not materialize and new financial goals are needed to restore them to wholeness.

Illustrations of Financial Crises

The path seems smooth and the way is clear for a while. There is not much money even though the traveler had been careful and disciplined. Suddenly there is a "blow out," a bump in the road that upsets everything.

Several illustrations explain. Toby, a single mother, is so disturbed about her ex-husband trying to get custody of their daughter, she cannot concentrate on work. Now she has lost her job from going to court so often. Peter's car needed repair, causing him to miss the rent payment again. Lelia, a young mother, feels rejected by her mother. She disapproves of her having a child and does not help care for the granddaughter. It is Easter and Lelia remembers that her mother did not buy her Easter outfits like the other girls had. So this year, Lelia used credit again to buy $300 of clothing at Penneys. It is most important to prove to her mother she can provide. She paraded her little girl in front of her mother's house. Todd is paid hourly. When recovering from a motorcycle accident, he did not get paid. He wants a short-term loan from the church. (Another motorcyclist received a large settlement from the accident. He wanted to know what to do with the money.)

Albert and Betty always have a back-to-school crisis. They would rather save face to their children than pay off credit card debt. Albert's oldest son starts college. His financial aid has not been received yet. Albert helps him buy $450 worth of books. Some of the interests on credit cards was over 20 percent. They were not dumb, just desperate to use credit. Betty's daughter started a job so Betty paid for her deposit and first month's rent on an apartment with credit. Now collectors are calling Albert and Betty for all payments due plus court costs which are in the hundreds each month. They could be jailed for a contempt of court order if they do not show up at the court.

Ellen's furnace failed in the cold of winter. She was already having trouble buying medicine. Susan is required to travel with her job, using credit as she goes. Instead of using the reimbursement for travel expenses she pays for insurance. Now she must visit her ailing mother in a distant state. She needs gas money.

Ethan was vice president of the bank. When it merged, he lost his job of 15 years. The mortgage payment is two months in arrears and the car payment is three months overdue. He is faced with moving. He does not want to leave the big church where he is the board chair.

Although embarrassing, these crises brings the individuals and families to the shepherd. Although fearful, they swallow their pride to seek counseling. The shepherd stops the bleeding and helps them get through the day. The shepherd directs them to emergency food and housing. Emergency food stamps are ordered through the Internet. The shepherd, at the least, gives them "one good idea and does no harm." The shepherd needs to reflect on their cases before suggesting further changes. That will come later. He or she must get their commitment to work on long-term changes. Someone could be assigned as a money coach or a mentor possibly from church. Otherwise, they will learn to manage crisis as a way of life and using the shepherd as a Band-Aid or a quick fix.

Budget to Control the Bleeding

Financial bleeding is stopped by a so-called "budget." The budget is a set amount for each category to control spending, for plugging the leaks. The tourniquet cannot be too tight or there will be an eruption because, regardless of the situation, money is needed for personal care, appearance, maintaining self-respect, and freedom in little things. A budget limits the amount used for addictions, for buying more collectibles, or for entertainment. A budget helps to break a habit of uncontrolled spending. (The reader can notice the word "a" not "the" budget because there are different types for the problem and personality of the client. See Chapter 4.) The budget plan eliminates the problem of deciding each time how much to spend. It reduces spending and increases debt payments for getting out of debt. The bleeding has to stop somewhere, somehow, and so the budget is an aid, not a noose. The budget counselor can suggest ways to reduce spending because the people in crisis see everything in a confused way, not seeing or hearing clearly. When the budget is set up, limits are set down for a period of time. Can I ? Should I? issues are discussed. Values and priorities are clarified. Spending is reduced so sharing with other people and giving to the work of God's kingdom can be increased.

The tourniquet stops the bleeding, which gives hope. Hope is unrealistic if the budget is unrealistic. **To stop bleeding:** stop restaurant meals, stop eating expensive foods or drinking expensive drinks, stop renting videos, use car only when combining trips, do more walking or taking the bus, stop newspaper, stop paying for features on cell phone, telephone or cable TV features not used often, eat only for survival not for entertainment, stop impulsive spending, turn down the thermostat in winter, and use electricity only for bare necessity.

Time is of Essence

Why did the crisis occur even if there were warnings before hand?   Reasons are: - Preoccupation with other areas of life.
- Thinking if they ignore it, it will go away.
- Not knowing that ignoring a problem usually costs more than trying to solve it.
- Not wanting to experience pain again.
- Fearing change.
- Lacking confidence to handle it by themselves.
- Not able to handle more than one task at a time.
- Not having been in the situation before or seeing anyone else go through it.
- Spending time fighting friends and family rather than the real enemy.

In crisis counseling, time has run out. The ideal time for help is past. While the crisis was coming, danger signs were ignored. People finally come for help. There is no time for complete data gathering, a committee meeting to review the situation, an assessment of the church's budget to see if it can help financially. Compassion is more important than policy. Support and options must be clear and strong. Urgent options are discussed. The counseling session is stopped in time before another office closes to get food for the children or before the deadline to appeal a case. Action must be taken before the crisis gets worse not waiting until a series of lessons are completed. Action gets people out of danger such as to a sheltered home for women and children. On the other hand, means are taken to stall for time such as preventing the marriage before terrible mistakes are made, the divorce to give time for reconciliation or sound judgments, the collection of bills that are not the person's, or repossession of the car. The car is hidden to prevent repossession so things may be worked out with the creditor. Since the time for house foreclosure has already been extended, options and contacts must be made quickly. Every day of postponement costs money. However, to have realistic plans which can be fulfilled, more data must be collected.

The shepherd assists in prioritizing since in a crisis people may be confused and clinging to outmoded thinking and deceptive or destructive feelings. However, the shepherd asks the individuals in the family what their priorities are. Family members may not agree. Do not always assume their priorities. Honor the people's feelings and situation without insulting. The shepherd is firm but kind.

A lay leader or mentor can be appointed in crisis ministry to do what needs to be done, i.e. take one to the hospital or arrange for immediate needs such as school supplies so children can get started on time in school. The lay leader stays with people to translate, find some food, get bus tokens (or passes,) get an emergency loan, arrange for utilities to be paid, or use some money from the "emergency fund."

One of the shepherd's tools is a list of agencies, their addresses, telephone numbers, eligibility requirements, hours and contact persons. A community crisis center should have this information. The shepherd gives information about entitlements and reasons why people fail to get them without making promises until details are checked.

The shepherd calling the agency may get the person's name higher on the waiting list. The shepherd can get the team members working to rescue those in crisis. This creates "a circle of love."

The team consists of family, community agencies, professionals, friends, clergy and other people. The shepherd has reference material which quickly provides information about the legal process, small claims court, and consumer rights. A diagram of the legal process shows where people are currently and what the options are. The shepherd helps prepare exhibits of current income and expenditures to take to the attorney or court. Confidence can be built by discussing questions that might be asked.

The shepherd helps people live with the consequences of past mistakes, failures in the past and how to handle them. Rather than taking loan consolidation or bankruptcy, a particular person can learn to handle a nasty call everyday, for example. The shepherd helps sort out what is urgent, major, and minor, not letting the client focus mainly on the minor. What change must be done now and what can be long-term?

Technical and Spiritual Responses

Responses must be timely, technical, and spiritual. Lou and Leona called Pastor Fern about their son who recently wrote an E-mail telling of his grave danger on a new job. Amos is in a third-world country and reports the "government is terribly corrupt and many are evil." Recently two of the men under his supervision were hacked to pieces while protecting the borders from smuggling. He is scared and tired of all the killings. Amos was complaining that his employer had not finalized his insurance package and he had not received the protective materials he needed. Pastor Fern, the crisis intervener, responds: "1) immediately get stop-gap insurance for Amos for loss of limb and disability; 2) pay for it since you have said you have power of attorney; 3) do not delay, do it now and write your son; 4) do not believe anyone who says, 'Do not worry, I'll take care of it.' Follow and check on the person's actions; 4) Remember God is a higher power than guns; and 5) write the 23rd Psalm, Psalm 91, and Psalm 103 to your son immediately." The spiritual as well as the financial crises is met with urgency, questions, and action to prevent more crises. Strength is in the Lord and peace is in taking some action.

The shepherd is called to save the lost, heal the financially ill, the captive in addictions, the tempted, the tormented, and those battered or broken by other people. The shepherd assists the grieving process which is necessary for financial renewal after loss of a job, change in lifestyle, law suit, etc.. The process is shock, grieving, remorse, and repentance. The counselor "gives permission" to grieve for a time, longer for some than other people. For the process to work, people need time to grieve. There are mistakes, misdeeds, and losses. Action helps the grieving. Some financial issues must be dealt with and not repressed because time will not heal otherwise. Some things have to become worse before they can get better. On the other hand, focusing on the next financial steps and helping someone "less fortunate" aid the grieving.

Time is needed to fulfill the consequences of bad decisions or wrong commitments. Time and practice are needed to overcome temptations. However, taking too much time can add problems and postpone grieving. The shepherd helps people make a crisis an opportunity for learning, for growth, for dependence on God, and for building character. They encourage people to pray continuously about everything (including financial affairs), and keep on praying. The shepherd affirms that God is with them in the financial decisions, changes, plans, and communication with businesses, creditors, and family members.

The shepherd must break into the crisis circle. Shepherds help people move to the resolution process, deal with the issues as they are able, and give time to accept reality. Then they can deal with financial issues. In the meantime, they are protected from performing irrationally or too quickly which would bring greater financial crisis.

Need for Warning

Shepherds have an obligation to point out the danger signs of an impending crisis. Do shepherds have an obligation to warn people? Yes, without forcing their values on them. They are obligated to tell them the consequences if they continue their patterns of thinking or behavior. People think they can just put a toe in the water and not be swept up. If they are swept away, they die in yielding to temptation. Sometimes, people blame the shepherd for not warning them: "Why did you not warn me about slipping into the hole or becoming captive to sin?" Their blood is on the shepherds for not warning them (Ezekiel 3:17-19).

"Crisis" comes from the Greek meaning turning point. The two Chinese characters for crisis are "opportunity" and "disaster." The shepherd assists people to go a different direction as well as meet the "challenge" of the crisis. Crises are times when people are often open to change. Therefore, opportunities to intervene that might have been rejected under calm circumstances are now accepted. As noted before, change is difficult and part of the client will not want to change or pay the cost. However, in a crisis, the "pain of NOT changing" becomes clearer and this is why crises are often necessary to spur change.

Prayer for the Journey to Financial Recovery

At the beginning, the prayer asks for hearts and minds to be aware of God's Presence. It gives thanks for the teaching of the Great Counselor who is "in the midst of the two or three gathered together in Jesus' name." The prayer request can be for the willingness to listen to the voice of God, to learn the principles of financial management and for seeking self-control. A blessing can be asked for the conversation that it will nourish the soul. Request can be to avoid the temptations and commercialism surrounding people. The prayer can ask for spiritual discernment as well as financial wisdom. Thanks can be given for the "Word" which teaches and inspires such as Proverbs 25:28: "Whoever has no rule over one's own spirit is like a city without walls."

At the end of the session, thanks is given for God's guidance, forgiveness for mistakes, and grace for imperfections in the use of money. Continued mercy and strength are asked for as one journeys through the financial valleys and up steep, rugged mountains.

The model is in Philippians 4:6-7 (NKJ): "Be anxious for nothing but in everything by prayer and supplication, with thanksgiving, let your requests be known to God, and the peace of God, which surpasses all understanding, will guard your hearts and minds through Christ Jesus."

◊◊◊ ⧗　⧗ ◊◊◊

Chapter 3. In The Valley of the Shadows, Financial Management in Times of Distress

God loves the people he created. People can choose to accept this love or continue to be in the valley of the shadows or in the crisis mode. Principles of financial management that reflect acceptance of God's love are inferred in illustrations of real people in this chapter. The shepherd can shed some light and guide through the valley of the shadows. Shepherds, counselors, and others "anointed to release the captives" (Luke 4:18) define the shadow or storm, why it came, and how to walk through it with financial management. The counseling session, as in a sermon, follows this format of *what, so what*, and *now what*. The shepherd motivates people to be willing to serve: lay leaders, people in the outreach ministry, chaplains, counselors, mentors, or volunteers with a servant's heart. When the counselor has developed a supportive climate and created willing hearts to serve those in need, someone will rise to answer the call. In the "priesthood of all believers" (as some denominations believe) people are assigned to walk alongside those in need, pray with them, deal with issues, aid in decision-making, give information, facilitate a resolution, and help them allow God to heal. Healing is possible with accepting God's love and grace.

The shepherd-counselor helps calm the storm, or at least, calms the person. Although the path is not made easier, the shepherd can help shoes to be stronger. If the person is depressed, discouraged and blinded to possibilities, the shepherd-counselor opens eyes to alternatives for walking up the mountainside. The counselor unleashes the stronghold for those caught in the thickets of credit, overspending, or addictions. The counselor helps those with paralyzing threats of danger and lifts the fallen from bad financial decisions and ignorance. The shepherd helps to unburden those crushed by too much materialism or those overwhelmed with responsibilities. Regardless of whether the problem is from external events outside one's control or from the person's mismanagement, the shepherd opens the gate and points to paths beyond.

The counselor coordinates or works on a team with the helping professional, social worker, parole officer, legal services attorney, insurance agent, trust officer, accountant, employee benefits official, and psychological or marriage counselor. Team members may be the State Attorney General, Family and Child Protection Services, Social Service Department at the hospital, neighborhood housing authority, utility company, food stamp office, meals on wheels, food banks, health clinic, career counselor, and visiting nurse. It may involve negotiating with creditors, landlords, attorneys and judges, employers, and hospitals. As Jesus fed the 5,000, the shepherd knows where to get food immediately and long-term, participating in the miracle. The shepherd participates in miracles beyond giving fish by teaching how to fish and, maybe, how to cook it.

Both men and women are spiritual leaders and helpmates. Both are responsible for financial management. If both cannot attend counseling, the shepherd works with one or the other. In some cases it might be a child. Someone has to take charge if the ship is off course or sinking and no one else is at the helm.

The shepherd counsels with empathy and understanding rather than legalism and judgement, leaving the way open for God's way and purpose - far bigger than imagined. Compassion rather than policy should be the rule. For example, definite answers and absolutes such as the simplistic "live within your means," "never use credit," or "women always stay at home rather than men," "spiritual leadership is always assumed by men," and "get rid of your son's dog since you cannot afford it" are inappropriate without explanation.

Sometimes, the individual or family may need to spend money on higher values and on celebrations; and sometimes it needs stricter budget control. Money is used to repair family break-ups, office politics, wounded hearts, shattered dreams, broken toys, and threatened health. When couples fight with money, the shepherd helps them fight in more constructive and less expensive ways, communicating rather than showing revenge or trying to get even.

Walking in the Storms

The path is smooth and sunny. Then suddenly shadows fall. A storm comes up suddenly. The dark side of money fills heart, soul, and mind. Storms come from decreased income from reduced hours, mergers, a lower-paying job or diminished return on investments. Most severe is a change in employment status. Adverse politics causes erratic spending behavior. A business may fail if the product or service is no longer purchased, economic/business conditions change, shortage of raw materials arises, and weather changes lifestyles. Borrowing ability may be affected. Change in economic cycles and conditions of the larger economy affect people more than their personal financial management. Yet, poor personal management brings on storms and shadows.

Other storms are billing errors, wrongful debt obligation, or defective merchandise. People may be a victim of unscrupulous or fraudulent advice, practice or scheme. Storms are loss of ability to fulfill job or home responsibilities because of physical disability or depression. A family may need to support a parent or someone else. An elderly or younger relative may move into the home, temporarily or in prolonged dependency. Premature death of a spouse or a birth of a child causes financial disruptions. An unexpected retardation or disability as well as illnesses and accidents affect income and expenses.

A lawsuit is a storm. So is divorce, whether unexpected or as a result of creeping disloyalty, selfishness, or financial mismanagement. The costs of divorce have driven many people into bankruptcy or financial depletion. Standard of living is lowered.

Housing repairs can spark a storm. Sometimes they could have been predicted such as furnace breakdown, roof, and appliance failures. Usually expenses are unexpected or underestimated. Price increase in electricity and property taxes are unexpected. Car repair is another storm.

On the sunny side, expenses connected with outstanding talent of a family member must be reckoned with income. The family recognizes outstanding abilities that need to be cultivated, but does not know how to provide it. Also, there are weddings or celebrations of friends, relatives, and children causing huge, irregular expenses. Fleeting joys are erratic. In the future the budget will balance if both saving and sharing accounts for irregular expenses are replenished from the times of celebrations and passages.

Counselors can help clients survive the storm by suggesting alternatives for solving problems or, at least, making them more manageable. Consumer education materials can be displayed and made accessible. Information booklets on topics such as consumer law, divorce, budgeting, reducing expenses, adjusting debts, or utility assistance can be given and discussed.

People often walk blindly into a storm. Though there were signs, they did not see the storm coming, and mismanaged their financial path. Now the darkness is upon a client. Counselors assist in changing the attitude toward what has happened. Although financial stability is threatened or ruined, abundant life can be found in God's love, peace, and provisions. What can the shepherd do to serve the lost, the bewildered, the mismanagers, the irresponsible, and the financially incompetent? First, they can see God in the midst of the storm. Things are not as bad as they seem when they know God is walking with them, meets them in their suffering; and is "in the midst of the two or three gathered together" while working on financial affairs. Second, when the shepherd and people understand the storm, options can be identified and solutions chosen. This gives a sense of peace. Financial renewal is possible. Character is built in suffering and change. The "refining fire" brings a bright luster of hope when reflecting the Light.

Financial storms or problems may be the result of misdirected worldly passions, poor management over time, insufficient income, or inappropriate spending patterns. Many people have no planning. They have only self-indulgences, lack of self-discipline, and ignorance.

Financial problems are related to other personal problems. They are sometimes the cause and sometimes the effect. Loss of employment and the accompanying financial stress may contribute to substance abuse problems. Alternately, substance abuse caused by behavioral problems can cause the loss of employment leading to financial crisis. Financial anxieties cause job, car, and home accidents, or at least, the loss of concentration on the job.

Symptoms of Financial Distress or Disorder

These symptoms include:
- Dishonesty about spending is on purpose or manipulative
- Addictions taking from basic needs of children or other family members
- Inability to make rent/mortgage payment
- Not answering the phone because creditors, etc. are after them
- No longer having a phone
- Not concentrating or listening to sermon because financial anxieties or job insecurity are interfering, dominating
- Reporting that they cannot pray or feel the blessing because disturbed about financial affairs, stressed out all the time, and irritable
- Spiritual malfunction which causes financial dysfunction
- Credit is maxed and there is no savings or source for an emergency or unusual, valuable, vital opportunity
- Not sleeping at night and not concentrating on work during the day
- Relying on overdraft protection by which credit is taken in larger increments
- Borrowing to pay debts
- Paying late fees, bad check fees, and over the limit fees
- Threatened or actual foreclosure, cut in service, loss of goods, or court action
- Perceiving credit as a resource rather than a debt.

Each day the financial shadows in the valley spread fear and build the storm. The shepherd-counselor is the non-anxious person. In light of the circumstances, the counselor could justifiably be anxious, but he or she directs this into useful activity. The Spirit gives courage to continue.

Fear Abounds

The Great Shepherd guides from the valley of the shadows to the table of the blessings. *"Although I walk through the valley of the shadows I will fear no evil for you are with me"* (Psalm 23). *"Fear not, for I have redeemed you; I have called you by name; You are Mine. When you pass through the waters, I will be with you; And through the rivers, they shall not overflow you. When you walk through the fire, you shall not be burned, Nor shall the flame scorch you, for I am the Lord your God"* (Isaiah 43:1-3). Fear is addressed in Psalm 103, Isaiah 43, and many other places. "Fear not" - the Great Shepherd is with people throughout the ages. The shepherd understands fear motivates people to do something about their situation, to come for financial counseling. Too much fear immobilizes and keeps them from walking up the rugged pathway. This fear of God is the foundation for wisdom. This is awe, reverence, awareness of God, submission to his authority, surrender to his will, primary allegiance to his kingdom, conscience, and motivation to follow commandments. Jesus said, "Do not be afraid of those who kill the body but cannot kill the soul. Rather, be afraid of the one who can destroy both soul and body in hell" (Matthew 10:28).

Financial Management Principles Inferred by Real People

Below are scenarios of fear and financial failure which describe predicaments and provide understanding of financial dilemmas. Inferred are suggestions for the shepherd to use if not stated directly. Nevertheless, resolving financial disorder and distress for any scenario uses a new plan or budget chosen from "chapter four." Completion of the budget on paper shows the reorganization and resolutions of problems or confusion.

Nancy and Nathan underestimate expenses because they lack experience, have few or no records, forget incidental costs and purposely minimize costs to justify expenditures. They do not even estimate expenses for making decisions or a budget.

Nancy continuously overestimates income by not calculating paycheck deductions and taxes withheld. She increases spending, not realizing the increase in wages or a bonus has been offset by inflation. Real income in terms of constant dollars, "purchasing power," has not increased while creeping indebtedness has.

Nancy and Nathan do not communicate about finances from the desire to avoid an emotional issue, inability to express oneself, or lack of concern. Overwhelmed with bills and expenses, Nancy and Nathan do nothing. They do not even open the mail from businesses and creditors. They are scared to death – a financial and a spiritual death.

Alfred is unable to say "no" to his children, sales pressures, and to himself.

He feels guilty about what happened in the past and is trying to reconcile past deprivation.

Lillie does not plan anything in her life. She tries but cannot stick with a plan. The plans are usually unrealistic anyway. Her spending is geared to desires, wants and peer pressure rather than to income. She has identified a lifestyle that she is determined to maintain no matter what. She uses credit to achieve and maintain her lifestyle regardless of whether it is supported by current income. She lacks a system for paying bills, a personal business system, or a way of keeping track of credit used or owed. She pays just the minimum on her credit card which will keep her in bondage forever.

Frank and Betty have not designated one person in the family as the "main manager" to control money flow, keep records, meet financial obligations on time, and communicate financial position. Therefore, "Everybody's responsibility is nobody's responsibility" and chaos results. For example, three members are using the same credit card account and make purchases unknown to the other members. No one is designated to make payments on the account in a timely manner. When someone does transfer funds, he or she has no idea of how much to cover in order to prevent creeping indebtedness. One member blames the other when in trouble saying, "I thought you were taking care of it!" Late payments have costly fees. These are costs for lack of communication and control.

Perry, similar to the majority, counts just the monthly payment and not total cost of purchases over a period of time. Perry's real total costs include upkeep, maintenance, fees, etc. in addition to credit. Therefore comparing total costs of various products or services is wise and efficient. Comparing cash versus using credit is this: Monthly payment X's number of months = Cost. Cost minus cash price = Cost of using credit. Total cost = cash + credit + maintenance fee + upkeep.

Marge buys and then tries to plan how to pay rather than vice versa. If she were creative and cared about frugality, she would consider alternatives to buying.

Taylor forgets to get promises in writing. She has even signed a blank form, at one time, believing someone who said, "We will fill it in later." Worse yet, she co-signed for a friend who did not pay the debt, and now Taylor must pay it.

Tom promises to pay more than his income allows. He is both scared and conscientious. Of course, he cannot complete promises. He should have been conservative in what he could repay.

Lewis lets pride and stubbornness prevent paying bills or solving a problem. When he gets mad at a business or landlord, he takes revenge by not paying for revenge. It just hurts him rather than them.

Aaron is weak at handling money. He makes mathematical errors and does not try to calculate the balance in a checking account. He does not keep his checkbook up-to-date. Aaron does not know the status of the checking or credit account so he pays fees for over drafts and writing bad checks. Some times, he is so desperate he does not care. He uses whatever source of income, he can find, thinking credit is a legitimate source.

Ruth seems to always get a lemon. She uses ineffective consumer complaint procedures. She gets mad and tells friends rather than asserting her consumer or legal rights.

Mavy is like many other people. She does not understand the credit process or how to control its use. She is incompetent in the credit world. Mavy maxes one card and switches to another card until all her cards are fully maxed. She uses store credit and finances her car with a high interest loan from a used car lot because it is convenient. If she were to calculate potential savings by comparing loans, her time would reward her over $200 per hour.

Michael, although brilliant in some areas and highly educated, does not recognize the danger signs of over-extended credit, loan consolidation, refinancing, or second mortgages. Comparing the original debt plan with proposed plans of refinancing or loan consolidation reveals higher interest costs. These cost more over time even though interest rate is lower. He could increase income and reduce expenses rather than use the more costly loan consolidation and new loans.

Esther uses money for emotional reasons. She makes up for past deprivation or insecurity. She boosts ego or soothes wounds. She seeks revenge by mismanagement, creating a sense of power, controlling other people, replacing responses of affection and appreciation, compensating for feelings of inadequacy, and impressing other people. If these emotional reasons for spending are understood and accepted by herself and her family, harm to them is negated.

Ben is a young man who uses credit to buy an old truck, which will need repair or replacement before the payments are completed. He has the skills to do the repair, not the mathematics skills to calculate costs of repairs. He is paying for a second car while repairing the first one.

Fred does not control expenses such as gambling, renting videos, entertainment eating, buying water and drinks, gas for the car, or telephone charges. He does not control anything else in his life.

Glen and Pearl do not have a cash reserve or credit for emergency use. They live at the edge and spend more every month than their income. They do not have even one month's income saved for emergency or opportunity, which would also cover the problem of underestimating expenses. Before they start investing, Glen and Pearl should have six months of income saved for covering time of unemployment, changing jobs, illness, accident, major appliance/car breakdown, care for someone, or required travel.

Ruth has conflict on the job. People cause her trouble. They are cruel and spread false rumors about her. Her healing and therapy is overspending.

Noble selfishly spends money before his family members' needs are met. For revenge, his wife spends more. She thinks, "Why cooperate when Noble does not care?"

Matthew thinks someone will bail him out, as they have always done in the past. So he is happy-go-lucky in financial management. Matthew, a loving and kind person, counts on help from parents, the system, and kind-hearted people.

Wyman has a compulsive personality. He is compulsive in gambling, drinking, smoking, eating, and spending in general. His behavior is addictive. He cannot control it, even if he sees the devastating results on his finances and family.

Sally and Sam experience creeping indebtedness by paying just the minimum on their credit cards, rather than paying off the amount owed each month. To cover bad checks, money is taken from the credit union's credit account. If the check is for $5.00 more than the checking account contains, $100 is transferred from the credit account, since transfer is in $100 increments. This is causing creeping indebtedness.

Dan and Donna neither utilize educational information nor professional advisors when needed. They do not realize that the benefits from these services would offset fees.

Blair blames other people for his mistakes and predicaments, playing the "blame game." He does not want to take responsibility with his own direction. Changing these patterns are challenges for the shepherd.

Peggy sees only failure and hopelessness for herself. Actually, she has good ideas. Peggy can be asked what she would advise other people to do if they were in her predicament. Then, she might apply them to herself. She does not realize her own power, confidence, and wisdom.

Patty has no goals or visions directing and disciplining her finances. Her lack of savings attests to this. When she identifies goals, she can change step by step to meet them.

Loss of Income. The loss is from loss of job, recently unemployed, laid off, fired, or rendered obsolete. People fear they will lose control, respect, and identity. When fired, Jake abused his spouse and children. He withdrew from group participation and feared meeting someone who would ask questions. In another case, Emily was so abusive to her husband when he lost his job that she forced him to leave early on the bus and come back after dark so no one else would know he lost his job. Her husband was not allowed to tell his children. Unemployed persons might consider doing volunteer work, thus maintaining respect and dignity as well as feeling needed and useful.

Fear of People. Susan learned fear from being bullied, belittled, and treated unfairly. Politics at the office caused Susan to overspend on little things, which became her therapy. She forgot to pay bills on time. She used her credit card for eating or drinking to escape pain. Expensive vacations were purchased with credit in vain attempts to heal the trauma from interactions and insults received at work. Susan transferred the abusive treatment to members of her family, making them scapegoats.

Making a Mistake. Families make mistakes and financially suffer from them. They have to work through the consequences. Many middle income families do not have financial space for making mistakes or have the ability to rebound from them. Because they feel incompetent or are lazy, they hire people to service house, yard, or car; use take-out food for parties; and tax preparers for work which they could do. Lack of skills makes them feel incompetent and frightened of making mistakes. They are scared of using the computer and the ATM. They cannot balance a checkbook. They have been caught by not reading the "fine print" and lost possessions. Practice can build their confidence.

Fear Strikes. Conversely to some other people, the Hares do not have enough fear or knowledge of consequences for not making payments on time. Over-draft fees and fees for banking accounts are exorbitant. When "lightening strikes," the Hares rightfully fear and experience the consequences. Expenses are large and inescapable such as taxes, college debts, child support, telephone bills, and large debts. Once the Hares were threatened with auto repossession. They do not know how to talk with creditors and to get out of debt. The Hares' entire lifestyle needs reevaluating to increase income, reduce expenses, and be efficient. Mainly, they need a better household business system for sending in bill payments to get there before the due date. In another case, the Martins suffer the consequences of fraudulently obtaining food stamp and Social Security payments. They could not meet their bills and fell into the temptation of dishonesty and stealing.

Being Enslaved by Credit and Captive to Debt Brings Fear. The Macys fear answering the phone because of creditors. They fear it will be disconnected because of high long distance bills which they cannot pay. If the phone is disconnected, they will owe the entire bill plus fees to be reinstalled. The Macys fear opening the mail. They do not know where they stand with the landlord or creditor. They are afraid the credit companies will catch up with them. Once they brought to the counselor a box of unopened mail and dumped it on the desk since they could not face it alone. The Macys are afraid of meeting relatives to whom they owe money. They are becoming afraid of everything. Like those described in Leviticus 26:36-38, they are wanting to flee, not able to stand.

Jason would rather be independent than take money from his relatives, who threaten with judgment on how it is spent. An option for Jason is to swallow his pride and live with parents since they are his last resort. Pride can be protected by writing a contract stating whether or not interest is paid, when paid, and how paid, through time, help, or money. Relationships can be protected this way. Jason convinces parents a loan to him will give them a higher interest rate than they could get elsewhere. If he buys a house from them, his parents could be the mortgage holder. If they require no down payment, they will enable him to get a start in homeownership.

Living on the Edge Financially. Krista lost her job and did not know how to adjust. An option is for Krista to baby-sit for her friend, who would then cut her hair. Krista uses the shepherd's help in getting a job.

For the Beavers a large, unexpected repair was needed so they could not pay other bills. "Running the race" for the Beavers is getting through the month with credit. The four percent starter rate on a new credit jumped to 24 percent. Their disposition and happiness revolves around payday. They fear having too many creditors or maxing out the use of credit. When they max out on one card, they just start another. The Beavers could fall off the cliff if an emergency occurs or income stops. They must make drastic changes right now for economic and spiritual security. They could stop eating out and eat peanut butter, eggs and beans. They could reduce the use of utilities. They could reduce any new purchases and postpone buying a car. They could look around for anything to sell. An option is suggested in Hebrews, "Therefore, since we are surrounded by such a great cloud of witnesses, let us throw off everything that hinders and the sin that so easily entangles, and let us run with perseverance the race marked out for us" (Hebrews 12:1 NIV).

Unable to Retire. Bob fears the unknown and hates his job. He does not have the tools for projecting retirement income and expenses although he could get the information from his benefits office. Someone with a financial calculator or computer program could crunch the numbers. By calculating the different incomes at age 59, 62, or 65 with different annuity benefits, returns from personal contributions and Social Security, and the decision on when to retire can be made prudently. When he sees the figures, an option to early retirement requires an attitude adjustment. If he changes jobs, he would lose too many benefits. Part of financial planning is to lower consumption now in order to survive an assumed number of years, or to choose an investment/retirement plan that keeps pace with inflation. Expenses do not necessarily decrease with retirement. Most will have to work after retirement. Possible or probable changes in housing are fearful and uncertain. Talking with the shepherd about projected expenses and the need to change lifestyle may be useful for those who would otherwise be making decisions alone. Value clarification must occur. To protect his back and his job, Bob decides to pay for counseling every week, go fishing on weekends, and hire house cleaning. For people without good pensions, the shepherd may suggest unusual employment plans involving service to other people such as a job which provides room and board. This could be a care-giver living in the home.

Threatened Divorce. Priscilla is deciding between her economic well-being and dependency upon an abusive husband. She has left him and is trying to survive. He calls her everyday saying, "How do you like being poor," to woo her back. She has a low paying job because previously he made her give up a better paying job with future prospects as a manager. He did not want her around men. As a child care worker, Priscilla can not live independently, own a car, rent an apartment, or pay other expenses. Now they are in marriage and family counseling which also costs money. He had to have a separate counselor because he did not respect a woman counselor enough to listen to her. The marriage counselor said the time spent in counseling is usually three months for a couple. For them, it would take a year because there are so many issues. The counselors have not yet addressed the marriage issues.

Problems with Financial Abuse. Children steal money needed for their things. Nell, a church member, was stealing from her mother, forging checks to get her boyfriend out of jail. Then she was jailed and left there by parents who did not visit her because they were so mad. A gift from a person at church was given for bail money in time to get her back to school.

In the Bower family there is financial abuse, bullying from adult children, and bullying grandparents. The Bowers cannot say no to children or to parents. An option for saying "no" to the children is telling them the financial counselor who calculated the budget said for them to contribute a given amount. Communication is easier that way.

The Florences have financial problems because they bail out children in another way. They pay off credit card debt so a child can get a job. They need to confront the children to accept consequences and take responsibility. This is called "tough love."

The Smiths had to fly at the last minute to a foreign country to "rescue" their child in an exchange program. The $4000 spent took years for the Smiths to recover financially. That started the 23 year pattern of having high credit balances, paying $400 more a month just for fees plus $800 for credit with home equity loans and credit lines. After a time of restricted spending and profit from sale of real estate, they became free of debt.

Abuse. How can the shepherd protect people in his flock from continued financial abuse, either from a child or a parent? How can people say "no" and keep communication open? Blanch hid money in bed with her when asleep. That did not even prevent stealing from her. On one day her granddaughter stole her credit card and also forged a check. The granddaughter faces eight years in prison. Some children beg for money until parents give in to their children. Others have children who are so desperate from addictions, surviving in their culture, or needing to get out of a severe problem that they will go to any means such as financially abusing an elderly parent, keeping him or her in captivity to pay their bills. The shepherd helps release the captive.

The abused need help in communicating and solving a problem. When a third party is involved, a change in behavior may solve the problem or it may put the abused in more danger. A person with no money to pay for services upfront can make an appointment with a shepherd or their social service counselor upon contingency of getting more money. The basic need for money is addressed. The shepherd can help write a letter to the abuser. Job counseling and addiction counseling for the abuser must be implemented. The shepherd could refer the person to a professional for help.

The problem is not only with the abuser. Sometimes it is also with the abused. Often, certainly not always, people abused financially do not know how to set appropriate limits and may facilitate or enable the "out of control" spending or financial demands. The shepherd may need to work with the abused to learn to set limits and to say "no." Enablers are often "people pleasers" who get their self worth by trying to make everyone else happy and do not know enough about "self care."

Children. The shepherd can give a positive prediction about expenses for children. By having a telescopic view, the shepherd shows that eventually financial pressures will lessen. (Unless children and grandchildren continually need their help.) Children are an investment in human capital. Generations can work together to provide economic security. One woman said she was extra agreeable with her children as she expected to live with them in old age. Many people find themselves poor or not "getting ahead" when there are dependent children at home. However, after the children are grown, parents do have a surplus of money. The Warrens came for counseling because they were bitter that they had worked so hard and were just above eligibility for college aid themselves years ago. Now their children were ineligible for grants and financial aid. Yet, the family was not getting ahead financially even with his professional job. The only advice the counselor gave was that while they were having children, they could not "get ahead" in investments. Their gifted children were their investments, their human capital invested in education. After their children's education was paid, money could go into retirement funds for the Warrens.

Costs. Costs of "living high" and the "high cost of living" eventually cast fear. Costs are overwhelming and confusing. John is distressed to the point of suicide because he can not pay his debts. He is afraid of losing respect from his children and his wife. He wants his children to be popular. He feels guilty he cannot provide what his friends and associates do for their children. John feels guilty especially at celebrations, holidays or special times to help children. His expectations are unreasonable. The peer pressure is too great. John would rather "save face" than pay off credit and debt. John's family is emotionally sick and lost. Their whole purpose is what they can get in this life and how they appear to other people. They are devastated by negative events. These attitudes could be changed by seeking God's purposes.

Control. The whole Baker family is out of control and acts erratically. They spend out of fear that certain member (s) will leave if they do not get their way. The breakdown of communication and the breakdown of finances are connected to the fear of the break-up of the family.

False Security. The Seamans' security is threatened because they think financial security and power will make up for not feeling accepted in society and will come from accumulating things like clothes, cars, etc. These only give comfort to the Seamans temporarily. Now they cannot afford to keep them, and are forced or threatened into bankruptcy. Worse, the Seamans fear their losing their conscience over taking bankruptcy. They seek counseling because they suspect they feel no disgrace. They do not even know the disadvantage of bankruptcy or know other options. Never-the-less, the Seamans will have to accept responsibility for consequences of past decisions one way or another.

Responsible With Insufficient Income. The Godfrys want to identify with a certain church on Sunday, want to be accepted and feel they belong to it. However, they cannot keep up with its expectations requiring money and other contributions. The Godfrys are conscientious in taking responsibility for church, community, Christian education, church camp, lessons, sports participation and keeping sidewalks in repair. However, income is insufficient for all of this. Fear is not based on mismanagement but arises from their sense of conscientiousness to fulfill responsibilities while lacking "good enough" income. An option is for the wife to return to paid work. One wife got a job waitressing on weekends. Their father got to know the children better.

Financial Aid. Tom and Paula both heavily used credit and financial aid to fund their education. However, their job and career did not meet their financial expectations. Paula wants to stay home with their children. Their credit history was a handicap in getting a job, mortgage, insurance, and even getting married since each brought debt to the fledging marriage. Tom and Paula are disappointed in each other since they cannot maintain the lifestyle they had in college. Reevaluating and defining standard of living is a must.

Depression. The "black dog" of depression haunts Winston. To ward it off he spends more than he can afford and then gets more depressed, continuing the cycle. Depression is one of the reasons he drinks heavily spending about $420 monthly. For Alice, depression keeps her from getting out of bed, from getting a job, and from preparing meals for her husband who is overworked already. Winston and Alice need to get a medical/psychological assessment for their depressions. The shepherd, husband, and friend must facilitate seeking employment which gives structure to life and something to think about rather than post traumas or their problems. They must name the one goal for each day. They need to praise God in corporate worship. Alice loves God. She has experienced the help of when in trouble, "Praise God." This applies to financial trouble as Alice has run up credit balances to over $30,000 for overcoming depression. A tight structure in repaying is necessary even if the depression still exists. In praising God, there is less fear, less pain. The financial path is clearer, more sunny when assisted in handling financial affairs; more depression is avoided.

Not Facing Reality. Fear haunts Kyle and Kate as they are not able or willing to face reality. Fear exaggerates the fear and consequences. The counselor helps sort out unrealistic fears. (Fifty percent of fears never come to pass.) To them, other roles and "saving face" with children or friends are more important than controlling expenses. They do not know how to say "no."

In another counseling session, Gladys complained that her husband Bill was buying beer for his friends when they went out on Friday night although he was unemployed and could not afford the dinner or the drinks. His response was "What is a man to do?" (Is the unemployed person who is buying beer for friends asking, "How can I keep the respect of my friends?") Behind the question was his need to maintain respect, dignity, and popularity.

In another case, the Serandoz were working with the shepherd-counselor in ways to reduce expenses. Their total costs of bowling on Friday nights included babysitter, dinner, extra rounds, drinks afterwards, and gas. The Serandoz decided to find additional employment just to fund the Friday nights, rather than cut out the activity.

Keeping up with the Jones. Some people fear of not keeping up with the "Jones" whether they are associates at work, a family in church, or relatives. The "Jones" may be a perceived lifestyle of the whole social class with which they identify, erroneously perceiving the need to buy or do things for acceptance. In reality, the "Jones" do not manage that way. The "Jones" show the appearances while not disclosing the details. People may withdraw or not attend church. Some know the technique of writing down where to keep up and where not to keep up with the "Jones." Some "Jones" cannot keep up with themselves.

The "Jones" have a standard package or standard of living which keeps increasing. Meanwhile, their real income or purchasing power is decreasing. Their standard package of goods and services is defined by their peer group, identification group, or the media. The standard package does not include sharing and saving, which ultimately causes havoc with their finances. The Jones cannot keep up with themselves! The Jones act out of habit and cultural patterns rather than experimenting with different solutions to solve unique problems and to seek God's purposes unique to them.

Loneliness. Loneliness contributes to fear and unhappiness. Yvonne resolves her loneliness in the buying process, where she is treated politely, feels important, and has pleasant interaction. The two problems of loneliness and commercialism meet. Yvonne meets the needs of loneliness in ways she cannot afford. The shepherd understands how Yvonne is trying to meet basic needs in financial behavior, which do not meet the deeper needs. Until these needs are identified, healing is difficult. Options presented by the shepherd are healthy, inexpensive ways to fill the void in search for God.

Finances are Subordinate. The Masons do not fear enough because they are preoccupied with other crises, problems, and goals taking precedence. These cloud the danger signs of impending financial crisis. They are not interested in financial affairs. They do not recognize the danger. They live for the present, for pleasures, for comfort, for lusts of the flesh, to keep a job, to pass the course. They just spend money until it runs out or use credit until it is denied.

Running out of Money. The bank calls Joan and says, "You have insufficient funds." Her fear turns into panic from not having enough money. Peter thinks money is everything and checks everyday to see what is in his account. Paul says, "Money is not everything but it sure keeps the kids in touch." Mary says, "Money is not everything but I hold my breath until the Social Security check comes in so I can breathe with medicine and my Bi-PAP."

The fear of not having enough money is keenly felt by those that pursue money as the supreme goal. They think they never have enough, "For the love of money is a root of all kinds of evil, and in their eagerness to be rich some have wandered away from faith and pierced themselves with many pains. But as for you, person of God, shun all this; pursue righteousness, godliness, faith, love, endurance, gentleness" (1Timothy 6:10-11).

"Living Above One's Means"

Shepherds accuse people of "living above their means." Why? Shepherds see credit problems, a nervousness about financial affairs, or a lavish lifestyle and assume people spend more than their ability to pay. The explanation is not that simple nor is the remedy.

A desired lifestyle dominates spending for goods and services. The lifestyle is expected and assumed by colleagues, relatives, neighbors, and church members. People will obtain and maintain lifestyle regardless of income level. Credit usage fills the gap. Reducing costs is rarely possible without a determined change in lifestyle. The lifestyle must be changed to obtain abundant life in Christ and to reduce anxiety dominated by the world's acceptable lifestyle.

Another explanation is that prices for necessities of personal care, homes, transportation, tuition, etc. have increased faster than real net income. Real net income is income after income, property, and Social Security taxes are subtracted from gross income.

The explanation of underestimating expenses has been cited as the biggest financial management problem. People do not estimate and plan for total costs involved in purchases ranging from a pet, house, to tuition. One purchase necessitates or triggers other purchases - a change of wants. Then there are upkeep costs, maintenance, repair, energy usage, etc. Real culprits are irregular, seasonal, periodic, yearly or semi-yearly, and unexpected expenses that are basic necessities. People do not save for these but purchase them as they must. So every month they are behind on bills and maximize credit. A list of things for which to save would document the need for planning. In addition saving is needed for emergencies and opportunities. But then current and regular expenses must be reduced to enable living within one's means.

Problems in Spending Geared to Wants Rather than to Income and Goals. Shepherds can learn from this case typical of many Americans. It shows the financial information and counseling processes necessary in fulfilling faithfulness. Sue observed that Bob and Nancy did not have a clue how to assess their difficulties or how to get started in changing financial management. They have simply geared their spending to wants, culture's standard, peer pressure, and customs rather than to income constraints. Bob and Nancy did not think they have to make decisions, prioritize, follow a budget, or have anyone dictating constraints. They have been able to do this with credit, parent's help, and negative balances every month. This is possible until one loses a job, a crisis occurs or they are in trouble with creditors. The American way of life is supported, on the average, by spending more than family income every month. Future income, which may change, beyond one's control, has been committed. Freedom seems now while bondage is later. If there is a loss of one of their jobs, they cannot maintain their consumption or obligations. They borrow more and fall deeper into debt and spiritual despair. Blaming each other, they "fight" or consider "flight" by divorce from the situation.

Bob and Nancy will end with owing three times what they originally spent. By paying only the minimum on debts including college debts, Bob and Nancy will pay for 17 – 20 years. Loan consolidation was the road to disaster since the psychological freedom temporarily enabled them to borrow even more. Now there are more fixed payments. Each year they borrowed for vacation before the previous ones were paid. Vacations were thought necessary to withstand negatives in their lives. However, the problem was not considering inexpensive ones.

Other dangers for Bob and Nancy's spending geared to wants rather than income are around the corner. After all, nations and most families spend for what is needed and wanted rather than making decisions to keep within a monthly balance. Most manage by crisis rather than by objectives: staying out of trouble, keeping a job, keeping a family, keeping a lifestyle, dressing for acceptance at school, etc. They stumble and fumble to keep moving, using credit or money from relatives when needed. They do not face the reality that "resources are limited and wants are expanding."

Dangers for Bob and Nancy include fighting and flight when reality hits. For Bob someone or something outside their control could drastically reduce his already limited income. They turn to credit as the answer and it is denied. They miss a great opportunity that would enhance life forever when they have no reserves to pursue it. They slip into bondage to business, companies, and things. They are harassed by creditors or relatives. Anxiety prevents sleeping and working. They pay more than necessary which eventually cripples their lifestyle. They are under the control and judgment of the lender or giver. Their obligations to the giver are not clarified or finalized. Since they are unaccustomed to prioritizing, they become neurotic. They do not know how to make decisions because in a decision, something desirable is given up. They do not know how to cooperate with each other and change to reach a goal. They do not have anything to show for the goal of retirement because they have not built a surplus through years by reducing consumption from a temptation to indulge.

Another problem with Bob and Nancy's spending that is geared to wants rather than income is definition and goals. Income is a vague concept rather than a flow of goods and services, measured by income. They have not geared consumption to any income whether gross, net, regular, take-home, discretionary, or decision income. Erroneously they define credit as income. When spending is geared to wants, ten percent for a tithe and ten percent for saving are not calculated. Without savings, when the crisis occurs they cannot continue their consumption without use of credit. Without money for sharing, needs arise and are met by more credit. Without tithing or some percentage, disobedience to God and spiritual weakness continue. Financial faithfulness is broken. Facing reality is gearing spending to income available without credit. Financial faithfulness is begun when spending is geared to sharing and to saving as well as to realistic income.

Walking through Valleys to Blessings with Mentor Programs

Financial management through the valley of the shadows leads to blessings of the tables. The shepherd walks with people to find abundant life in God's love, peace, and provisions. The shepherds are equipped for counseling, education, and inspiration by the content of this book.

One church encourages members to spend one hour in worship, one hour in study, and one hour per week in service either working at church or helping someone. The pastor in the church has built an attitude in people, who choose to do crisis or outreach ministry, of helping "those with less than they have." Help in financial management is given in everyday activities as this attitude is implemented. The pastor has built an attitude of searching for "those;" and God directs them to find "the least of these." The Scripture teaches, "A friend loves at all times, and a brother is born for adversity" (Proverbs 17:17). This service is fulfilled by Jean when she works with Sue, a teenage girl, in financial trouble. Jean, a churchwoman, is supportive of Sue who is working and caring for her brother in an apartment. Sue's mother who is on drugs keeps stealing from her.

Jean has helped Sue survive and grow spiritually by talking with her, encouraging her, getting her into an honor's program, helping her apply to college, getting the application in on time, helping her get a scholarship, and helping her get work-study. Jean invites her to lunch at her house. Sue has brought her friends and they have had lots of home cooked food and Christian and fellowship.

Some organizations assign a "mentor mother" to a high school teen mother. Another program matches up a mentor of an older woman with a younger one who has experienced similar obstacles. The mentor woman calls each week, suggests alternatives for accomplishing goals, is encouraging, and is informative, since she also had been in prison, on drugs, abused, discouraged and forsaken. Those in Alcohol Anonymous have a "sponsor" whom they must personally contact daily, not just leaving a message.

In the program called New Focus, a church member is assigned as a financial coach to work with people who formerly asked for money or were on welfare. Seminars teach financial management including obstacles to change. Scripture is studied for application in work attitudes, saving, and giving. Budget counseling and emotional support are provided. All families meet together with their coaches for dinner on Monday evenings and work individually afterwards. The shepherd can organize a program of "money coaches" or financial counselors equipped by studying this book.

Shepherds or mentors are assigned to befriend, support, and educate single-parents. They call each other once a week. Shepherds may go shopping with the single-parent to educate or babysit so the parent can go shopping. Then they sit with them at church and other fellowship programs.[10]

Resource Power for Those Who Have Lost a Job

Individuals who have become recently unemployed from plant layoffs, closings, downsizing, or relocations can be offered seminars, workshops, or counseling with the shepherd. Hopefully,

---

10   Covenant Presbyterian Church. West Lafayette, Indiana. 2009.

family members also attend. Meetings or "town hall meetings" are sponsored by the labor union, career development, recipients of a grant to help the workers in transition, agencies, or the local newspaper. As spiritual leader in the community, shepherds can volunteer to speak. Their effectiveness depends on providing concrete steps in transition and giving hope.

When a crisis occurs of any kind, people tend to blame themselves even if it is no fault of their own. The recently laid-off person may say, "If I had only taken that other job…". Some people concentrate on it as yet another evidence of their failures. They bring to mind the mistakes and inadequacies of their past. They may explode or go into depression as accumulation of past tragedies. They are stuck. The shepherd can guide them to reflect on past successes, their strengths, and victories. Develop strategies to keep moving in spite of life not being perfect or as wanted.

In a one-on-one counseling session, practical and technical steps in financial matters can facilitate psychological and spiritual changes. The Spirit is called for transforming the greatest resource - the power of the mind. An outline of the steps in sessions or seminars as a possible script for the shepherd[11] follows:

"**Face reality.** Your greatest resource is the power of your mind - to adjust attitude with the ability to change and retain what is important to you. Focus on your successes, not failures - on what you have, not what you do not have. Yesterday is a canceled check - gone and over. Direct energies, *time and money*, to restructuring your life, not on resentment and fear. You cannot do anything about the factory. You can do something about your personal corporation." Your greatest resource of the soul is the power of your spirit. Open up your mind, heart, soul, and strength to the Great Spirit for leading and peace. Rather than praying and wishing things will return to the way they were, spend energy on changes. Accept that things are not the way you want them to be or that they are not perfect. Yet, you are a person with strength for the new journey."

"**Set new goals and create new roles.** Keep the same values, if rooted in worthwhile soil. Focus on improving your self-image and confidence. Remember the past times in your life when you thought the earth would open up and swallow you but it did not. Call on the strengths from past successes to continue on now. Regain control and communicate with creditors, family members, prospective employers, rather than overreacting in demanding control. Be creative!"

"**Decide wants and tentative plans.** What do you want to do? Plan on how long it will take, how much it will cost and the adjustments for fulfilling your desires or goals. Seek advice from those without their vested interest. Ask those who are known to have Godly wisdom to pray with you."

"**Do a cash flow statement.** This is income _____, minus expenses_____, to get the balance_____ (surplus or deficit). Knowing your status, even if bleak, gives a feeling of security. Increase income, reduce expenses, be more efficient, and adjust lifestyle." Being efficient is your new job as well as comparison shopping or making things.

"**Increase your income:** Money and nonmoney, entitlements, community resources, money owed you, a hobby turned into a business, early inheritance, liquidating assets, selling of goods, exchanging goods and services with other individuals or families, bypassing the need for cash, Earned Income Credit (which can be received monthly or yearly after figuring income eligibility), food stamps, free or reduced lunches, and other programs. Eligibility can be checked on the Internet. When money

---

11   Flora L. Williams. Seminars given from 1970 to 2001. Interviews 2001-2009. Indiana.

is saved on food purchases, it is available for debts and necessities. Application for free or reduced school lunches can be made at any time during the year. Eligible families of four for free lunches are 130 percent below the federal poverty guidelines which is $27,560 ($2,297 per month). For reduced lunches it is $39,220 ($3,269 per month)."

"**Reduce expenses and change wants.** What would happen if you - Cut out? Reduced? Replaced? Put off? Postponed?" The quickest place to reduce spending is in the change from expensive food tastes, drinks, and convenience foods. Use of energy is another place."

"**Adjust debts.** Determine actual income and subtract minimum living expenses to get amount to pay creditors. Learn your creditors' policies. Write a letter outlining your plan to the creditor. It may even be a proposal to pay nothing until new employment is obtained. Keep a copy. (This used to work. Now some major creditors do not care and some will not even open letters.) Assume cooperation and ask to waive interest. If creditor will not adjust, learn to live with harassment. Have a job just to pay debts. Work off debts or loans from some people. If possible, take something back to the store or sell it. Use not for profit consumer credit counseling service. Beware of professionals who try to take your business, offer you loans, and sell you insurance or loan consolidation that you do not need. Some questionable credit counselors will charge you for talking with your creditors. Some attorneys will try to sell services you can do yourself."

"**Borrow with caution!** Borrowing is pouring gasoline onto a fire. Write a contract with family members if you do borrow from them. Pay more than the minimum to not be enslaved. Borrow against life insurance, pension, home equity, and savings. Use cash from any cash value life insurance. Debt consolidation is the road to disaster. Bankruptcy is killing a fly with a cannon. Alternatives: pay off little debts one at a time and go on a crash budget for several months."

"**Reevaluate Costs:** transportation, housing, travel, eating out, hobbies, insurance, or cable TV for examples. Use videos from the library, and change phone features for just the basic services. Eat well – bake a whole chicken, scramble eggs, and cherish dry beans cooked all day. Put some insurance or phones on vacation."

"**Make decisions in organized procedure.** First, list decisions in order. Second, jot down information needed to make decisions. Third, list steps to take. Pray for guidance and strength." "Take time to make a decision and count the costs of alternatives before selling out or bailing out."

"**Diversify.** "If given a lump sum settlement or severance pay, **diversify** in different types of investments and in different companies. If possible roll over to another qualified plan. Place a portion in 'hard-to-get-at' investments and other portions in liquid assets. Diversify your human capital investments. Take a course or learn new skills."

"**Develop a job search.** What are your transferable skills? List prospects, contacts, and times to check and recheck. Have someone review your resume. Role-play an interview. Do volunteer work while searching. This can look good on a resume. Remember 70 percent of the jobs are hidden. When people lose a job, some are interested in self employment or starting their own business because they think they would have more control. Many people want their own business, particularly if they have lost a job and think they will have more control. These people should be informed that 75 percent fail in the first five years. Steps for this decision include checking with someone experienced, getting help from a finance officer with your business plan, working with 'volunteers for starting businesses,' contacting Small Business Administration, calculating the costs (time and money), and learning to advertise."

"**Volunteer.** Meanwhile, volunteer in the community or state. This looks good on the resume as well as builds self-respect for contributing to someone, somewhere. Contacts while volunteering may lead to job prospects."

"**Champion change!!!** Write on one card 'what will change' and another 'what will not change.' Get everyone in the family to identify at least one change that would make the transition smoother and reduce expenses. This helps to face reality."

"**Build self-respect.** Reaffirm your self everyday as a child of the God who created you and loves you. Your creator will not abandon you as you seek new directions. Faith with hope will pull you through the valleys. Remember you were created for a purpose which moves in different paths at different times."

"**Deal with the respect of others.** This is a fear the recently unemployed faces because work gives the identity and the respect that all people basically need. One way to build or maintain the respect is to enumerate the economic contributions that one is making to the family and to the community. Tell them the useful and good things, no matter how small, that you are doing everyday. Love, emotional support, and care are assumed by family members. But respect can increase with naming the repair to house, yard, and vehicle; showing ways money is saved by doing rather than hiring (hair cuts, cooking), and paying bills on time. Another way is to call yourself a person who happens to be unemployed at this time rather than calling yourself an unemployed person. This is similar to getting away from the labels of calling someone a divorcee or a disabled person."

"**Be better, not bitter.** Respond to change by making it better, not fighting nor fleeing. Make a plan and list steps to take. A presumption masked as faith is NO action and thinking everything will be alright if I just pray enough."

"**Put crisis on the shelf a few minutes longer** each day. Think about something beside your loss. Do something concrete each day toward your new goals, new roles, and better methods of handling finances. Adjust in lots of ways and enjoy. Beware of needed adjustments in the family. For example, your spouse may say, 'I married her (or him) for better or worse, but not for lunch.'"

"**Conquer fear.** Accept it is normal to be fearful especially of the unknowns and uncertainty. Talk to God about your fears as Jesus did in the Garden of the Gethsemane. Talk to a trusted friend. The Chinese proverb says: 'When you share your joy, you double it. When you share your sorrows you halve them.'" Naming three options you have for now and the near future reduces fear, maintains respect and anxiety."

"**Be thankful in everything,** even in suffering, as this builds character. Be thankful for a time of unemployment to learn new things, to enjoy grandchildren, to reflect on life, and to restock one's character in worship. Develop sources of security and happiness not based on money." (Author's script).

Getting a Job or a Position with The Shepherd's Guides

In most unemployment situations, the solution is to get another job. The job search may be unfamiliar and intimidating for those who had been employed for many years. The church board chair who had been vice president of a bank needs pastoral help. He wants someone to look at his resume, since he had not done one for 23 years. The shepherd volunteers to critique it. Step by step the Lord leads the shepherd and the person in the job search.

The first step is identifying previously unconsidered talents, strengths, and past experiences transferable to new jobs. Next is to get an interview, not assuming someone is willing to hand a job to him or her. Let others know a search is in progress. They may have leads. The church family is useful in all circumstances. Some people "wait until their ship comes in, while other people swim out to the ship." When lining up an interview, the shepherd reviews and critiques the resume in content, format and appearance. The shepherd addresses the characteristics of a good interview and role-plays the interview. The shepherd may help fill out the application. The shepherd helps people persevere by conveying information about hiring processes and building confidence. Viewing the path of job search from different angles provides creative steps.

In identifying strengths, the shepherd probes for experiences, interests, and hobbies that can offer extra income or a new career. Perhaps self-employment, a second job, or temporary work can be used until the job is found. If one is skillful, one could work part-time making household repairs in the community. Baking, sewing, or babysitting could be used to supplement total income. Offering to till people's gardens or sawing their fallen trees is useful. The former banker could manage a non-profit agency which may be useful.

Interests can lead to the exploration of new areas. A desire to work with people may lead one to apply for a training program at a crisis center, or an interest in sales might encourage one to join a company's training program.Previous activities could be listed along responsibilities. Swimming or music skills could lead to teaching them.

Competencies are shown with the training and skills of every job listed with their duties and responsibilities. This includes training in volunteer work, odd jobs, home jobs such as landscaping, working at a booth in a festival, and paid employment. Babysitting experience could prove valuable in obtaining a job at a day care center.

God created each as unique individuals. People can create a job by developing a market for something needed and in demand at the time when no one else is supplying it. People can create a unique aspect, perform a unique service, or develop a unique product. Or on-the-other-hand, a temporary employment agency may be a good way to start. Searching on the computer opens possibilities. It has been said that 70 percent of jobs are hidden, not advertised. Creativity helps, as does flexibility. If a person is willing to work at flexible times and places, children may be allowed to accompany the worker or fit into relative's care. Women can choose jobs traditionally men's and vice versa. Men can choose nontraditional jobs. Nursing which is a career projected to be in great demand is no longer only for women.

The counselor can help people improve interpersonal skills, as it is *not* just the technical skills that employers seek. They want workers who fit into the group, and are good team players. An informational interview seeks to learn about the job or work organization. The shepherd can offer to give a recommendation. The resume can be delivered directly. The shepherd can prepare people for learning from interviews which may be numerous before a person gets the right job.

The shepherd helps sort out real from perceived barriers to getting a job. This may involve changing assumptions about roles in the family. The shepherd is explicit in explaining if Jill wants to save the family, she has to do her part. In Jill's case, this meant finding a job she thought was below her dignity as a "Southern Belle." (Jill's husband was required to attend counseling in the first place as an alternative to going to jail for stealing from the motel. The manager said he would not prosecute as long as Jill's husband would attend counseling sessions.)

Facing financial uncertainties may require prompting to get any job rather than waiting for the perfect match. Progress toward employment may require a temporary job while working at an apprenticeship program on the weekend. Temporary employment services may be the way to begin. It is tempting to solve the discomforts of unemployment by moving in with parents and doing nothing. In this case, one may need to get out of his or her comfort zone and have a structure for mental health as well as money. In some cases, getting more training may be worth the wait considering the added income and benefits in the long run. Long-term job goals may be too visionary, given the realities of the local economy. A parent can help with housing or even a loan which helps the unemployed know he/she is secure financially for a few months. This reduces the crisis of job search rejections.

Suggestions for the Search. Pray about the job search. Ask why God might want you to do this; and why God may not want you to do this. Pray during the interview and you will not be so afraid. Concentrate on expressing self clearly rather than impressing interviewer. The shepherd, members of the church, friends, and family members can assist in locating jobs, checking out employment trends, and even searching job listings. Places to look include the Internet, newspaper want-ads, the State employment office (an excellent source of information about job searching), government sponsored employment and training programs, private employment agencies although they may have a fee such as 10 percent of gross annual income, temporary help firms, labor unions, and the Chamber of Commerce. Check the "yellow pages" of the phone book, temporary help agencies, and go directly to businesses where employment is considered. One could ask for information even if nothing is advertised. In the process, a job might be created or another posted.

Application. Filling out an application is often required before an interview is granted. The application will become the basis on which the prospective employers will form their first impression. The fact that the shepherd will review the application or resume before submitting it gives courage, motivation to complete, and peace. Now many applications must be completed by e-mail. The shepherd can remind people of the following:

Do not leave portions of the application blank. Draw a line in the space or write N/A for not applicable. If it's impossible for you to answer a question, write "no answer. At least it will be clear you have not carelessly skipped it.

Prior to the interview, make a detailed record of your previous employment which will help you in completing the application. Your record should include:

former employer's name and address, employment dates, description of the work, rate of pay, name of supervisor, reasons for leaving, and references. Record your volunteer work, related experiences, education, and training.

Always have your Social Security number available for the application. Have names, addresses and phone numbers of references: character references, work references, and co-workers. First, check with those contacts to see if it is all right for you to use them as references.

If you qualify for at least one-half of the requirements for a job, go ahead and apply. You might say, "I know I am over the stated age, but I can do such and such." Or you can say, "I do not know such and such but I am willing to learn." Be enthusiastic about the job for which you are applying. Have a positive attitude! Do not dwell on the negative or talk about your problems. If you are not interviewed the day you apply for a job, return the next day! Show confidence in your own abilities.

The way to make a good impression is to never give up! Make every attempt to speak to an interviewer. Wait if necessary. Use a pen or computer, at the library (if you do not have one) and be very neat in filling out any applications. Be sure to spell correctly. Use a pocket dictionary, if necessary. Go to the interview by yourself to show independence. Interviewers look for honesty, abilities, intelligence, positive attitude, and self-confidence. The shepherd needs to discuss and role play appropriate language for the interview and on the job.

Two illustrations confirm the usefulness of helping with appropriate language. Ellie, from a disadvantaged family, was finally able, with the help of the shepherd, to get a job as a childcare worker. She was fired because her customary language was not acceptable for talking with children. No one had warned her. Jackie was interviewed by the search committee at church and assured she would be hired. When she was interviewed by a larger church group she used language considered vulgar and bathroom talk in order to be expressive and relevant to the outside culture she wanted to reach. The older people found it offensive and reconsidered the offer. No one had warned her.

To prepare for an interview, try to visit the company before the interview day. Look around for offices, restrooms, and check out type of clothing people wear. Dress neatly, appropriately and conservatively. You may need to buy (or rent) some items. The investment should pay off. Be sure hands are attractive with clean, trimmed nails.

Go to the restroom before the interview. While there, be sure hair is combed and clothing adjusted; and then do not fumble with them.

Avoid nervous habits: jingling change, scratching head, drumming fingers, cracking knuckles, or chewing gum. Do not smoke. Do not sit down until asked to do so. Sit up straight. Do not lean on interviewer's desk. Be on time; 10-15 minutes early is best. Look the interviewer in the eye. Take notes if you like. If a phone call interrupts, do not try to listen in. Ignore it or volunteer to wait outside. Do not check your watch during the interview. Do not use swear words or slang.

Let the interviewer lead the discussion by asking the questions. Give complete answers rather than one or two word phrases. Talk about salary when the interviewer brings it up. Do not lie. If there are problems, tell your opinion without putting other people down. Try to find out about the company before the interview (ask for booklets from human resources), then ask questions when the interviewer gives you the chance. Remember you may be judged on the type and quality of questions you ask. Among many good questions are: "Are there advancement opportunities? Are there training programs? How often will I be evaluated? What benefits are there?"

At the end of the interview, thank the interviewer. Ask if you can call him or her at a designated time and day. Shake hands as you look directly at the interviewer.

Managing the Job Search. "The job search is organized by making a time plan, a potential job checklist, and time schedule for calling the company after application and interview have been completed. One can keep checking back at a regular time schedule for openings. Ignoring the comment about we will call you, have an excuse to call and follow up by asking, "Did you get such and such?" and "What is the next step in the process?"

A "Job Search Tree" can be drawn with alternative lines of progress, decision, follow-through and action. The first step is identified, what to do there, and an alternative direction for a stand still.

Remember it is a job to find a job! Invest time and money into the search. Set aside time to enjoy life rather than feeling guilty about not spending all the time in job search. Join an unemployed persons' support group. Remember you are a person who happens to be unemployed at the time.

Meanwhile perform volunteer work for keeping up your morale, contacts for job leads, skill development, and adding to your resume. Perform work around the house, yard and car, developing skills and making contributions to family nonmoney and quality of life.

The Choice. Specificity helps to achieve goals. Decide how much more money is needed to meet expenses and the additional hours per week needed to earn that amount. Divide by expected wage per hour to know the hours required. Weigh the costs as a result of employment and find ways to reduce them. Increase net income by reducing work related expenses such as child care, work clothing, transportation distance, lunches, use of convenience foods and meals out. Examine transportation alternatives and schedules of family members. Gain confidence in handling overtime work, additional employment, new employment, a better job, or odd jobs. Improve division of labor and management practices at home, which affect job success.

Reducing wants and improving financial management may be more advantageous than earning more money. It is not taxed. Consider all types of costs: job related, family time, health, and loss of other interests.

Calculate costs of transportation, clothes, paying for benefits, etc. when comparing jobs. Reduce job-related costs. Overcome perceived barriers, get use to new roles, and assume inconveniences. The inconvenience of waiting for them saves money in not buying a car. The wait translates into $20 per hour, perhaps more than any job. Calculating into hourly savings also motivates school children to cooperate. A husband and wife may ask for different shifts in order to care for children, or advertise to exchange babysitting with one who has a different shift.

If Fired. If you are fired, apply for unemployment compensation even though you think you may not qualify. If you have been fired unjustly, because of discrimination or politics, you might qualify. Check with Legal Services or your union. Check the Unfair Labor Practice Law. Be honest when you apply for another job. Briefly state what you have learned from the experience and take steps toward self-improvement since the previous job.

A shepherd was talking with an individual who desperately needed a job since her husband was leaving the family and she needed to pay Habitat for Humanity for their house. She revealed that fear was preventing her from calling about a night shift job. She needed it because she was going to business college during the day. Why? She was afraid of rejection. She had been fired from the night shift. There had been a dispute. Now she was afraid of her supervisor. The shepherd said that 50 percent of worries never happen. Maybe the supervisor is not there. What is the worst that could happen? What would you do if that happened? The next step? (She would try another school system although the first choice was better for her using public transportation.) Fear was replaced with a more positive approach: "Be prepared to tell the director how much you enjoyed working there and what skills she had gained from the training." If her past was mentioned, she would tell what she *learned* from the experience and how she is different now. Her eighth and tenth grade children could stay with a friend at night since the neighborhood was too dangerous for them to be left alone. Prayer ended the session, thanking the Spirit to give her words to say during the interview.

Handling Office Politics – The Shepherd's Guide

Family financial problems and addictions are frequently cited in the news for their devastating effect upon employment. Less discussed is the effect of office politics upon financial management and family life. Office politics contribute to addictions and spending disorders. Finances become havoc when "politics" interfere with the basic needs for respect, caring for something or someone, a sense of achievement, security, a sense of identity, and the acceptance all of which work is supposed to fill. Committed Christians can serve God at their work place but this is hampered when "politics" interfere. (One can recall that Jesus' trial and crucifixion were a result of "politics" – jealousy, threatened change, power struggle, etc.). Since office/job treatment affects and causes financial problems directly and indirectly, the shepherd helps individuals handle "politics" rather to quit or retire early. The shepherd can help those with an adversarial attitude and help repair brokenness at work. The following suggestions can also improve family life.

The "principles"[12] for handling relationships on the job, which ultimately affect finances, are in the following script: "Learn the structure, power, protocol, and who really is in power. Determine if it's a competitive or cooperative system of management and adjust accordingly. Find out the unwritten job description. While at work, work; and while at home, think of home rather than mixing the two. However, arrange a hot-line for children to call you at your employment when they get home from school. Have another life, hobbies, or interests outside of employment. Have a way to release frustrations such as "working out," walking, pulling weeds, or home cooking.

Have a support group. (Counselors have counselors.) Associate with positive people. Persevere and certain people may leave. Perhaps you will last longer than they.

Change your attitude toward what happens. Realize you have good days and bad days. Hope you have more good days than bad days. Realize negative people, un-pleasantries, or disadvantages go with any job.

Do not talk too much. Do not listen too much to politics. Do not let talk or negativism get you down. Do not let other people pull you down with them. Do not always listen to someone who says, "If they did that to me, I would quit!" Realize there is a difference between friendliness and friendship. Beware a peer may become your boss someday. Do random acts of kindness and they may come back to you when there is a change in power or you need a favor from someone.

Decide who owns problems that arise. Do not take on other people's problems. Stay in control of yourself. Losing temper or labeled as a trouble maker will haunt you and cause a bad reputation. Be aware of bullies so they do not buffalo you.

Handle your fatigue. Figure out the causes and correct them. Ask what you are learning from the situation and other people. Be a passive observer. These approaches help mediate the pain from difficulty on the job. Manage your time. Stress management is time and goal management." (Williams' script)

Transition from Homelessness or Midlife Crisis

The shepherd will become an expert in "walking with people" in transition. The counselor's approach is similar when working with the "homeless" (those without addresses) and those

---

12   Script by Flora L. Williams in Seminars and Lectures. 1980-2001.

changing from one status to another, one country to another, or those recovering from a midlife financial crisis. First, determine if initial status (or level of living) was by choice or circumstances. Identify with individuals and their desired status in general, not all of the specific components of the new status (for example, determine if the individual wants an apartment and what kind of apartment). Realize that an individual is not "stupid." He or she thinks differently than some other people because of the current crisis, putting out feelers for protection, or having been treated adversely or dishonestly. Realize offers of assistance or advertisements may be interpreted as "cons." Funds may have to be managed for an individual such as a home-health aid paid by an agency, or other sources. The individual may get defensive and simply wait for the "balloon to burst." Do not overwhelm the individual with all needed decisions and adjustments at once. Help an individual to slowly adjust to a new society. Present assistance and information in an appropriate manner for those who completely resent and resist advice or criticism, which they interpret as a threat to their independence or an insult to their abilities.

The shepherd can assist people in qualifying for entitlements, medicine, services of employment agency, etc. in that order, sequentially over time. Assistance in completion of applications and submissions can be done by checking a rough draft and correcting spelling or grammar. Assembling necessary documents such as birth certificate, a copy of Social Security card for getting medical exam for Medicaid eligibility, and aiding in the "footwork" may be time consuming but necessary.

Build up morale. When people become frustrated and overwhelmed, list decisions or actions, without too many in one day. Reserve ideas and perceptions of what people could become in the future rather than pressing them into the counselor's mold or time frame. Personal goals may be developed when ready. The counselor's suggestions, stories of what other people have done, and information are helpful.

Assist people in fulfilling one goal at a time in order to handle change and develop ability to shift into logical differences in the new status. Work with objective facts and resources. Further, work with perceptions which include bitterness, disillusionment, confusion, expectations, and erroneous observations. Identify progress, not perfection, strengths not weaknesses, compliments not praise, encouragement while not taking over their responsibilities.

Referring

"Three sessions and then refer" is a frequently used policy in pastoral counseling. The shepherd can work wonders with skill, insight and the Spirit's power in three sessions. How does one know where to find a referral which will not cost more than the value received? How can the referral agency be checked out? In the shepherd's referral list the qualifications for assistance and costs are noted. Time of office hours must be given. If a helping agency only takes the first 20 who register, people under counseling should be informed to get there early.

The counselor helps people see that the short term cost of fees reduces costs over the long-term. People may balk at expensive counseling, although it is less than their monthly car payments. It appreciates their life, whereas addictions depreciate it. The counselor should not make promises of the help received. The counselor can help an individual make the call for an appointment. Usually, people are given three names from which they choose. If requested, the counselor can help assemble material for the first meeting including the reports and forms (financial balance and consumption problems) from counseling. This saves time and money at the first referral visit. The counselor needs to know if a referral letter is useful. Before sending any information to another professional, the counselor should get a signed release from the client. The professional referred to will also need a signed release from the individual to report back.

Over time, the counselor will develop relationships with referral sources. From reports, the counselor gets a sense of how clients are served by the referrals. Then, the referral can be done with more confidence.

A counselor becomes a better shepherd who knows the community resources and develops a working relationship with them. Some of them are the United Way, the Crisis Center, Neighborhood Housing, Child and Family Service Agency, Health Clinics, Consumer Credit Counseling Service, the State Attorney General, Area Council on Aging, Financial Planners, and other organizations. These can help locate other community resources and agencies.

A referral scenario might sound like this: Shepherd to person: "Have you thought about using the food pantry? This could free up money to pay other bills. Then when times are better you can contribute to the pantry." The shepherd tells how to check on entitlements. Shepherd: "Entitlements are government benefits for those who qualify. Your taxes partially fund when you are employed." The shepherd informs families on how to obtain scholarships or reduced fees from organizations such as YMCA, YWCA, Boys Club, Girls Club, and summer camps. Since clothing is important to young people or someone seeking a job, places such as discount stores, thrift shops, Goodwill, and Salvation Army are mentioned. Since families say they do not have money for fun together, the shepherd informs, "Here is Friday's newspaper telling of free activities. Did you know you can get videos from the library for free?"

When more than one counselor or specialist is working with an individual or family, the division of responsibility, roles, and length of collaboration are clarified and understood. Otherwise, confusion can lead people to use one against the other person or use the lack of clarity as an excuse for doing less themselves.

Prayer

"*Show me Your Ways, O Lord; Teach me Your Paths. Lead me in Your Truth and teach me, for You are the God of my salvation; on You I wait all the day*" (Psalm 25:4-5 NKJ). "*Good and upright is the Lord; Therefore He teaches sinners in the way. The humble He guides in justice. And the humble He teaches His way. All the paths of the Lord are mercy and truth, to such as keep His covenant and testimonies. For Your name's sake,…*" (Psalm 25:8-11 NKJ).

Prayer addresses the spoken and unspoken fears. Prayer is for options chosen and for removing barriers in accomplishing them. Prayer is for strength to change what can be changed, patience for that which cannot be changed, and wisdom to know the difference. Thanks are expressed for available resources within self, within family, and within community. Thanks are expressed for the Spirit's guidance and love in one's heart, soul, mind, and strength.

Financial Fitness and Faithfulness
Change Exercises

Write one change for each area for each week:

- Increase income, mobilize resources, exchange services or goods with someone _____

- Reduce or change wants and expenses _____

- Control credit _____

- Adjust or reduce debts _____

- Clarify priorities or change attitudes _____

- Plan or budget using a new format for one's unique personality and purpose _____

- Act effectively to realize consumer rights and responsibilities _____

- Improve household operational system _____

- Evaluate expenses of housing, transportation, educational funding, insurance, investments, and taxes _____

- Maintain or improve economic security by reducing risk or optimizing resources in diversifying income, skills, and investments _____, _____, _____

- Champion and handle changes or crises in consumption and lifestyle _____

- Communicate with others about finances effectively and efficiently _____

- Control finances and control life under God's love and wisdom _____

- Memorize a verse or phrase for spiritual replenishment. _____

◊◊◊ ⧗ ⧗ ◊◊◊

Chapter 4. Paths to Righteousness in Budgeting and Spending Plans, Analyzing Expenditures*

Vision, power, and control come from choosing the particular path, the spending plan, the budget. The plan implements changes in financial management to meet new goals, guide reorganization, and solve problems. Types of budgets and changes can be tried for a specified period of time and reevaluated. Frequently it is the control of the plan, not the plan itself, which is in error. In Mark 14:37, Jesus said the spirit is willing but the body is weak. The newest term describing people who have money problems, high financial distress, and poor financial well-being is "Budgetary Anarchy Disorder" (Ray Forgue). Budgets are an approach to bring order out of confusion. They bring discipline to plans. Reviewing all plans and choosing one clarifies the purpose for a new system based on unique problems and personality. This is required in the culmination of financial counseling for any and all individuals and families regardless of circumstance.

Reading these paths teaches and summarizes money mechanics, financial terminology, and choices.

THE FAMILY IN THE WORLD[13]

The purpose of "The Family in the World" is for those who want to see the function of money in a world perspective; financial management as a means to personal and societal development; the systems approach in action; or expenditures monthly, yearly, or over a lifetime.

The function of the budget is to bring relative order into the economic aspects of family life, from the point of view of its self-understanding. The perspective is that of the Family in Mission in and to the human enterprise of civilization. Outcomes are economic stability and spiritual joy in fulfilling God's purposes.

TOTAL INCOME Needed for Responsibility to Family and the World:
The Family Responsibility to the Family: Total $ The Family Responsibility to the World: Total $

The Physical Maintenance of the Family   **The Economic Stability of Society**

1	2	3	4	1	2	3	4
Housing	Utilities	Food	Health	Life Insurance	Other Insurance	Vocational Tools	Investment Savings
$	$	$	$	$	$	$	$

The Social Development of the Family   **The Political Security of Society**

1	2	3	4	1	2	3	4
Personal Appearance	Home Décor	Education Provision	Trans-portation	Income Taxes	Property Taxes	Misc. Taxes	Automobile Taxes
$	$	$	$	$	$	$	$

The Family Identity   **The Cultural Effectiveness of Society**

1	2	3	4	1	2	3	4
Celebration	Recreation	Vacations	Allowances Benevolence	Church Benevolence	Social Initiated Altruism	Family Savings	Cash
$	$	$	$	$	$	$	$

---

13   Adapted from materials of the Ecumenical Institute, Chicago, Illinois. 1970s.

SPEND, SAVE, AND SHARE

The purpose of the format using "Save, Spend, and Share" is for the anxious person or child who must first learn the basic uses of money. It provides simple envelopes for distributing and recording spending, saving, and sharing. It controls spending if a person stops when an allotted amount is spent. It does not work if a person plays games and transfers from one envelope to another when money is depleted. This system helps the individual or family to work with concrete rather than abstract concepts; develops habits of saving and sharing; helps people realize that if money is not saved for goals such as Christmas or gifts other plans will not work; and helps people understand that choices have to be made in light of expanding wants but limited resources. The balance reflects the reconciliation of wants with resources. Adults may expand categories to other areas with use of envelopes for other items. Financial peace is a result of having a balance in working with God's plan in economic reality.

Income
Expenditures

Save
-Save for taxes if withholdings do not equal taxes owed or self employed
-
-
-
-
-

Spend
-
-
-
-
-
-
-
-

Share
-
-
--
-
-
-

Total
Balance

ENVELOPES FOR CASH, RECORDS, AND RECEIPTS

Envelopes or jars labeled as follows may be used to plan spending, control spending, compare plan with spending, save for special purposes, and share:

Rent   Food   Taxes
Clothes/laundry   Transportation
School   Utilities
Personal   Special Savings
Allowances   Gifts and Contributions, Sharing

Here is an example of estimating expenses on the envelope, recording when expenses are incurred, and then comparing the estimated with actual expenses. Then new estimates or adjustments can be made.

Bus/Taxi/Car   Transportation

Put $ __30__ from each pay (or bus tokens) into envelope

Cost: Item:
____$1.50_____   _____Bus to Park_____
_____   _____
_____   _____
_____   _____
_____   _____

Weekly or monthly total.

NECESSITIES AND LUXURIES

The categories "Necessities and Luxuries" provide mechanisms for 1) clarifying priorities among family members; 2) planning for money needed in transitions, such as changing jobs, unemployment, retirement, or for returning to school; 3) teaching older children to think about the concepts of necessities and luxuries and 4) questioning patterns of spending; 5) deciding the minimum standard of living; or 6) learning to "skimp" on necessities in order to afford luxuries. Questions include what, who, and why to make changes. The disadvantages of this form are the omission of details and the reminder of when expenses will occur. Values are clarified when decisions are made, when choosing where to cut or reduce. Rather than a budget, ask where will you cut? Again, what else?

Income:
Expenditures:

Necessities
- Taxes unless working with net income
-
-
-
-
-
-
-
-
-
-
-
-
-

Luxuries:
-
-
-
-
-
-
-
-
-
-
-

Total:
Balance:
Needed:

FIXED, FLEXIBLE, AND SET-ASIDES

The concepts of "Fixed, Flexible, and Set-Asides" provide mechanisms to meet fixed expenses on time in order to avoid late fees; provide a basic master plan for reference when paying monthly bills; to have a monthly worksheet; evaluate where expenses have been underestimated; establish a fund for a special goal or vacation by setting aside or automatically deducting a regular amount each month; or evaluate which flexible expenses appear to be fixed. Budget items are frequently classified as fixed, flexible, and set-asides. Fixed are those that are regularly paid or that carry legal and/or moral obligations.

Ultimately, nothing has to be "fixed" in absolute amounts. Housing, food patterns, etc. can be changed. Items usually considered fixed are rent and mortgages, utilities, debts, insurance, and pledges. Of these, rent and mortgages might be the most difficult to change, but because they compose the largest percentage of budget items for many families, they deserve attention. Spending patterns for these expenses can be changed to accommodate evolving family goals. The purpose of the procedure is to spotlight fixed items to see if they are actually immovable or if steps might be taken to change them.

Flexible items include food, clothing, recreation, and personal care. Food is a peculiar expense. It is not exactly fixed, but some amount has to be spent for it. It seems to be a stable cost on an annual basis for any one family. From one year to the next, people do not readily change their food habits. Food is made up of many small items with diverse costs. Choices of items greatly influence the weekly cost. Variations appear from week to week although usually not for a longer period of time. Some food might still be on the shelves after one week and can be used during a tight money period. Money can be taken out of the food budget for other items by occasionally substituting inexpensive foods. Family members may enjoy baked beans once in a while but would complain if they had to eat them every day.

Set-asides may include an emergency fund, a revolving personal fund, and vacations. If a family budget is negative or the family anticipates big expenses in the near future, patient budgeting and extra set-asides are needed before an emergency fund can be accumulated. Even small amounts, habitually saved, will build up reserves. When the emergency fund equals two or three months' income, extra money can be placed into savings or investments. People are more likely to save for specific goals than general savings, so keeping separate accounts for each goal or fund may be encouraging.

If nothing else, this format can be used to list major obligations and taxes. Reference to this plan will be a reminder to have funds on hand to meet these obligations without late penalties.

ESTIMATED AND ACTUAL

"Estimated and Actual" are listed in order for individuals or families to plan by estimating expenditures. Then through keeping records, they can evaluate how accurately their estimates were. This information contributes to better planning. Problems with budgets and finances, in general, are due to overestimating income and underestimating expenses.

Income
Expenditures

	Due	Estimated	Actual
Contributions, Gifts, Charity			
-			
-			
-			
-			
-			
-			
Fixed			
- **Taxes unless working with net income**			
-			
-			
-			
-			
Flexible			
-			
-			
-			
-			
-			
Set-asides, vacation, savings			
-			
-			
-			
--			
Total			
Balance			

With the formats of "Estimated and Actual", expenditures are estimated prior to a series of paydays. At the end of each pay period, actual expenditures are recorded. This spending plan, if kept continuously, is a check on the budget estimates. Some questions such as "In what part of the year do various types of spending pressures occur?" would be answered. Over-and under-estimates are shown. The family is able to make adjustments to keep spending within income limits. Money can be accumulated, expenditures spaced, due dates changed for semiannual items, or spending reduced to maintain a balanced budget. Annual or semiannual expenses are prorated by pay periods to assure that funds will be available to meet them.

DEBTS, EXPENSES, SAVINGS, AND SHARING

The concepts "Debts, Expenses, Savings, and Sharing" or past, present, and future show progress from only paying off past pleasures or debts to paying current expenses and on to future savings. It shows how excessive debts affect future decisions. It can show percentages and dollars paid for finance charges. It encourages a healthy balance among past, present, and future needs. It motivates the repayment of current debts in preparation for future plans. It provides a mechanism for separation of financial accounting into debts and living expenses so that the debts can be handled by one person or paid by one job. This is an alternative to loan consolidation, which can be more costly over time. Analyzing the amount of interest paid over several months in a graph may motivate change.

Income
Expenditures

                                                          Due Date

Debts (Past)

    <u>Principal</u>   <u>Interest</u>   <u>Percentage of total</u>

-
-
-
-
-

Expenses (Present)

-
-
-
-
-

Taxes

-
-
-

Savings (Future)

-
-
-
-

Sharing

-
-
-
-

Total
Balance

INCOME AND EXPENDITURES:
Daily, Weekly, Monthly, and Yearly

The budget format with categories of "Income and Expenditures: Daily, Weekly, Monthly, and Yearly" provides realistic estimates of expenditures, saving, and sharing. It can prorate larger payments into smaller units (weekly or monthly). It provides records of when expenditures have been made to decide how much is used or needed to manage irregular income with irregular expenses; i.e., those made by a farmer or college student. It can be used to decide amount of allowances for family members, to stretch food stamps issued monthly but used weekly, and to plan or record for two months or two years either by date of income or by date of expenses. Personal allowances, although a small amount, are included in a realistic plan. Items to be paid from allowances should be clarified. Policies regarding allowances and advances should be established so that planning and control are learned. These budget categories promote realistic estimates, controllable.

Income:	Date		Date		Date	
Expenditures						
	Date		Date		Date	
	Estimated	Actual	Estimated	Actual	Estimated	Actual
Daily						
-						
-						
-						
-						
-						
-						
Weekly						
-						
-						
-						
-						
-						
Monthly						
-						
-						
-						
-						
-						
Yearly						
(semi-annually)						
- Taxes unless working with net income						
-						
-						
-						
-						
Total						
Balance						

BASIC MAINTENANCE, LIFE STYLE, AND HUMAN CAPITAL INVESTMENTS

The purposes of this budget "Basic Maintenance, Life Style, and Human Capital Investments" is to create meaningful categories; encourage investment in human capital or human resource development. It may help one to realize that "not getting ahead' may be a trade-off of the cost of education, children, or retraining. It questions the patterns of lifestyle expenses. It helps decide where and when to "keep up with the Jones" and where and when not to; encourage family members to satisfy "needs" with less expense; be reminded that lifestyle purchases or commitments take time as well as money expenditures; be creative; adjust creatively some expenses to be able to indulge in luxuries; and determine life insurance or support payments. If there is a trouble spot in the budget, it can be isolated and analyzed in detail.

Such category divisions are frequently used to decide who is to be given the responsibility for managing them. In two-income families, separate incomes can be delegated to specific categories. A complete separation of interests and concerns can cause conflict when members feel a category is unjustly listed as their responsibility. Couples with "his" and "hers" expenditures report as many problems as other families.

Income:
Expenditures

	Date_____		Date_____	
	Dollar	Percentage	Dollar	Percentage
Basic Maintenance				
-				
-				
-				
Household Operation				
-				
-				
Life-style Expenses				
-				
-				
-				
Living Expenses				
-				
-				
-				
Investment in human capital				
-				
-				
-				
Investment in financial capital				
-				
-				
-				
Contributions, charity, pledges, gifts				
-				
-				
-				
Total				
Balance				

PUBLISHED OR URBAN BUDGETS

The purpose of "Published Budgets" is to report average expenditures. Categories based on government research and expert analysis comprise this traditional format such as in the "Consumer Expenditure Survey." Survey expenditure budgets are updated from time to time and contain detailed estimates of living costs. They can be seen in the *Statistical Abstract in the United States* on the Internet. The categories are complicated but include all costs. Costs are listed by items not functions. Costs are reported as specified levels of income, age, composition, and locations. These budgets reflect spending patterns of statistical families and are not designed to be used as a guide for other families although clients request such information. When comparing costs with those of published budgets, the counselor should remind clients that costs vary according to their values and management ability. The counselor can assess other reasons why a client family has different expenses than the average by considering variations.

Percentages Comparison

The purpose of "Percentages Comparison" is to observe trends; to compare household's expenditure with national averages; to provide detailed expenditures in percentages for the inexperienced person; to provide analysis for estimating expenses if the family has the same values, composition and income; and to show the percentages for housing and transportation. The percentage distribution is not a guide for what families should spend. It can help alert clients to the possible proportions that other families are reporting and where they are underestimating. Costs by size of family, income levels, and region where they are living are reported in *The Statistical Abstract* available on the Internet. Families on the average are spending more than their income except for the highest income levels.

ANALYZING AND QUESTIONING EXPENSES FOR CHANGES

The Can Plan

The "can plan" is not really a plan. It is a method for everyone to report expenditures and then analyze – a plan for change. Change is motivated by **"We Can Do It"** attitude through crises or desires for new goals.

A can is on the table with pencil and paper to record the day's spending or to throw the receipts in it. If the computer program is used, it must be easily accessible for everyone to record spending, just inside the door and must be kept current. List every expense by categories useful to the household currently. Traditional categories are useful for tallying up expenses but do not answer the questions for change. Different formats could be used after analyzing. Lump together the expenses by the questions used to analyze.

Questions for recording and for change in financial management. Questions indicate usefulness of records: What is used for tax purposes? What ends arguments with parents, spouse, roommate, or children? What is a proof of purchase or payment? What is the reason for spending each item? Is it a good reason at this time? What are the grabbers, what are the leaks, miscellaneous, and what are surprises? What was underestimated? What is spent for past, current, and future satisfactions? How to build a saving account while paying off debts, and sharing? How does one calculate the emergency reserve of three to six month's expenses? What is used for re-planning the spending plan or budget? What shows more money must be available at what time? What was for sharing, giving or tithing? Who in the household is spending and needs to be spotlighted for a time? What were savings?

Where could waste have been reduced? What indicates there are more choices than realized previously? What were unintentional (spontaneous) purchases? What was spent out of habit, custom, or pressure from friends and were not really needs? What met long-term goals (or what did not meet long-term goals)? What added up to more than expected, a surprising amount? What was unexpected, an unusual expense at an unusual time? Why is the spending, saving, and sharing necessary? Where reduce or cut?

Evaluation. What did I learn from this? What will I change from this? (If not analyzed for change, keeping records is less productive than other uses for time.) What can be changed for now at least? Records need to be analyzed to make change possible.

In reality, no matter when people are asked to record or report, they will say this was an unusual week. Unexpected or rather unplanned expenses occur which drive people to use credit. That explains why they cannot save more. That is why they rob their church pledge. That is why they do not keep their vows to God, warned in Deuteronomy not to procrastinate. One purpose of a savings account is to provide for underestimated expenses and for the unusual. A unique system must be developed for the household which has irregular income and irregular expenses. A flow curve of income and expenses visually prepares for changes in spending. Recording can indicate pressure times.

A checkbook or credit record can reveal priorities and habits, time as well as money in reality, regardless what the person says. However, this simplified analysis can be unfair without asking *why*. There may be an usual circumstance or a business venture. Some items such as housing just cost more, some reflect past commitments, and some reflect another person's decision. Things that at first glance seem selfish may at a deeper analysis reflect worthy means to worthy ends. Even these can be reduced. Jane had large expenses for clothes and hair care, and a large phone bill. Conversation revealed she was not vain and frivolous, but was spending to be more effective on the job and redeeming people. She was calling regularly to elderly parents who lived in another state. She had a professional job where appearance was important for credibility.

Preparing for large or irregular expenses can be done by: prorating yearly expenses and writing in the check register the amount even if not paid, setting aside each month for yearly and semi-yearly expenses, automatically withdrawing to a special account that pays interest rather following the road of using credit to pay interest, or changing the due dates to different months to smooth out the flow of income and expenses.

Difficult and sensitive analysis. Questions to ask for determining change and spiritual or social development are: What expenses have been for making up for past deprivation but are no longer needed? What are for making a good appearance or impressing others? Which have been used to cover guilt? Prove your love for someone?

Spent because one does not know how to show love? Bargain? Bribe? Control? Power? Reduce boredom? Addictions? Are there less expensive ways to meet these needs? Is something so important that one will increase income to cover it and continue?

Fighting with money. Some couples use money or expenditures to "get even," show revenge, hurt or make another squirm, or spend for self since the other spent money for trips, having a good time, clothes, or for selfish reasons. Some "make up" after a fight with overly expensive means. Leveling the field may be a solution with less expensive ways to fight. A solution may be improving unselfishness. Allowing each to have some delights in life, or at least under his or her control, is another solution in the budget plan.

Change expenditures. Switching who pays the bills for a time so there is more understanding of budget demands is useful if talking does not show it. Previously a member may not even know there is a problem. Some members have not a clue what their expenses are. Get each member to do something or contribute something hoping to solve anxiety or insufficient income. Write it down for commitment. Involve everyone responsible for implementing a budget or financial plan in the planning so it is not sabotaged. Allow some money for each one to spend. Remember it takes practice, patience and perseverance. Build in rewards that do not cost money for cooperation in reporting and reducing credit use. Each person can write his/her contribution to the common good. The miscellaneous category is what needs examination and control.

Another **analysis that changes credit use** is diagramming the amount spent on interest and late fees separate from the amount of cash alone. Then a person could think what could have been purchased or given in generosity with this amount of interest. Diagramming over time encourages one to see progress toward reducing interest or debt.

On the other hand, seeing how amount deductable interest may reduce taxes helps in determining the real cost of a mortgage or home equity loan. When taxes are considered as well as interest, a different decision to buy, save, or share may occur.

Increasing expenses. Analysis can reveal which expenses should be increased. Examples are job related expenses, training for job security, capital development (savings and investment), repair to protect/maintain property, and education for changing job. Another analysis is where to reduce so that one can give, contribute or share more with others. What percentage to increase in sharing? Where to support work of God's kingdom?

"We Need a Budget"

What is behind the statement "We need a budget" has to be assessed to decide the type of budget or resolve the underlying issues. Is it controlling some member for whom criticism is for spending too much? Getting cooperation? Reducing fear that spending is out of control? Setting limits to live within income? Reducing interest paid for credit? Making ends meet? Wanting to save for security? Inability to say "no" to self or others? Having a guide to resolve uncertainty? Going through changes?

Remember the tool or word "Budget" has a different meaning for each family member.

SEASONAL OR IRREGULAR EXPENSES

One reason families are not accurate in estimating expenses is that they do not **record seasonal expenses.** (See form below.) They report difficulties are due to the week being unusual in expenses or sharing, birthdays, celebrations, repair, getting photographs, etc. However, most families report any week is unusual. There is always a season where different expenses are not routine. The season may be going back to school, holidays, spring planting, winterizing, vacation time, tuition, graduation, etc. Therefore, the following budget is useful. Each month money can be set aside for the seasonal or reduce other expenses. Automatic withdrawal from bank deposit to account for seasonal expenditures is helpful. Automatic withdrawal is helpful for pledges and contributions.

Most families manage by crisis. With **irregular expenses and irregular income,** families count on a smaller amount than those with regularity in timing and amount. The juggling act is a challenge. They need to congratulate themselves for doing as well as they do under the circumstances and uncertainties rather than to take the blame for an imperfect system. It is a challenge to meet needs of all members in spending, saving, and sharing the almighty dollar. Taking the hand of the Almighty Father in difficult times is a guide and blessing.

Seasonal or Irregular Expenses

January	February	March
April	**May**	**June**
July	August	September
October	November	December

MOVING OUT TO INDEPENDENCE WITH CHOICES

A Decision Tool for Independent Life-Style and Income Needed to Move Out

I. A. The purpose is to determine amount of savings needed for the time a person is moving from current residence. It is a tool to more accurately estimate expenses or income needed. It is a tool for deciding Amount of loan needed for initial expenses in a different situation. The amount depends on choices and life style.

    A. Estimate "decision income" (DeI) or income needed from a job to maintain life style:

        Project probable "gross income" GI_____

        Estimate "disposable income" DI after taxes and Social Security contributions_____.

        Estimate "take home pay" THP or "decision income" (DeI) is after deductions such as dues, parking fees, payments withheld, United Way_____ .

        Estimate "decision income" which is gross income minus disposable income minus these fees_____.

        An estimate is that Gross Income – 25% = "Decision Income." (Some estimates are 25 to 32 %)

    B. Choose expenses, saving, and giving to fit income **Or** income to cover them.

II. Initial expenses

	Low	Moderate	High	Yours
Phone installation	$ 30			
Damage deposit	250			
1st month's rent	250			
Electricity deposit	71			
Gas deposit	40			
Cable TV/Internet	20			
Food	100			
	$761			

III. Payments at end of 1st month

	Low	Moderate		
Phones/internet/TV	$23	$100		
Rent	118	100		
Electricity				
Gas				
Water/sewage				
Debts, college loans	50	100		
Saving	20	20		
Insurance	50	120		
Food	100	200		
Transportation	100	600		
Medical	40	120		
Personal/misc.	100	100		
Clothing	100	200		
Gifts/sharing/charity		300		
Entertainment/Education	80	500		
Work related	20	120		
Total	801	2,860		
Taxes	200	849		
Totals				
Income: Monthly	$1,000	$3,709		
Annually	12,000	44,508		
Hourly wage needed:				
	about $6	$22		

(However, earned income credit is available for employed low income people.)

FINANCIAL MANAGEMENT NOTEBOOK
SYSTEM: Plan, Control, Record, and Evaluate

A "Notebook System" can be used for planning, estimating and recording expenses as they are made, and for storing receipts. This system required a minimum of writing and calculating. "Working in the Book" is "Working on Finances" at a given time once a month or semi-monthly with paying bills at that time. This reduces the question whether something was paid or not. One problem is that credit cards may not have a 30 day cycle for avoiding late payments.

- The first page of a spiral notebook, left over from school use, should have goals and general financial plan.
- Pages can serve as dividers by paydays.
- Bills and "I owe you's" to be paid monthly, semiannually or annually can be placed in the pages by paydays. Looking ahead can remind one of expenses coming up. During pressure months, notes on what else to reduce can be made.
- Expenses can be summed as they are made by check, etc.
- Bills that cannot be paid this time are placed in the page divider for next time.
- Contributions or bills paid monthly are on a note and moved to next time
- The bottom half of the page can be used for recording miscellaneous expenses or those made by each family member, for special spotlighting an analysis.
- Expenses can be estimated on the left side pages to decide what to juggle.
- Utility bills can be compared over the months to motivate reduction.
- A reoccurring expense with only a one-time bill can be recorded as paid and repeated by actually moving the bill to ensuring payment periods. (Examples are monthly tuition, furniture loan, charity commitment, or a loan from a family member.) Sharing or contributions can be observed from month to month with the goal of increasing it over time.
- Insurance, savings, or charity contributions can be noted with actually moving the reminder to ensuing paydays.
- Amount paid, date paid, and check number should be written on the statement sent in as sell as on the part retained by bill payer that is kept in the notebook. The account number should be written on the check.
- Regular examination of bills and simple record of item in the notebook can catch errors and clarify what was paid when a payment and a new bill cross each other in the mail.

The notebook with the family finances should be organized and kept at an accessible place so that other family members could take the responsibility and become informed in the event that the chief money manager is suddenly unavailable or unable. Records can answer questions, project future expenses, and catch errors.

New Urgency For A New System: No Late Charges

A new type of budget or spending plan is needed for many clients due to the changing credit industry. New interest rates, grace periods, late fees, charges for returned checks, and various due dates make the handling of credit payments complex. Analysis of one client case revealed $128 of charges would accrue if credit card payments and utility payments were paid late. That amount is motivation to revise the system of paying bills to avoid late charges. The new system for paying bills on time can include:

Important is "when" to send in the check for the due date to be posted on time. If one credit card payment is late, the interest rate increases not only for that card but on all the other cards. These techniques may help:

Writing the date that the bill is due (when to send in) on the outside of the envelope in large figures.

Writing due dates (when to send) on the calendar by the "family business center."

Paying bills more often than once a month because of changing billing cycles.

Using the format designed for irregular income and irregular expenses, noting which week the bill is to be paid.

Accumulating enough balance in the checking account to pay bills as they are received.

Techniques, Tricks, and Systems that Work
for the Manager Through the Years
From Experience and Learning
List those provided by client

PLAN OR BUDGET GEARED TO PRIORITIES FOR DETERMINING INCOME NEEDED

	Two weeks Date:	Two weeks Date:	Two weeks Date:	Two weeks Date:
	$ %			
Sharing (Sh)				
Saving (S)				
Debt payment (D)				
Spending (Sp)				

Total=Sh+S+D+Sp _____

Net Income Needed _____

Actual Net Income _____

Surplus or Deficit _____

CASH FLOW ANALYSIS

	Receipt or Due Date	Income Estimated Total Monthly Date	Current	Revised	Amount Saved for Debt, Charity, or Investment
INCOME					
Net not Gross:					
Employment					
Spouse's Employment					
Real Estate					
Other Fixed Inc.					
Savings Income					
Securities Inc.					
Other Variable Inc..					
EXPENDITURES					
Housing					
Rent/Payment					
Electricity					
Gas					
Water-Sewage					
Phone					
Water Softener					
TV					
Repairs, supplies					
Furniture					
Taxes/Insurance					
FOOD					
Groceries					
Eaten Out					
TRANSPORTATION					
Payment/Bus					
Gas/Oil					
Repairs					
Insurance					
License					
Other Fees					
CLOTHING					
Laundry					
PERSONAL CARE					
Allowances					
MEDICAL					
Doctor, dentist					
Medicine					
Insurance					
OTHER					
Newspaper					
Education					
Tobacco, alcohol					
Recreation,					
Entertainment					
GIFTS/ CONTRIBUTIONS					
LIFE INSURANCE					
OTHER INSURANCE					
OTHER Child support					

SAVINGS INVESTMENTS					
TOTAL EXPENSES					
DEBT PAYMENTS					
TOTAL DEBTS AND EXPENSES					
BALANCE (Net Flow)					

FINANCIAL SUMMARY AND PLAN

Name: _____

Date: _____

Referred by:

Presenting Problems/Questions: (Real problems are clarified after further discussion.)

_____

Fears: **Other agencies or professionals working with:**

_____

Household Composition:

_____

Financial Position:

  Income (net monthly):   Source:

    minus

  Expenses:

  Debts: Type:

    equals

  Decision Income:

  Value of government services:

  Value of employee benefits:

  Assets (financial):

  Assets (personal):

_____

Creditor and legal problems (current and predicted)? *Harassment? Cut in service? Loss of goods? Court Action? Embarrassment? Immobility? Total due immediately? Cost above cash use?*

_____

Consumption and management problem: **Need for long-range planning:**

_____

Decisions to be made: (Then rank in order for solving.)   **Goals:** (Short-term and long-term)

_____

Information and resources needed to solve problems or make decisions:

_____

Compliment - Person's strengths, assets, experiences, good management:

_____

Spiritual assessment:

_____

Plan for person (steps to take): (short term-this week)Plan for counselor, educational material to give:

Plan (budget) from Chpt. 4 to implement:

_____

Plan for spiritual renewal: Scripture to read every day, hymn to sing, prayer with someone, etc.

Financial Planner's Guide:

FINANCIAL ASSESSMENT AND PLANNING

Client:_____Date:_____

Summary of Financial Position:
      Goals, objectives, values:
      Household Composition/Circumstances:
      Income flow and net worth position (wealth statement):
      Assumptions:
      Risk tolerance:
      Decisions and concerns:

Major Recommendations: (listed in priority order)

Standard of Living: (charity, cash flow, expenses, debts, life style changes)
      List by analysis of data, objectives, assumptions, recommendations (changes), implementation – for each area below also)

Sharing: (contribution, donation, gifts)

Savings: (cash reserve, investments)

Accumulations: (money, goods, business, real estate, education, retraining)

Protection: insurance, employee benefits, government benefits)

Financial Independence: (retirement)

Estate Planning:

Taxation:

Security: (spiritual growth, changes in source, job, business, miscellaneous)

◊◊◊ ⧗ ⧗ ◊◊◊

Chapter 5. Call to Change Financial Management through Counseling Paths

The shepherd under the direction of the Great Shepherd guides people in the path or picks them up from the pit. The shepherd's unique contribution is suggesting both spiritual and financial steps. The shepherd chooses paths for the unique individual and situation. The shepherd's own personality and beliefs affect the techniques used for financial change. The spirit in which the technique is used is more important than the technique. Theories or approaches do not have applicability for all types of problems. Purposes of this chapter are to equip shepherds to

– apply various approaches (theories) for changing patterns of financial management,
– discuss the resistance to change,
– identify dominant patterns (human nature) of change affecting financial matters,
– recognize underlying emotions affecting financial behavior, and
– know specific steps for change utilizing inspiration with financial management.

The counselor-shepherd knows that the presenting problem is rarely the real or underlying problem. Conversation begins with items perceived as "safe" to expose and used to test the waters for deeper exploration. The challenge is to work on one or two things that may be captivating individuals preventing them from moving to better financial management. The goal is to improve financial behavior so that greater financial stress is reduced no matter what the underlying cause. Financial management must be changed to prevent the spiraling downward of negative emotions and fears.

The counselor listens for subtle clues of hidden problems. The spouse might hint at something. Another clue is, when calculating cash flow, the balance indicates there are unexplained expenses. Total income flow minus total expenses and contributions equals net flow or balance (a cash flow statement). Counseling openers are: "I get the feeling there is something worrying you that is not easy to talk about." "You seem to have a burden on your mind. Would you like to tell me about it?" "You seem to be carrying a load of some kind. Would it help to talk?"[14]

Once the individual decides to commit to change, he or she must decide goals, desires, where to go, and results desired from use of money. Changes in destructive addictions cause financial havoc, affect employment, and diminish relationships. Only when individuals change their behaviors that have financial ramifications or change financial management can they change the outcomes. Unfortunately, many individuals expect different results just from wanting but not changing management. The counselor facilitates gaining freedom from captivity of thought, demons, and action through the power of the Spirit.

---

14   Howard Clinebell. *Understanding and Counseling Persons with Alcohol,, Drug, and Behavioral Addictions.* Nashville: Abingdon Press. 1998. P.312.

The overall goal of counseling is defined differently by shepherds. One definition[15] is to "empower persons to grow toward their God-given potential for full personhood, constructive relationships, joyful spirituality, and productive living including service to a needy world." Achieving the goal of abstinence or moderation in addictive substances and activities is a prerequisite for moving ahead financially. "Recovery involves the reconstruction of one's identity"[16] and step by step control of thinking, feeling, and doing. This corresponds to loving God manifested in financial management by one's mind, heart, and strength.

Underlying Emotional and Social Problems in Financial Management

Change in financial behavior occurs when deep underlying emotions, social deficits, and personality disorders are addressed. These affect financial management. Conversely, financial disorders and responsibilities add to distress and anxieties. Therefore, the admirable role of the shepherd is to address both domains. Emotional and social barriers need to be addressed *briefly* to free an individual or family to solve financial problems and develop new financial management. Dwelling on the latter areas actually will improve emotional and social captivity. For example, focus on resolutions not on the past or blaming. The shepherd can guide by saying, "You know, we do not believe in fixing blame. We just believe in fixing problems. Let us focus on fixing your problem. Then we can celebrate a Higher Planner in you."[17]

Enemies of God's Kingdom in the Culture. The shepherd can thank God for discovery of the predominant enemies in society which block opportunities for the individual "to share in the inheritance of the saints in the kingdom of light" (Colossians 1:12). The shepherd can help rescue individuals and families "from the dominion of darkness" and bring them into the kingdom of the Son" (Colossians 1:13). The shepherd can help them "be strong…against the rulers, against the authorities, against the powers of this dark world and against the spiritual forces of evil…" (Ephesians 6:10-13).

The predominant enemies are materialism, commercialism, and loneliness. These "alienate from God" and are enemies in your mind" (Colossians 1:21). They can cause erratic financial behavior, over-spending that brings on financial anxieties, and dissatisfaction with what one has or is. They determine unreal expectations and feelings of inadequacy that they try to resolve with using income but unsuccessfully. The shepherd suggests non-financial and spiritual solutions for bringing finances in order, reducing expenditures, and healing of the pain both financial and social.

Loneliness: Loneliness causes people to shop and buy things they do not even use. It causes addictions that destroy rather than help over time. Shopping gives them human interactions and helps resolve the fear of rejection by buying and having things. Spiritual solutions include walking and talking with God all day. Social solutions include finding or changing support groups, meeting basic needs of love and acceptance in different ways that do not require money, calling another lonely individual everyday to encourage him or her, having a hobby that is not too expensive, exploring unusual ways to get a job, perhaps a second job, for pay or volunteer, tutoring someone, and taking in a foster child.

---

15   Clinebell. Ibid. P.312.

16   Clinebell. Ibid. P.312.

17   Katherine Vessenes. Vestvert Advisors. Investment eCast. March 10, 2009.

Lack of Energy: Lack of energy and depression may be a physical condition as well as financial and social. All affect the psychological and emotional reasons for overspending or lack of control. Financial predicaments further exasperate the psychological affecting the physical. Never-the-less, physical conditions must be checked for diabetes, chemical imbalance, low sugar levels, low serotonin, low potassium, etc.

Also, the hurtful social interactions of words (curses), attitudes, and actions need to be identified. The social conditions affect expenditures and management because of the great needs to be accepted, to belong, to appear like the people with whom one identifies. For example, change from living like middle class to lower class is difficult and requires courage and self-acceptance. Yet, in the current economy, such change is necessary for survival.

The prescriptions in Psalm One, Matthew 10:40-42, John 4:10, 13, and Revelation 7:17 are for a "living tree planted by the streams." These bring blessedness, happiness, and productivity, prosperity, leaves not withering, God watching over us, and living forever. Connectedness and rootedness are the spiritual www: world wide web of God's word, God's works, and God's world of people who love God and respond by loving us. In contrast, the way of perishing is taking the advice in use of finances from wicked people, having a self-worth based on words of evil people, and succumbing to those who sneer at God. Courage is overcoming those who sneer at us when we believe in God, trusting his lead, and accepting his grace. Victory comes from marching to a different Drummer for purchases, sharing, and saving. People can move out of captivating situations.

Disappointment and Discouragement: Financial events as well as individual behavior bring disappointment and discouragement. These cause a momentary set back. Overcoming these is helped by having a listener to let off steam and identifying what is learned from them. Remembering Scripture and applying verses to personal financial management helps. Several that come to mind are Psalm 3:18 which assures that the Lord is close to the brokenhearted and saves those crushed in spirit; Proverbs 24:16 about falling seven times but rises again and again; and Psalm 34:19 about having many troubles but the Lord delivers a righteous man/woman from them all. The educated, counseled, and non-anxious individual concentrates on the next steps. Pray, "God, how should I feel? Think? Do?"

Depression: Listening brings awareness to depression symptoms. Depression is defined as the individual who has had two weeks or more of: feeling of captivity in a dark hole, not knowing the way out, loss of energy, loss of interest, or weight change. Does the individual see "shadows"? Feel engulfed by shadows? In the "valley of shadows" and cannot move on? The individual needs to tell someone and be taken seriously. He/she should either call a friend each day or have a friend call. The counselor identifies sources of referral, help groups, counseling centers, and asks a professional for help in biochemical depression.

One of the hallmarks of Bipolar Disease (Manic-Depressive) is that of the inability to handle money well. An individual suffering from Bipolar may spend without good judgment when in the mania phase. When in the depressed phase, the individual has much regret and remorse. There are many degrees of Bipolar and the disease may only be obvious to the family. An individual may cycle through the phases repeatedly. If the usual counseling does not help to make changes in an individual financial situation, a counselor should consider that there may be an underlying illness. Medical help is available and individuals do not need to suffer alone.

The counselor can appoint someone to sit beside or walk with the individual while doing financial tasks. A formal, legal structure is appointing or arranging for a "personal representative" to regularly assist in financial tasks. Immediate help includes setting up structure to be active, to work, to exercise or walk (with someone), and to help someone less fortunate. Write and implement three financial actions (even very small ones) that improve control over finances. Decide one task to complete each day. This in turns improves the spiritual, psychological and emotional well-being.

Naming items of gratitude help drive the demons of depression away since the place in the brain can not hold both at the same time. Apply each word of the 23rd Psalm to one's situation. Identify allegiances, fears, enemies, the blessings, and God's leading.

Grief: The shepherd saying "I understand" is not useful unless he or she has had the same type of grief. Grief is not a lack of faith. It is a process like going through a forest and chopping down trees preventing the journey beyond grief. One needs to build a focus replacing the loss. It is alright to keep a place in the heart for the lost one. Some hospitals help by making a memory box with things from the deceased baby. People handle grief in different ways and some helpful ways are: crying, acknowledging fears, having someone who listens, encouraging all types of options, not rushing into decisions, getting information, not feeling paralyzed so one cannot make decisions, realizing grief is a feeling and it may not be visible to others, controlling how one handles their other feelings although they are not ignored. When something triggers the grief, it can be turned into thankfulness that, at least, you have memories. Grief is an emotion like the ocean waves. They come when not expected. For some, an individual can walk through them, but for other individuals, they are overcome. Grief can turn into joy when people allow the Spirit to make a new creation by looking forward and not dwelling on the past. New financial management can occur when it is asked in Jesus' name (John 16:23-24).

Guilt: Managing guilt is as important as any stress. Some remedies are paying back double (Exodus 22:9), accepting consequences, (Exodus 34:7), guilt offerings (1 Samuel 6:13), confession (Psalm 32:5), and making restitution (Leviticus 5:16). Hope is assured when we draw near to God and are cleansed (Hebrews 10:21-23). Some people have guilt that is really not from their own doing and can be sorted out. Never-the-less, counselors can recognize the danger in spending or giving to make up for guilt. The counselor suggests creative activities in restoration of errors such as writing/making a birthday card rather than buying one. Also, activities are suggested to fulfill the longing "to make a difference" in the well-being of the world. This redirects use of money.

Many individuals by habit or by nature are selfish, shallow, thoughtless, and insensitive. An event or financial crisis can bring painful guilt to the sensitive individual. Otherwise, people ignore their guilt and blame others for financial mistakes. They keep running from guilt until they know the "pardoning grace" of a handshake from God. Then they are enabled to be what they were meant to be and handle finances.

Remorse: Remorse involves self-condemnation, conviction from God, guilt, and repentance. One needs a "turning in the path" or a change in direction in financial management. Recovering from remorse involves restitution for complete healing. Receiving forgiveness and grace fosters ability to change financial management. The counselor suggests that every time remorse engulfs individuals, they come up with a way to improve financial management.

Resentment: This can be harbored for years. Verbalizing helps, whereas retaliation may cause more problems. When resentment arises, they can turn it into thankfulness for gifts received from the individual or company. Naming the gifts helps overcome bitterness.

Sadness: This involves sadness of heart, mind, and soul. Cry as exemplified, "Jesus wept." Remember the promise that God heals the broken-hearted. (See Psalm 34:18 and Isaiah 61:1.) Make or buy a gift for someone who also harbors sadness.

Forgiveness: The shepherd can help individuals receive the gift of forgiveness from the Spirit. Another way is to remind individuals that Jesus forgives people in their imperfect state and, therefore, they can forgive others in their imperfection and hurt that they bestowed on others. Forgiveness is mandatory to move on whereas not forgetting is protective. Not forgetting some things makes an individual more aware of what may happen and to be shrewd for the next time. God's protection is to remember so that people can be armed with the shield of God when they go into difficult, dangerous situations with mean people and are thus prepared. Forgiveness puts the past behind and helps prevent over-spending to make up for past hurts, past depravations, and further hurts to others. Forgiveness, although it is difficult and takes time, is less expensive than harboring ill feelings that stifle and destroy. By revolving their life around God, forgiveness is easier when spouse, children, parent, supervisor, or job do wrong or deeply disappoint them.

Fear: Fear can motivate or immobilize. The right dosage of fear makes one move in spite of fears, to be on guard, to protect oneself, to have the adrenaline to make things happen, to learn from experiences, and to become stronger having gone through fearful experiences. This builds character.

When fears immobilize, the shepherd helps the individual to verbalize them. The counselor asks what the individual is afraid might happen. Naming the fears is a type of confession and helps in moving forward to handle financial matters in a time of fear. Identifying options reduces fears.

What are you afraid will happen? What are you anxious about? In the examples, there are fears of change, of losing control, of lack of respect, of not having enough food, and of taking care of debts. The shepherd can then provide technical information on the legal process, for example. Rather than just saying "pray about it," together the shepherd and the individual decide steps to handle the fears and the changes involved. They decide how to "work to direct and reduce worry. They define steps to change financial management, to move. Examples are how to effectively talk to creditors, how not to react too strongly to family members because of losing control, how to buy inexpensive food, ways to get another job, and developing income sources in retirement. The hope is for God's love to cast out fear.

There are those who have a habit of fearing. They should strongly say, "Stop that thinking. Get behind me Satan. Break a habit before it breaks me. I will give up one fear for lent. I can start the habit of running to the Lord to talk about fears." They can pray so earnestly, repeatedly, like Jesus did in the Garden of Gethsemane, until they are submitted to the Lord, not to fears! In Psalm 34:4, it says, "I sought the Lord, and he answered me; he delivered me from my fears." A "song in the night" may come as reported by several writers in the Scripture (Job 35:10 for one).

Healthy fear can motivate to change and get things done. One can fear God sufficiently to be respectful of the laws, be reverent, be in the Word, and be trusting. Fear sufficiently from experience and education to do something about finances, to be shrewd, to not throw pearls to swine, and to be aware of the wolves.

There are all types of fears. Some people fear everything. They even fear that they are sinning if they fear or worry. They cannot move, apply for a job, complete a contract, or make a phone call. They fear the shadows, their abilities to do finances, failure, and even successes. The shepherd shows how people can move in spite of their fears. This may require a financial makeover in which their source of security is changed. A change in lifestyle can be embraced, rather than feared, to overcome fear of economic disaster.

The shepherd helps identify ungrounded fears from real fears. Some fears are ungrounded and some are trivial yet they are weighting you down, making the travel cumbersome and fearful.

Patterns of "fight" or "flight" are analyzed. The shepherd suggests that the individuals talk with God about fears as Jesus did. Discussion can include how one is a slave to fear in some ways. They can write what will give them courage in spite of fears.

Near the end of the counseling session, steps for talking with God about fears are defined. One can recite every day while doing finances, "The promise that God is with us, will strengthen us, and uphold us" (Isaiah 41:10). Also, one could say, "The Lord did not promise life would be easy. He did promise to be with us each step of the way" (based on Isaiah 43:1-2, 5, 12). The counselor starts the first step, arranges for someone to go with the individual in a fearful situation, sits beside them when filling out forms, helps write letters, and encourages financial management in spite of fears.

Anxiety: Options for change are suggested by the counselor when the individual is blinded by anxiety and fear to see them. Fertile soil for growth is prepared by the counselor so that change can take root, birds do not devour the seed, others do not trample ideas to death, and the heat of pressures do not scorch attempts toward change.

The counselor either calms the sea and/or the individual. The shepherd as counselor is the non-anxious one with options. Walking with the individual makes the path easier and/or the shoes stronger.

The shepherd helps the individual know how to put a crisis on the shelf for 5 minutes today, 10 minutes tomorrow, and 15 minutes the next day, and on to control of emotions. The shepherd helps to set up a program of spiritual exercise, emotional rejuvenation for health, wholeness, and growth.

Ways to control anxiety include counting delights of the day and things to be thankful for each day. Other inspirational thoughts to control anxiety and any spending disorders because of it are: Gratitude drives demons away. Rest in the Lord. Breathe in and out "Into the arms of Jesus." Have peace in spite of anxieties. Change source of security from material and wealth security to ability to adjust. Reflect on what supported one through prior difficult times before which now can give strength and patience. Do something and talk with people who have information (Philippians 2:27-29). Humble self and receive the promise you will be lifted up in due time (1 Peter 5:6-7). Read Psalm 91, Psalm 23, and Philippians 4:4-8 over and over again. Have routines, regular schedules, and rituals for restoring power and peace. Walk through the fears, the valley of the shadows, to get to the blessings of the table (Psalm 23) to get a job, maintain a job, handle finances for children, handle finances for parents, retirement, etc. Turn some of the fears and anxieties into faith. Operate and make financial decisions from faith not fear and anxieties.

Worry: Some people need to worry more about their finances in order to be faithful stewards and make plans under the Great Counselor. The first stage of worry is accepting that worry is alright as a nudge from the Spirit to care and be concerned. Then an individual needs to decide what to worry about today and what to worry about later. Work instead of expending energy and time for worry. In other words, time, intelligence, and energy spent worrying need to be redirected to tackle one concern after another. As one gains success, hope and more success increase. Worry out of control or controlling people is the problem. In fact, if people were not anxious or worried about something, they probably would not do anything. They do need to improve, build the kingdom of God, and protect oneself and their families. People need those who will help fight off the negative emotions, the cancer cells, the lies, the criticisms, and injustices that distract from God's purposes.

Overwhelmed with Burdens, Responsibility: Financial burdens are different from others in that in addition to worries, fears and stress they include difficulties of information, process, and legal ramifications. Current families do not benefit much from the experiences of their parents/grandparents since there are new laws, procedures, etc. Since fear brings on procrastination, work needs to be designed to meet obligations in a timely manner. Responsibilities and financial burdens are lighter when shared in the "dual yoke" system. Yoked together, Jesus walks and works with you (Cara MacCallister). "Take my yoke upon you and learn from me" (Matthew 11:28-30).

Managing Stress: One way is to call on the Spirit, walk with the Spirit, and then work smarter and rest better, breathing in "Power" and out "Peace." Post Traumatic Stress occurs when flashbacks and nightmares come, sorrow is not resolved, and the past is the focus. Healing is necessary enough so as not to make erratic purchases or hoard. Healing is a process involving changing the response to the event or memories, forgiving, and focusing on Christ not the crisis. Find ways to heal the emotional damage and hurts without overspending or wasting money. As Isaiah 43:18 says, "Forget the former things; do not dwell on the past." The past can teach one to learn from financial mistakes and chalk it up to tuition for consumer education. Perhaps it is a habit of thinking about the terrible things that happened or a habit of poor financial management. Bad habits (and memories) need to be replaced with good ones or else as Scripture says seven demons more will fill the void (Luke 11:24-26). Exercise and use the artistic side of the brain to reduce stress. Sufficient stress is needed to pay bills and save money in comparison shopping.

Inability to Set Goals: Individuals go in circles emotionally and mentally when in a crisis. The counselor intervenes by asking them to choose from a list of possibilities what are their wants, desires, goals, efforts toward a goal, and steps for today (or tomorrow). Jesus said after healing, "Take up your bed and walk."

Anger: Anger keeps an individual in captivity if financial patterns and personal interactions continue which gave rise to the anger. The counselor identifies with the individual what makes him or her angry. They discuss what would be a sin in response to Jesus' words: "In your anger do not sin" (Ephesians 4:26). See where office politics, treatment of people, and past injustices or deprivation makes one angry, as a result money is spent to recover. Forgiveness is controlling the anger so that it does not destroy people or make relationships worse. If recently unemployed, the individual can be helped to fulfill another role in life. People can be encouraged to use the power of the mind. They can use energy of the emotion to change financial management.

Feeling Unworthy, Inadequate, Ashamed: The counselor helps the individual to concentrate on the strengths that helped him or her succeed in the past. The individual is asked, "What keeps you going" to identify inner strengths or friendships. Some people buy anything to try to cover feelings of inadequacy. The counselor helps develop inner strengths and capitalize on the gifts God has given. Together, they decide which hidden assets need to be developed and what can be emphasized to replace inadequacies. The counselor says, "Remember, 'The Lord does not look at the things man looks at. Man looks at the outward appearance, but the Lord looks at the heart'" (1 Samuel 16:7). God looks on the inside and loves you as you are. God your Creator wants to walk and talk with you about finances. You have beauty and strength not as the world judges. Keep saying all the time 'I can do everything through him who gives me strength' (Philippians 4:13)." When you look into the mirror, say, "I am made in the image of God. My job is to re-present God to others, not to buy into the demands of our culture and the passions of the flesh." The counselor discusses what it is to "die to the sinful use of money and be alive, a new creation in Christ" (Romans 6:2, 11, 14). The new creation listens to true messages of God's love, grace, and acceptability. The new creature identifies how these are reflected in changed financial behavior and management.

Making Decisions: The counselor assists in making one decision at a time. He/she asks, "Can you live with the worst that can happen?" He/she discusses what one is afraid might happen. What information is needed? The counselor grieves over the good choice given up for the one chosen. They discuss there are risks. They discuss how one succeeded before when there were risks. Risking in investments and financial changes may give a return against a guaranteed loss to doing nothing. They decide what is an option if the first choice does not work. They remind, as in any game, one wins some and loses some. The fears of making mistakes keep people from making a decision, paralyzes them. Someone may have told the individual a decision was stupid and the individual lost confidence to decide.

Need for Grace: Individuals are assured of grace and can learn from wrong decisions.. As Jesus was full of grace and truth, both grace and truth will set one free (John 1:14, 17). In John 1:16-18 are other promises of grace – one blessing after another and signs and wonders (Acts 14:2-4). People are saved by grace, not works (Ephesians 2:7-9). The message of grace is that after one has suffered or struggled, one will be restored and made strong, firm and steadfast (1 Peter 5:10-11).

Therefore, people can give grace to others and forgive them for their mistakes, their mistreatment, and trespasses against them. If people then accept their own forgiveness and grace, they are free. This financial freedom gives empowerment to change spending, saving, and sharing. They can learn to manage finances in new and liberating ways.

Love-based Approach: A Spiritual Program of Recovery

In the "love-based" approach, a spiritual program of recovery is embraced for changing from addictive behavior to becoming a new creation in financial management. Recognition begins the process of confessing, repenting, asking forgiveness, feeling the love of God through others, and showing love for others. The individual becomes committed to God, not to addictions and worldly passions.

The shepherd (pastor, compassion minister, educator, outreach director, mentor, helping professional, money coach, the support group, or the church fellowship group) provide unconditional love, love of the individual, and forgiving love. In surrendering, the defiant individual changes to accept help, guidance, and control from outside. Negative, aggressive feelings are replaced with love, friendliness, and peacefulness which make strategies for coping with problems possible.[18] These relationships give the courage to survive financial trauma or crises as a way of life and give hope.

Love combined with the Spirit creates and empowers change in small steps, one at a time, or in drastic changes. The Spirit moves heart, soul, mind, and strength. The Spirit sighs for them, because many in deep financial despair cannot pray for themselves (Romans 8:25-27). They cannot just say, "Trust God." They cannot just "stop doing or buying this or that." For some, the first change is to open the heart a little to receive the love. For others it is building confidence to communicate to family members and creditors.

Knowledge alone changes some people, whereas not others. Still, others are knowledgeable and willing while not *able* to change because of anxieties, fears, habits, un-acceptance by others, self

---

18   Ibid. P.359.

hate, guilt, and shame. Rather than self-worth based on performance, God's unconditional love comes from loving self as one is today and giving love, acceptance, and resources to others.[19]

Pain or crisis does not necessarily cause transformation or change. These can be the mechanism for the shepherd to facilitate opening "the heart of a person to the grace of God."[20] The theological premise for the transformation or recovery is the grace of God. The shepherd can create an environment conducive to change and hope. It is God's grace that makes this happen in His timing. The pain may have to get worse to make change happen. In other cases, the shepherd lovingly assures people "the worse is probably over." God will heal although not cure.

In moving from fear to love-based financial behavior, the counselor helps the compulsive spender or addictive person first see their search for happiness[21] was in things, possessions, wealth, and expensive habits or activities. To break this cycle of fear, the shepherd helps them see God's love expressed in different ways, even in the midst of darkness. Therefore, in addition to confrontation and practical techniques of intervention, the shepherd must have loving compassion.

In changing to a love-based approach, the focus is on the present – the newness, release, and relief. Peace is obtained when people experience God's transforming grace and the evidence of real change in financial management/behavior. In focusing on the present, getting through the day in a crisis, they move and think at higher levels than when possessed with negative thoughts or images of the past. Peace is acquired by practicing the Presence and self-acceptance.

The shepherd can direct steps patterned after "The Twelve Steps" spiritual program[22] which activate God's love in heart, soul, mind, and strength and love of neighbor as self. They are

(1) admitting financial affairs including addictions and desires are unmanageable; pain and buried conflicts are unresolved; overcoming denial;

(2) believing in a Higher Power to restore management and control,

(3) turning over will and lives to the care of God in total surrender;

(4) honestly searching their thinking, feeling, shame, guilt, financial wrongs, poisons, dominating fears, and worldly gods;

(5) admitting and confessing these wrongs and fears to God and to another individual in details, telling their story;

(6) preparing the soil of the soul for God to overcome temptations of commercialism, the negative influence of others, addictions, bad habits, poor management, financial wrongs;

(7) humbly asking God to remove these wrongs, obstacles and fears;

(8) writing a list of people who we have harmed or have harmed us in preparing the heart to restore communication and remove negative feelings;

(9) making amends to others wherever possible except when it would cause more harm or injury;

(10) admitting and asking forgiveness whenever we continue doing wrong or not trusting God to care for us;

(11) seeking in prayer and meditation to be sustained by God's love, to follow His will, to resist temptation, to fill the inner emptiness, and be Spirit empowered to continue rather than to use destructive and expensive means;

---

19   Ibid. P.73.

20   Ibid. P.148.

21   Ibid. Pp.68-70.

22   Howard Clinebell. Ibid. Pp.195-244.

(12) carrying the message to others and practicing the principles as God commanded: not coveting, not greedy, not having gods of the world; being honest, satisfied with God's love, and loving neighbor by sharing;

(13) affirming and enjoying our strengths, talents, and creativity not hiding these from ourselves and others[23]; giving thanks for everything including the things done right during each day with the Spirit's power and love;

(14) accepting that life is not easy and there are ups and downs on the path which are lessons for growth;[24] as the Lord is with us each step of the way; and

(15) taking steps to a) heal finances; b) organize lives; c) avoid (if possible) situations or people who are hurtful, harmful, or demeaning; d) have control under God's control; e) have commitment to change and f) have joy and peace from the God who saves.

Group Benefits

Love paves the way to recovery, provides ability to change and new ways for handling finances. The love of God touches the mind, heart, soul, and strength. The love of another individual enfolds the individual although broken in not feeling love. The love of a support group, an addictions group or sincere church fellowship, builds up the individual although ridden with shame. The love of God through others gives fertile soil for roots to survive the struggles of life and the fierce winds that uproot. The hardened heart, which turned away from God and turned to destructive behaviors may become receptive to the love of God and correction. With love from God and others, the Spirit as the Great Counselor guides, comforts the tormented spirit, and directs the changes necessary for hope and fulfillment of purpose. The Spirit helps the damaged individual forgive those who inflicted pain, were non-accepting or cruel, driving the wounded to addictions. The group's love helps to repair the irreducible worth as an individual, strengthened in growing competence. "Everyone needs the sure knowledge of being wanted, of belonging, and being united with others in a larger whole, rather than isolated and alone."[25]

Everyone needs to feel achievement is possible and to receive recognition. They need understanding and opportunity to share thoughts and feelings honestly, without judgment, with acceptance. The counselor or group can help change heart, soul, mind and strength in arranging for needs to be met in the counseling relationship. They try to find love by others seeing what they have or do rather than for whom they are, as they are. Their lack of love and feelings of inadequacy drive them to fear and fill the lack with fulfillment by desire for things, power over others, and greed. Media, advertising, and peers increase the sense of inadequacies rather than the Spirit setting ablaze joy and happiness. The need is to depend on God and God's love for self-fulfillment and security rather than on things, substances, and others.

Financial Management to Change Cognitive Behavior

---

23   Oliver J. Morgan and Merle Jordan (Eds.)   *Addiction and Spirituality – A Multidisciplinary Approach.* St. Louis, Missouri: Chalice Press. 1999. P.131.

24   Ibid. P.133.

25   Howard Clinebell. *Understanding and Counseling Persons with Alcohol, Drugs and Behavioral Addictions.* Nashville: Abingdon Press. 1998. P.60.

The shepherd is a "change expert" and is "an agent of change." The expertise in being effective is applying the approach for the unique individual, family, and situation. The approach contains assumptions of human nature in regard to financial behavior. The approach utilizes questions and responses that are effective in changing financial management. Below are various approaches (theories) that illustrate how these ways can change financial management.

Behavioral Based Approach. People have been conditioned to behave as a result of satisfactory responses to stimuli and reinforcement of those responses.[26] Change is possible by understanding one's thoughts, feelings, and financial actions. Focus is on the observable behavior and complaints of specific operational variables. Focus is on regaining or gaining control of thoughts, feelings and financial actions. The goal is to change the attitudes for the need to buy. It is also to meet the basic needs without going deeper into debt. An example of following through is to cut up credit cards to stop the automatic use of them. Changed behavior is reinforced by the satisfaction in feelings of control and reduced costs.

Techniques include using the interview and observation for behavioral assessment. Different structures for managing finances are implemented in the hope that changed attitudes will follow. Assertiveness training, including role playing, is useful for saying no to children, salespeople, and addictive behavior. Training in "thought-stopping" interrupts the connection between the stimulus and the anxiety.[27]

Applications to behavioral theory are readily seen. An individual buys a particular product, with some frequency, because the immediate consequence is a highly positive experience or reward such as increased status with using a particular brand. Or an individual may avoid saving money because the positive consequences are not immediate and perhaps present an immediate negative consequence, e.g. an empty pocket. The counselor shows rewards from the saving action and specific methods to both save and to reward "saving behavior."[28]

Insight Based Approach. Some people change when they receive financial or consumer knowledge, insight, and awareness leading to new understandings and acceptance of self. This theory assumes that chronological age determines awareness, insight, capacity to enjoy life, and contributions to others.[29] Youth make mistakes and some learn from them. Others need a crisis to create desire to learn or change. Others are unable to change with knowledge alone.

The shepherd in financial counseling stresses thinking-doing-feeling, in that order, to reduce financial stress. What an individual thinks about, he or she becomes. Thinking about Scriptural instructions rather than pressure of peers or advertisements will lead to action and then feelings of control and joy, fruit of the Spirit can follow. In contrast, when people operate from negative feelings that dominate such as obsession with comfort, fear, and feeling of inadequacy, action may not happen. Feelings cannot be trusted. The heart can be deceptive. One needs to grow in recognizing truth based on reality in the economic system and the word of God. There are facts of

26   J. F. Burke. *Contemporary Approach to Psychiatry and Counseling.* Pacific Grove, CA: Brooks/Cole. 1989.

27   Burke. P.166.

28   C. J. Pulvino, J.L. Lee and C. E. Foreman. *Communicating with Clients: A Guide for Financial Professionals.* Paramus, N. J.: Prentice Hall Information Services. 1987. Pp. 56-58.

29   Burke. 1989. P.384.

how the legal system works, how the credit system works, and what current economic conditions affect people.

The counselor helps erase erroneous thinking, inadequate thinking and gives information – the facts. The counselor stresses **changing the structure and methods** and in so doing assumes hope and courage will follow. Especially in crisis, the "doing options" give hope. Otherwise, fear and defeatist attitudes will not move an individual along. Attitude adjustments then can follow information, thinking, and doing. The support for this counseling approach is "Love your God with all your heart, soul, mind and strength." So thinking, doing and feeling are involved.

Structure is implemented. The shepherd can appoint someone to sit beside or walk with the individual while doing financial tasks. A formal, legal structure is appointing or arranging for a "personal representative" to regularly assist in financial tasks for someone. Immediate help includes setting up structure of a budget, to be active, to work, to exercise or walk (someone with you), and to help someone less fortunate. Write and implement three financial actions (even very small ones) that improve control over finances. Decide one task to complete each day. This in turns improves the spiritual, psychological and emotional well-being.

Cognitive Approach. The counselor's goal is "cognitive restructuring" of perceptions, attitudes, beliefs and expectations. These may not have been readily observable. Techniques for changing behavior assume people learn vicariously by observing others and seeing the consequences.[30] The goals are to replace irrational and faulty reasoning with more realistic patterns. Change requires observation of financial models, stories of other people and consequences of their reasoning, and practice with verbalizing self-statements about money. The counselor does not push values down the throat. Rather he or she shows alternative thought patterns and the possible consequences such as always living beyond one's current income. Different ways of living, consuming and managing finances, as well as thinking about finances are shown.

Approach of Transactional Analysis. The counselor observes the mode of behavior to determine if a change in taking responsibility is necessary. The personality is assumed to be ego states of exteropsyche or Parent, archaeopsyche or Child, and neopsyche or Adult. Although each of these states is available, the Adult as a computer directs behavior realistically by calculating possibilities and probabilities in the financial arena. However people want strokes, attention and recognition. Therefore, money is spent, saved, or shared to get these. People play games, also, of which "some are unconscious manipulations of social transaction" having negative consequences.[31]

Financial behavior follows an advertising or commercial script or a consumption pattern written in the individual's head which he or she thinks they are to follow and fulfill the role in life. The script may be followed unconsciously. The counselors help the script to be rewritten for glorifying God and appropriateness for the individual's financial situation at the time.

An example of inappropriate ego state is where the client, acting as a child, wants to place all financial responsibility on the counselor, acting as a parent. Counselors sometimes are guilty of assuming the parent role rather than fostering an adult-adult relationship.

Humanistic-Existential Approach. The individual is assumed to be growth-oriented and capable of taking responsibility. The motivation for growth is based on the innate human capacity

---

30   Burke. Ibid.

31   Burke. 1989. Pp.248-249.

to achieve self-actualization after sufficient needs at other levels have been satisfied. Maslow[32] described these levels as biological and safety, social in identifying one's identity and establishing meaningful relationships with others, and psychological in the search for meaning, purpose, values and goals. Expenditures represent these levels which may be excessive. The counselor helps people meet their needs in less expensive ways.

Techniques for change involve the therapeutic relationship and emotional insight into stage of development. The counselor builds trust in the client to find their own awareness of conflicts and assume responsibility for change.

The counselor provides information for increasing the probability of making a decision and the predominant level of motivation based on Maslow's need hierarchy. Then the client can exert reasonable effort to affect the economic environment when he or she has a sense of control over personal business or consumer affairs. The counselor facilitates acquisition and development of resources to move the client to self-actualization under God's control and further to glorify God and share or act for the neighbor's good.

Person Centered Approach. Financial healing resides within the individual rather than in the power of the counselor in the person-centered theory and so is considered "nondirective." The counseling experience is described "as a shared journey in which both therapist and client reveal their humanness and participate in a growth experience."[33] Change is facilitated with the counselor relationship when it is genuine, empathetic, and unconditionally positive.[34] Yet the counselor assumes people have a vast potential for understanding self and for resolving their own problems.[35]

Techniques for change include questions and comments to assist the client to clarify the situation. Comments are: I notice a frown, You seem confused, Tell me what's going on, and Please go on. Paraphrasing shows the client how he or she can be understood and how items can be clarified or corrected. Summarizing periodically helps. To commit to change, the counselor can say, "It appears that you need or want to do some things differently if you want to solve the problem of….. Do you agree? What have you decided you must change? Brainstorming may be useful. The client chooses solutions and is helped to be very specific in financial solutions. The counselor may ask, "What do you mean by…? Then the client prioritizes the list. The plan cannot be finalized if the client does not know exactly where the money is spent. Although a temporary plan can be identified, the client will have to keep track, record and observe spending over a certain time period. Assessment of the spending gives a basis for taking greater control and planning more realistically. Although the client is assumed trustworthy, the process of planning and controlling expenses may be new to him or her. Planning and controlling may have been nonexistent in other areas of life. Therefore, the healing, the guidance and the power of the Spirit are essential in the change process.

The Logotherapy Approach. The assumption in this theory is that free will is expressed in both action and attitude. The primary motivation of humans is to have meaning in life. An inborn

---

32   Burke, 1989. Pp.385-386.

33   G. Corey. *Theory and Practice of Counseling and Psychotherapy*. 3rd Ed. Belmont, CA: Brooks/Cole Publishing Co. 1986. P.103.

34   Burke. Ibid. P.385.

35   Corey. Ibid.

desire of all humans is to be meaningfully engaged in life [particularly work] and that meaning must be discovered individually.[36] Happiness is the result of a meaningful life. This assumption is in contrast to Freud's assumption that pleasure is dominant in motivation and to Adler's assumption that power is dominant. Therefore the techniques for change include finding meaning through completion of financial tasks, giving to missions, and choosing productive activities. The counselor helps individuals focus on projects and solutions rather than analyzing why the behavior, financial problems or past mistakes occurred.

Adlerian Approach. The nature of humans is considered self-centered with a dominant method used in interacting with others and spending. The nature of problems involves the feeling of powerlessness and inappropriate methods of meeting needs. Self-centeredness is overcome by motivating the client "to do something for society, choosing to display social interest."[37]

After gaining insight into the client's early life, lifestyle, private logic, confused goals and maladaptive behavior patterns, the counselor moves "the client toward specific changes of financial behavior by establishing new goals and encouraging the client to move in directions that benefit both client and society."[38]

Application by Poduska[39] states, "Counselors face not only the task of helping clients resolve their immediate financial problems. They also help them cope effectively with personality characteristics that dictate how they manage their financial affairs. The determination of the dominant interaction method or the client's first priority [superiority, control, pleasing, and comfort] is one of the most useful tools in determining financial treatment."

Superiority "manifests itself through a desire to buy the best whether one can afford it or not,…use of particular brand names and labels, and prestige of the store. Reference groups of the client with a 'superiority priority' are those 'who appear more successful than themselves…'" "Insight therapy is used by confronting clients with the real purposes in purchases (spitting in their soup) by pointing to consequences, prescribing paradoxical intentions, and establishing 'goal alignment' of sufficiency among family members."

Control priority manifests itself by "not giving into the urge to purchase what could be categorized as wants, luxuries, or the frills of life…" and therefore "impulse buying is absolutely forbidden," existence is miserly, saving is exaggerated, and surroundings are austere." Some believe that the one who controls the money controls all (others, distribution of inheritance, family income, and outcome), and may be secretive about income and net worth, overly insured, and inflexible in their plans. "Counselors help 'controllers' to see themselves as educators more than dictators, to 'catch themselves' when criticizing others or passing judgment on other's imperfection in spending." This insight can allow them to gradually change their perspective.

"The **pleasing priority** is manifested by purchases to avoid rejection and the belief that money can buy love and acceptance. Some individuals may buy gifts "to gain recognition and affection, lending money to neighbors when their own family is in need, not asking for repayment, co-signing loans, inability to say no to requests made by family members, or buying for the attention of sales

---

36   Burke. Ibid. P.290.

37   Burke. Ibid. P.231.

38   Burke. Ibid. P.231.

39   Bud Poduska. Financial Counseling Using Principles of Adlerian Psychology. *Individual Psychology*. 41. 1985. Pp.136-145.

persons." Processes used by the counselor include "examination of the true basis of interpersonal relationships, motivations of buying and lending behavior, and paradoxical intentions."

Clients with **comfort priorities** "tend to be self-indulgent and to make little or no discrimination between wants and needs," or may be impulsive buyers by reducing the stress of "frustration of not having what is desired." Stress is reduced by refinancing loans, taking out additional loans, consolidating existing loans, obtaining cash advances, delaying payments on less stressful bills, or declaring bankruptcy. "Since clients are often evasive about providing information, the counselor: 1) suggests the real purpose of their behavior is unwillingness to assume responsibility and 2) builds up client confidence in their ability."

Comfort clients may expect the counselor to solve their financial problems in a short period of time whereas the problems have developed over a long period of time. One technique is to urge clients "to act as if" they were someone they admired who was "financially solvent, significant, not arrogant, but vital." "Comfort-oriented persons…resist structure or limited corrective programs" and therefore, "remedial programs…should not be too austere." Alternatives for increasing income rather than reducing expenditures are more effective.[40]

The Approach of Dominant Predispositions.

Poles wave the flags for allegiance and financial behavior. Within a family, individuals are drawn in different directions and hence the conflict and uncertainty. Some individuals are bi-polar and hence confused whether to save or spend. The two conflicting and dominant poles are 1) achievement and risk taking for growth, change, and excitement and 2) security, stability, and reserve. The counselor helps the individual or couple become aware of motivations. The counselor helps extremists have balance in financial activity. The counselor helps the client move from one to the other as needed for courage to advance and expand resources. Too risky of individuals are helped with sensibility to have a reserve. God asks people to move in faith with investing resources and making changes. God also asks people to be content with his good gifts and find happiness in the Lord rather the world's way of achievement and risky thrills. On the other hand, people are asked to risk all for the work of the Lord and get a return on their investment.

The basic need of achieving or expanding wants can be channeled, redirected, substituted toward the purpose of God. Money can be spent in Jesus' name and for his sake. The basic need for security and a lighter burden can be found in trusting God and his provisions. Therefore, selfish control and anxious miserliness in use of money can be channeled, redirected, to the "neighbor's good" and expanded work for God's kingdom, not fearfully saving, retreating from assertive missions, or not generous.

The theme in Jesus' teaching is total surrender to God's will. He acknowledged that the "spirit is willing but the flesh is weak" (Matthew 26:41). He taught that those who seek to save their lives will lose them. He warned that the gift, talents, or money must be used or they will be taken away. He showed the cost of discipleship. He promised that when individuals and families seek first the kingdom of God, their needs will be added to them.

Although the dominant desire is "I surrender all" to the Lord and Master, habits of previous predispositions, human weakness, and the lures of the worldly pleasures dominate financial behavior. Paul explains this well in Romans 7. Habits, natural inclinations, commercial programming, peer pressures, and hunger have to be surrendered. The challenge of counseling is moving people to desire spiritual growth and security in God undergirding financial decisions and behavior. The

---

40   Poduska. Ibid.

shepherd counselor facilitates movement under the guidance of the Spirit of God. The submitted heart, desiring to live and have meaning in Jesus, ultimately will resist the desire of cultural trends, habits of spending, and addictions.

Since the individual has a dominant predisposition, problems are seen through the individual's lenses. The lenses may be quite different, even opposite of the counselor. Resistance to change as assessed by the counselor may be a function of the individual not perceiving a problem as the counselor perceives or fears.

The counselor must be cautious in identifying the dominant predisposition because the observation may be moods, personality, and different cultural background rather than different predisposition. Never-the-less, focus can be on the problem solution rather than analyzing predisposition and the whys of the problem.

Facing Reality and Responses to Counselors about Financial Management

The goal of reality counseling is to help individuals or families learn effective ways of acting, buying, saving, managing, and communicating to meet their needs, needs of the community, needs of the church, and to glorify God. The techniques are to gain a commitment to change, set goals toward which the individual/family will work, establish priorities in goals, plan for attaining the most important goals, learn to overcome obstacles, implement the plan, evaluate the results, and replan or move on to the next goal.

People change management patterns, consumption, or savings when their skills improve. They change when they gain knowledge or information on financial procedures or products. Therefore, the counselor presents procedures for better management, consumption, and saving that are appropriate for the unique personality and situation of the client. The counselor provides experiences for skill building. The most difficult task of the counselor is to change the willingness of the client, which is based on different emotional reactions.

Improved plans will not be utilized unless the counselor assesses the willingness, addresses stated and unstated barriers, and applies techniques or words to modify behavior. Unstated barriers are erroneous beliefs and emotional reasons. The counselor must recognize that stated comments may reflect rational thinking whereas unstated reasons reflect erroneous thinking, faulty beliefs and anxiety. The counselor must address underlying erroneous beliefs. For example, the counselor can ask, "Suppose you did not spend this money, what would be the bad thing that would happen?"

The individual has to care enough to make changes. The counselor has to care for the individual enough to assess why there is resistance to change and then empower change. The counselor can assess barriers to financial suggestions by responses that are unstated as well as stated.

1. Barrier: Stated, "You are right and we really want to change". Unstated when out of the counseling office, "We have just bought more time and now that the creditors, etc. are off our backs we can continue to do whatever we want to do."

Response: "This month you are off the hook and maybe next month. Unless you make drastic changes, creeping indebtedness will catch up with you. Bad credit ratings, bad checks, etc. will be on your credit report for seven years. A worse emergency or opportunities will come along which you will not be able to utilize credit for them. Control your money now or you will be controlled by it. Your economic security will be diminished as you cannot get more credit, you will not be able to use services to which you are accustomed, you will lose some possessions, or you or your relatives will be harassed. Eventually, your boss will be notified and your status or job will be in jeopardy."

2. Barrier: Stated, "I have worked so hard or have been victimized now I deserve something for me." Unstated, "I must make up for past deprivation, working so hard, or sacrificing for other people for such a long time."

    Response: "I know that you do deserve rewards and you have worked hard and suffered much. I also think that you deserve to be in control of your own affairs, to be master of your own finances rather than be enslaved by a new type of slavery that of indebtedness or addiction to such buying, gambling, or some set course. You have achieved success in so many areas of your life. Finances and the control of spending is yet one area over which to master - to be in control. You have succeeded so much that you have no fear of failure - thinking that nonmanaged finances will not destroy you. Do not set yourself up for failure. Be wise in financial matters also."

3. Barrier: Stated, "I think I should do such and such" or...silence... Unstated, "I can do whatever I want to do." "No one is going to tell me what to do."

    Response: "You can do whatever you want to do, go anyplace you want, or not do anything. We are creatures of choice. You have the right to make your own choices, choose your own destiny." "I have the responsibility to show you the consequences of your choices. (Show the individual if he/she is a visual type. Tell the individual if he/she is auditory type. Tell a story and involve the individual if he/she is the kinesthetic type.) I would deprive you and be guilty if I did not warn you of possible consequences of various choices. It takes more effort and concern for me to explain consequences than to just let you go on your merry way without informing you."

4. Barrier: Stated, "I cannot save now. I have too many expenses. I am just trying to survive now." Unstated, "Why should I save for the future when it is so uncertain and I am so anxious about today?" "My family needs the money now."

    Response through scary facts, philosophizing, computer printouts or discussion: "Drastic changes in lifestyle now are necessary for life security throughout your later years. A sense of security is felt from the ability to save for utilizing opportunity or emergency. Do not defy statistics. Everyone will have a crisis at one time or another, of one type or another, that will be lessened when there is a financial reserve. The first financial planner, Joseph in the Old Testament, advised people to save in the good years for the lean years. For thousands of years, we have had business cycles, good and bad times. The Rule of 72 can be applied by dividing 72 by the inflation rate which will project the number of years for the purchasing power of fixed income to be halved. If you want to maintain purchasing power, returns from investments have to be higher than inflation rates. If you start now by saving for example $100 a month you will achieve the amount for a reserve fund that later will take $1,000 a month and in many more years will take $5,000 a month. If you do not have a fund that increases with inflation, when you are in retirement you will have to plan how to decrease consumption and lower standard of living. That lowered lifestyle and insecurity are more difficult to accomplish than planning to save now. Financial independence comes from planning, saving, and sacrificing now so that you have choices later. Otherwise, you are moving to time of life of perceived no choices."

5. Barrier: Stated, "I cannot save now. We are just getting started....We cannot save now. We have a child who has lots of expenses....I can not save now. I finally have a chance to have a little fun." Unstated, "I spend more time planning a vacation than planning my finances." Planning the use of money is a bore. I do not want to. My wife and I always get in an argument when we talk about money."

Response: "When you have a crisis or when you retire, if I, as a financial advisor, leave you alone, you will say to me, "Where were you when I needed you years ago? Why did you not make me start prioritizing things? Why did you not make me start the habit of setting aside 5 – 10 percent since you could see down the road and I was so busy with career, family, and fun? Now my family will suffer. Why did you not show me the consequences of just one choice - that of a new car versus a used one so that I could have everything and still save?"

Role play: Ask where participants want to be in X years? Then pose situations of "what if?" Show the possible events, the possible choices, and the possible changes in the economic/business conditions and life stages.

6. Barrier: Stated, "I do not think it will work..." Unstated, "Why try? It never works out right anyway." or "I really do not want to take the effort to change myself, someone else, or something."

Response: "Maybe the plan will not work - that is true. The plan will certainly not work if you do not try. The risk of improvement (or greater return from repositioning assets into a more risky investment) is taken versus a guaranteed failure (or loss in the return of assets due to inflation)."

7. Barrier: Stated, "It is really a good idea. I like it, but my wife (husband or kids) will never go along with the plan."

Response: "Take leadership. Have a meeting. Explain your idea in definite amounts for a specified period of time. Allow unjudged, uninterrupted responses. Elicit cooperation from the view of how each can contribute to family income and resolving a problem. Present it as a challenge to one's creativity. Elicit their ideas until the ones chosen are their own."

8. Barrier: Stated, "I cannot get my spouse to handle employment." Unstated, "My husband (wife, or child) is a bum, lazy, or scared to meet the public." "I am resentful that he/she will not help out financially." They have all kinds of excuses.

Response: "At this time the person probably is not able to work (or stop compulsive spending, or cure alcoholism) because of emotional illness, fear of failure, fear of getting hurt, or addiction. The person has to want to change and be willing to seek professional help." An individual might ask his/her spouse or child, "What would you like to do dear - this, this, or that?" This identifies alternatives and goals, gets a commitment from the individual when feeling like it was his or her choice.

Response: "Suppose he/she does not want to _____. What are you going to do? You may have to assume that he/she will not change and you will have to plan and continue accordingly."

9. Barrier: Stated, "I cannot help spoiling my children. I work to give my children opportunities that I never had. My children cost a lot." Unstated, "I cannot say no to my children." "I am afraid they will not like me or will leave me if I do not give in. I do not want them to think poorly of me."

Response: "The greatest gifts to children are the ability to make choices, to have faith in something other than material possessions, to be self-reliant and resourceful, and to know the value of money. By not saying no, you are setting up your child for failure. Communication about money can be learned and practiced. Expect resistance to change. Be persistent. Do not say, 'We can not afford this or that.' Rather say, 'If we choose this, we cannot have that. We choose this for now. We are in control. Even if I had a million dollars, I would not buy such and such.'"

10. Barrier: Stated, "I have cut the budget everywhere I can. Bankruptcy seems the only answer." Unstated, "I do not want to change lifestyle." "I really do not want to go bankrupt. It seems to be the last resort." Client is unable or unwilling or lacks knowledge of options that a checklist could provide.

Response: "There are advantages and disadvantages to bankruptcy. Most people are not aware of the debts that are not discharged or the consequences for getting certain types of future jobs or future loans. Bankruptcy, in many cases, is using a 'cannon to kill a fly.' Ultimately, nothing is fixed. There are drastic changes if you really want to prevent bankruptcy. You can increase income, reduce expenses, and reorder priorities. Let us look at some options. What is the worst that could happen (with this or that option)? Some changes are more healthy. Time will help in acceptance of some changes. In fact, let us set up a time table for trying some changes."

11. Barrier: Stated "I do not see how we can get out of this financial mess even with reducing expenses and paying creditors less than the minimum payment." Unstated "We have this new house, young children, vacation plans, good auto, and contributions to charity that we cannot relinquish." We have the standard package considered respectful and what our friends/relatives have. We are scared because we have gone beyond the limit on credit and cannot pay current bills." "We want financial peace of mind."

Response: "You have arrived with new house, etc. Enjoy them. Now a new era of paying for them awaits you. You can survive a few years without credit, like some do for four years of college to have a more financially secure life. Defer gratification because you have it. Enjoy your dream. Your investment now is in your house and children. Then after a few years and you have cleaned up the "financial mess" you can fulfill other dreams. The ultimate in financial peace of mind or economic security is the ability to adjust. Let us write ways you can adjust for four or more years and identify ways to modify the standard package. What is the worst that would happen if you cut out selected items of expenditures? Let us examine errors in your thinking of what might happen. Let it be a challenge to your creativity."

"There are always people who have more and those who have less. If you want to be miserable always compare yourself with those who have more. Even if another family (Or the child at weekend visits with parent in a divorced situation) does or buys something that we do not, we have different resources, different priorities, and policies."

"You would not respect me as a parent if we were to go bankrupt or have to move because I did not have the stamina to say no, to be in control. My job as financial manager in this family is to make decisions, monitor, and protect assets. So please help me to perform my responsibility. I am showing you the example of strength of financial discipline rather than regrets by poor management because I care enough about you to provide financial security through choice and control."

Parents or spouses may not have the ability to communicate the knowledge of how to discuss finances, or the willingness to address difficult issues. Thus the reason for lack of communication needs to be assessed in assisting clients to better communicate and make decisions with family members. Sometimes, written ideas or statements of financial positions are easier to communicate on paper than audibly. A client could use the approach of stating that the financial advisor suggested such and such for your consideration and response.

12. Barrier: Stated, "I need a budget. Will you give me a workable budget?" Unstated, "I spend more than my income," or "I am in trouble with my creditors,'" or "I am scared because of overwhelming costs," or "I feel out-of-control in handling my finances," or "I cannot say no to my children."

    Response: "Why do you think that you need a budget?" "How do you handle your finances now?" "Where do you feel that your spending is out of line? Out of line with what?" "Who is spending ..., how much ..., for what ... or whom?" "Let us write down your expenses, analyze them, and then set up a financial plan or budget with a format and system for control, appropriate to your need and personality that will work for you." (See Chapter 4.)

Recommendations to Change Based on Knowledge, Willingness, and Ability

Questions for assessing barriers to change financial behavior and management before recommendations can be made are:
1. Is the individual **unknowing or unaware** of alternative behavior or paths to solution?
2. Is the individual **unwilling** to change even though he/she is knowledgeable?
3. Is the individual **unable** to change, even though he/she is knowledgeable and willing to change?

The individual has to be willing to face reality and change. Barriers to willingness must be identified. Lack of knowledge and inability to change are possible barriers to willingness to change. Individuals generally are not aware of their unconscious motives. Counselors are not aware of the client's need for affirmation. Barriers can be understood with financial remedies.

A few illustrations confirm the analysis. Many people are knowledgeable of good food and eating habits but are unwilling or unable to change. Most smokers know the harmful effects of smoking and are willing, but the barrier of inability prevents changes.

The barrier of being **unknowledgeable** can be explained. Individuals may not internalize knowledge if the information is not presented at a cognitive level compatible with their mental ability to comprehend it. They may also fail to acquire knowledge if the information is not presented in the predominant method of information processing. For example, knowledge is internalized more quickly if it is presented in a visual method to an individual who predominantly processes information visually, in an auditory method to an individual who predominantly processes information through hearing, or in a kinesthetic method to an individual who predominantly processes information by hearing stories, arousing emotions, or active involvement.

The counselor's role is to present knowledge that is relevant to solving financial dilemmas and promoting change. Counselors will better communicate this information to individuals by considering both their comprehension level and information-processing system. For an example, in providing an interpretation of the credit rating and the possible implications of the facts, a computer-generated display could be used for a visual presentation, while a fear tactic to stress the serious implications of facts could be used for an emotional presentation.

The barrier of **unwillingness** can be explained. The individual may be unwilling to change when he/she 1) has other, more pressing priorities, at the time, 2) has preconceived ideas and strong values that are contrary to the alternative recommended, 3) has a role that interferes with implementation of alternatives, 4) has a lifestyle or religious belief that dominates consideration of the alternatives, or 5) has a relationship with another individual(s) who does not want him or her to change and is expected to please that individual. People important to the individual who do not want the individual to make changes must be identified.

The unwillingness to change is a deliberate, rational decision made by the individual. Therefore, the counselor addresses the factors influencing the decision with a rational approach, upholding the client's self-respect and freedom of choice. However, the shepherd may want to address the spiritual issue of disobedience to God.

Some individuals, on the other hand, have a combination of both unwillingness and **inability to change**. Individuals who are also unable to change must be approached in a different way than those who are only unknowledgeable or unwilling. The individual's inability to change is a reaction to severe emotional anxiety that makes the individual unable to change even if they want to, are willing, and are knowledgeable. Individuals are unable to change if they cannot face reality due to 1) erroneous beliefs, 2) the new alternative is too upsetting or painful, or 3) the new alternative is too new to absorb.

As counselors know, the first reactions to crises are a "blocking off," a denial of the existence of the crisis, and an inability to look at new alternatives. Acceptance of the situation and ability to consider alternatives are later in the sequence of reaction to crisis.

Other reasons that individuals may be **unable to change** are that they have

(1) emotional anxieties dominating over rational action that knowledge and willingness would direct otherwise, 2) habits that are so ingrained in which responses are automatic and feel natural, good, and comforting (It is hard work to change habits because this process is anxiety producing.), 3) societal pressure such that a change does not fit into life at the time (For example, meeting the needs of other people or one's children is more important than changing credit use.), 4) depression syndrome that stifles hope and energy needed to meet the demands that new alternatives would command, 5) preoccupation with another crisis that is overwhelming ("You cannot worry about the pot on the stove boiling over when the house is on fire."), 6) allowed societal pressures, such as advertising, to dominate, 7) a comfort zone in which they want to keep rather than expand (The individual is unable to handle the conflict and anxieties that expanding the comfort zone with new alternatives would create.), 8) lack of discipline, 9) environmental pressures all around and they are trapped or hindered from stepping out onto new paths, or 10) emotional needs that are more fundamental than handling the change, i.e. need for self-esteem, respect, love, and physical provisions that are insufficient to permit working on new changes.

Techniques for Overcoming the Barrier of Inability

General techniques that the counselor can encourage individuals to use in making financial changes and taking action are:

- Become aware of inability to handle new alternatives and to change. Realize problems seem so overwhelming that one alone cannot do everything about them. Identify one concrete task to be accomplished each week.
- Join a support group, perhaps specific to the problem, such as alcohol/drug abuse, overeating, overspending, or single again.

- Pursue activities and thoughts, from a list, that are not expensive, reducing emotionality.
- Commit to an underlying philosophy, goal, purpose larger than oneself, or new purpose in life.
- Develop a wider purpose in life, a broader cause, or a mission.
- Change the major purpose in life.
  - Serve others and have compassion, acted out in deeds, for others.
  - Fulfill emotional needs in less expensive ways.
  - Write down commitments, leave a copy with the counselor, and post one at home.
  - Have accountability to someone for promoting progress, not perfection.
- Stop thinking in a certain way out of habit, be deprogrammed, or stop the tape running in the brain in order to create new thought processes or more positive attitudes.
- Obtain stress-management techniques and practice them.
  - Exercise and change the daily scenery to overcome depression.

The Challenge

The challenge is to act on the correct assessment to facilitate overcoming barriers to change. The difficulty is discerning when an individual is truly unable and when he or she is merely unwilling. The individual might claim the former, when it is really the latter. Further investigation by listening is necessary. The challenge demands the ability to communicate the counselor's concern about individual ability to implement recommendations. The challenge to the financial counselor is to have the skills to properly

1 Know the individual by the perceived or real barrier to change,
2) Present knowledge in a way that the individual can understand,
3) Establish a relationship and utilize strategies that provide motivation to overcome unwillingness,
4) Provide some counseling with appropriate techniques to overcome the inability to change which are congruent with the individual's value system,
5) Know efficient and effective strategies to implement change, and
6) Refer people to other professionals for deep-seated emotional problems.

Risks are involved in referring. There is the risk of referring people to others as an easy path for the financial counselor rather than to take appropriate measures to assist in a timely and effective manner. There is also the risk of erroneous referral for congruence with the approach. A risk occurs when a referral means more expense, especially when financial difficulties were the cause of the problem in the first place. A benefit/cost assessment must be the basis of recommendations for referral. The financial counselor can attempt several cost-effective measures to reduce the inability to change.

Some are embarrassed to seek counseling. Some are too proud to expose weaknesses or fears. So confidentiality must be assured. Counselor Wenger tells every client that he sees, "You are one of the healthiest people in the community because only the healthiest are gutsy enough to ask for help and work at tough issues of change."

Conclusion

The Master Teacher and Counselor demonstrated effective techniques for encouraging people to change. He was not successful one hundred percent of the time. Jesus' technique was story telling and parables. On some occasions, He was more direct. Sometimes the personal application and response were left up to the hearers. Jesus did say the Spirit would give the meaning of the story and inferred that the Spirit is what brings about change. The counselor can show rather than tell through stories what other people have done. Contemporary stories would be meaningful.

The counselor identifies options, many which would be heretofore not considered. The individual chooses. Not to choose is also a decision.

Many individuals are afraid to change and/or inexperienced in coming to a decision. The shepherd works with these resistances as well as the ones cited above in determining knowledge, willingness, and ability. The shepherd gives both fear and hope in motivating change. Scary facts and dire consequences of continued behavior that others have experienced are described. Hope is shared. Hope brings energy to move.

Encouragement is given by identifying the strengths of the individual. For others, they can repeat all day long, "I can do all things through Christ who strengthens me." "Waiting" upon the Lord is listening to where God is asking an individual to change. Then in application, one change for the week with commitment is concretely planned. The change may be a different structure in financial management or a control of some buying or habit. It may be a change that moves toward more love for God and neighbor through a change in financial behavior.

Complete counseling includes a discussion on how others may resist the individual's change and how this might be handled. Prayers can be for the courage and strength to change, remembering that God is walking beside them in the new adventure.

Prayer about Change:
"Serenity Prayer" by Reinhold Neibuhr

God grant me the serenity
To accept the things I cannot change;
Courage to change the things I can;
And wisdom to know the difference.

Living one day at a time;
Enjoying one moment at a time;
Accepting hardships as the pathway to peace;

Taking, as He did, this sinful world
As it is, not as I would have it;
Trusting that He will make all things right.

If I surrender to His Will;
That I may be reasonably happy in this life
And supremely happy with Him
Forever in the next.

Amen

◇◇◇ ⧗ ⧗ ◇◇◇

Chapter 6. Financial Management Unique to Life Stages

If shepherds are to be sensitive and useful to people's financial management, they need to know the relevant financial issues occupying minds and hearts at various stages. Some decisions and financial management tasks naturally involve advice from the shepherd such as going to college, divorce, and funeral planning. Shepherds are most knowledgeable and interested in their own stage. Information in this chapter can assist financial management beyond what they have experienced. Then, sympathy, advice, and encouragement can be real.

Since the decisions and management at one stage affect other stages, the shepherd can assist in preventing disasters or ill preparedness for the next stage. Tasks must be completed sufficiently to move to another stage with ease rather than financial dis-ease. Prayers, support groups, daily communication, and sermons can include thankfulness and petitions for wisdom and strength to handle family life tasks and financial management for every stage. Illustrations used by shepherds for every stage affect their credibility.

The stage of family life dominates expenditures and predicts financial decisions and tasks. Other influences on money use and credit are: *dominant* needs, *dominant* values, and *personality* types. Education and income are important influences and help to explain variations. Cultural scripts, peers, and advertising exert tremendous pressure. Patterns in past generations as well as current lifestyle influence financial behavior.

Possible outcomes from the shepherd's assistance are: increased economic security, economic stability, maximizing resources for opportunities unique to the stage, smoother interactions with others or businesses, and delight in fulfilling God's purposes.

Decision-Making

The shepherd is called to assist with decisions. In addition to technical information, the shepherd can shed some spiritual light on making decisions. Spiritual growth can accompany maturity in making economic decisions. The shepherd's first responsibility frequently is addressing the decision-making. The shepherd facilitates decision-making by identifying issues and showing how decisions might impact future stages. The individual or couple in financial stress often sees things through fuzzy lenses and goes in circles when describing dilemmas. The counselor organizes or interrupts circular discussion and thinking by clarifying the decisions and prioritizing them by their urgency and dominance. Some of them are directed to the back burner. One or more are addressed when sufficient information is gathered. People are released from the bondages of cultural influences and commercialism. Creative decision-making under the Cross liberates people from bondage.

Using a good decision process does not guarantee good outcomes or success. It does reduce the risk of error. It can give some peace in trying. Taking risks and failing can be forgiven. Not trying is a sin.

The decision process is completed by asking: "What is the worst that could happen? Can one live with that?" Many cannot bring themselves to make a decision without this approach. Is there an alternative that is acceptable other than the first choice? If the outcome is not satisfactory, what are other options? Does the decided outcome meet the goal? How does it seek first the kingdom of God, and/or the commitment to follow Jesus? What is the "due time" to complete the decision? How can people gain control and follow through under God's power and love?

The shepherd is aware that what seems irrational is rational in the mind of the client given the circumstances, perspective and resources. Conflict is inevitable among those making the decision because of their unique processing, personalities, priorities, and differences of opinion of how and who should make the final decisions. The shepherd shows grace by allowing alternatives that give fun and joy and is mindful of people's fears. Decisions are difficult because something desirable is foregone in choosing the alternative. "Opportunity cost" is, therefore, in every decision.

The shepherd teaches cooperative decision-making. The shepherd assists the family in reaching consensus by communication and commitments. The shepherd helps clarify who or what is controlling people's decisions. A part of God's plan, discernment as well as decision-making leads to humble obedience. The Spirit is asked to guide the specific steps. Principles of decision-making under the Master Principal are:

- Having a conducive time and place for making decisions;
- Concentrating on direction of the process, knowing "due time" needed to complete decisions (not getting side-tracked);
- Attacking the problem, not the person; avoid name calling or bringing up negatives of the past;
- Analyzing patterns of decision-making, assessing whether these are appropriate for now; (Patterns in the family with titles are: 1. the "traditional-dominant" person makes the decisions for all, 2. "social rational" or "bureaucratic," 3. "democratic problem-solving," 4. "egalitarian" approach, 5. "exchange-specialist" approach where each has a unique expertise for making the decision, 6. "permissive free-form," or 7. "fatalistic," depression approach.)
- Developing a "decision tree" where each choice branches out to other choices, for each section at a time;
- Assigning an individual to get sufficient information for making a decision; (Overload stifles decision-making.)
- Determining a specific, designated time to try out the decision with a promised re-evaluation;
- Involving all people in the process who are responsible for carrying out the decision;
- Designating one member of the family or group to carry out parts of the decision, realizing "everybody's responsibility is nobody's responsibility;"
- Brainstorming to get quantity, then quality, and then creative solutions;
- Comparing prices and services of at least three places or companies which expands possibilities and gets the best value for the money;
- Working on decisions and meeting wants sequentially over time, not equally or simultaneously (or, letting them go, under submission to God);
- Using computer analysis or stories of what others have done and adapting them to one's unique personality and circumstances;

- Sorting out alternatives by writing them on cards, and then stacking the top three and the bottom three;
- Maximizing satisfaction by seeking one alternative until a better one is found;
- Dividing decisions into a series of smaller units and deciding just within a particular unit until that goal is accomplished;
- Using intuition which is conceptual and holistic;
- Using guidelines as to what is available, what is representative, and what is in line with belief as to what God would want, what Jesus did, cross-checking with Scriptural agreement;
- Allowing people to argue to clarify how they feel;
- Asking what is the worse that could happen in the decision and if a person can live with that; identifying next steps if that were to happen;
- Showing how lack of communication results in no decision, which is a decision; thus leading to events or expenditures by default rather than by design.
- Discussing how someone might sabotage the decision, taking preventive measures, and then praying together.

Singles Labeled as "Independent Stage"
(Individuals at any age)

The stages with ages are prototypes to identify economic issues. Some would be uncomfortable with the stages and identified ages and would prefer to look at this as the "trajectory" of life. Everyone moves along through stages. However, life circumstances will change and individuals move between the stages. For instance, a person does not marry, but adopts a child. Another person marries, does not have children, and then becomes single again at some point in life. The age of the adult will influence the financial tasks as well as the responsibilities for dependents and sharing of life with other adults. At every stage, the financial management task is deciding to increase income, reduce expenses, be more efficient, and clarify priorities to make changes.

Predominant values for many singles are independence, self-reliance, individualism, and survival skills which influence spending and sharing behavior. Many decisions are made haphazardly until bad experiences help them compare prices and reorganize financially. The financial tasks unique to many singles include having goals in general and objectives in specific amounts for sharing, saving, and spending. Many singles were intentionally living when they were working for educational degrees and beginning employment after graduation. Now, as singles, new goals must be clarified as they fulfill new roles or much time, effort, and money may be squandered. Then, as time passes and new events occur, they regret that they had not saved for emergencies or new opportunities including more education or changing jobs. They impulsively buy to feel a longing for new excitements and adventure including travel. Frequently, vacations and travel are funded with credit and they are still paying for them when next year's vacation time comes again.

Another financial task is choosing charities, adopting a child, maybe in a foreign country, supporting a niece or nephew, or choosing pets to fulfill the longing to share and help others. They make decisions about charitable contributions. Singles are free to do short-term mission trips which expand their world view.

Parents often continue to *rescue* children, particularly daughters. They often do not consider them "grown up" because they are not married. Single women particularly and historically will marry with financial security in mind as well as for emotional needs. Some postpone financial maturity if they continue to live with parents. They may not develop skills needed in managing finances, tax filing, choosing insurance, investing, cooking, and maintaining house and equipment. However, there is less motivation to plan and less concern about insurance than other areas. Since housing expenses and rent are higher per person, other items have to be foregone or credit is overused.

Singles need to maintain credibility insurance with their employment for times of disruption. They need to develop transferable skills for increasing job security. Many begin careers or jobs with start-up debt and college debt. Some will need to have two jobs to recover from debts, past financial mistakes, expensive vacations, and college loans. The second job gives expanded social interaction and financial peace of mind even though hours at work are increased. A second job can transition to a new career or job. They must learn to balance other interests with work demands. Singles need to secure a source of steady income, several sources of income to diversify the risk, and income that increases faster than inflation. Decisions about transportation and housing needs must be based on take-home pay which is, disappointing and surprising, 25-35 percent less than gross income. It is realistic to give oneself an allowance for the miscellaneous or unplanned. Although some singles spend to make up for past deprivation and others to reduce boredom, they eventually need to simplify living so that expenses are less than net income to allow for saving and sharing. The Spirit can motivate them to live simply so that others may simply live. A reserve of three to six months income allows for unexpected changes due to job lay off, accident, illness, forced change of housing, appliance or car repair, travel, and underestimating expenses. After the reserve is met they can begin risky investing which usually yields more.

Life insurance is necessary if one's death or reduced income would be an economic loss to someone. In the case of singles, hardship would fall on co-signers of debt or loans. Disability insurance is more important than life insurance for this stage and for the next ones. Buying insurance at a young age reduces the costs of the premiums and guarantees insurability.

Singles should establish and maintain a support group, find a church family, or do volunteer work for establishing friendships. Recent graduates have reported that not having contact with other like-minded people was the disappointment or loneliness associated with a new job in a far-away place from college or home. Happiness comes from not only what the group can give to oneself, but what the individual can contribute to the group. A trusted friend is an asset. Some trust in God and feel Jesus as a friend who sustains life and prevents destructive addictions. Jesus Christ can be the director on their board of advisors. Other advisors selected, contacted, and named before a crisis occurs are physicians, counselors, attorneys, accountants, financial or credit counselors, and ministers. As well as continuing to develop personal resources, singles need to mobilize community resources. They may need a second job which meets several needs.

The financial dilemma with many singles is that their desired lifestyle is similar to that of two income families. A case study explains: Jane, middle aged, has to move because her son, with whom she has been living, is getting married to a woman with two children. Jane has a secure business job with $38,000 income. She has a good used car and two credit card debts for clothing. Her only addiction, she says, is eating too much. She has been looking at houses around $100,000. She has no money for a down payment. She shows the pastor her reported expenses to get his advice and encouragement. Jane trusts the pastor because she tithes regularly and wants to do

God's will in this decision. The following figures are those Jane gave and demonstrate her low-income status as these are the minimum someone in her state could spend. They also demonstrate underestimation of expenses.

Net monthly pay			$2,110
Tithe		$320	
House payment (proj.)		600	
Car Payment		330	
Insurance for car		87	
Utilities	Gas	45	
	Water/s	20	
	Electric	75	
	Cable	35	
	Cell ph	67	
	Telephon	45	
Credit Cards			
	JCPenney	30	
	Merrick	24	
	Orchard	37	
	Mid Vel	40	
Gas for car	Amex	100	
Dad's cable		37	
Fixed Expenses Total			$ 1,892
Flexible Expenses Total			figure $218 (insufficient)
	Food		
	Personal Care		
	Gifts		
	Insurance		
	Miscellaneous		

The mortgage is the question, not the house Jane can afford because of possible sources and amount of the down payment. If she wants a more expensive house, she can increase the down payment to afford the mortgage. A larger down payment can reduce the mortgage and, thereby, increase the cash flow. The projected budget was for a $75,000 mortgage, approximately. The shepherd suggested ways to get money for a down payment: early inheritance, borrowing from her 401K plan, sending self-addressed stamped envelope to ex-husband requesting some help since settlement had been unfair, borrowing from her aunt, who would get a higher interest rate than from other sources, although lower for Jane than other sources, going on a crash budget for a few months, not using credit to get her score up, getting a second job until down payment is acquired, selling a collection, and using her tax refund of $1,400 (although in the past she had used this to pay for license plates and Christmas debt). She qualifies for the Mortgage Credit Certificate which benefits her for a lifetime.

By analyzing her expenses above, possible reductions are: the $600 payment contains interest that is tax deductible, Cable TV could be reduced or eliminated, the cell phone could be reduced or eliminated, and her brother could share half the payment for their father's Cable TV. The unexpensed balance $218 is for food, clothing, personal care, and gifts. This is an unreasonable and underestimated amount since she has not kept track of spending. These items have been purchased by credit cards and, therefore, the credit probably will not be reduced. She has been paying just the minimum required which is about two percent of the balance. (Some banks are now increasing this to four percent.) Mistakes to avoid would be consolidating debts including college debt if she had these and buying appliances of a new house on the mortgage debt.

Since she has a good job, advantages of home ownership are the interest deduction by itemizing, the mortgage exemption, and the independence she desires. She assumes she will have a one and a half percent salary increase which is equal to the inflation rate (price increase). By her paying the mortgage with fixed dollars. It will become a smaller and smaller percentage of her income as it increases.

The above projected budget seemed plausible with reductions including reduced food expenditures. As other Americans have experienced, gas for the car and utilities may increase causing inability to meet all her bills. She knows health insurance and gas for the car will increase. Energy reduction is a must including planting trees, using double draperies, and utilizing an automatic thermostat set for the changing times of the day. Sequentially, she can plan to obtain the new house one year, landscaping the next, furniture the next, and so on. Clothing purchases can be put off, and she can have a new look with accessories or putting outfits together in new ways. Gift expenses can be reduced by giving poems and letters. Since Jane is a perfectionist and has high standards, wanting to do everything right, she must continually ask herself what is adequate rather than what is ideal.

However, Jane's realtor convinced her to buy a small $97,000 house which requires three percent down payment for first time homebuyers. A special program called "$1 Move-In" was convincing with lender or developer paying first year's insurance and closing costs. The payment would be $630 per month. She figures with the MCC and only paying back the interest on the 401K borrowed money, she would get a tax refund of $500. The money squeeze will be in the second year when she has to pay the mortgage insurance since she had less than 20 percent down and the tax refund does not cover her license plates and gifts. She will continually live above her income by using credit for food and new things for the house and yard.

From Jane's illustration we can see how a family on this average income *would use credit to live continually beyond their means.* The family is vulnerable to unexpected expenses or accidents. Jane has no savings other than employer pension. (If the scenario had been a larger family, it would have more expenses and be forced to have two or more earners, a second job, or reduce the tithe.) She wants to be faithful to her tithe. She will not even use it temporarily for the transition because she does not want to get out of the habit or jeopardize her blessing from giving. Jane is contributing time to work at her church as part of her tithe. In some churches, this is not acceptable.

The shepherd discusses the alternatives if Jane cannot keep her house: These included renting a room, moving her mother in with her to help pay the expenses, and getting another job on Saturdays. She will have to keep her old used car rather than buy a better one.

Beginning Families Labeled as "Adjustment Stage"
(Parents' ages 18-26 plus)

By definition, every stage has financial adjustments. Some individuals are better at decision-making than others. The counselor emphasizes that decisions will be made *for* them if they are not active in the process of deciding the desired outcome early. This stage has the task of establishing a family identity, a system of division of work, and financial management appropriate to them rather than some perceived prescription of how to operate as a family business. The President of their business can be Jesus Christ which guarantees sound practices rather than selfishness, unconcern, or damaging control. The stresses from surviving and succeeding at employment can interfere with family communication time. Severe job anxieties can interfere with sound financial practices.

Working at marriage is a job. Saving money by performing household tasks such as cooking, cleaning, etc. is also a job. Since resources are limited and wants are expanding, demands on limited resources are great. The couple can be happier if they simplify life and financial management, are disciplined, and are efficient. Due to inexperience, these take practice and perseverance which is aided by prayer. Beyond meeting current needs which seem overwhelming, time to identify short-term and long-term goals will aid in getting out of debt, saving, and sharing. Experimentation on less expensive eating habits and use of utilities is required for most couples today. Consumer mistakes, if learned from them, can be considered education. The marketplace and credit are complicated and terribly deceptive so couples in this stage must learn quickly to protect themselves from disaster. A current problem for many couples is deferring gratification. For example, many do not want a "starter home" or an old car and so they buy more than they can afford. Builders and lenders are a major part of the problem as they do not provide the education for sound decisions.

Life insurance is necessary if the spouse's death or reduced income would be an economic loss. Insurance is necessary for the spouse who is caring for children because the surviving spouse would have to curtail education, reduce employment, or hire someone to take care of them. Term insurance for protection, not saving, is a must. A slightly higher premium is necessary for guaranteeing insurability. Buying insurance at this young age reduces the cost of premiums. Disability insurance is even more important since this likelihood is greater than death at this age.

Young Children "Accumulation"
(Parents' ages 18 - 33+)
This Stage may be Grandparents with Young Children

Financial problems are easy to identify because they are so prevalent in today's society. What is not easy is how to talk about money and to resist the use of credit for needs, let alone wants. Conflicts between couples arise over what are needs and wants, necessities and luxuries, adequate versus ideal, current versus future purchases, gambling, pornography, hobbies, criticism over how much the other is spending, and fulfilling expectations of lifestyle or standards. Creeping indebtness and captivity to debt not only devastate finances, they affect relationships. Frequently one member does not know there is a problem or understand what all the expenses are. The challenge is to control spending and have a reserve while maintaining each other's dignity and respect for judgment in financial decisions. The challenge is difficult for this stage with the real needs and temptation involved in rearing children, child care, household furnishings, equipment, toys (for children and the grown-ups), and housing. Wants are expanding while resources are limited. This causes many families to live beyond their income. For some, it is out of necessity and for others it is out of ignorance, desire, or defiance.

Both a husband's and a wife's incomes are committed to fixed expenses in most families. Special accounts for education, vacation travel, and Christmas gifts can be built by automatic deductions from wages. If the goal is to have a reserve of three to six months in case one spouse loses a job, funds for that should be saved before more furniture or a newer car are purchased. Today's needs often seem more important than building a reserve, getting out of debt, or having long-term goals. Time and money in education or job security benefit the family more than spending at this stage. The question is what can only be done now. Some will skimp on necessities to have the luxuries. The urgency is to control addictions, bad purchasing habits, and inadequacies that cause overspending before finances are devastated.

God's power can be realized also by education, wise decision-making and practical steps. For example, whether income is adequate or not depends on the size of the mortgage, number of children, number of vehicles, gambling, and living simply. As the family expands in number and ages, the need for larger housing is felt. Currently, one member in the family is working just to cover housing expenses, contributing about 40 percent of the income as housing is 40 percent of total consumption (income).[41] Whether there was a monthly deficit or surplus was dependent on the ratio of housing expenditures to income in Williams' research. The housing purchase is so major that decisions are facilitated by knowing the facts and options. (Therefore, these are covered in more depth in Chapter 8.)

Life insurance is crucial in this stage as well as in others if there would be an economic loss or debts to those left after a death. It is less expensive to increase life insurance to cover mortgage than to buy mortgage insurance. Term insurance premiums are less than other types of insurance. Individuals should not be misled into buying insurance for: savings features, duplicates of what they have, or buying more than needed. In health, auto, and property insurance, the higher the deductibles paid, the lower the premiums. Disability insurance is more necessary for young families than life insurance. Workers have employee benefits, perhaps, or Medicare disability in which they can pay for deductibles rather than long-term disability insurance or instead of it. However, it is difficult to prove need for disability income without attorneys who specialize in this. (Pamphlets and Internet information on Medicare and Medicaid are available.) Savings can be acquired for emergencies in paying the deductible. Many people work in order to obtain health insurance for their families. At least major medical insurance or "stop-gap insurance" should be covered by families who do not qualify for Medicaid. Programs for low income people are increasing income eligibility levels, and currently many families are taken off the program which is causing greater financial hardships. Low income families may go to clinics, use resources for designated illnesses, check if doctors or dentists take charity cases, or ask before going to the emergency room if the hospital gives free treatment based on its use of federal funds in building the facilities.

The question of children's allowances comes in this stage. When a child can keep from losing money, he or she is old enough to have an allowance to learn money management since he or she will be spending money anyway. Clarification of what the money is for and what will happen if the money runs out are lessons learned. To estimate and decide categories, expenses can be clarified in daily, weekly, monthly and yearly expenses. Envelopes can be used for spending, saving, and sharing. The parent remains strong in not bailing out the child if he or she runs out of money, given that amounts were realistic. A lesson learned is that each does some tasks without pay which contribute to family well-being and happiness. Other tasks may be for hire and therefore paid.

---

41   Flora L. Williams. Housing Expenditures: Trends and Difficulties. *Proceedings of the Association for Financial Counseling and Planning. November 1999. Pp.115-132.*
Flora L. Williams. Financial Difficulty Measured as Monthly Deficit: An Empirical Analysis of Associated Factors. *Consumer Interests Annual.* Vol.43, Pp.118-123.

To reinforce the responsibility, allowances can not be given before routine tasks are done although they are not tied to a specific task.

Probably the most important financial decision for young families is the choice of housing *location*. This affects price of house, taxes, access to child care, transportation costs, need for one or two cars versus public transportation or walking, resale, church, social opportunities, schools, and environment. Now with the price of gas and vehicles, choosing so one member can walk, take public transportation, car pool, or drive short distance can save thousands of dollars over the years. The effect of the neighborhood and pollution upon children's development is more important than anything.

Grade School and Junior High Children "Expanding Stage"
(Parents' ages 25 – 36 +)
This Stage may be Grandparents with Grade Schoolers

Time management responsibilities are difficult because of conscientiousness in fulfilling employment, parenting, managing/doing household business/work, community citizenship, and church responsibilities. Energy and simplicity comes from having all of life revolved around God. Self-control and creativity in use of money come from the infilling of the Spirit.

Decisions are difficult because something desirable is given up in the choice. Limits to good things are required since there are more demands than resources. For example, rather than saying, "We cannot afford this or that" we can say, "We choose this for now." This latter statement explains to children, spouse, relatives or businesses, "We are in control of our choices not custom, advertisement, or peer pressures." "At this time, we are choosing sequentially rather than having everything equally at the same time." This approach is more honest and trustworthy. It keeps communication open rather than depressing when saying, "We cannot afford this." It represents having thought through choices and what is most important for now, what can be obtained later, and what makes a difference in the improvement of life. Important lessons in finances can be conveyed to children in this approach: deferring gratification or deferring to others. Even expenses, celebrations, and gifts for certain family members can be done sequentially over the years because items or education costs more, rather than treating members equally. This allows members to be treated equally over time. The benefits are equal although the expenses are not. Income is distributed based on need, not who earned it (production).

Conscientious families strive to be good citizens for keeping their homes, property, and sidewalks in good repair. They want to provide education, camp experiences, and contribute to church and professional endeavors. The money does not stretch far enough. The challenge calls for more creativity, efficiency, time contributions, and reducing expenses in areas, like doing services for oneself. Some things and activities can be deferred until the children are raised. Many families are financially stripped themselves until children are independent. Wealth accumulation or retirement funds may not be possible in this stage. Their investment in education is human capital providing accomplishment and security. The conscientious family has to decide what God expects rather than what the reference group expects. Obligations are to develop youth with hearts and skills to contribute to communities. Community resources are mobilized in this development.

Jim was conscientious and asked to see the counselor about finances. Jim was told to bring his wife Jane, which was the policy for counseling. Jim said it would not be necessary since he made the financial decisions and Jane was busy with the children. The counselor insisted. To summarize, the conclusions of the counseling were that the finances would be turned over to Jane who wanted to learn to use her computer, so that Jim could concentrate on his job. To get the truck brakes fixed, Jim would drive around until he found a mechanic that needed his garage signs repainted. This exchanging services was a way the family increased income to solve financial stress.

High School Youth "Middle Stage"
(Parents' ages 32- 48 +)
This Stage may be Grandparents with Youth

Family income is frequently at the peak when both husband and wife are employed. However, expenses peak also. If one spouse loses a job, since both incomes are used, it can be devastating. Sometimes decisions, including divorce decisions, are made in the stage with infant children when expenses are in the one digit category ($1-9) not realizing grade school children's expenses are in two digits ($10-99), high school children in three digits ($100-999), and college/training expenses in four digits ($1,000 plus). If an escalator clause both for inflation and ages is built into the divorce decree, stress is reduced in several ways.

Over time, families have felt they were not "getting ahead" because prices have increased faster than real spendable income, their purchasing power. Credit appears to solve the problem temporarily but has long-term consequences of bondage. If credit is "maxed," an accident, misjudgment, or important opportunity can be more devastating since credit is no longer available. Saving face with one's children seems to be more important than paying off debt or not using credit. It is difficult for youth not to participate in school activities or to not wear new or name brand clothing because of income shortages. However, one of the greatest gifts to give children is the challenge of resourcefulness and creativity rather than just spending. "Credit as the answer" often begins in this stage under the guise of student financial aid rather than considering options for funding higher education.

Calculating the youth's contributions to family total non-money income may motivate cooperation. For example, cooking a meal at home or taking a hard cooked egg for lunch saves the family X dollars. Multiplied by weeks and months to estimate the yearly total is convincing. Waiting to be picked up saves hundreds of dollars by not buying another car and, translated into dollars per hour, would contribute more than any part-time job could pay.

Grandparents often help underwrite financial shortages in many families. In other families, the couple in this stage has responsibility for grandparents as well as children.

A family council meeting seems mandatory for this stage with the rapid transitions, need for planning, and required cooperation in work and finances. Even though the family is organized in various ways of authority or leadership, it needs cooperation in making some decisions and following through on them. Suggested guides are to have decisions at the regularly scheduled meeting not just in passing by or with a whim, equality and mutual respect (everyone has a chance to be heard), agreed rules, deliberated jointly, and reciprocal responsibility as components for success.[42] Agenda items include minutes; allowances, deposits, and withdrawals; calendar, transportation, baby-sitting, mealtimes, old business, new business, and future plans, especially for

---

42   Rudolf Dreikurs, Shirley Gould, and Raymond J. Corsini. *Family Council.* Chicago: Henry Regnery Company. 1974.

fun together. Some families cannot work with such formality. On the other hand, working under chaos is neither pleasant nor effective.

Divorce Decisions

The shepherd is challenged to help those in the flock through the storm of threatened and actual divorce. Both spiritual and economic information are useful. The call to faithfulness in finances with God and to the family is heard by the shepherd. The shepherd can guide in considering options in the path: keep fighting, flight, or make it better.

The storms in marriage cause damage to personal financial management, credit, and wealth accumulation. It reduces cooperative efforts, encourages erratic financial behavior, and addictive spending. The financial behavior, the financial irresponsibility, and the financial troubles are frequently the cause for a divorce. Divorce represents "flight" from the situation rather than solving them. Expectations of lifestyle are not met. Consumption patterns and ways of solving problems are perceived inadequate. Therefore, if financial affairs could be corrected or a new structure initiated, other dissatisfactions could be addressed. Furthermore, when the financial aspects of divorce are carefully managed, future crises are lessened, and, perhaps, the couple may reconsider changing their management system and themselves rather than splitting. The financial aspects are addressed here for the shepherd to help identify benefits of staying together and costs of divorce. The shepherd also helps explore the benefits and costs of living apart. The study of this is urgent since much is affected by these questions. Divorce affects economic well-being immediately and long-term.

Shepherd counseling is important since the far-reaching effects, people affected, and financial decisions are rampant. The shepherd may be working with only one spouse as the other has already left emotionally with no return policy. The dream of regaining harmony, tranquility, safe place for emotions, affection, and wholeness is just a dream which the shepherd helps replace with other dreams. Moving forward with financial concerns, detailed here in the reading, the shepherd helps the individual trust God will be with him or her in the decisions. The goals in counseling are making transitions smoother, equitable, healing and preventing future crises.

The shepherd explores the cost/benefits of saving the union by redemption and changes in the social system, communication, and financial management. These are tried before changing the people in the system. For one reason, divorcees who remarry often find the new spouse is no better nor worse, after awhile, than the previous one. The grass looks greener on the other side, but as King David found out, the grass is not greener and belongs to someone else. Often individuals in divorce are trading one set of problems for another, rather than working with known problems. The ex-spouse is never out of one's life as long as there are children. If they did not learn to communicate before divorce, they have to afterwards. So why not learn before?

Therefore, the shepherd encourages alternatives. (Pastor Clyde would get a late call from a desperate individual or couple wanting counseling right now. He would suggest their going to sleep and counseling with him in the morning. By then, frequently, they could not even remember what they were fighting about.) Other suggestions are:

Separate for a time to better estimate costs, adjustments and trade-offs.

Change employment by one or both in type, place, hours, or shift.

Invest more quality time with spouse.

Change role responsibilities around the house.

Practice forgiving and forgetting.

Compliment spouse each day.

Change expectations of the other person or of a lifestyle.

Change policies, procedures, method of handling finances, and leadership style.

Study how marriages succeed by reading, seminars, and group counseling.

Participate in individual, marital reconciliation, and/or divorce counseling.

Listen to yourself as on a tape recorder to hear how you come across to the other.

Get medical help or belong to a support recovery group.

Be honest and stop secretive living; stop having secrets that are pernicious.

Shepherds can give suggestions that have worked for couples and are worth a try: Spend energy on changing rather than fighting. Change the system of division of labor. Change self rather than trying to change the spouse. Think if you were treated as you are treating your spouse now, how would you feel? Act and pretend as you want it permanently.

Other suggestions are be the non-anxious person. Lower your voice in conversation, criticism or requests. Compliment the person everyday. Show respect. Tease, joke, and have new fun together. A hug a day will help. An arm around the shoulder disarms hostility.

Be the best you can be without being a wimp or a leech. Get through the day. Pray. Do not nag, beg, criticize, plead, or be willing to do anything to get the other person back. Face addictions. Get in a support group. Do not be a co-dependent. Do not force a decision. Give time for change with forgiveness and patience. Maybe not all the big changes will occur, but a few may survive the storm and erase the shadows with Sonlight. Time for repair is needed.

Allow the Spirit to guide, direct, and work. Forgive, forgive, forgive, and forgive as God has forgiven us. Remember, you are imperfect and yet God's love is always with you. As you have received grace; give grace to the other person – "in sickness and in health." Center life on Jesus Christ, not the spouse or another person who is imperfect and will disappoint you. Give grace as God gives grace and salvation.

Consider working at marriage as a second job, which will pay dividends in happiness, and actually reward you in money saved from exit fees. Work at loving a person because it is work even if the spouse is not so loving and you harbor bad memories. Couples move toward more love or toward more separation.

Change the financial management system. Change the type of spending plan thereby saving "money and marriage." Beware that some persons who have been normally gracious now suddenly grow horns when it comes to personal finances.

The shepherd suggests social-psychological remedies while identifying financial considerations. The former may take years. Financial action must be done immediately as can seen below. Attempts for changing persons can be tried before trotting off to the divorce court. In so trying, a person feels less guilty the rest of life for trying another route, even if the marriage was dissolved.

The shepherd should be knowledgeable of common causes with alternatives to try to remedy the disruption before dissolution:

If addiction of substance, process or activity abuse is the problem, try....................

If distrust, secretive behavior is the problem, try...............

If lack of communication, ways of solving problems, an unsafe place to share emotions is the problem,...........

If a person just left emotionally,...................physically,......................

If involved in pornography to the point of adultery,.................

If person is mean, abusive, ...

If person is a leech, selfish, rather than a helpmate,..................

If person is irresponsible (or conflicting) in spending,.....housework,..............

If person is socially incompetent (does not know how to converse, does not learn from experience, marginal intelligence, inappropriate behavior and remarks),..................

If disappointed with standard of living, lifestyle, expectations, rituals, finances,................Begin by asking "are my expectations realistic?" If they are not, then that is the first thing to change.

If person is unfaithful, has an affair,..................

If disrespected, unloved, unappreciated, and ignored,..............

If bored,..................

If "it is the thing to do," friend says to do it since she does not want to see you succeed...

If your spouse just quits, gives up, never talks to you and you are tempted to look elsewhere for something better,...........................

The shepherd must be prepared for one spouse to be closed to reconciliation. One spouse may have emotionally left long ago, even privately prepared the finances to his or her own advantage. The "willing to work on it" party needs encouragement to walk through it with God anyway. God calls to "lay it all down" at His feet, letting God have control. Can the person do that if he or she is a believer? This is casting all cares on God since he cares for us (1 Peter 5:6-7). If all is given to God, the manipulating spouse has less to manipulate.

Mediation Approach

A shepherd should know the process of **"mediation"** for referring persons or actually performing the service. The **mediator** is trained to deal with conflict. Mediation is helpful when each partner starts to make independent decisions and the other becomes more distrustful and estranged. In contrast to mediators, attorneys are advocates, negotiators, and litigators. Persons are often advised to communicate only through attorneys. Since divorce is a legal matter, most attorneys are trained in the legal process and issues, not personal problems or family therapy.[43] In contrast, **"mediation"** addresses the underlying problems for the common good rather than greed for one.

"Mediation is a voluntary process in which parties to a dispute, with the help of a neutral third party, explore ways to negotiate their differences and reach a satisfactory resolution."[44] Although this is not marriage counseling or therapy, mediation "emphasizes the family as a system and restructures patterns of communication . . . and . . . encourages parties to take responsibility for resolving their own problems and to depend less on professionals."[45]

The **mediator or shepherd** helps develop sense of control under the Spirit's control by a balance of power between the parties, full disclosure of family finances, outside assistance with financial and budgetary matters, referral to community resources and referrals to support groups or career counselor. A schedule of meetings is outlined, and the parties are asked to fill out budget

---

43   F. M. Kusnetz. Divorce Mediation: Help for Families in Crisis. *The Houston Lawyer*. Sept.-Oct. 1988. P.33.

44   Ibid. P.34

45   Ibid.

forms, prepare lists of assets and liabilities, and produce documents showing the present value of each item. For some, this task is sobering, as they learn the realistic parameters within which they will negotiate. The couple defines issues and formulates agreements. The **mediator** builds on success of easier issues in order to build confidence for the more difficult. In some cases, an accountant, an appraiser, or a child psychiatrist are included in the work. Therapists and attorneys are consulted as needed in the process. Mediation may be suspended temporarily while experimental living and/ or financial arrangement is tested before a final decision is reached. A memorandum of agreement is prepared by the mediator to take to their respective attorneys. The attorney prepares the court order. Many **mediators** reserve the right to review the order before it is signed to ensure it reflects the agreements reached by the parties. The attorney for a party in mediation plays an important role - giving advice, protecting legal rights, suggesting possible resolutions, and helping to ensure the mediation process is fair.[46]

Reaction *to* Divorce

The shepherd assesses unique reactions to divorce to assist people to make decisions and adjustments. Common reactions to crises such as denial, mourning, and indecision as well as anger, rejection, or revenge complicate the decision-making process and underlie many property squabbles."[47] The shepherd-counselor helps overcome barriers of not knowing, not being willing, or not being able to cooperate, take action, or make decisions. People may react with depression, loneliness in losing a partner, loss of identity, while others are relieved a relationship is over or want to escape. Some people are determined to make it on their own and may even be arrogant. Others are confused with changes in lifestyles, careers, friends, schools, in-laws, churches, and many other facets of life.[48]

The shepherd-counselor reminds people going through divorce, as in most crises, emotions may cause missed payments, financial mistakes, lapsed insurance payments, or erratic spending. People are helped to focus on financial issues of immediate concern as well as long-term consequences.

Looking at Costs *before* Divorce

Planning for divorce takes time and knowledge, perhaps more than marriage planning. "Look before you leap" into divorce is just as crucial advice as in the marriage decision. Planning for divorce needs expert help since a business, a legal unit, as well as a social relationship is dissolved.

Looking at current costs compared to the costs of living separately or responsible for two households must be done accurately to calculate all types of costs: major, minor, related, material, social, and emotional. Looking before you leap examines three years' of previous income. Current records of expenses are needed to accurately estimate expenses with a changed situation. Projected costs for different ages and stages of the family life cycle are calculated. Parents need help in projecting costs for the children, otherwise they will underestimate. Many expenses for years before preschool require roughly one-digit expenses. For grade school they require two-digit expenses,

---

46   Ibid. P.35.

47   O'Neil. Ibid.16.

48   M. A. Hompertz. The Institute of Certified Financial Planners. Greater Chicago Society Newsletter. 1988. P.3.

for high school they require three-digit expenses, and for college years, they require four-digit expenses or higher.

The shepherd helps the person or couple calculate financial information for divorce made carefully, equitably, and efficiently to plan rather than panic. Resources are identified and actions suggested for reducing future crises. The shepherd may have time only to hand a list of questions to take to the attorney. The list contains decisions, considerations, and incidental division of responsibilities that the couple may not have been aware. Financial information is obtained from previous years' tax returns, reviewing insurance policies, requesting copies of credit reports, and analyzing employee benefit summaries and statements. One could use several months of check registers and credit card statements, perhaps using a spreadsheet for expenses. Expenses are usually greater than estimated or expected and, therefore, should be increased before signing a financial affidavit. When couples look at how income, expenses and future responsibilities are affected, reconciliation may become the attractive solution.

Looking at time expenditures, such as family services provided, and goods produced, documents non-monetary contributions. Special contributions such as work, which added to the appreciation of the house, should be noted for fair settlements.

The counselor tries to present a realistic picture to those contemplating divorce: Most women experience a decline in standard of living while men increase theirs. Monies "needed" are separated from what is "wanted," what is "ideal" from what is "adequate." "Goals need to be realistic and reassessed frequently, as changes may occur rapidly, especially in the early period of divorce."[49]

People sometimes are advised to handle a bad marriage long enough to straighten out any credit. In other cases, an effort must be made to get an irresponsible spouse's name off of certain credit cards. Since filing for divorce deteriorates credit ratings, credit should be established in each party's name before filing for divorce. Some community property states have protection for both parties to continue credit availability and to keep both spouses' Social Security numbers on the credit records.[50] "...Separating couples should immediately close all jointly-held open-ended credit lines such as home equity lines of credit and credit cards, and notify existing creditors in writing of their impending divorce."[51] Titles on property may need to be transferred, rather than liquidated for equitable distribution.

Savings in separate accounts need to be built up for the period of transition. Job skills and secure employment, ideally, can also be assessed and established before divorce. In the modern divorce system, economics rather than guilt is the criterion and witnesses are appraisers, accountants, and financial planners. A spouse may hide assets by denying the existence of an asset, transferring to a third party, claiming offsets - assets exist but were diverted, claiming asset was lost or dissipated, or creating a false debt.[52]

Costs *during* Divorce

The shepherd reduces the temptation to make irrational decisions because of an urgent desire to accomplish the move quickly rather than consider the impact on the future. The stress

---

49   Hombertz. Ibid. P.3.

50   O'Neill. Ibid. P. 160.

51   O'Neill. Ibid.

52   C. A. Wilson. *The Financial Advisor's Guide to Divorce Settlement- Helping Your Persons Make Financial Decisions.* Chicago: Irwin Professional Publishing and International Association Association. 1996. P.34.

and strain of divorce may cause an individual to act out of hurt, frustration, and a desire to get it over with rather than to do what seems best for all involved, since some people in this time of crisis lose confidence, self-control, and the ability to function. The role of the financial counselor is crucial in helping people make decisions, plan rather than panic, and regain a positive self image. Although an individual going through a divorce is concerned about the immediate, the financial counselor identifies decisions affecting the intermediate and long range.

Tasks in the divorce process seem overwhelming to some. The shepherd-counselor identifies decisions and their priority, information needed for each decision, and resources available. One resource may be a support group in the community for emotional support. The shepherd-counselor, who holds a less vested interest, is understanding of the individual going through divorce. In many cases, neither the individual's family, the church, nor the lawyer is understanding or is afraid to get involved. In other cases, a relative or friend may be giving erroneous advice. The shepherd-counselor supports options and not making a hasty decision, including forcing a spouse to choose too soon. The shepherd knows that most all couples have times in the desert, in the valley, of questioning. Support is provided by objective, factual, and effective methods. A telescopic vision of cost/benefits provides support. Support is given to help the individual regain control over economic affairs such as cash, savings, expenses, and durable goods plus the confidence in his or her ability to make decisions.

Time of separation may need to be lengthened to make arrangements for protecting credit, rights, property, future income, and future security. The spouse who does not "sue" can take time to bring the divorce to fruition. Therefore, time as needed to get information and to make decisions without pressure can be utilized. The shepherd-counselor helps the individual avoid acting out of panic or making decisions until ready.

Working with the Attorney

The lawyer is the advocate and executor of documents while the shepherd helps individuals reduce costs by identifying issues before consulting with the attorney. The counselor gives awareness of possible fraud and deceit. The financial counselor's advice involves expenses, income, debts, taxation, ownership of property, contributions, child support, pension rights, restitution, and insurance. The financial expert can figure the present value of a pension or perform other technical services. Additional costs of joint custody can be identified.

In choosing an attorney, credibility and integrity are the most important criteria. Some attorneys may keep things "stirred up because they earn more money that way."[53] Obtaining a lawyer involves cost comparisons, fee arrangements, services provided for fees, support of the individual's unique situation and gender, and previous services. Although sharing one attorney appears to save money, it is ill advised because of the attorney's advocacy role. "While not illegal, one-lawyer divorces are ill-advised and can be considered unethical."[54] The individual filing for divorce chooses the divorce court with the advantage of choosing a supportive judge, or one who considers non-monetary contribution and recognizes the time cost of raising children.

Calculating Costs

The shepherd or financial counselor helps people weigh the short-term costs and benefits versus long-term ones. Other assistance is encouraging control and reduction of living expenses;

---

53   Wilson, Ibid. P.15

54   Ibid. P. 16.

finding temporary inexpensive housing; estimating current and projected expenses of raising children, household operation, upkeep and repair of the house, retraining if needed, children's college or training, and retirement.

The counselor raises questions of how college expenses will be provided which is part of the divorce agreement. Accurate costs of raising children include seasonal and miscellaneous expenses such as club/sports membership, payment for telephone calls, or transportation to the absent parent. Identifying all types of costs is crucial. Otherwise, the stress and expense of trying to increase child support in the future usually cost more to go back to court and get agreements changed than the new award. Another question is who should spend money or time on an elderly parent(s).

Costs of children include both: 1) direct or monetary, and 2) indirect, time, or monetary cost, which the counselor prepares with individuals or attorneys. Diary methods and/or statistics prepared by the family economics research group of the U. S. Department of Agriculture on the cost of raising children can be used. Techniques of "time value of money" are applied and assumptions stated in projecting costs. An agreement to increase support according to cost-of-living increases or significant changes in income of either parent is ideal. The calculation of total family income and contributions of each parent will promote a more equitable child support division. Income considerations begin with a definition of what is income - current and projected - and who has contributed to income. Pensions, Social Security payments, future inheritances, and rental, business, and non-money income are types of income needing technical and legal treatment. Both gross and net income calculations are necessary. Contribution to the total family income is calculated using various methods of estimating the value of family services and lifestyle decisions which made accumulation of wealth possible. The child support obligation of each parent is based on the ratio of each parent's income, the percentage of time the child spends with each parent, and the amount of alimony paid to the custodial parent.

There needs to be a check, recording, and enforcing system to prove alimony or child support is paid. This can be done through the court. Wages can be garnisheed. If payments are in arrears, arrangements can be made to deduct these from assets liquidated at a later time, such as the sale of a home. Every state is required to enforce payments. Measures are withholding wages or a state tax return; putting a lien on real estate or personal property, and notifying credit bureaus.

Family Services

The value of family services includes depreciation of human capital when a parent stayed at home and the time for child education, child or parental care, hostessing, etc. Values of family services and household production are calculated to determine the amount of spousal support used in restitution and alimony. These values are calculated by different methods such as the "opportunity cost" method, which is an advantage for those of higher educational and occupational backgrounds, or the replacement cost method, which is an advantage for those with larger families. The contributions of one spouse to the other spouse's education and training can be considered along with family services. Calculating the enhanced earning capacity of the major wage-earner spouse and the depreciated earning power of the other spouse may be more important to equity than calculating the value of family services.[55] Direct costs of education and training paid by

---

55   E. S. Beninger and J. W. Smith. *Determining Child and Spousal Support.* Dearfield, Ill. Callaghan and

one spouse is also a contribution to income and considered in spousal support, restitution, and reimbursement. Cost of education or rehabilitation after divorce for a spouse can be considered in some cases.

Credit

Creditor policies and collection procedures must be known. Ownership of debts must be clarified. Division of responsibility for debts is only enforceable by the divorce decree and between the couple. Creditors will try to obtain payments from whomever's name is on the debt or from the individual for whom they have an address. The decree states who will pay which debt and within what period of time although that does not assure compliance. If one spouse fails to make a payment on a secured debt, the creditor can pursue the other. Just because it is a decree does not mean it will happen. "Legal decree and the final outcome are very different things."[56] For unsecured debt, separation agreement needs to include a "hold harmless" clause. This indemnifies the nonpaying spouse. The paying spouse gives the nonpaying spouse the right to collect not only all missed payments, but also damages, interest, and attorneys' fees if payments were not made. Without a hold harmless clause, the nonpaying spouse has the right to collect only the missed payments "If a spouse files bankruptcy before, during or after divorce, the creditors will seek out the other spouse for payment of marital debt - no matter what was agreed to in the separation agreement."[57] While married, they can file for bankruptcy jointly, eliminating all separate debts of the husband, separate debts of the wife, and jointly incurred debts.[58]

Asset Settlement

Whereas, property is divided just once, career assets continue to produce income regularly for years. With software, income flow is shown for each individual. When it stops the adjustments have to be made in transferring assets for equity. These can be considered in the settlement. *Divorce Plan TM Software* is one such software available from Quantum Institute for Professional Divorce Planning, Boulder Colorado.

Equity and reasonableness are used in dividing those assets and dividing the property acquired during marriage through joint effort, those which increased during marriage, and those investments in earning ability. Inheritances can be divided. In some cases inheritances may be outside the "joint ownership" arena. However, "spouses who have wasted or dissipated family assets are sometimes penalized for this economic misconduct in support calculation."[59] Assets and property which require no division are identified as those acquired prior to marriage, by gift or inheritance, or after degree of separation. Division of community property varies depending on duration of the marriage; pre-nuptial agreement between parties; age, health, occupation, amount and source of income, vocational skills, employability, and liabilities of each spouse; needs of each spouse; whether the property settlement is in lieu of or in addition to maintenance (alimony); present and potential earning capability of each spouse and retirement benefits.[60] Alimony

---

Company. 1989.

56   Wilson. Ibid. P.145.

57   Ibid. P.148.

58   Ibid.

59   Beninger and Smith. Ibid. P.3-66.

60   E. Brandt, L.K. Fox, and K. Hardcastle. *Making Financial Decisions when Divorce Occurs.* Bulletin No.

trusts and annuities are useful to recapture provisions and restrictions associated with children; to provide longer direct-support payments; to be used for unallocated family support "without making income taxable to the grantor;" and to continue payments after the payee's death.[61]

Insurance

Insurance needed is "stop-gap" insurance, insurance on the ex-spouse, and continuation of health insurance benefits. One ex-spouse can own a life insurance policy on the other to protect child support payments and other projected expenses. To generate the stream of maintenance income, the recipient spouse should either own the life insurance or be an irrevocable beneficiary.[62] This will help ensure payment of premiums and provide benefits for tax treatment, secured by a fidelity bond. Disability insurance, based on the payer's ability to earn income, is also important.

Taxes

Financial counselors can learn consequences in divorce settlements from the Internal Revenue Service Publication No. 504 *Tax Information for Divorced and Separated Individuals*. Tax implications of child support and using the children as tax exemptions need to be addressed. Unless otherwise specified, the tax exemption usually goes to the parent who has physical custody of the child for the greater portion of the calendar year. The exemption can be traded back and forth with a written waiver or IRS Form 8332 and it can be divided among the children. The child must be in custody of at least one parent for more than half of the calendar year. Who will take the head of household filing status must be decided. It is available for those who are divorced, who provide more than half the cost of maintaining the household, and whose household is the principal home of at least one qualifying person (child or other dependent) for more than half of the year.[63]

Pension

Methods for dividing pensions are based on the specifics of the employer's retirement plan, the buyout or cash out- award in a lump sum settlement, and deferred division or future share of benefits. The biggest mistake in dividing pensions is the "failing to anticipate death" and what happens if either party dies before the non-employee gets the whole share of the pension.[64] With an income distribution approach, a spouse may file for "qualified domestic relations order" (QDRO) for the pension plan. The value is established at time of divorce and recorded with the pension administration so the spouse receives the pension plus interest, which belongs to her or him. If a second wife also files, she has priority over the first wife. Another approach might be to have stock certificates moved to the broker's office, who then follows procedures for dividing them according to the settlement into two new accounts. To receive Social Security benefits under the spouse's work record, these apply: divorced for 2 years, married at least 10 years, and is 62 years of age or older.

733, University of Idaho Cooperative Extension Service.

61   Beninger and Smith. Ibid. 5-7.

62   Wilson, Ibid. P.129.

63   Wilson, Ibid. P.134.

64   Ibid. P.73.

Housing

Most people make housing decisions based on emotions and immediate family concerns rather than ability to afford all the costs of housing on income after divorce, qualifications for a new loan, and "opportunity costs" of having money invested in the house versus income-producing assets. Also, they need to consider actual market value of the home based on current appraisal, the interest rate and monthly payment under their existing mortgage compared to what is currently available if they purchase alternative housing; "comparison of current and real estate market conditions and conditions the parties are likely to encounter if they remain in the family home and sell at a later date," and imputed rent which is money paid as rent if not living in one's own home.[65]

Equality and consumer rights support provisions such as the woman can keep the house and make payments on it. In unusual instances, the children may keep the house, and the parents rotate staying there. Another issue of equity can be raised if one spouse is required to take out a loan to buy a portion of the house, paying large amounts of interest, while the other can pay child support payments over time.

Renting frees the individual to have money in liquid assets rather than invested in a home, particularly during the period of post divorce economic transition. It also frees one from responsibility of unanticipated maintenance and repair expenses as well as allowing greater geographical flexibility.[66]

Division and Fairness

If the couple does not decide, the judge will decide for them. Couples usually arrive at a better division of household items than a judge. The judge may order a count of items and divide by two; or order selling everything and the money distributed equally. The couple can define fairness. Decisions can be based on a 50/50 division of things by value or by number, cash rather than things, taking less than 50 percent if their share is all cash, more interest in future security than in present assets, or more interest in an unequal agreement to compensate for the larger earnings of one of them now.

Management after Divorce

The shepherd helps the individual deal with anger, bitterness, remorse, guilt, and adjustments in well-being. General well-being is affected by financial management, community or informal support groups, church fellowships, friendships, and relatives. Bitterness is reduced when each is thankful for the gifts of the marriage they did receive including children, good times, travel, and awareness of human nature.

Children are critical of the divorce decisions and may say nasty things. Others are critical of their mothers or fathers for allowing the divorce to happen. The conflict of living in two alternative households with different rules becomes apparent. Others find after divorce more tranquility, more control of the financial situation, and eagerness to learn new roles, new goals embracing the future with less conflict.

Communication should be direct rather than sending "messages through children, relatives, or mutual friends."[67] One parent cannot assume the other parent knows the details and reasons for

---

65   Beninger and Smith. Ibid. P. 2-2 and 2-3.
66   Ibid. P.2-2
67   Brandt, et al. Ibid. P.23

expenses. Records of payments made and received are important concerning child support and can aid future decisions. Child support payments made by check have the canceled check as proof and the check forwarded to the prosecuting attorney's office will be recorded and sent to the parent.

Confusion and conflict in resource management of stepfamily households are based on divergent meanings of fairness, interpretations, and implementations. Another conflict is differences in attitude toward meeting current household expenses and "future allocation of assets" such as inheritance. Another problem is balancing obligations to support children of a previous marriage that are consuming assets that they eventually would receive.

The shepherd can assist individuals to consider ways to increase income in various ways including exchange with others. Discussion can include ways to reduce or change expenditures, acquire and control credit, adjust debts or financial obligations, and organize a new system of household and financial management. Divorce usually changes lifestyle. Individuals champion change by useful techniques: identifying what will not change as well as what will change, putting the crisis on the shelf for longer periods each day, using energy to be better rather than bitter, having mottos to modify behavior, communicating with confidence, and taking the hand of Jesus. A crisis can be an opportunity for personal growth if faced optimistically. It takes time, practice and patience to adjust. Rituals, schedules, predictability, intimacy, church, and grandparents are useful resources for adjustment and growth. Most individuals require several years to recover emotionally from divorce and some never do except by the grace and love of God of which the shepherd reminds them. Individuals can continue in their new *chapter* of life as new creation in Christ with new policies, new procedures and new purposes.

Remarried or Blended Families "Readjustment Stage"
(Parents' ages 20 – 48 +)

Just as in other stages, children have to learn that there are families who have more and those who have less, different families have different policies, different spending guidelines, and different consumption patterns. Therefore, children in two different households have to learn to adjust and not be resentful or disrespectful of the less fortunate parent since guilt and stress are hurtful, harmful. Divorced people learn that the ex-spouse is never out of their lives when there are children involved. If they did not learn to communicate about finances before divorce, they must learn to afterwards.

Decisions as to who will pay for the small, incidental expenses such as long distance calls or large ones like camp or lessons are so difficult that in the conflict the child gets nothing. Children should not be victims because parents cannot decide who is going to pay for a particular expense. Child support is usually just enough to pay a babysitter so the parent can work. Regularity of child support has to be enforced and there are legal avenues for this. In the single-parent families, scholarships can be sought for group activities and education. Insurance may be available from the ex-spouse.

Financial planning and record-keeping are sometimes more complex for blended or remarried families than others. The Spirit-led parent has to learn to work with combining incomes from various sources rather than the messy way of playing games, bargaining, and fighting with use of money and about money in order to secure funds needed for children.

Older Youth "Launching Stage"
(Parents' ages 45 – 56 +)

While the "young adult" wants independence, the need for dependence while in college or in job transitions necessitates decisions and policy changes. New communication patterns and tasks are established. If the young adult is employed, perhaps he or she can pay for house cleaning or for the electricity. Some parents find it difficult to say "no" to certain expenses or to ask for more contributions from a youth's meager wages. Writing these requests may be easier than face to face confrontations. The counselor can be blamed for asking for more contribution. The youth can be shown how reducing certain of his or her expenses would make contributing more to the household possible. The desire to live more simply could solve financial problems.

If money is borrowed or early inheritance is obtained, a contract clarifies obligations and protects trust and communication. Otherwise, the young adult never knows when he has completely repaid the loan, feels judged every time he/she spends money, and knows if interest is paid or not. Consider this example: Betty and Paul borrowed from their mother and promptly paid it back so when their brother David asked for money the mother quickly consented. However, David's wife wouldn't let him pay her back. The mother expected repairs on the house every time David came to visit in lieu of interest. The visits got fewer and fewer and relationships between mother and son became more and more strained.

"Doubling up" of two or more generations may be the answer to the high cost of housing, particularly as utilities consume a higher and higher percentage of family expenditures. Creative arrangements to consider are building or remodeling a house funded by two generations. Separate quarters, baths, and entrances can be arranged. Temporary or permanently, grandparents can help with the children and their studies. Parents can have a nicer home with pensions helping to support it.

The Shepherd's Role with the Youth, Wanderers, and Nomads

Young people want adventure, independence, change of scenery, acceptance, respect, to feel worthwhile or contribute something worthwhile, and to develop a skill or ability. The shepherd or youth minister has a role in helping youth while in high school or nomads who move around without family to meet these needs and wants. Many times they are ignored since shepherds only help those attending their classes or meetings. The marginalized and irregulars are missed and not inspired. Possibilities for them are not presented.

The challenge is to encourage, to point to directions, and to assist those who confused and lonely. Many feel incompetent and unworthy. They do not have family support. Their family may feel rejected or threatened if they were to get more education or change social class. They only have poor or un-ambitious role models for behavior. They have never been out of their community. Their high school grades were low and maybe they have not graduated. Savings for college is nonexistent and since they did not have money enough for high school, cannot imagine how they would go to college even with scholarships to pay for living expenses and incidentals. They assume they have no future.

Therefore, the shepherd can tell stories of the paths that other youth have taken.

First, shepherds can show the importance of completing their GRE degree. They can include them in a church mission trip. They can help them find work for a mission in distant lands. They can work one year in Brethren Volunteer Service or the Peace Corps. They can help them find a local job and go on mission trips during vacations or time off. They can volunteer for disaster relief in a different location or with local organizations assisting the less fortunate. Other possibilities include an apprenticeship program but now many require some vocational training or military experience. Shepherds can show respect and not assume everyone has to go to college. They can give them a job at the church, which shows faith in them, or help find a local job that is hidden or unusual. Working at certain fast food chains provides fringe benefits and even retirement plans. Others promise no benefits. Shepherds can help them know how to explore various college or trade school funding.

The Shepherd's Warning

The shepherd should warn youth and recent graduates that they will be asked to think and do things in a job, college, and the military that break their baptismal vows and violate their steps in following Jesus. Therefore, the effect of a choice in a job or the military should consider allegiances and responsibilities before joining, not just the wage or benefits. Encouragement for resisting and to persecution from decisions is in 1 Peter 5:8-11: "Be self-controlled and alert. Your enemy the devil prowls around like a roaring lion looking for someone to devour…". The temptation to choose activity for making more money or getting a promotion is "selling your soul."

College or Trade School Funding Decisions and Encouragement

For two generations, the decision was how much financial aid a student could get. Getting the maximum or more than needed was encouraged because of its low interest. Parents encouraged financial aid which allowed them to purchase new cars. This made possible spending on wants. Graduates are surprised when prospective employers pulled credit reports, insurance companies raise premiums, mortgage lenders are skeptical, credit rates are higher, and prospective marriage partners look the other way. Even advancements in the military are in jeopardy. The experiences of people unable to pay all their debts and the fact that Social Security benefits can be garnished demonstrate their difficulties. Tax refunds can be attached to pay the debts. Now with experience and an uncertain economy, alternative ways to fund college are more important than ever. The sources of private funding are being reduced in this economy. Getting a loan after the first year is not guaranteed these days. Colleges that provide financial aid are required to provide counseling but this is after college debts are decided, usually.

The shepherd encourages by telling alternatives for funding:
- Parents can help out as an investment in human capital. Parents can plan to have other debts paid off so that cash is available for college expenses.
- Parents can save for at least the first year by using Section 529 Plan or Series EE bonds with tax advantages for student's education.
- Parents and students can save for at least the first year and then together can work an extra job to accumulate for paying for second year, with debts reduced can pay for third

year, and with scholarship and work-study programs can complete college with a minimal amount of loan.

- The parents could postpone getting a new car, expensive trips or house remodeling until student graduates.
- Parent can buy apartment building in which student(s) reside and manage and then sell it after students graduate.
- One parent can be employed at the college or university to get student discounts.
- Students might take an early inheritance.
- Students can combine community college with state universities or private colleges. Or they can choose a career which the community college provides. Some universities are extending the opportunity for students attending a community or technical school to participate in viewing games or belong to fraternities and sororities. Religious groups on campus are inviting them also.
- Students can extend time of college with internships, work-study, and cooperative education programs.
- The youth can join any branch of the military for four years afterwards which he or she through the GI bill will receive free tuition for four years at any state university or other college up to the state university tuition, and for some masters programs. In addition $1,000 per month will be paid for books, supplies, and living expenses.
- Student can join national guard, ROTC, or reserves.
- Use tuition assistance from father or mother being a disabled veteran.
- Students can be employed and take fewer courses per semester.
- Students can use Pell Grants. These are need-based grants to low-income undergraduate and certain post-baccalaureate students – full and part-time in college and vocational schools. Family incomes can be up to $60,000 but most go to families below $30,000. In 2009 to 2010 the award ranges from $609 to $5,350. Different assessment rates and allowances are used for dependent students, independent students without dependents, and independent students with dependents. Check on the Internet for Pell Grants or collegeboard.com.
- Students can use the loan forgiveness programs for entering selected programs, teaching in selected areas such as the inner city for a number of years, practicing medicine in selected areas for a number of years, and others.
- Work in the Peace Corps and AmeriCorps which also provide tuition assistance for undergraduate and some graduate programs as well as provide service credit for some employment.
- There are numerous scholarships available, many of which are not advertised. For example, there are scholarships for left-handed people, first of a family to go to college, and for maintaining a certain grade average. Search in the "un-claimed" scholarship folders which are plentiful.
- Spend hours in researching and applying for grants (not paid back) and scholarships. Although the rejection rate may be high, the one or two obtained will be worth the effort which can be translated into a high hourly wage rate.
- Students can find resources, scholarships and grants from community groups,

- employers, etc. Check with parent's employer. Read the material in the high   school counselor's office. Study the material in the college financial aid office. Search for these with www.fastweb.com.
- Rather than government guaranteed programs, check for scholarships, loans and grants from colleges, banks, corporations, civic programs, professional organizations, and religious organizations.
- Get a loan from an individual which may give a greater interest return to the lender than other investments. It is also an investment in human capital with faith in that person.
- Students can live at home and commute. The whole family might move to be close to college. Participation in organizations on campus is still possible and important.
- Some "study abroad" programs may be less than one year at the college.
- It is possible to take extra courses in order to graduate earlier.
- Student can take employment that pays for more education, master's degree, etc.
- Live with an elderly person near campus and provide services such as care of house, yard, and shopping in exchange for room and board and use of vehicle.
- Students can be a residence hall counselor in later years.

Encouragement for Incurring College Costs

Education is worthwhile. It appreciates rather than depreciates compared to vehicles and other things. No one can steal a degree. It gives a sense of accomplishment. It facilitates communication with others with higher education when working in leadership roles.

Parents can estimate that state universities or community colleges may not cost much more than their expenses for the child's early years with child care costs, private schools, food, and utilities consumed by student when at home. An encouragement of using financial aid for those who have no other option is that education remains for a life-time, opens doors to employment, and returns are greater than other investments. The temptation is to borrow more than absolutely necessary for additional lifestyle wants, thereby decreasing lifestyle in the future.

Avoid Going into College Debt

College students lose financial freedom from committing years of repayment and reduced options for employment, insurance, mortgages, marriage possibilities, and peace of mind. To avoid over-extension, first it is the desire not to go deeper or overly in debt. With this attitude, search time for other funding can be worthwhile. A common problem is overestimating income and underestimating expenses. Frequently, students get enough aid for tuition but cannot continue because of incidental expenses. They get the financial aid or loan check after they have to use credit for books and supplies. This starts a cycle of short-term credit and creeping indebtedness that become long-term debt. They do not estimate high enough for miscellaneous. However, this may cause overuse of financial aid and guaranteed loans. Or they do not control spending and soon debt controls them.

Short-term debt becomes long-term if not repaid in a timely manner. The Higher Education Act of 2001 encouraged loan consolidation and extended time, which is a curse rather than a blessing. Using credit and loans for convenience, out of habit, without thinking of alternatives reflects a "credit card mentality."

Other remedies are choosing a lifestyle that is adequate although not ideal, belonging to organizations that are less costly, and resisting social pressure to party. (Sometimes students spend about $400 a month for beer.) Students could control costs by doing own laundry, cutting each other's hair, limiting long-distance phone calls, and not using credit for food and drinks.

If students do borrow, they should plan to repay very soon. They may get an extra job to maintain lifestyle. They can change expectations of college and its social life and still have a satisfying experience without burdens that last a lifetime. Pray for resistance to easy credit, creditors on campus, receiving gifts to sign up for credit, and contributing to organizations which allow them to advertise.

Students may be having crises in passing courses, social life, health, or family. They do not recognize the danger signs of too much credit use and financial vulnerability. They are meeting today's needs rather than controlling debt now for future needs.

Maybe for the first time, students confront social discrimination, which drives them to spend money they do not have. A real challenge is to develop their own strategies for these issues without spending too much money. They can find a group where they do "fit in."

(See Chapter 11 on credit for more vital information for students.)

Encouragement after College

The shepherd counselor encouraged Joe and Gerri, a couple who had lost freedom after college due to huge college debts. It would take four years for them to get out of the mess. Specific steps were identified. The counselor encouraged them to remember the four years were what they successfully used to get through college. Therefore, they could gain freedom after four years of sacrifices, frugality, bare bones necessities, hard work and calling on the strength of the Lord. Although mistakes and too much spending occurred in college, now they can live on memories of those past enjoyments. Enjoy what they have now. Now there is a chance for Joe and Gerri's redemption and following their dreams.

A decision to buy a used economy car rather than a more expensive one takes discipline and resistance to temptation. The difference can be applied to the college debts. Another decision is to resist the temptation of consolidating debts that funding agencies and advertisements suggest. Sure, the monthly payment is lower because of extended time but the total cost over time is greater. Shorter loans are consolidated with longer ones which increases the total time. A third suggestion is to meet wants sequentially rather than equally at one time. Upon graduation and a new job, the temptation is to have everything all at once rather than sequentially over the years: deferred needs, independent housing, glasses or contacts, expensive vehicle, expensive vacations, clothes, hobbies, trips and gifts for weddings, expensive recreation, and over spending on hobbies. A suggestion may be a part time job for paying college debts.

Retirement Decisions "Contracting OR Expanding Stage"

(Parents' ages 50-67)
(See Chapter 12 for details and expansion of retirement decisions.)

Decisions about retirement are probably more difficult than other decisions unique to life stages. Planning is done with assumptions about uncertainties. The economy is volatile with uncertainties about investments and employer retirement plans. Health and life expectancies for years after retirement are uncertain. Ability to be employed somewhere or somehow after retirement and spouse's employment are variables. Expenses and sources of income are uncertain. The inflation rate affecting prices is uncertain and measured by the Consumer Price Index. They are based on a selected, standardized "market basket" of goods and services. People buy items that are not measured or price increases may be greater than reflected in the CPI.

Most people are advised to estimate 30 years to live after retirement. (Up-to-date life expectancy tables that are gender and race specific can be found on the Internet. For example, an individual at age 60, on the average has 24.2 more years to live. Of course, parents and grandparents' longevity, general health, and risk factors influence one's longevity. (See *Vital Statistics* of the United States.)

Analysis of Expenses in Retirement

Some expenses will be reduced while others will increase. Decreasing are work related expenses, hopefully credit card debts, college expenses, furniture and self-determined items. Increasing are medical, vacation trips, and gifts. Either the family must have income that increases with inflation (price increases) or it has to adjust consumption expenditures downward.

An estimate of surplus or shortages at different years can be determined by writing expenses on paper or using a computer program. The inflation rate is assumed for increasing expenses at future years. A factor from a mathematical table for given years and given rates can multiple the expenses or the Internet financial calculator can be used. Then the next column can be projected income.

The rule of 72 can be used to determine how many years until purchasing power (real income) of a "fixed income" is halved: 72 divided by assumed inflation rate equals number of years. (72 / 4 percent = 18 years when purchasing power is halved).

Analysis of Income in Retirement

A pencil and paper analysis or a computer program can identify different income sources at early retirement, normal (67), late (70), and if one spouse dies. For example, Social Security benefits, life insurance, and inheritances vary at these times. The *number* of income sources gives a sense of security more than the *total dollar amount*. Development and diversification of income sources can be started now for future use. Sources include Social Security Income, Supplemental Security Income (for low income aged, blind, and disabled,) savings, investments, annuities, employer plans, rental property, business interests, inheritances, liquidating assets, selling things, and exchanging goods and services among neighbors, relatives, and friends. The Employee Benefits Office may have benefits as well as information about the qualified retirement plan. Planning to serve a home or organization for room and board is another type of income source. The American Association of Retired People and the local agencies have information for employment after retiring and for volunteering.

Checking on employer benefits before and after retirement is a must for decisions, especially because of false impressions for early retirement motivations. For example, a teacher may be told she can retire with full benefits. However, the benefits are not identified. The teacher may get a pension, but it is reduced since taken out early and Social Security is reduced for all of his or her remaining life. A benefit is participating in the group health plan. However, the teacher will be required to pay a larger health insurance premium.

Retirement planning involves checking on accuracy of Social Security records, availability of employer plans, profit-sharing, and self-administered plans. A reminder to those who are giving a bequest or inheritance is to have their wills updated. A reminder to those who have life insurance is to have beneficiaries updated.

Most people will have to work after retirement, a fact impacting retirement decisions. Therefore, developing and diversifying skills now will give a sense of security.

Although early retirement sounds desirable for various reasons, the long-term effects on long-term income may be devastating. Estimates for most people are that by working 10 extra years, which add to the retirement account causing the fund to last longer, they will need one-third less for retiring.

Lou's comparison of early with later retirements show the process for comparing incomes at different times. Note the change in Social Security income at various stages. Note the increased income from a self-directed savings plan and from an annuity with compound interest factor.

Age	Years of Service		Average of Highest 5 years		Factor	Annual State	Total Pension Benefit
59	28	x	$53,509	x	1.1%	$16,480	$21,854
	Own contribution		55,980	x	9.6	5,374	
	Social Security until age 62					-0-	
62	31	x	58,026	x	1.1	19,787	
	Annuity	71,820		x	10.03	7,203	
	Social Security estimate					11,470	$38,460
65	34	x	62,624	x	1.1	23,421	
	Annuity	91,661		x	10.55	9,670	
	Social Security estimate					14,340	$47,431

The challenge is to decrease consumption now for saving for retirement years if a deficit is shown on the worksheets. Also, it is to commit a percentage to the work of the Lord and sharing with others as first priority, the practice of faithfulness.

The shepherd assists people to handle undesirable aspects of work as an alternative to early retirement which would reduce or lose benefits. Counseling for creative changes involves changes in attitude, stress counseling, taking more vacations, changing work requirements and physical demands at home, or modifications in job descriptions at employment. Counseling can encourage new group or community participation.

Bob and Nancy went to their attorney to process estate planning including up-dating their wills. Putting the farm, their largest asset, in someone else's name was difficult because they had sacrificed everything and persevered through depressions, crop failures, and uncertainties to keep the farm. Their reluctance changed when actual figures shown to them indicated that without planning and changing ownership they would pay more in estate taxes than they had paid for the farm over the years. When the estate planning was completed, the attorney looked squarely at Bob and Nancy and said, "Now that your financial future is secured, what have you done about your spiritual future?" Bob and Nancy began attending church and dedicated much of life to the work of the Lord after that.

Transferring Wealth

Wealth needs a broader definition for management in this stage.

Wealth for Developing and for Passing onto the Generations.[68] Human and financial capital is composed of several dimensions. These are the goals of resource management and indicate practices that build value. Each aspect can destroy or enhance the others if not managed throughout the life stages.

"Spiritual": The mission, values, core purposes and shared meaning that are the foundation of the family, and the approach to wealth. The relationships to each other expressed as telling the family story (faith) to the next generation.

"Financial": Resources to reinvest and support a comfortable lifestyle, and ability to manage and sustain investments productively.

"Human": Developing the character, skills and identity of each heir to understand how to manage wealth, to find important work, and to live in a complex, difficult and demanding global environment.

"Family": The ability to stay connected within the extended family, to compromise and work together, and create caring, positive and productive relationships....Expressed as generating respect and trust by regular communication; healing past misunderstandings and hurts; and ability to listen and learn from each other.

"Structural": Structures to manage the family wealth, to make decisions, to get competent advice, to manage family businesses or investments, and to steer them in a volatile environment.

"Societal": Commitment and a sense of respect, compassion and connection to the suffering and concerns of others, taking a place of service within one's community, and using resources to support the future of the planet. (Jaffee)

(*See Chapter 12.* "The Light Side of the Money Trail" for terminology and steps in saving, investing, retirement, and estate planning.)

After Retirement "Senior Stage"
(Individuals or Families with ages 65 – 85 +)

Depending on attitude, health status and prior income, this stage varies in income security and in opportunity to continue contributing to the "greater good." An individual can continue productivity if another one believes in him or her, has faith in him or her, and someone gives this opportunity. The author's research has shown that people with disability, now called "Differently-Abled," contribute "services in-kind" such as exchanging baby sitting services for other services between families. They also contribute creative arts and are "prayer warriors." When someone asks for the elderly's advice, he or she feels they can contribute their wisdom and experience

Whereas many seniors are independent and enjoy life to its fullest, some are dependent on an adult child. In our society, many women are caring financially, physically, or in decision-making for a parent for a longer time period than the parent cared for them. Already some advertisements are appealing to the daughter about meeting her mother's health needs, for example. Relations and financial planning in earlier stages with this realization can make a smoother transition to this stage. Grace in finances and love in communication can maintain dignity, respect and contributions to the greater society.

---

68   Dennis T. Jaffee. Six Dimensions of Wealth: Leaving the Fullest Value of Your Wealth to Your Heirs. *Journal of Financial Planning.* April 2003. P.74

Although planning for this stage is difficult due to uncertainties of personal health, children's and friends' activities, and government programs, most face downward consumption in job-related expenses, taxes, and physical activities. Upward expenses are in health care, recreation/travel, and gifts. Out-of-pocket expenses have increased for insurance, house repair, eating out of the home, and utilities plus gasoline for vehicles. Many have to choose between food and fuel. Many cannot afford out-of-pocket expenses for medicines or medical insurance.

Of all the programs for low-income persons, the largest has been Medicaid for long-term care in nursing homes for those who have liquidated all their assets. Many are considering private insurance for long-term care. For this decision, other sources of help such as family members, use of community programs, and live-in help are assessed as well as the percentage that need long-term care more than two months, currently about 30 percent. Premiums, as also true for life insurance, are lower if started at a younger age. A program illustration, showing decision issues for most insurance options, is long-term care for active and former federal employees and their families, as long as they are in good health. Premiums depend on age, features such as daily benefit, benefit period, waiting period for benefits, percent of home care, and automatic compound inflation rider. This plan does not have discounts for excellent health, married people, or nonsmokers like other plans do. To qualify for benefits, the individual is unable to perform two or more activities of eating, dressing, bathing, and toileting. Premiums vary from $114 a month for three years to $140 for five years to $191 for a lifetime. The illustration gives features, benefits, and premiums as a model to set up a worksheet for comparison shopping with private plans. Worksheets for comparisons are useful in decision-making for all types of insurance, purchases in general, financing, etc.

Lifestyle and standard of living must be reevaluated and changed as in previous stages when there are financial problems or income shortages. With reduced purchasing power on fixed incomes, reevaluation and changes are mandatory. Budgets based on what is adequate versus ideal or necessities versus luxuries are rewritten for giving a sense of security and assistance in control over spending. Rather than panicking, individuals calculate hidden costs, total costs, and costs of alternatives. For example, hiring someone to do maintenance in and around a house may be less expensive than buying a condominium where the maintenance fees increase periodically. Using community resources may be less expensive than moving to assisted living. One resource is wearing a "life-line" pendant around the neck which is connected to the hospital which has the names of emergency friends (or the sheriff) to help in an emergency or danger. For a few dollars per month the senior continues to live independently because of the feeling of security with the pendant.

"Late-life" financial issues are complex because credit companies continually change their policies and billing cycles, retirement accounts have different rules and some seniors are not aware of all the resources they do have. Shepherds can guard the elderly by knowing their attorneys, caregivers, and financial planners with whom they may need to discuss their personal finances. Shepherds also need to monitor their activities for theft, mismanagement, or fraud. They can help organize "important papers." The shepherd can do these activities or see that they hire a "bill payor" or "representative payee" who is authorized to receive monthly benefits or money from Social Security, Veteran's Affairs, or pension plan which is deposited in a joint account. A trusted volunteer may do these activities for little or no pay. The church can be a clearing house for volunteers or set up the program initially. The shepherd should beware that children and other people having taken over the finances or paying bills may erroneously or purposely keep the elder in the locked position once they started. They may financially abuse or squirrel away money from the elder. An arrangement with a relative may work whereby a trusted friend financially manages for the relative in the local community in exchange for the relative caring for the friend's parent in the far away community. A contract needs to be written for clarifying rights and responsibilities.

The AARP Bulletin[69] suggests ways to help a parent long distance: Personal management includes making a budget, monitoring accounts and paying bills online. With a joint checking account, copies of statements can be sent to both for checking deposits and check writing. Have cash, pensions, Social Security, IRA withdrawals, stocks and assets in one account with check writing and credit card services. Arrange for automatic payments of bills such as utilities or rent. Get a joint debit or credit card for groceries, drugs, clothing, etc. which will send statements to both parties. Those who serve as "power of attorney" or personal financial representative should have a family member on the account.

A call to Eldercare Locator 800-677-1116 can provide information for local resources. Senior services in the requested community include legal assistance, day care, home health care, financial aid, nursing homes, local Area Agencies on Aging, Meals on Wheels, and programs unique to the locality.

As in other stages, people are victims of scams and rip-offs and, therefore, need warning. The elderly have frequently been advised to get a new car, new siding or roofing under deceptive persuasions. They have parted with antiques at a low price due to con artists, some of which consider themselves Christians.

Decisions for elderly care depend on personal assets, status, occupation, health, family and heirs' composition and age, and lifestyle desired. Resources for care of the elderly which can be mobilized are:

Government programs and community resources. (Ask Area Council on Aging)

Income from Social Security, investments, pensions, inheritances, rental property,

insurance funds from tax deferred annuity or single premium life insurance, reverse annuity mortgage, farm, or business, Supplemental Security Income for low-income aged, disabled and blind.

Family care. (A member might even retire to care for the elderly person.)

Housing Lease-back

Accelerated death benefits

Long-term care insurance

Home equity conversion plan

Home owner equity account

Having a renter share current housing.

Income could be from reverse mortgage, adjustable rate mortgage, shared appreciation, and deferred loan plans. A "reverse annuity mortgage" enables qualified homeowners over the age of 62 to convert the equity in their homes into cash and requires no repayment as long as they live there. Reverse annuity mortgage plans are attractive to some people because it gives them more perceived control. The homeowner can decide how to spend the money received in payment. No agency or institution mandates that the funds must be allocated for a particular use. Reverse mortgages can supplement income to the elderly who have insufficient income to support current consumption.

The reverse mortgage allows older persons to borrow from their home's equity. Taking out a reverse mortgage does not mean that the lender "gets" the home. The person taking out the reverse mortgage remains the owner and is still responsible for property taxes, homeowner insurance, and

---

69   Ellen Hoffman. "Managing Money from Afar." *AARP Bulletin.* June 2003. Pp.21-22.

repairs. When the loan is terminated, the owner or heirs must repay all cash advances plus interest. The owner can never owe more than the home is worth. Cash from a reverse mortgage can be received as a lump-sum payment, monthly payments over a fixed period of time, monthly payments over the remaining lifetime of the borrower if the home is used as principal residence, a credit line that allows the owner to decide how much cash to get and when to get it, and some combinations of the above. Payments are tax-free, considered as part of a loan.

Advantages and disadvantages of these various sources need to be researched and weighed. If a non-paying renter lives in the home and does maintenance, shopping, etc. in lieu of rent, a contract needs to specify responsibilities and rights.

Stage of the Final Journey

The shepherd may be the first to start plans or maybe the only one alongside the individual during the final stage. He or she is alerted to various needs through visits during illness or a call in time of an emergency. The shepherd needs to study and have prayerful input into decisions for controlling medical treatment, appointing a qualified individual to make decisions such as the "health care representative," disqualifying someone to make medical decisions for another, "advance directive" documents to protect rights and having someone speak for the individual when unable or no longer able to understand medical issues. Directives for decisions are explained in the Health Care Consent Act, the Living Will Act (about life-prolonging treatments), and the Powers of Attorney Act (acting for an individual in many situations). Advance directives and organ donation information are in the wallet or purse and communicated to appropriate people. Other decisions are preplanning and prepaying for the funeral and burial.

Preplanning the Funeral

Death is "slipping away to sail upward with the Divine" (Williams). This final journey is sometimes filled with difficult financial decisions. The shepherd walks with the family in faith, by faith, for faith, and with financial faithfulness in life's transition from life through death to more abundant life for survivors. The shepherd guides the grieving process and gives suggestions for the funeral that inspire faith and reduce financial stress. Phases, ways of working through, and display of grief vary with individuals. The usual shock, disorganization, volatile emotions, guilt, sense of loss, and loneliness are barriers to making sound financial decisions. The shepherd with the shield of information and love can increase the meaningfulness and reduce the financial mistakes, potential scams, and future stress.

Advantages of preplanning, especially with a spouse, are relayed by the shepherd. These are: planning rather than panic; planning today and tomorrow; planning together, not alone; planning with rational thinking, not just emotions; and comparison shopping with less emotional appeals or reactions.

Preplanning tasks that the shepherd can guide are: writing names of family and friends to be notified of the death as soon as possible, individuals notified for various reasons, their clergy, names of funeral director and financial planner, where important papers including estate planning papers are, who is appointed executor or executrix, will and trust information, bank accounts and credit cards or debts, government documents, insurance policies and benefits, investments, distribution of things, who is given special consideration in ceremonial arrangements, if an open casket what is placed in hand or beside them in the casket, favorite hymns (poems), favorite Scriptures or Bible stories, preferences for location of ceremony and final disposition, and where copies of forms and instructions are located.[70] Preference of body to be buried, cremated, or donated for medical research should be stated.

Encouraging the individual to tell one's life story gives the strengths used throughout life. The shepherd can discover the cues and orchestrate them into the funeral service. Rather than the shepherd's agenda, the deceased individual has preplanned the agenda by his or her wall hangings, plaques with Scriptures, books, good deeds done for others and services, sayings to others, words of wisdom given to others, favorite songs and poems, financial contributions, social contributions, accomplishments and awards. Also, include things and activities that gave them interest and purpose to life, what they loved to do, children, and missionaries for which the individual supported. The purpose during the service is to show and tell who the person was, what gave them meaning and direction, and the gifts they gave to the world. Even learning from some evil individuals how not to live is a gift. Opportunity for people to express gratitude for the individual's life is meaningful. Sometimes the "open microphone" gets out of hand so some people plan for expressions to be made before or after the funeral.

Disadvantages of Preplanning

Disadvantages are comfort for those who have not preplanned. A disadvantage is that rather than preplanning, preneed arrangements, or prepaying, some people think it is therapeutic for the survivors to make the funeral arrangements since it allows their involvement in saying goodbye, not making it just a routine experience. Decisions made at the time of death are a part of the grieving process. Not a disadvantage, others think having the details decided and written is a gift to the family and expresses wants of the individual's last big decision. Arguments, anxieties and fights among siblings or others are prevented and expenses are met.

Consumer Rights and Responsibilities Applied to Funeral Planning

As in other decisions and financial management, basic principles are: Delegating, not relinquishing control of finances. Avoiding pressure to do something that does not feel right. Comparing goods and services and their prices. Knowing the options, the alternatives. Asking questions. Calling over the phone for itemized prices. Calling two or more funeral directors even though it may not be comfortable or convenient. Usually directors want to quote their cheapest price over the phone. Sometimes in the display rooms, customers are shamed into buying more expensive items. At the time of need, they could take a third, less interested, party with them when purchasing. As in other purchases, a good steward asks what is "adequate" versus "ideal." Other considerations are: buying "respect" not "prestige;" buying "transition activities" rather than compensating for guilt; buying with an information base rather than just an emotional base; maximizing resources by getting the best use of money; knowing the consumer laws and when told something is a law, asking whose law. It may be just their policy. Considerations include exercising rights to see itemized lists; resisting sales pressure and determining the vested interest people have in the decisions; empowering self to empower others to make life's transition a quality, growing experience by simple planning and participation in decisions.

---

70   A packet of pages designed to "Get it Together" are available from Chaplain Myrna Long Wheeler, Hillcrest Retirement Community. 909-392-4354. 2008.

Lack of knowledge about funerals promotes hasty, erroneous, and wasteful decisions. Knowledgeable consumers buy in line with their values and resist sales pressure. They prevent abuse, fraud, and misrepresentation. They question whose vested interests or agendas others have when purchasing goods and services. They allow values (religious preferences) to affect decisions rather than customs. Knowledgeable consumers separate laws from business requirements, although a funeral director may try to blur them.

A booklet "Consumer Redress and Assistance" is available with information from the Funeral Service Arbitration Program, P.O. Box 27641, Milwaukee, WI 53227, 1-800-662-7666. Also, contact the Federal Trade Commission or state Attorney General.

The Federal Trade commission Funeral Rule (1984) states that provision on a funeral cannot be based on the purchase of certain products including a casket. The customer must be told that a casket is not required in the case of cremation. Nationally, about 15 percent of those who die are cremated. This is increasing. Embalming is NOT required by law in any of the 50 states. Exceptions are in time and transportation.

A major funeral expense is viewing and what goes with it such as embalming, other services, use of viewing room, transfer of body to funeral home, refrigeration (per day), clothes, clergy, flowers, and music. The death expenses outside the funeral service are cemetery costs which include spaces, opening and closing the grave, monuments, burial vaults, mausoleum, overtime labor charges, and frost removal.

The Question of Prepaying a Funeral or Not

Prepaid Funeral Plans (about 25 percent of all funerals) are through special savings account, insurance policies which dominate the industry and "Totten Trusts." States have a law to protect money through these trusts should the funeral home become bankrupt. (States vary in details and names.) Money is placed in banks authorized to hold the trusts. One may change the funeral home, merchandise, or services purchased. This money is not counted as part of probate or as an asset for welfare eligibility consideration. At the time of death, the money is paid to the funeral director with whom pre-arrangements were made. The IRS has ruled that income from the trust is taxable to the creator of the trust (i.e. the consumer).

One can prepay through a state-regulated trust by paying the funeral director who will invest the money and use it for the funeral. One can buy life insurance from the funeral director who buys a policy. One can deposit money into a bank account with a Totten trust payable to an individual named at time of death.

Advantages of Pre-paying the Funeral

Pre-paying avoids the increased cost due to price increase, inflation; avoids troubling and costly emotional decisions; is a gift to the survivors by knowing what you want and having set aside money for your final arrangements. In the Totten trust, although you pay taxes on the income, the money escapes probate. Life insurance checks are made payable to the beneficiary, not the funeral home.

Disadvantages of Pre-paying

The funeral director invests a percentage of the prepaid money, from 100 percent to 50 percent, depending on the state; one does not have control of the prepaid money; one is committed to a particular funeral home and tied to a particular locality; one could make your own arrangements such as buying term insurance or having a bank account designated for funeral expenses and earn the monies for yourself over time; setting aside money in a savings account with a higher rate of interest has the best choice; and survivors are prevented from participating in the final arrangements considered by some people therapeutic and necessary. Without prepayment plans, expenses are paid from current operating budget, survivors' benefits, or state funding.

A savvy consumer will check for maintenance charges and service fees that reduce the amount available to pay funeral expenses. Other checks include seeing if the trust earns more than the costs of the funeral and who would receive the difference - the survivors or the funeral director. One can check for reciprocal agreements with other funeral homes around the country. One should find out the refund arrangements in case he or she changes one's mind.

Limiting Costs and Personalizing the Funeral or Memorial Service

The services, content of sermon, music, group participation, and special effects that the people involved do want must be respected, not just the pastor's preferences or experiences. Hopefully, they will want to know the options before making their decision.

Costs for a traditional burial, including embalming, steel casket, and concrete vault buried in a cemetery can exceed $10,000.

An option is a "green burial," costing less than $2,000 in which the casket is made of a biodegradable product. Cremation is another option. The costs for pick up fee, service fee, cremation fee, and simple urn can range from about $1,000 to as much as a traditional funeral with full service, vault or digging a grave.

Options can be mentioned by the shepherd that are available although not readily known or told such as:

- Viewing and visitation can be in a church or private home.
- Friends and family can be received at church or home without casket present.
- Funeral ceremony can be a church, a private home, or other meeting place.
- Selecting an inexpensive or moderate priced casket. (Illustrations are: minimum plywood is about $300, minimum steel about $500, basic steel with crepe interior and adjustable bed about $1,000, standard steel about $1,300, polished wood about $1,500, oak with crepe interior about $2,000 to over $6,000). These prices vary state by state. Be sure prices are for casket only. Funeral services are sometimes included in the price of the casket.
- Renting a casket in the case of cremation.
- Having a friend or relative provide the music. (An example of fraud was when the deceased had prepaid for the music and then a friend provided it who was never paid.)
- Buying flowers directly from the florist, having friends and family provide them, or doing without. (An example of fraud is when flowers are prepaid, but so many are sent by friends and associations that the funeral director does not buy them.) So if the deceased made arrangements with the director, check on current status. Check itemized list with prepaid arrangements.
- Giving a donation to charity as an alternative to sending flowers.
- Checking on price list if any items are double-listed or counted, or different than discussed previously.
- Establishing a scholarship in memory of the deceased instead of sending flowers.

- Providing guest books, acknowledgment cards, and programs from less expensive sources.
- Giving honoraria directly to individuals who provide services.
- Recording the ceremony yourself, if one is desired.
- Using personal cars rather than limousines and flower cars.
- Not using a police escort.
- Asking friends and relatives to serve as pallbearers.
- Filing for death benefits to use for the services.
- Asking a family member or close friend to write the obituary and send the death notice to the newspaper. (Information for the obituary can be provided in the preplanning done by the individual. It includes name, birth, date and place, parents and their birthplaces, maiden name, spouse's name, survivors, career, religion, residence, memorials.) Newspapers and college alumni departments for sending information is done in the preplanning.
- Obtaining death certificates on one's own.
- Using clothing owned by the deceased instead of purchasing new clothing.
- Writing thank you cards.

After the death, surviving family members need immediate access to funds lasting from three to six months because of delays in collecting death benefits and probating wills. Avoid making final decisions when pressured or uncertain. Allow a year to complete them. Meanwhile, preserve the inheritance of each family member. Get comfort from the gifts and memories that live beyond the loved one who "slipped away to sail upward with the Divine."

Communicating the Move for Parents, Changes and Fears

Presented through the eyes of Jill for the ears of the Shepherd

1. When you recall working with your parents about their housing transition, what emotions, pains, regrets, satisfactions were aroused ?

    Love pain was present because it was a 40 year move with much history. Sadness was aroused for both children and parents. I actually had no regrets because we approached every situation with saying, "We need talk about the alternatives. The current situation is not an alternative. The situation is not working now. We have to find a way to change for you and for me." We had a good relationship of tough emotional things as long as we dealt with love and compassion. We were straightforward. Because of the good relationship, we could deal with the tough, hard issues. We had satisfactions and joy that we could talk and work things out. We have no regrets even with the hard, sad things as we look back

2. What do you recall are the main issues in working with parents in their housing transition?

    For us it was safety with equipment in bathroom, in kitchen, and in the stairs. Mother's mental capacity changed and we had to have things so they did not get hurt. Their mobility was changing. They had problems with walking. So they needed walkers and other things. They had to be open to change structures, move furniture, and get more space. Dad, because of his lung capacity, had chairs so he could stop and rest. He had to think how furniture and equipment could assist him. We had to reevaluate their housing in relation to the services they needed. They had to question how far were the doctor, grocery store, and whatever they needed so they could drive themselves. Dad could drive at the beginning. At the end, my sister did all the driving. I had to think about driving in various ways. When it is in a larger community, while there are more services, the traffic and other kinds of things were harder to get back and forth because of safety. Once they moved back to the small town, there were lots of people driving around with limited driving mobility and so we did not worry as much. There were a series of housing transitions: to the big house in the larger community, to farm house in community, to nursing home near the farm house, to clear across the state next to one of their daughters. We had to decide where housing involved safety, mobility, and moving to one location to fit the needs. Every transition changed their social community which was an important issue. For them, it never was a real financial issue, just a perceived one. For other parents, the financial issue is a big one.

3. What did you base their housing decisions on?

    Someone living nearby, sell of current property, depletion of assets, least expensive, familiarity. In preretirement and early retirement state we had two places – 125 miles away. When issues started coming, they were traveling back and forth. The main issue to them was loving care that two places could not continue. They had to choose among three alternatives: the large house, the farm, and a new place. Current situation was not acceptable and she had to tell them in a loving way. Together, they said no new place such as a house in larger community or farm house. They each wanted the opposite. Her message to them was, "Our family has always made tough decisions. You have talked things out and come to a decision. Do you want me to help with that or do you want to. A new decision must be made. We cannot avoid it." They said, "We will make the decision." She said, "Very good. Merrill and I will help you move." We let them talk for a week and did not mention it again for a week. Next time she said, "What are you talking about, what are the problems, and what are things you like about each? What do we have to do to change?" For the big house, there were changes in steps, hand rails, and retrofitting. She knew that Dad knew that. Mother said she wanted to be near her grandchildren. Once we realized that my sister, who had children, worked out ways they could do things together if they were at the farm house. When mother expressed what she wanted and her fears, they were able to work out to help her be around children more by being near a beginning elementary school..

4. As you recall, what happened or when did you realize you, as an adult child, had to start treating parents as dependents? That you needed to help them?

    She realized mother's limitations. She could not keep up two houses. Dad was o.k. because he just went back and forth. Mother had to figure out food each time in different locations, how to care for the house each time, and she was wearing out. (Traditional system) Now later, we realized looking back that we as children figured things were going on. Mother was beginning some dementia. We saw her struggle to take care of things. Dad protected her and did not share all that was happening around the dementia. They had a system of protecting each other. Jill as a child was only seeing part of it. The insiders were Mother and Dad. The outsiders were making judgments. As a child, she was closer looking in than were others in the community. As a child, I found solutions for what was going on. Another person who was more on the outside was giving unhelpful opinions. To find out information, one has to find out what is going on in that family. It took three years to make the decision, as time enfolded. One needs to know what was happening at that time. Emotions get in the way for seeing what was going on. Dad was protecting Mother. Dad probably came to the decision. She did not know it was Dad's decision but she said it was o.k. Because of her dementia, she knew she had to have help.

Jill took two weeks of vacation and went to the big house and started packing. Merrill came a week later to help at the end and actually helped in the transition of moving, unpacking and setting up their house. By this time, Dad was elderly. He was in his late 70s and early 80s. Merrill did work for them, giving lots of help which can be called human capital, emotional capital, and financial capital. (He paid for his own trip there.)

5. What fears did you sense on their part? On your part? How were fears of the unknown manifest?

I do not think they had fears. They were comfortable. My fear was that if I had forced a decision and while it looked like the best decision given the circumstances, my fear was that it would not be the best for them. She remembers talking her fears through with her husband. There were the parent couple system and her couple system. From our inside situations and the link between the two, the decision would turn out not to be the best even though we thought it was the best decision available.

Their fears were of absence of children and mental capacity. These realities developed later within three to four months when mother was having trouble doing basic things. Lack of mental capacity had a pattern in dementia reflected in planning and getting a meal together. Dad protected her which was even more evident when they were in a new place. When Jill came to visit she could see all the problems occurring.

6. How did you maintain their independence, their dignity, their self-respect, and their sense of   control while controlling and directing their steps in transition?

Jill knew that she still wanted a strong couple system for them in making a decision. They needed to feel it was their decision. Her role was to discuss decisions before they were implemented. She did not want to change the couple system but brought it out so she could know about decisions they were making.

She often said we just need to talk about the alternatives. She said, "Have you thought about…?" Then she would give a new alternative and come back with the question, "What do you think about…?" She would list all the alternatives including the new one. It was her way of keeping them empowered and the decision their own. Her sister Susan had a different approach and situation. She was caught in the middle with young children and elderly parents. Susan would get frustrated in using her own human capital, own emotional capital, and own money to assist her parents. A decision may take more from each of them. A bad decision would impact their lives. Therefore, the decision had to minimize their own decisions and resources. The difficulty is about the use of available family resources.

7. How did you keep communication open and non-threatening? What other words would you use with your parents?

I would ask them, "What have you thought about doing?" I would talk about alternatives. I would always find words to support the good things for which I agreed. I would minimize the things I did not agree with. If I told Dad "no" and confronted him, he would get angry. I praised him for the good decisions he made. If he made a decision with which I would not agree with, she would laugh and say, "Dad, that is your decision. I would have done this and that. Yet, it is your decision." In 90 percent of the time, he would come around to her alternative. Otherwise, when her sister confronted him and told him what she thought, he would say what he was going to do. After that, when my sister and I realized what was happening, we talked things through before presenting them to the family.

8. What problems with siblings entered in the decisions and transition?

When you have siblings that come from different points of view and having different levels of resources for parents, there needs to be a plan for those resources. She and her sister provided human capital, the emotional capital and doing things out of own pocket. After parents moved to the farmhouse for five years, for every five weeks, Jill took weekends to fly out, 600 miles, and rent a car to help work things out. She would call her brother, 1,500 miles away, on any big decisions and talk over any alternatives. She would ask him if he saw others. She was blunt to ask him to support the decision finally made and needed him to support the decisions. Decisions were tough enough that she did not want someone who had not provided human or financial capital to provide alternatives that would not be suitable for the situation. He did have emotional capital. So she wanted knowledgeable people to be supportive and especially those who would be talking with the parents. His talking with his parents did provide emotional capital, social capital, and support.

9. What information did you need?

Dad said several things after the fact, after mother's death. If we had known the amount of dementia and issues of health, maybe we would have made other decisions. I knew that during the final stages and at the end, but not at the initial housing decision. We wanted to be very open about what we were doing and why. With more information, we could have made another decision along the way. These are satellite decisions along the way.

10. What resources did you use?

Human resources, financial resources, human capital, her education, knowledge of how to deal, information from community such as what kind of doctors in the community and things for daily living.

11. Did you consider alternatives to housing transition such as live-in homemaker/ health, caregiver, and using community resources? Were these available?

Yes, we used housekeeping services and physical care services.

12. How does one make decisions – directing the new path of life's journey for elderly or ill, dependent parent?

Carefully, lovingly, and with respect.

13. Do you think the statistics are true that a daughter will take care of or help with decisions of her mother more years than the mother took care of the daughter as a dependent?

Yes, my guts tell us as our lives get longer. It is longer than the 18 years. She senses it is "yes."

14. What questions need to be asked? Did you ask? So what do you say are the questions to ask professionals?

(Since this is the first and only experience of most adult children, they do not know the questions to ask or the issues.) See questions above.

15. What is the role of the pastor (or shepherd) in the housing transition and the changing relationship between adult child and dependent parent?

For her, a pastor's role is to sort out questions asked by the family or information shared by family members and to sort out where information is coming from: within, the couple parent or from child's view of parent. The pastor is still the outsider. He or she needs to understand whether the information is from parent couple system or child system.

16. What did the pastor do or say that was useful, creative, and sensitive?

She asked three questions every time they had to make a decision: "Will this alternative make a difference? Do we have the resources to use for this decision? Most important, are we willing to use those resources and carry forth with the decisions." If not a yes for all three, I must walk away from this situation. I have seen parents so torn up that they cannot help or do anything. They cannot function if they cannot do it. It is very sad and they cannot function in that situation. It is very sad when they do not have resources to do. There were times we had to walk away. It took a long time to come to that level of thinking. Some would say that is cold but she said it was sensible, rational, sensitive, and loving. She had had her own situation which included a loss of a sister later.

The pastor's role depends on closeness of the pastor to the family. He or she could play different roles. The pastor cannot tell the family what to do. He or she can help them find alternatives. The role of the pastor may be to initiate church educational classes or support classes on housing decisions. People need visitors to help them in transitions. The pastor is to open eyes to see the needs. The pastor can grieve with the individual and family when leaving a lifestyle and something comfortable they liked. It is usually not a happy time. Amount of grieving or acceptance of changes depends on who they are.

17. What did the pastor do or say that was NOT useful, creative, and helpful?

I could imagine the pastor saying things that put a strain on the parent-child relationship. For example, "You're the parent. You have the right to make decisions even though the child has to come to help." Better to say, "I see that there are lots of decisions and lots of resources for looking for the best decision. Sometimes, when there are few resources, one has to make the best decisions out of poor options."

It is hoped that pastors, counselors, and others assist in a manner that strengthens the decision-making and provides emotional strength to those who have to make the decisions. The issue is how, where, and when help is provided as an outsider. It is looking to the inside to see how one can strengthen the resources that are inside. These include physically, spiritually, emotionally, and financially for questions on where to get funds. These include how to extend or substitute resources. It helps them to use finances better or to substitute.

18. What would you do differently if you were to do it again?

Nothing, because we did the best we could with the resources and knowledge at the time. We are not people to live life in regret. We live each day and go forth.

We have been discussing the scenario of choosing the path of parents. It is much more complicated when there are two parents with different abilities at the time. Then, as time goes on, one is left alone so the initial decisions have to involve the sequential, probable situation of the other.

19. What perspectives and steps in the path were considered, should be considered, in assisting with the telescopic view in mind?

Focus on parent with greatest need first and then resolve issue with second parent because the second has more emotional, health, and human social resources. Focus on the greater need before the second. A balance of what needs are addressed is important because one cannot focus on all of it at the same time. Every situation is unique.

20. What situations, events, decline of health, etc. occurred subsequently that you did not expect?

Broken bone, broken hip from a fall and he was primary caregiver. Continuum of decisions. Thinking of housing, a continuum of what can become. Realize things will not remain the same. When mother was first into the nursing home, it was very tough. Father called and said, " I cannot do this anymore." So we went into nursing home with her and arranged for a couple room. This was a short-term decision because he hated it so bad. She needed the care with increased dementia. However, the nursing home is a good place for someone with a strong, good mind. Dad would take her out for two days a week. Since that seemed a bad decision, he decided to remain on the farm and drive into the nursing home from the farm to feed her everyday. Eventually, the domino effect of moving clear across the state, again into another nursing home together, caused him to move out and go back to the farm. He was there a month and then to apartments connected to near where his daughter lived. They had lots of services. Jill flew to the farm and talked with her Dad, but he decided he was not taking the apartment. Before the weekend was over, he decided to take it. He worked through the decision until he told her it was the best thing. The decision had been made earlier. Jill's sister had paid a check but then he wrote a check and her sister got her check back. Jill's job was to help him come to that decision which he did on his own. He lived near her sister for two years. Her sister made his meals on wheels every night because he did not like the meals connected to the nursing home.

21. How typical was your case?

We feel blessed among families who have a history of working together. There is no physical or verbal abuse, no alcohol, or sexual abuse patterns. There was a pattern of respect for everyone. Parents were married over 50 years and had long-term marriages of their children. Long-term marriages work on their problems, celebrate together, and learn to live with what you have. If people do not expect a lot, they are not looking for a lot. If they expect to live together, they do live together.

The issue is not just the aging of America, but the distance between where families live. Jill said to her parents that we do not want any surprises. Her dad told her everything. Therefore, when he passed away, Jill and her sister could deal with it. Her dad wanted to have control. She just wanted to have conjunction with him. Some parents want to be in control and want to be the decision makers without understanding the impact of the decisions on more than their couple system – the child system and in later years, the entire family system.

◊◊◊ ⧗   ⧗ ◊◊◊

Chapter 7. The Shepherd Marries the Couple: Premarital Counseling for a Journey of Love and Business, Communicating About Money

The shepherd guides the couple in righteousness as old paths are merged. The pastor-counselor equips the couple for the journey of both a love union and forming a new business, a new partnership. This transition can also be a time of spiritual development. Premarital sessions are designed to increase faith, faithfulness, communication about money, financial information, and commitment to sound financial management practices.

Theology for the Journey

The shepherd can stimulate interest and growth in vital subjects pertinent to personal and marriage success using the following ideas: Keys to success for family happiness are having the <u>S</u>pirit, <u>S</u>ex, money <u>S</u>ense, and absence of <u>S</u>in. Sin is three types: commission, omission, and disposition. Disposition refers to personality which includes relating to a person and not ignoring him or her, mannerisms, conversation, and demeanor. Any of these sins can separate a person from God as well as the love and respect of the other. Any of these sins can block the gifts that could be received from the other. Any sins, by definition, lead to a destructive path. Any event or finances of the past that have not been resolved "sufficiently" will eventually, if not currently, disturb or dissolve the new marriage. Facing them, naming them, and planning one step toward resolving them in premarital counseling will assist in building spiritual wholeness. Expectations may be modified upon understanding what baggage, mistakes, or fears the other person brings to the marriage. Common examples are extreme anxieties because of negative experiences of parents, bad habits or addictions not controlled yet, and huge debts from credit use or financial aid. As Solomon says, "News of debt can ignite all kinds of emotional issues related to trust, security, power and control."[71] Happiness begins with forgiveness. It continues with action.

When a person's life is guided by the Spirit and drinking from the "Living Water" all needs are not dependent on another person. When the Lord rather than one's spouse is on the pedestal for worshipping, the spouse is accepted and loved with imperfections, mistakes, and shortcomings. When one's center of life is God's love, he or she can accept the other person with the gifts brought to marriage and not expect all of life to be from him or her. One sees in the person the gifts as gifts from God, not all of life. When one sees the other as a gift from God, the good is seen. The good is enjoyed in humble gratefulness rather than thinking constantly what is not good, trying to reform the spouse. Disappointments and errors can be handled on the journey when one or both keep focused on God.

---

71   Syble Solomon. Life Wise. 421 West Blackbeard Rd., Wilmington, NC. 28409. 2008.

Keys to success are forgiveness, not seven times, but 70 times 7, and learning from mistakes. Forgiveness of the other person is easier when one realizes how much God forgives one's own weaknesses, sins, temptations, and imperfections. As we receive God's grace, we give grace to the other. Love is received from God and reflected in one's behavior toward the other person.[72] Trusting God to restore relationships is a key. Rather than panicking, one or both can pray and plan when there is a problem by asking, "What is the next step?" When trouble comes, "turn your eyes upon Jesus" and he will direct your paths.

The famous survivor of Nazi persecution Cory ten Boom asked, "When your train is going through a dark tunnel, is this the time to jump out? Or are you going to trust the Engineer to pull you through?" Couples can expect valleys and mountain top experiences. Faith in each other as well as in God can pull them through. The challenge is not to not have problems nor to avoid them. Everybody and every couple have problems. The challenge is how to solve the problems. How to solve problems is an area of disagreement. The pastor-counselor should be listening and watching for controlling behavior. Couples may need to be taught new methods for solving problems and managing resources of time, energy, material things, and money.

The story of the "Beauty and the Beast" gives a model. By treating the person as one would have them be, that person becomes as one would have them be. Love and respect, not curses, can beautify a person. One approach for improving the situation is to go through the day pretending and acting in married life how one would want it to be. Perhaps it will become that.

Habits can keep a marriage afloat or drag it down. Couples should start good habits at the beginning such as patterns of eating together, throwing trash (all kinds) in the bin, walking together, having daily devotions together, saying please and thank you, sharing work, comparing prices, saving money, acknowledging each other's gifts, presence, and rituals developed or desired. Habits for living together are difficult to change after periods of time. A key is to compliment the person every day even though it may be hard to do on some days. It may be just on his smile or her cooking a particular food. Learn the languages of love described by therapist Gary Chapman, recognize them, and check if the other is receiving what is desired. The language may be in actions, in words, or in touch. Thinking of the other person before one's self causes one to speak the other's language. Some say the key to success is to affirm in simple words the love for the other. One can practice the language of respect: complimenting and encouraging, recognizing the gifts or helping to develop the gifts. Although a successful marriage is not guaranteed, the risk of failure is reduced when habits and patterns are developed.

Contrary to opinions of a novice, one has to work at loving another person because any one is imperfect and disappointing at times. Keys for a marriage to work successfully include having prayer, practice and perseverance. Transforming one's self rather than changing someone else is not easy. "Jesus looked at them and said, 'With man this is impossible, but not with God; all things are possible'" (Mark10:27 NIV).

A Chinese proverb warns "Before marriage keep both eyes open. After marriage, shut one eye." Loving is not always easy because "one eye has to be shut" at mistakes, irritations, temporary insults, personal quirks, weakness, and faults. The other eye is looking for what is done right, and doing more at it rather than focusing on problems. It is work **not** to say everything one thinks, bite one's tongue before speaking, be easily irritated, keep score, raise one's voice unnecessarily, and spend money for self before putting others first. The challenge in families is dealing with

---

72   David Henderson. Sermon Notes. Covenant Presbyterian Church. West Lafayette, Indiana. 2005.

the "mosquitoes" rather than the "elephants" – the irritating little nuisance things - more than the big values and purposes. The "mosquitoes" are the management or mismanagement of little tasks each day such as kitchen manners: each clearing the table and cleaning the counter. Management includes habits such as turning off lights when a person is done with them. They are keeping themselves and the near environment clean and attractive.

Marriage can offer a new beginning to walk with the Lord as the couple walks with each other. The old journey may have been filled with thoughts of the bad things that have happened, dominating perspectives and dispositions. The old walk may have been filled with addictions and resentments passed onto the new spouse if not forsaken and forgiven. Destructive reasons for marrying have to be examined and eliminated. The new walk should remember the good things that have happened, rather than the bad, dominating one's thoughts, heart, and soul. With a focus on Jesus, the newer walk focuses on doing good things for others, random acts of kindness, and glorifying God. The journey continues with this healing power and love in action not just words. This is grace. God is faithful and fills the path with joy and peace as the couple is faithful to God, to each other, and to their finances.

The love language is shown in actions. One example is performing little or big household responsibilities. Surveys[73] of disagreements in families at different times have shown the same conclusions: Household tasks or division of labor including responsibilities were the highest source of disagreement. Finances were a close second or first in other research. Involved in these disagreements are expectations and standards in the home about who does what and when. Organizational systems are an issue especially when each comes from a different system. The first household task is to decide on a system that is unique and appropriate for the new couple, i. e. who does what task for daily living. Couples should feel free to change their system as circumstances of family life change. A new structure can be established and better attitudes toward its use will improve. As in other areas of married life, keys are patience and the realization that systems will continually evolve out of the situation and out of love. A key is to be unselfish and a help-mate, a team member, not a leech nor a slave.

Sex is a gift from God to be enjoyed responsibly, kindly, and unselfishly. This is "heaven with you." Guard from any sexual expressions which would give rise to jealousy. After centering your life on Christ, your spouse is first before anybody, anything, or any purpose. This is the first rule for togetherness. No secrets kept. No deceptions. No dishonesty. No selfishness. Pernicious in the love union and in the business enterprise are selfishness, greed, and harboring secrets. Hiding assets and not reporting expenses are symptomatic of other problems. Give words to reassure the person's acceptance and to reduce anxieties and fears they may have. Then the gift remains pure and full. The challenge is to overcome boredom by centering life on reflecting God's love not seeking pleasures in obsessions with possessions or immoral living.

Premarital Counseling in Financial Management

The pastor or shepherd can financially educate by presenting in a class or on a one-to-one basis useful experience and practical wisdom of the ages. Sensitive areas are discussed openly. Stimulation to think about financial management is intertwined with spiritual concerns. Several

---

73   Flora Williams. "Financial Disagreements and Difficulties from Selected Studies." Unpublished paper. 2002.

selected ideas follow. Each brings to the marriage some money sense. Each brings some burdens, extra baggage that has to be disposed of to make the marriage trail easier. If a person is in love with money rather than the other person, obstacles in the path abound. On the other hand, each contributes a type of non-money income which contributes to a higher quantity and quality of life than is individually possible. Marriage is committing to a third job – managing financial affairs, that of household maintenance, cooking, shopping, yard care, and car care. Handling conflicts is a job in itself as conflicts are inevitable.

Various studies give insight into potential pitfalls.[74] One study reported that 14 percent of couples fought over their overspending whereas 6 percent reported arguing over one's "penny-pinching." Over half of the respondents in another study reported "arguing a lot about money." One study reported the additional car caused the monthly deficit. Another said that addiction or gambling was the problem. Several studies reported that creeping indebtedness overtook those who were complacent or thinking the monthly minimum payment would suffice. Financial problems were evidenced in warnings of having utilities turned off, late house payment or rent, not affording to keep equipment in repair, inability to save, not buying what children want, and overusing credit until there was no more. One large study reported conflicting areas were similar in dysfunctional and successful families: finances 70 percent, household management 64 percent, personality disagreements 63 percent, sexual adjustment 59 percent, sharing household tasks 56 percent, personal habits 43 percent, and religious matters 27 percent just to mention a few areas. Several studies have reported similar percentages.

The challenge for couples is sustaining a love relationship while entering into a business relationship, a partnership, an economic union. Policies and procedures for grievances must be established for when, not if, things go wrong and failure occurs. The business policy as well as the love union policy is foremost "honesty." For either to succeed, honesty and trust must prevail. Therefore, honesty and trust policies must be enforced as the foundations for beginning anew after brokenness. Policies are enforced by confession, repentance, asking forgiveness, recommitment, and starting anew. This is what marriage as a "new beginning" is all about. Why? What is the alternative? Hurts accumulate and erupt in explosive behavior or withdrawal. Distrust and suspicion increase. When the policies have been broken, healing and repair must happen or the marriage, as well as personal hope and happiness, will die.

Because there are too many temptations, trials, and weaknesses, the newly formed company needs a president and CEO. Although Jesus can be the board president, the couple has to choose its board members. The couple has to set new goals, some that are personal and some joint. Although the transition may be difficult, people can develop peace, love, and strength.

The company's assets include financial knowledge, taking advantage of consumer rights, awareness of the wolves, and managing to pay all bills on time to avoid costly late fees. Keeping records will provide a more accurate estimate of expenses. Record keeping is not the same as planning. Expenses must be analyzed and changed after record keeping to be useful. (See questions and techniques in Chapter 4 on budgeting.) Savings are needed for meeting the problem of underestimating expenses and for unexpected opportunities or crises. The key is control and balance of expenditures, saving, and sharing. Sharing expenses are usually underestimated because the couple does not calculate costs of giving gifts, honoring celebrations, weddings, gifts, giving to the poor, and birthdays. For the marriage to succeed, some couples need to control addictions,

---

74   Flora Williams. Ibid.

hobbies, collections, impulsive buying, and the urge to satisfy every want. Over time, the love and respect from each other and from God help meet psychological and social needs so that destructive spending does not dominate.

Before it is too late, couples can have a strong foundation of financial knowledge to guide them on their way. According to an old saying, "Experience is a good teacher, a fool can learn no other way." The key for the newly formed family company is to invest in financial information, consumer savvy, and effective management. The key for success in this business venture is to reevaluate priorities, meet goals sequentially, and have money for each as well as together, if possible. Having one main manager in selected areas seems to work better than having everyone manage. Another old saying is "Everybody's responsibility is no one's responsibility." Switching roles to pay bills from time to time teaches necessary skills and promotes understanding of pressures or strain. One idea for the controlling person is to allow the freer one a certain amount to manage separately. Rather than feeling threatened that the other person is controlling, that partner can thank with appreciation that the person cares enough to care, remind, clean, pay bills, and help the other person to take responsibility.

Building Blocks for a Foundation for the New Love Union and the New Business

The couple in the premarital counseling session can decide from the following lists the discussion issues for the given session and what can be discussed at the next session. If both do all the talking, they need to learn the control – the art – of listening. If both are silent, they need to learn how to express themselves. Both skills are vital for the new business or company. Therefore, questions in the areas from which each chooses for their unique interest in forming the love union and a new business are suggested below. Questions identify needed information and building blocks. Taking turns in selecting and answering the questions begins a pattern of communication. Issues, misunderstandings, and ignorance are faced. Gifts of increased understanding are exchanged. Facts for success are learned in discussion with the pastor-counselor. Of course the pastor-counselor is aware the couple may not be honest or self-aware. Nevertheless, answers are structures to begin the building with a firm foundation. Through practice and perseverance, attitudes and hope can follow structure rather than having all healthy attitudes in place before beginning the union.

Forming a New Love Union

The following questions can guide discussion with depth and reality as well as educate.
1. What are your hopes for forming a love union?
2. What are you afraid might happen?
3. What have you done before when something turns out differently or disastrously? (How do you solve a disappointment? A problem?)
4. What secrets do you need to share?
5. What secrets or area of secrets do you agree are best left unshared?
******
6. What would you do to "work" at your marriage?
7. What would you do during the day to have exciting, passionate, and gentle sex at night?

******

8. What daily disciplines would you have to increase the Lordship of your life, serve a Higher Power, or meet ultimate purposes?
9. Describe a typical day desired with designated his, hers, and our time?
******

10. What would be difficult to forgive in the other person?
11. What day is trash day? (Day each week to throw away hurts, suspicions, evil thoughts, bad memories). As most communities have weekly trash pick-up, couples can have one.
12. What day is resurrection day? (Day each week to "make up"? Start anew? Say I am sorry? Forgive?) As the Sabbath is honored to restore the soul, it can restore the couple.
******

13. What "love language" would you expect from your spouse? How do you feel loved?
******

14. What are the gifts you bring to the other?
15. What are the "mosquitoes" in your marriage? (irritations, flaws, habits)
16. Why is arguing good? When is it uncontrolled?
17. What are examples of "I statements" you want the other to hear?
18. What are you going to do each day to be filled and directed by the Spirit?

Forming a New Business, a New Partnership in Finances

Questions can face the delicate and difficult issues rather than just hiding the unresolved past, preconceived perspectives, and ignorance that may cause difficulty in a marriage. They identify basic management tasks in the new business. These questions move the couple beyond generalities to specific roles and action:

1. What needs to be brought to the board meeting of the new company biweekly or bimonthly meeting?
2. What is your financial story, i.e. money use in your family, meaning of money, "easy come-easy go" or "financially challenged?" (Without knowing the story, one may be too critical or too uncaring.)
3. How have finances affected your self-worth, school or job performance?
4. When or where have you over-spent to make up for past deprivation, boredom, to be respected, to solve office politics, to make others happy, to make yourself happy, and/or to impress others?
5. Is there some addiction or uncontrolled spending you want coaching on? Need help with?
*****

6. If you received a $100,000 insurance or inheritance, what would you do with it? (The answer helps clarify values but action is the real clarifier.)
7. What is your attitude toward credit or borrowing, the amount of debt load to assume?
8. What have you learned or skills developed from handling finances?
*****

9. Who is going to be the main manager and pay the bills on time?
   (Why would it be good to switch periodically who pays them?)

10. How are you deciding who will do what tasks or take responsibility for the house, yard, car, etc.?

11. What type of household organization (system) do you want to try? (Patriarchal or matriarchal, rational bureaucracy, communist, democratic, equalitarian, exchange, permissive, or fatalistic) (See descriptions below.)

12. When will you schedule a "business meeting"? What day every two weeks or monthly?

13. Where will be a business center with important records, insurance papers, bills due and bills paid, stamps and envelopes that are accessible? What needs to be copied?

*****

14. Describe your "standard of living"? (That for which you feel deprived if you do not have and are willing to work for?)

15. What are your "rights" to uphold? (Consumer rights to information, safety, recourse, protection, disclosure, honesty, justice)

16. What do you consider your responsibilities? What new skill or task do you want to develop to contribute more to family non-money income?

*****

17. What are your definitions of "necessities" versus "luxuries"? How might these differ from your spouse's? How could you "skimp on necessities to have the luxuries"?

18. How could you better estimate expenses and make decisions on what to change (cut or add?)

19. What is wrong with basing decisions on housing and transportation on the monthly payment rather than the 60-40 rule? (60 percent of total cost is the payment and other related costs are 40 percent.)

"What is Wrong with the Following Action?"

A problem exists when one sees something as a problem and the other one does not. There are basic principles and facts needed for a business to succeed. The following questions ask for specifics which reveal level of understanding and predictable, maybe erroneous, behavior. They deal with the crucial tasks of financial management. Contents below are for a brief session in financial and consumer education which help a marriage succeed:

1. Paying just the minimum on a credit card bill?

2. Taking Loan consolidation?

3. Continuing the same spending patterns you had before marriage?

4. Avoiding discussion of a problem such as the other spending too much?

5. Having his and hers budgets?

6. Keeping records and not doing anything about them? What use is record keeping?

7. Basing decisions on the monthly payment? Spending more than disposable or take home income each month?

8. Deciding on gross income rather than decision-income?

*****

9. Planning too rigidly? (Missing opportunities, reevaluating after a designated time, new information, and new resources).

10. Not budgeting for possible "unexpected" expenditures that you should "expect" each week, month, or season?

11. Trying to keep up with, or down with, or impress your friends?

12. Buying prestige rather than transportation?
*****

13. Receiving financial assistance from relatives without a contract?

14. Using money to fight, to handle hurts, or get even? (illustrate)
*****

15. Saving some money *after* everything else is paid?

16. Giving to others or some worthy cause *after* everything else is paid?

Are You Ready for Love and Economics? Or Where is Development Necessary?

The shepherd can lead discussion on these topics:

1. What evidence do you have that you are mature enough to successfully handle marriage? Immaturity is always wanting everything you want and not thinking of the other person before yourself. Maturity is evidenced by acting as a team member or help-mate and encouraging. Maturity is learning to handle conflicts in a way that honors each other and honors God, attacking the issue not the person. So, maturity is listening and expressing self rather than impressing another with one's power and importance. As St. Francis of Assisi said, "Grant that I may not so much seek to be understood as to understand." Maturity is discerning the other's needs, not calling names, prioritizing and limiting decisions for the session, choosing what is important to be upset about and what is not, and talking in loving and non-anxious tones. Talking about finances conjures up emotions that other areas do not. Maturity moves beyond "angry recriminations and excuses prompted by who spent how much on what."[75] The choices are to fight, flight, or make it better. The choice is to respond rather than react.

2. For what are you the most thankful in your future spouse?

3. If you were to apologize today for something what would it be?

4. What unresolved issue(s), traumatic experiences, or rejection need to be faced and expressed as you continue the journey together?

5. What area of disagreement has already "reared its ugly head" and needs to be faced to continue on the journey? (Possible areas are financial support, household work, affection, respect, commitment, honesty, personal space, sex, shared activities, problem-solving, security, mother-in-law, biorhythms of alertness, and sleepiness.)

6. What needs do you expect to have met in other ways than from the spouse (such as intellectual, social, spiritual) and how?

7. What do you have, do, or spend that needs better control or discipline?

Reality Game for Real

Financial despair and hateful disagreements come from differences in expectations, smashed dreams, selfishness, not reconciling expenses with income, underestimating expenses, and overestimating income. These usually result from inexperience, lack of records, or purposely avoiding

---

75   Brian J. O'Connor. "Honey, Let's Talk Money." *Journal and Courier*. July 4, 2005.

reality. Couples blame each other (or one does all the criticism) for not enough income or for not shopping more carefully, not controlling addictions, or not managing the cash flow. Without goals or priorities, money is spent for whatever and whenever which eventually brings unhappiness and financial failure. Sometimes couples split because one does not know there is a problem or because one/both do not know where to adjust. Therefore, investing time in learning financial management can bring dividends in happiness and monetary return. To manage, values are clarified. Necessities versus luxuries are known. Differences are exposed. Weak mathematics ability is revealed and helped. The need for increasing income or reducing expenses (which may be more controllable) is suggested. One person's "needs," may be the other person's "wants." Income can change over time and with events. Reduction in specific expenditures can be temporary. Acquisitions can be sequential over the years. One person's wants may dominate for a designated time such as retraining. Then the other person's needs are considered priority in due time. Selfishness is out of the question although individuals may have to overcome it. The money flow emphasizing one, then the other, at different times can give a total satisfaction over the life span. Both can work and buy "smarter not harder." Gifts brought to the marriage are creativity and ability to be "content in want or in plenty."

A useful exercise is having each person estimate the monthly dollars which they feel are "adequate" or which are "ideal" for various expenditures, saving, and sharing. Then each adds them for the total. Dividing by 2000 hours gives an estimate for the hourly wage(s) needed, after taxes and fees required. If a person or couple are not paid that much, they have to decide where to cut expenses, how (where) to increase income to cover perceived mandatory expenses, or change expectations. Otherwise the continual "living beyond their means" gets them into credit trouble. Sometimes, couples have become divorced because one is unhappy with not meeting expectations or lifestyle desired.

If too rigid, the budget will not work nor followed through. For any budget to work, money for personal care and freedom to spend must be included for each person.

Estimates are usually inaccurate until experience with living in a new situation or community has been acquired. Keeping records of spending, saving, and sharing as a couple shows *actual* versus *estimated* for facing reality and where to exercise more control and adjustment. Records can reveal *creeping indebtedness* before disaster sets in.

This reality exercise in completing the list below can educate and increase communication about money matters and help to make decisions. The exercise gives insight into the other person's expectations, past financial experience, and information for marriage success.

Expenses	His estimate		Her estimate		Revised Together
	Ideal	*Adequate*	*Ideal*	*Adequate*	
Housing Rent/payment					
H. Taxes & insurance					
H. Utilities					
Furniture, equipment, repair					
Telephones, computer					
Television					
Videos, CDs, magazines					
Food & groceries – in home					
Food & drinks – out					
Vehicle payment, bus					
V. insurance, taxes					
V. gas, oil, repair					
Clothing					
Personal care, hair					
Personal allowances					
Personal health, workout					
Medical visits, checkup					
Glasses, contacts					
Medicine					
Health Insurance					
Child or elder care					
Child support					
Job costs – work related					
Life Insurance					
Vacation (prorated)					
Gifts and contributions					
(Prorate annual gifts for month)					
Entertainment					
Debts, loans – short					
Debts, loans – long term					
Savings, investments					
Other annual items					
(Prorate for month)					
Monthly Total					
X's 12 = Annual					

Divide by 2000 hours
  For hourly wage after taxes needed

Deficit or surplus with
Current Income after taxes

Choosing a New Household Management System

Various household management systems differ in organizational structures, money distribution, power, interactions, divisions of tasks, and sense of control. Eight types are described below from which couples can choose.[76] The first two are characterized by families who manage by tradition. The third through sixth are characterized by participatory processes. Seven and eight are by crisis management. Examination and development of a system for the unique couple is important because each person may have come from a different system and assumes roles and distribution of money which are foreign to the other person. The structure may not be acceptable for the new marriage. Conflict about roles as well as distribution of money have been causes of divorce. Past experiences and preconceptions need to be resolved.

1. *Autocratic, Traditional, Authoritarian, Patriarchal or Matriarchal System.*
   In this system the authority figure makes the decisions and enforces the roles that are clear and prescribed. The most efficient does the most important jobs. Tradition, responsibility, productivity, accumulation, and power are emphasized. Money is distributed according to whom has earned it.

2. *Social, Rational Bureaucracy, Cooperative*
   In this system the individual is important depending on contributions to overall objectives. Husband's career is most important. Wife serves family needs and advances husband's career. Specialization contributes to efficiency in work roles. Money is distributed to advance husband's career and family objectives.

3. *Communal or Familistic, Sharing*
   Welfare of the family is emphasized with use of "we" not "I." Everything is shared under collective leadership. The most efficient and productive does the most work to meet the needs of the least able. Money is distributed to benefit the entire group's well-being.

4. *Democratic, Rational Autonomous*
   Objectives and decisions are conditional rather than absolute, decided by problem solving, and discussed to meet individual needs in meetings such as a "Family Council."
   The individual is assumed to be best judge as to how to manage and perform tasks. Money is distributed based on agreement and consensus to advance growth and development of each. Cooperation is assumed.

5. *Egalitarian, calculating*
   All members are treated equally with equal status. Decisions and division of tasks represent minimum role differentiation. Work is divided for equal responsibilities and rotated even if one person is more capable and efficient, initially. Money is distributed in equal proportions with his and hers budget.

6. *Exchange, Laissez-faire, Market exchange (quid pro quo), Specialists, Competitive*

---

76   Flora L.Williams and M.L.G. Paixao. 1993. Effects of the Resource Management System in the United States and Brazil. In R. von Schweitzer (Editor). *Cross Cultural Approaches to Home Management. The Private Household.* Vol. 18. Campus Verlag, Frankfurt am Main, Germany. United States: Westview Press, Pp.233-255.

A member's own interests are sought and fulfilled by exchange, "trading off," and bargaining in roles, tasks, jobs, and money use. The assumption is that "As each member seeks his own interest, the benefit will be for the good of the whole" family (Adam Smith, 1976). The individual is assumed to be the best judge of his own goals, time, ways to manage, what to do, etc. as long as others are appeased and the family survives. Division of tasks is based on specialization and, therefore, members are highly interdependent on each other. Money is distributed to persuade activity or bribing. Persons are paid for their tasks.

7. *Permissive, Change-Prone, Free-Form, Expressive*

Objectives although few are in free form and change as new interests appear. In some families, objectives change when consequences are considered rather than following conventional standards. There are no definite roles, division of labor, or decision making patterns. These change at different times with changing composition of family responsibilities, work outside the home, roles, and psychological needs. Members do what they enjoy and feel like doing when they want to rather than following prescriptions and demands. Jobs are done by those who care about them. Individuals are accepted for what they are as persons rather than on position or income earned. Money is distributed according to whims and wishes, desires and crises, until it is gone or until next pay period, by whomever is interested and finds excitement in spending.

8. *Fatalistic, Non system or non-structure, Nonproductive, Non-cooperative*

Confusion and ambiguity are the norm. Group objectives and roles are ignored. Responsibility is minimally undertaken. Management is by crisis rather than objectives. Morale and productivity are low. There is parental disassociation from directing children's behavior since a parent (s) may be mentally ill or alcoholic, or absent. Money is distributed according to whom happens to think about it, irregular in paying bills, given in mixed messages to requests (sometimes yes and sometimes no for the same thing), and used for addictions or overcoming depression/rejection of others.

Communication Comedy of a Real Couple

Both eager and excited, Jeff and Amy come to the required premarital counseling. (Or at least they pretend to be eager.) They both look intelligent, act "put together," talk intelligently, and appear up-to-date. However, they are not really hearing because they are:
- thinking about other things,
- in a transition in their life and everything seems fuzzy,
- have a mindset – are hearing something else,
- hear the first statement or first part of the statement, assume the rest of it, and do not listen to the second statement or second part,
- have a lapse in memory, or
- get side tracked easily since they cannot focus or concentrate very long for one reason or another.

Shepherds as well as parents, doctors, and spouses have to continually ask, "What did you hear me say?" not "What did I say?" in loving, firm, and sympathetic tones.

Jeff and Amy at a Later Time

Amy, in her nightgown, called to Jeff, "I need to talk with you" out of the upstairs window because time was so urgent. It was obviously urgent for her to call from the window half dressed. However, he did not answer. He went upstairs to the computer and the time was short. The Credit Union was going to close within a half hour. She said, "Go get money for our trip out of the Credit Union." He said, "We do not have any money" although they had previously discussed it. She had told him that they did have money set aside for a trip in the money market account and money from interest on insurance. He had not heard her since he had a certain mindset. He did not think they could afford a vacation trip although she needed to get away from job stress. He did not think of alternatives. He went on to say, "We can not just take money from our money market. (This showed his lack of information.) She had to say, "We can take the interest out." "How much?" This was a snap decision without discussion or estimating expenses. Of course people usually underestimate expenses especially if they are trying to persuade someone to buy or spend. Here is an example of managing by crisis, rather than by objectives. He said, "We have never set aside money for vacations." His poor memory was a result of job preoccupation or poor listening habits. She said, "Yes, for years I had money withdrawn by the Credit Union into a separate account for the children's church camp and family trips before our saving funds went into our checking account." Poor communication and management were again covered up by sufficient money and one person having some money sense.

Choosing between a Christian and a Conventional Marriage[77]

Language of Covenant
"I take you to have and to hold, from
this day forward, for better or for worse,
for richer, for poorer, in sickness and in health,
to love and to cherish; and I promise
to be faithful to you, forsaking all others,
until death do us part."

Language of Contract
"You will deliver to me the
agreed upon supply of goods
and services according to my
terms and to my satisfaction.
Failure to do so will result in
breech of contract and render
this contractual arrangement no
longer binding."

"We have a picture of the perfect partner, but we marry an imperfect person. Then we have two options…" (Grant Howard).

Tear up the **picture** and
   accept the **person**
Look to God for satisfaction, take time to find
Spouse brings one closer to God

Tear up the **person** and
   accept the **picture**
Look to someone else, have affair
Verbal attack or retreat; hurt back

---

77   Excerpts and adaptations from selected sermons by David Henderson, Stephen Kirk, Ron Hawkins. Covenant Presbyterian Church. Lafayette, Indiana. 2002-2005.

Grow in demonstrating my love	Focus on what other needs to do
All needs met in Jesus Christ	Look to spouse for all needs met
Expect spouse to fail to meet all needs	Keep tract of disappointments
I will fail spouse in meeting all her (his) needs	Assume spouse exists for me
Free to forgive and love spouse regardless	Harbor hurts, disappointments
No-matter-what promise to never walk away	Break promises and vows
God has given spouse to love and serve	Partner fails to meet needs through
God meets partner's needs, in part through me.	selfishness, insensitivity, discouragement, unkindness, distraction, busyness, unfaithfulness.

"A good marriage is a union of two good forgivers," said Ruth Bell Graham. "Go all out in your love for (each other), exactly as Christ died for the church – a love marked by giving, not getting," said Eugene Peterson. Paul in Philippians 2:3-5 said, "In humility consider others better than yourselves. Each of you should look not only to your own interests, but also to the interests of others." Your attitude, in other words, should be the same as that of Christ Jesus. Henderson[78] said, "In the Christian view of marriage, forgiveness is absolutely indispensable and nonnegotiable. It is perhaps the single most important gift one can give his/her partner, the gift (the grace) of withholding from each the punishment and anger that they rightly deserve, and giving love, acceptance and a fresh beginning instead." But how? "It hurts when we are slighted or overlooked. It is painful when we are missed. It builds resentment when we are insulted. The only way to extend full and repeated forgiveness is if we have experienced that sort of lavish, outlandish, undeserved forgiveness ourselves. And that is exactly what we have in Christ. Through his death on the cross, he purchased our forgiveness and gives us the gift of a second chance - every time."

Ten Tips to Help You Talk to Your Honey about Money
By Syble Solomon[79]

"The Big Day is coming up! As you prepare for your wedding, take the time to do something that will help you prepare for your future life together. It may not sound romantic, but sit down and have a good talk about money. Couples who communicate effectively about money can usually communicate about anything!

Did you know that money issues in a marriage are inevitable? Money has consistently been named the number one cause of conflict in marriages whether couples said they were happy and satisfied with their marriages or not and whether they stayed married or got divorced. Since money problems are predictable, be proactive and get talking before you walk down the aisle. The more you understand each other's habits and attitudes about money, the fewer misunderstandings you will have in the future. In fact, your ability to talk about money and manage it is the best predictor of a solid marriage!

Here are ten tips to help you get started:

---

78   David Henderson. Covenant Presbyterian Church, Lafayette, Indiana. October 13. 2002.
79   Syble Solomon. Life Wise. 421 West Blackbeard Rd., Wilmington, NC. 2008. www.moneyhabitudes.com

1. **Just do it!** If you are uncomfortable or suspect your honey may not want to talk about money, acknowledge that it feels awkward and you are both in new territory. Sharing information about money and understanding each other's priorities builds trust to lay a strong foundation for your future so it is worth the effort to have the conversation. To get started, find a time and place to talk where you can relax.

2. **Reminisce.** An easy way to begin is to just share your memories. Remember the first time you bought something with your own money? What did you buy? How did you get the money? Here are some other ideas of stories you can share:

   - Talk about your first job and the ones that followed. What did you do with your money?
   - How did you get money as a child and a teen? What did you do with it?
   - When you were a kid, did you think you were richer or poorer than your friends or others in your family? Who did you know that you thought was really wealthy or really poor?
   - Were you expected to contribute to or pay for class trips or projects when you were in school? What about going to a prom or on a date to the movies?

3. **Think family.** Growing up, how was money talked about in your home? Do you know who paid the bills and how big financial decisions were made about buying a car or house, investing or saving for the future? If there were arguments about money, what usually caused them and how were you involved? How would you know when your parents disagreed about money? Were you encouraged to live simply and be content or was there a sense of competition to keep up or outdo others?

4. **Look around.** Did your immediate family seem to have a different lifestyle or values than your extended family or other people in your neighborhood or community? Did they encourage you to fit in or to get more education, have more or be different? Are your lifestyle and values now in sync with your parents, siblings and old friends or are they different?

5. **Enjoy life.** How have you spent your money for fun in the past? Has anything changed? What have you done for fun and pure enjoyment that doesn't cost a penny? In the future, how do you see spending money on entertainment, fun and recreational activities?

6. **Face your fear.** What is your biggest fear about money? If you can, share the story of what caused that fear.

7. **Share the past.** How would you describe your financial past? Do you have a history of saving, investing or going into debt? Have you ever declared bankruptcy or had major credit card debt? Did you save up for big ticket items or pay them off over time? Are you used to buying the best and newest clothes, electronics, cars, etc and how have you paid for them? Have you significantly changed anything about the way you manage money now than you did in the past? What caused the change? How much debt do you currently have?

8. **Clarify expectations.** What would it take for each of you to feel financially secure? How much money does it take for each of you to feel independent and meet your needs? How do you both feel about giving to your church, charities or to help friends and family members? How much debt are each of you comfortable having month-to-month? How do you each use credit cards? What lifestyle do both of you project having in five years? Would it help to discuss a

pre-nuptial agreement if either or both of you have assets, financial concerns, children from previous marriages or other financial responsibilities?

9. **Talk money.** How much do each of you earn and how much is deducted for retirement and taxes? Are there investments, bank accounts, bonds and other financial assets? What do each of you own and owe? What financial obligations do you each have?

10. **Have a system.** How will you manage money as a couple? Who will take responsibility to pay bills, stay knowledgeable about investments and monitor the general flow of money? Agree that both of you will stay informed. Will you merge all your money and have everything in joint accounts, keep everything separate or a combination of both? Will expenses be split 50/50 or by the percent of what each person earns? What if one person is not working—will that person have his or her own discretionary money? How much will you spend without talking to each other first?

Did you notice that only No. 9 actually talks about numbers and personal finances? Communicating about money really means communicating about life experiences and values. It builds trust, openness and honesty—a great foundation for a long, successful marriage!" (Syble Solomon).

Managing Disagreement and Conflict Over Money Within Couples

Sharon M. Danes, Ph.D., Professor, Family Economist,
Family Social Science Department, College of Education and
Human Development, University of Minnesota

Pastor or shepherd counseling in finances works with the whole person, both couple and family history – resolved and unresolved. Financial counseling with couples also has a social dimension about disagreements or conflicts. Counseling with couples has a third dimension - an emotional dimension - because each individual within the couple has grown up with attitudes, feelings, experiences, and beliefs about money that have been with them all their life. Many were learned very early in life when they were a child. To further complicate matters, couples often choose a partner who is a complement to them on many characteristics, including how they manage and use money.

The foci here are on strengthening communication during difficult times and presenting a problem-solving model to assist couples in managing disagreement and conflict over money. Before a pastor-counselor can be effective in assisting a couple with money problems, a discussion about strengthening communication in difficult times is useful. Often, by the time a couple seeks assistance, they have had heated arguments about money, maybe unstated. Strengthening communication in difficult times has these key points:
*   The two-way part of difficult communications
*   Showing respect in communication
*   Making criticism productive
*   Silent communication
*   Positioning oneself in one's circle of influence

Problem solving with the couple about money problems has a number of steps. First and foremost, there needs to be agreement that there is a problem by both members of the couple. It is not possible to problem solve if only one member of the couple thinks there is a problem with money. Once there is agreement that there is a problem and both parties are willing to work on that problem, then it is important to agree on what that problem is.

Both parties may have indicated that they are willing to work on the money problem. You cannot assume that they both are perceiving the same problem. So first identify, separately, what is the problem. Then, agree as a couple on the importance of that problem. After that, it is possible to identify the feelings tangled up within the problem and to uncover the factors contributing to the problem. It is only at that point that the alternatives for solving the problem and agreeing upon the alternative(s) to try can be attempted. If the prior steps are not accomplished, the problem solving process will most likely not be effective.

The Two-Way Part of Difficult Communication

When there are concerns about money, we are often intent on figuring out how to get our message across. That is a one-way approach to communication. Effective communication incorporates active listening along with message giving. It is just as important to hear what is said between the lines or behind spoken words by the person with whom you are communicating as it is to state your message in ways that can be heard by that person.

Active listening focuses on both the message content and the underlying feelings. It involves joint problem solving. It means listening to the content of what is said, acknowledging the emotion behind the words, and providing feedback on both. It fosters open communication and good relationships.

Showing Respect in Communication

Respect is important in communicating with others. Saying something respectfully will be more productive. What exactly does that mean? It means instead of constant criticizing, point out what needs to be done. Instead of using "put-downs," state a message in a more positive way. For example:

Instead Of Saying...	Try Saying...
That's stupid	I do not see it that way
That's not true	Where did you get your information?
You forgot to say--	I'd like to add—
What a dumb idea	How would that idea work?
You're wrong	Here's another way to look at it

Put-downs and constant negative criticism can interfere with others' ability to hear a message. To motivate people, try rewording your message. Notice that the statements on the right acknowledge that you are open to further involvement in the problem solving process.

Make Criticism Productive

Most people consider criticism entirely negative. Criticism should include both positive reinforcement and a statement of what needs to be improved. However, most people have only experienced criticism in ways that are blaming and shaming. We are usually not taught to give criticism in positive ways.

You may have heard that it's important to use "I" statements in communicating (for example, saying "I feel angry" instead of "You make me mad."). But an "I" statement can be just as blaming and shaming as a "you" statement. A productive "I" statement should:

- Use "I" rather than "you"
- Include a feeling word
- Include a cause of feeling

Also consider indicating specifically what is needed to alleviate the problem at hand, and/or end with a question that targets the discussion toward addressing the concern causing the problem. Here is an example of "you" and "I" statements addressing a money issue where one member of a couple does the primary record keeping:

> **"YOU" STATEMENT:** *You bought that $200 tool and you never told me.*
>
> **"I" STATEMENT (WITH THE SUGGESTED COMPONENTS):**
> *I would feel more secure about managing the finances if I weren't surprised about a major purchase. Can we agree on a maximum amount of money, like $50, that we can spend without discussing it first?*

Here is another example of a "you" and "I" statement. "You always spend too much money!" is a "you" statement that is often heard by financial counselors when counseling with couples. This "I" statement is much more conducive to a continued line of open communication: "I feel afraid when I cannot pay all the bills. Let's figure out ways we can reduce our expenses."

Keep in mind that "I" statements, while often helpful, are not appropriate in every circumstance. They are just one approach to problem solving. Practicing communicating with respect, if done with sincerity and persistence, will increase the willingness to problem solve. Here are examples of other "I" statements that you might suggest in your financial counseling sessions with couples:

Instead of saying:	Try saying:
You fail to see what I mean.	I do not think I explained that well.
You misinterpret me.	I think you see it differently than I meant.
You didn't do this right.	This wasn't finished the way I asked.

Silent Communication

Remember that all communication is not through words. In fact, 7 percent of any communication is the words that are said, 93 percent in the body language. So actions do speak louder than words. Be careful that you are not saying one thing and reflecting a different message through your actions or body language. If you tell someone you are not angry but your face, neck, or ears are "red" with anger, which message do you think the person will receive?

Position Yourself in Your Circle of Influence

A critical aspect of communication is that you be in your "circle of influence" rather than your "circle of concern." The circle of concern consists of those things over which you have little control, but which concern you. The circle of influence contains those things over which you have control. If you are frustrated and angry, you most likely are in your circle of concern. Ask yourself, "What is it I do have control over?" The answer to that question will help you get back into your circle of influence where you can problem solve. You cannot change others, but you can change the way you communicate. Remember the physics principle that "for every action, there is a reaction"? If you practice some of the principles of communication in this piece, over time you will begin to experience an impact on those around you.

Managing Disagreement & Conflict Over Money

Worksheet 1

Money management is much more than financial record keeping. As adults, you have many attitudes, values, and feelings about money that you have brought with you from your families in childhood. Many of those are so deeply a part of oneself *that one does not even realize how they impact money* decisions or actions and reactions to what family members do in terms of money.

For many reasons, including those just identified above, disagreement or conflict about money sometimes arises. Disagreement and conflict are not the same. Disagreement is a difference of opinion while conflict is more threatening. Disagreement is usually restrained and fairly calm; conflict is a clash of feelings and interests that can be unreasonable and angry.

Hopefully, one can address money disagreements before they become conflicts. Before one can begin to manage conflict over money, the parties involved must be willing to work on the problem. When a person is the only one willing to recognize and try to solve the problem, then he or she can only address the situation in ways that person can control. Adjustments are in the view of the situation, involvement in the situation, or reaction to the situation.

Once there is agreement to work on the problem, the conflict management process can begin. Below are some suggested steps one or both take to begin to address a disagreement or conflict about money. To begin to manage value or role conflicts about money, the people involved must agree upon the problem, identify the feelings tangled up within the problem, and then identify and agree upon alternatives to tackling the problem. Each person involved in the disagreement needs to complete Steps 1 through 3, individually, and then discussion needs to occur among the parties involved.

Step 1. State the problem to be solved in one sentence. Take time to think about this because what people argue about often is not the real root of the problem.

_____

_____

_____

Step 2. Have you written the problem in an "I" statement rather than a "you" statement? This means that persons have stated the problem in terms of they feel, not only in terms of what the other person has done. An example is writing a statement of need such as, "I feel anxious and frustrated when bills come that are bigger than we can pay in a month," rather than, "You always spend too much money."

  a. If you cannot seem to write it in an "I" statement, go to Step 3 and try to identify your feelings. Then rewrite the statement in an "I" form.

  b. If you have written the problem statement in an "I" form, go on to Step 3 to begin to identify the feelings involved.

Step 3. Identify the feelings you have relative to this problem. Several feelings have been identified for you but there is room to write other feelings you may be experiencing. Circle the number that best describes the intensity you feel on a scale from 0 to 5.

a. Not at all angry	0	1	2	3	4	5	Very angry
b. Not at all frustrated	0	1	2	3	4	5	Very frustrated
c. Not at all anxious	0	1	2	3	4	5	Very anxious
d. Not at all confused	0	1	2	3	4	5	Very confused
e. Not at all resentful	0	1	2	3	4	5	Very resentful
f. Not at all _____	0	1	2	3	4	5	Very _____

Step 4. Now get together with the other person(s) involved with the disagreement or conflict. Do you all view the problem in a similar manner? If you do not, all parties involved should complete **Worksheet 2: Conflict Management Involves Uncovering Factors Contributing to the Problem**. That worksheet may further assist you to identify the issues involved in the problem.

Worksheet 2 starts with having all parties involved indicating the points of agreement. We often get so caught up in the problem that we do not realize the points on which we do agree. The questions under "Points of Agreement" are to get you thinking about issues on which you might agree.

Under "Points of Disagreement", use the questions identified under "Person 1 Viewpoint" to help you target the specific parts of the conflict where there is disagreement. The questions are there to help break apart the tangled emotions that may have surfaced over the money conflict.

After answering the questions in Worksheet 2, discuss the points of agreement and disagreement from each party's view. Remember that it is just as important to hear the other person's view as to get your own view across to the other person. The objective of the exercise in Worksheet 2 is to agree upon what the problem is so that alternatives can be pursued.

Step 5. Once there is agreement about the problem to be solved, the feelings and their intensity have been recognized, and the needs of each person have been identified regarding the conflict, alternatives to begin to solve the problem can be identified and investigated.

List below the possible alternatives that might begin to address the problem at hand.

Alternative 1:_____

_____

_____

Alternative 2:_____

_____

_____

Once an alternative has been decided, set a time to review progress toward a solution. Doing so gives a chance to try another alternative if the first solution doesn't work, or, it gives a chance to celebrate if the first solution worked.

This process is about <u>managing</u> conflict rather than <u>resolving</u> conflict. Resolving conflict implies that there is an end to both the problem itself, and the feelings surrounding it. Managing conflict involves redefining or restructuring the part of the situation that is causing the tension. There may be some remaining tension and disagreement as new approaches are tried for managing the conflict. Managing conflict is a more realistic way when thinking about challenges over money that develop in families. When people spend as much time together as they do in families, disagreements and conflict are part of the normal course. That's especially true when the money available is suddenly reduced. So it is important to have realistic expectations about conflict management.

Worksheet 2. Conflict Management Involves Uncovering Factors Contributing to the Problem

Statement of the problem:

Points of Agreement:	What are the hopes and positive ideas?	What is most important?	Who should do what?	What are some possible options?	Who is assisting in positive ways?

Points of Disagreement:	What is it you need to reduce emotional intensity related to the problem?	What do you want the other person to understand about your position?	What parts of the problem are your responsibility?	What parts of the problem do you have control over?	Who is interfering with whom?
Person 1 Viewpoint					
Person 2 Viewpoint					

Developed by Sharon M. Danes, Professor, Family Social Science Department, College of Human Ecology, University of Minnesota.

The Nature of Money Disagreements and Conflicts

There are a number of reasons conflicts arise over money. They may arise because of lack of communication or miscommunication. There may be a value conflict that involves opposing attitudes or beliefs. For instance, one spouse may have been raised in a family where siblings always help each other during difficult times. The other spouse may believe that when siblings are adults, they take care of their own problems. Money conflict may arise due to discrepancies in expectation about role performance. One person may believe that men should be the ones to handle money while the other might believe that each should manage what they earn. Often in money conflicts, there is no right or wrong answer. The couple has to decide what works best for their situation. There is one point, however, that is very critical. Unresolved disagreements over money fester over the years and eventually affect the relationship.

This section has presented information and a structure for a financial counselor to use in counseling with couples about money conflicts. Financial counseling is not just about finances. Counseling has a social dimension in that there are interactions between the two individuals within the couple. The dynamics within this dimension are best described by the physics' principle that states, "For every action, there is a reaction." It is best to have both members of the couple when doing financial counseling because of this social dimension. However, if that is not possible, then keep in mind that any suggestions you make to the one person will have consequences when those suggestions are incorporated into the couple system. A third part of the financial counseling with couples is the emotional dimension. Money sometimes elicits strong emotions, some of which people aren't even aware of at a conscious level. Those will need to be acknowledged in the problem solving process, as well, for it to be truly effective. (Sharon Danes).

Prayer

Great God of the universe! Creator God of everything beautiful! We praise you and thank you for the creation of this marriage union. We praise and thank you for being present in our lives and in the discussions today. Thank you for the gift of each other here and for the gifts each gives to this new venture on the journey of life. We pray we will be receptive to your guidance in all our ventures including financial decisions, household management, and social interactions. Thank you for your everlasting love and we pray it will be reflected in the love for each other, our kin, our friends, and our neighbors. Forgive us when we fail in our promises and intentions. Keep us forgiving others as you have forgiven us and help us show grace to each other. Now as we receive your blessings, help us to receive your wisdom and power. We pray that we will be open to your comfort in times of misery, your joy in the delights of life, and your directions in everyday decisions. Give us the strength to persevere, to be patient, and to practice sound resource management, in the name of Jesus. Amen.

◇◇◇ ⧗ ⧖ ◇◇◇

Chapter 8. Leading to Greener Pastures and Still Waters through Financial Management

Learning to purchase well and buy with basic principles will *maximize* resources. Knowing some options for reducing major expenses and taxes *equip* clergy, compassion ministers, educators, financial counselors, helping professionals, money coaches and others appointed to "release the captives." Financial management and consumer education can lead to greener pastures and still waters. The shepherd can assist the confused, bewildered, and scared in providing information about buying, managing income, scams and frauds, and assessing standard of living for changing lifestyle. The shepherd can help to reduce hazards and risks along the way. Correcting steps on the path or using wise initial steps in buying complements spiritual development. Information can reduce frustration thereby releasing energy to "seek first the kingdom." Embarrassing mistakes, spending more than necessary and a lavish lifestyle can diminish one's witness for abundant life in Christ. However, grace and forgiveness for errors or mistakes are possible. Learning replaces stress. Brokenness in finances can be healed.

Many people want the shepherd to wave a magic wand when they are in financial trouble because of "overspending" due to addictions, habits or poor judgment. They are hoping everything will be alright by trusting in the Lord. This is a presumption masked as "faith." The reality is that the Lord wants them to use their mind, heart, soul, and strength to make wise buying decisions or to make drastic, upside-down changes not only in spending patterns but also in housing, transportation, jobs, and doing work at home.

The Shepherd is justified in providing consumer education so that more money can be shared, contributions to church programs increased, and support of missionary efforts revitalized. These contributions are increased through better buymanship and changes in lifestyle. Good buymanship is a part of faithful stewardship. Hazards and mistakes from ignorance or habit move people away from green pastures and still water. The road to economic security, the Promised Land, is bumpy and uncertain even when following good principles of financial management and buymanship.

Opportunities to Educate

Education can be conducted through counseling, coaching, classes, and sermons on overcoming obstacles to seeking first the kingdom. At the end of a worship service when shaking hands or in casual conversation, as well as a counseling/teaching session, people will bring up what is on their mind if given a chance to talk. In passing, a couple may say they are looking at houses. That is a chance – three seconds or three sentences to give them three ideas that will help them be good stewards of resources, wise and shrewd, in their decisions.

Pastor Lee met Eric at the Farmer's Market during periodic visits. On one visit, Lee gave him a book. This time Eric said he was looking for a job now that the farmer's market season was over.

Pastor Lee mentioned the temporary employment agencies with their addresses like Manpower, the State Employment Office, and Workone.

Another opportunity for the shepherd is during visits when one of the family members is ill or in the hospital. The patient may have grave concerns about ability to pay, wills, estate planning, or being taken advantage of. Advice in the form of a few facts or actions to take can be comforting. Ideas presented below, prompted by the Spirit, can aid decisions and dilemmas.

Financial counselors can use the holistic approach and apply implications of spiritual needs and commitments to Christ, finding abundant life, addressing addictions, and replacing destructive or expensive habits with healthy, frugal ones. What would an individual think of his or her medical doctor who was addressing a hurt elbow and did not notice the cancer growing on the cheek? The argument for the comprehensive approach is supported. Even though the individual brings up one concern, the financial coach can care about all aspects as one concern affects other financial decisions. Other plans or decisions could sabotage the current concern if not addressed. Other fears or mistakes could prevent working on the current concern.

Since risks of making the wrong decisions are so great, the shepherd needs to help people understand how to prevent or reduce risks. Informational pamphlets can be distributed to people they are counseling. The shepherd is not expected to know all but can at least know where to find information and have some available. Pamphlets and websites are available from educational organizations, Publication Services of the Federal Reserve System, State Cooperative Extension Service offices available in every county, Consumer Resource Center of the federal government, and other institutes. They have a wide variety of information available, free of charge, for which clergy, helping professions, financial counselors, money coaches and others responsible for change can distribute. For example, information about leasing a car is available at http://federalresearch.gov/pubs/leasing/guide.

Hazards Along the Way

Trust and hope in the Lord are mandatory for the journey because of events and circumstances beyond one's control such as amount and type of income. Also, the temptation to be out of control in finances rather than under God's control is everywhere. Particular hazards on the way are unemployment and underemployment, reduced purchasing power, divorce, creeping indebtedness, creeping envious eyes leading to luxurious spending, daily needs which overwhelm, not being prepared for emergencies, and not knowing how to adjust spending and income rather than borrowing.

Hazards to greener pastures and still waters are business cycles, increased expectations while real net income is decreasing, risk of accidents and illness, and mistakes in major purchases. Hazards exist in every sphere from not doing the mathematics, not calculating total costs, and not being savvy in choosing goods and services. Another hazard is falling prey to deceptive advertising, scams, and frauds.

The purpose of education and planning is to reduce the risks of errors as there is no guarantee that faithful followers will have a life of ease. In fact, believers are called to count the cost and give their all. The purpose of education and planning is to reduce the potential pitfalls that even faithful followers will experience.

Hazard on the Road - the Wolves

In Matthew 7:6 Jesus advised, "...do not throw your pearls to pigs. If you do, they may trample them under their feet, and then turn and tear you to pieces." In all areas of life, people need God's wisdom and discernment. The guidance of the shepherd is to help people realize that offers and people in sales, professions, and churches are not always as they appear or are presented. The shepherd needs to help people get out of traps and out of control by manipulative people.

Preventative Action

The shepherd can assist people to recognize the wolves in sheep's clothing. Consumers can be urged to "investigate before investing" in any purchase or service by calling the state's Attorney General, Office of Consumer Affairs, Consumer Protection Agency, Insurance Commission, state Banking Commission, Postal Inspection Service of the U.S. Post Office, or the Better Business Bureau. The credentials of the individuals, their state licensing, reputation, and education should be checked. Checking with previous customers can be helpful.

Looking at a contract can raise questions. The contract can be changed if both parties initial each change. To prevent accusations of practicing law, the counselor must not fill out the forms. The counselor helps write letters to creditors, landlords, doctors, children, etc. The counselor helps the consumer discern where the "evil one" is breaking the law. The counselor can accompany an individual to court or another official interaction to give moral support. The counselor can refer to the *Consumer Action Handbook* (www.ConsumerAction.gov) which lists contacts for problem resolution and information and manuals such as *You and the Law* or information sheets available from local legal services or legal aid. It is very useful to have consumer affairs and legal professionals in the church or community who can ask questions free of charge on behalf of the consumer.

The balance of the account must be checked to see if double charging or other errors have been made. Also important is the time period in question and "statute of limitations" to correct fraud or errors.

Frequent consumer complaints involve cars and light trucks. Some transactions are unscrupulous and although legal are "flim-flam." For major repairs such as body work, more than one estimate whenever possible in writing is helpful. The work to be done without your authorization needs to be clarified. One should not sign a blank repair order. The same principle for home repairs applies. No one would want anyone to do major surgery on his or her body without a second opinion. So major surgery on one's pocketbook should not be done without a second or third estimate. If the first two estimates do not agree, one can keep getting estimates until he or she knows exactly what needs to be done and how much it should cost.

Great harm occurs when a crook or friend steals an identity, using one's Social Security number or a friend uses one's Social Security number or other identification cards. The Social Security number should not be given unless required for income tax records, medical records, credit bureau reports, college records, loan applications, and vehicle registrations. A warning is to not give S.S. number for personal checks, orders over the phone, credit card offers, club memberships, identification for store purchases and refunds, address labels, and general identification purposes. (Camera phones can capture and steal identities.)

Who are the scam artists, identity thieves, friendly persuaders, and those who deceive? They include unauthorized insurers selling phony health insurance. One can contact the state insurance department and sponsor about unregulated plans and names that approximate names of real insurers. (See www.dol.gov/ebsa and www.insurancefraud.org.) Victims number over 150,000 with over one billion dollars of unpaid medical bills. Americans lose an estimated $10 billion to investment fraud annually. Health frauds and quacks try to pass themselves off as legitimate professionals.

Credit fraud thieves pick receipts or carbons out of the trash and clerks make extra imprints of credit cards. Advance fee loaners "guarantee" a loan for a fee in advance but legitimate ones do not guarantee. Checking account cons magnetically encode a bank draft and empty accounts when verifying account number for easy or low-interest credit.

Housing repair scams deceive people into thinking they need repairs, improvements, or replacements, but the job is often not done after payment has been made. Overpriced water treatment systems sold by companies prey on fears and make unfounded claims about their products. Companies will test water for free, and then they will pressure to sell their systems. The "unscrupulous" solicit gullible people by mail and e-mail especially those on limited incomes and the elderly. They are told to send $20 or so for the fee to continue seeking information for sweepstakes, a fee to claim prizes, or a fee for the non-compliant person who fails to claim stated amount.

In Matthew 10:16 Jesus warns, "I am sending you out like sheep among wolves. Therefore be as shrewd as snakes and as innocent as doves." In Matthew 18:7, "Woe to the world because of the things that cause people to sin! Such things must come; but woe to the man through whom they come!" More than one in ten Americans fell victim to fraud as reported by the Federal Trade Commission in 2004.

Fraudulent E-Mail requests are: Fake web sites and e-mails that attempt to trick consumers into divulging valuable personal information such as bank accounts and credit card numbers, Social Security numbers, passwords and personal identification numbers. These are called "phishing" schemes. Thieves purporting to be government agencies or companies and financial institutions with which one does business ask for personal information later used for unauthorized withdrawal from bank accounts, paying for online purchases using credit cards, or even selling personal information to other thieves. The FDIC's name has been used fraudulently.

According to the survey by the Federal Trade Commission in 2004, people between ages of 25 and 44 were the most likely fraud victims with 11 percent compared to 4.7 percent of those 65 and older. Top ten frauds were: Advance-fee loan scams (4.55 million victims), buyers clubs, credit card insurance, credit repair, prize promotions, Internet services, pyramid schemes, information services, government job offers, and business opportunities (.45 million victims).

Other wolves in sheep's clothing are more subtle. Some credit counseling firms use their non-profit status to mislead consumers into paying large fees for questionable services, taking their own fees before paying creditors, and including unnecessary expenses on the debt service such as the mortgage. Time shares and others who do not present all the fees and increasing costs until after the contract is signed are other examples of wolves looking for easy prey. These sales rushed to be made the same day of presentation usually with no business card so they cannot be called later.

Friendly Persuaders

An example of persuaders is those encouraging students to borrow rather than considering other alternatives. They think of their own benefit by encouraging too high a car/truck payment or do not negotiate to reduce the price by adding unnecessary fees. Counselors have reported that the biggest problem causing over-indebtedness was the "new car syndrome."

Perverse persuaders are anyone who persuades people to put their trust and security in false gods. They are deceptive. They promise satisfaction and happiness in a product or service which is not deliverable. Others who pretend to have the individual's best interest when it is to their own benefit include clergy, doctors, dentists, financial planners, peers, and relatives. People should ask whose vested interest it is. Who benefits – the buyer or the seller, the patient or the doctor/dentist, the book seller or the reader?

Children should be taught that specific advertisements, sales people, and billboards are deceptive. Advertising, repetitive exposures, and appeals to half-truths are others. Tell them, "They are trying to get your money from your pocket." There is more than one way to "pick pocket" someone. Advertisements can be analyzed for their appeal to basic needs such as belonging, love, respect, and power. People can learn early not to be deceived by false claims or false promises. They can learn not to fall into traps set for them.

Sales pitches are fast talking speeches, often a series of questions to which one answers yes including would you like to own, and then, hook you in the emotion of the moment. The **sales tactics to be aware of** are: encouraging impulse buying, creating a need, appealing to a basic need and emotions, making it difficult to say "no" to salesmen, children, or parents, smooth and fast talking so one cannot ask questions, insisting on a purchase right now because of cost advantage, asking a series of questions that are automatically answering yes until the final one which asks how one is going to pay – cash, check, charge or to sign here, without reading the long contract. This hooks a consumer into buying it now. Other pitches are giving nebulous answers to questions about costs, offering guarantees of "lifetime" which do not clarify whose life, containing easy credit plans, noting "services across the nation" rather than specifying the areas, not being able to contact the salesperson later, and making one feel dissatisfied with his or her present situation. One of the most important defenses is to ask oneself if it is needed or just a want created by someone else. Remember, if something sounds too good to be true, it usually is. One should be suspicious if he or she has to act now, cannot get an address to ask questions tomorrow, or see a "bait and switch" job. One needs to be savvy in false claims and assumptions such as using a condominium "x" times per year.

Elderly Abuse

Financial exploitation sometimes involves an addictive relative who demands money and threatens/carries out violence if refused. Theft is commonly committed by hired helpers, caregivers, or family members who rationalize their stealing. Some do not receive medicine because the money is hidden by the thief family member or other caregivers. Other abuses the shepherd might prevent or catch are astronomical fees charged for services, unscrupulous fees by attorneys for hearings, and judges committing people to guardianships without first assigning attorneys and hearings.

It is recommended to victims who are suspicious to tell someone one trusts such as the shepherd. The shepherd can help the elderly secure financial documents, protect ATM cards, credit cards, and checkbooks by putting them in a secure place. The shepherds who visit and observe encourage the elderly not to share information with those who do not need it or are untrustworthy. Intervention by law enforcement is often sufficient to frighten and stop criminal behavior. Other suggestions are on the Internet – www.aarp.org. If necessary, the shepherd can call the county Department of Social Services, Area Office on Aging, and Adult Protective Services.

As a pastor, Kathy Reid, Executive Director of the Association of Brethren Caregivers, promises to pray for healing and wholeness for victims of emotional, physical, and financial abuse by their caregivers. "Just naming the issue breaks down walls of denial and allows people to grow spiritually." She affirms that education about problems and community resources has an impact.

Saying "No"

Christians and well-meaning people are victimized as well. They are kind, generous people who cannot "kick a person out the door" and say "No." They cannot say no to their children. The counselor can role-play with a vulnerable person to practice.

Jesus warned about throwing pearls to the swine who would devour us. By friendly persuasion or "dressed in sheep's clothing," the evil ones or the "swine" are trying to get one's money. Homeless children in some countries must steal a certain amount each day or be beaten by their master at night. "Keeping from evil or the evil one" is such a problem that Jesus included it in his model prayer.

Pastor Lois intercepted the purchase of a truck by her father-in-law, an elderly man. He had been sent a card saying he needed a new truck and it was now time to trade in his old truck and he was on his way. The purchase would have been disastrous, given his financial situation, and his truck was perfectly fine for him which he kept till his dying day.

It is generally best not to make donations by phone unless one knows the solicitor. If a telemarketer asks for donations, the savvy consumer investigates to see if the charity is registered with the state charitable solicitation office or the Better Business Bureau. The Evangelical Council for Financial Accountability is another place to check since it does a guaranteed annual independent audit.

Rapid Response if Victimized

One can call immediately after checking credit card receipts and payments against your monthly bills. Call first and if not cleared up, put it in writing. Question in writing any doubtful charges on your bill. Call credit card issuer immediately if it is thought someone has illegally used the card and follow up with a letter. The law provides that one is not responsible for any unauthorized charges from the time reported. If cards are used before you report, the maximum loss is $50 per card.

The shepherd is aware that many are victimized but also understands that most are too embarrassed about being conned and defrauded to discuss it. Nobody wants to admit being a fool, being taken. The shepherd can ask, "What mistakes do you think you made?" Again the shepherd works with the emotional and the technical. The shepherd can help find the deadline date for breaking a contract, the deadline for appealing a court case, the process for stopping credit card theft, and procedures for becoming freed from abuse. These are situations that call for urgent response.

Reducing Risks on the Road - Insurance

Insurance has been one way to reduce risks, but the current and expected premium increases are now a crisis in themselves. Auto insurance is required, but some take the risk of not having it.

Not everyone can afford the cost of health or required auto insurance. So they do without and risk their financial well-being.

An illustration of increases is Betty's insurance. Betty's group health insurance, which is her joining with others whose employers do not provide health insurance, is $500 per month this year but will go to $800 next year. (Campus pastors and missionaries also have a group plan with United Health Care with a slush fund.) Mary is paying $460 per month on a net income of $1300 a month. If anyone in her group has a large claim, payments will increase greatly next year. For many families, insurance premiums are half the monthly net income and increasing.

What are some options and what are people doing about these new phenomena? Some are changing jobs purely based on the insurance out-of-pocket expense or the percentage self pays toward the premium. Some buy only major medical insurance. Others are paying the medical expenses for daughter or granddaughter out of pocket. Some are not getting married so that the grandfather can pay for the daughter's expense of having a baby. Some use the well-baby or women's clinic for the poor. Some use the emergency room as the health care provider with knowing the limits per month for eligible free care. Some get a list of doctors who will take so many charity cases per month. Some ask the church to take up a collection or give out of the compassion fund when there is a medical or health related need. Some will have to give up smoking, eating out, long distance calls, etc. to pay for the increased costs. Some will not buy the medicine prescribed or cholesterol and blood pressure medicine needed and assume the risk. Some will get sick and survive, others will not.

A health insurance option for low income children is CHIP. This is available through Medicaid and expanded in 2009 (not to be confused with Medicare.) For seniors, the SHIP is a national volunteer counseling program for seniors with questions or issues about Medicare. www. medicare.in.gov.

Life insurance as well as health insurance is provided by some employers, professional associations, private companies, and state associations for those not eligible elsewhere. Thus, comparison of premiums and benefits is vital. Then comparisons of benefits with various deductions and exemptions must be made.

Consumer Reports magazine reported how a family could save $800 for the same coverage depending on which auto insurance carrier they used. A customer should check the company's rating. Also, there are discounts for multiple car plans. The deductible is the amount paid out of pocket before the insurance company pays. As the deductible goes up, the premium goes down. As the deductible (part you pay first) increases, the premium decreases. Therefore, calculate costs of premiums against deductibles you are willing to absorb to see on average what would be financially advantageous. Premiums charged depend on credit scores, previous claims paid, and tickets received.

Most people need at least the minimum health insurance as "stop gap," temporary insurance, or major medical. Even with standard health insurance plans, increasingly there are problems with getting full payment. People need to submit more than once and keep trying to get the payment that was initially denied. The poor and elderly often do not do this. They have difficulty arguing their case clearly. Perhaps the shepherd or mentor can assist with these negotiations. New plans and offers, costs and benefits can be compared on a worksheet for current and proposed including exemptions (which are often in the small print).

Term or burial insurance is usually the least expensive, the minimum life insurance to carry if the death of one would be an economic hardship to others. An "economic loss" includes a student with high debt someone else would have to pay only if co-signed, someone paying for household services and childcare upon death of the mother, and protection of flow of income of father or ex-husband. It is against the law to market insurance as a saving since other types of saving give more return. Also realize insurance premiums have administrative fees. The premium increases as features increase but guaranteed renewability feature may be worth it. In regard to insurance for a child, the only advantage is the guaranteed renewability at age 21, a gift to them, or in case the child has a handicap or illness. Permanent life insurance, in contrast to term insurance, can be a resource to tap when in trouble by cashing in the insurance or using the cash build up rather than borrowing more money. For most people, disability insurance is needed more than life. As investments go up, need for life insurance goes down.

Insurance contributes to one's economic security and independence. Events happen that are outside one's control as observed and noted in the "Random Walk" theory. Insurance and self-management can reduce negative effects of these risks. Avoid extras such as credit insurance, extended warranties, replacement, and service contracts.

As investments go up, the need for insurance goes down. If there is no one who would suffer an economic loss upon death, life insurance is not necessary. Some individuals have duplicate insurances and are paying more than necessary. For a house, rather than mortgage insurance, increase term life insurance to cover default through death. Check with lender to cancel mortgage insurance once the 20 percent of home equity has been met.

Choice of Deductible for Car Insurance

The deductible depends on analysis of driving history, willing to be preventive, and have assets available such as saving to pay on claims. Ways one can reduce the premium costs of insurance or reduce the hazards that cause damage are:

- Increasing personal savings and take the highest deduction one can afford when purchasing coverage.
- Practicing defensive driving. Insurance companies investigate if their customers have a reckless-driving or drunk-driving conviction within the past five years.
- Using an anti-theft system in the car.
- Not driving when sleep deprived or on certain medication.
- Not letting radio or friends be a distraction.
- If one must use a cellular phone, getting a speaker adapter. Drivers who are talking on the cell phone have four times as many accidents.
- Maintaining vehicle in good mechanical condition. Keeping tires in good condition. (This lack caused a tour van accident in which the author lost her hand. The driver slammed on the brakes rather than guiding the van safely on the road.)
- Practicing safety and take precautions in your living habits and all that you do within your home or apartment. Engaging in risky sports can contribute to increasing the insurance premium you pay.
- Keeping health problems down by having periodic physical checkups, practicing discipline in dietary control and healthy eating choices, getting daily exercise, avoiding tobacco use, and promptly taking care of all health problems or abnormalities.
- Buying insurance to protect yourself only against losses that would be financially catastrophic.
- Shopping around – do not assume all insurance companies charge the same. Insurance rates vary widely and some insurance can be purchased directly from a company bypassing an agent and commissions.

Divorce Insurance

Divorce insurance prevents financial disaster since divorce wrecks financial well-being as well as marriage. Effort toward protecting and maintaining a marriage is necessary for emotional, spiritual, and economic well-being. The risk of financial disaster from divorce can be reduced by better decisions, attitudes, and behavior. The asset or the perks from marriage can be enhanced by communicating with one's spouse, developing a unique household management system, solving problems rather than fighting or flighting, practicing forgiveness, and protecting family relationships. Working at marriage can be considered as one's primary job. Decisions and management should be conducted realizing that divorce can still happen. Even with the best of efforts and conscientious behavior over the years, unexpected turns of events happen. (See Chapter 6 for Divorce.)

Diversification of Income and Savings or Investments

People have reported that a sense of security comes from having a variety of sources of income more than the amount. God wants people to use their talents in caring for their skills, materials, and investments. Diversification is the key for security. God maintains us when we use the God-given skills to work for money and to have money work for us. With the risks involved, security comes from diversification in market types, companies, short-term, and long-term investments.

Hazard on the Road – Change in Business Cycle

The first financial advisor in recorded history was Joseph in the Old Testament who noticed that there are cycles of good years and lean years. He was the first financial planner as he advised saving during the good years for the lean years. Cycles occur roughly every seven years. Many people in surveys have reported that what kept them from getting ahead was increased prices. Business cycles affect people more than making a good budget. When people are shown the cycles, they understand and are motivated to plan and save accordingly. On the other hand, they may become more generous when they see victims of natural and business disasters who could not have planned for or prevented such disasters.

Increased Expectations and Decreased Value of Dollar

Real income changes are based on reduced salaries and purchasing power of the dollar adjusted for inflation. Perceived and actual economic security of Americans is threatened. Many are bewildered as to why they are "not getting ahead", why they are in extreme debt, and why they are unable to meet their expenses. The financial problems of many families are due to their decreased real net income to which they have not adjusted, while their expectations and standard of living have increased. Analysis in any area confirms the increased expectations as to what is considered "a need." One can easily observe increased expectations as to what makes up "the good life" in telephone/communications, landscaping, vacations, and housing (from no garage to one car garage to two garages to automatic door openers). Children feel deprived if they do not have a cell phone or a trip to Disney Land or World, for examples.

Examining job related expenses, gas prices, and fewer employment opportunities in addition to changes in purchasing power and increased taxes provide an expanded method to assess compensation and income adequacy. Recession conditions during the years have decreased the real income of low-income workers and middle-income professionals. This forces a decreased standard of living, unprecedented for generations.

Real net income was calculated by adjusting for both price increase and tax liabilities. Since 1967 is the base year, later salaries are reported in "constant dollars" or the purchasing power based on that year. Constant dollars or the inflation effect was calculated by dividing current salaries by the Consumer Price Index for a series of years. With 1967 as a base year equaling 100, the beginning teacher salary (West Lafayette, Indiana) in constant dollars or purchasing power was $5,750. In 1982 the beginning salary in constant dollars was $4,650 although in current dollars, it was $13,638. Before calculating additional purchasing power loss to taxes, real income decreased by over $1,000 with inflation alone. Although current salaries of beginning teachers increased to $23,216 in 1992, in constant dollars salaries were only $5,944 and $5,559 in 1996. In 2005 beginning teachers' salaries were $33,000 but adjusted for inflation after increased taxes and Social Security were less than in 1967. Yet, expectations and spending are based on gross incomes not adjusted for inflation.

Two earners are now required to purchase what one could in 1957. In addition, increased income has placed earners in higher tax brackets showing the effect of the income tax "bracket creep" on real income. (The Index for given years can be obtained on the Internet on the Bureau of Labor Statistics.)

Graphs reflecting increased gross income since the 1970s, increased net income by about half as much, and decreased real net income which was lower than the beginning point provides understanding of the dilemma. The Consumer Price Index is used to measure changes in prices for identical goods and services identified in a particular market basket. Sometimes the fair percentage increase for a pastor's salary is determined using the increase in the Consumer Price Index. This may not be what the pastor actually buys. This applies to other professionals.

Many people base their attitude toward income adequacy on their increased gross income rather than on their real net income figures. They plan on what to buy and increase spending based on their salary raises without realizing that the increased income already has been offset by increased prices.

Credibility Insurance

Credibility insurance, or proving one's character on the job, is a protection against loss of job. If one has credibility insurance, if there is a family or health problem, disruption to personal life, or special need accommodations, one can gain special accommodations. You do not buy this, you earn this. One has proven loyal and diligent in the past. One has gone the "extra mile" or "out of the way" to help the boss or company. The reputation is not being "a trouble maker." Protection against loss of job includes having diversified skills, getting extra training, letting the supervisor know what one has done, and willingness to adapt on the job. When finding a new job, identify the skills and responsibilities that transfer. Acquire credibility insurance while:

- During college and working years—live and work responsibly. Carry your part of the load daily and be aware of how you can assist others, teachers and supervisors. Look for ways to do extra!
- At your employment, arrive early and be organized to take on the day's activities. Especially in the beginning, be involved in reaching your company's goals, not just your own.

- The evolving work environment requires staying current and ready with new skills. Be knowledgeable on current issues in one's production or profession.
- Be creative and willing to modify or change methods of working and focus.
- Participate in a "flexible spending account" which is money set aside before it is taxed. They can cover required education for credibility insurance, health costs not covered by the group health insurance such as dental or vision, and the 20 percent co-pay for which one is responsible after insurance pays. Thus the actual cost, because of use of pre-tax money, is lower.

Income Needed along the Road

When Mark Twain was asked how much income is enough, he replied, "Just a little bit more." The natural tendency is to expand wants as income increases. Standard of living by definition is just above our level of income and keeps expanding. More money, however, will not solve a mismanagement problem. Some spend and borrow without thinking much. They just follow the deceptive heart. Others pay more than necessary by not comparing prices or waiting or not using credit. Income from "money working for you" could be increased by changing investments and/or the institution.

Income by definition is a flow of goods and services. That definition expands the possibilities. Money is a medium of exchange. Its value fluctuates with the times. Nevertheless, money represents someone's time and sweat and, therefore, needs to be handled carefully and frugally as a steward of this gift from God. When expanding the concept of income, the shepherd can help find ways to sustain life by suggesting community resources, exchanging goods and services with others, providing goods and services non-commercially at home, and employee benefits sometimes chosen in lieu of salary increases because of tax benefits.

The common complaint is that there is not enough money for repairs. Human nature suggests the counselor begin at a different point than the presenting problem. For example, Emma's refrigerator quits and she demands that the church get a new one for her. The basic problem is food preservation so other alternatives should be explored. An icebox outside in winter may work. A small dorm sized refrigerator may solve the problem. Buying non refrigerated foods is another. Reconstituting dry milk is another. In another situation, Nancy said she needed a new kitchen floor because there was hole in it. Nancy was conscientious and needed the beauty from fine house accessories. A rug covering the hole solved her problem.

Non-Money Income

Non-money income (flow of goods and services) is necessary when money income is reduced or non-existent. **Exchanging goods and services with others may be the answer.** Return from providing services in the home and care of individuals may be unpaid and bring non-money income. This is a flow of goods and services for the well-being of those in the household. The choice may to be to purchase goods and services or to do-it-yourself to save money so that more may be shared. This care involves knowledge, skills, and desires to sustain life and give quality of life to those in one's care. A common problem is unfinished projects caused by procrastination on house maintenance due to budget restrictions, lack of confidence, or other pressing issues.

An attitude of stewardship and careful production are God-given commandments. However, the choice of what to do or what to hire depends on the mission God has called one at that particular time. If we did everything ourselves, businesses would be out of business. A lifestyle change may be necessary for putting God's work first. This includes God's standards not those of magazines or makers of household products. One has to work smarter rather than harder to fulfill faithfulness to God, church, family, and community.

An example of providing non-money income is waiting for someone one-half hour per day because of sharing a car. This is translated into non-money income by figuring what an individual would be paid for the equivalent money saved. If having only one car for the family saved $400 per month, the waiting time would be translated into the equivalent of earning $20 per hour. The money saved could be invested and yield thousands of dollars over a number of years. Examples:

Household Work – Yields Non-Money Income in Services and Goods at less dollar cost –

	Saves
Cooking and lunches	$300
Comparison shopping	100
Hair cut and set	20
Laundry and clothes repair	100
Painting, repair, etc.	50
Juggling time with 1 car	400
Paying bills, taxes	75
Preventing late fees, Bounced checks, etc.	100
Total	$1,095

Finding ways to increase non-money income will probably make a bigger difference than increasing money income for many people. Besides, **it is not taxed.** An increase in non-money income means a change in behavior. An increase in money income can mean one has more money to manage, or dig oneself into a deeper hole in which to fall. Some pay 100s of dollars in interest.

Employee Benefits

Knowing and using employee benefits is a way of increasing total income. Many such benefits are not utilized. Employee assistance at one's workplace often has many valuable resources. It may have tuition assistance and counseling programs as well as information on payroll changes. One example is by taking a tax deferred annuity each month, more take home pay is actually available. (See illustration in savings and investment Chapter 12.) Another is paid for counseling services. Matching investment funds is another benefit. College scholarships may be available. Prepaid legal counsel may be available, but as in other benefits, the employee must enroll by a specified time.

Many employers promise no benefits, no advancements, and no wage increases. Other employers offer some level of employee choices and tradeoffs such as increasing salary or giving a benefit (which has a tax benefit over increasing salary). Others offer these for those fortunate to compare when choosing a job or position: medical insurance, life insurance, dental insurance, maternity/paternity leave, retirement plan, training and/or education, company provided or subsidized child or parent care, flexible work schedule, paid sick leave, paid vacation, paid legal counseling, and paid financial advising.

Money Income Sources

(See Chapters 2, 9 and 14 for complete listing.)

Community Resources as Expanded Income

At the least, shepherds have at their finger tips the lists of community resources, agencies, programs and scholarships such as those for summer camp. Government and non-profit agencies are sources for benefits and assistance for individuals. Accept what is rightfully available and provided through public, private and college assistance programs. People through their payment of taxes have participated in contributing towards these benefits. They are entitled to them and can contribute back to these agencies and assist others in getting resources needed when they are able after a financial hardship. Government or community resources, parks, concerts, schools, roads, recreational facilities, financial aid for college, loan forgiveness programs, and employment assistance expand opportunities.

Tax Credits and Breaks

- Energy efficient purchases and home improvement for energy reductions.
- Child care assistance, Child Care Credit or Dependent Care Credit. A percentage of childcare or disabled care expenses is used to reduce taxes due if filing. A $500 credit is available to couples with an adjusted gross income of $110,000 or less or singles with adjusted gross income of $75,000 or less for each child under age 17.
- Tax Credits for hiring specified employees.

Contact IRS (www.irs.gov), school counselor and financial aid offices, and www.finaid.org for details, clarification.

Tax Credit – Money is refunded annually or by pay date. It is a direct reduction, dollar for dollar, from one's tax liability. Examples are:

Earned Income Credit which is available to those individuals who have earnings from a job and their modified adjusted gross income is less than a pre-specified amount. Check with the state and federal IRS or a current tax guide for information on qualifying for this credit and the qualifying amounts.

Tax Breaks for Higher Education include:

Going to school while you work -- Workers are allowed to exclude up to $5,250 of employer-provided education benefits from their income. This assistance must be for undergraduate courses beginning after June 1, 2000.

Community Service Loan Forgiveness. This provision excludes from income student loan amounts forgiven by non-profit, tax-exempt charitable or educational institutions for borrowers who take community-service jobs that address unmet community needs. This applies to loans forgiven after August 5, 1997.

Tax Credits and Deductions Available for Higher Education;

Student loan interest can be deducted for interest paid in the first 60 months of repayment on student loans. This deduction is available even to those who do not itemize their deductions. The maximum deduction allowed is $2,000 for the year 2000 and increases to $2,500 in 2001 and beyond. The deduction is available for all educational loans to students, parents, guaranteed student loans, and loans from private lenders made after August 1997, when the new student loan interest deduction became law. It applies to the 60 months of repayment eligible for the deduction. Consult with current tax law or a tax advisor for adjusted gross income requirements.

Education IRA. For each child under age 18, families may deposit $500 per year into an Education IRA in the child's name. Earnings will accumulate tax-free and no taxes will be due upon withdrawal if the money is applied to pay for post-secondary tuition, required fees, books, equipment, and eligible room and board expenses. Consult current tax law or a tax advisor for adjusted gross income requirements and other eligibility guidelines.

IRA Withdrawals. Since January 1, 1998, taxpayers may withdraw funds from an IRA, without penalty, for their own qualified higher education expenses or those of their spouse, child, or grandchild. Qualified expenses are limited to tuition, fees, books, equipment, and room and board.

HOPE Scholarship Tax Credit. This tax credit applies to the *first two years* of college or vocational school training. Students receive a 100 percent tax credit for the first $1,000 of tuition and required fees, and a 50 percent credit on the second $1,000 for a maximum allowable credit of $1,500 per student per year. This applies to fees not paid by a grant or scholarship. Consult current tax code or a tax advisor for adjusted gross income requirements and eligibility guidelines. The current plan replaces the Hope Scholarship Credit with the American Opportunity tax credit and offers a maximum of $2,500 toward college tuition and related expenses for 2009-2010.

Lifetime Learning Credit. This is a tax credit applicable to college juniors, seniors, graduate and professional degree students, and to adults who want to go back to school, change careers, or take a course or two to upgrade their skills. A family will receive a 20 percent tax credit for the first $5,000 of tuition and required fees paid each year through 2002, and for the first $10,000 thereafter. The Lifetime Learning tax credit is available for tuition and required fees less grants, scholarships, and other tax-free educational assistance. Consult with a tax advisor or current tax code for additional specific guidelines. Look for tax advice and up-dated credit limits at www.irs.gov. You cannot take both Hope and Lifetime Learning Credits the same year.

Federal Income Taxes and Deductions. For information and instructions call 1-800-TAXFORM for free copies of Publications *A Student's Guide*, 508 *Educational Expenses*, and 520 *Scholarships and Fellowships*.

Keep records of certain expenses when beginning your job search for possible tax deductions if you itemize when tax filing. Job search expenses include travel to interview, unreimbursed expenses to interview, overnight stay, resume preparation, and others. See IRA Publication 17. Possible deductions include: job search expenses, moving expenses, and qualified (required) education after graduation.

Other income deductions include major medical expenses, mortgage interest, professional dues and memberships, tax-preparation fees, charitable contributions, and state and local taxes. Mileage to attend required meetings of church official work can be deducted. Donations of car, clothing, appliances and furniture can be deductions. Deductions of expenses for a room primarily used for business or day care services can be deducted. Of course, there are tests to meet the deductions such as employer does not provide the space, clients meet in the house, and service is provided in the home. Self-employed versus employees can deduct various expenses or insurance. Tom, who was a truck driver, revealed through conversation at the financial clinic that he had not been deducting his insurance nor taking depreciation on his semi.

Prepaying by saving money for a future expense or taxes seems wise but may not be if one considers money could be gaining interest when not used before it is absolutely needed. Withholding more from taxes so that it is a forced saving to get a larger refund seems unwise if withholding less would have prevented use of credit.

The Challenges in Spending

The challenge in counseling is assisting the individual not to be "penny wise and pound foolish." Glorifying God and serving for one's neighbor's good is defeated if all the time is spent worrying about saving pennies. Stewardship is not controlling and reducing expenses only. The shepherd will encourage some to spend more money and buy services, education, and habitat for the larger purposes in life. Celebrations such as when Jesus was anointed with precious perfume can be celebrated with joy, humility, and opportunity to bless a unique time. For example, Tim had heard his parents talk so much about reducing expenses that he did not tell them about the honors dinner they had been invited to attend. Tim's parents were disappointed because they could have skimped somewhere else to be able to attend this celebration. Relationships and spiritual growth are the goals. The challenge continues as the shepherd helps explore ways to meet the larger purposes with less money, with no money as in exchanges, and doing for oneself. Some need to tell Satan to get out of their spending and their spending plan. Creativity under the Spirit's guidance will direct the steps in planning, organizing, shopping, saving, sharing, and convincing others to cooperate.

Faithfulness in financial management is good stewardship and is reflected in smart management. Good management is "effective" and "efficient." Effectiveness is doing "right" or buying the right things the right way. Efficiency is getting the most satisfaction with the least resources. What is "right" is individualized under the Lordship or the Sovereign Power in one's life, not under others' directives. This is seeking righteousness.

What is "right," the values or priorities, are clarified when individuals or families decide what to cut out or, usually better, what needs to have a limit or be under control. Another guide is asking what would happen if this or that would be cut out. If nothing or less disastrous than something else, it can be cut out. Also, people can ask what can only be done at this time and what can be done later. They can consider how buying something glorifies (reveals) God or denies him. The buying of certain things may break baptismal or marriage vows. The counselor can return the list of current expenditures several times until the necessary reductions are made. Equally important in deciding what is "right" is what needs to be added for sharing (tithing for some), saving, and spending.

The natural tendency is to expand wants for some people when they are bored. They like new styles. The problem is that for one want to be fulfilled, other wants must be met – a chain of wants. Some are the creeping desires for more luxurious living. Creeping indebtedness can be a silent killer. Each month less and less of the monthly credit bill is paid off. Over-draft protection for a check written when there are insufficient funds becomes a loan in increments of $100. The worst killer is loan consolidation or refinancing because total costs over time are greater even when interest rate/payment is lower and after the pressure is off, more credit is assumed, but this time with more fixed payments.

People can activate "no call" list. People need to role play and practice saying "no" to sales pitches, addictions, and family members and saying "yes" to creative ways to meet needs – all types – social, emotional, physical, economic, and spiritual.

Comparing Before Buying or Traveling

When asked by reporters what the single most important shopping strategy was, Professor Williams answered "comparison shopping." A gift to God is giving time and personal energy by comparison shopping and consumer frugality so that more money can be given to the work of the kingdom. The savvy consumer has a shopping dilemma in that buying too cheap a product may wear out sooner and then the replacement results in more expense. On the other hand, paying more for features in appliances, equipment, or vehicles that will never/rarely be used can be considered wasteful. For example, buying a refrigerator with water and ice dispenser that will rarely be used, or optional features in telephone services can be considered wasteful. This chapter is focusing on product comparisons. Equally mandatory for good stewardship and economic security is comparing services, savings and investment opportunities, and employee benefits in choosing jobs.

Comparing interest rates, various terms, and years of the loan reveals thousands of dollars difference. Even a small interest rate difference on a home loan can reap great savings. The return on the time comparing and searching for slight differences yields thousands of savings probably greater than low and moderate income families would ever realize from other investments. One frequently overlooked comparison is paying for services to maintain current home and yard to that of the maintenance fee required in a condominium or other housing.

Compare Total Costs: Interest, Upkeep, Utilities, Over Time

Short-term cost with long-term benefit is the guide for buying appliances, furnaces, etc. More energy efficient models may cost more at the beginning, but the savings over the year in utilities would pay for the higher initial cost. This guide must be stated because of many examples of schools and churches who compared only the initial costs. They incurred short-term benefits with long-term costs. Short-term cost with long-term benefits is buying an energy efficient furnace and other appliances versus short-term benefit with long-term costs.

The initial cost of an appliance or equipment may be lower as compared with another choice with a higher energy efficiency rating, but it may cost more in the long run. Miller school made this mistake when buying a furnace without calculating the long-range costs.

Comparing "total" cost by calculating delivery charges, installation fees, upkeep, accessories, and replacement of parts shows the total. Comparing places among dealers and banks on interest rates are part of the process. Comparing cash versus credit calculates monthly payment by number of months and subtracts the cash price. The reason comparison shopping is so wise is that it slows down impulsive behavior. The consumer has to think about the purchase rather than being caught up in the emotions of the moment or the season. Comparison shopping educates one about features, questions the thrill of owning, gives one a chance to think carefully, and reduces money that could be used for other needs and delights. Comparison can include making or repairing by oneself rather than buying or hiring.

Comparing the total costs of a given activity/event with another for the same/similar benefits is part of the stewardship process. Jim and Elva find recreation, meaning in life, and something to look forward to in their Friday night bowling. Analysis of their total cost revealed dinner, drinks, game, extra round, drinks afterwards, babysitting, and travel to and from. Rather than cut out the event since it was expensive, Jim and Elva decided to increase income to cover it. Elva became a waitress on Saturday night which gave the income and time for Jim to become more acquainted with the children.

Principles of Buying

Wise buying practices include: Looking one day and deciding on the next. Buying items when reduced in price. Learning what a true special is versus a sale, off-season, after-holiday, periodic sales, or just marketing gimmicks to mislead one to think it is a bargain, especially when the purchase is not based on real need. Others are:

- Use credit when money can be saved in the long run.
- Record checks or credit card purchases in the check register (or a small notebook for credit) before writing the check or using the card.
- Plan for how the item can be paid for before it is purchased. Figure the extra dollars for using credit now and consider if those extra dollars would be better used for something else or to wait and pay cash.
- If the contract is too difficult to read or understand, have someone knowledgeable review and read it for the consumer. It may say wages can be garnished without going to court or automatically taken from savings account or tax refund.
- Never sign a contract with blanks left unfilled. Draw a line above blank if not filled in.
- If changes are discussed in a contract, have both parties initial the changes in the lines of the contract.
- Realize that price is not always an indicator of quality. Example is when name brands are on sale, store brand items are still less costly. If $4.00 is saved on canned foods each week for one year, total savings are $208.
- Get information from friends, magazines, and catalogues, local Cooperative Extension Educators, Consumer Action handbook (also on Internet,) Consumer Information Center, Pueblo, Colorado 81009 (or on Consumer Information Center on the Internet,) and Consumers Reports. Get information on scams, leasing a vehicle, buying a used car, etc. from Federal Trade Commission on Internet: www.ftc.gov.
- Know that you can cancel an agreement within three days. Always keep a copy of the agreement. Check on policy and procedure before signing an agreement.
- If product is technical and expensive, consult an expert you trust.

Analyzing and Reducing Food Costs

The shepherd can guide the reduction of food costs whether it is required from a recent unemployment, loss of income from pensions, reduction of debt load, manage as a newly single parent, being a newly independent on one's own, or freeing up money for more generous giving and sharing. The shepherd can say in casual conversation, "I have found that a way to reduce expenses is...." Or the shepherd could set up cooking classes and seminars on reducing expenses. Changes in food purchasing is a part of changing lifestyle or, at least, changes in style of food and home preparation. Reducing food costs is sometimes the only place a family can make changes. The changes can be fast although some family members may resist and are slow to learn new eating habits and preferences.

The United States Department of Agriculture and Family Economics groups have published food plans with estimated costs for thrifty, low, moderate, and high food levels. The estimate is that three of ten families would meet the recommended dietary allowances on the low cost food plan. The low plan costs are adjusted for size of household, age, and updated with price change. Eligibility for selected programs for the poor was based on three times the thrifty food cost, assuming a third of income is spent for food, and three times the low for other, near-poor families. Food stamp allotment is based on the thrifty plan. The plans could meet nutritional needs depending on shopping skills, preferences, routine eating, cooking skills, and compatibility for simple, repetitious foods. The problem with food stamps is stretching the food over a period of time, especially if there are teenagers. This demonstrates choices in styles of eating. Many choices abound with ways to maximize nutrition. An example of good stewardship is maximizing the nutrients with a given dollar amount such as $3.00 for a breakfast for donuts, soft drink, and coffee versus toast, egg, and orange juice which provides the vitamin C and protein and keeps one full longer. Observation has revealed families could save between $70 per week to $700 and more.

Rather than making elaborate menu plans or impulse buying at the store, the guide could be to buy what is on sale and plan meals around that. Buy in quantity for use over a month. Set a budget for food and designate certain foods off limits. Or reduce frequency rather than cut out entirely. Most people save money by not shopping when hungry and shopping less frequently, maybe once a month. Emergency items like peanut butter, dry beans, and dry milk can be stored. When on a trip, people can take supplies for eating one meal without purchasing it from a restaurant.

The family may use the food pantry periodically. This reduces costs or may be a vital part of survival. Money saved can be applied to credit card debt or the mortgage. In their mind, they can commit to contributing to the pantry later. Free breakfasts and lunches can be used if eligible. Some schools are distributing food to take home.

Even city dwellers can plant some greens in pots. With enough space, berry bushes can be used as part of the shrubbery. Decorative vegetable plants can be mixed with flowers such as parsley, chard, endive, cabbage, lettuce, and tomatoes. Individuals and families can exchange services for vegetables or fruits grown by others. Classes could be conducted on other creative means.

Some families have set up cooperatives. Others have organized car pools to drive to discount food stores.

Other techniques for reducing food costs are: choosing different types of food but with same nutrition, getting protein from inexpensive sources such as eating beans every other day, fasting on some days, reducing portions, omitting soft and hard drinks, buying items on sale, buying store brands, cooking and preparing lunches, not buying chips, not buying processed foods (ready to eat), shopping by comparing cost per serving since there may be more waste on some that initially appear less expensive, comparing cost per protein units, buying what is on sale, and having rules such as buying fruit only when less than $1.00 per pound, and having "pitch-ins" rather than eating out. Avoid expensive packages and conveniences. Compare sizes for price differences. Usually when forced to reduce costs, eating the basics is more nutritious and healthier. These options can save between $80 through $500 per week for food for a couple.

Not drinking soft drinks saved Eleanor 1,000 calories a day and almost $1,000 a year. Not drinking Starbucks coffee saved Tom over a $1,000 a year. Boiling beans all day provides protein and opportunities to save and share. Cooking a whole chicken in the oven with potatoes placed beside it reduces costs. Some would argue that it takes time. Waiting in a restaurant in a formal atmosphere also takes time. This is the response for those who say they are too busy and do not know how to cook.

With a plant closing or lay off, people may panic about possibly not having enough to eat. With severance pay or last paycheck, insecurity can be reduced by buying from a list of high nutrition and low cost non-processed, minimally packaged-foods. Potatoes rather than chips, for example, require cooking and some consumption control, but are more nutritious. Six dozen eggs can last for awhile. At least, the worry about not having enough to eat is reduced for a time.

In comparing cost per protein rather than by pound or package, the costs ranged so widely the notes are worthwhile. (A bar table would be effective.) For example, starting with the lowest for one fourth of a day's protein for the average man, dry beans was 15¢, beef liver 19¢, eggs, large 20¢, peanut butter 26¢, chicken fryer 27¢, hamburger 29¢, turkey 34¢, tuna 38¢, ham, whole 41¢, American cheese 42¢, beef, chuck 44¢, round steak 44¢, frankfurters (hot dogs) 50¢, pork roast 56¢, ocean perch, fillet 59¢, sirloin steak 64¢, pork chop center cut 70¢, beef rib roast 73¢, bologna 74¢, pork sausage 94¢, and bacon, sliced 103¢.

Sitting across the table from each other at a financial counseling conference were Maslo and Flora. Maslo was a young African-American male working in family services with the Army. Flora was an elderly, white female working with a university clinic. They slyly exchanged their counseling secret to be "teaching the client to cook."

Buying food with high nutrition at lowest cost is only half the problem. Organizing the food supply, storing it properly, planning the use and distribution of it over time, and creative use of left-overs are challenges especially for hungry people. For example, not letting people drink orange juice or sodas as an unlimited supply. Yet, they need to manage it so they receive vitamin C every day. (The story is told that some mothers give their children more soft drinks than milk. Some do not know orange drink does not have the vitamins that orange juice does.) Some people purchase water when running the tap longer before drinking it would give fresh, safe, and less expensive water. The talent and the gift to the household is having someone manage the food supply, stretch the food stamps, limit the intake, watching to prevent spoilage, etc. As in finances in general, one main manager to guide and control the kitchen works better than everyone buying and eating whatever, whenever.

Some of the greatest gifts given to children are learning to defer gratification, cooking skills, nutritional knowledge, and responsibilities for financial management, self reliance, and dependence on God as provider and sustainer. Home activities can be structured intentionally to develop these gifts rather than the buy, buy, buy mentality with credit cards. Another gift is to learn ways to be entertained rather than through eating entertaining food. Some question why fellowship is always involved with food when most people get enough calories.

Maggie complained to the pastoral counselor that Aaron, her unemployed husband, was spending money they did not have. He would meet his friends once a week and buy them all beers. At that point, Aaron threw up his hands and exclaimed, pleading with the counselor, "What is a man to do?" The counselor perceived behind the question was: How can Aaron receive admiration and friendship? How can Aaron maintain his self-respect and dignity he felt when he was employed but now has lost?

An individual may decide and enjoy skimping on necessities in favor of having luxuries in certain types of food. A so-called luxury may be redefined as supporting a favorite missionary.

The shepherd or money coach understands that many retired and poor people eat out once a day as their daily food because they are lonely, do not have cooking facilities, energy or knowledge. As in other areas, therefore the shepherd helps them find the least expensive such as "meals on wheels," senior citizen shelters, community meals, church pot-lucks, simple/low overhead places with no soft or hard drinks, and buying food requiring no cooking such as peanut butter and cheese. Some of these feed the emotional as well as the hunger and other physical need for a retired or low-income people.

Grocery Bags Of Similar Food In Different Styles Or Forms
Illustrate Savings In Food-Style Choices
(Shows process and choices with relative prices that can be updated)

Bag One		Bag Two	
8 qts. Non-fat dry milk	$4.49	8 qts. fresh milk	$5.50
1 lb. margarine	.89	1 lb. butter	2.04
12 oz. cornflakes	1.35	12 oz presweetened	1.89
8 c. uncooked rice	1.99	8 c. pre-cooked rice	2.70
1 can mackerel	.79	I can salmon	2.89
1 can stewing tomatoes	.69	1 can whole fancy toms.	.85
1 can store brand green beans	.57	1 can name brand beans	.81
½ lb. raw potatoes	.45	½ lb. potato chips	1.09
1 can frozen orange juice	1.67	46. oz. can orange juice	1.99
1 dozen medium eggs	.55	1 doz. large eggs	.75
Total Bag One	**$13.44**	**Total Bag Two**	**$20.51**

Greater than these $7.00 savings can be shown for other choices in regular purchases. Calculating the relative savings for the total number of bags over a month or year would motivate changes and preferences by family members. If one spends 30 minutes comparing prices whether among brands or different food-styles and it saves ten dollars then this translate into a wage of $20 per hour.

Child Care Arrangements

Both the poor and the affluent may require child care from someone other than a parent. In America and other countries in the world grandparents historically provided this. Now-a-days, the grandmother is employed around the world more frequently and to an older age. With "welfare reform," mothers are to be employed to receive government benefits. Provisions with state and federal funding for child care are available within limits, paid on a sliding scale fee. Alternative child care arrangements need to be weighed for the effect on children. Many parents do not know the options. People perceive negative effects of some child care arrangements whereas in reality there are positive effects. For example, some grade school children have their increased understanding and skills as they help younger children in a day care.

Just as in any other decisions of employment, the net return is after health and fringe benefits subtracting taxes, gas, clothing, child care, and work related expenses. However, the wise manager looks at benefits and costs over a period of time. For example, the net return may be zero while there are child care costs for just a few years, but with salary increases, training, and job security, returns would be much greater over a longer period of time. Benefits include psychological, health insurance, and the opportunity to serve God as well as financial benefits. If an individual is not employed, costs might increase because of anxiety, stress from not working, failure to meet basic needs, fear of survival, and inability to provide children's education. So with more demands upon time and energy with two or three jobs and parenting, one has to work smarter not harder, be efficient with housework, and have quality interactions among family members. John and Jane have different shifts, but when Jane was not working they were fighting about finances. Now they share child care responsibilities. Two single parents could also have different shifts and share child care responsibilities. A nonemployed spouse could start a day care center in the home. When choosing housing location, the supply of babysitters or grandparents is a consideration.

The myth of more meals out, thereby increasing costs of a working mother, needs to be de-mythed. If a spouse works because of family needs or wanting to share more, why would he or she waste it on food? The myth of a wife's job actually costing rather than contributing can be de-mythed in realizing the earnings help to buy the clothes or the hair care she would need anyway. The challenge is to decrease child care expense. There are some jobs that a parent can take children with him or her.

Remember in child care and education, responsibilities should be delegated, not relinquished. The home maintenance, supervision of studies, cooking, and cleaning have to be organized, but all can learn and share in these survival skills. You are responsible for the quality of life at home regardless of who is employed at how many jobs. Parents need to be complimented for their creativity in handling responsibilities, keeping it all together, getting the family to church, and contributing to social concerns. It is a real challenge but their strength comes from the Lord. Singles, parents, grandparents need encouragement whether working outside the home, in the home, or both as their mission field, working "as unto the Lord."

An illustration of creative arrangements follows: Leona taught at the university, but one class ended after her two children got out of preschool. One semester a college student took Ben to swim class until Leona had her lunch hour. Another year the preschool teachers let them stay a half hour longer and dropped them off at the public library where they waited quietly until their mother came. Years later they reported that the time of reading books unsupervised was the best time of the day.

Jane lived in a neighborhood where Rene and other elderly people lived. Rene thought walking across the street to baby-sit was an answer to prayer. The children loved her as a grandparent although she was strict. Getting help with housework is wise while children are young since they cannot help enough with chores. It helps the employee and helps the employed mother. What the couple or single parents decide to do is between them and God, not what others such as in-laws may dictate.

Research has revealed that the effect of the mother's working was a result of attitude and child care arrangements. If the child perceived the mother was working to get away from him or her or because the father was a failure, negative results happened. But if the child perceived the mother had gifts to use and was contributing to their needs and wants through income, the results were positive. Positive attitudes and work methods of a mother are transferred to children regardless of employment status. One problem of employed mothers was having time to supervise children's work and study assignments.

Analyzing and Reducing Transportation Costs

The President of the National Foundation for Consumer Credit said most people would get out of financial trouble if they would get rid of one car and stop gambling. Credit counselors for years have said the main reason for financial trouble was the new car syndrome. With transportation, there are many choices to compare. Control is resisting persuasion by glitter and romance. One can buy transportation or prestige and respect associated with it versus getting these basic needs met in other ways. Further, the price of a new car could buy all the furniture and appliances desired in a starter home. The rule of diversification can be applied when a lower priced car means having more money for vacation travel. Related costs of owning a car are 40-50 percent of total transportation costs and become more crucial, as everyone knows, as gas prices increase.

Matt wants the family to get a new car. They can afford the payments but not the other costs: insurance, taxes, upkeep, etc. Further, postponing the purchase means money in the pocket every month the current car is kept. Funding for college is settled by saving the $300 difference per month between having an extra car/truck or among vehicles. The dilemma is how long to keep an old car needing repairs before it becomes too costly or more to keep repaired than a different one. One advantage is that the individual knows the old car but not the risks of a different one. The cost of inconvenience in sharing a vehicle or a youth waiting to be picked up can be calculated in an hourly rate of saving. The projected saving from waiting, since the family has only one car, is probably greater than from any paid job one could find.

Larry ordered the tire rim but the store wanted $45 to install it. Another place wanted $15 but he could do it in a friend's garage for $6.00. Larry ordered the rim for his tire but compared the labor cost and installed it himself.

Reducing costs can include comparison shopping for insurance, taking the higher deductible for lower premium, comparing prices for gas and oil, accelerating and stopping smoothly, planning trips so errands are combined, or on the way to somewhere else. Reducing the risk of buying a lousy used car is worth the fee paid to have an independent mechanic exam it before purchase.

Cutting Costs of Transportation

Years ago when the author started doing credit counseling, the agency with whom she worked said the most prevalent problem with family finances was the American dream of having a new car. To afford it, payments were extended beyond the time in which repair would be needed. A car might be repossessed so the individual is paying for two cars – one with a remaining balance on a car that was repossessed. Paying over 60 months the buyer may owe at some point more money than the car is worth. On a 72 month loan the car has been paid for once at the 36-month time. On the other hand, keeping an old car is advantageous because even if there are periodic repairs, one knows what the problems are. Every month of keeping it running is money in one's pocket.

Having one vehicle rather than two reduces not just the payments but taxes, insurance, etc. If only one vehicle is not maintenance free, have a back up of another vehicle or have someone who can take one to work or the child to school in an emergency. A church might organize a pool of people who can transport others to work in an emergency or on a short notice. Choice of housing location so one or more can walk, take transportation, or car pool is advantageous. When borrowing for a vehicle:

- With a larger down payment, the loan amount is smaller.
- Interest rates can be lower with a down payment and good credit rating.
- If borrowing against one's saving, the interest rate can be substantially lower; therefore, it pays to build up savings before buying a vehicle.
- To compare insurance premiums for comprehensive, collision, disability, and credit life insurance which vary among the different agents and a dealer, lenders, credit union and a bank. Credit life insurance is not required nor is it necessary; and it may be already covered by one's life insurance at less cost.
- Premiums are determined by the year, make, model, geographic location, miles driven, and drivers. Collision insurance costs less as cars or trucks depreciate. Most advise to drop collision insurance when the car or truck is very old as the insurance may be greater than the car is worth.
- Reductions of premiums are possible with multi-car insurance, age, academic records, low mileage, or good driving record.
- The homeowner's policy may cover contents of the vehicle and so duplicate coverage is not necessary.
- Notify the insurance company if one car is sold or a driver leaves the household.
- The largest deductable possible on insurance can be taken to reduce premium if one wants to and can afford the risk.
- It is advantageous to have all insurance with one company such as housing, renter's insurance, and vehicles.
- The insurance may be less costly is paid annually rather than in installments.

Comparison shopping includes buying from the owner versus sales people. It includes comparing value given for trade-in with price one could get by selling the car to someone. The prices on the Dealer Sticker can be negotiated which are the suggested retail price and options of dealer mark-ups, additional dealer profit, dealer preparation, and undercoating. One can comparison shop for the best interest rate offered by dealers, banks, credit unions, private owners, insurance companies, and leasing. The differences in vehicles can be compared for their principal (cash price), interest and finance charges, insurance, license, gas usage, parts and upkeep, and safety. Savings in any area can be compared to other uses of money in general. For example, alternative use of money by buying a small, low maintenance vehicle is a trip overseas, trip plus clothes, charity contributions, savings, and education or training to secure employment. Differences in prices of the vehicle or from an alternative method of financing could be put to savings. For example, the present value amount of $6,000 saving would grow, with compound interest at 8 percent, to $27,966 in 20 years.

Analyzing and Reducing Housing Costs

People most often buy with the heart rather than the head. Having a quality house or apartment in a quality location is important for relationships and child development and aesthetic living – beauty all around. However, the creative, industrious person can make a habitat beautiful and delightful, turning a substandard living quarters into quality. The state governor's wife (an ordained pastor) decided to keep the house in the inner city and make it her mission to befriend the neighbors, plant trees and flowers, and improve the safety.

A talk with a financial counselor could save thousands of dollars or to help one to see alternatives. Comparing interest rates could reduce thousands on the mortgage. If one chooses quality housing that stretches the budget, plan to cut elsewhere such as the electric use, transportation, entertainment, travel or dinners. Bob and Nancy sought the financial counselor's advice at the clinic before they purchased the house of their dreams because they were conscientious and wanted to be sure they could afford it. The counselor gathered the data on take-home income, projected salary increases, expenses, amount for down payment and plans for the future. This included sending a daughter to a nearby university. Using the 60/40 rule where 60 percent is for mortgage payment and then dividing by the factor in the amortization table (rather than multiplying to get payment for selected number of years at given interest rates) and multiplying by 1000, the amount of mortgage they could afford was estimated. Right now they could barely afford the mortgage for the house they had seen, but the counselor told them they would have tradeoffs now and in the future. They could only buy used cars, reduce travel, cook meals and take lunches, and the daughter would have to live at home while going to school. They were not listening – their heart was set on a particular house.

People buying with the heart, not the mind, purposely ignore some costs or are usually not given all the different types of costs. Using the mind, the decision is difficult because there are tradeoffs from the different costs. Housing costs in one way or another. If not in money, it costs in space, beauty, neighborhood, access to schools, access to work via public transportation, need for repair, utility costs, energy efficiency, privacy, tranquility, ease of maintenance, opportunity for self-expression in yard or house, and flexibility for changing lifestyles or stages.

When tax implications and deductions are considered, the monthly payment is actually lower since most of the mortgage payment goes for interest in the early years of the loan. The deductible interest reduces taxable income but is lower for those with lower marginal tax rate. In addition, there are homestead and mortgage exemptions from taxes. People need to be reminded of the deadline to file for these. The cost may be higher than anticipated when property taxes are higher. People are surprised the second year of ownership when taxes such as property taxes increase substantially and they had not made provisions for the increase. They are higher because taxes were prorated when one buys and they did not see it the first year. Current programs to supposedly assist first time home buyers may have a second loan built in to be paid over the years which actually increases nonflexible costs. Depending on location and improvements, the house may appreciate and be sold at a return greater than other investments.

How Much House Can One Afford?

Don and Lucy were told they qualified for a $250,000 house by the lender – clearly a false and deceptive statement. The lender did not even check on unusual or other expenses nor clarify amount of interest paid for more expensive houses. Rules for lending may be out of date given the cost of related items such as utilities, upkeep, and property taxes. If there is 20 percent or more for a down payment, owners are not required to have the Private Mortgage Insurance. Since the amount of down payment determines mortgage, the question is how much mortgage one can afford rather than how much house.

With the cost of vehicles and gasoline, the mortgage one can afford as a percent of income varies with location from employment and retail or hospital services if they are required. Assuming one's wage or salary will increase and mortgage payments are fixed, the argument for buying more than one can afford at the time is valid. If the size or the neighborhood becomes inadequate or undesirable, a move would be more expensive than buying more initially.

A single person in a higher tax bracket may benefit from the deduction from a mortgage payment. Initially, most of the payment is interest. If the location is right, the starter house can be used for "trading up" or an investment with return. Mobile homes usually depreciate like automobiles. If the house needs improvements for quality living or resale, the return from "sweat equity" can be calculated. Susie found that refinishing the woodwork, stair repair, and decorating returned greater income when the house was sold after 10 years than any employment she could have had, and she was home with the children full time. Darin bought a small rural house listed at $88,000. With 20 percent down, his twice/monthly payments were $250. Darin built or renovated a sunroom into his office by adding insulation, mini blinds, a ceiling fan, and a gas heater. This added 200 square feet to living/working space of 1,200 square feet. (Indiana Department of Environmental Management says one could benefit by adding insulation if the current one is less than seven inches.)

Initial Cost of Home Ownership

The larger the down payment, the lower the monthly payment and the lower the total cost over the years. However, with the interest deduction from income taxes (higher for those in a higher tax bracket) it is advisable to make a lower down payment than is affordable and invest the difference. Since one is paying a lower mortgage payment, one would insist on not using credit for other purchases. Never-the-less, a larger down payment (20 percent) qualifies one to not have to purchase Private Mortgage Insurance and one can get better interest rates. Comparing rates is important but just as important is to reduce other credit and postpone credit purchases such as a new vehicle so one qualifies for the lower interest. The closing costs are substantial and have put many couples or single people over the edge financially. Therefore, rather than make hasty decisions, it is worthwhile to compare financing, closing costs including points, and lenders. Consumers may think they are too busy to compare but since several thousands of dollars are at stake, the return is greater than their hourly compensation. For example, if they spend $1,200 less and it took six hours to compare, the return is equivalent to $200 per hour.

The shrewd buyer compares the total cost (interest and cash price) of buying appliances separately with having appliances included in the thirty year (or whatever) mortgage. Comparison of providing a larger down payment to investing some of the amount earmarked for a down payment fulfills the principle of diversification. In addition to tax deductions received from interest paid with a larger down payment, the choice to invest part of a possible larger down payment may give security over the years.

Reducing Closing Costs

The down payment may have been saved and a reasonable, competitive interest rate obtained. However, many families have found the closing costs became a problem and upset other financial plans because they had not allowed for them. Closing costs can be as low as 2 percent and as high as 10 percent of the mortgage loan amount. Costs vary due to local customs and negotiations between buyer and seller which should be specified in the sales contract. It is possible to have an agreement in which the buyer pays all closing costs or one in which the seller pays all. Fees usually paid to the lender at closing are:

Loan origination fee

Loan discount points (a one time charge which can be negotiated depending on market conditions. (Price, interest, inclusions, when delivered, etc. can be negotiated.)

Appraisal fee to determine whether the value of the property is sufficient to secure the loan

Credit report fee

Assumption fee which the buyers pay for processing if the payments on the seller's loan is taken over

Advance payments if lender requires interest on the mortgage from day of settlement to beginning of period covered by first monthly payment, mortgage insurance premium for first year's premium or a lump sum, hazard insurance premium required to pay for year or bring proof that buyer has paid for such a policy

Escrow accounts or reserves if lender will be paying the property taxes, mortgage insurance, and hazard insurance

Title charges

Recording and transfer fees

Additional charges of surveyor's fees, charges for termites and other pest infections, and other inspections

Miscellaneous fees.

Down Payment Possibilities

There are "contract programs" where little or no down payment is required and individuals rather than institutions sell the home. A couple may sell a home quickly with no down payment and low interest since they want to move to Florida, so the individuals become the mortgage holders. A parent may loan the money for the down payment to a child who buys the parent's home as an investment and charges the parent rent, maybe just breaking even which helps the child's tax liability and get the home out of the parent's estate for tax purposes.

By having a larger down payment, an individual could easily save over $50,000 over time affording a nicer home than otherwise, with the ease of a lower monthly payment. There are programs for "first time homebuyers" where a down payment is not required. There are programs which require no down payment, but remember, the total cost is still higher. In deciding on a house, it is the mortgage not the price of the house which affects affordability. Therefore, possible sources of a down payment to reduce the mortgage are:

- Cash from checking and savings account accumulated by deferring spending on other items
- A second job for designated time
- Accumulated payroll deductions for a specified number of years
- Retirement fund from previous job with understanding of not returning to the job
- Withdrawal from retirement fund
- Sale of stocks or bonds and/or used as collateral for cash borrowing
- Pension fund which allows for house purchase
- Gifts from relatives or early inheritance with a contract stating if any repayment
- Cash value of life insurance and/or cash value of dividends
- Advances from or borrowing against future bonuses

- Equity loan "swing loan" on real estate being sold (sometimes secured)
- Borrowing against valuable personal property such as jewelry, collections, cameras, tools, and equipment
- Borrowing against savings account balance and/or certificates of deposit
- Selling some personal property such as vehicles, goats, elephants
- Use work equity with labor and materials done on property and credit toward purchase price
- Income tax refunds
- Corporate cash advances (relocation fees) when corporation is transferring employee – a transfer bonus
- Assignment of interest or dividend income to be earned
- Additional savings from earnings between date of offer to purchase and closing transaction by a crash budget or drastic change in lifestyle.

Property can be purchased without a down payment. These include using a contract for sale direct with seller, having a land contract, leasing with option to purchase with a portion of rent going toward purchase price, assuming an existing mortgage, using the Veterans Administration mortgage, using Farmers Home Administration (FmHA) for qualified moderate income rural families, pledging savings by seller or third party to lender, using an existing property owned as collateral to purchase another, buying with use of a balloon payment scenario and no monthly payments but just a periodic lump (long-term preferable) (this can be dangerous because of change in circumstances later,) and using option to buy at a specified date allowing for some appreciation to accrue with the right to assign or sell option and/or property.

The 60/40 Rules

The 60/40 Rule, so to speak, was observed in local surveys and national data. The results of the calculations can affect decision-making. Although most people think of just the monthly mortgage payment, the total housing cost is divided by about 60 percent (50 percent recently) for the payment and 40 percent for the remainder of the costs of utilities, maintenance, landscaping, and taxes. Also, one person in the family is employed to pay for the house since income of one spouse is about 40 percent of the total income and housing is about 40 percent of total expenditures. The author's research further documented that a monthly deficit (negative cash flow) was correlated with expenses higher than 40 percent, number in family, and number of vehicles. This is an example of "living beyond one's income" which resulted in higher stress and expense.

Rather than using the realtor's or lender's guidelines of debt to income for qualifying for a loan, the 60/40 rule would indicate an affordable lower mortgage. Calculate how much is available for overall housing and than choose a 60 percent monthly mortgage payment. Of course, a larger down payment could mean a more expensive house. A longer term also lowers a lower monthly mortgage payment but considerably more interest is spent over time which is tax deductible.

The choice is theirs, but if they overextend on housing, they need to realize they are committing someone to work just for housing. Credit cannot cover forever other expenses and vacations. They are locked into expensive payments, utilities, upkeep, and taxes. With creativity, they could expand current space with visits to the park, for example.

Applying the 60/40 Rule. To be realistic about how much mortgage (not house) one can afford use this worksheet:
1. Write money available for total housing costs

Or 25 percent of monthly gross income _____

2. Multiply by 30-60 percent to estimate mortgage payment depending on assumption
X .60_____

3. Divide by factor in amortization chart _____

4. Multiply by 1,000 to estimate affordable
mortgage (house value minus down payment) X 1,000 = $_____ .

Steps to Meet the Threat of Foreclosure

When foreclosure threatens, **adjustments** have to be made. Reducing expenses or increasing income to make timely payments protects one's credit score. There may have been warning signs of the threat which people have ignored and adjustments postponed. Some people plan to walk away from the home, doing nothing since their credit rating has been destroyed anyway. Adjustments include these: **Doubling up** of generations to share expenses, taking in a boarder, rearranging or remodeling the house for two families, taking early inheritance, using **Reverse Annuity Mortgage** (home equity conversion) for monthly payments, **borrowing against the equity** of their house but not repaying as long as they live there (a government-backed loan program for 62 ½ year olds or older), using **Housing Lease Back** (selling to an heir for investment) but living there with a small rent, loaning the down payment to a child who buys a house and rents to the parent, and **arranging with the landlord** to paint or other services in lieu of rent or a reduction in rent. There are programs for mortgage **loan modifications** under Veterans Administration or Federal Housing Authority. Loan modification programs are available where the loan term is extended with missed payments tacked on at the end or the loan terms such as interest are modified. It may change the mortgage on an adjustable rate to a fixed rate. There may be a processing fee.

Scams with foreclosures are now being reported. They even call themselves "counselors." (See Foreclosure Rescue Scams on the Internet.)

The best option for some is to sell the house. (See ForeclosureResources for Consumers with links to local resources.) The lender usually gives a specific amount of time to find a buyer and pay off the amount owed on the mortgage. If one cannot sell the property for the full amount, the lender may accept the amount received in the selling price, even it is less than amount owed. The Internal Revenue Service can explain the taxes owed on the difference between amount you owe and the amount able to pay back. (Some forgiven loans can be considered income and taxable.)

A qualified buyer may be allowed to **assume** (take over) the mortgage. The d**eed-in-lieu of foreclosure** is a step to "give back" the property to the lender who forgives the balance of the loan. There may be tax consequences and restrictions such as the requirement to try to sell the home at a fair market value for at least 90 days.

The Shepherd can guide steps[80] **in meeting the threat of foreclosure:** When the family is unable to pay the mortgage or have not paid, the first step is to review the loan documents. Then call the lender. If the lender will not talk with the family, then contact a housing counselor who is certified. A list of counseling resources can be found at NeighborWorks and on the U.S. Department of Housing and Urban Development (HUD) website or 800-569-4287. A short-term solution is needed because of missing one or two months due to illness is a temporary plan for paying missed

---

80   The Federal Reserve Board. "5 tips for Protecting Your Home from Foreclosure." www.federalreserve.gov/pubs/foreclosuretips/default.htm. March 10, 2009.

payments. One possible step is **reinstatement** by paying a lump sum by a specific date to make up the back payments. **Forbearance** is a temporary reduction or suspension of mortgage payments for a short period, after which the lender creates a repayment plan. A **repayment plan** includes a portion of the past due payments each month until payments are current. **Partial claim** may be filed by the lender if the mortgage is insured by a private mortgage insurance firm. Some provide a one-time, interest free loan to bring the account up to date. This loan is due when one refinances, pays off the mortgage, or when the property is sold.

A Case Study. The Quincys were emotionally distraught because of "foreclosure proceedings" on their house. They were behind in the payments on a secured loan. They lived entirely on Social Security. Other information prompted the counselor to refer them to an attorney. The attorney filed legal papers to halt the imminent foreclosure and filed a lawsuit against the loan company for compensatory and punitive damages for "unconscionable" lending practices under state statutes and case decisions. A judgment for $1.5 million was rendered in favor of the Quincys against the company for its act of loaning money to people on a fixed low income under circumstances where it was certain the loan could never be repaid and the home would go eventually into foreclosure. (See Chapter 11 on credit and debt.)

Prepayment of Mortgage Decision

At first glance paying off the mortgage sooner would seem to be advantageous by saving thousands of dollars in interest. Of course, the shorter the term, the less interest is paid. Also, one can save interest by making one or more extra payments a month or paying more on the principal. A lump sum payment or inheritance can reduce the interest dollars. Of course, paying off a mortgage earlier than contracted reduces interest paid. But this is only part of the story.

A flippant, simple answer is not sufficient for determining financial results in 30 years from paying off the mortgage early, paid in half the time, or reduced in interest by adding to the principal each month early in the scheduled contract. This decision is a strong example of money management taking into consideration the 5 M's – *m*athematics, *m*anagement style, *e*motions, *m*ajor life issues, and other family *m*embers. One is advised to not trust "feelings" only. They can be deceptive. One is advised to trust "faith" and to use one's mind to calculate dollars gained or lost.

Considerations in the decision are: Tax deductions of interest paid, mortgage exemption in taxes, saving the differential of prepayment versus the 30 year term, using credit for a mortgage over time allowing cash for other things, diversifying use of income to house and investments, tithing rather than paying loan off early, paying for college rather than paying off the loan, and continuing the payment pattern into retirement fund after the mortgage is paid off early. Comparing the interest dollars that are saved with interest dollars earned by investing the prepayment differential shows families what the results would be by investing rather than prepaying. However, taxes are paid on interest earned by saving or investments, the amount varying depending on the individual's tax bracket and return on savings.

Some advise to pay, sequentially, the family's debts, to have an emergency fund, to pay off house early, to build savings, to have investments, to save for retirement, and then to give generously in that sequence. Problems exist in using this process for the majority of American families. Demands are greater than income at the early stages of family life and they resort to using more credit since income is tied to large house payments. An emergency fund or savings need to be started immediately when married because of underestimating expenses, emergencies, and opportunities. Savings need to be built while paying off credit. The time for the sequential build up is not sufficient to meet college expenses, even in part. Saving for retirement is possible if begun in the first stage because of the "magic" of compound interest. Generosity and sharing with other people need to be a way of life, a way of trusting God to provide from early years to later.

Advantages to the longer term mortgage such as the 30 year versus the 15 year are: Mortgage payments are fixed and become cheaper dollars with inflation. In most families the need for a higher cash flow is higher than it would be in 30 years. If income increases by wage increases, different jobs, and promotions, the percentage of income going for mortgage decreases. This justifies buying a more expensive house initially than one thinks one can afford if income is sure to increase. People may be able to get a substantially lower interest rate for buying a vehicle when they have savings. They borrow their own money at a lower rate of interest and as they make payments they replenish their savings. Taxes are reduced by deducting the interest paid on the mortgage. Many people need this tax deduction. Also, there is a county mortgage exemption which helps reduce property taxes as long as there is a mortgage. The savings which would have been used for prepaying provides a larger emergency or opportunity fund. Using money for both mortgage and investments meets the principle of diversifying assets. Economic security and financial peace of mind are increased with diversification. Rather than tying up an inheritance or extra dollars each month instead of paying the higher mortgage prepayment, there is some flexibility for changes. A mortgage loan is probably the cheapest loan an individual has. Stretching out the mortgage for 30 years versus 15 for a reduced monthly payment increases total interest but increases cash flow in the earlier years. Since the interest is tax deductible, the cash flow allows the consumer to have cash to use for other expenses which would offset his or her increased mortgage interest. Therefore, a smaller payment permits one to pay cash for other expenses including clothes, vehicles, and college tuition. On the other hand, planning for college or retirement can include having the mortgage paid off. The amount initially going for the mortgage is now available for college and retirement. The spread between interest paid on the mortgage and interest earned from investing the differential is not the sole criteria for the decision. Even at the same rate (4 percent versus 4 percent), *interest earned is greater because "debt does not* compound whereas *savings does."*

The **decision to prepay or not** depends on the need to have
- Security based on diversification of assets,
- Accessibility of invested funds to pay a mortgage payment in time of inability to pay the mortgage,
- Feeling of ownership free and clear,
- Sufficient income or cash flow to pay non-mortgage costs,
- Liquid assets versus non-liquid assets (house paid) which are difficult to obtain in a short period of time without depreciable loss,
- Money working for the family (savings, investments) as well as the family working for money, and
- Positive outlook for future economic conditions. (If one has an adjustable rate mortgage, the interest rate will fluctuate and may be lowered in recessionary times.)
- Researches found that "better financial results accrue to some borrowers when they select a 30-year mortgage coupled with a simultaneous investment plan rather than a 15-year mortgage term and subsequent investment plan. Further, the financial benefit associated

with a 30-year mortgage increases as the borrower's marginal tax rate and risk tolerance increase."[81]

Refinancing

Even with a lower interest rate, if the time is extended, the interest cost will be more. An example of a deceptive practice: usually the reduced monthly payment at various interest rates and the months to pay are quoted but not the total cost over time with the added fees. The cost of refinancing could be invested. **Months to recoup** the cost of financing are figured by dividing the cost of refinancing by the monthly reduction of payment. If the cash flow is deficient, people can make drastic but temporary reductions elsewhere and/or get another job until they are out of the pit financially. Otherwise, they are just digging a bigger hole with creeping credit captivity.

Taxes and Housing

The federal government has promoted homeownership by providing significant tax benefits. Therefore the monthly payment of principal and interest are not as much as one observes without the tax advantages. The deduction from interest alone may save thousands of dollars in federal income taxes. (Use Form 1040 – the long form.) In the first year as homeowners the points paid to the lender are also deductible. Property taxes are deductible, and for some jurisdictions, moderate and low income homeowners qualify for full or partial property tax abatement. Moving expenses can be deducted if they were job-related and other requirements are met. Costs of repair and operating expenses as well as annual depreciation allowance can be deducted for rental property. Capital gains deferment from selling a home at a profit varies with the law from time to time. For tax purposes when selling a home, accurate and complete records of the cost of improvement should be kept for determining the increased "basis" on which taxes may be calculated.

Energy Use and Reduction

Many families, as predicted by a Consumer Affairs Conference research report years ago, will find their energy costs for home and car are 50 percent of their budget. The old government surveys of consumer expenditures no longer apply and they never were "prescriptions" or guidelines for individuals and families but results of surveying what they actually spent. Expenditures depend on values and management but expenditures are also a result of past decisions, irrevocable expenses, and the fact that some things such as housing just cost more. The averages can be found in the Internet reports of the Bureau of Labor Statistics.

Now that health insurance is about 50 percent or more for some people's income and that energy, utilities for the house, and gas for the car are over 50 percent, reductions in other expenditures are mandatory for survival and still keep the commitment to share. One can concentrate on the

"energy hogs" and make drastic changes. This translates into money saved. Compare energy use by noting the "Energy Guide" label. Estimated kilowatt hours per appliance can be multiplied by average cost per kHz to estimate monthly cost. The average estimated kHz per month for appliances are: water heater 350, air conditioner 321, range 109, food freezer 109, refrigerator

---

81   Peter M. Basciano, James M. Grayson, and James Walton. Is a 30-Year Mortgage Preferable to a 15-Year Mortgage. *Financial Counseling and Planning.* 17,1. 2006. Pp.14-22.

99, clothes dryer 83, dehumidifier 77, light bulbs 72, furnace fan 59, ceiling fan 45, television 37, dishwasher 30, microwave 16, radiant heater 14, humidifier 14, frying pan 9, coffee maker 8, iron 5, hair dryer 5, radio 2, clock 2, toothbrush 1.

For air conditioning, energy reductions include planting shade trees around the outside of the house, pulling shades down or adding more layers of draperies, tuning off lights, using fans, installing a thermostat that adjusts temperatures 24 hours for seven days, taking showers and air drying for cooling oneself, and air drying clothes. For reduction in heating costs, techniques include designing window placement to absorb the sun's heat, using double panes or plastic covers in winter, keeping a lower thermostat but getting warm with shower or cooking, using space heaters or light bulbs for areas, shutting off infrequently used rooms, stuffing or taping cracks, wear warmer clothing, bed covers reflecting or preventing heat loss, and window treatment. The electric or gas utility may do an energy audit for free or refer clients to a qualified professional, thus saving hundreds of dollars a year.

Compact fluorescent light bulbs use 67 percent less energy and last up to 10 times longer. Lights account for 20 percent of a typical home's bill. (IDEM) Indiana Department of Environmental Management

For appliance reduction of energy, use oven only when more than one item is cooked, wash dishes or clothes only with full loads, turn off burner before finished cooking, and place a message at light switches "Be bright – turn off light." A breakfast that saves human energy, motions, and utility energy is "egg in the basket." The bread is placed in the skillet and the egg placed in a hole torn out of the bread. It is turned once. Toast and egg are eaten together. Another is the meal with the meat cooked in a skillet, turned once, and then vegetables are added. Potatoes are placed in the skillet at the beginning.

Tax credits are available for installing certain energy saving appliances and home improvements. Check for current opportunities and limits.

Other Utility and Energy Reductions

It is estimated that most families could reduce expenses by at least $50.00 per month. Here are suggestions:

Turn water heater to a lower setting (120 degrees).

On cool days, turn down thermostat and put on sweaters.

Install automatic thermostat that pays for itself by changing settings for various times of day and for days of the week.

Turn off appliances and range immediately when not in use and turn electric burner off before food is quite done or served.

Hang up clothes, etc. to avoid using the dryer and provide humidity for the house.

Be sure the registers for supply or return air are not blocked.

Keep closet doors closed.

Shut off rooms or the registers in rooms rarely used.

Detect drafts and openings and use weather stripping, caulking, rolled up rugs, or rags to cover wind or cold air flow.

Insulate attic, walls, basement ceiling, and crawl space.

Regularly replace furnace filters and tape leaks in ducts.

Insulate all duct, electrical outlets, and switches with plug kits.

Change water usage by using a different method of showering. Turn off water sooner at the sink. Sixty percent reduction in water usage can be obtained by turning off water while brushing teeth, repairing drippy faucets, installing low-line shower heads, and faucet aerators according to the Indiana Department of Environmental Management 2009.

In the heat of summer without air conditioning, shower but air dry.

Install glass door enclosures on fireplaces.

Install an additional layer with bed sheets on an extension rod in windows.

Locate compressor units of central air conditioning and heat pumps in shaded area.

When replacing a roof, choose light colored shingles to reflect sun's heat.

Run kitchen and bath exhaust fans only for eliminating water vapor, smoke and odors.

Wash clothes when only a full load or wash dishes when only a full load.

Eliminate sediment from water heater which insulates the heating element.

Locate water heaters close to places of use. In sprawling ranch house, have two water heaters. (The counselor noticed extreme cost of utility for a small house. Upon questioning, the water heater was located in a garage and not insulated. Moving this saved her $50 per month.)

Use smallest practical diameter for hot water supply pipes and reduce the volume of trapped water.

Use telephone during times when rates are better. Change telephone features for unique usage, overseas, and frequency for reduced rates.

Apply for energy assistance and obtain the weatherization program. "Weatherization measures reduce average annual energy costs by $218 per home," reports the Weatherization Assistance Program. Typical measures include tune-ups and repairs to heating and cooling systems, replacing appliances, installing insulation, reducing air infiltration, and replacing with candescent lighting. Area IV agencies may have their own crew or private contractors to do the installation. Priority services are for the elderly, people with disabilities, and families with children. People who qualify are those within 150 percent of poverty level. For a family of one, that is $15,600; for two, it is $21,000; for three, it is $26,400; and for four it is $31,800. Some states have a source of funds for those needing housing, needing house repairs, or school supplies such as the Township Trustee in Indiana.

Housing Cost Reductions

The shepherd can suggest these changes to reduce costs: Build a house or buy a duplex with two living quarters (kitchens, bath rooms, thermostats, and entry ways). This is an advantage for the recently divorced individual who has to downsize from a house. The change is not so drastic as otherwise. This could save money for a single individual who uses an inheritance to buy the house and the renter in the duplex pays enough to cover the duplex house payment. This enables a young family to have a larger home while a parent (usually) combines his, hers, or their income to buy the house, to be close for both care of parent or babysitting for children while maintaining independence.

The shepherd can help check eligibility for public housing, public assistance programs, senior citizens' programs, federal subsidy for low-income groups, or emergency grants from county, state or federal government. In rural areas there are Farmers Home Administration housing programs. The interest is lower, there is an approved house plan for lower construction costs, and there are other benefits.

The shepherd can help find Title 8 housing or encourage a landlord to get on Title 8 because of the assured payments. To be eligible, the income is to be 80 percent of the median income in the area. The government pays the rent and the low-income individual pays one third of his or her income regardless of rent price.

If the assessed value of property is higher than one thinks reasonable or the individual is not the typical occupant for using the house, the assessed amount can be disputed. This will lower property taxes.

To avoid taking out a second mortgage for maintenance and repair, set aside 2-3 percent monthly of the house market value. Establish a savings account for these large but inevitable occurrences.

Proceeding with Consumer Rights

The covenant in the market place is "Consumer Rights and Responsibilities." Public policy is necessary to "regulate private greed." Market transactions work more smoothly when built on trust, responsibility, and honesty. Because of the brokenness and abuse, Consumer Rights were established by President John Kennedy in 1962, but consumers, businesses, advocates for the poor, financial counselors, clergy, helping professionals, and educators must enforce them. The **Rights** are:

- To make an intelligent choice among products and services
- To have accurate information on which to make a free choice
- To expect that the health and safety of the buyer is taken into account
- To register dissatisfaction, and have a complaint heard and weighed.
- The Right to Service was proclaimed by President Clinton in 1994.
- To provide convenience, courtesy, and responsiveness to consumer problems
- To insure that products and services offer quality and performance levels claimed by them.

Customers have a right to complain, say no, and question insurance companies. People make large financial mistakes but can be forgiven through accepting the consequences, working through them, counseling, prayer, and asking others to forgive them. The clergy, financial counselor, money coach and others responsible for financial change can help write letters of complaint. They can assist by knowing the process for resolving disputes and by shepherding them. The least a counselor can do is to have the client check for errors in Social Security statement of benefits and all three Credit Reports. This reduces the hazard of identity theft.

Shepherd's Role in Consumer Questions. The shepherd promotes peace and justice in the interactions of consumer and business or professionals. Isaiah 26:7 says, "The path of the righteous is level; O upright One, you make the way of the righteous smooth."

The shepherd provides information and procedures about the use of legal services available to low income consumers and of the small-claims court. Read and analyze letters or notices for false threats or promises, fake information, frauds and deceptive practices. The shepherd can suggest alternative solutions to problems with other consumers, landlords, businesses, or professionals. Suggestions include: Refer appropriate concerns to consumer affair offices, state attorney general, legal services, and mediation services. Itemize expenses incurred in obtaining legal services. Be sure to attend a court notice to prevent contempt of court. Suggest alternative procedures to prevent foreclosure, eviction, repossession, and utility cut offs. Know the statutes of limitation for action from a good reference.

The shepherd may have to give steps for obtaining child-support payments: writing letters, harassing, getting wages garnished, going through court to have a record, etc. Explain wage garnishments and situations where lack of income and some types of debt make the individual possibly "judgment proof." (See Chapter 11 on credit.) The shepherd may help decide whether it is worth chasing "bad money" with "good money." The shepherd may have to help the individual realize that his or her being stubborn about a grievance is only hurting oneself not the company. One may need to swallow his or her pride and proceed.

The shepherd can help in a complaint situation by having people write information and collect documentation, empowering them to contact the party involved to discuss the problem with an authoritative representative, and writing letters. The shepherd can advise on writing an effective letter that contains what the complaint is, what will satisfy consumer, who arbitrators are, what the rules are, where they are against the law, and what the company should have done or can do. Make copies of warranties, contracts, sales receipts, canceled checks, billing statements, sales brochures, sales advertisement, model number, serial number, and account number with company. Fair solutions are to repair, replace at a reduced price, or other action.

Communication in Uncertain Times (A Summary)

The shepherd can give advice, teach and encourage. These are gifts to individuals and families when they and/or the economy are in trouble:
- Seeking new opportunities to become resourceful.
- Having the goal of getting more with less.
- Learning to make choices.
- Teaching people to be thankful for what they have instead of wanting more.
- Increasing contentment by comparing with the less fortunate rather those who have more than they do. (There will always be children with more money and children with less money.)
- Teaching the value of money based on someone's sweat, if not currently, another generation's.
- Sharing with others rather than just keeping things, hope or money to themselves.
- Realistic personal allowances with clarified expenditures (and not bailing them out).
- Not leaving children in the dark about what is going on. Adjust level of information depending on their age.
- Showing them there are choices or alternatives.
- Saying "even if we had a million dollars, we would not buy such and such."
- Saying, "If we choose this, we do not have that," or "We choose to spend our money this way for now." This is better than saying "We cannot afford that," which brings negative responses especially when they see money being spent for other things.
- Discussing the reason a child or spouse wants something to discern the underlying need.
- Keeping routines and celebrations to help children and spouse feel secure.
- Assuring children the difficulties are not their fault.
- Reassuring by statements such as, "Times are hard now, but will not last forever. We (or I) will always care for you."

Fear abounds in uncertainty. Confusion abounds in the conflict between commercialism and commitment to an abundant life in God's love, peace, and provisions. The change from seeking abundance in goods and services and wealth to a lifestyle seeking joy and contentment in God's ways is difficult in the details. Yet, people are called to be shrewd in business dealings and decisions. They are warned not to throw their pearls to the swine. These responsibilities in uncertain times require more communication among all generations – young, old, and in between. It calls one not to be seeking good feelings alone. It calls for making wise decisions about goods and services, when and how to buy them to serve God's kingdom. It calls for diversifying sources of security and skills including those around the home, yard, and travel. It calls for tighter holding of the hand of the Heavenly Father as we journey down the uncertain road.

◇◇◇ ⧗   ⧗ ◇◇◇

Chapter 9. **Not Enough Pasture For the Poor With Us**

The shepherd leads his or her people to greener pastures and quiet waters. For some there is not enough pasture, not enough grass. They are in want. The shepherd may be the pastor, priest, rabbi, compassion minister, educator, financial counselor, mentor, helping professional, money coach, distributor of funds, or outreach leader. The purposes of this chapter are to sensitize shepherds to the predicaments of the poor, identify resources available to them, present possible programs for implementation, and show ways to give hope.

Shepherds are called to *do more* than observe, characterize, analyze, and plan a program to ease their guilt. "The Spirit of the Lord is on me, because he has anointed me to preach good news to the poor…" (Luke 4:18). Outcomes are energizing, encouraging, and empowering for both shepherds and those on the path.

Shepherd's Role – Anointed to Give Good News to the Poor

Jesus replied to the disciples when they told him that John the Baptist was in prison, "… Report…the good news is preached to the poor" (Matthew 11:4). And "If you want to be perfect, go sell your possessions and give to the poor" (Matthew 19:21). He acknowledged, "The poor you will always have with you, and you can help them any time you want" (Mark 14:7). Deuteronomy 15:11 tells us, "The poor shall never cease out of the land: therefore I command thee, saying, Thou shalt open thine hand wide unto thy brother, to the poor, and to the needy, in the land." The Psalmist in 82:3-4 directs: "Defend the cause of the weak and fatherless; maintain the rights of the poor and oppressed. Rescue the weak and needy; deliver them from the hand of the wicked."

Shepherds and the more fortunate are called to care and to share. The shepherd can equip those seeking grass to find new pastures. Our prayer includes "our": "Give us our daily bread." Then the Great Shepherd guides for alternatives through talking and referring to the list of community resources. Many shepherds say they do not know how to talk with poor people, probably because they have not visited them, been around them, or included them in the church family as sisters and brothers. The biblical judgment is clear that if we ignore our brother's need, we do not love God as we proclaim. Churches are trapped in middle class America culture and have strayed away, in many cases, from the original mission of preaching good news and giving to the poor.

Out of necessity and faithfulness to the call, the shepherd needs to network and develop working relationships with agencies. These include, for example, the crisis centers, family shelters, and the Salvation Army because they are trained to work with the low-income and have set up good referral and networking systems with other agencies such as pharmacies, landlords, Food Finders, and legal services. They know how to get funding. So rather than the shepherd or church duplicating the efforts, the shepherd can increase communication with other charitable and advocacy organizations. However, the shepherd needs to look for the lost, those falling through the cracks.

Definitions of Poverty

The following poem[82] expresses the issues and how many define poverty:

I'M POVERTY

The masses.
I'm just one of many.
I'm grouped.
I'm not a person, I'm a category
I have problems that are different,
They are mine alone.
They are not the same as everyone else's,
But who cares?
Not the social worker,
I'm a serial number;
Not the sociology student,
I'm a statistic;
Not the taxpayer,
I'm a dollar sign;
Not the congressman,
I'm not a constituent.
They lump me, sum me,
Treat me in generalities.
If it's characteristic of a few,
It's characteristics of all.
No one cares about me,
No one knows me.
Will anyone ever listen to me?
Will there ever be a time when
I'm treated as an individual?
Maybe, but as always,
There's so little hope.

"**Absolute**" **poverty** measures are consistent over time and between countries. It is measured by less food than is required to sustain the human body. It is consuming less than 2000-2500 calories per day. With "absolute" poverty, people lack basic needs to function. In America and other countries, many people, especially the elderly, are forced to choose among food, utilities, and medicine.

By definition there will always be "the poor," since "**relative**" **poverty** is those having less than 50 percent of the median income in a country. Companies and schools are designed for the middle income way to function, so having less than the median income is a hardship. Some students afford schooling but cannot graduate with the expenses required in the ceremony. Relative poverty as percentage of the median income is an index of income inequality. People become unhappy with what they have when they see the majority having more.

There is the "**statistical**" **poverty** which is used to administer most means-tested programs, based on cost of food for various age groups and composition of families. To get the threshold the

---

82   Martha Nall. Graduate student of Flora Williams. Purdue University. 1974.

cost of food for the particular family composition is multiplied times three. This threshold assumes a third of one's income is spent on food costs for a "thrifty" food plan, thus inferring many needs other than food will be unmet. Research of people spending this amount for food has revealed only one of ten actually meet the Recommended Daily Allowances for nutrients. Only one of three on the higher "low cost" food expenditure plan is estimated to meet the RDAs. Shopping and cooking skills as well as knowledge of nutrition are required to meet RDAs at this spending level.

Different agencies, tuition assistance, school lunches, and other programs use different percentages of this poverty level or threshold. For example, the Weatherization program for providing energy efficient remodeling uses the eligibility of 150 percent of the poverty threshold. The U.S. Census Bureau's poverty threshold categorized individuals and households as poor in 2006: one person $10,294, two persons $13, 167, four persons $20,614, nine or more $41,499. In 1980, a one person's threshold was $4,190. As food costs change, the poverty levels change. More details and percentages below poverty for states can be found on the Internet *Statistical Abstract*. A good discussion of poverty can be found on the Internet by typing in low-income.

The worst kind of poverty is absence of hope. The primary purpose of churches is to share "the good news" which is a message of hope. The advantage of churches which provide non-profit services is that they can implement day care centers, housing and youth development programs, job training and placement, food shelves and feeding programs, health clinics, etc. along with hope.[83] Government grants can strengthen the ministry.

Who are the Poor Among Us?

It may be those in a church when they cannot pay the salary of the pastor. It is a grandmother who has to provide for grandchildren when the parents will not or cannot. They may be those on maternity leave, laid off, or injured. It is a college student who gets a scholarship while not having enough money for the living expenses, books and incidentals to stay in school. It is the small Amish grocery store owner whose utilities are $19,000 every two weeks for refrigerating cheese and meat in rural Indiana. It is the elderly couple who have to sell their home because they cannot pay the $5,000 increased property taxes. It is the family where both parents earn minimum wages that do not cover the rent, food, and transportation. It is the family where the father has been sentenced to prison, and, therefore, the whole family is sentenced in the deprivation and the struggles that ensue. It is the young woman who works two low-paying jobs just to sustain herself, leaving little time for church participation. It is the beggar who comes to church for a handout pretending it is going for expenses rather than drink. (In one case, four years later he makes the public confession, joins the church, and continued to invite others to attend.) It is the nursing home resident whose assets have been depleted and now is on Medicaid. It is the single mother with responsibilities she cannot meet, now in danger of losing her child because the social worker sees that her pantry is bare.

Is there a culture of poverty with generations continuing the "cycle"? Some perceive there is a culture of poverty with attitudes and lifestyle and they would answer "yes." Some researchers say "no." They would argue that the only thing in common is that their income is low; or non-existent. Therefore, a more compassionate response is to refer to such people as low-income rather than poor. Others appropriate labels are "those less fortunate than we are" or the "disadvantaged." A new term is "financially challenged." However, higher income families with too many demands,

---

83   Joy Skjegstad. "Starting a Nonprofit at your Church: Drawing more Resources to Meet Community Needs." *The Alban Weekly.* Issue: 250. May 11, 2009.

ignorance or inabilities can also be "financially challenged." Many people will be low-income at one time in their lives. In other words, some people are in and out of poverty as employment, marriage, and other situations change. To address the issue of labeling and different types of poverty, family economists at the Federal Reserve Board use the phrase in their research "low-income and poverty."

Policy makers decide on levels of inadequacy for receiving benefits. When asked how much is enough, Mark Twain replied "Just a little more." Wants expand with income and the challenge continues. More money alone will not solve a mismanagement problem. Observation reveals that income adequacy is dependent on the number of vehicles, size of mortgage and number of children.

Discrimination or Insensitivity

Is there prejudice or discrimination against the poor? Some shepherds demonstrate this by lumping all people of a certain class, vocabulary, and manners into a stereotype and avoiding them or quickly referring them to others. Other churches have met the challenge and purposively include all socioeconomic levels. In some religious groups, socioeconomic status has been leveled in their common purposes. Particularities of people are accepted when the focus is on Christ rather than people as in a social club who must meet certain standards.

Jim, a junior high student, feels discrimination at school. Although he excelled in sports and was excellent in basketball in junior high, a chance to participate on the high school team was denied because he came from a poor neighborhood. He did not have the "connections" and was perceived to not have the extra money for uniforms or other aspects of the team culture. **Ann** was affirmed throughout high school. However, she was not prepared for socioeconomic discrimination in college and exclusion from sororities. In response, she drastically overspent with credit to fit into the college culture.

Sue is a single parent with daughters 15 and 18. She feels the prejudice when the pastor talks only of families in the usual sense and emphasizes families. She is not invited to dinner by other members as the couples are. Although she works at two minor medical administrative jobs, she teaches the Awana group in her church. This keeps her attending that church. Financially and emotionally, she struggles severely to pay the bills. A new pair of shoes is only possible about every 18 months. She knows using credit would be devastating since she can only meet basic, reduced expenses month by month. Her daughters feel the discrimination in subtle ways. Her daughter is working while still in school and receiving vocational training. Sue plans for her daughters to continue living at home so that they will not have to struggle so much. Sue does not want a handout. She wants encouragement as she struggles as a conscientious mother. She needs compliments for managing so well. She wants friendship in the church which would enhance her strength. She keeps going to church reassured that "Jesus is her friend."

Only 50 percent of church attendees are in families as stereotyped or typical. Other people are "nomads" or singles. Singles frequently feel excluded in some churches. Singles are students, not yet married, those in the military, divorced, transients, wanderers, and the elderly. The wanderers may be the shepherd's own children. Some are in the church family. They are the ones who cross people's paths but are ignored by the mainstream of people and not given leadership in the churches.

Single Parents

In both the Old and New Testaments, the mandate is clear to care for the widows and orphans. In our society, they are widows in the churches, wives of military men serving abroad, women without emotional and financial support from anyone, wives of incarnated husbands, and widowed wanderers or homeless. Orphans are the homeless children and youth, those without any parental guidance or support, those with the absence of one parent/grandparent or both, and those ignored by the church and school.

With the onset of "welfare reform" and stringent work requirements, many single-parents do not have time for formal counseling. The results of the "reform" are that some parents are working over 60 hours at two jobs. However, in brief passing, one good idea and encouragement would be useful. Positive personal benefits and income have improved. The concerns for their children remain. The parents have fears about limited time with their children, problems with supervision, and school performance. They report family life is in chaos and time management for household work is a problem.

Dual-parent families have problems similar to single-parent families when a spouse is absent much of the time, is not supportive, is not present to relieve the other parent of care of children or household tasks, or does not give information useful in decisions. Usually two-earner families have more income than single-parent families. Dual-parent families also need acceptance at church in spite of poor appearances and guidance in raising children. They may also need mentoring and skills for everyday activities.

A challenge for the church is to serve in such a way that "Those who have never been told about him (Christ) will see, and those who have never heard of him will understand" (Romans 15:20-21 NLT). It is estimated that 95 percent of single parent families do not regularly attend church.[84] An outreach ministry or a Compassion Circle Ministry, for meeting the practical needs of low-income single parents may include help with: Affordable, quality child care; maintaining an affordable, safe car or having a network of friends or church people to provide transportation when the car needs repair; affordable, safe housing; budgeting and money management; education, job training and career options; affordable, quality professional services and medical care; mentoring for parents and children; food and clothing resources; and spiritual and emotional support.[85] The story is told of an individual seeking help, prayers and counseling from 10 to 20 churches without success. Now centers are established that include financial counseling, financial assistance, food, pregnancy testing and counseling, job training, and pastoral counseling such as Mercy Tree Ministries in Buford, Georgia. These are usually larger churches with a larger "workforce." Pastors or shepherds of a small church need to network with others who can help.

Interventions in the Poverty Cycle

Some generations of families remain in a cycle of lifestyles, attitudes toward education, multiple health problems, and absence of hope from lack of positive role models or religious influences. These are in contrast to those "in" and "out" of poverty or low-income at various ages or stages of the economy. This cycle can start at any point (as can be shown on a circle): the lack

---

84   *Money Matters.* "A Pioneering Opportunity for America's Churches." Crown Financial Ministries. Issue No. 322. December 2004. P.7 1-800-722-1972 or Crown.org/Shop for ordering manuals for church use.

85   Ibid.

or absence of proper food, health, role models, motivation, education, opportunity, employment, and hope. Government initiatives attempt to break the cycle with education, housing, and food programs. Shepherds can mobilize resources provided by the government and give hope with spiritual guidance.

The Shepherd's Intervention in the Poverty Cycle

Shepherds can help break the poverty cycle by assisting at any point on the circle directly or indirectly. The "worst" kind of poverty is absence of hope, which Jesus discussed as being poor in spirit. Jesus' work on earth verified that both physical food and spiritual foods were important and said those carrying on his work would meet both. Since hope gives energy, people can attempt the other aspects of the cycle. Shepherds can inspire courage and provide the process for obtaining other aspects of the cycle.

The author of Hebrews reminds: "Do not forget to entertain strangers, for by so doing some people have entertained angels without knowing it. Remember those in prison as if you were their fellow prisoners, and those who are mistreated as if you yourselves were suffering" (Hebrews 13:2-3). In discussing the ministries of the early apostles, Paul reminds: "All they asked was that we should continue to remember the poor, the very thing I was eager to do" (Galatians 2:10).

The shepherd can encourage the individual to take action with courage. At the minimum, the shepherd can pray with the person and provide information about referrals and agencies. Other activities and encouragement can be delegated to deacons, mentors, compassion ministers, educator, money coaches, or other individuals to handle. Some churches have a program designed for the helper, "new shepherd" that has been recovered or restored in the past to take this responsibility as a mentor. Accountability is built in the process regardless of who shepherds.

Possible assistance by the shepherd, compassion minister, educator, mentors, etc. are:
- Getting a job perhaps through people in the church.
- Giving advice on how to change appearance or language for the new culture involved with a new job.
- Caring for an elderly person's home, food and yard in exchange for use of car and housing.
- Sharing an apartment or house with someone, becoming a housemother or housefather.
- Finding a group home.
- Exchanging services or tools with other families. An illustration of exchange is Bob's case. Bob needed his brakes repaired but did not money for that. He had a painting service. The counselor suggested he find a mechanic who needed his sign repainted or a new sign in exchange for repair of the breaks.
- Increasing income by renting a garage or barn, getting money owed them, getting early inheritance.
- Arranging for Carrier Alert for mail carriers to check on them daily, buying or having someone buy for them a pendant that is connected to the hospital in case of crime, falling, emergency, etc. These last two items can allow persons to stay in their own homes and gives a sense of security.
- Informing people of details of programs available from lists self-developed or available from community resources. The shepherd encourages them to apply for assistance, meeting the due dates.

- Utilizing nonprofit consumer credit counseling services, HUD relocation services, State Cooperative Extension Service, and homeless prevention programs.
- Explaining agencies with locations, times, and brief qualifications written clearly.
- Assisting in filling out forms.

Assistance is needed considering that only about 50 percent of those qualified for food stamps actually get them.[86] "Nationally, only 15 percent of eligible families use child care subsidies made available to them through the state welfare system."[87] A high percentage of qualified people do not use state insurance programs for prescriptions, Medicaid, EIC (Earned Income Credit), or professionals who would take "charity" cases. Many college scholarships go unused. Why? They do not know they qualify, they do not have the forms, they feel the small amount of food stamps received do not justify absence from work. They are embarrassed and they fear filling out forms. In the counseling office, the shepherd can start the process and remind people to follow through. Starting the process or a phone call increases the likelihood of following through. Reluctance can be overcome when recipients are told how their taxes have already paid for the assistance or will when they are working again. Reluctance to use a food pantry may be overcome by suggesting that some day recipients can contribute to the pantry.

- Warning people of possible hassles, insults and obstacles in getting assistance.
- Providing transportation or giving bus tokens.
- Assigning or connecting a money coach or mentor to an individual who needs assistance in changing everyday patterns, i.e. cooking, budgeting, and shopping behavior. Education, accountability and encouragement occur on a one-to-one basis. The Nutrition Aid program found success was enhanced when the Aid or "coach" himself or herself had been in poverty and successfully moved on to educate others.
- Arranging for the individual or family to be a part of a support group, New Focus, or a church group.
- Participating in Habitat for Humanity.
- Arrange for transportation to thrift stores or Goodwill to get clothes for employment.

The individual may need assistance to safely get out of a group, gang or association without getting killed. Support is needed to say "no" to friends who are pressuring the person to buy certain things, do certain things, or continue addictions.

The Shepherd as Part of a Team

A good shepherd is a good networker and part of a team. Shepherds who have extremely busy schedules, already, can set up programs from the many possibilities new shepherds to lead. They can mobilize resources in the individual, family, and community.

The team is composed of directors and counselors of community agencies prepared to assist in meeting the material and spiritual needs for all types of people. Getting acquainted informally and formally can clarify what each has to offer. The tools include regular contact with key players, brochures, up-to-date lists, etc. .

---

86   Flora L. Williams. Effect of Policy Change upon Reallocation of Resources: The Case of the Food Stamp Program. *Review of Social Economy*. Vol. XLV, No. 2. October. 1987. Pp. 200-208.

87   Thomas S. Weisner, Christina Gibson, Edward D. Lowe, and Jennifer Romich. "Understanding Working Poor Families in the New Hope Program. *Poverty Research News*. Vol. 6, No. 4. P.4.

Referrals

During the certification process for WIC (Women, Infants, and Children,) the health professional is required to make the appropriate referrals to health and/or social services. These may include, not limited to, First Steps, Healthy Families, Early Head Start, Head Start, Cooperative School Extension, Food and Nutrition Program, Community Action Program, Workforce One, Township Trustees, Childcare Assistance, Food Pantries, Families United, Drug and Alcohol Abuse Centers, Planned Parenthood, Christian Nursing Services, Women's Resource Centers, and Health Departments. The health professional is also required to refer participants to the Department of Family and Children Services if they appear to be eligible for Medicaid, Food Stamps, and/or TANF (Temporary Assistance for Needy Families).

Referral goes both ways. The shepherd refers people to agencies and agencies refer their clients to churches for spiritual and social programs. The shepherd assures the people under his or her care that the church welcomes participants involved in agency programs, since most recognize the importance of the holistic approach. A brochure can be distributed to this effect. For example, welcome would be those in transitional housing, prisoners on parole, those in a mental institution, vocational rehabilitation, disabled, those limited in outside activities because of receiving disability, those under house arrest, etc. Most of these people do not feel welcome or comfortable in most churches, although the Scripture tells of inviting them to the banquet (Matthew 22:1-14, Luke 14:12-14). The banquet is the worship service, social life of the church, ball team, pot-luck dinner, and the entertainment. Beggars can be brought into the fold, into the banquet, not just referred to another agency or a clearing house for agency participants.

Invitation and Assistance

The Scriptural mandate is clear. "But when you give a banquet, invite the poor, the crippled, the lame, the blind, and you will be blessed. Although they cannot repay you, you will be repaid at the resurrection of the righteous" (Luke 14:13-14). When it is time for the distribution of inheritance prepared since the creation of the world, the King will say, "Take your inheritance, for I was hungry and you gave me something to eat, I was thirsty and you gave me something to drink, I was a stranger and you invited me in, I needed clothes and you clothed me, I was sick and you looked after me, I was in prison and you came to visit me" (Matthew 25:34-36). When the righteous answered, "When did we do this?" the King replied, "I tell you the truth, whatever you did for one of the least of these brothers of mine, you did for me."(Verse 40) or "Whatever you did not do for one of the least of these, you did not do for me" (verse 45). In Acts, there are several references to giving to the poor, in Galatians 2:10 to remembering the poor, and in James 2:6 comes a warning about insulting the poor.

Some helping professionals only know their agency's service and not what is available from other agencies. Hence, the shepherd's need to work with the team approach and willingness to learn. Shepherds of any type need to go the second mile showing possibilities outside their scope of services. For example, beyond the usual seeking of financial aid, one can seek the unusual scholarships available, assistance from a parent's employer, an individual who would start a scholarship, or internships created for the first time. One could start at a community college and later transfer to a more expensive one. There are now scholarships for first time students of their family to attend college.

There is a story of an engineer laid off from the steel mills who had a daughter with unusual skating ability. He could not continue the lessons, clothes, travel, etc. He found a local organization to sponsor her as the pride of their city.

Government Intervention in the Poverty Cycle with Programs

The shepherd has a list of programs and resources with office hours, telephone numbers, and eligibility to direct those who ask for any type of help, or do not ask. The shepherd may receive clues that information on addiction programs is needed. To not embarrass or reveal a secret, the shepherd can say, "We go through the list as routine for everyone and have brochures on various programs. You would not want us if we were a medical doctor to assist in a bad elbow and ignore the cancer growing on your face. Therefore, we take the holistic approach." A possible list or brochures are:

- Supplemental Security Income for low-income elderly, disabled and blind. Individuals can receive both SSI and Social Security if benefits are low enough
- Individual Development Account (IDA) for low-income people to save and receive $2-7 return on the dollar. Loans through area councils on aging for education, housing, or starting a business.
- Food Stamp Program with expedited stamps order through the Internet and available within five days or the monthly food stamp program.
- Free school lunches, reduced school lunches, and breakfast. Application for these can be at any time.
- Food banks and food pantries operated by unions, churches, and other community groups. Reports show that food stamp requests have doubled in the last year (2008). By using food assistance, money can be freed for other bills for which help is not readily available. When suddenly unemployed, people wonder what they will do. Handing them a list of low-cost and high-nutritional food that can be purchased and will last for a month can be helpful. Learning to cook can help avoid that whatever money is left is not gobbled up at a fast food place. (Example: Buy potatoes rather than potato chips and six dozen eggs for the month to stretch food stamps.) Shopping savvy can be learned. See Chapter 8 on "Leading to Greener Pastures."

Financial counselors in family services in the military, in consumer credit counseling services, independent services, and in university clinics report that teaching clients to cook and to carry lunches is most valuable and helpful in reducing expenses. Lists of food ideas for stretching food stamps as well as encouragement are helpful. Ideas for meals for those without refrigeration or cooking facilities can improve health, save money, and encourage.

Just as Jesus had to tell the disciples how to feed the masses, the shepherd can encourage someone to give the gift of taking hungry people to the food pantries. Just as for other programs, the shepherd can inspire those to give a special ministry in mentoring, "walking along with," filling out forms or providing transportation to get public and church assistance. Resources in the community include the following:

- Well-being or women's health clinics, monthly visit to emergency room of hospital, free vaccination at fire station, etc.

- Housing assistance, Neighborhood Housing Association, getting subsidized housing or Section Eight housing, or providing Section Eight housing as landlord. (In this program the low-income pays one-third of income regardless of the amount of rent.)

- Unemployment Compensation.

- State Employment Offices and services.

- Job Corps, free education and training program for youth 16 to 24, helps youth learn a career, earn a high school or GED, find a job, and maintain a job.

- Legal Services, Legal Aid.

- Temporary Assistance to Needy Families (TANF).

- CHIP (Children's Health Insurance Program) through Medicaid initially but expanded for higher income families in 2009.

- Women, Infants & Children (WIC) Program.

- In Child Care Centers through the Division of Family Resources funded by federal and statement dollars for child care on a sliding scale fee within limits of space and funding.

- Community Health Clinic with mental health or psychological counseling at a university, military base, or in the local community.

- Alcoholics Anonymous, Smokers Anonymous or Over Spenders Anonymous.

- Student Military Health Center.

- Job Corps for evaluation, counseling, training, and career preparation for youth aged 16 to 24.

- Public libraries for computer use and programs. Check out free videos.

- Pell Grants for students with low-income. (See Chapter 6 on Decisions.)

- Tuition assistance. (Purdue University offers a "Promise" program whereby a family of four under $40,000 (for example) promise students can graduate debt-free.)

- Scholarships for camps, recreational activities, memberships, music lessons.

- (The father took his 10 year old to meet the bus on time for summer camp. Unhappily he learned then he was supposed to register a month earlier. Therefore assist people to know the due dates for enrollment.)

- Sources of clothes such as Goodwill, Salvation Army and some churches.

- Church sponsored program such as Love, Inc. with volunteers to check the vehicle before taking it to a mechanic.

- Weatherization program usually through the Area Council on Aging which installs energy efficient construction and products or does upgrades to improve energy efficiency.

- Furniture and appliances from used items stores, second-hand stores, and Habitat for Humanity stores.

- Local banks and credit unions to make available free, no-minimum-balance savings accounts that participants can use.

- Free activities for fun as a family, advertised in libraries, the Friday edition of the newspaper, and participation in church classes and activities.

New programs are being created in this economy's crisis. Communication about availability is confusing. Some government programs and benefits have been cut or reduced because of government policies and lack of funding. Some under the stimulus package have increased such as Pell Grants and buying a house. Some funded by endowments are lost because of reduced return on investments. The burden of helping those in crisis and in need will shift more to the churches. To survive the current crisis, all segments of society need to unite, communicate, and pull together. Individuals will need to contribute more to food banks and pantries.

Income Sources and Resources

Supplemental Security Income

This is a federal program for aged, blind, and disabled with limited income and resources. Rules change and program cuts occur. Therefore, the counselor needs to know enough to ask questions and to know someone who knows. A case study explains some procedures and issues for counseling: **Jim** who is disabled asked if he should try to get better employment. Jim is receiving $512 per month from the SSI benefit plus Medicaid and Food Stamps. If he earns more than $1,089 through employment, Jim would lose SSI and Medicaid. His withholdings from his paycheck are temporary since he will receive an Earned Income Credit. As with other programs, there are formulas used in deciding how much more an individual can earn without losing benefits. (There are asset limitations also.) In counting income to get SSI, the first $20 per month is subtracted, the first $65 of earned income is subtracted, and half of the amount over $65 per month is subtracted. In Jim's case, for illustration, assuming 40 hours per week or 160 hours/month, he could make $6.81 per hour and get SSI and Medicaid. For 100 hours, Jim could earn $10.89 per hour. If he earned $8.00/hour for 160 hours, Jim would earn $1,280 and lose SSI and benefits. If he worked half time, 80 hours/month, and earned $7.00 per hour he would earn about $560 per month plus keep half his SSI of $250 for a total of $840, which is more income than he currently has.

Temporary Assistance for Needy Families

TANF is a state grant program administered for emergency assistance, work-related assistance, job opportunities, and basic skills program. There are many rules and regulations for compliance. Usually the program is limited to no more than two years. The program requires individuals to sign a Personal Responsibility Agreement (in Indiana). For a minor parent residing with a parent, the agreement is not having more children, children getting immunizations, ensuring regular school attendance, raising children in a safe environment, not using illegal drugs, participating in all employment and training, not quitting job, not committing fraud, developing a self-sufficiency plan, and complying with all requirements. Violations result in sanctions, such as loss of cash benefits and Medicaid. Some people would rather die or not take sanctions than change. They do not want a job which is unappealing. They are hoping for jobs that do not exist or are out of reach.

Earned Income Credit

EIC is a refundable federal tax credit, state and federal, available for low-income working people. Unclaimed funds remain in the U.S. Treasury. A survey of a college class taught by the author revealed that many are eligible while not aware of it. If at least one person is working and family income is below $39,783 for the 2007 year (filing jointly with two children), they could receive as much as $4,716. A single person with income under $12,500 could receive a maximum of $428. EIC can be received monthly by contacting the employment business office. Up-to-date guidelines for income and size of family are available.[88]

Tax Preparation

Several volunteer agencies that provide free tax preparation can be cited. Some low-income families lose money by insisting on rapid returns or paying preparers who can advance the refund. These arrangements, however, charge an extremely high percentage of the refund. Some projects help people open bank accounts for direct deposit of their tax refunds. The Tax Counseling Project uses trained volunteers at convenient locations. Contact tcp@centerforprogress.org.

Legal Services or Legal Aid

The shepherd can distribute brochures describing legal services available to low-income individuals and families. Free legal representation or advice may be available in civil cases. The shepherd can know the attorney and paralegal and what specific legal services the programs in the community provide. The pastor may have professionals in the congregation who may give their services, part of Pro Bono responsibility.

The shepherd should be aware of and have available free informational material, making sure it is from a legitimate source. Legal Aid and Legal Services offices, Pro Bono programs, local bar associations, and court programs may provide advice, referral services, or even representation in certain cases. Courts in some areas have even been involved in the creation of self-service legal forms for use by unrepresented litigants. Of course, as shepherds refer clients to available resources, he or she must be aware of the danger of the unauthorized practice of law. It is easy to do more harm than good, despite the best intentions.

In Indiana, brochures and materials from Legal Services are available for several areas of law: public benefit (Medicaid, Disability, Supplemental Security Income, and food stamps), landlord tenant law, consumer law, and family law. Just knowing the law and citing it can help deal with landlord-renter disputes. The shepherd can get pamphlets and books to have available for those in trouble.

Of course, due to the great need, free legal representation is most often not available. However, in the case of domestic violence, many providers have identified this as a priority for assistance.

Information about Small Claims Court are available. Fear is reduced by knowing the potential steps, action, and costs involved. Action is prompted by knowing what could be done. One counselor had a client who had his antique car hit and the small claims court decided against him. The counselor looked in the manual and saw that the next day was the final one for the client appealing the case. He did, and this time he won.

---

88   See Publication #596. "Earned Income Credit (EIC)" for detailed examples, eligibility requirements, and advance EIC in the paycheck. This information is available on the Internet by typing Earned Income Credit.

Health Care

The shepherd knows how to make direct contact with doctors and dentists who take charity cases. At the least, the shepherd knows the public health or community nurse who can be helpful in where and how to obtain medical services, vaccinations, financial assistance for certain chronic illnesses, sliding fees for psychiatric services, free baby clinics, etc. Brochures can be obtained about Medicaid, low-income insurance, Medicare, Disability Benefits through Social Security, State Children's Health Insurance Program (CHIP) and other government programs. The shepherd needs to have a direct contact, maybe an attorney in the church, who can answer questions about process. Many people depend on stop-gap, short-term, or only major medical insurance. Many low-income families also depend on the use of emergency services. Low-income under Medicaid are allowed to use these free of charge, once a month in some states. If not on this program it is usually less costly to use "Urgent Care" than the emergency room in most cities.

Notwithstanding their low wages, uncomfortable work situation, and/or enduring pain, some people are employed just to get health care benefits for themselves and their family members. A high percentage of low-paying jobs do not provide any benefits. A proposal to expand Medicaid to include low-income businesses is currently underway.

Hospitals built with federal funds are obligated to treat low-income within limits of quantity served. The problem is to ask for this program before treatment begins. There be a small sign that says "Hill Burton funds." The shepherd needs to alert those under his/her care about these and inform them of the procedures.

Comparison shopping is illustrated in Ellen's search for prescription drug coverage. She met the income eligibility requirements in her state. The computer program asked her to type in her prescribed medicine. From several possibilities, she chose Medicarix. It is a state insurance program with a monthly fee of $13.10. The most she pays is $1.05 for a generic medicine and $3.60 for the name brands. Some pharmacies in retail stores advertise cost of any prescription medicine for $4.00.

Housing

Professionals, part of the team, in Neighborhood Housing, Subsidized housing, Housing Development, and the Farmers Home Administration for rural families have or know of low-income housing programs. These contacts are valuable and also educate the shepherd in the eligibility of these programs. Counselors can learn on the job about services, qualifications and processes as needed. Shepherds need to know enough and care enough to give alternatives when someone asks a question or seems to need a service, even if they do not ask. For instance, contacting the director of the agency and explaining the individual's need can possibly place him or her higher on the list for housing. Response to a radio talk show about housing for a single-parent, the only answer was "to pray about." Alternatives in this book could have been used in the response.

One counseling mandate is to consider housing that is on a bus line to employment or within walking distance for at least one member of the family. This could reduce job-related expenses and should be considered in choosing a job.

Educational Intervention in the Poverty Cycle

Most people receiving food stamps receive little, if any, education about shopping, preparation, storage, and cooking food. Although this seems an obvious shortfall of this government program, the shepherd or church outreach director can suggest resources available through the local Cooperative Extension office, nutrition aid program, or a few publications. Most people could save hundreds of dollars per month if they shopped wisely, cooked creatively, and enjoyed boring, repetitive basic foods. Some simple rules for financial survival would be: no alcoholic or soft drinks, no processed foods, no fast foods, no bottled water, and no chips.

The discovery years ago that "the poor pay more" still holds true today. Low-income neighborhoods and remote rural areas do not have supermarkets and bargain stores. The use of credit stores, payday lending, rapid cash, etc. results in paying more for services. Buying in small, uneconomical quantities costs more. Lack of cash precludes taking advantage of good garage sale bargains. Quality lower-cost items wear out faster and the need to be replaced. Greater costs are incurred when people are subjected to fraud and deceptive practices. These include "bait and switch," referral selling, misrepresentation of prices, and substitution of inferior goods. Local, small retailers, often low-income themselves, are financially hurt when people buy from discount stores or in quantities from large stores.

Giving More than Money

The church or the shepherd can give more than entitlement programs. With "welfare reform," the theme is "from welfare to workfare." The theme changed from government dependency for well-being to personal responsibility, from thinking entitlements to meeting mandates to employment. The themes reflect the United Nation's motto of "Give a man a fish and you feed him for a day. Teach a man to fish and you feed him for a lifetime." This is a theme for counseling when helping people to deal with both crises and material deprivation as a way of life. The policy, the mandate, when giving something to someone, the beggar at the door, a church member in need, or anyone is to offer some education and spiritual hope. Although brief, the shepherd's words, love and respect can change lives and actions.

Employment Intervention in the Cycle

Federal and state agencies and Job Corps exist to work with hard-to-employ individuals. They provide training or arrange referrals to temporary employment agencies. Testing and evaluation are part of the program. Counseling to maintain a job is given. Most agencies are eager to tell of their services and work with the shepherd as a team member on a particular case. A prospective employer may be more willing to take risks with marginal people when he or she knows the shepherd is providing some support also.

Temporary employment has resulted in jobs for other low-income people. They are subject to the chronic problems of low wages and job instability. Workers, especially single parents, may have everything going smoothly for months and then something "blows up." There is a legal custody problem, a health crisis, or emergency household repair. Work life is so disturbed that the job is lost.

Mobilizing Resources

The goal of the shepherd is to mobilize resources of all types within the individual, the family, and the community. The shepherd carries a two-edged sword to pierce poverty. On the one side, the shepherd inspires, informs and trains members of his or her group or church to seek programs for which to volunteer. On the other hand, the shepherd counsels directly, one to one, to anyone who comes down the path. (Perhaps the person was sent by God or an angel disguised.) Therefore, ideas below are utilized for both. Mobilizing resources includes mobilizing individuals in the church to seek programs for the poor, the young, and the elderly to alleviate suffering and give hope. Many individuals are seeking counseling, education, and activities in a church to alleviate their trauma or loneliness, whereas in seeking to help the poor they help themselves gain purpose and fulfillment. For example, church members can volunteer for the Community Transition Program administered by the corrections department of every county where court-ordered participants are helped to get jobs, eye glasses, a bike and contact with other agencies.

Mobilizing Resources for Marvin

Marvin walked into the employment agency. The application form asked him about his transportation and where he lived. Since he marked "none" and his residence was 20 miles away, the employment counselor denied any help. Marvin's path took him to the pastoral counselor who asked him other questions and pointed out possibilities. Personally asking questions gives more information than formal procedures. His health, strengths, resources, interests, and abilities were revealed. Marvin had walked 20 miles from the neighboring city to the employment office. He was repairing an old car which would soon work. He had an aunt in the city with whom he could stay for a while in return for repairing her windows and doing other odd jobs. He was flexible in learning new trades. His honesty and shyness had prevented him from marketing himself earlier, but with the pastoral counseling, identifying his strengths and employment possibilities, he became successful.

Setting Policies about Giving to Strangers and Members

Policies the church or agency set are guides and vary with beliefs, interpretations of Scripture, experience and resources. Diversified and contradictory policies are:

1) Leaders in outreach programs or the one distributing funds require accountability and responsibility, demonstrating "real" need on the part of the poor. They give or share with those who demonstrate real need and are responsible and accountable, proving worthiness of help. They expect changes, and deny continual requests. They may quote Jesus when he said, "Take up your bed and walk" or "Then neither do I condemn you, Jesus declared. "Go now and leave your life of sin" (John 8:11).

2) In contrast, other church policies are based on Jesus' example of not documenting income before he gave help. They help those who do not ask although they appear to be in need, regardless of their lifestyle. They reach out as Jesus reached out to the fallen, and the unclean. They just give money with no questions or strings attached. They err on the side of compassion taking the risk of being bothered or taken advantage of. They are reminded that Jesus was thanked by only 10 percent of those he healed (Luke 17:15-16).

3) Another controversial policy is to give some education and spiritual uplifting along with money. The policy is to express that sharing is in the name of Jesus. With the gift, they exclaim how all gifts come from God and that He is working in their lives by this gift. The policy is to help them rejoice over the good things God has done and tell others.

4) The conventional 80-20 rule in management is to spend 80 percent of time on the 20 percent of the people that are "important" or contributing to church, whereas Jesus' way is working with

and giving to the "least of these." Ask, "Who is God sending me today?" rather than thinking what a nuisance this individual is.

5) Accountability is required as a policy. Arrangements or persons are set up for accountability. This requires growth in the Body, however. With a "sense of entitlement," money that is given is spent on wants. Then requests come for rent money or medication. Those who do not want accountability move on.

6) Some people carry oat bars rather than money to give to beggars.

7) In Brazil, homeless children are beaten by their master if they have not stolen or acquired enough for the day. Knowing something of the system in which the poor person operates helps one to determine his or her personal response. One time, Matt gave his sandwich to a child who tapped him on the elbow. Promptly, the booth owner gave Matt a free sandwich.

8) Policies for procedures for a program need to be established. The first time someone requests assistance from the compassion fund, for example, no questions are asked. Then, after three times, counseling and referral are required. The mercy minister gives time, energy, and knowledge not just money. Usually checks are written directly to landlords, utility companies, pharmacies, etc. However, giving $25 is not going to help much in a $400 utility bill. A call to the utility company can indicate effort is being made.

9) Does the heart have suspicion and skepticism or does it have compassion? In other words, when one sees someone begging or asking do we say "no" because we would be supporting fraud or deception, or do we say "yes" because we share as part of family, bringing the beggar into the fold (the banquet).

Bottom[89] wrote, "He is always there during daylight hours, standing near a busy corner. Near him is a crudely lettered sign that reads, 'Unemployed. Homeless. Please help." Most who pass turn their heads and ignore his plea. Some say, "He's too lazy to work. He probably takes his money to the nearest bar and spends it on liquor.' My wife is one of the few who gives him money. She refuses to judge him. 'Begging is not an easy way to avoid work. He's there on the hottest and coldest days as well as the rainy days, with nothing to shield him from the weather. And he's humiliated because more people make abusive remarks and even laugh at him than offer him help.' The thought was that the poor represent an opportunity to give in love as God gives to us."

10) A policy may be following the nudges of the Spirit in hopes it is part of a larger plan even if we are not sure what it is. Christ may be working in the crisis. **Mary** recalls her time in Africa as a missionary. She was helping Mbodie, a young man, in his marriage to his fifth wife. His rented car was impounded because it broke down and daily he was charged by the rental agency. Mary finally paid for Mbodie to get his car back. Results? Although Mbodie has not become a Christian, although two of the wives have and are taking their children to church. Mary thinks God prompted her pay the car expenses. She stays tuned to the Spirit for deciding who to help.

10) A policy may be based on the assumption that there are people who are "takers" and those who are "givers." One could judge and say we will only help the "givers" and who are responsible. As one person said, "They are in our church as we know them as 'brothers' and can trust them." (That there are no "moochers" in some families in the church is a false assumption.)

11) A policy could be to help the "takers" become "givers." The policy may include that the joy of earning income eventually is the real joy, not just getting. It assumes anyone can work at something

---

89   Raymond Bottom. *The UpperRoom*. June 23, 2004. P. 61.

and be productive. It is supporting the "Protestant Work Ethic" and has not room for other lifestyles.

12) A policy could be that the "givers" would also give hope, education, and responsible activities to those whom they give. Young children and especially youth (and older people) who are backwards or irresponsible would be given some responsibility for someone or something in the church or group setting. They can feel accepted and mature in the responsibilities. They would follow the teaching in Acts 3:6: "Then Peter said, 'Silver or gold I do not have, but what I have I give you. In the name of Jesus Christ of Nazareth, walk.'"

Sharing Church Resources for Strangers and Members

Traditionally in some churches there is a "Deacon's Fund" to help those in need. Others have an "outreach fund" or "Mercy Ministries." Some call the leader "Administrator of Compassion Funds." Some have "Stephen Ministers."[90] Many churches support financially the centers where funds, counseling and mentoring are available. Others set up counseling sessions, such as in New Focus, where lessons are taught, trained volunteers are financial coaches, and some money is given. Some have "Bread of Life Ministry," which provides meals after surgery or a hospital stay. Some get people to use community resources rather than giving money directly, such as Meals on Wheels.

The Spirit leads the way for counselors to provide timely resources and organize those in the church to be prepared for emergencies. An illustration is the "Back to School Crisis." A few procedures are: Arrange for free school lunches, check early with township trustee (or whoever) provides books and supplies, get clothing at thrift shops or discount stores, trade goods and services with friends, and belong to a cooperative. Other examples of practical help are staying with children after school, arranging car pooling for taking children to school, getting vaccinations and physical examinations from community referral nurse or paramedics, paying partial car insurance, and advising parents to start a schedule of healthy sleeping and eating a week before school starts.

Some families report that they "get by" while not having money for "fun together," entertainment, and camp. Here is where the counselor can point out the free activities listed in the newspaper, using free from the library rather than buying videos, and scholarships from the YWCA or YMCA. Some need to be encouraged to cut out channels on the TV. Computers are available in the library for school assignments.

In surveys, mothers report family and friends make everyday lives more manageable. One woman stated, "The people in my church, especially the pastor and his wife have been very helpful. They have kids, and they go through all the same things…they can give you a good objective opinion about things to do."[91]

Sharing the Gifts

Members in the group have gifts to share with the less fortunate if they are asked to sign on a list, perhaps annually. They may share if asked by the director of outreach in the church or a local organization which coordinates (clears) these activities. Examples are: cutting hair for someone

---

90   The Stephen Ministry provides training and organizing lay people to provide one-to-one Christian care to hurting people in and around the congregation.

91   Elaine A. Anderson, Bonnie Braun, Linda Oravecz, and Juloie Kohler. "Rural Motyers Soeak: About Relationships." Maryland Policy Brief. 2004.

seeking employment, diagnosing car problems before it is taken to a mechanic, repairing a door or roof, inspecting an electrical problem, providing foster child or elder care for a difficult individual, sharing a row of vegetables, cleaning house for a few hours, providing emergency child care, taking someone to work at the last minute when the car fails, helping a child with school work, giving $50 for an emergency, providing transportation in emergencies, taking someone to the gas station for necessary fuel, installing or planning energy conservation measures for the elderly, taking a family member to visit someone in prison, praying for another or grieving with them, boarding a stranger in the house for the night, volunteering at the homeless shelter, driving the person to the hospital in another city when needed, and providing other gifts that are their specialty or involve their time.

A compassionate prosecutor did not file charges on a poor man with a large family as long as he was in financial counseling sessions. He had made promises to pay in emergencies and when he was relocating. The motel manager, food establishment, and gas station attendant trusted him. He did not repay since he had not enough money.

The Shepherd Guides in Counseling

As reported from the experiences of a family shelter program, most of the people on low-income assistance do not receive psychological or financial counseling enough to change patterns. The shepherd with basic counseling could fill this gap rather than quickly refer them to counselors who charge a fee. The shepherd could mobilize professionals or skilled workers to donate time to counseling, have a list, or call them for those who need it. The shepherd should understand the crisis intervention process. He or she should notice symptoms of post traumatic stress and intervene for positive changes. Available sources of counseling at low or reduced fees in the community should be provided. The shepherd of the flock cares for the ones that stray, even the wanderers, even those in his own family.

Low-income families may have someone with a special need for which they cannot afford help. One may have psychological disorders or be extremely gifted. They do not know where to obtain affordable services. As a team member, shepherds know where free or sliding scale fees are available. They also know members in the congregation who can donate a few hours per month. The local Family and Child Protective Services usually offer programs and counseling on a variety of subjects.

How can the shepherd support Evelyn, a church member, who recently has assumed the care of her two grandchildren? First, by understanding her financial pressures and emotional strain. Then by praying with her, reading Psalms together, and mobilizing church or community resources as Evelyn grieves and makes financial decisions. Evelyn was in shock and felt beaten herself as she saw her daughter come into the courtroom in shackles. It was as if she were in shackles. Evelyn's daughter was sentenced to 20 years for cocaine dealing. The whole family was sentenced in one way or another. At first she got $200 month from TANF. Then she got a job as a receptionist at a beauty salon since she was to care for her grandchildren. She participated in a first time home buyer's program. The state made the down payment and paid the closing costs. Since her husband died in Vietnam, she got a Veteran's Administration loan at 5 ½ percent. Her house payment is $670 per month including insurance and taxes. She used the food pantry at first. She qualifies for a day care subsidy of $85 per week per child. However, as in other programs that sounds good but only a few slots are available. For $8 a month she is on Medicaid, certified semi-annually. Now she is off of TANF and receives no child support from the children's father, no WIC, and no food stamps. She was able to enroll her junior-high grandson in a sport. (Usually the uniforms and fees make this prohibitive.) It is too hard to manage extra curricula activities for both children. Evelyn tried getting support from the YMCA, but she found the application was too intrusive and revealing. Fortunately, a local university had an eight week sports program free of charge. She heard that the Brian Fellowship is a resource for grandkids.

One way to get started in financial counseling is to ask the client to list income and expenses. Otherwise, the presenting problem may take too much time and conversation will go in circles. The real problem may surface in the listing of income and expenses. A negative balance is a problem in itself but it gives an opportunity to question what unusual expense is occurring and why. The type of income can reveal the client's situation. Some people have income they do not want to disclose that would explain a negative balance. Not knowing expenses is also revealing. Detailed records may have to be kept for a week to analyze where possible changes can be made. Records of expenses form a basis for discussion, not judgment. However, they may reveal lifestyle, ignorance, real struggles, and items that could be substituted by something less expensive or acquired in a different way. Rather than cutting out, limitations or substitutions can be tried. An example was when Sally's expenses revealed an enormous amount for soft drinks. The student-counselor erred when she said, "Cut this out." Visiting in a non-threatening way with another counselor, Sally revealed that she had been an alcoholic and her psychiatrist told her to substitute drinking Coke. The wise counselor told Sally where she could get Coke for less than where she was buying it.

Sometimes counselors need to be more compassionate than mathematical when discussing what to "cut out." The family may be down to the bare bones and cupboard may be bare, so he or she must be careful not to insult them further. Think twice before saying, "Get rid of the dog" when that is the only friend the poor boy has.

Although the counselee starts with the "presenting problem," the counselor responds at a different point. The counselor starts at point further back or at the real, non-verbalized question behind the presenting problem. For example, if the refrigerator has broken down, the request may be for replacement. The basic problem is safe storage of food. Then alternatives are addressed including non use of a refrigerator.

The shepherd or designated leader for the outreach ministry assists individuals in getting a job. Announcements can be made to the church family, which has prospective employers or jobs could be created at the church or member's businesses. Individuals with low-income themselves can be effective in working with the poor.

The shepherd or leader for outreach needs to help people learn social skills and responsibilities of a work environment. Their language may have to be modified. Time schedule may have to be adjusted and controlled. Taking insults and bad humor may have to be overcome. Proper appearance may have to be shown. Office politics, unsympathetic employers, criticisms, and emotions have to be handled. New employees experience non-acceptance, being laughed at, bullied or ridiculed even if they do not admit it. They need to be taught acceptable responses to these affronts such as abstaining from hitting another co-worker. In some jobs such as day care, a person should be warned to not use foul or substandard English. On the other hand, helpful steps include establishing a telephone check at a designated time when children return from school, with the supervisor's permission.

Conversation that Counts, Cures

The "way" to talk to poor people is first with the orientation that whomever you are talking with at the time is the most important in the world. You can learn from anyone. Some can explain the "system" to you. Some have street smarts. You can pray, "God, what are you trying to teach through me? How are you, God, working through them to come to me?" After you have heard their story, try to get past that. Ask, "What can we do beyond that?" (However, those who have been deeply wounded do need to be listened to enough that they feel "heard." Then try to get beyond hearing the same story week after week by deciding what to *do* differently. Ask "What is the real story?" Let them know that you have been in a crisis, and it has not always been so easy for yourself. The choice is to sit and stew (a pity party) or to take action. Ask what they *think* could be changed. Analyze barriers and how to overcome them. Give them opportunity to set goals. Give them something else to focus on.

How do we talk to the poor? Just like to our peers rather than *down to them*. The words come from the heart, so first we have to change the heart to think of the stranger as one of us – not *them and us*. It is tempting to quickly turn away when seeing a disabled person. We first have to think of them as "differently-abled." They are people who happen to have a disability. When the professor saw Sara with her badly scarred faced sitting across from her in the office, the temptation was not to say anything about the obvious. When the professor asked what had happened, Sara explained and said her mother had taught her that internal handicaps were harder to heal than external ones. She was glorious and victorious. Humor in any conversation helps to break any uncomfortable or tense feelings.

In conversing, be *matter-of-fact*. Ask "How is their day going?" "How is life treating them?" Not "How are you? How are you feeling?" Ask "What is the good news?" "What is the bad news?"

Responsibility with Money Issue

Is responsibility taught or is it caught? Does the church or agency give responsibility to people who otherwise would not have the opportunities for responsibility? The shepherd or leaders can say, "We give you this responsibility" rather than "Here is a job to do." Shaking hands with very young children and involving them in activities, such as taking up the offering or serving refreshments, starts the process. When Luke was complaining to his father that sitting in the chapel before church was boring, David said, "See what you can do to help." This started the orientation of what we can give to the church (or others) rather than what the church (or others) can do for us. Teaching responsibility to someone may involve the creation of a new self-image, and a new role for him or her. When failure or mistakes occur during this process, the counselor or supervisor can simply say, "I am not giving up on you, and neither is God." The counselor reviews with the person what went wrong, what went right, and what needs to be changed.

The counseling question is how to get people to take responsibility. Related questions are how to help one to change when he or she does not want to change or refuses to get a job. The dilemma is trying to help them get a job when the job does not exist and, further, most employers would not want to hire them either. The shepherd is in behavior modification work, although he or she depends on the Spirit to do the changing. To find the reasons for resisting change, the shepherd can ask, "What are you afraid will happen?" In working with the poor as well as others, shepherds help put out fires for some and light fires for others to get them started. As well as a shepherd, the pastor, counselor, social worker, or money coach is a "resource readjustment consultant." One can promote change by substituting new roles, new goals and habits rather than saying, "You must stop…". The client's comfort zone must be expanded. Some may need convincing that it is easier to go to work than taking time and energy to "work the system." Talk in terms of opportunities not problems. Build on past successes, not failures. Create a possibilities list. Ask "What have you thought about doing?"

The shepherd can explore why a person is irresponsible, has destructive habits, spends money foolishly, or is a problem for main stream responsible citizens. Is the person unknowledgeable of what is acceptable behavior? Is the person unaware of how the behavior is affecting others or his/her financial soundness? Is it a social habit? Does the person choose to identify with a parent who is also irresponsible and perhaps in and out of prison? Does the person want independence and freedom from others "directing him or her" so that he or she will not take responsibility for self or for family. (This behavior can be seen in some homeless persons or those that change residences or jobs often.) Some people fear success and choose failure as safer and allowing others to care for them. Is the person mean and does not care? The analysis of the behavior will help the prescription for developing responsible financial behavior. It will direct the guidance.

Rather than following the poverty cycle described above or following Jesus, some people do not want hope. They just want survival. Their need for education, and many have it, is "street smarts" and "working the system" rather than working for pay. Generous people have to decide whether to share although the irresponsible person never becomes self-reliant since the person is in a different economic and value system.

A successful mentoring program in a high school was designed for every student to have a mentor. Volunteers of all ages met the student once a month over lunch. As sometimes happen, persons do not avail themselves of such opportunities for growth. One girl never showed up her freshman, sophomore, and junior years but did her senior year and benefitted from it. This example shows that one should not give up on another.

The Master Counselor dealt with the problem of irresponsibility. After he redeemed the woman and accepted her in love and grace, he said, "Go and sin no more." This illustration demonstrates that Jesus was "full of grace and truth" (John 1:14, 17, Colossians 1:6, 2 John 1:3). The challenge is to confront people with the truth of being responsible in a clear, strict way and at the same time showing mercy and grace in a loving way. Also, the teachings of the scripture make clear there are boundaries and limits for responsible living with discipline to develop it. Some professionals would say boundaries, limits, and discipline are the way to develop responsibility. People need to accept and fulfill the consequences of irresponsibility or mistakes. These certainly can be applied to financial management. The challenge is that some people do not learn enough from their mistakes or failures to alter behavior. The Master Counselor taught boundaries, consequences, and the need to change. In John 5:14, he said "See, you are well again. Stop sinning or something worse may happen to you."

The goals of teaching people to share and to take responsibility could be met with this simple procedure: When giving money, goods, or services to someone, discuss possibilities and opportunities for returning some kindness to someone during the coming week. The recipient may suggest a service, activity, visit, watching, cleaning, carrying, or helping someone in return for the gift just received. It could range from picking up trash to playing checkers with an old, lonely man. This sharing gives a different way of being productive and builds self-worth of the "beggar" who does not want only a "hand-out" but a "helping hand." The sharing attitude is developed as people "work together."

Spirituality, Hope, and Welcoming

Since all "families face trials, tribulations, transitions, and tragedies over time" what helps some to get through these challenges better than others?[92] Research has revealed that life satisfaction was positively associated with 1) frequency of attendance at religious services, 2) frequency of participation in religious activities other than services, and 3) getting strength and support from God, receiving help from prayer, and seeking God's guidance when making important life decisions.[93]

Can the shepherd see beneath the hardened faces and outside appearances of those wandering on the path of life that they need guidance although they have an air of arrogance and independence? Some are limping or walking through the shadows of survival. They are walking to the soup kitchen. They are the poorest and most unfortunate making their way to food or to outwit the system. Some have addictions and health problems. Some are out of work. Some are stranded on the road without funds. Yet, all these are children of God with multiple problems. Rather their problems are different than our multiple problems. Some are emotionally or mentally ill, streetwalkers, who in years past would have been institutionalized.

The shepherd or outreach minister can walk with a person who has been battered, scared, broken, or ill to rise again and again to go on again in spite of negative feelings or conditions. Some days the person is depressed, does not get up, does not go to work, and misses an opportunity. The person may be in the line searching for a "hand out." But God placed an opportunity in front of the shepherd and the people in the church. So they cannot "blow it" even if the wanderer has blown or missed opportunities.

The shepherd can do that which other agencies are not doing such as giving spiritual food, hope, and worship with fellowship of believers. Agencies can advertise these spiritual and fellowship opportunities. Along with food, cards with the addresses and telephone numbers of shepherds and churches can be handed out. The shepherd can provide devotions at the family shelter or arrange for young or old people to volunteer these. Eleanor has a cooking class, distributes food they prepared which lasts for several days, followed by a Bible study. Some experience and enjoy this for the first time.

Shepherds Meet the Challenges with Diverse Programs

Pastor Griffith,[94] at the First Central Church of the Brethren in Kansas City, explains: The shepherd has people who coordinate a clothing closet for women with need in newly acquired jobs, cooperate with Project Hope and Eagle ministering to pregnant and parenting teens, create a playground for area children, donate monthly to the Metropolitan Lutheran Ministries, sew lap robes and gowns for Cancer Action, hold weekly Bible studies and monthly craft classes in Central Park Towers, a low-income, high-rise building, and is involved in community efforts to make it a safer and more enjoyable place to live.

---

92   Bonnie Braun and J.R.Marghi. Rural Families Speak: Faith, Resiliency, & Life Satisfaction among Low-Income Mothers. *Michigan Family Review.* Vol. 8, Issue 2. Fall 2003. Pp. ??

93   Ibid.

94   Caring for the Poor in our Midst. A Congregational Resource of the Church of the Brethren General Board. 2003.

Boyer describes[95] expanding a church-based half-day program for pre-kindergarten youngsters into a full day by partnering with Head Start. Each child receives at least one meal. Members of the congregation read to the children and each child may check out one book per week from the church library.

Brumbaugh-Cayford reports from Colorado[96] their giving by collecting "spare change" each Sunday for Habitat for Humanity, Habitat International, the Food Pantry, and to hunger grants made through the Church of the Brethren Global Food Crisis Fund, and a special need identified annually within the congregation. In addition to local gifts, they collect disaster relief kits. One year they sent these to those losing jobs because of the 9-11 destruction. The youth cook a meal for migrant workers.

Price reports that they have no formal policies for deciding who gets help.[97] Clothing is available five days a week. Only the recipient's name is asked. For food distribution, recipients are asked name, address, and phone number, plus size of household. Usually records are kept so patterns of need may be seen. The only criterion is expressed need, not proof of need, because the church wants people to know they are "important and loved." They reason that "Christ was willing to be taken advantage of in order to help people understand his great love for them." Their deacon board administers the home mission fund.

Heishman[98] reports that temporary housing and an hour a week of counseling to the homeless "was like offering someone aspirin when what they really needed was to be rushed to intensive care." They expanded and used "an intensive care" model in addition to buying old houses and restoring them. Now six buildings with sixteen apartments and four staff members are supported by eight partner congregations in Harrisburg. Since 200 families came each Friday for groceries, they invited them to morning Bible study. Some came to Sunday morning worship. One man for whom they provided transportation to an evening Bible study provided marvelous and valuable services for the church – shattering preconceived stereotypes of homeless men.

Rolston reports[99] moving from a morning program to a full day daycare program using scholarship monies, federal and state block grants, and the Child Care Food Program. In addition to a playground, there are a woods and a small garden.

Hostetler[100] reports youth serving meals to the homeless in a neighboring city and conducting the evening's chapel service. Forty members have spent a week ministering to children in Puerto Rico as short-term missionaries. One of the children came to live with a Bremen, Indiana family. Other activities include: annual "mission fairs," raising money for "If a Tree Falls..." (restoring God's creation in some of the poorest regions,) assistance in community food pantry and Meals on Wheels, youth's work in the Hope Rescue Center, work trips to assist city agencies, and the pastor serving as director for Salvation Army who responds to calls each week.

Still other shepherds report regularly sharing about the church's work for peace and justice, deacons' every-member visits for responding with mutual aid to members and friends of the church, retired persons volunteering every year at the Brethren Service Center, and special offerings for agencies and ministries to the poor.

---

95   Ibid.
96   Ibid.
97   Ibid.
98   Ibid.
99   Ibid.
100   Ibid.

Wolf[101] reports his church organized "Faith in Action" program. When receiving a call, they would first give "emergency support." Then an appointment would be scheduled to go to the home, assess the situation, offer budgeting and counseling, make referrals, and provide incentives toward self-help. They also participated in the Bosnian refugee settlement. They team with the community's umbrella organization which trains volunteers to interview potential recipients.

Humbert and Hostetter[102] report that a Bible study group decided to have lunches available at the church all the time. In the uncertain economy new programs evolve.

Some **congregations** include a budget line for community emergencies with the staff authorized to disburse certain amounts. Others make arrangements with local businesses so that assistance can be given by a telephone call or simple voucher. Some churches arrange with the office of a grocery store for a food gift certificate which is picked up at the store. The office sends a monthly bill to the church. Through a local clergy association, a fund was developed to which member congregations contribute. Vouchers are then arranged for each member congregation with gas stations and fast food restaurants. The clergy association writes one check to each business each month.[103]

Volunteers at a **Midwestern church** are financial coaches for those with a Habitat for Humanity house. Hours of participation count as part of the required time in building their house. A special class is held for those facing foreclosure. The poor in this program have multiple problems – health, disabilities, drugs, unemployment, trouble with the law, transportation breakdown, erratic behavior, insufficient income, children's uncooperative behavior, mistakes such as not studying when in school, marital disruption, etc. However, the lectures by some people at some times are out-of-date and irrelevant since study material they use is designed for middle income, "normal" families. Teachers are mostly unaware of their decisions and struggles because they have never experienced life as these folks have. Some of the coaches are prejudiced. Other money coaches *taught some basic management on a one-to-one basis.* Participants are polite since they are required to attend to avoid foreclosure. Nevertheless, changes were made and encouragement received because of sharing in the group, prayers, and the power of the Spirit. The pastor who heads this compassion ministry demonstrated compassion and gave a relevant interpretation of Scriptural guidance for financial management and grace for the impoverished. As shepherd, he has to inspire and educate the coaches.

The **Elwoods** redeemed a dark time in their lives when their son was arrested and imprisoned. As friends "came along us" they brought prayer, consolation, friendship, and more closeness to the Word. God opened the opportunity for the Elwoods to "come alongside" men who were released from prison to start life over with nothing. They brought the men to church, drove many hours to help them find work, and baked birthday cakes for them. Their mission and great joy is trying to help this segment of society become renewed, successful citizens by accepting them, showing grace and mercy, and assisting in financial management. (Within a year many had gone back to prison for parole violations and other reasons.)

Wilson reports on a program where he delivers meals to homeless youth in a large city out west. They also provide counseling and activities such as "midnight basketball."

---

101   Ibid.

102   Ibid.

103   Ibid.

Scenarios for Education and Action

WIC – Women, Infants and Children [104] - A Case Study

For the church, WIC could mean Winning in Christ. The federal WIC is a special supplemental food program offered to women, infants, and children up to the age of five. The program is sponsored by the United States Department of Agriculture and was established by Congress through the Child Nutrition Act of 1966. WIC is available in all 50 states. A participant must be income eligible (at or below 185 percent of the poverty level), have a nutritional or medical risk factor, and live in the state in which services are provided.

When a participant comes into a WIC clinic, she/he is screened for income and must provide verification of residency and identification. The participant then sees either a Registered Dietitian or a Registered Nurse. The health professional will then complete anthropometrics and check the hemoglobin level if necessary. A 24-hour food recall is taken and discussed for adequacy of each of the food groups from the Food Guide Pyramid. The health professional will then discuss any other necessary nutritional or breastfeeding questions and/or needs. The participant then receive WIC checks that can be redeemed at grocery stores and/or pharmacies for items such as milk, cheese, juice, beans, peanut butter, eggs, cereal, tuna, carrots, and formula (if necessary). Subsequent nutrition contacts are completed at least every three months.

Kelly had been on WIC in a more urban county for three years before she came to the WIC clinic where I am employed. She moved to this more rural county and was not sure of any of the resources available. Kelly is married to Bill and they have three children.

Kelly and Bill got married in their early 20's and decided to start a family. Bill had a factory job and was laid off. He then worked at a fast food restaurant. The family had two more children and decided they could not provide for their family financially. Bill and Kelly then moved in with her sister. Bill and Kelly found employment at a local fast food restaurant. Kelly was fired after two days for tardiness. Bill is still employed there and Kelly is seeking employment.

The family receives Food Stamps, TANF, and Medicaid. Bill first came to the WIC clinic to transfer to this county. They were out of formula and the WIC checks did not start until a week after he came in. I referred Bill to the Women's Resource Center and provided him with directions to get there. The Women's Resource Center provides free pregnancy tests, a 24-hour Care line, information on pregnancy, adoption, and abortion, post-abortion counseling, maternity and baby clothes as well as furniture and supplies, and on-going support. I also referred him to the Salvation Army for any additional food items that they would need to purchase. The Salvation Army provided assistance based upon need and size of family. Monies that are not going directly to an individual go to a merchant. These monies can be used for lodging, meals, rent, groceries, transportation, healthcare, clothing, and the like. There are also disaster funds available for individuals who have experienced flooding, fires, or other natural disasters. Funds are acquired through Christmas bell ringing and the funds stay in the county.

Kelly then came in for a medical update on her none month old baby, Ray. Ray was behind in immunizations. I suggested that Kelly take Ray to the Well Baby Clinic sponsored by the Christian Nursing Service in order to get caught up on those. The Well Baby Clinic provides medical care for children from birth to 18 years for sick child care, newborn follow ups, immunizations,

---

104   Kristine Seward Frier, RD, CD, Lafayette, Indiana. 2006.

and physicals. Services are free, and care is provided by a nurse manager, volunteer doctor, and volunteer nurses. Kelly also said that they were getting low on food. I also referred Kelly to a food pantry sponsored by a local church.

About two months later, Kelly came in to recertify Jorden for assistance. Jorden is three years old. He is delayed in speech. Mom can barely understand his words. Kelly had a bad experience with First Steps and did not really think that she would like help. First Steps provides services to children who have developmental delays up until the age of three. A free evaluation can be completed and services are based on a child's needs. I gently explained to Kelly that if she were to get speech therapy for Jorden now he would have an easier time in kindergarten. Kelly then allowed me to make the referral to the Cooperative School Extension. CSE serves children from 3-21 and provides special education services.

Kelly had come in on a later date to speak with our Food and Nutrition Program representative. She called me over to discuss housing. She felt as if her family was imposing on her sister. I then referred her to Habitat for Humanity as well as the Department of Housing and Urban Development. Habitat for Humanity is a non-profit ecumenical Christian housing ministry that partners with families to build or renovate houses. Habitat participants are involved in the building providing "sweat equity" and make payments for the materials used. HUD is a federally-funded rent assistance program for low-income families, elderly, and disabled person. Kelly and Bill decided that there were more housing resources in a more urban area and have since moved to another county. I have not seen the family since.

The Prisoner and the Sentenced Family – A Case Study

"To be sure, it was altruism that propelled me to Kansas City as a participant in "Mennonite Voluntary Service. Retired from a career in editing and pastoral ministry, I now awaited a new job description and made a two-year commitment as full-time volunteer." Muriel T. Stackley

In the array of local service possibilities, "Arts in Prison" (AiP) sounded like a good match. Funded by private donations, corporations, and grants, AiP is a nonprofit, tax-exempt organization that facilitates personal growth through the arts for the incarcerated and their families. For two years my tasks with AiP as "Operations Coordinator" included contact with local congregations, public presentations, office work, and—most important for this essay—accompanying and assisting teachers and choral conductors inside the walls of Lansing (Kansas) Correctional Facility, the principal institution where AiP works. (AiP also offers classes in writing, gardening, guitar, painting/drawing, and drama.)

My contact was with (1) men who were rejoining the "general prison population" after time in isolation, (2) men who are in Maximum Security, and (3) men in Minimum Security, with a sub-set called Therapeutic Community. The first group, in successive weeks, ranged from 20 to 40, and received well the subject matter: music appreciation (listening and discussing). The second and third groups were choruses, singing (in four-part harmony) a variety of music wisely chosen by their respective, seasoned conductors.

Assisting in these three settings soon taught me two lessons: First, our society's poverty is a parallel universe to its prison system, and second, in contact and conversation with these incarcerated men I received more than I gave. Goodbye, altruism. My education and empathy expanded exponentially.

The first lesson is borne out of this stunning statistic: with five percent of the world's population, our country has twenty-five percent of the world's prisoners. State and federal prisons in the United States house around 1,500,000 people. Local and county jails add to that number. Two-thirds of those incarcerated are convicted of nonviolent offenses. Ninety-five percent of those incarcerated will be released.

As I write, my county Wyandotte in Kansas is rushing to create adequate re-entry services for people who "have done their time." Those services run the gamut: virtually *everything* is needed by people exiting prisons. Even where there is a family to receive a parolee, that family is itself often needy. The array of agencies coming forward must cover food, clothing, employment, apartments, round-the-clock availability for emergencies, and regular check-in services for the duration of parole. Add to this the unrealistic but pervasive "not in my backyard" attitude of many communities—unrealistic in that with the ripple effect surrounding upward of two million people, few communities in our country are untouched by this phenomenon. My wish is that hesitant communities might discover—as I did—that in giving they receive.

In Wyandotte County, service agencies and local businesses are compiling success stories in this regard, spreading the conviction that prisoner re-entry ministries are economically viable as well as necessary. Here and in every community these agencies and businesses merit our support.

Where I sit, a non-staff volunteer, I continue to be persuaded that the fine arts in general and our organization in particular have a bearing on this subject and on prisoners and former-prisoners. Inmates who have participated in arts programs while incarcerated have a lower rate of recidivism than those who do not participate. Some make the disclaimer that participation is self-selected, and that such individuals *choosing* to participate are naturally more likely to "make it" on the outside. It *is*, however, documentable, that where arts programs are mandatory for prisoners, that prison has fewer disciplinary incidents.

It has been my pleasure and benefit to learn to know about 150 of Kansas's 8,500 prison inmates (2,500 of them in Lansing). Over its ten-year history, my agency, Arts in Prison, has touched many, many more. I wish that *all* who are inside the walls could pick up song books, paint brushes, writing journals, guitars, garden trowels—any of which would help shape their lives upon release and ameliorate the impact of the poverty that awaits many of them.

Salvation Army Fights Poverty[105] - A Case Study

The Salvation Army provides several emergency services and crisis intervention in a new brick building with a large parking lot in the central, older part of Lafayette, Indiana. This crisis organization helps 4,000 – 5,000 people a year in the community of 150,000.

Family Crisis Shelter. On the window of the door (one of three) are telephone numbers and times for emergency assistance. One of the three doors is always open for the 24 hour emergency assistance for family shelter. There are three rooms that house 15 people. Usually there are five families, depending on the composition. A stay is for 30 days possible. At the end of 30 days, the situation is reevaluated and extended if an earnest effort is shown for working on self-sufficiency. Facilities are modern, pleasant, and organized.

The families in the emergency shelter usually need food, housing, jobs, and child care. Sometimes they are referred for counseling, although this has not usually been successful.

---

105   Interview with Shirley Blaville. Salvation Army. Lafayette, Indiana. 2005.

Sometimes they have lied or had issues about their situation reports the director. Participants are required to have four or five contacts with potential employers every day. They do gripe about the employment search requirement.

Families have heard of the shelter from calling the Crisis Hotline, the Internet, and word-of-mouth. Families have come from out-of-town and other states because of the good reputation of the Lafayette Salvation Army. When they request shelter they have to provide date of eviction, when they have been at the shelter before, and the time spent on the waiting list.

The families who stay at the shelter are the homeless types. Among the **reasons** they need the shelter are: Family and friends will not allow them to continue staying with them anymore. The landlords do not want freeloaders anymore with the wear and tear on overcrowded rental housing. The family was renting subsidized housing where their rent increased. The family on HUD or Section 8 housing was kicked off, and then found it very difficult or impossible to get back on these programs. When credit checks were made, it turned out that they had bad credit. They could not get subsidized housing in the first place. Others had to pay 60-80 percent of their money in rent and could not afford it.

The four paid employees for the 24 hour emergency shelter work in three shifts. They work three to five days a week. Funding for the shelter comes from grants, fund raising projects, township trustee funds, FEMA (Federal Emergency Management Assistance), and the United Way. The Lafayette-West Lafayette community, with major university churches, companies, factories, sororities, fraternities, and other caring individuals, is more generous and helpful than many other communities in the nation. The programs have been presented on national television as a model community.

Other Emergency Services and Programs. Other services the Salvation Army provides are food and clothing on Monday, Wednesday, and Friday mornings, transportation, assistance with utility bills, school supplies, tools, steel toe boots, drugs, appointments with doctors, and summer camp for children. Appointments are made for many of the services to avoid waiting in line. Before appointments were instituted, 30 people waited in line at 6:00 a.m. but staff could only help 12. Telephone numbers for setting up appointments are posted on the door window at all times. Currently there is a waiting period of about four weeks. A maximum of $150 is given for the year of receipt, not the calendar year.

Summer camp is offered for children with different times for different ages and specialties such as music camp. The cost is $40 for the five day overnight camp. Activities include religion, skills, crafts, horse back riding, and swimming. This is funded by United Way. There is no income basis for participating. Children raise money by selling candy. The Salvation Army also provides Christmas gifts and visits to nursing homes and shut-ins at Easter.

In November, cold-weather clothing, blankets, and other winter supplies donated by the community are distributed. Transportation assistance provides bus tokens or passes, money for gasoline, and referral to a volunteer mechanics group, Love, Inc. which is a local branch of World Vision. Also available is help with utilities such as water, electricity and gas as well as contact with utility companies for programs or assistance, holding off disconnections. (Chronic problems requiring $900 - $1,000 for reconnections cannot be solved.)

Much of the service involves telephone communication with other agencies, landlords and pharmacies, working on behalf of those requesting assistance. The participants sign permission that the director can speak on their behalf.

By use of a computer the assistance to each family from Salvation Army and other agencies is recorded. Abuse of the system is therefore reduced. As the director said, there is not enough money. So rules and timing frequency of assistance have to be enforced.

These services have a full-time paid director and a 20-hour part-time assistant director. Volunteers from other churches also donate time for the services. Services are funded 100 percent from United Way and food/clothing donations presented annually, monthly, or weekly from community residents. Food Finders provide the food.

The director of the Salvation Army services told about the joys and the difficulties in her work. Shirley was exuberant and eager to share. She was sympathetic with those requesting assistance since the majority were in tough times. She has befriended them and they have confided in her. She gives and gets lots of hugs as well as crying on the shoulder. She has been invited to the "goodness celebrations" but cannot go. She does rejoice with them when they get a job, graduate, or have weddings. Many come to say "thank you." She has even been asked to be a God parent (which of course, she cannot accept.) She concentrates on seeing the good people, the good jobs, etc. because other aspects are there.

When Shirley started working, many people were rude, name-calling, demanding, swearing, and screaming. She does not allow that now. She will ask them to leave with such behavior. She has even called the police at times.

Unfortunately, there is not enough time and money to give to those requesting help. Some do try to pull the wool over her eyes. She does not take the work home emotionally. She realizes anyone could be in trouble. "Anyone could be in need."

She goes the extra mile to work with churches and vice versa. Some have special collections for the Salvation Army and they work together in other ways also.

She goes the extra mile for someone who is really struggling and, for example, may extend the time in the shelter or give more food. One such individual was Sue who had had six back surgeries from an accident on the job. The settlement was being fought. Shirley was a good sounding board for Sue to express her feelings. Now she comes to say thank you.

Shirley is happy to be a witness to Jesus Christ. Although she is a Catholic working for Salvation Army, her priest thinks what she does for the people is wonderful. She "feels special." She feels "blessed to be working here." The overall management of the Salvation Army is good, she thinks and knows.

Ryan Works With Homeless Children Who Teach Him[106] - A Case Study

Ryan, a college student, directs volunteers, distributes food, and befriends homeless children and those with extremely low-income. The program is described at www.cem.org. The Center for Student Mission is a nondenominational para-church agency, located in major cities. Ryan says the average age of the homeless in the United States is seven years old. In Houston it was nine years old.

During the summer months, Ryan takes 12-14 middle school and high school students, who have paid a fee to rent the church, with him to distribute lunches, sit and talk, and play games with about 30 homeless children. They meet in the playgrounds and shelters. Contacts have been made through the Boys and Girls Club, Homeless Shelters, the Salvation Army, Government programs, and Star of Hope. Different organizations, including New Kids Care, Kids Meals, Interfaith Ministries, and Elderly Refugees, have prepared the sack lunches. Program participant take a route each day looking for receivers.

Ryan and the students play basketball with the children. They play Uno and other card games. They play pool at the pool hall and paddle ball. The girls braid hair and play games. They build things. Mostly, as Ryan says, they just hang out with the children and give them intentional attention.

The children are under stress, so Ryan says the volunteer just go into the city and love the children. He could not always change them. But by loving them gives God a chance to work. When the children's needs are met and they are loved, they respond with extreme gratefulness. Ryan has heard amazing stories of changed lives. "It is awesome. It is cool." The children are similar to the students, who also have heartbreaking stories, struggles and faith.

What have Ryan and the volunteer students learned? They have learned to love and be loved in return. When they showed they cared, the children expressed how much it meant to them. They appreciated their just showing up, sitting down and talking with them, laughing with them, and being there. They learned to not be afraid when they were with them. At the end of the time, the children thanked them for coming and talking.

The biggest thing Ryan learned is how to love and be loved in return. When the situation seemed dark and hopeless, God would be ready to do something. God was very much at work in the streets and in the inner city. God took spray paint and made something beautiful of lives that had been wounded, torn, and frazzled. God directed Ryan to spray paint the ugly, make it beautiful, and make it greater. The children were reaching out to the volunteers and others. They were helping others become transformed. They were reaching out. They ministered to the new groups coming into the city.

Ryan said he learned the students and the children all have different life experiences and so we can minister and serve different people in different ways. Ryan's advice is to look for people that God places in our lives. God uses untrained people (like the apostles), the scum of the earth, and the little people. These children gave Ryan more than he could give them in the blessings he received. God is willing to touch those with scars and wounds and make them beautiful, glorifying God even in the brokenness – such a blessing. Ryan learned first and that God allows people who

---

106   Interview with Ryan Kreider, Columbia City, Indiana. 260-244-4921. 2006

do not have much to "bless us back" spiritually. This was an eye-opening experience for Ryan in his summer work. Ryan felt God's presence when in the children's presence.

The summer before this Ryan was at Nashville handing out sack lunches. He saw across the street a bum, a hardened Black American, obviously struggling. The man came across and hugged Ryan while saying, "Brother, I cannot wait to see you in heaven." That was a life-changing event for Ryan, which led him to start making himself available to be used by God. Ryan says we do not even know how God will use anyone, if they are open to the Spirit. What matters is acting on the Spirit's nudge. Sometimes God prompts you to talk to someone. You do not know ahead of time what you would do. It is a lifetime opportunity. In just being there and available to them, God allowed it to happen.

Ryan ends with the plea that God needs more workers. There is such a harvest while the workers are too few.

In Retrospect

Many people emphasize independence, self-reliance, materialism, accumulation of goods, and building wealth. These are their measure of success and maturity. Frequently, these are manifested in selfishness, envy, and greed. These attitudes are counter to giving to the poor. Therefore, we can rejoice in organizations and programs whose purpose is sharing and assisting the poor. We can be thankful for systems set up to distribute wealth and develop vehicles for sharing. We can be appreciative that there are such dedicated people in charge of programs. Many of us are not in contact with those in need. If we were, we would be more apt to share. If we understood the struggles of people, we would be more generous. Illustrations and examples help us to be more motivated to share. We can be spiritually and socially uplifted to hear of the good and generous volunteers and contributors. Hearing of the good programs and networking in the community is encouraging. Telling the stories confirm that churches, social agencies, schools, businesses, industries, students, and medical and health services work together to alleviate suffering. The stories confirm it takes a village to raise everyone.

Consciousness of the more wealthy needs to be raised. University students, while getting an education, can also learn to think of other people's needs through service projects, outreach or volunteer programs like some institutions have initiated. Community life is composed of sharing with everyone. We can learn from those struggling and we can learn to provide services better.

The need to provide services by networking with other agencies can also be illustrated by its neglect. One program worked with Habitat for Humanity people in danger of losing their homes. Not once were the services of Salvation Army explained, nor of other emergency agencies, Earned Income Credit, or food stamps. Someone who had been in poverty and now advanced could have taught better lessons than the department chair of a university with research experience in an unrelated subject, using outdated material. The material with Scripture verses was not up-to-date or relevant to the poor clients' struggles. Some of the teachers were "clueless" about financial problems of the poor, having neither been in poverty nor managing their own finances.

A political and sociological problem phenomenon that needs to be recognized in program planning is how extended families often work together for housing and transportation. Government subsidies and programs actually discriminate against households with several generations and income spread around the extended family.

Psychologically, one can see different types of make-up and spirit among the less fortunate. Dark circles show around the eyes of many of those mistreated, abused, sick, and struggling. Others have a joyous spirit, seeing the humor in things amidst their crises and struggles. Still, misfortune, disappointment, and pain are written on their faces. Pastors, educators, helping professionals, mentors, counselors, and volunteers can hear stories of failures and defeat when reading between the lines. There are also victories in seemingly impossible or cruel situations. The problem for shepherds is enough time and concern to listen and give practical steps in managing resources. Most do not even give encouragement. On the other hand, many poor have done better with what they have than others could have done. We can learn from them. Many need to be complimented on how well they do with managing life as a series of crises. In fact, beginning workers do learn from the underclass about how to get around the system, about the law, and about street smarts.

Members of the middle class have historically been conditioned to think that people can pull themselves up by their own boot straps. Sensitive counselors know some people who do not have boots with straps and can help them find boots.

As a culture, we tend to blame victims and the poor for their situations. They do make mistakes and wrong turns. Many are shortsighted when it came to education. For example, a young man had received a Pell Grant for going to community college which did not require repayment. Then he got drunk and partied so much he did not study and complete school. Now he is required to pay the loan back. Others have addictions, sicknesses, and learning disabilities. Many do not have good role models, do not receive encouragement, and the practical guidance on how to succeed.

Research has documented that regular church attendance and spirituality are the most important factors for rising out of poverty.[107] Churches that combine material outreach with spiritual development would seem to do as the Master Teacher would have done. Jesus was concerned for all people as he taught about the material needs, the wellness, and the hope that give energy which comes from God.

Prayer Directed by James I and 2[108]

Lord, as your people we do not much listen to your Word as information. We want to be your people to do as it says. Our desire is that we give expression to our faith in the ways your Word invites us. It calls us in our speech. It guides us to listen, slow to speak, and slow to anger. In our care to needs of those around us, help us to look after the orphans and widows in their distress. In the manner in which we accept **all** people into our presence, help us to not show favoritism to those who are wealthy and help us not to discriminate against those who are poor. Form in us a poverty of heart that moves us to a posture of dependence upon you. Make us rich in faith. Help us to keep the royal law of love you have given us through your Son to love our neighbor as ourselves. Your Word says that with mercy we keep the law. If we stumble at just one point, we are guilty of breaking the whole of it. Help us as we are invited here to speak and act as those who are going to be judged by the royal law of love, that law that gives freedom. We believe that we will be judged without mercy if we are not merciful. We believe mercy will be our judgment. So, then as your people make us gracious people, loving people, attentive to the needs of

---

107   Research from forthcoming from papers presented at a conference by the National Center on Poverty.

108   David Henderson. Covenant Presbyterian Church. Lafayette, Indiana. March 1, 2009.

others, submitted, dependent people to your conforming our lives to your loving purposes. Even as we invite you to do this work in us, we confess we are incapable. We cross the line, we have failed you, come up short, and blown it with you. We have sinned against you. We thank you for the encouraging expression of love that was on your lips and took on flesh, came to us, the word of God made flesh to die in our place that we might have new life and forgiveness in you. We put our faith and trust in you. We thank you for how the way you have been merciful to us. Make us a merciful people and as others come before us with needs, we pray that you would allow us to not to respond by saying, "Go and we wish you well and be well fed," but that you would move us to put practical tangible expressions to our care and concern. That we would provide clothes and food and time to care and encouragement. Allow us to be willing to let our lives get messy for the sake of demonstrating the mercy of God. Your desire is that we would believe in you. What you require in us is belief made expressive in our lives. Allow us the embodiment of your love in this world for your people, for those you place around us, that we might glorify you and give expression to those you place before us. **Amen**

◇◇◇ ⧗ ⧗ ◇◇◇

Chapter 10. **Out of the Snares of Spending and Gambling Addictions**

Misdirected Search

Probably everyone has some type of addiction as everyone has some type of imperfection, brokenness, or incomplete surrender to God. A misdirected search for wholeness, meaning in life, joy, or relief from pain may end up with gambling or other addictions. Compulsive behavior and obsessions with possession attempt to fill the empty void that only Christ and his redeeming love can fill. Compulsion to spend or gamble does not assure more love, better self-esteem, healing the hurts or regrets, or reducing stress in daily living. The compulsion is a search for comfort, power, winning or to overcome loneliness, shame and anger. It can be a result of disappointments or being fearful. Obsessive compulsive disorder is characterized by not distinguishing the important from the unimportant. "Addiction is a misdirected spiritual search."[109] Some have addictions of collecting things or doing things that require money. By revelation of the Spirit and questions, shepherds may recognize these.

Things and substances are substitutes for the real thing and they are expensive substitutes because they may cost one's family, career, savings, financial stability, life, and/or one's soul. Dependency on substance and process addictions involves the chemistry of the body, the ability to think clearly, habits and relationships. The shepherd guides the individual's heart, soul, mind, and strength to search for wholeness and recovery with the Great Physician directing the path.

Addicted individuals come from all walks of life. A **college student** came to his pastor begging for help. He could not stop buying even though it was making his parents suffer emotionally and financially. **Jim**, a hard working factory man, periodically has to get his **wife** from the mall since she cannot stop buying. Then they have to return things. **Bruce** cannot stop for gas without getting lottery tickets. **Mary** is held by gambling's hold and uses both hands to play two slot machines at the same time. **Amy,** a religious individual who regularly reads Scripture and goes to support groups, keeps buying clothes she does not wear and cannot find among her cluttered things. She has not recovered from devastating politics on the job, low self-concept, obesity, and depression. She suffers from Post Traumatic Distress Disorder. Her professional husband's salary doesn't stretch as they are $32,000 in credit card debt. **Oscar,** a professed conservative Christian, asked his parents to pay off his debts from travel so he could get a job. Then he continued to buy and buy for his hobbies and travel. He had expensive tastes in furniture. Now the debt is higher than ever. His job is uncertain. **Beatrice,** who directs the shelter for battered women and helps them daily, finds her therapy and relief from continually buying all types of clothes, food, and things.

---

109   Oliver J. Morgan and Merle Jordan. *Addiction and Spirituality*. St. Louis: Chalice Press. 1999. P.66.

The National Endowment for Financial Education reports, "On any given night across the country at Gamblers Anonymous meetings sit doctors, lawyers, business owners, executives, and bank presidents."[110] Older Americans who have money and time are showing an increase in gambling to reduce loneliness and boredom.[111]

More Explanation of Addictions

The "addictive thought system" holds on to past deprivations, grievances, and worry about the future – enough money or being liked. The culture, the media, and society tell people they are short on something, lack something, are never enough, or are incomplete. This system tells people they need more money, nicer possessions, better car, expressive clothes, and external excitement in buying, gambling, and expensive recreation. Advertising and television confirm these feelings and offer endless pursuits to fill the void and release of pleasure.[112] The media is a reflection of "our own collective state of mind." People are under the illusion that something external "outside of us" brings freedom, power, and love.[113] Happiness is thought to be in obtaining the substance, possession, person, or excitement. Actually the result is fear; as the compulsive "search for happiness in people, things, and substances results in the vicious cycle of fear."[114] Fear is in not being good enough, in being rejected, not being loved, and in being bored. When this fear is confirmed in words and reactions of family, friends, students and work associates, ways to distract from the pain are sought. Lack of love, respect, and self-love drive people to seek escape, deviant behavior, or some form of addiction.

The Power of Addictions

Substance and process addictions are those intakes and activities which demand more and more to satisfy an individual's cravings, longings, and emotional highs. They are uncontrollable in that an individual cannot stop using them even though they are damaging to family relations, family finances, work behavior, job security, and physical or mental health. The addict is one who is consistently unable to make behavioral changes despite negative consequences. The addiction takes precedence over other values and activities. The individual is compelled to follow through on the desires and passions of addictions as though a driving force moves toward the addiction rather than healthier choices. People who are addicted are under the illusion that something external will bring the freedom from pain, healing from past hurts, release from trouble, removal of bad memories, and escape from fear. Many addicted people fill the natural void of emptiness and of rejection by using a substance or an activity. Then there is a chemical change in the brain that reduces the control mechanism. Gerald May defines true addictions as "compulsive behaviors that eclipse our concern for God and compromise our freedom, and that they must be characterized by intolerance, withdrawal symptoms, loss of willpower, and distortion of attention."[115] Other characteristics are self-deception, release of pleasure, hopelessness, denial, repression, rationalization, distortion, mind

---

110   National Endowment for Financial Education. Helping the Problem Gambling Client. Supplement to the September 2000 issue of the *Journal of Financial Planning*.

111   Ibid.

112   Ibid. Pp.196-223.

113   Morgan and Jordan. Ibid. Pp.65-66.

114   Ibid. P.68.

115   Gerald G. May. *Love and Spirituality in the Healing of Addictions*. HarperSanFrancisco. 1988. P.37.

playing tricks, delaying tactics, hiding, crippling behavior, and collusion. In summary, addictions are a disease of the body, mind, and soul.

The Power of the Spirit

An addict is one who "is consistently unable to make changes in…behavior despite increasingly negative consequences in all or some areas of life: medical, legal, relational, economic, vocational, emotional, and spiritual."[116] Morgan and Jordan call this situation as being in sin, "disconnected from God, self, and others in a profoundly emotional way."[117]

The longings, the *thirst*, the desire to be loved, respected and accepted are attempted to be met by accumulating more and more, by uncontrolled spending, by the buying process and the products. Frustration and discontent eventually result when longings are not met as the world dictates rather than from the Living Water (Psalm One). "The fear of need, when the pantry is full, is the thirst that is unquenchable" (Kahlil Gibran). Some people do not believe Jesus when He says, "Everyone who drinks this water will be thirsty again, but whoever drinks the water I give him will never thirst. Indeed the water I give him will become in him a spring of water welling up to eternal life" (John 4:13-14 NIV).

Recovery involves learning to love God more than all else. Attraction and aversion addictions differ from true addictions in the degree of tragedy and destructiveness. They "impede human freedom and diminish the human spirit."[118] The difference is between choosing or doing and being compelled. Many attraction addictions are based on the motivation to love whereas those compulsive addictions are based on slavery. Understanding how enslavement happens helps in the recovery toward freedom and love.

Saint Augustine said that God is trying to give good things to us. We do not receive them because our hands are too full of addictions to receive them. Addictions fill up our hearts, minds, attention and strength which otherwise would be filled with grace.[119] Grace is "the dynamic outpouring of God's loving nature that flows into and through creation in an endless self-offering of healing, love, illumination and reconciliation. It is a gift that we are free to ignore, reject, ask for, or simply accept."[120] Grace is ready to transform and empower us even in ordinary situations. Miracles are nothing other than God's ordinary truth seen with surprised eyes."[121] The Spirit changes the desire. The hand of God intervenes in recovery. One of the fruits of the Spirit is self-control.

Some people are addicted to gaining other people's approval in order to feel good about themselves. They have a habitual way to seek approval and so experience great stress when rejected, feeling bad about self.[122]

A simple solution to ending addiction is to quit it, not engage in the next addictive behavior, and not indulge in the next temptation.[123] This is a result of spiritual growth. The best explanation

---

116   Morgan and Jordan. Ibid. P.66.

117   Ibid. P.196.

118   May, Ibid. P.38.

119   Ibid. P.17.

120   Ibid.

121   Ibid. P.155.

122   Ibid. P.37.

123   Ibid. P.177.

I can understand for recovery is expressed this way: "It is simultaneously the expression of Christ-with-and Spirit-in us, sharing our suffering and restlessness, creating and empowering and living in and through the very cells that make us, preserving our freedom with intimate love in everything we do and are."[124]

Gambling

Gambling and overspending are two of the many addictions that are an escape from fear and pain, search for power, and need for acceptance. Internet gambling is increasing due to accessibility, affordability, anonymity, convenience, escape, immersion, dissociation, dis-inhibition, event frequency, associability, interactivity, and simulation. There needs to be protection of the vulnerable, regulation of Internet gambling in the workplace, electronic cash, and unscrupulous operators.[125]

Gambling types are increasing and include casinos, sports betting, slot machines in pubs and bars, telephone betting and gambling over the Internet. New gamblers are increasing faster than ever with the video slots at home. Horse races, lotteries, bingo, dice, sports events, and the stock market are gambling opportunities. Six percent of individuals are estimated to have a gambling problem during their lifetime.[126]

Gambling usually interferes with attention to spiritual growth and interest in giving to church or charities. Why else is it considered a problem? Problem gambling is defined as behavior which disrupts one's life physically, socially, mentally, emotionally, maritally, legally, and financially. Although it seems less serious, it may become compulsive or pathological gambling. Studies report suicide attempts among pathological gamblers from 17 to 24 percent.[127]

Gambling is a problem, as is overspending, when it uses money earmarked for essentials, disrupts the plan for financial well-being, and prohibits any sharing with others. It is a problem when it destroys inheritance income, family heirlooms, or dips into a child's college fund. It is a problem when the tax refund, unemployment income, trust income, cash advances from credit cards, and home equity lines of credit are depleted. It is a problem when checks are sent for reimbursing travel or house repairs but are used for gambling. It is a problem when it destroys family relationships and breaks relationship with God and becomes the god of one's life – motivating thoughts and actions. The stages begin with excitement from winning and reduced stress from work, family, or loneliness.[128] Then the losing stage is when the gambler is preoccupied with gambling, bets are more frequent, loses are "chased," credit cards are maxed. Personal property is pawned or sold, at a fraction of its value, or investments are depleted. In the desperation stage all life falls apart – health, finances, and relationships. Some turn to crime. Others lose hope and become depressed. Others were depressed in the first place which started the gambling. Money is viewed as the tool to keep in action; not the traditional view as a means to buy necessities, a way to meet goals, security, and freedom.[129]

---

124   Ibid. P.180.

125   Mark Griffith. Internet Gambling. *CyberPsychology and Behavior.* 6, 6. 2003.

126   National Endowment. Ibid.

127   The Editorial Team of Medic8® Family Health Guide.

128   National Endowment. Ibid.

129   Ibid.

Pathological gambling has been studied in its neurobiology, epidemiology, and phenomenology realms. The question is whether it should be treated as an addiction or as an obsessive-compulsive disorder.[130]   Pathological gambling is associated with financial consequences. Gamblers have twice the amount of debt as non-gamblers, disruptive family life, group participation, and negative emotional well-being.[131] Pathological gamblers, after their hitting bottom, and their families can face reality and become receptive to help.[132]   In addition to Gamblers Anonymous, there are thirty-day in-patient rehabilitation options. They use "multidiscipline treatment teams that integrate psychological assessment, medical and psychiatric treatment with group psychotherapy."[133]

One research reports support for any specific treatment modality is still limited.[134] Cognitive-behavioral treatments were the most effective. Genetic contribution to gambling is weak.

Barriers to treatment include availability, stigma, cost, uncertainty, and avoidance.[135] Other studies report barriers as control bias, predicted control, illusion of control, expectancies of gambling, and perceived inability to stop gambling.[136]

Suggestions to clinicians for treating pathological gamblers are addressing cognitive distortions and exposure to cues whether real or imagined.[137] Cognitive restructuring therapy identifies false beliefs and replaces these with realistic understandings.[138]

In 1999, three million adults were considered problem gamblers reported the National Opinion Research Center. They reported that 15 million were "at risk" gamblers. An Illinois Gamblers Anonymous reported an average of $113,640 of gambling related debt, an average of $215,406 over a lifetime, and 18 to 28 percent of the males had declared bankruptcy. Other studies report that financial pressures, job loss, marital difficulties, etc. associated with pathological gambling leads to health problems, depression, and suicide.

Gambling, of which there are many types, is called behavioral, process or activity addiction. It is described as "destructive patterns of obsessive thinking coupled with compulsive behavior."[139] It takes more and more energy and attention. Mental health, relationships, and fiscal viability are affected and gambling gains increasing power in people's lives. They lose voluntary control over gambling. By definition, gambling is an addiction when people cannot stop in spite of destruction to their values and well-being.

---

130   Timothy Fong, M. D. Pathological Gambling: A Clinical Guide to Treatment Psychiatric Publishing, Inc., 2004.

131   Michael Hodge and Angela K. Moore. The Financial Consequences of Pathological Gambling. *Proceedings of Association for Financial Counseling and Planning Education,* 2003. Pp. 98-108.

132   Ibid. P.132.

133   Ibid. P. 134.

134   Tony Toneatto. Assessing and Treating Problem Gambling: Empirical Status and Promising Trends. *Canadian Journal of Psychiatry.* 49, 8. August 2004. From America Online.

135   Author unknown. Factor Analysis of Barriers to Treatment for Problem Gambling. *Journal of Gambling Studies.* 20, 2. Summer 2004. Abstract on-line.

136   Namrata Raylu. and Tian Oei. The Gambling Related Cognitions Scale. *Addictions.* 99, 6. June 2004. 6.

137   Hermano Tavares, Monica Ziberman, and Nady, el-Huebaly. Are there Cognitive and Behavioral Approaches Specific to the Treatment of Pathological Gambling? *Canadian Journal of Psychiatry.* Feb. 2003.

138   Ldouceur et al. Correction of Irrational Verbalizations among Video Poker Players. *International Journal of Psychology.* 1989. Pp. 43-56.

139   Howard Clinebell. Ibid. P.119.

Whether the gambler is non-pathological, emotionally vulnerable, biologically based, or impulsive, there are common elements.[140] Gambling creates excitement, dissociation, and increased heart rate. Cognitive distortions include "illusions of control," and the "gambler's fallacy." Cognitive behavioral therapy addresses attitudes about control, luck, prediction and chance. Education about odds and probability is useful.

Encouraging "patients to identify times when they have applied appropriate coping strategies and problem-solving skills to other areas in their life" is useful.[141] Developing management skills and activities is useful. Commitment to long term goals and focus are important for improvement.

Gambling money comes from pensions and Social Security for the elderly who cannot recover financially. Even so, they gamble to escape loneliness, loss of a spouse or other loved one, or a frustrating illness. Many of the poor become hooked with the desperate attempt to gain money. Middle class males gamble to repay huge losses.[142] Some squander life savings, equity in their houses, use other's money, and plan to repay with winnings. Suicides sometimes result when they cannot pay. Some gamblers turn to crime such as robbing a bank for the desperate addiction for gambling. Others use pawn shops and pawn family heirlooms.

Awareness

To raise awareness of compulsive gambling as a mental health problem, wristbands are being sold to raise money for health-related charities by employees in member casinos nationwide.[143] The National Council on Problem Gambling offers referrals in all 50 states. (Call 1-800-522-4700). They characterize problem gambling as "a need to bet more money more frequently, and restlessness or irritability when attempting to stop." "Behavior continues in spite of mounting, serious, and negative consequences."

How to Know if the Person has a Pathological Gambling Disorder

Some signs of problem gambling are[144]:
- Constantly thinking about and preparing for gambling sessions
- Gambling more often and playing higher stakes to "win back" lost money
- Gambling during work or when expected home
- Gambling to escape from stress and pressure
- Getting into debt from gambling and lying to borrow money to gamble
- Using illegal means to finance gambling
- Neglecting family and other responsibilities

If five of the following symptoms are present there is a problem:[145]
- A preoccupation with gambling
- Excessive gambling despite heavy monetary losses
- A need to gamble with more money to achieve the "thrill" of winning

---

140   Teasell and Ballon. Ibid.

141   Ibid.

142   Ibid.

143   Liz Benston. benston@lasvegassun.com. Las Vegas Sun.

144   The Editorial Team. Illinois Institute for Addiction Recovery. 800-522-3784. 2002.

145   Ibid.

- Repeated attempts to control or stop gambling
- Irritability or restlessness due to repeated attempts of control
- Gambling as an escape from stress
- Lying to cover up gambling
- Conducting illegal activities, such as embezzling or fraud to finance gambling
- Losing a job or personal relationship due to gambling
- Borrowing money to fund gambling.

Signs of pathological gambling in the workplace include continual tardiness from work, unexplained absences or disappearances, reading gambling related material, long lunch hours or breaks, frequent request to use phone, borrows from co-workers, requests for advances in salary, credit card or loan billings mailed to work, family inquiries about salary, requests pay rather than vacation time, theft of company merchandise, use of petty cash to float overnight loans, falsifying expense accounts, arranging card games for money, and organizing office pools and/or sports pools.[146]

The Shepherd's Guide through the Valley of Gambling Addiction for Recovery

The Spirit can direct individuals to someone who will help overcome it since, by definition, they cannot do it alone. Shepherds can help turn an individual around to face God, not the cultural programming or inner turmoil. God is seeking to restore wholeness and health. The shepherd assists the Great Physician, the Great Shepherd in re-directing addictive, problem gambling, pathological gambling, and compulsive behavior in controlling, not curing.

Recovery is seeking new options, replacing the addiction with new longings especially the longing for the God Spirit infilling the soul. The entire family has to be involved. Others have been co-addicts in various ways. They have faulty beliefs in both culture and basic beliefs that have to be changed.[147] Denial has to cease. Secrets have to be exposed. Energy must be spent on changing rather than fighting. Personal management must be assumed. Respect and dignity usually need to be increased. The prognosis for pathological gambling varies with people. Control, rather than total cure, is possible as long periods of abstinence are possible.[148].

A combination of treatments is recommended and useful:
- Individual therapy, long term counseling with the shepherd.

- Medication, long-term from psychiatric evaluation.
- Group therapy self-help group programs such as those using the "12 Step Program," and other support groups
- Educational classes
- Couple therapy
- Family therapy
- Psychiatric evaluation

---

146   Liz Meszaros. Impulse Control Disorders. Gale Encyclopedia of Medicine. December 2002.

147   Patrick Carnes. *Out of the Shadows*. Center City, Minn.: Hazelden. 2001.

148   Liz Meszaros. Ibid.

- Gambler's Anonymous, Debtor Anonymous
- Financial counseling, credit counseling services, financial planning

"The pastor brings together family, friends and other concerned persons, creating a support network for each member."[149] This network in turn "engages and empowers the individual to grow and change in a positive way." [150] The ARISE model is "designed to protect and enhance the long-term nature of family relationships, while at the same time removing the addiction from controlling the family."[151] All must agree to empower the individual to make changes and not shame or humiliate him or her. The ARISE process is telephone coaching, two to five face-to-face sessions with or without the individual to mobilize intervention network strategies, and setting limits and consequences in a loving way.

Several resources are the National Council on Problem Gambling, Gam-Anon, Compulsive Gambling Society, Gambling Problem Helpline, GamblingHelpER.com, and the Salvation Army's Oasis Centre for Problem Gambling. "The Good Shepherd Restoration Ministries has established a Christian, addiction support group to help those that are compulsive gamblers. It is similar to the 'Twelve Step' programs …but encourages participants to confront their issues in light of the Christian faith." Jesus Christ is their only source of strength – the 'highest power.' Recovery is one day at a time. The group facilitator is a committed Christian, a recovered gambler, and an advanced student of the Bible. The model fosters exchange of views, spiritual growth, and responsibility for life choices, understanding of the addictive behaviors and consequences, and a saving knowledge of Jesus Christ."[152]

One of the "first steps in dealing with an addiction is to find the motivation to change." Understanding the emotional trigger that creates the addiction is useful. "Compulsive shoppers are harboring pent-up emotions, especially anger, and shopping may feel like a release for that anger."[153]

Hope for recovery depends upon accepting God's grace. The spiritual recovery process that has proven most successful is based on the Twelve-Step program.[154] Therefore, the following is adapted for addictions:

(1) admitting addictions and desires are unmanageable; pain and buried conflicts are unresolved; overcoming denial;

(2) believing in a Higher Power to restore management and control;

(3) turning over will and lives to the care of God in total surrender;

(4) honestly searching the thinking, feeling, shame, guilt, wrongs, poisons, dominating fears, and worldly gods;

(5) admitting and confessing these wrongs and fears to God and to another individual in detail, telling our story;

(6) preparing the soil of the soul for God to overcome temptations, the negative influence of others, addictions, bad habits, poor management, wrongs;

149   Intervention Services. The Illinois Institute for Addiction Recovery. 1-800-522-3784. Rick Zehr. Eric. zehr@proctor.org. 2002.

150   Ibid.

151   Ibid.

152   Ibid.

153   CONCERN. Baptist Memorial Health Care Corporation. 2005.

154   Morgan and Jordan Ibid. P.131. Also see www.gamblersanonymous.org/recovery.html and www. spenders.org.html. On-line. 2009

(7)   humbly asking God to remove these wrongs, obstacles and fears;

(8)   writing a list of people who we have harmed or have harmed us in preparing the heart to restore communication and remove negative feelings;

(9)   making amends to others wherever possible except when it would cause more harm or injury;

(10)   admitting and asking forgiveness whenever we continue doing wrong or not trusting God to care for us;

(11)   seeking through prayer and meditation to be sustained by God's love, to follow His will, to resist temptation, to fill the inner emptiness, and be Spirit empowered to continue rather than destructive means;

(12)   carrying the message to others and practicing the principles as God commanded: not coveting, not being greedy, not having gods of the world. It is being honest, satisfied with God's love, and loving neighbor by sharing;

(13)   affirming and enjoying our strengths, talents, and creativity not hiding these from ourselves and others[155]; giving thanks for everything; and recounting the things we did right during each day with the Spirit's power and the love of Jesus Christ – giving thanks for that too;

(14)   accepting that life is not easy and there are ups and downs on the path which are lessons for growth;[156] while the Lord is with us each step of the way; and

(15)   taking steps to: a) heal finances; b) organize lives; c) avoid situations or people who are hurtful, harmful, or demeaning; d) have control under God's control; e) have commitment to change and f) have joy and peace from Jesus Christ who saves.[157]

Recommended Financial Management Actions

The shepherd may be one of the first to detect money problems and gambling addiction in the conversation of individuals who comes under the guise of other problems. Casually at first as most begin, people safely say, "We sure have money problems." When asked to explain, a financial crisis, high or rising debts, huge gap between income and expenses, possible house foreclosure, and threatened bankruptcy reveal the severity. These are still just the tip of the iceberg until the shepherd is seen as trustworthy and knowledgeable. The problem from pathological behavior is still to be diagnosed.

Steps and strategies are undertaken and structures set up even before the gambler is healed.[158] First, the access to cash and assets must be "sealed off" or limited. Both partners must agree to the strategy. The financial control must be turned over to the non-gambling spouse or another trusted one. Asset control must be shifted to the non-gambler. Someone is appointed to pay household bills other than the gambler. The gambler is given a small weekly allowance. Expenditures are reported before getting the next allowance. People are warned not to restrict or cut off the gambler's access to money if he/she would become abusive, violent, or suicidal. Protective measures may need to be in place.[159]

---

155   Ibid.

156   Ibid. P.133.

157   May. Ibid. P.39.

158   National Endowment. Ibid.

159   Ibid.

Financial consequences have to be clearly explained such as additional taxes, decreased possibilities for meeting goals, poor credit rating, and debt problems.

Spouse, relative, or friends must be discouraged from co-signing loans or bailing out the gambler. Taking loan consolidation or bankruptcy are also discouraged. Credit cards should be hidden, cancelled, or cut up.[160]

Personal identification numbers on bank debit cards and line accounts need to be changed. Valuables need to be stored in a safe-deposit box. Sources for cash ("stashes") which the gambler is trying to hide need to be identified, whether unreported credit card, money, pawned jewelry, unreported pay from work, secret bank accounts, individuals, or loan sharks.[161]

The gambler's credit report needs to be reviewed for obligations. Also, check for a post office box used to hide transactions, and errors. Tax returns may reveal 1099s or W-2s for undeclared income. Underreporting of income is common, however.[162]

A spending plan or budget needs to be reestablished, realistic, and putting welfare of family, not debts, first. However, expenses have to be reduced to free up money for debts. Savings are treated as priority. Extra sources of income or tax refund should be saved or invested, not used to pay off debts. This provides emergency funds not an easy way to get out of debt. The gambler must agree to give oversight and implementation to someone else. Checks are given to this trusted individual to deposit if income cannot be automatically deposited.[163]

Large sums of money need to be protected from the gambler's addiction and mistakes, and for protecting others. Non-spouses should never comingle a gambler's property with their own to prevent creditor's going after their property to satisfy debts. "A transfer of a gift to a third party in which the gambler retains a limited interest may protect an asset from being squandered."[164] The counselor can arrange for spousal consent for loans or hardship withdrawals from tax-deferred retirement accounts. If the accounts are easy access, the gambler can withdraw assets, pay the taxes and penalties, and put them in someone else's name. Traditional pension plans should be annualized not taken as a lump sum. Someone else should own the life insurance policy on the gambler's life, put it in an irrevocable life insurance trust, or irrevocably gift the policy. The ownership of the annuity should be transferred or the payments annuitized. The titles on investment accounts should be changed such as to the child under the Uniform Gifts to Minors Act. The gambler should not be the custodian. The beneficiary of inheritances should not be the gambler, put in a trust, or disclaimed. Gambling winnings should be put into irrevocable trusts or used for household bills, not used to pay off debts.[165]

The gambler should help determine the monthly amount to pay creditors. Then the gambler contacts the creditors for reducing payments, thereby taking responsibility. The gambler could work through a legitimate credit counseling service. A conservative amount needs to be promised for repayment even if it takes longer because 1) it reminds the gambler of the nightmare created and 2) quick payoffs may drive the gambler to return to betting. The gambler may need to have a second job just to pay off gambling debts.

---

160   Ibid.

161   Ibid.

162   Ibid.

163   Ibid.

164   Ibid.

165   Ibid.

Family members may need to be counseled for several reasons. They may not have been aware of the problems and need to be supportive of changes in financial management. They erroneously may think they can control the gambler's behavior or are "enabling" the gambler. They may have developed inappropriate management habits in response to the gambler's problems. The addictive individual can also get addicted to excessive giving (for approval) at the expense of good management.[166]

The Shepherd's Guide in Summary Steps

The shepherd can assist and
1. Pray with the individual who has an addiction or compulsive disorder that the empty void be filled with the love of Christ directed to the service of others.
2. Redirect (replace) the futile search for healing and wholeness through the path of God's purpose under the Spirit's leading.
3. Inspire a closer walk day by day, hour by hour with Jesus Christ.
4. Set up a support group or family members with their better understanding of the addictions and ways to control them.
5. Refer and implement the beginning steps of other professional services and reading materials including help on the Internet.
6. Implement changes in the financial structures, habits, management, and budget arranging for accountability for changes to someone.
7. Involve the individual in helping the young, elderly, the lonely, poor or deprived children.
8. Design church worship services, sermons, and programs following the Twelve Step Program.

---

166   Ibid.

Gambling Recovery 12 Steps Prayer[167]

First Step Prayer

Dear Lord, I admit that I am powerless over my addiction. I admit that my life is unmanageable when I try to control it. Help me this day to understand the true meaning of powerless. Remove from me all denial of my addiction.

Second Step Prayer

Heavenly Father, I know in my heart that only you can restore me to sanity. I humbly ask that you remove all twisted thought and addictive from me this day. Heal my spirit and restore in me a clear mind.

Third Step Prayer

God, I offer myself to Thee to build with me and to do with me as Thou wilt. Relieve me of the bondage of self, that I may better do Thy will. Take away my difficulties, that victory over them may bear witness to those I would help of Thy Power, Thy Love and Thy Way of life, May I do Thy will always![168]

Fourth Step Prayer

Dear God, It is I who has made my life a mess. I have done it, but I cannot undo it. My mistakes are mine, and I will begin a searching and fearless moral inventory. I will write down my wrongs, but I will also include that which is good. I pray for the strength to complete the task.

Fifth Step Prayer

God, My inventory has shown me who I am, yet I ask for Your help in admitting my wrongs to another person and to You. Assure me, and be with me, in this Step, for without this Step I cannot progress in my recovery. With Your help, I can do this, and I do it.

Sixth Step Prayer

Dear God, I am ready for Your help in removing from me the defects of character which I now realize are an obstacle to my recovery. Help me to continue being honest with myself and guide me toward spiritual and mental health.

Seventh Step Prayer

My Creator, I am now willing that you should have all of me, good and bad.

---

167   From http://www.geocities.com/southbeach/strand/2512/12step.html. GamblingHelpER.com. 2006.
168   Ibid. Page 63 in A.A. Big Book.

I pray that you now remove from me every single defect of character which
stands in the way of my usefulness to you and my fellows.
Grant me strength, as I go out from here to do your bidding. Amen[169]

Eighth Step Prayer

Dear God, I ask Your help in making my list of all those I have harmed.
I will take responsibility for my mistakes, and be forgiving to others as
You are forgiving to me. Grant me the willingness to begin my restitution.
This I pray.

Ninth Step Prayer

God, I pray for the right attitude to make my amends, being ever mindful
not to harm others in the process. I ask for Your guidance in
making indirect amends. Most important, I will continue to make amends
by staying abstinent, helping others, and growing in spiritual progress.

Tenth Step Prayer

I pray I may continue: To grow in understanding and effectiveness; To take
daily spot check inventories of myself; To correct mistakes when I make them;
to take responsibility for my actions; To be ever aware of my negative and
self-defeating attitudes and behaviors; To keep my willfulness in check;
to always remember I need Your help; To keep love and tolerance of others
as my code; And to continue in daily prayer how I can best serve You, my God.

Eleventh Step Prayer

Dear God, as I understand You, I pray to keep my connection with You open
and clear from the confusion of daily life. Through my prayers and meditation
I ask especially for freedom from self-will, rationalization, and wishful
thinking. I pray for the guidance of correct thought and positive action.
Your will Higher Power, not mine, be done.

Twelfth Step Prayer

Dear God, My spiritual awakening continues to unfold. The help I have
received I shall pass on and give to others, both in and out of the Fellowship.
For this opportunity I am grateful. I pray most humbly to continue walking day
by day on the road of spiritual progress. I pray for the inner strength and
wisdom to practice the principles of this way of life in all I do and say.
I need You, my friends, and the Program every hour of every day.
This is a better way to live. **Amen.**

---

169   Ibid. Page 76 in A.A. Big Book.

Overspending

Whether a human weakness or a mental disease, over-consumption is increasing according to some reports.[170] At least one psychiatrist at Standford is reported to treat compulsive shoppers with an antidepressant. Researchers believe that compulsive shopping is a mental disorder often as devastating as drug addiction or pathological gambling.[171]

People go into debt for tens of thousands of dollars. Estimates are between 1 and 5 percent have the mental disorder and average $20,000 to $27,000 in credit card debt. They tend to go to crowded stores, with activity, tension, and excitement.[172] Many are not interested in the things, just the tension with agony while wrestling to control impulses and then a sense of relief followed by depression, despair, and guilt.[173]

A German psychologist Emil Kraepelin defined excessive shopping as an illness called "oniomania" or price. Others call it "the ordinary pleasures of living getting out of hand, with people starting out as a recreational shopper." Susan McElroy, a psychiatry professor, says it is a problem when "irresistible, intrusive and/or senseless" and shoppers find it difficult to think about anything else.[174] The disorder is impulse-control like pathological gambling or binge eating, feeling a distinct high, which rush keeps them going back for more. They suffer acute withdrawal symptoms when not shopping, thinking about the deals being missed. Credit cards act as enablers. And credit-card debt is greatly underestimated. Credit cards "decouple" the pain of paying from buying, and, therefore, it is easier to splurge.[175] "Wild spending" occurs during the manic episode of a "Bipolar Affective Disorder."[176]

Another type of over-spender is the hobby shopper.[177] Others are bargain hunters who are impulse buyers with clearance or other sales. Destructive patterns have occurred for those who *use credit rather than a budget.* Many overspend because shopping is their form of entertainment. Holiday compulsions can also be an issue. Some people are drawn to "getting to zero" literally and figuratively so if there is money in the bank they have to spend it.[178]

Addictions in overspending may reflect the attribute of *grandiosity.*[179] The clothes, car, and other possessions of the over-spender support the need for feeling grand and important. Sometimes, the grandiose is a self-enamored behavior, a protective armor to hide self-rejection, lack of ego strength, crippled self-esteem, and the need to put others down.[180] There is the addiction of wanting bigger and better. Difficult circumstances provide a sense of entitlement of "I deserve this." They think they have worked so hard or been a victim that they deserve gifts for themselves.

---

170   David Futrell. *Do You Shop Too Much? Money Magazine.* CNNMoney. October 31, 2003.

171   Ibid.

172   Melanie Therrnstrom. "Spending Sickness." *New York Metro Xcom. No date.*

173   Thermstrom. Ibid.

174   Ibid.

175   Ibid.

176   Newsletter. 5, 1999. Allied Psychological Services.

177   Village News. Dec. 12, 2002. On-line. Compulsive Spending.

178   Thernstrom. Ibid.

179   Howard Clinebell. *Understanding and Counseling Persons with Alcohol, Drug, and Behavioral Addictions.* Nashville: Abingdon Press. 1998. P.66.

180   Ibid. P.66.

The culture calls addictions "sickness." Theology calls it "brokenness in our sin." God calls it idolatry.[181]

Debtors Anonymous in the UK report[182] debting is a disease, progressive in nature, which cannot be cured. It can be arrested, controlled. They struggle from crisis to crisis with being broke constantly. Debtors feel they are plain "no good" when in reality they are sick people in which simple programs have proven successful for recovery. Some ignore debts hoping somehow they would be miraculously paid. Some are compulsive spenders, buying things neither wanted nor needed. In contrast, there are those who have a disease of finding it impossible to spend on themselves. Their vision of themselves is they are not "good enough" at home, work, in social relations or in the world in general. There is not enough out there for them.[183] A sense of impoverishment is all they see and do. Some of these withdraw into a dream world, fretting over money, and avoiding responsibility.[184] They feel unworthy of anything.

Individuals so desperately want a lifestyle that they really cannot afford that they buy it without facing consequences for the long term. Others are not disciplined in anything at all. Others feel so unloved that they buy a present for oneself. Like other addictions, individuals know the behavior is wrong. They want to do it anyway. Buying is an obsession with the "fix" that is controlling one's feelings and does not last. Talking to oneself about this helps. Buying will not increase feelings of self-worth permanently. Stop substituting symbols or idols for the real thing is the new message. God defines one, not the possessions, is the realization that starts the road to recovery.

How to Know if the Person Has a Problem?

Overspenders Anonymous suggests indications that someone needs help: Running up excessive bills and debt, unable to handle finances, buying things because of depression or need to bolster self-esteem, sneaking new purchases into the house, not needing what is bought, feeling compelled to shop and buy, rarely using things you buy, and not remembering what was recently purchased.[185]

The Illinois Institute of Addiction Recovery states that, "It is universally agreed upon that addictive disorders are characterized by the following: Recurrent failure to control a behavior, increased tension prior to a behavior, and pleasure while experiencing a behavior." Signs and symptoms the IIAR suggests are:

- Shopping/spending habits causing emotional distress or chaos in one's life.
- Having arguments with others regarding shopping or spending habits.
- Feeling lost without credit cards.
- Buying items on credit that would not be bought with cash.
- Spending money causes a rush of euphoria and anxiety at the same time. (Increased tension prior to behavior and pleasure while experiencing it).
- Spending or shopping feels like a reckless or forbidden act.

---

181 Ibid.

182 Debtors Anonymous in the UK. www.denbtorsanonymous.org. 2004.

183 Ibid.

184 Eric Feber. *Virginia Beach Beacon*. June 2, 1996. P.8.

185 Debtors Anonymous in the UK. Ibid.

- Feeling guilty, ashamed, embarrassed or confused after shopping or spending money. Many purchases are never used.
- Lying to others about what was bought or how much money was spent.
- Thinking excessively about money.
- Spending a lot of time juggling accounts and bills to accommodate spending. (Four or more of the above indicates a problem with shopping or spending.)

Compulsive spenders are[186] "people who use spending to ease symptoms of depression or anxiety and may feel a need to spend more often, with increasing amounts of money. Effects may include insomnia or excessive sleeping, guilt and shame, deeper depression, anxiety, helplessness or anger at overwhelming debt, restlessness or extreme irritability. The cost of compulsive shopping can lead to writing bad checks, theft or other illegal activities designed to maintain cash flow. Severe guilt and depression may lead to suicide attempts." Shopping temporarily fulfills emotional needs, such as those from feeling unloved, insecure and isolated.[187]

Most references report the common signs of compulsive spending as Debtor Anonymous[188] does:

- Lack of a list for planned purchases,
- Shop without knowing if funds are available,
- Spontaneously buying at the checkout stand,
- Usually buy extras at grocery stores or gas stations,
- Lack of comparison shopping for features and prices,
- Not considering long-term impact,
- Browse mail orders, Internet or stores without a purchase plan,
- Shop from the shopping channel,
- Brags about "great deals" bought,
- Have unworn clothing, unread books, unused tools, unused equipment, etc.
- Rationalize sale items,
- Buy for others since cannot justify buying for self,
- Hide purchases from others,
- Buy and return purchases for enjoyment,
- Use shopping to cheer self, calm self, feel elated,
- May feel or not feel regret, remorse, or shame after purchasing,
- Have someone criticizing or worrying about your spending,
- Takes pride and jokes about one's erratic spending patterns,
- Has belief system of able to fix problems in life by purchasing, and
- Lose job or relationship because of spending.

Other signs[189] are that the consumer cannot remember what he or she did or bought. They are in denial that there is a problem. Most say, "I can stop anytime." Most have an "intense, overwhelming desire to have things and riches with thinking about these all the time." Shopping is the primary activity-of-choice. The person lied about the purchase. A friend's purchases have

---

186   Family Service – Consumer Credit Counseling Service in Health Forums.com. May 17, 2002 (on line).

187   Ibid.

188   Group #252. Debtors Anonymous, General Service Board, Inc.. Debtors Anonymous Intergroup (On-line). Northern California. P.O. Box 920888, Needham, MA 02492-0009. 781-453-2743. 2004.

189   CONCERN. Employee Assistance Programs. 1503 Great Road, Suite 120, Mountain View, CA 94040. Internet on-line. 2001.

been put on credit card and cash collected from them. The person feels nervous and guilty after the spending spree. Others would be alarmed if they knew spending habits. The person feels hopeless and depressed after spending money. Some do not even know the current status of their financial position.

Debtors Anonymous[190] warn that for debtors there are two roads at the decision crossroads. One road "lures you on to further despair, illness, ruin, and in some cases, mental institutions, prison, or suicide." The other road is "a more challenging road, leads to self-respect, solvency, healing, and personal fulfillment." The warning signs on the road to disaster are: unhappy about life; distraction from daily work; affects a reputation; lowered self-esteem; gives false information to obtain credit; makes unrealistic promises to creditors; fear that employer, family, and friends will find out about indebtedness; not considering the rate of interest required; expect negative response in a credit investigation; break a strict regimen for paying off debts when under pressure; and think one is superior to others and when given a "break" will be out of debt overnight.

Dr. Engs[191] observes, "Shopoholics, when they are feeling out of sorts, shop for a pick me-up. They go out and buy, to get a high, or get a 'rush' just like a drug or alcohol addict." "They often buy things they do not need. Holiday seasons can trigger shopping binges among those who are not compulsive the rest of the year. Many shopping addicts go on binges all year long and may be compulsive about buying certain items, such as shoes, kitchen items or clothing; some will buy anything."[192]

She suggests these ideas to prevent "shopping binges:"
- "Pay for purchases by cash, check, debit card.
- Make a shopping list and only buy what is on the list.
- Destroy all credit cards except one to be used for emergency only.
- Avoid discount warehouses. Allocate only a certain amount of cash to be spent if you do visit one.
- "Window shop" only after stores have closed. If you do "look" during the day, leave your wallet at home.
- Avoid phoning in catalog orders and do not watch TV shopping channels.
- If you are traveling to visit friends or relatives, have your gifts wrapped and call the project finished; people tend to make more extraneous purchases when they shop outside their own communities.
- Take a walk or exercise when the urge to shop comes on.
- If you feel out of control, you probably are. Seek counseling or a support group." (ENGS).

"Impulse control disorders" involve loss or lack of control.[193] There is anxiety in these situations which is relieved or diminished. Inability to resist this action regardless if it is harmful

---

190   http://www.debtorsanoymous.org/help/questions. htm. June 6, 2009.

191   Ruth Clifford Engs, Professor Emerita, Department of Applied Health Sciences, Indiana University, Bloomington, Indiana 47405. 2005. Author of articles and books concerned with alcohol, drugs, tobacco, social reform, and clean living movements. The above is reprinted from On-line 2005, Jewel Taylor's S.T.O.P. On-line support for Over-Spenders.com. 2004.

192   Ibid.

193   Liz Meszaros. Gale Encyclopedia of Medicine. Gale Group. December 2002.

to self or others is the characteristic. Impulse control disorders are diagnosed when symptoms of other medical and psychiatric disorders have been ruled out.[194]

The Shepherd's Guide through the Valley of Overspending

The shepherd counselor by assisting in spiritual development cultivates the fruit of the Spirit of self-control. The shepherd assists in reordering priorities, establishing loyalties to "Seeking first the kingdom," and sorting out the influence of the love of Jesus shown to others in responsible actions. The love and acceptance of Jesus, the shepherd, and the church fellowship replaces the futile attempts to fill the empty void and need for love and respect from compulsive buying, not buying enough, seeking favor of others through giving, and addictions. Recovery with practical steps are variations on these themes.

On balance, most agree that "out-of-control spending" is actually a disorder that can be treated.[195] It is an impulsive-control disorder with a defined condition so that it is an official, insurance-covered psychiatric disorder.[196] Reported in this article is that first the behavior has to be stopped. The answer is simple – "quit it, not indulging in the next temptation.[197] It may be simple, but not easy. Withdrawal from one leads to another hard emotional work. Taking the crutches of neurosis away may lead to a psychosis for some.

Donald Black, a University of Iowa professor, suggests tough love is more effective than pills with cutting up credit cards, no checkbook, not shopping by self, having only one debt card, and resisting the automatic drive to shop. Taking pleasure in the things already obtained is also a change.

Debt consolidation will not work as people have with them psychological freedom to go buy more. In a year, they are even in greater debt with more fixed payments and over time are paying more interest even if the monthly payment was lower than before. More income as in a raise may just hide the problem. It may encourage more overspending rather than facing reality. Debt consolidation with some credit counseling agencies is helpful if the specialized counseling they provide includes specialized counseling for addictions.

Debtor education may be required for those that are irresponsible, just as required for irresponsible drivers. Volunteer programs are in effect. Others may be funded with tax money because of the cost to society by those taking bankruptcies. Overspending is greater now than ever as people struggle with the economy and loss of jobs. Others need psychiatric help in overcoming the addiction, Consumer Credit Counseling Agencies report. People are urged to join a support group, many on-line, to get the self-help. They are to talk about the subject, that one has a problem, and help other compulsive debtors achieve solvency.

Theological or Biblical Considerations

The Creator has a unique purpose for each individual. It is not to increase the passion for possessions. If an individual wants to change, he or she can submit to God not one's cultural

---

194   Ibid.

195   Melanie Thernstrom. "Spending Sickness." *New York Metro.Xcom.* Date?

196   Ibid.

197   May. Ibid. P.177.

passion for directions. Individuals can look to Scripture, not advertisements for authority. They are empowered with the Spirit, self-control, longsuffering, and joy. When people slide off the path, their Creator can talk and walk with them. The Spirit can challenge, redirect, and energize. They continue talking with their Creator as they walk into the store, the car lot, use the internet, view television, and trade with others. They can learn to value simplicity. They can continue to pray "Keep us from temptation" and "from the evil" which may be the programming, the lure, and the advertisements that would lead them in devastating directions.

1 Timothy 6:9-10 says, "People who want to get rich fall into temptation and a snare, and into many foolish and harmful desires that plunge them into ruin and destruction. For the love of money is a root of all kinds of evil. Some people, eager for money, have wandered from the faith and pierced themselves with much grief."

Psychological Considerations

To identify "compulsive spending behavior," more has to be sorted out than *what* the expenses are and *when* they occurred. The *why of behavior* has to be determined. Basic needs that are trying to be met by spending have to be determined. Suggestions for meeting these in less expensive, more constructive, and more fulfilling ways have to be identified. Basic needs, those that drove the individual to misdirect the search, include social, psychological, material, health, and spiritual needs.

To treat "obsessive-compulsive behavior," or "disorder," medication and cognitive behavioral therapy are used. The hypotheses is that the orbital cortex located at the underside of the brain's frontal lobe is overactive for those with OCD.[198] An increase in serotonin is needed so serotonin reuptake inhibitors are used to inhibit the uptake of serotonin back into the pre-synaptic neuron by clogging the passages. Thus an increased amount of serotonin is in the synaptic cleft between the neurons and every once in a while, serotonin will be absorbed by the post-synaptic neuron.[199]

Cognitive-Behavioral Therapy builds the individual's faith in one's own rationalization skills, i. e. reasoning ability and instinctive responses to certain events. The goals are to reduce fear, refraining from acting out rituals, and reducing catastrophic and exaggerated thinking.[200] The Therapy attempts to "reduce excessive emotional reactions and self-defeating behavior by modifying the faulty or erroneous thinking and maladaptive beliefs."[201]

Immediate solutions to concrete problems are "solution-focused therapy" or "practical behavioral constraints" which the financial planner and shepherd-counselor can suggest. The success of treatment or therapy can be measured by "whether the client can withstand the frustrations and limitations" in a given period "without buying, gift giving, or using other ways to 'purchase' self-esteem."[202]

---

198   Joseph Xiong. Obsessive-Compilsive Behavior and the Types of Treatments. Serendip. Jan. 7, 2002.

199   Ibid.

200   Brenda Teasell and Bruce Ballon. Centre for Addiction and Mental Health, Problem Gambling Project. 416-535-8501 ext. 4550. 2008.

201   Ibid.

202   Stephen Montana. Compulsive Spending. Lukenotes. 111, 1. Saint Luke Institute. 2008.

Impulse Buying: Tool to Follow the Spirit or Disaster for Finances

An impulse may be a nudge from the Spirit to help someone or buy something that makes for better stewardship. It may be a prompt to buy something useful for one's mission in the future.

Impulse buying is **helpful** when it is a part of a general objective and will not undermine more important objectives or expenses. Impulse buying is helpful when it is truly a bargain or will help increase income. A bargain is only a bargain if the price is reduced and it is needed. Being a bargain is the lure for some addicts. Impulse buying is helpful when it is a part of a realistic goal, although the specific time was not determined.

Impulse buying is **harmful** when other, more important expenses cannot be met. Satisfaction is less than it would have been with more careful thought before spending. Impulse buying is harmful when it is prompted by fear, worry, hate, revenge, loneliness, or anxiety. Usually, these purchases give only temporary satisfaction and longer-term dissatisfaction because of less money to spend for other things. Harm is caused when impulse buying upsets the financial management plan or debt payment plan.

Reducing Impulsive Spending

The shepherd can combine power from the Spirit with suggestions for changing resource use or structure to reduce "impulsive" behavior. The structure can be changed although the feelings and the basic needs have not been met yet. Getting candid cooperation and honesty is not easy. With practice, the habits, feelings and hopes can follow the structural change. These actions can stop the "bleeding" or "leaks" in the budget:

- Do not take credit cards with you.
- Go on fewer shopping trips.
- Think through "decision making steps."
- Stop to think what else is foregone in this purchase.
- Sleep on the decision – the larger the purchase, the more the nights.
- Allow a certain amount for each family member to spend as desired - no more.
- Develop desires for experiences rather than things. Seek activities and diversions that do not cost money.
- Ask someone to support you in self-control and discipline. Call him/her before purchasing or take someone with you.
- Seek professional help if a family member or yourself has a compulsion to spend, gamble, or feed an addiction.
- Use on-line support groups and educational information. (See GamblingHelper.com)
- Keep most of your money in checking or savings accounts. It safer than carrying around cash. The process of writing a check or withdrawing money may make you think twice before purchasing.
- Use cash if seeing your money makes you stop to evaluate its use in terms of what other purchases will be foregone in this use.
- Look one day and decide the next day.
- Check three places or services to compare prices.
- Plan first, then purchase. Many problems arise when something is bought without sufficient thought as to how the bill will be paid.

- Do not take tags off of clothes until you wear them. If not worn in two weeks, take them back to the store.
- Get through 24 hours without yielding to your addiction.
- Reward self (without spending money) when a specified time has elapsed without impulse spending or behavior.

Guide for the Shepherd

The shepherd in counseling, casual conversation, sermons, and support groups can assist in recovery, control and prevention of addictions. The shepherd can guide thoughts. People with patience, practice, and perseverance can change thoughts. They can learn to trust their faith, not their feelings. One way is lifting up the right people to compare with, because when people constantly compare with the wrong people, they never allow love to set them free.[203] Children should be taught there are always people richer and others who are poorer than themselves. Who you compare with will make you content or dissatisfied. The choice of one's reference group will influence one's psychic income. The desire to please God can replace pleasing others "by buying things with money you do not have to impress those you do not like." Through sermons and Scripture study, people can change their reference group. The Scripture has a lot to say about being a child of God, being adopted, working in the kingdom, and serving others.

The shepherd assists people to deal with judgment. Pain, which drives some people to addiction, is based on perception, beliefs and past experience. People who have been judged or perceived negative judgment are sentenced to feel guilt, low self-esteem, and feelings of inadequacy which may contribute to addiction and overspending.[204] The shepherd can help an individual redefine himself/herself in the sight of God. The shepherd can reverse the negative judgment to acceptance and forgiveness.[205] The shepherd gives opportunities regularly and frequently and in special ceremonies to ask forgiveness and feel the assurance. Every week individuals can repent and then be washed clean and feel the love of God (Ephesians 5:26). This "sends an invitation to love and puts wind in our spiritual sails."[206]

The church service and fellowship meetings can be designed as support groups for people with imperfections. Acceptance and respect as well as love expressed in these groups can change behavior. The shepherd guides these groups and stresses the purposes.

By guiding spiritual growth, the shepherd can reduce addictions to the core by filling the spiritual longing through worship: prayer, music, church fellowship, conversation and counseling. The church can be a safe place to be real about brokenness.

"The feeling of yearning for something more is…a misdirected spiritual longing."[207] Since the basic yearning is for God, love, acceptance, caring for one another, loving and being loved, these can be felt in church fellowship. The search for these can be through serving others and, especially, those less fortunate.

The shepherd can present the truth in counteracting the culture and correcting faulty thinking. The truth will set people free from the addictions of "counterfeit gods." Conformity

---

203   Morgan and Jordan. Ibid. P.64.

204   Ibid. P.64.

205   Ibid. P.65.

206   Ibid.

207   Ibid. P.66.

and obedience to material goods, beauty, wealth, and status refute "inquisitiveness, originality and spirit."[208] A choice to be committed to Christ or to self must be made because energy to work for the Kingdom, i.e. the poor, the lost, or helpless and to care of oneself is limited.[209] A decision is made to trust God to care for us.

Pastoral counseling for problem gambling is available in J. W. Ciarrocchi, 1993, *A Minister's Handbook of Mental Disorders*, New York: Pauline Press. Also in the *Journal of Gambling Studies*, No. 9, is the article by J. W. Ciarrocchi and D. Reinert about family environment and length of recovery for gamblers.

One of the fruits of the Spirit is self-control. Spiritual experiences and growth can develop the self-control. Shepherds can help this in counseling for related causes: depression, anxiety, weak task persistence, and a variety of health problems.[210]

Giving thanks and praying constantly are Biblically based. These techniques are critical to improve self-worth, change moods, and have healthy relationships with others. The shepherd can suggest counting on ten fingers every night or writing every day the positive events of the day, the accomplishments, positive aspects, things done right, small blessings. This exercise "engenders positive self-fulfilling prophecies."[211]

The shepherd can address imperfection, human weakness, and the fallen state of people. The shepherd must stimulate "hope" in the Lord. A writer explains, "Grace is our only hope for dealing with addiction, the only power that can truly vanquish its destructiveness." In failing and hopelessness, people can honestly and completely turn to God for his grace.[212] The shepherd can use reality-counseling theory because "addiction to power, money, or relationships can drive people to distort reality just as much as can addiction to alcohol or narcotics."[213]

Searching for fulfillment in "our longing for God" through power and possessions will eventually lead to disappointment. May suggests the more one seeks God through things, the "more abnormal and stressful it becomes to look for God directly."[214] Since the shepherd as prophet takes God to the people and as priest, takes the people to God, he assists in transformation. *Transformation of desire*, as Fitzgerald uses it, can then take place in the lives of the addicted.[215]

The shepherd can help people replace bad habits with good habits, loneliness with the presence of Christ in their lives, the need for distraction from psychic pain with being in his loving presence. The key to changed behavior is "seeking first the kingdom of God and then these things will be added." This is choosing to trust God to "cover" one's real needs.

The shepherd walks with individuals through the valley of death. The individual dies to oneself, old pains, old ways, old habits, old pleasures, old lifestyles, and old friends that would lead them down the path to destruction. Death of old ways is painful but is necessary for rebirth, new ways, new habits, new pleasures, and new joy in the Lord. In addition to saying, "I am going to quit or I am going to control my spending," the author suggests saying, "I am going to suffer and

---

208   Ibid. P.113.

209   Ibid.

210   Ibid. P.183.

211   Ibid. P.186.

212   May. Ibid. P.16.

213   Ibid. P.50.

214   Ibid. Pp.92-93.

215   Ibid. P.95.

die. The Suffering Shepherd is walking beside me, I will be led to greener pastures. The new path will be difficult but I have stronger shoes. I will be restored. In the presence of my enemies, the addictions and chemical dependencies, my cup will run over with joy." (Williams)

Power of Referral Source: Consumer Credit Counseling Service[216]

Consumer Credit Counseling Service suggests,[217] "Spending sprees may be triggered by boredom, loneliness, and/or depression. Some individuals over-spend following breakups with spouses or lovers. Consider the following characteristics of compulsive spenders:
- Shopping brings the pleasure, and then guilt removes the pleasure.
- Shopping temporarily fulfills emotional needs, such as those from feeling unloved, insecure and isolated.
- Compulsive shoppers have to shop.
- Some purchases are never used.
- Compulsive shopping leads to debt, bankruptcy and/or problems with family members.
- The addiction to spend causes feelings of anxiety, guilt, and remorse.
- Understanding the emotional trigger that creates the addiction is necessary. Budget counseling, debt management programs, and/or professional counseling may be appropriate measures.

The following steps to curb spending are suggested:[218]
1. "Prune your plastic portfolio.
2. Begin to clean up your current credit card debt.
3. Begin to find suitable rewards to replace the over-spending "high." (Williams, the author suggests that these are small rewards but the feeling sought needs to be the real thing – in Christ alone.)
4. Seek the support of others working through their addictive behavior in group meetings.
5. Be good to yourself in ways that will not increase your debt or guilt." (CCCS)

Power of On-Line Services

Griffin-Shelley[219] encourages: "Resisting urges gets easier with time. Initially, most over-spenders need to do what alcoholics have to do -"think through a drink." In other words, before you spend, especially impulsively, you need to think about how you will feel afterwards. If you think that you might have second thoughts or regrets, do not spend!

"Another important step is to avoid "people, places, and things." All addiction recovery focuses on these issues. For over-spenders, "people" can be a friend who likes to go shopping. A "place" could be the mall by yourself. "Things" could be credit cards or sales. If you are not safe when you are alone, do not be alone. Go to the mall with someone. Tell them in advance why you are going, what you are looking for, and how much you plan to spend. Keep them informed while

---

216   Consumer Credit Counseling Service of North Little Rock, Reprinted on Over Spenders.com. on-line 2005. Family Service Agency, 628 West Broadway, Suite 300, North Little Rock, AR 72114. 501-372-4242 – Ext. 318.

217   Ibid.

218   Ibid.

219   Dr. Eric Griffin-Shelly has worked with addictions for 20 years. He is author of Sex and Love: Addiction Treatment Recovery. The above is reprinted from On-line 2005, Jewel Taylor's S.T.O.P. On-line support for Over-Spenders.com. 2004.

you shop and do not let them wander off and leave you alone. If you are tempted to shop online or on television while you are home alone, call someone. If this is not enough, get up and go to a meeting or to someone else's house. Have an "I'll do whatever it takes to stop" attitude. Ask for help. Write in your journal when you are alone. Educate yourself about overspending. Go online and get support. Identify your "triggers" and find ways to manage or avoid them. As you progress in your recovery, it will get easier and become more natural. Some day, if you stick with it, you will get the wonderful reward of being able to help others-when you give it away, you get it back ten fold." (Griffin-Shelley)

OVER SPENDERS, registered Debtors Anonymous group #450, is a forum on-line for compulsive spenders and debtors to "share their experience, strength and hope with each other that they may solve their common problem and help others to recover from compulsive debting." This group uses the twelve steps, traditions and tools of Debtors Anonymous as a suggested program of recovery from compulsive spending and chronic debting. "Today numerous D.A. members come to us from court programs and counseling services. Some arrive voluntarily, others do not. After a member has gained some familiarity with the D.A. program through attendance at meetings, he or she organizes a Pressure Relief Group, a meeting to relieve any financial or other kinds of pressure the member may be feeling and provide support for recovery. The meeting consists of the member and two other members of the fellowship who have been solvent for three months and who usually have more experience in the program. The group meets periodically to review the new member's financial situation. Professionals who work with debtors share a common purpose with Debtors Anonymous: to help the compulsive debtor become solvent, and lead a healthy, productive life."

Power of Scripture and Prayer

Whittaker[220] from Kansas illustrates how people who are collectors can become obsessive. No matter how much they have, it is never quite enough. She reports, "I collect children's dishes. I stopped counting after I had 200 sets. No matter how much I had, there was always one more that I wanted. My appetite was insatiable; I was as obsessive as an alcoholic, a drug addict, an overeater, or a gambler.

As my collection increased, the prices escalated. Soon I was spending more money than we could comfortably afford.

One day, in my daily devotions, Luke 12:15 jumped out at me. "Take care! Be on your guard against all kinds of greed; for one's life does not consist in the abundance of possessions." (NRSV) I realized that I had become a slave to my possessions and that I needed to rethink my priorities. I prayed for strength to overcome my problem: "Dear God, help us set priorities, and strengthen us to resist temptation. Amen."

As with any addiction, I had to detach myself from temptation, so I stopped visiting antique shops and internet on-line auctions. When I was tempted, I asked myself, 'Will this satisfy me, or will I want more?' Only by prayer have I been able to find the self restraint to overcome this problem." (Whittaker)

---

220   Arleen Whittaker, Kansas, *Upper Room*, November 22, 2004.

Over Spenders' Twelve Steps to Recovery[221]

"1) We admitted we were powerless over spending and money and that our lives had become unmanageable.

2) Came to believe that a power greater than ourselves could restore us to sanity.

3) Made a decision to turn our will and our lives over to the caring God, as we understood God.

4) Made a searching and fearless moral and financial inventory of ourselves.

5) Admitted to God, to ourselves and to another human being the exact nature of our wrongs.

6) We were entirely ready to have God remove all these defects of character.

7) Humbly asked God to remove our shortcomings.

8) Made a list of all individuals we had harmed and became willing to make amends to them all.

9) Made direct amends to such people wherever possible, except when to do so would injure them or others.

10) Continued to take personal and financial inventory and when we were wrong, promptly admitted it.

11) Sought through prayer and meditation to improve our conscious contact with God, as we understood God-praying only for knowledge of God's will for us and the power to carry that out.

12) Having had a spiritual awakening as a result of these steps, we tried to carry this message to compulsive spenders and to practice these principles in all our affairs." (Over Spenders, Debtors Anonymous group #450, On-Line)

---

221   Over Spenders Anonymous. 2000. http://www.spenders.org/about.html 2009.

◊◊◊ ⧗ ⧗ ◊◊◊

Chapter 11. **Caught in the Thickets of Credit and Debt**

The Shepherd's Guide to Assist Credit Management

The call to break the chains of credit and debt is found in Isaiah 61:1: "The Spirit of the Sovereign Lord is on me, because the Lord has anointed me to preach good news to the poor. He has sent me to bind up the brokenhearted, to proclaim freedom for the captives and release from darkness for the prisoners."

In the valley of the shadow of debt, pastors, educators, mentors, financial counselors, helping professionals, and others responsible for change will encounter a complex world of credit, a dark world of predators, the monsters of mismanagement, people of ignorance, and people captive to credit. Many people are captive to credit due to their own fault because of poor decisions and also because of unscrupulous, assertive creditors. The credit industry admits they have contributed to consumer disaster, maybe one-third of the time or more. Believing they are victims of how parents taught them, how social groups caught them, and how creditors bought them, hurting consumers fail to admit their lack of knowledge, blaming others for their credit predicaments. The shepherd's role is to warn about the wolves.   Jesus said to be as wise as serpents but harmless as doves. Therefore, the shepherd can teach a better way of living for those who want freedom *from*:

1. captivity *to* becoming new creations,
2. victimization with credit *to* becoming victorious,
3. ignorance *to* becoming enlightened, walking in the light of facts, figures, laws, and knowledge of the credit process,
4. being undisciplined and irresponsible *to* becoming disciples,
5. being out of control in every sphere in life *to* being under God's control, (The fruit of the Spirit becomes manifest in credit use. The Spirit makes one loving, happy, peaceful, patient, kind, good, faithful, gentle, and self-controlled (Galatians 5:22-25)).
6. being driven by wants and myths *to* living in the real world with purpose and intention.

The shepherd notices and questions danger signals, suggests changes and encourages new living, buying, saving, and giving. Credit information as addressed below can be shared. On the other hand, some people have lived through many crises and have lived for a long time in many different cultures. The shepherd can learn lessons and details of the law from them.

The importance of counseling in credit or debt use is obvious when the signals show the depth of financial despair. The shepherd usually hears a safe, presenting problem whereas the deeper problem involves changing the heart, soul, mind, and strength of the individual. Action must be taken to solve life threatening situations. The skill to find the deeper problem by asking simple financial and social questions to reveal the danger signals: Credit card balance over $20,000, more than 20 creditors, not opening the mail, not answering phone calls, not having a phone, dishonesty with spouse about finances, not talking about finances because there is too much pain, not sleeping at night, finances affecting employment, contemplating suicide over finances, contemplating divorce because of finances, embarrassment about the lack of giving and failure in finances, getting notices of housing foreclosure, not paying bills because of accelerated payments, not communicating with friends or relatives because not able to repay them as promised or co-signing and then payments were not made, and not participating in contributions or offerings. Other signals include impulsive use of credit cards, accounts not being paid on time, accounts paid with minimal amount or defaulted entirely. Payment on mortgage or rent is defaulted. Family relies on overdraft protection for checking accounts or paying bills. Insurance is insufficient for the financial expenses from a vehicle accident, a medical problem, disability, damage to dwelling, personal liability, or loss of income earner. Other danger signals include using credit to pay credit (i.e., cash advance) or paying interest on interest, using credit for day-to-day expenses, and the amount of net income going to debt increasing each month.

Credit is a way to financial freedom for some but the way to bondage for many. It is misunderstood and overused as a tool to expand opportunities and provide for emergencies. Overused credit can commit one to years of struggling to climb out of debt, distracting from important issues and missions. When credit is maxed out and an important opportunity or crisis occurs, it is too late and one is trapped.

Employers, insurers and landlords pull credit reports. One's credit rating or amount of indebtedness can affect future promotions and new loan rates. Problems with one's credit card can affect the interest rate charged by other cards. "Credit card companies giving away cards are like drug dealers giving away nickel bags of crack cocaine."[222] Credit is a problem for many and a helpful way to live for other people. The challenge for shepherds is to understand attitudes toward use of credit and consumer behavior as well as credit processes to assist people.

Reasons for Captivity Help Prescribe the Release

Who? When? In a recent study, distressed consumers reported their most pressing money management issues were making mortgage payments or paying for housing (reported by 16 percent), paying down debt (13 percent), making ends meet (17 percent), paying for health insurance or medical expenses (16 percent), fuel or energy costs (9 percent), and job uncertainty (6 percent).[223] The National Foundation for Consumer Credit reported in 2008 that 40 percent of young adults were delinquent on bill payments and 10 percent of adults had missed a mortgage payment in the last year.

Reasons people overuse credit or misuse credit vary greatly. The following underlying reasons must be assessed to assist individuals or families in getting out of debt and getting finances under control:

- Living above one's means. One cause is spending geared more to a desired lifestyle not current income. People are purchasing what they want or consider necessary, respectable, regardless of whether or not income is available to spend for it. This is considered necessary for people to feel accepted by their peers, to meet job related expenses, to meet

---

222   Stephan Bailey, CEBA, LUTCF, RFC. Debt Has Become an Addiction. *Journal of Personal Finance.* March/April 1999. P.1.

223   2008 Retirement Confidence Survey. Employee Benefit Research.

church obligations, to be a responsible citizen in the community, or to be able to afford the American standard package of goods and services. Keeping up with the Jones encourages people to live above their means by using credit. The problem today is that some "Jones have trouble keeping up with themselves." When credit is maxed out by continually living above one's means, an emergency or opportunity may come and people are trapped by thinking the use of credit is always the answer. People fail to see "another way of living" without credit.

- Unaware or not caring about danger signals of spending patterns or using too much credit. They can only handle one crisis at a time, or they lack knowledge and experience.
- Using credit for everything in order to get points to use for other purchases, i.e. cars or flights.
- Not tracking credit use, unaware of the grace period, and unaware of the billing cycle.
- Not knowing the credit process, the credit world, and reading the fine print.
- Underestimating all related expenses and the upkeep of purchase. Thinking only of the monthly payment and not the total cost over time.
- Not saving for irregular expenses, unexpected repairs material and medical, and yearly expenses not having been prorated for monthly payments which are paid by credit.
- Failing to compare prices or waiting until prices are lower.
- Meeting basic needs (emotional, social, physical, material, and spiritual) through overspending since they are not being met in other ways.
- Not being able to say "no" to family members, businesses, friends, and attractive advertisements.
- Fulfilling expectations to save face with spouse, parents, children, or social group.
- Not having the energy or knowledge to save money by cooking as an alternative to using credit. For example, ordering pizza using a credit card and having it delivered.
- The goal to be "debt free" is not as important as other goals or needs.
- Fear of getting older, of losing out, of missing something, or of loneliness.
- Would rather die than change consumption level.
- Unwilling to wait to purchase things and do things one after the other rather than all at once. For example, buying furniture and appliances all the same year.
- Having high standards that dictate having the "ideal" rather than "adequate," now. One has bought into "having all you can have."
- Thinking they have worked so hard that they deserve the American dream.
- Thinking more is better with spending rather than spending creatively. Thinking the good life is a lot of goodies, i.e., that a good Christmas is getting lots of good gifts.
- Overly optimistic in thinking they will always have a job, get raises, and will never get ill, divorce, or that no unexpected break downs will occur.
- As get raises or promotions, increase spending or have a better car.
- Love the fast pace and the excitement of living on the edge. Shop to overcome boredom.
- Responsibilities for grandchildren, parents or others are more important than being "debt-free."
- Proving to others that they are acceptable and deserving of respect.
- So involved in another life crisis that they do not see the "credit crisis."
- Mentally ill or disturbed, depressed, or mentally challenged.

- Uninterested, uninformed or too lazy to manage a checking account or have had mistakes in past which do not allow them to use other methods of payment.
- Undisciplined in most areas of life and credit use is no exception.
- Combination of loss of job and income, medical expenses with or without health insurance, increasing calls or letters from creditors, increasing debts, and anxieties affecting productivity on the job and family relationships.

Trying to qualify for a loan is a bad mistake that many people make. Institutions use a debt to income ratio to determine qualifying for a loan. Results are erroneous in many cases. Ratios are misleading because commitments other than debt are not carefully considered. People are not being accurate or truthful about their debt load and level of income. The institution may not check for accuracy. The total cost of a house or vehicle is not accurately calculated because often only the monthly payment is considered. The monthly payment may be only 50-60 percent of the total cost because of the cost of upkeep, utilities, gas, insurance, licenses, etc., purposely ignored or underestimated. These tricks used for getting a loan can bring captivity to credit or debt. To qualify for a loan, people may postpone other loans until after qualified for the first loan. After obtaining the first loan, they apply for other loans. In a way, this is deceiving the initial or the first loan of the true obligation intended by the debtor.

Commercialism defines consumer needs, whereas in reality commercialism makes consumers feel dissatisfied with what they have. It is not a level playing field because the consumer is competing with specialists in advertising and marketing. Self-control in the face of pressure of commercialism is an ongoing challenge.

Why the Shepherd Should be the First to Know

The shepherd can see the situation objectively whereas an anxious person is emotionally driven. The anxious person goes in circles in thinking and conversation. The anxious person may not be listening to counselors. The person has been persuaded by unscrupulous dealers and attorneys who have their own vested interests, benefitting themselves rather than the client or customer. The advantages and disadvantages of options may not have been considered before the troubled one jumps for help. The process of each option may not be known until after the troubled person commits to one, which may not be the best alternative. The provider or program may misrepresent itself or just list the advantages. Information gives tools to assist in making decisions before the trouble hits and choosing an option to get out of financial trouble. A valuable resource on many topics is the Federal Trade Commission, 600 Pennsylvania Avenue, N.W., Washington, D.C. 20580. 202-326-2222, www.ftc.gov. The shepherd or money coach can provide questions to ask before committing to a solution.

Costs should be estimated before making a decision. Myths and misinformation as well as scams should be talked through. The shepherd should know enough to help others work on ways out of credit captivity. Most of all, the shepherd can give support to use wisdom in choosing and have courage to avoid pitfalls of the wrong path. Talking to the shepherd before talking with other professionals is showing spiritual fortitude. Prayer also moves one along.

What Those under Shepherd's Care Do Not Know Does Hurt

Those in financial trouble can be more motivated to pay their bills, or decide which bills to pay, if they are aware of what will hurt them if they do not pay. The shepherd can use the worksheet below to analyze the consequences. In some cases nothing will happen because that person is "judgment proof" in that Social Security benefits and retirement funds are restricted on garnishment limits, there is nothing to be repossessed, the person is not employed so their job is not in jeopardy, and the debt does not involve services which could be "cut off."

In bankruptcy, an individual does not know which debts will be discharged until after the attorney and filing fees have been paid. Debts can be listed and analyzed to determine whether bankruptcy will help before a public record of bankruptcy is made. Alternatives to bankruptcy can be suggested by using the procedures described below:

Alternatives to loan consolidation might be considered once the individual understands what most people do after loan consolidation: get more in debt with more fixed payments, for a longer period of time with even more stress than before.

Using a home equity loan does pay off debt but over a longer period of time. This sets up another fixed payment. "Increased borrowing to solve a debt problem is like pouring gasoline on a fire" (author unknown.) Taking a second mortgage increases the risk of losing one's home.

How loan consolidation and credit use cost more can be calculated. Even choosing a counseling agency can hurt if people they are not aware of the unscrupulous procedures some agencies use. Self-administered programs can work using the procedures discussed below. Ways to handle medical debt can be explored rather than feeling helpless and turning to bankruptcy. The shepherd can even suggest ways to handle mortgage foreclosure without panicking and giving up. Through prayer, the individual and shepherd can plan how to get out of the pit of financial despair.

Recognizing the Steps to Captivity under the New C's

Once upon a time credit worthiness was determined by the three C's - Collateral, Character, and Capacity to pay. The C's of credit are different now because of companies marketing to people they know cannot pay, to the uneducated, to the poor, and using deceptive lures to hook people into a lifestyle of debt. The C's today are described:

Capital – Credit expands opportunities. The ability to get credit for developing human and financial or business capital is a personal asset. Borrowing can lead to a higher standard of living than otherwise possible. Credit can be a hedge against inflation, i.e., payments are made with cheaper dollars. The payments are fixed although prices for identical items keep increasing.

Convenience – In today's world, credit is necessary for guaranteeing hotel rooms, meeting emergencies, etc. It can also be a way of tracking expenses because most people do not have a system for doing so. It is a method for transferring funds or purchasing over the Internet. Individuals who are authorized users on parents' credit cards can use them in an emergency or for the purchase of necessary goods and services.

Credit remains a convenience only if the monthly payments are made on time and the loans are paid off rather than allowing them to escalate. Managing convenience includes protecting the strips on the cards so they continue to work. The magnets if close together or one reads right to left and the other left to right may be disabled. Also, have more than one card in case the bill has not been paid on one or one is blocked from use in a foreign country without prior notice.

Creeping Indebtedness – Paying the minimum while the balance continues to increase illustrates creeping indebtedness. Paying less and less toward a high balance, while the interest increases, leads to creeping indebtedness. Balances keep rising, as increased expectations lead to spending more than income. It is easy to understand why one does not "get ahead." In addition, with late fees and missed payments, it is possible to actually owe more after several years of minimum payments.

Commercialism – Commercialism and advertisements make consumers feel dissatisfied with what they have or what they do not have. Credit's answer is to spend money whenever you need to resolve a problem or meet a need. "A frog will be boiled before it jumps, if the temperature is turned up slowly" (author unknown).

Crime – Although credit may not be recognized as unlawful, it can be thought a crime because it is morally reprehensible to knowingly extend credit to people who are unable to pay, are unaware of the credit process, who are unaware of other alternatives when desperate. It is a crime to provide credit to those who have a gambling problem or an addiction which will lead them farther into the pit of financial despair. It is criminal when credit cards are used to buy lottery tickets or when poor older people make unnecessary repairs with credit.

Curse – A curse falls upon the consumer when all available credit is maximized and then a real emergency occurs. Credit in the hands of irresponsible people is dangerous and can be disastrous. Future employers may perceive credit problems as an indication of recklessness and not entrust one with company resources if one can not manage one's own. One of the curses of credit is that a person no longer needs to think, plan, and set priorities. Instead, one passively accepts all that credit can buy. Signing up for a credit card to get a free-shirt (or whatever) is not a good reason. It could be the most expensive t-shirt ever bought!

Dangers in the Credit Path which the Shepherd Should Warn

Conflicts in the Path

A "contract" may reduce conflict when loaning money to family members. The contract should clarify interest, if any, and the pay-back schedule. It may state whether this is an early inheritance or not. Also, the contract should clarify if it can be repaid with work or services.

Severe conflict occurs when identity theft happens among family members. Imprisonment may result in addition to hostile relationships. Most identity thefts occur among family members.

Piggybacking is the name given for including family members on the primary owners' debt/loan. It is the practice of signing on an individual with poor credit rating and low credit score as an authorized user to an account of an individual with good credit. Some consider this mortgage fraud and it encourages consumers to commit fraud. Irresponsible members may break up the family over finances. Getting a payday loan or co-signing for a family member often causes problems. The shepherd can help with reconciliation. The consequences of behavior must be accepted, if the child or spouse is to grow.

Some do not understand the obligations of co-signing for someone else. It is hard to say no when that person has done a favor for them in the past. The loan appears on both maker's and co-signer's credit reports. A co-signed loan will be included when calculating the debt-to-income ratio. Delinquency is also reported on the co-signer's report.

Family relationships may be weakened or disrupted when one member is discovered to bring into the marriage a large amount of debt. Mistrust may result. Peace in the valley will occur with a plan, control, and time.

Co-signing a loan is an activity condemned in Proverbs. Here is the dilemma: A friend has helped Jim move to another state and resettle. Now the friend asks Jim to co-sign a loan. The friend could not pay so Jim nearly loses his farm to meet the obligation to the loan. It is hard to say "no" to the friend. The loan goes on both the maker's and co-signer's credit report.

Awareness of the Wolves, Scams and Frauds

It has been said that "white collar crime" dwarfs street crime. Mortgage fraud, scams, payday lending, and other crimes are rampant in the news. Many lending agencies are fraudulent because they purposely target and make loans to those they know cannot repay. Their poison is affecting all of society.

Some people and companies advertise bankruptcy services are nothing more than high priced scams. As for other businesses, one should be skeptical and check with the Better Business Bureau, the State Attorney General, and the Consumer Protection Office in one's state.

The Federal Trade Commission and the Internal Revenue Service have warned that some credit counseling firms may be using their non-profit or tax-exempt status to mislead consumers into paying large fees for questionable services. Abuses involve hidden or extra fees. Check with the State Attorney General and the Better Business Bureau. For more guidance on choosing a credit counselor call 877-382-4357 the Federal Trade Commission or write www.ftc.gov/bcp/conline/pubs/credit/fiscal.htm.

Another scam is a telephone call to investigate the account or lower card interest rates when in reality all they want is more information in order to steal someone's line of credit. One should hang up immediately. One should never click on 9 as they suggest.

Prohibited debt collection practices include making threats of violence, using publishing the list of consumers, using obscene or profane language, or repeatedly using the telephone to annoy. They cannot falsely imply they are attorneys or government representatives, work for a credit bureau, misrepresent your amount of debt, infer papers they have sent are legal forms, indicate papers are not legal forms when they are, or threaten arrest if you do not pay. However, these prohibitions do not apply to the initial grantor of the loan. Indebted consumers and those who were once in debt are targets of Junk Debt Buyers.

Another scam proliferating the Internet is the "debt elimination scam." They charge borrowers substantial up-front fees and commissions based on the total amount of debt to be forgiven. They use fake financial instruments and bogus tactics as well as false claims. They claim to take advantage of loopholes in the system to eliminate mortgage or other debt for an up-front fee. Borrowers pay significant money without eliminating or reducing indebtedness but increase the risk of foreclosure or legal action. All this can have negative effects on credit rating and score.

Schemes to be reported to the FBI which are in violation of the Fair Debt Collections Practices Act include: Those re-aging accounts, misreporting the legal status of a charge off or discharge in bankruptcy, misreporting the "open date" and "date of last activity" on an account, provide multiple listings of same debt, and collectors pretending to be lawyers.

Credit repair clinics promise miracle cures but usually leave consumers victims of fraud. Their fees range from hundreds to thousands of dollars. Everything that a credit repair clinic does legally can be done by consumers for free or at minimum cost. They misrepresent in that no one can legally remove accurate information from a credit report, any consumer can dispute inaccurate information at no charge, and everyone loses by distorting credit histories.

Phishing, the online fraud by crooks passing as a legitimate business resulted in a loss of $2,320 per victim, whereas identity theft by friend, relative or neighbor resulted in $15,607.[224] One must guard against deceptions that get consumers to disclose credit card numbers, bank account information, Social Security numbers, passwords, and other sensitive information.

People are ashamed to reveal that they have been victims, but the pain is great. The attorney general in the state or the government agency dealing with fraud and scams is the place to start for any redress or legal process. The most frequent fraud found in the Federal Trade Commission survey (2004) were advance-fee loan scams, buyers clubs, credit card insurance, credit repair, prize promotions, Internet services, pyramid schemes, information services, government job offers, and business opportunities.

Payday lenders make uncollateralized loans ranging between $100 and $500 which the borrowers agree to repay within two weeks.[225] The annualized interest rates typically are 400 percent plus. Therefore, many become entrapped in revolving short-term debt. Short-term emergency loans and financial counseling to change long term behavior are needed. Consumers end up having to roll over their original loan to extend the time to pay for another two weeks. Two weeks pass and another rollover is necessary. More money is owed to pay off the interest than the original amount borrowed. Payday loans are considered "predatory lending," but the industry claims they are doing consumers a favor because banks do not want to serve this clientele. Some people are addicted to this kind of borrowing. Others have maxed their credit with mainstream lenders. Many people would not take a payday loan for themselves but do for a friend in serious trouble. They are not able to discern and say no. Payday loans are risky, especially those obtained over the Internet. Some people have maxed their credit with mainstream lenders and have no choice. Their problem is building savings and improving credit histories.

Cleaning up the Credit Path

A young man asks, **"How can I keep a clean credit record?"**
- If bad debts are completed in 7 years and bankruptcy in 10 years, follow through to get them off the credit record.
- Prevent identity theft which occurs mostly among friends and relatives.
- Reduce credit inquiries.
- Prevent having non-sufficient funds when check writing.
- Have a bill automatically paid by the bank or credit union so it is never late.
- Watch the grace period and changing billing cycles. Grace periods vary by banks. Billing cycles are becoming shorter.
- Write on the calendar when to send a payment, not when it is due so posting, as done by some companies, is completed before the due date.
- Keep a record by writing down every credit transaction.

---

224   International Consumer Federation Education (ICFE). E-News. February 3, 2005.

225   John P. Caskey. Payday Lending. *Financial Counseling and Planning.* 2001. Pp.1-13.

- Concentrate on avoiding late payments, insufficient payments, and missed payments which create huge fees and penalties. These result in owing more than originally owed even if paying some on the principal.
- Guard against over-draft protection which takes from checking accounts in increments of $100s.
- Periodically use the credit line or card that is available and pay it off within due date to prevent fees or a lower score from under-use.

Matthew was denied a small loan because he had not used his credit card at the credit union. He had no debts. Another time, years later, his employer's credit union issued a card with additional services. Although Matt never used the services he was charged for them as well as a delinquency fee because he had not paid. The error was corrected on Matt's insistence but the negative activity remained on his credit record until Matt convinced the bank to remove it.

Check Annually and Correct any Mistakes in the Credit Record

The first step towards victory over the use of credit is to get credit reports and resolve any errors (see forms below). Insist that the errors be corrected. If one finds incorrect information, complete a dispute form to have it corrected. Correct but negative information cannot be removed. Make sure the incorrect information is removed from all three credit reporting agencies.

One annual report from each of the three credit reporting agencies is free. More reports will cost unless one has been denied credit, denied insurance, adverse action has occurred because of it, one is a victim of identity theft, unemployed, or is on public assistance. States have different policies. All three reports from all of the "Big Three" are necessary. Estimates are that over one-third of reports have errors and information that needs to be cleaned. Access to review your credit report from any of the three is available from www.annualcreditreport.com. However, as of 2005, there were problems with this federally mandated free credit report site because of close misspellings which were imposter domains. The primary fault was that credit bureaus were blurring lines between what was free and what had a fee. TransUnion selected consumers to share information with affiliates and partners. Be sure to watch for any pre-checked marketing or newsletter offers. Some educators suggest consumers call or mail rather than use the Internet. The toll free number to call for reports is 877-322-8228. Request that only last four digits of the Social Security number be displayed on the reports mailed to you. Do not give out e-mail address to obtain the free credit report.

Equifax www.equifax.com (800-685-1111) www.investigate.equifax.com

Experian www.experian.com (888-397-3742)

TransUnion www.transunion.com (800-916-8800)

Trans Union, Consumer Relations Center, P.O. Box 2000, Chester, PA 19022

TRW/Experian, National Consumer Assistance Ctr., P.O. Box 2104, Allen, TX 75013-2104

CSC Credit Services, Customer Assistance Center, P.O. Box 674402, Houston, TX 77267-4402.

The credit report is often called "the second resume." Protecting credit and one's rating is like protecting one's life so it can protect in emergencies, illness, and during temporary need. The credit rating is one's reputation. Employers, insurance carriers, lending institutions for home ownership, creditors, prospective spouses, and leasing agents check one's credit rating. It can affect job prospects, ability to obtain loans at lower interest rates, ability to buy a house or other large items, ability to rent an apartment, and reduced income due to garnishment of wages or tax refunds.

Getting out of Captivity, Out of Bondage, Out of the Pits

Individuals need to communicate with the shepherd, now equipped to do financial counseling, creditors, doctors, landlords, the Internal Revenue Service, credit and financial counseling services. They should not simply ask "What can I do?" but rather try to get ideas, procedures and policies. Each has own vested interests including the shepherd.

Then empowered by the Spirit, individuals can set up a plan that is best for them. They know more about their own situation and possibilities than others do. Possibilities include:

1. Return merchandise, car, furniture, etc.
2. Sell goods, possessions, collections.
3. Allow repossession although may have to pay the difference owed between the loan and the auction price received.
4. Hide or cut up credit cards.
5. Collect on debts owed to you.
6. Make hard and fast rules not to use credit for things that will depreciate before they are completely paid. Not using credit for food. (Using discipline to eat a peanut butter sandwich rather than ordering a pizza and paying for it for years.)
7. Calculate number of months to go on a crash budget, having severe restrictions and reductions with adjustments until total payments are manageable. Show it on a graph. Studies reveal that the average family would need an income increase or expense reductions for 11-12 months to get to the equivalent of a total payment on a loan consolidation, but save thousands of dollars and have less stress.
8. Get a second or third job to pay the credit and loans. Someone in the family gets a job and with working so much does not have time to spend money.
9. Ask for early inheritance with a contract not to increase this debt or ever get back into debt.
10. Pay twice the minimum on time.
11. Do not incur new debt, new creditors, or new loans.
12. Reprioritize debts to pay based on various methods: One method is based on what happens if it does not get paid? These are: Harassment, loss of goods, loss of services, court action (garnishment, judgments), accelerated payment and total due all at once. Reconnect fee and all past loans may be due before obtaining service again or at a different location. Nothing may happen depending on the type of debt and situation/income of client.

Other options to decide priorities are:

Whether it is secured status versus unsecured (having collateral, co-signer). These debts need to be distinguished since they are handled differently if not paid and in bankruptcy adjustments.

Legal action taken or inevitable, possible judgments, garnishments of wages or bank accounts.

Interest rate increase or finance charge.

Implications such as harassment at place of work or telling one's supervisor.

Danger of losing goods or services or the value of assets.

Creditor policies. There may be an option to pay debt all off if early payment which reduces the interest.

The Self-administered Program for Getting Out of Debt

By being an assertive consumer, one can ask questions and make a plan to get out of debt. The mortgage is always paid first although arrangements can be made to catch up by slightly paying more or paying every two weeks without penalty.

A self-directed program for getting out of debt includes:

- Determine who really owes the credit/debt. Be aware that creditor/medical billing strategies include making one think one owes the bill when someone else does, one may have borrowed for someone else, or the insurance company owes the bill.
- Realize the divorce decree is ineffective. Companies collect from whomever they have an address.
- Find out creditor/debtor policies, past practices, and adjustment rules if possible.
- Determine minimum budget. Sum and show total net income from all sources.
- Show balance which may actually be negative.
- Calculate a conservative amount for payment. Decide debt priority. Note if secured versus unsecured, i.e. has collateral or lien against it.
- Have a summary statement of adjusted income, minimum fixed expenses, amount for distribution, and proposed payment framed with lines on the letter.
- Find out who makes the decisions at the creditor agency. Go higher and higher up the authority ladder until you find a policy maker who can make the decision. (Example: If possible, talk to the doctor before the collection agency receives the bill.)
- Find out the "pay-off" amount. Negotiate or make a decision about the amount to pay. Be assertive. Inform the creditor what you are going to do. Do not ask what can I do?
- Know some debts may have already been written off by the company or business as bad debts.
- Write creditors regarding the proposed payment. A form letter with a blank address (area to be filled in) informs creditors there are more than one and so they are lucky to get the proposed payment. Request that interest be waived. In the letter say, "I assume interest will be waived."
- Proposed payment to creditor should be conservative so that it can be consistently paid. Some troubled people promise anything to get creditor off their case and then they cannot follow through.
- Pay proposal as written and on time, consistently.
- Keep copies of everything.
- Propose a payment monthly or bi-monthly for one's remaining life, although very small.
- Negotiate an amount to write-off the debt.
- Propose beginning payments after getting employment.
- Pay in full on alternate months to prevent creditor actions.

Starting with the smallest debt/loan starts the process, giving a sense of control and hope as larger and larger debts are tackled. Number of debts is reduced and spendable income increased by beginning with smallest and paying it off, even though the extremely large one has the highest interest and payments are not reduced. By rapidly gaining more control, the largest can hopefully be handled in time to prevent more legal action. Most families find it encouraging to pay off the smallest debt first and then paying the second smallest and so. For the family with problems, their credit rating is in jeopardy anyway. So paying off the smallest ones as fast as possible prevents some problems. This may prevent them from going into collections. Then larger amounts can be applied to the largest debts.

The self-administered plan, as well as others such as credit counseling service requires a savings plan while paying off debts. It requires sharing in one way or another. The goal is to move from paying all expenses from past satisfactions to have some money for current situations and then some for future delights.

Another family member may have to get a job just to pay off debts for awhile. Even if one family member gets another job just to pay off debts, it may cause more peace since it is progress on the road to getting out of debt. While at home without additional work the couple may be fighting or stressed out about finances, so time apart may be more peaceful.

The self-administered program does not go on the credit record for 10 years like bankruptcy and is not public as bankruptcy is. Bad debt stays on credit record for seven years. The debtor may have to follow through after seven years to make sure it is removed.

If harassment remains a problem, the assertive consumer informs the creditor that they are breaking the law. The law is to protect against collection agencies. The original grantor can still harass the debtor. It is unlawful to use obscene language, call persistently to irritate or annoy, call at odd hours or at work, and call relatives or friends without permission.

A financial counselor suggested to a poor woman at home with a child to tolerate harassment and to take a nasty call every day. This would be her job, because using bankruptcy would be more expensive.

Examples to work off debts include providing labor such as painting the house. The debtor may be hired to collect rent payments in an apartment complex. Individuals may buy a used vehicle and put the difference in paying for a new vehicle toward a debt. Arrange a new payment schedule in time and amount with creditors by writing them the new plan and follow through with the new amounts, asking them to waive the interest. Paying off a debt early may reduce the total amount owed through negotiation.

Loan Consolidation – the Road to Disaster

In loan consolidation, bills and accounts are paid with one large loan. This reestablishes credit rating, reduces calls from creditors, seems easier to handle since only one payment needs to be made instead of several at different times, simplifies record keeping, and reduces past interest and penalty. But what really happens to most people after loan consolidation is "the rest of the story."[226] They get into more debt.

Loan consolidation would seem to reduce financial and psychological stress, whereas in reality, after some psychological financial freedom, it may cause more stress and costs more in the long run. Loan consolidation is a short term fix. If the user continues to add credit to existing debt with now increased number of fixed payments, it becomes the road to disaster.

In consolidating, one may be tempted (and encouraged by the lender) to borrow more than the original which adds to the total cost over time on overuse of credit. The persuasion to borrow more than the original says, "You probably have other expenses or needs coming soon which this loan could cover and make life easier."

---

226   Flora L. Williams. Costs and Benefits of Loan Consolidation. *Financial Counseling and Planning.* Vol. 10, No. 2, 2000. Pp.62-72.

Loan consolidation increases stress, rather than reduces it; encourages borrowing more than is absolutely necessary; postpones solving a problem with reconciling expenses to income; and increases interest paid over time, even with a lower interest rate. A large fee may be required to set up loan consolidation and if it is included in the debt over time, it increases the rate of interest. This could have been applied to paying off debts. Other dangers with loan consolidation are: With relief of lower monthly payment made through consolidation, individuals or families are tempted to incur additional obligations. They add non-interest bearing accounts to those consolidated which now become interest bearing. They now have a fixed payment in addition to other payments that were previously more flexible. They pay longer even with a lower interest rate in order to get the monthly payment lower and, therefore, pay more over the long run. Some debts may have just a few months left to pay but with consolidation they are included with the longer ones. If they decreased expenses for a few months and increased to pay off debts, total of the original loans would be reduced. Several debts will be paid off in a few years compared to a consolidated payment which will last for 15 to 20 years or more. (These are shown in the table at the end of the chapter.) The cost of 10 years versus 20 years for a student loan is shown below:

Cost of Consolidation Table

Amount Owed	Years	Payment	Payback	Interest	Years	Payment	Payback	Interest
Student Loan	10				20			
$9,000		$109	$13,800	$4,080		$75	$18,000	$9,000
17,000		206	24,720	7,720		142	34,080	17,780
30,000		363	43,567	13,568		251	60,240	30,240
50,000		605	72,600	22,600		418	130,320	50,320

The payments for 20 years are lower with consolidation but, as shown in the last column, the interest is increased by thousands of dollars. The difference between interest paid for the four debts in 10 versus 20 years are $4,920; $9,360; $16,672; and $27,720.

Bankruptcy – Using a Canon to Kill a Fly

Bankruptcy gives the freedom, the peace with grace to start over again if debts are discharged. It prevents house foreclosure and with the "automatic stay" stops harassment. Arrangements with the lender to keep the house must be made. Types of bankruptcy include Chapter 7 "Straight bankruptcy" also called "liquidation," Chapter 13 "reorganization," Chapter 11 for businesses, corporations, and partnerships, and Chapter 12 for family farmers.

Chapter 7 Bankruptcy

In Chapter 7 property is sold to pay bills. House and certain other assets are exempt. Social Security and retirement income are exempt. Enough is left to get started again. Debt that is secured (by property or collateral) and unsecured debt are treated differently because secured loans are repaid by property being returned. A trustee is appointed who collects all the non-exempt property from the debtor, he or she sells the property, and distributes the proceeds to the creditors. Exempt property is returned to the debtor. In cases where there are no assets to lose, the discharge process is faster. Reaffirmation arrangements are made so that car loans and mortgage payments continue. The co-signer still has to pay.

An attorney arranges the bankruptcy by filling out the forms listing assets and liabilities. Of course, he or she wants to be paid up front. Payment is made whether or not discharge is allowed or one is "judgment proof." The judge, after a hearing, assigns a trustee to decide which debts are to be discharged. Some people may be "judgment proof" as defined above. Some debts may have already been written off as bad debts. Some may have listed debts which are not really theirs.

The advantages of bankruptcy include the automatic stay on foreclosures, repossessions, utility shutoffs, and other creditor action. However, creditors may encourage continuing payments in order to keep certain possessions. An up-to-date reference lists the exemptions and how income for bankruptcy is calculated. After bankruptcy is taken, if the debtor makes a payment, the debt obligation is reinstated.

The disadvantages of bankruptcy are that it does not discharge student loans unless they were private loans, child and spousal support, wages for employees, secured debt, those debts one wants to keep because one wants to continue using the property, those debts one forgot to list on time, and income taxes. Bankruptcy stays on the record for 10 years. It may hurt parents' (or others') credit rating if they co-signed in the past and can keep one from getting a mortgage for a house, credit at reasonable rates, a job, or promotion especially in financial institutions.

Student loans are not discharged except under certain conditions. Private student loans that are not government backed can be discharged. Other conditions where student loans may be discharged include paying them back would cause undue hardship to self or those dependent on the debtor. Undue hardship is inability to maintain a minimal standard of living and paying for significant length of extended time that is impossible. The debtor has to show effort to pay which is usually repaying for five years before filing. Since bankruptcy cannot be taken for another eight years, it is advisable to be sure it is needed at this time. There are other ways less expensive to solve over-indebtedness than bankruptcy.

Bankruptcy costs about $700 to $1500 since there are the attorney fees, filing fees of $500 to $700, and fees for the two classes before filing and after hearing with the judge. For most people these dollars could have been used to pay debts.

The latest Bankruptcy Act requires the debtor to obtain Certificate One from counseling classes 180 days before filing. Then Certificate Two is required for classes in financial education after filing but before debts are discharged. The bankruptcy trustee handles applications for the classes. The Bankruptcy Abuse Prevention and Consumer Protection Act of 2005 requires budget or debt counseling and financial education.

The new act allows a request to change to Chapter 13 which is a consumer reorganization or debt repayment rather than a Chapter 7 liquidation bankruptcy. Abuse of Chapter 7 filing is considered when not paying 25 percent of nonpriority unsecured debt or $6,000 or $10,000 whichever is less if 60 times current monthly income would allow it. Current monthly income excludes Social Security income less allowable deductions defined by the Act.

A debtor may not file another Chapter 7 for seven to eight years or a Chapter 13 for four years after filing a Chapter 7 discharge and two years after filing for Chapter 13. New provisions include: asset interests in an automobile cannot be separated if purchased within 2 ½ years prior to bankruptcy or consumer goods within one year and no longer can landlords use the automatic stay provisions but can proceed with eviction processes.

Warren and Tyagi[227] report that many families do the right thing by filing bankruptcy. The major causes for 90 percent of the families in their study were divorce, disability, major health problem, or a job loss leading to financial disaster. It was their last ditch effort to provide for the children. They reported "two-income families have very little hedge room."

Chapter 13 Bankruptcy

In Chapter 13, disposable income is expected to repay debts. Disposable income is current income minus qualified expenses and cost of health insurance, domestic support obligations, charitable contributions, and necessary business expenses. The debtor has to meet the "means test" to take Chapter 13 to reorganize debts. Regular income is required. If a debtor's income is above the median income for those in the state adjusted for family size and inflation, Chapter 13 bankruptcy is required. In Chapter 13, debts are paid off and discharged after payments are made for three to five years (Insolvency Act of 2001 extended the time to five years). Chapter 13 is a repayment plan supervised by the assigned bankruptcy trustee. If debts cannot be repaid in three to five years, they are not included in the plan. Debts included in the Chapter 13 plan now have no or reduced interest. The highest interest rate that can be charged on a secured debt is 10 percent which is probably lower than the debtor had been paying. If the value of the item is less than the debt amount, the difference is paid as unsecured debt.

The trustee is paid a fee for distribution and services. Called "bankruptcy for those with regular income," the debtor's income goes to the trustee through garnishment or a court arrangement. Payments will not be missed this way. Several forms are filled out in detail. Debtors are advised to have an attorney, although much work needs to be done by the debtor. Secured creditors versus unsecured creditors are handled differently in repayment. Therefore, debts are first analyzed by whether or not they are secured. There are meetings of creditors, court hearings, and written details of transactions. A budget is determined for deciding how much to distribute to debts. Debtors report to the trustee. If the budget is too strict, difficulties in following through on the plan occur and the plan has to be forsaken.

Co-signers are protected in the Chapter 13 plan. They receive an "automatic stay." It is not advisable to merge a business or develop a business with a relative after setting up Chapter 13. Otherwise the Chapter 13 plan may be revoked. Bankruptcy stops harassment. Creditors must adhere to the repayment plan. They are prohibited from collecting claims from the debtor.

Handling Medical Debt

Generally, doctors, lawyers and dentists accept partial payments and even settle for less than what is actually owed on the bill. Sometimes, it is necessary in working out a repayment plan to talk with the professional directly, as opposed to the receptionist. One should try to get on a payment plan which helps the debt to stay unreported to credit bureaus. The plan may be small amount to be paid for the rest of one's life. Contact the billing department so that unpaid bills are not put into collection and they do not start charging interest.[228] If not contacted, they may legally refer the account to the collection agency. Medical debt can be reported to the credit bureaus, as well as a collection agency or an attorney for legal action.

---

227   Elizabeth Warren and Amelia Warren Tyagi. The Two-Income TRAP: Why Middle-Class Mothers and Fathers are Going Broke. Basic Books. 2003.

228   Griffin. Credit Bureau Experian.

Ways to handle medical debt are suggested in this SmartMoney article[229]: Check for errors in billing including duplicate billing for services and supplies. One county hospital lost their records so they billed people and waited to see who would respond to correct errors. Be sure the insurance is paying its share. If there is a dispute between doctor and insurance plan, the doctor will eventually bill the patient. Continue to check on the insurance company especially if the bills are not paid. Perhaps they have the wrong billing code. Negotiate the best billing code when making the appointment. The Medicare rate could be 50 percent less than full price. Use the state indigent fund or a fund available because the hospital was built with government funds. Ask the doctor or hospital financial counselor for help on which program one might be eligible. This is best before receiving treatment even in emergencies. Check on assistance from nonprofits which usually help with specific diseases (see www.patientadvocate.org).

If the bill is sent to collections by mistake, get a letter from them so that the error does not go on your credit report and negotiate with collection agencies who sometimes may settle for one fourth or one half of the bill.[230]

A true story illustrates how a shepherd can be helpful. Juan and Maria were worried. Being recent legal immigrants, they had no health insurance. Juan had unexpected heart problems that resulted in a huge hospital bill. To Pastor Betty's surprise, one call by her to ask the hospital about setting up a payment plan for Juan and Marie resulted in the forgiveness of the whole bill by the hospital.

The common experience has been reported[231] of a woman having $100,000 in medical bills from cancer even though she had health insurance. Through assistance from the medical provider and a credit-counseling agency, the debt was reduced to $8,000.

Selecting a Credit Counseling Agency

Credit counseling agencies vary but use similar names. The advantage of using their services is that a third party works with creditors on the client's behalf. They can negotiate a lower payment and frequently reduce interest. One check is sent to the counseling agency and they distribute the money to the creditors on the plan, communicating with them on the client's behalf. Working with the agency is recorded on the credit report but it shows an attempt to pay. The advantage is that the non-profit agency gives education and requires that one not use any more credit. They usually help the client to cut up the credit cards so they can no longer use them. This is in contrast to loan consolidation and self-administered programs which after relieving some pressure, encourage more debt.

Be leery of counseling agencies that infer they are non-profit or for-profit but have questionable procedures. These include collecting payment that all goes to the agency first before distributing to creditors, charging for making the mortgage payment (which some family member could pay), charging excessive fees, collecting large sums of money in advance, making promises they can not keep, and not including education as promised. Check the agency's certification. Call the Better Business Bureau, the State Attorney General, the consumer protection agency, or the state's consumer affairs office on the legitimacy and performance. Talk with satisfied customers.

---

229   Ibid.

230   Detweiler. Credit.com

231   Stacey L. Bradford, "Digging Out of Medical Debt" in SmartMoney. Internet. August 7, 2008.

Contact the National Foundation for Credit Counseling www.nfcc.org. For the nearest Consumer Credit Counseling Service, a non-profit, near the client call 1-800-388-2227.

Contact the Association of Independent Consumer Credit Counseling Agencies for services available: AICCCA.org. Check with the attorney general of each state on the legitimacy of these agencies and a list of the many others who promise to do things they do not fulfill and are unethical.

For InCharge Institute of America and Its Family of Financial Wellness Companies, call 1-888-734-6205 for Profina Debt Solutions for English speaking. Call 1-800-565-7525 for Spanish speaking. Use www.incharge.org. www.profina.org. www.concordcredit.org.

Facing Reality by Knowing the Credit Process

Individuals get into trouble because they do not understand the process and types of credit including calling cards. Revolving credit (credit cards, lines of credit) requires a minimum amount to be repaid each month, but there is no fixed time to repay. Installment loans require a fixed amount (including interest) to be repaid monthly over a pre-set period of time.

Perceiving credit is money gets people into trouble. Just thinking it is debt, not a resource, unless paid in full each month, changes some people's use of it. Credit implies that goods, services or money are received in exchange for a return promise to pay a sum of money at a later time. When all credit is used to its limit and a bigger crisis or greater opportunity occurs, the tragedy is that there is no credit available. Credit spends future resources without making choices about priorities, without deciding what is adequate versus ideal, having now rather than waiting until later, having convenience rather than saving money. Students report that when they think of credit as a debt they are less likely to use it.

A clause which goes unnoticed by many cardholders allows the bank to make subtle changes in fees, terms and conditions. Then if the cardholder uses the card he or she agrees to the proposed change. Changes to monitor include monthly maintenance fees, balance transfer fees, cash advance fees, fees for late payments, and fees for sending in less than the minimum payment.

Some people do not know there is a lien on their house for unpaid taxes until they get into a greater problem. Experience has revealed that three IRS counselors need to be contacted since different answers are received from them. Try, try again! Repayment of taxes can be negotiated. Tax refunds will be used automatically for unpaid past taxes without notifying the taxpayer.

When to use but not abuse is the question. The best advice is to borrow to increase human and material assets knowing there will be a return worth the extra cost of interest. Develop credit literacy and know the credit process. Know the rules and policies of the credit card and store charge cards. For example, over-limit fees can range from $20 to $29 dollars each month until the balance is reduced to less than the limit. The average amount for a late fee is $29.00.

The cure for captivity is to understand the credit process. It includes calculating the cost of credit, using real interest rates and totals. It requires comparison shopping and changing credit use to reflect careful, thought-out decisions. It requires control in buying by resisting commercialism and reconciling expenses with income. Comparisons should be made on prices, features, and interest rates. If one never carries a balance, one should look for the lowest annual percentage rate (APR). If never carrying a balance, one should look for a card with no annual fee. If a high user, one should look for suitable perks (e.g. rebates, airline miles). All users need to be cautious of short-term introductory—or "teaser" rates. If an individual misses a payment or is late, the interest can go dramatically higher. Introductory offers have time frames, so watch carefully. Individuals can negotiate interest rates by calling to ask for a lower rate.

Paying more than just the minimum reduces a mountain of debt and saves thousands of dollars over time more than is usually estimated. A typical minimum monthly payment is 90 percent interest and 10 percent principal. For example, by paying the minimum (2 percent) each month on a card with an 18 percent APR, paying off a $2,000 purchase will take about 19 years. It will cost more than $3,862 in interest, so a $2,000 purchase will end up costing more than $5,800!

Bankcard Holders of America (www.bankcardholders.org) gave this illustration of 18 percent interest and the payment of 2 percent of the balance:

Amount	Pay-off period	Interest costs	Actual cost
$1,800	22 years	$ 3,800	$ 5,600
3,900	35	10,100	14,000.

In Cathy's comic strip, she wanted to buy a sweater because it was on sale – 30 percent off. Her friend explained to her the cost when it hits the 18 percent credit card. A department store's interest rate is often higher. If one has $2,000 on the credit card with a $40 annual fee and pays just the 2 percent minimum, it will take 24 years to pay off, including $4,396.50 in interest on top of the $2,000 charge.

The Public Interest Research Group's survey asked students how long it would take to pay off a $1,000 credit card debt at an 18 percent APR, if only the minimum balance is paid. Using a generous 3 percent minimum payment (most credit cards require less), only 20 percent of all students guessed the correct answer - six years. In addition to the $1,000 paid off, the student would also pay $559 in interest. A $2,500 debt could take 34 years to pay off, with total payments of over $10,000, including $7,500 in interest.

Paying an amount above the minimum regularly reduce the time and cost of pay-off significantly. For example, paying an extra $20 per month on the above purchase would cut payment time to about 6 years and save over $3,000 in interest.

Comparing Fees for Credit

The main comparison is on interest rate annually. The APR is stated for ease in comparison. In the fine print, other fees may be stated. Annual fees are often charged for the use of the card. Late fees (sometimes applied to payment only one day late) can cost $30 or more. Over limit fees are applied if one charges more than the pre-approved amount. Transaction fees may be applied when an individual takes out a cash advance.

Rates for cash advances are different from those for purchases. Fees are charged for using credit cards at different ATM locations. When a payment is late, the attractive initial interest rate usually jumps to a much higher rate.

Calculating Interest

A number of methods are used to calculate the interest, including basing the interest on the average daily balance or on the outstanding balance at closing. Knowing the method of calculating interest is useful to choose the best payment method. The reason to know the method of calculating interest is that with the method of average daily balance the sooner one sends in the payment the better. Know the policies of and way of calculating interest by various lenders.

A $1,000 balance @ 18 percent interest over three years with regular payments like a car loan and debts with an add-on interest method would charge about half of the principal amount in interest of about $500.

An example of the average daily balance method: A $600 payment was made on the 15th day of a 30 day billing period. Interest is charged on the average amount outstanding. Since $800 was outstanding for 15 days and $200 for 15 days, average daily balance was $500. One month interest is $7.50, at 1-1/2 percent monthly interest rate (18 percent APR). The sooner a payment is sent, the lower the average daily balance and therefore the lower the finance charge.

Knowing the type of student loan is useful for paying the debtor. In a subsidized loan, students pay part of the interest. Interest starts when one starts paying. In an unsubsidized loan, students pay all interest which starts accruing when the loan is taken out. The sooner one pays off the debtor the better. The ability to defer is not a blessing. It is a curse. The number for borrowers' tracking their accounts is 1-800-433-3243. The Student Default Hotline is 1-800-621-3115.

The difficulty in handling credit payments today is billing periods for different companies are different and the grace periods are different and getting shorter. When bills are delinquent, the time for charging late fees is different than before and for different companies.

Identifying the Grace Period

A grace period is the time when no interest is being charged for new purchases. This varies by creditor and may change without the individual knowing it. Grace periods, which vary by company, usually do not apply when a balance is carried on the card. In general, grace periods are getting shorter.

Making Payments on Time

The consequences of missing the due date include raised interest rates on future purchases for all credit cards. The fine print allows card issuers to garnish wages without going to court. Getting behind on payments can result in harassment from bill collectors and even court action. There is a worksheet below for analyzing the consequences.

Understanding Statements

It is important to check every statement for correct information, including purchases, credits and payments. Reminder: Act quickly to correct errors. Keep receipts and other records. Always notify card issuers of change of address.

"Card Hopping." Shift the balance to a card with a lower APR when the old one rises, but be sure to cancel the first to avoid fees. Adding new cards to take advantage of lower interest rates may have a short-term benefit, but be sure the permanent interest rate is also advantageous. If a payment is late, the interest rate rises. Always close the "old" card to avoid having too much open credit. Card hopping can be more trouble than it is really worth unless one is committed to following through as necessary.

Calculating the Cost of the Loan

After several years of paying on a loan with missed payment fees, late fees, and paying just the minimum, the total owed has increased. Total cost of credit equals the payment amount times number of payments minus the cash price. (This is obvious but emphasized here because of the neglect and abuse in calculating cost of credit during the buying decision.) Financial calculators on the Internet can be useful.

Cost of credit = (Payment amount X Number of payments) – Cash price

Examples: Paying for a $6,000 car at 18 percent over three years:

Cost of credit = ($250 X 36 months) - $6,000

Cost of credit = $9,000 - $6,000

Cost of credit = $3,000

Example 1: If one pays only $20 a month on a $1,000 credit card bill with 19 percent interest, it will take one 99 months to pay it off. The total amount is $2,720. Using credit will cost an extra $1,996.

Example 2: One charges $500 on a card with 13 percent APR and pays only minimum of $10 a month. It will take 72.4 months or about 6 years and the total amount paid will be $2,168.33.

Example 3: $20,000 in a loan will cost $28,488 when paid back over 10 years at 7.5 percent interest rate. Interest charges are $8,488. The same $20,000 loan costs $24,046 when paid back over five years at 7.5 percent. Interest charges are $4,046.

Example 4: Paying the minimum on a credit card at 18 percent interest and a $40 annual fee will take 24 years to pay it off. The individual will have paid $4,396.50 in interest on top of the $2,000 charge. **All student loan interest paid qualifies for the Student Loan Tax Deduction ($2,000 for 2000 tax year and $2,500 per year after that).**

THE DOLLAR COST OF CREDIT ON A $1,000 LOAN

(This is shown to emphasize the importance of comparison shopping for credit and loans' rate. It shows how length of term increases interest.)

The Add-on Interest Rate is:	Interest in Dollars Over Various Number of Months				
	12	18	24	30	36
6%	$ 60	$ 90	$120	$150	$180
8%	80	120	160	200	240
10%	100	150	200	250	300
12%	120	180	240	300	360
14%	140	210	280	350	420
16%	160	240	320	400	480
18%	180	270	360	450	540
20%	200	300	400	500	600

Challenges for College Students

Use of credit cards is one of the biggest problems for college students although they may not think so at the time. More students drop out of school because of credit and debt problems than poor grades. Suicides over credit and financial problems of students have been reported.

The easy credit, creditors on campus, and Financial Aid encourage students to borrow resulting in their captivity. There is intense marketing of credit cards to students, they are easily available and the marketers are very persuasive. New scams arise quickly. The Higher Education Act of 2001 encourages loan consolidation and extending the time to pay. When they do not get the aid on time to buy housing, books, and supplies, they use credit and get more financial aid to cover short term credit. Short term credit turned into long term debt and consolidation digs the hole deeper and longer.

Over time, students are encouraged to borrow more than needed without counseling about alternatives. Easy credit on campus, as well as availability of student loans, encourages more debt. Financial savvy people consider changing the concept of what the standard package of college life considers adequate; working part-time; going to community college and then transferring; working to control credit for reports to prospective employers, insurance, and housing; getting an early inheritance, going through poverty for a few years; searching more for scholarships (there are many unclaimed scholarship and scholarships for unusual circumstances such as left handedness and first time college goers in the family); thinking of the future rather than managing by crisis; getting parents to help; combating commercialism; and not spending so much for drinks/beer. Choosing a major that will have debt waived for working in remote areas or certain occupations may be helpful. Other suggestions are in chapter 6.

A good credit rating is as important as good grades when graduating and seeking employment. A good credit rating may be needed to qualify for graduate school financial aid.

Repaying Student Loans

These are typically easy to get, but--with few exceptions-- they must be repaid beginning six months after leaving school. They are helpful to responsible students. Upon employment, buy a good used car and pay back the debt rather than buy a new car. Get information on the Direct Repay and Great Rewards programs for discounts and retiring the debt earlier at www.collegeboard.org. If the collection agency finds the debtor and the debtor refuses to pay, the Justice Department takes over to get the debtor to pay. The worst practices are paying just the minimum, consolidating, creeping indebtedness, and not being willing to defer gratification.

Beware of "Too-good-to-be-true" plans. Credit postpones solving the problem of keeping expenses below income. These cost more over time even at a lower interest rate if one consolidates. The best advice is to reject the buying frenzy dictated by the media. The enemy is the pressure to rely on credit and then to consolidate. "Redefine the good life your own way. You have worked and studied hard to get into college and you deserve to be in control with financial peace of mind rather than buy with credit every pleasure, activity, or material thing desired, for now anyway. Protect your future financial freedom and the flexibility of choice with wise use of credit." (Williams)

College students can defer paying student loans until 5 – 6 months after graduation, unless they claim hardship or are going back to school. They can deduct interest for 50 months, depending on the loan, and need to check with the originator of the loan. They need to find out if the interest is deferred or if is still accruing same as other credit/debts. Maybe it has not reached them and meanwhile interest is accruing.

Mother and daughter came to the financial clinic with the question of how to reduce their assets so the daughter could get more financial aid. **What is wrong here?** First, it is the wrong question. (A basic counseling principle is to sort through the questions that need to be asked. Another principle is to examine what is behind the question. An astute counselor starts at another place than the "presenting" question.) Obviously with fewer assets and parental income, the more the student can borrow. Obviously, the more one borrows the more one has to pay back. When asked how not to have such large student loans, the first answer is not to go into debt. Another answer is to consider ways of increasing income which include employment, going to a local college and then transferring, early inheritance, checking out scholarships at the office of financial aid and the Dean's office, and using parents' help. At one time, parents encouraged student's borrowing because students receive a lower rate than the interest rate they would have to pay for a new car, etc. Parents, as well as students, need to defer gratification for some purchases for a few years. One can have good experiences and enjoy college without all the standard package items considered "ideal."

The availability of student loans is changing. The number of companies offering loans has greatly reduced and so students "seek private loans to fill gaps left from scholarships and limited state and federal support."[232] Lenders are not as interested in unsecured debt which has a 2-4-year "lag in repayment." Fees for missing payments have increased. Lenders may not want to make commitments for more than one year.

A **college graduate** comes to the financial counseling clinic because her job is in jeopardy. **Why?** Judy works at a bank and employees are not allowed to have a bad credit rating. Judy graduated from college five years ago, the first in any of her family to acquire a higher education.

Upon graduation she spent money to buy eye glasses, clothes, car, apartment, furnishings, meals with colleagues, trips to weddings of friends, and hair care which all cost more than her beginning salary. To buy all these, many which were job related, she used credit. She was managing by crisis just as she had during college years. After graduation because she was concentrating on the new job and caring for her dying mother, she did not pay her college loans. At graduation they were $8,000, but now with late fees, missed payments, and loan consolidation the total debt was over $20,000. Although a remedy of a second job would be time and energy consuming, she was spending leisure time worrying about her finances. With a few lifestyle changes, she could be out of debt in four years. She needs emotional support to defer gratification for four years (which is the time she was successful to manage college). Changes, for a set time, with a goal that seems possible, give hope and energy.

A **middle aged pastor** has filed for bankruptcy. As reported in the newspaper she had assets of $181,000 and liabilities of $73,000. Whether or not further action was taken beyond the filing, the report affected her credibility and effectiveness to witness to some people. Yet her case is easily understood. She had student loans from undergraduate school plus loans for graduate school all encouraged by the financial aid office without giving alternatives. She had consolidated some of the loans. Then she had a nasty divorce which is a frequent cause of bankruptcy. She had expensive attorney fees for the divorce. She had travel expenses from changing churches. Other expenses included furnishings and supplies for a new apartment, new clothes for her professional position as pastor, new car, photographic equipment which she used for church activities, travel to visit

---

232   Lauren Tara LaCapra. August 11, "Student-Loan Woes Hurt Upper Middle Class." www.mainstreet.com. 2008.

elderly parents, travel to conferences and seminars for continuing education or enrichment, tithing, utilities, gas, and food. Her church no longer provided health insurance. She had several chronic illnesses that needed attention in order to continue her employment. Eventually, she obtained some insurance through another denomination that was relatively inexpensive.

One Sunday from the pulpit, she confessed her difficulties and stress. She said she had made mistakes and was embarrassed. She asked for forgiveness and grace. She asked for prayer as she would be going through the bankruptcy process and court hearings. Several weeks later she shared her joy that all her debts were erased. A great burden had been lifted.

What debts were repaid? Since she kept the car, what are the payments? (She is taking the bus to and from work rather than driving.) What things did she return? What assets were liquidated to pay some debts? Did she use her retirement income, which is usually exempt, to pay some college debts? How could her college debt be discharged unless she had private loans? (Private loans may have picked up where Sallie Mae, government backed student loans, and U.S. Department of Education "direct loans" left off.) When does she go to the educational class required of bankruptcy filers? Or is she taking it on-line?

Victory in Managing Credit

Preventing Foreclosure

Foreclosures occur after a homeowner stops making payments and the lender initiates legal proceedings to force the sale of the property. To prevent foreclosure the shepherd needs to have a reference from the legal services or neighborhood housing authorities that diagram the legal process. This shows options, points of intervention, times between legal actions to recover house, and sources of referral. Special arrangements can be made when the loan is secured by the Federal Housing Administration or Veteran's Administration. Possibilities include reinstatement (getting the money together to pay arrears when necessary in the legal process), forbearance (scheduled increased monthly payments beginning with a large first payment), deferment, refinancing (worthwhile if interest rate is at least two percent lower), assignment of the mortgage to HUD, recasting, deed-in-lieu of foreclosure, and re-amortization.

With some lenders, an individual might perform labor in keeping the house maintained or may provide services or repairs in lieu of rent. Other ways to continue payments may be to take in boarder(s), rent the house to someone else until they can start making payments, or to double up with another family/grandparents. Perhaps an individual could agree to add $100 or $200 to the current payment until the delinquent amount is met. Maybe the individual could pay every two weeks without a late penalty. A financially able child may purchase the house as a tax sheltered investment and rent it to parents for a small amount (or "sell-lease-back").

Some consumers are fraudulent and plan to leave a house while owing on it. However, the reasons for today's high loan default rates are: predatory lending practices, including high fees on refinanced loans, and high interest rates; economic hardship such as a layoff, high medical bills or other calamity; death; marital problems; excessive obligations; mortgage fraud; and lending practices that lure first-time home buyers into assuming more debt than they can afford.

Upon notice of foreclosure, first contact the lender. Many banks are willing to work out arrangements as they are aware of the current economic conditions and admit they were part of the problem. However, options are not available if the lender was in the subprime market and did predatory lending. These lenders want to repossess and serve papers again. Other homeowners are victims of high pressure tactics and unscrupulous lenders. They choose poor management such as putting new appliances on the 30 year mortgage. When variable rates increase, borrowers owe more now than what the property is worth. They can not sell the house for what they owe.

HUD (Housing and Urban Development) and Consumer Credit Counseling agencies have certified counselors. Be sure the counselor is HUD certified. They may suggest ways to keep out of foreclosure. They do a budget analysis by identifying normal living expenses, look at controlling indebtedness, and determine net income. They suggest using tax refund and taking more monthly withholding from income taxes. The first priority as other counselors will say is the house payment. One must contact the mortgage holder. The worst thing is to ignore the lender or last collection efforts. Let the mortgagor know there is a problem. Depending on the circumstances different remedies can be made. In a repayment plan, more cash is sent each month until caught up. In loan modification, the mortgage is extended for 10 – 15 - 30 years. Overdue payments are transferred to the end of the loan. Interest rates are lowered as are the monthly payments. The best advice is to not move out of current housing because there would be fewer choices. On the other hand, there are advantages of renting if one has the deposit. Homeowners will still owe on the house.

Improve Credit Score

Some consider the credit score a mediocre measure of behavior or worthiness because it is based on the lender's decision. Never-the-less lenders use the score for determining whether to grant credit and at what rate. Businesses, institutions, and companies routinely check credit reports and scores of prospective employees. The vantage score is developed and used by national credit bureaus. Credit unions may have their own system. The score is lower for the individual who does not use credit. It is lower for one who checks on the account too often.

Thirty-five percent of the credit score is based on late or missed payments, foreclosures and bankruptcies. Although credit reports are free, there is a charge fee for getting the credit score. These reports must be checked for accuracy. About 30 percent of the score is based on amount owed in relation to credit limit. The best advice is to keep account balances below 50 percent of credit limit. Ten percent of the score comes from new inquiries for credit cards, loans, and other requests. Fifteen percent comes from length of time credit has been managed (average age of accounts). Keeping an older account helps to balance newer credit. (See Chapter 8 on preventive foreclosure.)

Change Attitude and Behavior

The caveat is "Control credit or it will control you." The danger is that credit can enhance a person with immediate pleasure but can destroy and enslave for years. To change credit use may require de-programming and rejecting the buying frenzy dictated by the media, advertisements, television and certain cultures. The enemy uses pressure to rely on credit and then to consolidate. Victory is gained through redefining the good life and marching to a different drummer.

Getting out of captivity means changing from the credit mentality of "I can have anything I want, anytime, from anywhere." Control of the plastic card means making choices. It is saying "no" to some things and people and "yes" to other things and people.

Another caveat is to "Protect your credit as you would protect your life." In fact, the lack of credit control does affect the life and death of one's financial life, as well as the physical life in an emergency. Changes in managing credit may be necessary. Setting up loan payments to be made electronically with direct payroll deposit or transfer, late fees can be avoided. Making a calendar with due dates or posting date (if it can be found) and noting when payment is to be sent is useful. Not only are late payment fees charged but the interest rate may rise if a payment is missed. Mistakes and late payments on one credit card can affect the rates on other cards and on one's credit score.

The first step out of captivity of credit is having the desire to get out. The second is to change one's purpose for living, way of loving, and way of spending. One cannot expect different results from the same financial behavior. Every area has to be examined for minute changes including mode, method, and use of such things as utilities, eating, trips, etc. As the rich young man who asked Jesus what to do to inherit eternal life, individuals gain release from their captivity by leaving things and the past behind to follow sound teachings and to start serving others. Discipline is involved in seeking first the kingdom (reign) of God, trusting these other things will be added.

Disciples do not eat food needed for tomorrow. A college student told the author that his mother said, "Borrow all you can because they cannot get blood out of a turnip." Some think the answer to a money problem is borrowing more. In contrast to the prayer "Give us our daily bread," people seem to be demanding "Give us tomorrow's bread to eat today." Rather than taking more credit, people need to consider alternatives for increasing income, reducing wants, being more efficient, changing expectations, and being creative.

Avoid Credit

The victory is in avoiding credit where possible. Counselors recommend cutting up cards leaving one or two for emergency. In case the one does not work due to lack of payment, say in a foreign country, or the magnetic strip has worn off, a second emergency card is useful.

People could avoid credit on many purchases by not going there, not being persuaded by advertisements, not getting caught up in the excitement of the moment, and not stopping for an expensive latte on the way home from work.

Save

A major reason that credit is "over used" is that people "underestimate expenses." People do not save for emergencies, irregular and seasonal expenses. They do not have funds for the unexpected expenses, which occur every week for many people. In surveys, consumers will usually say, "But this was an unusual week." They do not realize house or vehicle payments are about 60 percent of their total costs because related upkeep, taxes, insurance, repair, etc. are 40 percent or more. Their decisions were made on the monthly payment rather than total cost.

People could refocus on doing for oneself, repairing, keeping old things longer until they are out of debt, and find ways to reduce expenses. They could have separate accounts, deposited monthly, for annual taxes, vacation, Christmas, or education. They could consider exchanging goods and services or doing cooperative buying among friends and neighbors. Where and how change must occur is written down and referred to daily.

Credit could be avoided by not overestimating income. People do not realize "decision" or "disposable" income is much lower than gross income. They use pay raises for new things rather than realizing inflation has already spent the pay increases.

Change Priorities

To get out of captivity and make decisions, priorities have to be identified. By definition, resources are limited. Credit control is learned by a willingness to give up something desirable to make a better choice. Priorities can be decided by asking questions about what is most important. Questions to ask are: What will improve well-being over time, what is healthier, what can only be done at this time in one's life, how much can be done at this time of one's life, and what will make one more effective in serving God's kingdom? Certain expenses can only be met at certain times in the stage of family life.

One question to help decide priorities for time and money is "What will happen if one does not have this or do this?" In contrast, ask about the competing want or the possibility of not using credit. If nothing will happen or is less beneficial than something else, this is what can be cut out.

Credit control is choosing when, from whom, and for what to use credit or a loan. Control is thinking of alternatives for funding rather than automatically flashing out the plastic card or taking a quick loan with high interest without comparing interest rates.

Timing is everything for many endeavors and these are times when credit or a loan comes to the rescue. Worthwhile endeavors are those for which a harvest or return is sure. Payoffs can be in material gain, spiritual renewal, or work of the kingdom. Seeds have to be planted at certain times to multiply. A business endeavor has to expand to provide the product or services in a timely manner. Skills and training for developing human capital have to be obtained at certain times of one's life. A trip to rescue a daughter cannot be put off. The opportunity to share is now and recuperating financially can be postponed till later.

A telescopic vision is useful. Using credit at certain times of one's life and recuperating from it at other times is making a decision (having control) rather than using it all the time without thinking. When using credit or a loan for *a* worthwhile purpose, individuals and families must think what can be foregone or postponed for awhile. Some families do not have money even for basics when there are dependent children, but they will have ample in later years. On the other hand, acting out of love, grandparents are burdened by caring for children of irresponsible or incarcerated children. For some, the high cost of credit, which is used, is the cost of surrendering to the Cross. Life may never be easy but is lived in the promise (comfort) of God's presence, healing the broken-hearted, and providing guidance for getting daily bread.

Changing desires, lifestyle, and not buying into America's Standard Package may be the answer to get out of credit captivity. The challenge is how to change lifestyle or how to get similar satisfaction and security with less expense. This involves better management of credit and debt. It is natural to want to increase one's standard of living and to have the American lifestyle. Let it be more natural to seek counseling and education to manage credit and debt. Give up captivity to addiction and ignorance. Let the fulfilling of spiritual needs and generosity be part of financial management and the standard of living. Paul in Romans 12:2 says, "Do not conform any longer to the pattern of this world, but be transformed by the renewing of your mind." Credit use, loan behavior, and lifestyle are changed in minute and in drastic, large ways. Wishful thinking will not renew the mind or change behavior, but disciplined action and control will.

Encouragement needs to be given to everyone. Otherwise, people will fall away from teaching and quit, saying as some of Jesus' disciples said, "This is too hard to follow" (John 6:60-66). An individual says, "I worked so hard so I deserve nice things, vacations, parties, etc." One can encourage him or her by saying, "You worked hard and you deserve to be in control of your credit, to be master of your financial fate." Individuals could be reminded that it took four years to get their degree or training so now take four years to get out of debt. List the wonderful things and vacations they now have and enjoy them before buying anything else. If they have children but not the savings, clothes, etc., for themselves, remind them they are investing in human capital. Someday they will be able to make "ends meet" and save for their retirement.

If credit use has been geared to custom, friends, past, future, television, culture, and despair to the detriment of finances, these identities may need to be changed. Purpose and focus in life may have to be changed. Roles in life may have to be reprioritized. Rather than one's life revolving around car, hobby, pets, occupation, etc. it can revolve around accepting God's love and sharing it with others. When life revolves around God's purposes and seeking first his kingdom, one is not so devastated when loss of job, income, or denial of credit occurs. One's source of security from using credit has to be changed to relying on inner resources in tough and uncertain times.

Prayer

In the Lord's Prayer, the phrase "Keep us from evil, or the evil one" can refer to deceptive, unscrupulous credit granters who are thinking of their own benefit rather than those in the best interest of the customer. The prayer includes help to not be misled or misdirected. Prayer can help one to listen to God who whispers options.

There is promise of victory. Measure progress, not perfection, so that one does not become discouraged. The prayer for better financial behavior is like what Paul said in Philippians 3:12, "Not that I have already obtained all this, or have already been made perfect, but I must press on to take hold of that for which Christ Jesus took hold of me."

The spiritual formula and steps for action for victory in financial and credit matters was the theme of Annual Conference of the Church of the Brethren in 2008 for renewal in life: "Surrendered to God. Transformed in Christ. Empowered by the Spirit."

Tools and Case Studies to Educate and Use for Decisions

Case Study Using Loan Consolidation Worksheet

A. Current Program

Creditor's Name	Address	Phone	Annual % Rate	Remaining Balance	Monthly Payment	X	No. of Months[1]	=	Sub-total	+	Balloon, Other Costs	=	Remaining Total Payback	Prepayment Penalty or Payoff Cost	Current Monthly Interest	Total Interest
						X										
						X										
						X										
						X										
						X										
						X										
						X		=		+		=				
TOTALS for current program						X		=								

B. Consolidation Programs

															1st Mo.	
						X		=								
						X		=								
						X		=								

Case Study Using Loan Consolidation Worksheet

A. Current Program

Creditor's Name	Address	Phone	Annual % Rate	Remaining Balance	Monthly Payment	X	No. of Months[1]	=	Sub-total	+	Balloon, Other Costs	=	Remaining Total Payback	Prepayment Penalty or Payoff Cost	Current Monthly Interest	Total Interest
VISA			18%	$1,282	$52	X	31						$1,612		$20.00	
Department Store			18%	1,715	102	X	20						2,040		36.41	
Credit Union			12%	2,540	281	X	10						2,810		30.10	
Department Store			18%	375	47	X	9						423		6.00	
Department Store			18%	296	25	X	22						550		4.65	
Department Store			18%	221	22	X	11						242		2.00	
Mother-in-Law			8%	2,500	200/yr	X	48	=	800	+	2,500	=	3,300		17.00	
Dr. Smith			0%	160									160		0.00	
TOTALS for current program				$9,089	$546[2]	X	9 to 31	=					$11,137		$106.16	$2,048

B. Consolidation Programs

			Annual % Rate	Remaining Balance	Monthly Payment	X	No. of Months	=					Remaining Total Payback	Prepayment Penalty or Payoff Cost	Current Monthly Interest	Total Interest
Credit Union/2nd Mortgage Security			16%	$9,089	$167	X	120	=					$20,040		1st Mo. $121.19	10,951
Credit Union/2nd Mortgage Security			16%	9,089	283	X	48	=					$13,584		121.19	4,495
Finance Co./2nd Mortgage Security			21%	9,089	206	X	84	=					$17,304		159.06	8,215

[1] A financial calculator with amortization calculations will show number of months left so that the current program costs can be obtained.

[2] **In 11 months the $546.00 payment would be reduced to only $196.00.**

Case Study Using Loan Consolidation Worksheet

A. Current Program, Jan. 1993 (as of 2/2) Creditor:	B. Interest Rate	C. Principal Balance (PV)	D. Monthly Payment (PMT)	E. No. of [1] Months	F. Monthly Principal Portion $(D_1 - G)$	G. Monthly Interest Portion $(B/12 \times C)$	H. Remaining Total Payback $(D_1 \times E)$	I. Prepayment Penalty or Payoff Fees	J. Total Interest Over Time $([H - C] - C)$
1. Equity Loan	11%	$10,721	$193[F]	78.3	$93.87	$98.64	$15,072.75	0.00	$4,350.92
2. VISA	13.5	941	200[B]	4.9	189.36	10.64	980.00	0.00	38.58
3. His Signature Loan	11.99	4,464	150[F]	35.5	105.36	44.64	5,325.00	0.00	861.37
4. Educational Loan	11.99	3,538	200[B]	19.6	164.62	35.38	3,920.00	0.00	382.06
5. Her Signature Loan	11.99	5,042	206[F]	28.2	155.84	50.42	5,816.53	0.00	774.93
6. VISA	13.5	4,995	200[B]	29.5	143.56	56.44	5,900.00	0.00	905.20
7. Farm Loan	7.15[1]	24,994	192[F]	135.8	43.08	148.92	26,073.60	0.00	1,079.60
8. VISA	19.8	4,774	144[B]	48.4	65.22	78.78	6,969.60	0.00	2,195.13
9. Loan on Retirement	8.75	4,868	70[B]	96.0	34.51	35.49	6,720.00	0.00	1,852.00
10. Department Store	21	850	100[B]	9.3	85.13	14.88	930.00	0.00	80.00
11. Department Store	21	1,536	200[B]	8.3	173.12	26.88	1,660.00	0.00	1,124.00
12. Master Card	15.48	1,917	47[S]	58.5	22.27	24.73	2,749.50	0.00	832.50
13. MasterCard	15.9	4,274	106[B]	57.5	50.87	55.13	6,095.00	0.00	1,821.00
14. Department Store	21	448	95[S]	5.0	87.16	7.84	475.00	0.00	27.00
15. Department Store	21	772	280[S]	2.9	266.49	13.51	812.00	0.00	40.00
16. Dentist	0	1,400	150[F]	9.3	150.00	0.00	1400.00	0.00	0.00
17. First Mortgage	6.375[1]	103,634	801[F]	219.5	250.44	550.56	157,822.22	0.00	72,188.22

[1] Assuming no additional purchases or cash advances are made.
[F] Fixed payment.
[B] Budgeted or arbitrary payment.
[S] From billing statement.

TOTALS for current program:

		C.	D.	E.	F.	G.	H.	I.	J.
All:		$179,168	$3,334	2.9 to 208.5	$2,051.01	$1,252.68	266,657.19	$ 0.00	$88,487.95
All except #17:		75,534	2,532	2.9 to 135.8	1,798.83	703.42	90,834.97	0.00	16,299.83
#1 thru #6:		29,701	1,149	4.9 to 78.3	852.6	296.16	37,014.28	0.00	7,313.06
#7 thru #16:		45,833	1,383	2.9 to 135.8	407.26	946.22	53,820.69	0.00	8,986.77
Consolidation of #1 thru #6:	10%	32,000	335	180	68.00	267.00	60,300.00	Fees for new loan 174.00	28,300.00

(Since this is a home equity loan, subtract 31% of interest paid for tax deduction)

Comparison Process: Calculate months until original debts #1 thru #6 would approximately equal payment of consolidation loan. In this case, in 29½ months the total monthly payment for #1 thru #6 would be about $343, and in 35½ months would be $193 for the remaining 42.8 months (42.8 + 35.5 = 78.3 months) compared to 180 months on the loan consolidation.

What Will Happen if this Bill is not Paid? What will Hurt Person?

Bill or Debt	Harassment	Cut in Service	Loss of Goods (Repossession)	Court Action Garnishment (seizure)	Total Due Now
1.					
2.					
3.					
4.					
5.					
6.					
7.					
8.					
9.					

Garnishments are creditor garnishment, replevin (chattel mortgages), foreign judgments, child support, IRS levies, Bankruptcy (Chapter 13), and miscellaneous. In earlier times, an individual would be fired if there was a garnishment. Now a column on the company payroll form is ready for a check mark since it is so prevalent. People sign that wages can be garnished without going to court.

Will Bankruptcy Help or Not?

This is a tool to analyze, before filing, whether or not bankruptcy will help.

Debt	Yes (Bankruptcy will Discharge)	Maybe (Depends on Amount of Equity)	No (Bankruptcy Will Not Discharge)
1.			
2.			
3.			
4.			
5.			
6.			
7.			
8.			
9.			

Is Loan Consolidation the Answer?

YES	NO
When property is saved and one learns from experience to be disciplined or does not incur additional debts.	If psychological freedom of smaller monthly payment encourages more debts.
If it pays the balance and stops paying only the minimum on debts and not incurring additional debts.	If it is a second mortgage, because both first and second mortgages must be paid regardless of circumstances and are inflexible in amount and timing.
If it stops the pattern of revolving charges which are never paid and purchases continue to be made with higher interest. If it stops "creeping indebtedness."	If loan consolidation includes no "interest bearing accounts" (medical, attorneys, relatives, collection agencies).
If it prevents bankruptcy which goes on one's record for ten years, and limits certain future loans or job opportunities.	If it contributes to "creeping indebtedness," more debts with higher portions going to interest than principal.
If all debts have higher interest rates than a consolidated loan would have, and the consolidated debt can be paid off in the same amount of time as the previous debts.	If using the house for collateral causes stress when payment is late or other expenses increase.

Sample Letter to Creditors

February 13, ____

        Re: John D. Doe
                  Main St.
                  Lafayette, IN 47905
                  Account No._____
                  Total indebtedness:_____
                  Number of creditors:_____
                  Net income:_____
                  Minimum Living expenses:_____
                  Proposed Monthly Payment:_____

Dear Sir or Madam:

John D. Doe, a young man with a family of five, is working with me on his budgeting and debt problems. Mr. Doe has told me that medical expenses and a divorce had caused problems with his financial management. Mr. Doe is now willing and able to make some changes to overcome his financial difficulties. His present wife, Jane A., is beginning to work part time. A realistic, minimum budget has been set up for their living expenses and a program of payments has been developed.

We are asking each creditor to accept a reduced payment to be applied on the principal for several months. Amounts will be increased as possible until the total debt is paid. Mr. Doe plans to begin sending payments to you on <u>(date).</u>

We hope that any present or pending legal proceedings be stayed. Please inform us of the correct balance due.

We assume your cooperation and sincerely thank you for it. Please indicate on the form below if this plan is acceptable and send it directly to Mr. Doe.

Our counseling, budgeting, and educational service is free of charge to our clients. We accept referrals.

                    Very truly yours,

_____   _____

Client who has asked counselor   Financial Counselor
to communicate for him or her.

Name of creditor:

Acceptance of payment plan: _____ Yes _____ No
Remarks:

Please send statement of balance due to: John D. Doe
                                  123 Main St.
                                  Lafayette, IN 47905

CREDIT REPORT "REQUEST" FORM

(Not all creditors report to the same agency. Send a request to each credit reporting agency.)

Type or print clearly. Provide all requested information.

_____ Please send a copy of my PERSONAL credit report.

_____ Please send a copy of our JOINT credit report.

_____ A check OR _____ money order is enclosed (if required).

_____ I/We were DENIED CREDIT, EMPLOYMENT, or INSURANCE within the past 60 days by:

_____
(Name of firm)

Because of information contained in my/our credit files at your agency. A copy of the letter of denial is enclosed. I/We understand a copy of my/our credit report will be sent without charge.

Date _____ Daytime Phone (_)_____

Full Name _____
          (last)   (first)   (middle initial)   (Jr., Sr., 2nd, etc.)

Current address *_____

Mailing address _____
             (PO Box, etc. if different from street address)

City _____ State _____ Zip _____

Previous Addresses (past five years) _____

_____

Marital Status _____ Spouse's First Name _____

Your Date of Birth _____/_____/_____ Spouse's Date of Birth _____/_____/_____

Your Social Security Number   _____ - _____ - _____

Spouse's Social Security Number   _____ - _____ - _____

Current Employer _____

Spouse's Current Employer _____
                            (if joint)

Your Signature _____

Spouse's Signature _____

* Attached is verification of my current address and a copy of a current billing statement from a creditor, a copy of a utility bill, or a copy of a driver's license).

CREDIT REPORT "DISPUTE" FORM

TRANS UNION CREDIT BUREAU
Consumer Relations Center
PO Box 390
Springfield PA 19064-0390

www.transunion.com

EQUIFAX CREDIT INFORMATION SERVICE
P.O. Box 105873
Atlanta, GA 30348

www.equifax.com

EXPERIAN
National Consumer Assistance Center
PO Box 949
Allen, TX 75002-0949

www.experian.com

Name _____ Date of Birth _____

Address _____ Home Phone _____

_____ Work Phone _____

Social Security Number _____

I dispute the accuracy or completeness of the following items that appear in my file:

Signature _____ Date _____

Company name   Account #   Comments

_____   _____   _____

                                                    _____

                                                    _____

_____   _____   _____

                                                    _____

                                                    _____

                                                    _____

                                                    _____

_____   _____   _____

                                                    _____

                                                    _____

                                                    _____

                                                    _____

Included is a copy of credit report.
Thank you for your assistance in investigating the accuracy of this information.

CREDIT CONTROL
(Do you control credit, or does it control you?)

Ask yourself these questions:

		Yes	No
1.	Do I need it now? (If you need it, you must have it to function as a human, in your job, or in social affairs)	____	____
2.	Is it worth the extra credit cost to have it now?	____	____
3.	Is it worth the risk of losing the money I have put into it if I don't meet the payments?	____	____
4.	Will this purchase help achieve a family or a personal goal?	____	____
5.	Is the interest cost reasonable?	____	____
6.	Will I still be using the purchase when I have finished paying for it?	____	____
7.	Will this purchase meet with family approval?	____	____
8.	Am I buying from a fair and honest person or firm?	____	____
9.	Can I buy it without committing an anticipated increase in income?	____	____
10.	Is my use of credit cards reasonable?	____	____
11.	Do I make payments on time?	____	____
12.	Have I been able to pay charge card statements in full and thus avoid finance charges?	____	____
13.	Can I make these payments without skimping on necessities?	____	____
14.	Do I have an emergency fund to take care of unforeseen expenses?	____	____
15.	Is my credit good enough so that I can borrow in case of illness or emergency?	____	____
16.	Are my job and health prospects good?	____	____
17.	Have I avoided dipping into savings to meet regular expenses?	____	____
18.	Am I _always_ honest with spouse (or self, if single) about my expenses?	____	____
19.	Do I avoid borrowing to pay off other credits or debts?	____	____
20.	Am I always current in rent and utility payments?	____	____
21.	Are my assets greater than my debts?	____	____
	T O T A L	____	____

Add up "yes" answers to determine how much credit you can afford and control. Give yourself 1 point for every "yes" answer.

9 points & under

Stop and wait to make a decision. Any one of these may cause trouble enough. But the more "no" answers, the more questionable is the use of credit.

10 - 15 points
Proceed with caution.

16 - 21 points
Go ahead.

319

Comparison of Annual Percentage Rates for Consumer Credit[1]

Financing Agency Type of Loan	Annual Percentage Rates[2]	
	Approximate Range of Rates	Common available rate in local community
Cash Loans		
Borrowing on life insurance	5-12%	
Credit Unions	9-21%	
Commercial banks—secured personal loans	12-15%	
Commercial banks—check credit cccounts (unsecured loans)	7.3-18%	
Finance companies—operating under state small-loan laws	18-36%	
Pawn shops—under state laws or municipal ordinances	24-40%	
Illegal lenders—often called "loan sharks"	42-1,2-200%	
Revolving Charge Credit		
Commercial banks—general-purpose credit cards (Visa, etc.)	6-21%	
Department store and other special- pupose cards	12-21%	
Installment Credit Agreements		
New cars	5.75-15%	
Used cars under two years old	6.25-24%	
Used cars over two years old	7.25-36%	
Recreational vehicles	6.9-21%	
Appliances	18-24%	
Home equity line of credit	8.75-21%	
Retirement fund as collateral	8-18%	

[1]Credit formula for comparison when factor is unknown:

$$APR = \frac{2 \cdot D \cdot P}{F(N+1)}$$

APR = Annual Interest Rate
D = Total dollar cost of credit
P = Number of payments per year (usually 12)
F = Dollar amount financed (borrowed)
N = Total number of payments

[2]In addition to interest, other finance charges, annual fees and late fees vary.

◇◇◇ ⧗　⧗ ◇◇◇

Chapter 12. **Light Side of the Money Trail**

Even "if your wealth increases, don't make it the center of your life" (Psalm 62:10b). The premise of this book is that the center of one's life is doing God's will, seeking first the kingdom of God and his righteousness and other things will be provided, caring for the good of one's family and neighbors.

The shepherd, regardless if a pastor, compassion minister, educator, outreach director, financial counselor, mentor, helping professional, money coach or others responsible for change, can guide with techniques, information, and illustrations. The shepherd can give a few suggestions and direct the person to another professional before money is squandered or misdirected. The purpose is to equip (educate) the shepherd in asking the questions and on where to find information, not to know all the answers. The shepherd guides, and is not the expert.

A Balanced Life is a Blessed Life

The shepherd guides people toward seeking a balanced life. A balanced life is a blessed life. Blessing is happiness, peace, contentment, and fulfillment. A balanced life directs resources to spending, sharing, and saving. Individuals direct money to past satisfactions (paying on debts), current satisfactions, and future satisfactions. They distribute income to meet spiritual, social, emotional, material, and physical needs. They plan for self and others. They invest in both human and material capital. They diversify skills and investments. People work for money and have money working for them.

The challenge for spiritual security based on financial security is to have a balance between spending, saving, and sharing. If one of these is insufficient or overly sufficient, it will draw on the others causing severe stress, if not disaster.

To keep a balance, an illustration of using contact lenses is useful. Some people use one contact in one eye for distance and the other for near sightedness. To seek balance, they first contact God. They focus one eye on the future and the other on meeting their present needs. They focus one eye on seeing where God is working and the other on where to work their hands for God's work. They focus one eye on the everlasting love of God (eternal life) and the other on how to encourage others each day. They focus one eye on wealth building and the other on caring for the earth's resources. They focus one eye on following God's purposes and the other on everyday decisions requiring discipline. They focus one eye on building job security and the other on building skills to adjust if they lose a job. They focus one eye on seeing the "wonders and signs" and the other on watching their resources grow. They focus one eye on achieving a balance and the other on not wasting resources.

Illustrations of centering one's life on wealth building are many. Some advisors would suggest paying off the mortgage early or having a 15 year term mortgage. The mathematics show huge amounts of dollars saved on interest. However, the balanced life considers the losses in this decision. Cash freed by a longer term mortgage for many families would enable them to provide educational, social, and recreational opportunities in lieu of saving the interest. Examples of opportunities include music lessons, group participation, travel, family vacations, visiting grandparents, correctional and medical care, and giving to worthy causes.

Scriptural Basis

One of the first advisor/planners to guide was Joseph in the Old Testament who observed the cycles of prosperous years and lean years. He advised saving for the lean years which included distributing to the poor neighbors and foreigners who had a famine and had not saved ahead. (Genesis 41:33-58). Then, in Proverbs, advice includes: "He who gathers money little by little makes it grow" (13:11). "He who ignores discipline comes to poverty…" (13:18). "A good man leaves an inheritance for his children's children" (13:22). "Diversification of assets is advised in Ecclesiastes 11:2: "Give portions to seven, yes to eight, for you do not know what disaster may come upon the land" and attitude in 5:19: "Moreover, when God gives any man [woman] wealth and possessions, and enables him [her] to enjoy them, to accept his lot and be happy in his work – this is a gift of God. He seldom reflects on the days of his life, because God keeps him occupied with gladness of heart."

Jesus gave financial advice and spurred action in his famous parable (Matthew 25:14-28). The kingdom of heaven is like being entrusted with property. Some responded by putting the money to work but one servant was afraid and hid the money. To those faithful with a few things whose money gained interest, the Master said, "Well-done, good and faithful servant! Come and share your master's happiness."

Throughout Scripture are warnings about seeking first the riches as gods, as displaced longings, as greed, as supreme allegiance, and ignoring the poor. Financial faithfulness is using good business sense in stewardship of wealth whatever it's source. All are gifts from God, whether earned by oneself or as an inherited gift.

Worries and Risks

Although the title is "Light Side of Money," it is not all light, free from worries and risks. Persons who have had adequate income, who have saved and invested, and who have contributed to a retirement plan may still be rightly anxious with worries and risks. Some are paralyzed with fear to make decisions due to disastrous experiences in the stock market. Their financial prospects are bleak due to investor losses, lower income from investments, a lack-luster economy, job insecurity, low interest rates (lower than inflation rates), being able to afford to retire and retiring later than desired, scandals in corporate accounting, fraud in management, self-dealing in brokerage firms, and a myriad of confusing choices. Their questions are how to protect life savings from healthcare costs, how not to outlive their money, about probate, and how does one avoid being double taxed on assets. On a different scale, people are worried about burial expenses, last medical bills, remaining debts, final taxes, and nursing home expenses. People worry about fluctuations in the value of their stocks in response to company, political, and regulatory circumstances, the stock market, and the economy. Stocks with greater return may have the risks when their value declines because of not being FDIC insured, no bank guarantee, nor insured by any government agency. Loss of retirement benefits as previously promised is a worry and risk as documented by current news reports.

Traveling on the light side of the money trail, the faithful see money not as the be-all and end-all but as a tool for the work of the kingdom and quality of life as the Light directs. Jesus viewed wealth as a spiritual issue. He said, "How hard it will be for those who have wealth to enter the kingdom of God!" (Mark 10:23) and "It is easier for a camel to go through the eye of a needle than for someone who is rich to enter the kingdom of God" (Matthew 19:24). The temptation not to maximize it for the glory of God and the neighbor's good, out of inertia, is only one issue. In Jesus' day, people also thought having more would solve their problems, bring more happiness and everything would be all right. The health, wealth, and success theology is prevalent today. However, many know being faithful to God has its cost, persecutions, inevitable natural calamities, and sicknesses.

People have the desire to save. They know it is a necessity. Although they know why it is important, most Americans do not save or invest. They try to maintain the standard package of goods and services even if it means everyone is employed and credit is maximized. The problem is knowing how and where to save and invest especially since it is in the control of someone else or the economy. The challenge to the shepherd is to motivate people to reduce current consumption and change habits in order to meet future obligations if one loses a job or retires.

Credit and credit history need to be changed, if not already in individual names. These separate sources are invaluable for investment possibilities, business ventures, retirement, widowhood, divorce, and for meeting emergencies in case the spouse's or child's credit is unavailable or has a bad record.

Cost, loss, and risk are reduced with timing. Now is the time to start a saving program even while reducing debts. Now is the time to begin estate planning with ownership of property. Now is the time to note fees in comparing different investment opportunities and for setting up trusts. Now is the time to note the penalties for early withdrawal. Now is the time to encourage people to remain in a job to realize full benefits from pensions or qualified plans and Social Security. Now is the time to help people change other aspects in their lives rather than leaving a job or retiring too soon. Now is the time to control the fit of anger or flight from a bad situation.

The shepherd can remind those with whom he is counseling to be mindful of timing and take action. For example, there are due dates for rolling over assets to get higher rates, for signing up for more life insurance with only a small increase in premium, for enrolling in a health care plan, for changing plans, for withdrawing without penalty, for working to receive full benefits, and for signing up for profit sharing plans. There are due dates for getting funds for first time home buyers and for installing energy saving equipment for a tax credit. This is fulfilling the Proverbial wisdom: "Be sure you know the condition of your flocks, give careful attention to your herds;" (Proverbs 27:23).

Financial planning and investing do not guarantee success for any of the desired objectives. They do reduce the risks from doing nothing. They give a sense of control. Savings and investing reduce the risk of depending only on working for pay as they provide income by money working for its owner as well. We pray for God's guidance but results many times are based on "luck" for a particular job or a particular investment and the state of the economy. This "luck" translates into jobs, spending behavior, and decisions based on "confidence." Consumer confidence affects trading and buying from each other, moving the wheels of industry.

Why People Do Not Save

Many people do not save because today's needs are more important than tomorrow's wants. They are in a crisis management mode. Basic needs including the psychological and emotional needs are not being met. Saving face to the children or community (church) standards is more important than the invisible, long-range actions of saving/investing. Actions become visible when crises occur from not saving for emergencies or opportunities, however. Some people are caught in the short-term, immediate gratification net. Others do not have the discipline and control for anything including setting aside a portion of income daily and monthly.

Feeling and being adequate now are more important than future adequacy. Coveting, which makes comparisons, contributes to the feelings of inadequacy. Commercialism and peer pressure make a person feel inadequate, i.e. never enough to wear, show, use, or enjoy.

Excuses

Excuses include these: "I can't afford to save." "I'll save what's left over at the end of the month." "I'll worry about that..." Later....After graduation....When I get a job." "Saving takes will power. Saving means total self denial." "It's just a couple of bucks, what good will that do?"

The shepherd as counselor learns, as do financial planners, that people need "hand holding" along the paths of fears and decisions. People need reassurance as the value of housing is decreasing and utilities are increasing. People wonder if they can retire or continue to give. Reassurance can be shown in calculating projected income sources and expenses. With interest assumptions, persons can see the income flow from pensions, rental property, businesses, investments. They can see when there will be a deficit and adjustments that need to be made. They can discuss how they could live with the worse case scenario. They can have peace of mind in knowing what the options are. They can have peace in knowing what control they have with repositioning assets and for their loved ones when they die. The shepherd guides through reluctance to movement. In reality, you probably *do* have the money to save. You *can* start saving right now. It does not take a lot of money to make a big difference. It does not mean your life will be dull and boring. Saving is generally insured and the return is known whereas investing is more risky, but the return could be greater.

Procrastination

When shown the cost of procrastination, people may be motivated to reposition assets or start a savings program. In comparing rates of return, the cost can be translated in lost income every day that changes are not made. The cost of waiting can motivate the start of a savings program. (For every day a tax form is not turned in, money is lost from the potential use or saving from a tax refund.)   Another example is saving $3,000 per year at 5 percent, starting at age 30, would yield $143,000 at age 55 (or if started at age 40 the amount at age 65). But the cost to wait one year to start is $16,000. With $143,000 saved, the annual income received to age 85, assuming both principal and interest are being consumed, and earning 5 percent per year, is $9,302 per year.

Motivating People to Save and Invest

Many people who are the visual type could be motivated by seeing the visible lines on a graph of how savings grow. Others who are the kinesthetic type hear the heart-wrenching tales of those who did not save and change their behavior. Others who are the audio type can be motivated by talking about their fears and hearing the results of a pattern of saving.

People following the Master Teacher actively invest and watch their savings grow, not bury and hide them. This requires effort, getting information, scrutiny of spending money currently, identifying goals, and using numbers. It takes risk and willingness to move out of one's comfort zone. It involves the work of trusted professionals for calculating and implementing.

Why Save? Save or Sink

Why to save would seem like an unnecessary question, except the majority of people do not save. On the average, saving is three percent rather than the ten percent recommended by planners and by Nehemiah for the Levites (10:38). In fact, most families spend beyond their means which means spending more than income, with most families having a monthly deficit. (See Statistical Abstract on the Internet showing income levels and amount of deficit spending.)

Saving contributes to independence and economic security by providing for emergencies and *un-forseen* and *foreseen* opportunities. **Reasons for saving** are:

- Allowances for underestimating expenses which is common for most people
- Income taxes and business taxes, taxes that must be estimated and paid quarterly to prevent a penalty
- New eye examination and glasses, dental examination and work
- Seasonal expenses, college tuition (for at least the first year and then each year)
- After graduation "start-up expenses" and "start-up businesses"
- Security deposit on an apartment or down payment on a house
- Security deposits on utilities
- Getting a car, truck, bicycle
- Dress clothes for interview and employment or uniforms
- General investment funds for capital accumulation and additional income
- Retirement
- Estate transfer such as paying inheritance tax so the property or farm does not have to be sold to pay taxes and to distribute equally among others

Emergency funds:
- To cover the deductible on car insurance, renters/homeowner's insurance
- To cover the co-pay on medical plan and for medicine
- For maintenance and repair on vehicle
- For repair on a roof or furnace
- To cover minimum expenses when laid off that unemployment insurance does not

Opportunities:
- Education and retraining
- Travel for job interview
- Travel for visiting parents or children, for rest and leisure
- Discounts for cash
- Maxing the down payment (less that is financed, less interest paid, more money saved)
- Get No-fee checking with a high enough minimum balance
- Ability to "stock-up" when an item goes on sale (thus, saving even more money)
- Avoid service and finance charges by paying insurance premiums annually
- Annualizing costs for services, rather than monthly, saves money
- Wedding or participation in weddings of friends.

Most of these are considered necessities. Therefore, one can see why people use credit to obtain them because they have not saved for them.

Choices in One Stage of Life Determine Choices in Another Stage

The shepherd has telescopic vision for the money trail. What is available for the later stages of life is based on actions taken at beginning stages. The choices are human assets, material assets, investments, securities, real estate or private use houses that are liquidated for income, lifetime maintenance, or changing residence. Charity contributions continue and gifts to others increase in the last stage for many people. Possible income and resources for **retirement** are:

- Social Security Income, Supplemental Security Income for low-income aged, disabled or blind
- Earned Income Tax Credit if employed and earnings are below guidelines
- Pension, 401-K, Individual Retirement Account
- Accelerated life insurance benefits
- Reverse Annuity Mortgage getting $300-500 monthly from equity on home.

The advantages of home equity conversions: No repayments as long as borrower stays in the home. Borrower cannot be forced from the home to repay the loan. Income payments are received income tax-free. Payments are not counted as earnings for Social Security or Medicare purposes. Payments continue for the life time of homeowner. Counseling is required. Disadvantages are: Homeowner's death, entering nursing home, or changes in residence initiate repayment of a reverse mortgage. Total payments may exceed value of the home A forced sale due to death or an early move may occur to pay off an outstanding balance. Value of the estate could be reduced or eliminated.)

- Sale-lease back of home usually to a relative and pay a small rent to new owner.
- (Advantages: Lower transaction costs which make it less expensive to initiate than the equity conversion. Ease of transferring assets to heirs and the "one time exemption from capital gains tax" on a personal residence. Flexibility in agreement to meet desires and needs of seller and buyer including amount of down payment and net amount received by the homeowner. Disadvantages: Availability of a suitable buyer who wants a long term investment. The need for the lease-back to be a legitimate business transaction. Deductibility of mortgage interest is lost.)
- Veterans Home to live and veterans' services.
- Community government subsidized housing or Title Eight Housing (pay one-third of income for rent).
- Church provided housing (Many are in financial trouble now and are asking members to save in middle years for after retirement years. Many, if they were to save, could not contribute to church as they do currently.)
- Government and hospital services in home if income eligible and sliding scale fee such as Meals on Wheels, Homemaker-Home Health Aid, Community Nurse, Life-line Pendant for emergency help, community health clinic.
- Family or friends take individuals into their homes and care for them. (This may be doubling up or persons retiring early and/or not being employed to care for them. There may be a tax credit for dependent care for the employed person.)

Knowledge Motivates One to Save

Compound interest is exponential. It is advantageous because it is interest on interest on the principal. Below are the accumulated regular deposits for a selected length of time at 5-1/2 percent interest rate.

Length of time accumulated	Amount Regularly Deposited						
	$5	$10	$5	$20	$25	$50	$100
	Accumulated Funds						
6 months	$ 30.39	$60.80	$91.19	$ 121.58	$ 151.97	$ 303.96	607.90
1 year	61.47	122.98	184.44	245.91	307.38	614.80	1,229.50
2 years	125.75	251.58	377.33	503.08	628.82	1,257.73	2,515.38
3 years	192.97	386.07	579.04	772.01	964.98	1,930.09	3,860.05

Other examples that can motivate changes are:

A. Reduce smoking (or some other item) by $5.00 per day. This results in $150 saved per month or $1,800 saved in 1 year, but with compounding interest would yield over thousands in several years.

B. "Buck A Day" saved during four years is $1,460.

 Be a millionaire for $8.53 per day at 10 percent for 35 years (retire at 55)

> $108,970 cash out of pocket
>
> $890,954.61 is the investment return earned.

C. TDA or Tax Deferred Annuity

Through the tax deferral advantage of a TDA, individuals may be able to meet their savings goal and still have the take-home pay needed to meet budget responsibilities. The following example compares the impact on take-home pay of saving $3,000 through a tax deferred annuity versus saving $3,000 in a financial institution on an after-tax basis. The TDA approach leaves $442 more take-home pay for the year.*

	With TDA*	Without TDA*
Gross Pay	$28,600.00	$28,600.00
TDA Contribution	3,000.00	-0-
Taxable Pay	$25,600.00	$28,600.00
Less: Federal Income Taxes	$1,417.50	$1,867.50
State Income Taxes	734.40	836.40
Social Security Taxes	2,187.90	2,187.90
Savings Deposits	-0-	3,000.00
Take-Home Pay	$21,260.20	$20,708.20

Techniques in Saving

By definition, savings has liquidity in funds and is readily converted to cash without loss of principal. Investing requires marketability with a market for buying and selling.

The shepherd may be the first to know whether or not there is savings in the household. The clue is there is no savings because a cry for help in a crisis comes to the shepherd. Another clue is an expectation of inheritance coming because of the death of someone.

- When money is received from "where-ever," put some into savings first.

- Set the bar for savings goal in dollar figures. Write it down.

- Have a spare change jar into which coins are tossed (pennies, nickels, dimes). Quarters are for laundry, vending machines, and tolls.

- Pay oneself first by putting a regular amount in savings when one sits down to pay bills. Do not rely on "saving what's left over." Use payroll deductions.

- Reduce impulse buying and save by resisting hype and advertising and "Point of Sale - Impulse Purchase Displays." Shop from a list - only buy what is on the list. Compare prices and methods as a way to save money on decisions. For example, E-commerce and catalogs are not always the cheapest because of the added shipping and handling.

- Plan ahead a little to save money by avoiding: Late fees, Finance charges, Access fees at ATMs, Bounced-check fees, Convenience fees/prices.

- Be Positive - save *FOR* something, rather than denying oneself. Think of it as "buying the future." Have an envelope with a picture of the savings.

- Have a savings account at the same time while paying off debts.

- Be frugal with current expenses, hobbies, collections gifts, and worthwhile experiences. Every time resistance wins in eating out, remind oneself that one can be entertained in less expensive ways.

- Compete with someone (siblings) for "most money saved" over some time period (week, month, semester).

- Over-withhold from one's paycheck. Then put the tax refund in savings. However, this money was not getting interest while held by the government.

- Join an investment club for studying and pooling income to invest.

- When or if one gets a raise, save all or at least half of the increase to one's paycheck.

- Set up an automatic payroll deduction: When the paycheck is deposited in the bank or credit union, a regular amount is withdrawn into a savings account (s).

- Set a saving goal in dollars for short-term, intermediate, and long-term.

- Sell collections, art, durable goods, equipment and supplies not being used.

- Continue making payments into special accounts with the money previously used for debt payments.

- Buy no load mutual funds by regularly contributing to them when paying household bills.

Frequently, the goal of having savings equal to 3 to 6 months of expenses is recommended before investing. If one loses income, the 3 to 6 months is the time you could hopefully get another job, recover from an accident, get well, or move. Of course, if there are parents to go home to, can quickly find another job, or never have an accident, not as much is needed for savings. It is better to put it into investments.

Places to save are money market accounts, certificate of deposits, U.S. savings bond (monthly purchase), and piggy bank. Everything else can be considered an investment. A good mix of stocks, bonds, real estate, and annuities make a well-rounded portfolio. Checking account is *not* for savings since it is too easily accessed. Check with several institutions for types of savings and compare rates of return. Use the savings as collateral and to get a lower interest rate for vehicles, etc.

People report a higher sense of security from having several sources of income. Although some sources give small payments, the respondents feel more secure with a variety than if only one source provided a greater total.

Savings and Investments for College Funding, Retirement, and Estate Planning

Investments are assets purchased to generate income or appreciate in value. Included are formal education or training (human capital investments), personal residence, a house that you repair/remodel and sell or rent, stocks, bonds, real estate, collectibles, art, coins, stamps, beanie babies, etc. They provide income and give economic security as your "money is working for you" and you are not just working for money, living paycheck to paycheck. You work hard for your money. Make sure it works hard for you or your favorite charity.

There are tools the shepherd needs to know sufficiently to be able to ask the questions of parishioners, clients, those in one's ministry. They, in turn, can work with the financial planner, advisor, consultant, trust officer, accountant, life insurance underwriters, and/or attorney. They can be aware of biases or favorites of the professionals. They can know the advantages and disadvantages of the various tools.

Life Insurance - The type of insurance obtained depends on current needs and goals. Since these change from time to time, life insurance programs need to be evaluated periodically. Generally, life insurance is needed if one would be an economic loss to someone. Some are overly insured. Term life insurance buys protection only, not savings. For most, it is worthwhile to pay a higher premium to include the guaranteed insurability clause.

"Accrued cash value" of Permanent Life Insurance can fund a policy in later years. The policy can be continued as term life insurance for a specific need or time. The policy can be canceled and the cash value used to buy an annuity. If life insurance is no longer needed for protection, the cash value accumulated can supplement retirement income through an annuity or investments. Life insurance can provide funds for paying state taxes on inheritances by survivors.

Universal Life Insurance - A way to solve financial security, wealth transfer, charitable giving, estate and legacy planning issues.

Single Premium Annuity - A one-time lump sum is deposited into an account with no further deposits. This could provide for survivors. Premium varies with age.

Tax Advantaged Investing - Utilizing accounts that are tax-deferred so assets grow without a cost until withdrawn, i.e. IRA, 401K.

Lump sum distribution - When a person leaves a firm, the employer may make a lump sum distribution of your 401K assets with mandatory two percent tax but taxes can be avoided by rolling over money into an IRA or other retirement plan – with limits for people over a certain age.

If born before 1936, a 10 year averaging can be done.

Individual Retirement Account - It is tax-deductible for lower income workers or those not covered by a company pension plan. Upon retirement, can take in lump sum, withdraw in installments or place in an annuity. (Check tax consequences of options.) The tax advantage of an IRA is that it can be stretched through children's and grandchildren's lifetimes. Managing IRA assets are easier with consolidation. The original allocation in an annuity income can be changed even after receiving income. If annuitized, no changes can be made. In an **Education IRA,** the contributions are nondeductible (to a limit) but the eventual withdrawals are tax-free.

Keogh plans - Contributions are made if self-employed, even part-time, starting a business or turning hobby into money-making.

Roth IRA - Contributions are not tax-deductible but accumulate without being taxed. They are withdrawn tax-free. Investors can switch from an IRA to a Roth IRA when modified adjusted gross income is below $100,000. After five years, $10,000 can be withdrawn tax- and penalty-free for education or qualifying first time home buyers.

Annuity - This provide a guaranteed income for life, purchased from insurance companies with lump sum proceeds of an IRA or company pension or with cash surrender value of a no longer needed life insurance policy. The decision to be made is whether payments continue to a dependent spouse.

Variable annuity - Annuity that has separate accounts so one can invest in a variety of funds. Interest earned changes with "stock market," the economy. Watch expenses or compare them with the insurance company.

Tax-sheltered annuity - All annuities enable one to have assets grow without taxes until withdrawal. Assumption is that tax bracket is lower when taking out payments. This is not true for some people because they no longer have deductions and the tax brackets of the future cannot be predicted. Generally, it is always good to have a portion of one's portfolio in products that defer taxes.

Section 529 College Savings Plan - Contributions and earnings grow with federal and state income tax-deferred. Withdrawals for qualified education expenses are completely federal income tax-free. A plan can be set up for anyone that will have educational expenses and the beneficiary can be changed at any time. Maximum amount of contributions vary from state to state. Also, the state tax credits vary. In the majority, the maximum exceeds $200,000.

Matching Programs - One sure recommendation is for a person to participate in any matching program of the employer. For example, if the employer matches the person's contribution of $100 to a profit-sharing plan at the 50 percent match, the person has $150 working capital in contrast to $68.60 if he were to invest on his own after taxes.

Tax Exemption - Some investments may be tax exempt or even provide a tax credit to encourage support for particular research or enterprises. Recommendations vary depending on the Internal Revenue Service ruling and/or investment performance.

Growth versus Income - Some assets become more valuable as they grow and produce income. For others, the value of shares changes because of the economy and the demand upon them. Other investments expand as they are regularly or periodically added to the principal working for returns. The time frames and liquidity needs are critical. Diversification in all types of investments is still the answer, especially in an uncertain economy.

Strategies in Investing

Some familiar strategies are:

- Have some liquid assets that can be quickly converted to cash without loss of principal (checking account, savings account, money market). Generally, a person should have 6 months of living expenses in liquid assets.

- Have some that are nonliquid such as real estate and art so that one is not tempted to take it out and spend it.

- Have some with marketability which is the ability of the asset to be readily purchased or sold such as stocks (securities sold and bought in the NYSE, NASDAQ, AMEX and other markets both domestically and globally) and bonds (issued by corporations, municipalities, government that have par values and coupons paying interest semiannually). Less marketable are Indian war clubs of the 18th century, precious stones, and antiques, for examples.

- Have an income return now or when the asset (equity) grows in value and can be sold. Total Return, one measure of investment performance, is determined by adding the change in price (gain or loss) and the income (either interest or dividends). For example,

- (gain or <loss>) + (interest or dividends) = Total Return

- (10% appreciation) + (2% dividend) = 12% Total Return

- Compare returns on types of investments and on financial institutions. The Credit Union National Association President reported in 1999: "Simply by shifting funds from a bank to an equivalent account at a credit union, consumers could earn billions of dollars more in annual interest" (Consumer Federation of America).

	Bank	Credit Union	Difference between the Bank and Credit Union
Checking	-0.51%	-0.28%	0.24%
MMA	-0.71%	-0.21%	0.50%
6-mo Cert	-0.51%	-0.07%	0.44%
1-Yr Cert	-0.63%	-0.11%	0.53%
5-Yr Cert	-0.82%	-0.22%	0.61%

Data Source: Bank Rate Monitor

- **Know names of types** of instruments which are cash and equivalents (bank accounts and CDs), fixed income (bonds and mortgages), equity (common and preferred stock), commodities (Grains and Oilseeds, Metals and Petroleum, Wood, Hybrids -stock options, convertible securities, index options, commodity futures contracts, derivatives), and Mutual funds that hold many different stocks.

- **Let tax implications help** you choose investments.
  There are tax-qualified investments that grow tax deferred and contributions may be deductible. Penalties for withdrawal before age 59 1/2. Examples are IRA -Individual Retirement Account; 401(k) or 403(b) in which the employer sponsors retirement, and

Keogh SEP and SIMPLE for self-employed persons to put aside 15 percent before tax for retirement.

Non-tax-qualified investments have no tax penalties for withdrawing money. You pay taxes on income and capital gains. Examples are bank accounts and brokerage accounts. Non-qualified accounts can be in stocks and mutual funds among other types of accounts. (One can have non-tax-qualified products that have penalties such as taking money early from a one year CD.) Some bonds are tax exempt and therefore their return is higher at the same rate than a taxed one.

- **Tax exemption benefit** – Example, Peggy is in the 28 percent federal tax bracket and considering a tax-exempt instrument with a 6 percent yield. She would need a taxable yield of about 8.33 percent to match the tax-free yield. If the interest is free also from federal and state tax rate, her combined marginal federal and state tax rate is 35 percent. She would need a taxable yield of about 9.23 percent to match the 6 percent triple-tax-free yield. The formula for comparing **equivalent yields** follows at 7 percent tax free, 45 percent tax rate: Tax-free interest divided by (1 – marginal tax rate) = Equivalent yield in taxable interest.

- Tools of **"Rules of 72"** motivate changes as they show
    1) How many years to double savings or investment at an assumed rate of return. Examples 72 / 9 percent = 8 years to double your money. 72 / 6 years = 12 percent needed to double the money.
    2) How many years it takes to cut the purchasing power of a fixed income in half at an assumed rate of inflation. Example 72 / 5 percent inflation = 14.4 years to halve the purchasing power. This motivates moving away from fixed income/bond investments. This can motivate savings behavior. *This indicates the need to decrease wants or be more efficient.*

- The technique of **Dollar-Cost Averaging.** This is investing the same amount of money in a security on a regular schedule (such as monthly) without regard for market conditions. Since the amount being invested is always the same, more shares are bought when the price is low, and fewer when the price is high.

- Time and market fluctuations can work if a person is patient. Emotions can cause panic which erroneously push selling or greediness by chasing high returns. Web sites for more information are www.ici.org (The Investment Company Institute) and www.aaii.cpom (American Association of Individual Investors.)

- An individual can learn the basics by watching, listening, reading, surfing, and taking some classes. Belonging to an investment club is useful in which members do research and share information. Statistics show most individual investors underperform the market due to lack of planning, emotions and chasing returns. Advice and implementation are most helpful from a financial counselor, planner, advisor, or broker.

The best predictor of future behavior is past performance but it is no guarantee of future results. Rarely does the same asset class lead in returns for consecutive years. The range of annual return for the asset classes between 1926 and 1997 was a high return to low return according to Ibbotson Associates:

Small company stocks	-58.0%	to	142.9%	
Large company stocks	-43.3	to	54.0	
Long-term government bonds	-9.2	to	40.4	
Intermediate-term gov. bonds	-5.1	to	29.1	
Cash	-0.0	to	14.7	

Cost of Delay

The advantage of that initial year of growth, when the power of compounding is the greatest, can be calculated. This motivates persons to get started. When a person saves $1,000 per year beginning at age 30 at 5 percent, he or she will have $48,000 at age 55 and $66,000 at age 60, and $90,000 at age 65. If he waits one year to get started it will cost him or her $5,000. For example, in 20 years at 8 percent, the cost of a one year delay with monthly investment in a Thrift Savings Plan of $25 is $1,416. With a monthly investment of $200, the cost of delay is $11,327.

Diversification

One diversifies for increased economic security and reduction of risk. Risk is diversified by having several different investments to counteract the risks of business risk and failure, management risk, financial downturns, market changes, change of interest rates, and purchasing power changes due to inflation (prices change). The impact of purchasing power risk is shown in the table illustrated below.

An investor who places $10,000 in a 10-year certificate of deposit, earning 5.0 percent per year.[1,2]

End of Year	CD Value at End of Year[1] (5%)	Purchasing Power at 3% Inflation Rate[2]	"Real" Value of CD	"Loss" Due to Inflation
1	$10,500	97.09%	$10,194	$ 306
2	$11,025	94.26%	$10,392	$ 633
3	$11,576	91.51%	$10,594	$ 982
4	$12,155	88.85%	$10,800	$1,355
5	$12,763	86.26%	$11,009	$1,753
6	$13,401	83.75%	$11,223	$2,178
7	$14,071	81.31%	$11,441	$2,630
8	$14,775	78.94%	$11,663	$3,111
9	$15,513	76.64%	$11,890	$3,624
10	$16,289	74.41%	$12,121	$4,168

Over the 10-year period, inflation reduces the purchasing power of the investor's dollars by more than 25 percent. Income taxes, ignored in this example, further decrease the investor's net return.

---

[1]   Assumes a 5 percent annual after-tax return, and that interest is reinvested at the same rate of return.

[2]   To calculate, divide previous year's percentage by (1+.03). Example: 1.00/1.03=.9709; .9709/1.03=.9426.

Choosing the Characteristic of an Investment

Choose investments to reflect risk tolerance and "characteristics" that match individual needs and desires:

- Safety of principal (amount contributed to invest), preservation of capital
- Liquidity
- Expenses
- Income generated now and at retirement, yield (earnings on deposit), fixed rate, change with market rates, inflation protected
- Growth favored (deferral or relief)
- Freedom from care or management attention, management ease
- Tax status, tax favored, tax eliminated, tax deferred
- Collateral value for loans
- Protection against creditor's claims
- Legality.

There are tradeoffs among these. No investment includes all these desired characteristics.

Working with an Advisor or Other Professional

"In the multitude of counselors there is safety" (Proverbs 11:14). The shepherd can give peace by helping people work with professionals who are trustworthy. The shepherd suggests people interview financial planners to make sure they are comfortable with them and trust them. People can purchase from a discount broker if confident and well informed on investments. Advertisements are in selected newspapers like Wall Street Journal. The mutual fund prospectus should be read. People should know the risk factor of investments before depositing money into them. They should know how to withdraw money and the cost of doing so before investing in a specific product.

An accountant, financial planner, Certified Financial Planner, Registered Financial Consultant, financial advisor, financial consultant, Chartered Financial Consultant, pension officer, stock broker, insurance underwriter, and/or an attorney are required to state the advantages of various arrangements and to implement the changes. These professionals will need more details to do the "number crunching" but general ideas here show the decisions and issues involved.

The shepherd urges the person to examine and move on the path to estate planning. Believers of the Way "trust in God." This is done partly by having professionals in whom they trust. This can be done by setting up trusts including charitable giving trusts.

It is illegal for an advisor or shepherd to help eliminate assets within three years of nursing home care in order to become eligible for Medicaid. However, attorneys may be required to establish eligibility for Social Security disability. Documents or documentation that assets are under the limit or have been exhausted for nursing home care need to be provided.

Ethically, the shepherd names at least three trustworthy professionals to work with from which the person can choose. Conflict of interest on the part of the shepherd must be avoided. These should be certified or registered people with experience and education. They will explain fees and describe the services rendered. They should be interviewed to verify similar beliefs. They should give names of satisfied clients you may contact.

In any "fiduciary" relationship, the financial professional fulfills the "prudent man" procedures. These are research, revision, record keeping, recommending changes, and performing "due diligence" conduct.

The individual is responsible for the plan and should maintain control. This is prefaced by a statement that professionals and individuals agree on. "Alternative plans with supporting computer-generated information are identified from which you can choose to meet your objectives and solve financial problems. These are based on the information which you have provided, given assumptions, your current stage of family life cycle, current economic conditions, and tax policies. If any of these conditions change, the financial plan needs to be examined and revised."

Socially Responsible Investing

Individuals should make sure the financial planner/consultant understands their views and are willing to adhere to them on socially responsible funds or specific companies that may produce services or products that you oppose. "Social choice investing" considers conscience in investing in companies that make bombs, sell tobacco, receive income from gambling or alcohol use or military weapons, discriminate in hiring practices, exploit labor, use slavery, use unfair business practices, produce unsafe products and services, pay their CEO millions, or damage the environment. Desired is an attractive rate of return while investing in companies that work on community development and quality of life. Other desires may be employee relations, appointment of women and minorities, and philanthropic activities and community relations. "Social screens," of various degrees, are used to exclude investor concerns for choosing accounts. Comparison of returns from socially responsible choices show less than average for some and more than average for others.

Retirement Planning
(See Chapter 6 for other issues, tools, and illustrations.)

Major issues in planning for retirement are estimated income allowing one to retire, health insurance which takes a huge chunk of retirement income, alternatives to retirement, transfer of private business, and volunteering to share wisdom as well as a purpose for getting up each morning. Many people are psychologically, socially, and emotionally ready to retire. They cannot wait because each day at their current job is stressful, tiring, and their work not appreciated. They are not prepared financially to retire. Some eagerly want to prepare for retirement and the steps are outlined below for decisions and financial management for the next journey of life. Stories below have dealt with the issues. They can provide estimates and expectations.

Jesus told a story about a man who wanted to retire early and spent all his time building wealth for it. In Luke 12:15-21, when Jesus was asked to be a judge or an arbiter, he responded: "Then he said to them, 'Watch out! Be on your guard against all kinds of greed; a man's life does not consist in the abundance of his possessions.' And he told them this parable: 'The ground of a certain rich man produced a good crop. He thought to himself, 'What shall I do? I have no place to store my crops.' "Then he said, 'This is what I'll do. I will tear down my barns and build bigger ones, and there I will store all my grain and my goods.'" And I'll say to myself, 'You have plenty of good things laid up for many years. Take life easy; eat, drink and be merry.' "But God said to him, 'You fool! This very night your life will be demanded from you. Then who will get what you prepared for yourself?' This is how it will be with anyone who stores up things for himself but is not rich toward God."

This story sounds like the yearning for early retirement and concentrating on amassing wealth for it. However, possible messages are to not hoard, not keeping all to oneself, be willing to share, designate the beneficiaries and be active in retirement with sharing wisdom as well as wealth.

Then the story is told of Caleb who hated his job and first just wanted to quit but then his financial advisor warned: Check on the time required to receive full benefits from your company. Check on what the company means by saying "when you retire you will receive full benefits." It may only mean you can participate in the company's supplemental insurance but you have to pay $50 or more. The benefits over the years would be worth hanging on to your job. You could try attitude adjustment. The fee for counseling would be offset by wage increases or increased benefits. The large concern is having health and disability insurance. Also, check on your vested contributions and when there is a penalty for early retiring. Meanwhile, if the company has matching fund opportunities use it to the maximum. Put as much money into the 401K plan (403B for non-profits) as allowed. Get a new hobby, take more trips or vacations, and join a prayer group. If the physical work at the job is too demanding, check on therapy and hire any manual work done around your house and yard. Try different methods of work, get a cushioned mat to stand on, examine the relationship of posture or heights of chairs/tables, and lighting or colors at your workplace.

Rather than retiring, if the person is a professional, for example a pastor, he or she needs a spiritual advisor or a mentor for listening and venting his or her feelings. Talking with other professionals can help prevent burn out. The professional can find a side job. One became a part-time chaplain. Another was a chaplain for truck drivers on the interstate. Another one rode with the police officer to give them moral support.

In retirement planning, shepherds can alert people to possible volunteering. These can be in areas that they have had experience or a whole new life which they can learn. One possibility is with CASA, Court Appointed Special Advocate, available in 50 percent of the states. The advocate is a court advisor on behalf of a child. The advocate is a voice of the child explaining what care the child needs, when to go back to his/her family or how to handle punishment. This volunteer provides patience and love the child sorely needs. Another possibility is a parent in a group home. Retirees can be hosts or hostesses at a large retail store or tour directors. They could assist their adult child with business responsibilities. The shepherd can share other informed possibilities from a list.

Chris' story is successful and demonstrates some income and insurance decisions. As a high school graduate she began a beauty shop. As owner, she was making $70,000 per year which she ploughed back into the business. So she did not lose money in her investment as other people did in 2008-2009. She retired at age 62, collected Social Security, and took a salary as she continued to work in the beauty shop. Her daughters and granddaughter became managers and received a higher wage than others and thereby inheriting the business with less tax consequences. She receives a wage of $14,000 to keep under the limit for Medicare taxation. With the additional $18,000 from Social Security, she has a comfortable income, although it is half what she had before retirement. Her Medicare income is taxed 100 percent, one dollar for every two earned, after earning $14,000 between the ages of 62 and 66. The tax rate decreases after age 66 and is 85 percent of the Social Security income as well as the earnings limit increases.

Before retirement she spent $1,500 per month for health insurance since she had had cancer. She now pays $300.00 per month for supplemental health insurance. She wants to buy life insurance for protecting her husband's income source from her being employed. He is disabled. The insurance would cost $350 per month at her age.

Louis wants to have purpose in his life after retirement because his work had given him meaning, respect, and purpose. Now what? Many opportunities exist for Louis to share his wisdom and experience. Some are listed with the local volunteer bureau and visitor's center. Many are listed on the Internet under Volunteering in America. Disaster relief possibilities abound. The American Association for Retired People can provide much information with details. Volunteers of America received $33.5 million in grants to provide housing for low-income seniors and people with disabilities in five states. Schools at all levels including colleges need volunteers. Senior citizens are desperately needed to mentor and tutor children in the public schools. Part of the national program AmeriCorps patterned after the Peace Corps, seniors are needed for tutoring and mentoring. National nonprofit, spiritually based organizations providing local resources can be found at www.voa.org near one's home. There are older Americans needing support to live healthy, safe, and productive lives as they age at home. Representative payees are needed who do the finances for elderly or incompetent persons. The area council on aging can provide contacts. Time for volunteering was a trade off of more than an hour a day watching TV. Adults who never volunteered spent an average of 436 more hours per year watching TV than adults who volunteered.[233]

Mary Lou realizes that retirement with a fixed income and since a small amount means she will have to change her lifestyle. She can depend on going to the emergency room for medical care allowed once a month for Medicaid people. However, since she is not on Medicaid, it would be less expensive to go to urgent care facility. If she were a veteran, she could use the VA hospital for some illnesses or treatment. Other possibilities are dental colleges, beauty colleges, or women's clinics with volunteer doctors and reduced fees. She can buy groceries on the days that give senior discounts.

Ellen could not afford medicine or health insurance before retirement. If she were on Medicaid, she would receive prescription benefits and physician's care. To become eligible for Medicaid as health insurance, her assets have to be below certain limits. Financial advisors who recommend "spending down" so people can become qualified are fined and imprisoned if less than three to five years. The time period to "look back" for divesting assets or reporting the value of assets can be seen on the Internet. The check is very rigorous. Anyway, some physicians do not take Medicaid patients nor do they take those on Medicare. Some physicians charge Medicare patients a fee for doctor's visits above what Medicare pays. Medicare has a prescription program Part D separate from Medicare health insurance. Ellen is on a state program for seniors in which she pays $5.00 a prescription whereas her sister with higher income in another state pays $78.00. Ellen's sister Flo is enrolled in a group plan of supplemental health insurance in which she pays $370.00 per month. After insurance, Flo her retired sister, pays $400 or more per month for medicine. This includes a very limited dental and optical coverage. Ellen contributes in other ways than volunteering. She has purpose in baking cookies to distribute to group homes in her community.

Questions that Summarize Readiness for Retirement

Can you answer "yes" to the steps and decisions in these issues?

---

233   Volunteers in America website. May 30, 2009.

1. Do you have a savings account for retirement? _____
2. Do you have a supplemental retirement account through employment? _____
3. Are you decreasing your debt load so you have no debts when you retire? _____
4. Have you accumulated furniture, equipment and supplies?_____
5. Have you listed all income and expenses at various ages? _____
6. Will you have a plan of employment after you retire? _____
7. Can you modify your housing for less upkeep, greater mobility?_____
8. Do you accept that Social Security will replace about one-half
   if earnings are $20,000-40,000 and one-third if $50,000-60,000? _____
9. Did you request an Earnings & Benefit Statement from Social Security? _____
10. Did you get an approximate pension report from employer's business office? _____
11. Will you be the recipient of a bequest? (Is their will up to date?) _____
12. Is there life insurance on the person providing you with income? _____
13. Are you a beneficiary on someone's insurance policy? (Updated?) _____
14. Are your investments diversified or have several sources of income?_____
15. Have you upgraded or diversified your skills for employability? _____
16. Could you get a reverse annuity mortgage based on home equity? _____
17. Have you discussed retirement possibilities with your family? _____
18. Can you find community, state, and federal resources to help you? _____
19. Are you disciplined in diet, exercise, and medical check-ups? _____
20. Have you organized your financial records (advisors, insurance, etc?)_____
21. Do you keep spending and tax records for assessing possible changes? _____
22. Can you liquidate assets or sell unneeded goods? _____
23. Do you have a reserve fund for emergencies, travel, or opportunities? _____
24. Can you adjust spending downward as prices increase on a fixed income? _____
25. Are you prepared for long-term care expenses or people to assist in need? _____
26. Do you know where your health insurance will come from if retiring before 65? _____

Assumptions and Risks Used in Planning

Objective statements are required of financial planners. Assumptions must be stated and utilized whether in a self-directed plan or a financial planner directed plan. Other assumptions used in choosing savings vehicles, repositioning assets, retirement planning, and distribution of assets should be stated. What are your goals, given your age and circumstances? What assumptions do you have for life expectancy, considering your health and history of parents and siblings? What interest rates for returns? Yield from investments? Marketing prospects for investments? Liquidity possibilities? Inflation rates?

In 2001, the U.S. Census Bureau forecasts the average 65-year old man will live to age 84. Most women at age 65 will live to 88. If assumed retirement is 65, he has 19 years to live without a *salary* income. On a fixed income, expenses have to be decreased with the assumed inflation rate. Life Expectancy Tables and information are available on the Internet. One can see at given ages the years remaining on the average.

The average is what? Statistics report averages, but an individual should read the footnotes or explanation of what is average for what group. Averages can be the mathematical summation divided by number of cases. Average also can be the mode (most common number) or median with 50 percent above and 50 percent below. Another interpretation of statistics to understand is what "faster" means. When one group's life expectancy is increasing faster than another's, one should remember percentage increase is a function of the starting point. If one group has a low number initially, the increase in number shows a large percentage increase. Comparing increase in numbers rather than percentages yields a different interpretation. Therefore, one should question the use of the term average and how increases are calculated. Interpreting the economic conditions by a former President was erroneous. When he said fewer people were collecting employment benefits, he assumed conditions were better. In fact, the unemployment payments and terms had expired and that fewer people were receiving them.

Assuming that housing costs in retirement will not increase because the mortgage is paid off is erroneous. Property taxes, maintenance, and utility costs keep increasing. Alternatives are to move, modify existing housing, or rent a part of the house. If the house is shared with a live-in helper, policies must be clarified and a contract written.

Assuming Medicare will cover all medical bills is erroneous. Supplemental health insurance is necessary to fill the gaps because Medicare generally pays less than half of health care bills. Those not on Medicare may qualify for Medicaid.

On the average, reports of family expenditures by age in the Bureau of Labor Statistics (Internet) show some expenditures decrease after 65 while others increase. Those that increase include gifts, travel, and medical care.

Assumptions of growth and health of companies or industries are based on history, demand of consumers here and abroad, and analysis of the economic cycle. For example, in 2008 McDonald's stock increased in value because eating at expensive restaurants declined sharply.

An assumption is that planners can assess the risk tolerance of individual clients. It is critical that the investor completes a risk tolerance questionnaire for the planner. If the investors do not understand the questions, they must proactively ask for explanations. A portfolio of all risky investments provides an average higher rate of return. A mixture of risky and more secure would provide a lower overall return but is conducive to sleeping at night. Handling risk is hard work but the effect of "no" decision making is unfaithfulness. Faithfulness is working hard through uncertainties and risk for what is best for loved ones, the best charities, what is the best use of money now, and the best management of human and material assets. Setting specific goals with numbers is hard work but this is the basis for "planning."

Investment vehicles are assessed in their risk of loss of principal (losing all or what was contributed initially), risk of potential for appreciation, and risk of purchasing power due to inflation. Then there are market risk, business risk, and financial risk due to uncertainty of firm's use of debt to finance operations. Industries have pioneering stage, expansion stage, and stabilization stage. A humorous recommendation for investments is to buy a sick calf that you know is going to get well.

Hotchkiss[234] writes that "The parable of the talents…is about risk. The "good" servants whom the master rewarded for managing his money wisely were daring and adventuresome. The "bad" servant was the cautious one. He invested, so to speak, in federally insured bank deposits with a guaranteed return of zero. Today such investments do worse than that – because of inflation, a guaranteed investment can be expected to lose value." He has learned that the nonprofit world with boards, staff, and volunteers need "to act as if the mission were more important than safety, harmony, or comfort."

---

234   Dan Hotchkiss. The Stewardship of Risk. The Alban Institute. March 3, 2007. P.1.

What Will Income and Expenses Be? Utilizing a Worksheet

A worksheet can help estimate income sources at various ages for each spouse and for when the spouse dies. Debts can be listed and shown when these drop off so more cash flow is available. Living expenses can be listed by fixed, variable, gifts or contributions, and work or business related. The surplus or deficit is estimated. This helps determine early or delayed retirement. A revised plan can show planned changes, changed expectations, and new goals for meeting retirement needs.

RETIREMENT ANALYSIS

	Husband Yes No	Wife Yes No	Current Value	Vested Yes No (If yes, how much contributing now?)	PRESENT				REVISED			
					Age 65	62	Other	When spouse dies	Age 65	62	Other	When spouse dies

Estimated Monthly Income

A. INCOME
1. Pension plan with employment
2. I.R.A.
3. Keogh
4. State Teacher's Retirement Plan
5. Pension benefits from previous employment
6. Profit Sharing Plan
7. Deferred Compensation
8. Federal Pension
9. Social Security
10. Tax-Sheltered Annuity
11. Savings/Investments
12. Other Savings/ Investment Programs

Total Income   Monthly   Yearly

B. Debts
1.
2.
3.

C. Living Expenses
1. Fixed
2. Variable
3. Gifts/contributions
4. Work or business related

Total Expenses   Monthly   Yearly   Balance

D. Surplus or Deficit

Estimated Monthly Expenses

How Much Do I Need to Save? Utilizing "Time Value of Money"

The time value of money tools utilizes techniques of compound interest in calculating present and future values of money. Techniques can use either formulas, tables, financial calculator programs, or computer programs. These can be found on the Internet. The formula using the assumed interest rate is $(1+i)^n$ where "time value of money" is the "n" in $(1+i)^n$.

Betty wants to know how much she needs to save to have $2000 per month at age 55 to retire. (The answer by using the time value techniques is either $761 or $1,780.65, depending on assumption, per month.) The counselor asks these questions:

1. When do you start pension? When do you start Social Security? Age 65 (NOW this age has increased) (before this time there would be a reduction in benefits)
2. What is your age now? 43 When do you plan to retire? 55
3. How many years do you need $2,000 per month? 10 years until pension begins
4. Do you want to use principal as well as the interest?
5. What other sources of income do you have or want?
6. How do you plan to maintain purchasing power or level of living at retirement?

Assumptions of counselor:

- $2,000 per month will have less purchasing power at age 55 than now.
- Must use present and future values of compound interest
- Treat interest rate as inflation rate using the table of how $1.00 left at compound interest will grow to find how much is needed to maintain $2000 purchasing power
- Inflate $2,000 for X years to maintain purchasing power OR
- Assume $2,000 is protected from inflation by built-in increase in investment (interest) rate so do not inflate.

Steps for counselor:

(1.) Show the value of $2,000 in 12 years when she will draw Social Security. Use table or program "What $1 due in future is worth today" or the "Present worth of $1." This is $1.

Assuming 8 percent, $2,000 would have the value of $794 in purchasing power.

(2.) Inflate the value of $2,000 using table or program "How $1 left at compound interest will grow" to maintain purchasing power.

Inflating the value of $2,000, the date of retirement, $5,036 is the amount needed to maintain purchasing power.

(3.) Find amount needed to pay out periodically using table or program "What $1 payable periodically is worth today" or "annuity."

* If $2,000 the amount needed is $173,304 to pay out $2,000 per month for ten years.

* If $5,036 the amount needed is $405,500 to pay out $5,036 per month.

(4.) Determine amount to save periodically using table or program "sinking fund" and "periodic deposit that will grow to $1 at future date."

If one uses $173,304 value, one would need to save $761 per month.

If one uses $405,500 value, One would need to save $1,780.65 per month.

* If she were to live off the interest and not use the principal, she would need to save approximately **eight times** as much.

More explanation to use the appropriate table, formula, calculator, or Internet program:

A. **Future value of $1. Amount of $1 left at compound interest. What $1 invested today would be worth at the end of the time period.** One program would be used if, for example, you inherited $12,000 and just kept it at a given interest rate. <u>OR</u> if you earn $12,000, you can calculate the increase in salary needed to keep up with inflation.

B. **Future value of $1 annuity. Amount of $1 deposited periodically. What future value of regular deposits of $1 would be.** Another program is for periodically depositing money monthly or yearly.

C. **Periodic deposit that will grow to $1 at future.** Another program is for determining how much to set aside to have a certain amount in the future.

D. **Present value of a future $1. What $1 due at end of specific year in the future is worth today. (Discounting value)** Another program is for determining what $12,000 in future dollars is worth in today's purchasing power value.

E. **Present value needed for providing a series of amounts in the future.** Another program calculates $12,000 paid out annually over 5 years in today's dollars, how much is needed initially in a lump sum.

F. **Partial payment from an annuity worth $1 today; a partial payment on a loan worth $1 today.** Another calculates paying off $12,000 (car) during 5 years (paying back with cheaper dollars). How much would you pay monthly?

Can I Retire Early? *(See chapter 6 for illustrations of retiring early.)*

When a person retires early, high earnings of the last few years may be missing from Social Security estimate, account or report, which influence the Social Security benefit for the remaining life. Social Security benefits for those younger than 65 (67) are reduced by ? ___ percent for each month short of full retirement age.

To help make decisions on working a few more years to receive a higher benefit, call 1-800-772-1213. Ask for form SSA 7004. This gives wages and taxes credited to one's account and an estimate of retirement benefits payable. (Years of lowest earnings are excluded.) Social Security benefits can be seen in pamphlets available in public buildings or on the Internet which show reductions for early retirement, increased benefits for delayed retirement, benefits to spouses, disability benefits, and other valuable information. For example, people born in 1943 or after will receive 8 percent (.66 of one percent per month) increases over full retirement benefits for delaying receipt of Social Security.

Be sure people sign up for Medicare at age 65 (a few months before) even if they decide to delay retirement. When starting retirement benefits after age 62, contact Social Security in advance for finding the best month to claim benefits.

Full benefit for a spouse is one-half of the retired worker's full benefit. This is reduced (37.5 percent at age 62) if spouse takes benefits before age 65, unless spouse is taking care of a child under 16 or a disabled child. Benefits are 50 percent regardless of age. The years between child's age of 16 and when spousal benefits are available are called "the widow's gap." (See Chapter 6 for more on retirement decisions, tools and a case on early retirement.)

The shepherd can suggest alternatives to early retirement if it would be detrimental to long term economic well-being. Other changes can be made to relieve the emotional and physical stress of a job. Examples are hiring help for home responsibilities, being more efficient, using labor or back saving devices at work, interviewing a stress counselor, having diversions and vacations, gaining spiritual strength, and establishing new goals for working and for roles outside of working hours.

What is the Employer's Retirement Plan?

The plan administrator can provide a summary plan description. However, questions to ask are:
- What will the pension be at voluntary early retirement? 65? 70? Earlier?
- Is the plan insured? By whom? For what?
- Are there payout options? Lump sum? Annuity?
- Are benefits guaranteed for life?
- Are benefits reduced when one takes Social Security?
- What benefit options are for survivors? Before retirement? After retirement?
- What determines survivor benefits to collect benefits?
- Can employer change or discontinue plan?
- How many years to become "vested"? Is employee currently vested?
- Can credit be transferred to another's plan?
- Is there a cost-of-living adjustment in retirement benefits?
- Are there disability payments? For how long?
- Can additional contributions be made to the plan?
- What are the pension fund decisions?

A "joint survivor" or "single life" is a decision. "Joint life pension" is assumed unless the spouse signs a document permitting her/his exclusion. Most people do not shop for an insurance alternative. The difference between using the "joint life" pension and "single life" and using the extra to pay for term insurance or single premium annuity for the surviving spouse is shown below as an example:

Single Life monthly benefit	Joint Life benefit	Monthly difference	Cost per month of life insurance	Annual Savings
$2,000	$1,600	$400	$200	$2,400 ($400-200 X 12)

People need to be reminded if they choose the "joint life" option and the spouse dies first, they cannot go back to the employer and change to "single life." Buying insurance eliminates that problem.

Estate Planning

What If I Were to Die Tomorrow?

This is the question asked of people to examine if their soul is right with God. It is used to encourage people into making changes so they can be assured they will be with the Lord now and for eternity. The question is asked here to examine if their financial house is right for kin or others for whom they feel responsible. The questions to be settled are: Who would get their property? Will the church or mission continue without their support? Who would be the guardian of their children? Will survivors be provided for in an equitable manner? Will spouse have adequate control of the family business? Will some of the property be forced into a public sale because of a disagreement among heirs? Can there be a priority sale to specified family members? How would their debts, loans, and credit cards be paid? Will the co-signer be able to pay the loans? If there is no credit insurance on these, will life insurance cover them?

Can the spouse and children remain in their home if the income earner dies? Is there enough insurance for the spouse to continue working or get more training for a better job to support the family including dependent parents? Is there insurance on the spouse who cares for the children so child care can continue? Does each spouse own the insurance policy on the other so the face value is not in the estate for the deceased? Are there provisions for an irresponsible person or one who has disability? Does the survivor, who needs to pull business and personal finances together for distribution, know where the important papers, policies, reports, documentation, and certificates are kept? Does someone know what kind of funeral or memorial is desired? Answering these questions are the steps to financial peace of mind through estate planning.

If my parent died tomorrow, how would property be distributed? Any member of the family may need to take some steps in estate planning. The above considerations apply as the shepherd assists people to get organized, manage their assets, pay debts as part of retirement planning, and distribute property. Tax refunds and Social Security can be garnished to repay guaranteed student loans (up to 15 percent).

Probate costs - The court supervises transfer of a decedent's assets to rightful beneficiaries, and the payment of debts, taxes, and expenses. Costs are 4 to 10 percent of the assets of the estate. Most states require minimal involvement with courts when assets subject to probate are under $60,000. (One needs to check the current minimum for a given state). Avoiding probate means lower costs and faster settlement. Non-probate property includes assets transferred by contract rather than by will. They include insurance proceeds not payable to the estate, retirement plan benefits, personal pension plans, annuities, and assets owned jointly with right of survivorship. Other property not going through probate are things already passed to named beneficiary, things given prior to three years before death, government co-ownership, and assets placed in a living trust. Living trust is more costly to prepare than a will but it avoids probate. The savings are to beneficiaries only and there is no public knowledge of disbursements.

Inheritance tax - A state tax in 16 states levied on inherited property when received by heirs. It is based on value of property and relationship of the heir. The tax is paid out of the cash available in the estate or sold inherited items usually at an auction. Some children are forced to sell the family farm to pay inheritance taxes. A survivorship insurance policy can be bought to pay the estate taxes if set up more than three years before death.

Trusts - Gifts and transfers at death are made outright to beneficiaries or put in trusts. Trusts are placed with a person or bank (trustee) for the benefit of another as specified in the document creating the trust. A living trust is useful if one lives in a probate expensive state, if the settlor desires third party asset management, if the settlor becomes incapacitated, needs multiple estate administration to be easier, or wants some cost savings at time of death. The disadvantages are greater up front costs, no provision for death tax savings over a will, and could use financial power of attorney as a lifetime issue.

Testamentary trusts - These are created under the terms of a will and are effective upon death of the grantor. They are designed to provide money or asset management after the grantor's death.

Irrevocable Life insurance trust - The trust is the beneficiary. At death of grantor, the trust receives funds to pay the taxes.

Irrevocable Living Trust - This gives away assets to reduce taxes. It is modified by the grantor during his/her lifetime, which bypasses probate and estate taxes. The grantor gives up the right to control of the property, change beneficiaries, and change trustees. The trust pays the income tax due. The fee for setting up the trust ranges from $750 to $2,500. A typical will is much less expensive at about $200-500.

Estate Planning Begins

Estate Planning begins when a child is born as the will needs to be updated, particularly naming a guardian for the child. Deciding on the guardian is the number one reason couples do not have wills. Otherwise, if one parent dies the other one has to go to court, as state appointed guardian, to ask permission on how to spend the money on the child. If both parents die, guardians named will more likely meet preferences of deceased.

Estate planning begins when property is accumulated. Titles can be joint, or if separate, gain tax advantages for settlements from asset accumulation. For example, the husband should own the insurance policy on the wife and the wife on the husband so that proceeds do not go into the deceased estate.

Estate planning begins when property, insurance, collections, certificate of deposits, stocks and bonds are acquired and beneficiaries named. Otherwise, if the state distributes the property, requiring liquidation or sale, the deceased and survivors lose control, preferences designated, and value due to taxation. The assumption of estate taxes is redistribution of wealth as the founding fathers did not want large wealth to amass to a few families as it had in Europe.

If the family is content with how the state will distribute the property, that is all right. If their religious convictions or desires direct otherwise, they should do some planning. Mr. and Mrs. Farmer were reluctant to do the planning suggested because it meant giving the farm away to relatives before they died. Through depressions and crop failures, they had sacrificed everything else to keep the farm, so it was difficult to imagine giving it away, out of their control. They changed their mind when it was shown on paper that without planning the estate would have more taxes than they originally paid for the farm. They were shown how putting the farm in a trust and receiving income from it gave them both control and income.

Estate planning begins with collecting **important papers**, making copies, storing in a safety deposit box, and informing a person where they are kept. Included in important papers are birth certificates, marriage certificates, baptismal records, adoption papers, citizenship papers, passports, abstracts and deeds, mineral leases, bond and stock certificates, armed service records (need discharge papers for veteran benefits) (Form DD214), school degrees, Social Security numbers, and divorce decrees. Other papers to save are credit card numbers and who to call in case they are lost, insurance policies and agents, attorney's name, banking records, trustees, name of trust department involved in estate planning.

Receipts of major improvements to the house should be kept for years. These will be used for eligibility and proof of expenses when value of property purchased and at sale are made. Records of tax deductible items are also kept. (Jane showed her family the receipt from child care and said it was worth $20 in tax credit.)

Other items are heirlooms and valuables with photograph and appraisal, household inventory of purchase records, serial and model numbers, and warranties or guarantees. Personal property items and who would receive them need to be listed. An option is labeling the items with the name to receive them.

Medical history, medical doctors, accidents, immunization including tetanus, family medical history which could be used for possible inheritance or recurring, employment history, educational history including training experience, conferences, seminars, community activities, volunteer work, and special recognitions and honors.

Employment history includes employer, supervisors, responsibilities, dates, and references. Educational history includes schools, diplomas, honors, scholarships,

For estate planning purposes, real estate can be listed for type of property and acres, location, year acquired, cost, how titled and the market value. Other personal property ownership needs to be identified for purposes of estate distribution. Stocks and bonds are to be named, date when purchased, exact name of owner, face value and purchase price. Life insurance, in addition to company and policy number, can be identified whether double indemnity, face amount, owned by husband or wife or jointly, cash value and any outstanding policy loan, exact name of owner insured, and beneficiary on policy. Mortgages, other real estate debts, and personal liabilities with date due and amount remaining to be paid should be written. Liens against personal property for unpaid debts or taxes need to be known. A record of taxable gifts should be available. Financial information is available on income tax returns. It is recommended to keep tax returns five years. Retirement benefits are documented in detail such as pensions, profit-sharing, deferred compensation, annual benefits for both spouses, amount invested, retirement income, death benefits, contracts, partnerships and corporation agreements, and divorce decrees.

IMPORTANT RECORDS

Organize records and list important papers. It may be wise to make duplicate copies of some of these papers. Store the papers in a line-proof place, a bank safe deposit box, for example, or keep in another residence. You will need to develop some of the lists. Others you do not need.

<u>Important papers:</u>

<u>Where kept:</u>

    Birth certificates ——————————————————————————————————
    Marriage certificates ————————————————————————————————
    Baptismal records ————————————————————————————————————
    Adoption papers ——————————————————————————————————————
    Citizenship papers and/or passports ——————————————————
    Abstracts and deeds ——————————————————————————————————
    Leases ———
    Bonds and stock certificates —————————————————————————
    Armed service records ————————————————————————————————
    School degrees ———————————————————————————————————————
    Social security numbers and information ———————————————
    Divorce decrees ——————————————————————————————————————
    Wills (Have a copy at home because a safe deposit box,
        in event of death, is closed unless court order opens it. Check state regulations.) ———

<u>Other records:</u>

    Financial advisor's name: ————————————————————————————
        Plan: ——
    Social worker's name and number ——————————————————————
    Insurance policies - life, auto, medical —————————————
    Insurance agent's name(s): ———————————————————————————
    Attorney's name(s) ———————————————————————————————————
    Credit card numbers - Addresses, phone number of creditors to notify if card is lost. ———
        Tax returns - Save all records for deductible expenses such as
        medical services and prescription drugs.
    Major improvements - Save receipts for capital gains purposes ———

    Banking records
    1.   List of savings accounts - ownership, account number, location ———
    2.   Cancelled checks - keep for seven years ——————————
    3.   Certificates of Deposit ——————————————————————————
    4.   Name of trust department that may be involved with estate planning ———
    Safe deposit box - Keep a list of the contents and give a copy of the
        list to someone else. ————————————————————————————
    Household inventory (Keep in safe deposit box)
        Heirlooms and valuables - Photograph these and have appraised
            for current value. ——————————————————————————————
        Purchase records
        1.   serial and model numbers ——————————————————————
        2.   warranties/guarantees ——————————————————————————
        3.   price ———
        4.   bill of sale or receipt with date of purchase ———
    Medical history
    1.   major illnesses ——————————————————————————————————
    2.   medical doctors and addresses ——————————————————————
    3.   accidents ———
    4.   immunizations including tetanus ————————————————————
    5.   family medical history - possible inherited or recurring
            illness such as mental illness, Tay Sachs, etc. ———
    Employment history - Employer, address, salary, job
        responsibilities, dates, supervisor, references ———
    Educational history - Schools, diplomas, transcripts, honors, scholarships ———
    Experience or training - Training programs, conferences, seminars, community
        activities, volunteer work, special responsibilities ———
    Special service recognition, awards, honors ——————————

Descent and Distribution

Descent and distribution of property is *by* title, operation of law (i.e. Joint Ownership), contract (life insurance, 401K, 403b), will or trust, and intestate (decided by the state). The state will appoint an attorney who will see that property goes to the spouse and children equally. Therefore, analyze how property is currently owned. If desires are different than how the state would distribute property, one must change the title, write up a contract, and/or have a will to revise distribution. Pension and insurance will go to the named beneficiaries. Periodically, these need to be reviewed and updated. The tax advantage of different arrangements for beneficiaries of one generation compared to another need to be examined.

The Will to Be Updated

When there are young children, the mother or father, or someone must be appointed guardian so that the state appointed guardian does not have to go to court (or established official) to get permission to spend money for them. For older children, if one or more are incapable or irresponsible, safeguards and arrangements need to be mentioned. An executor (executrix for female) or personal representative is appointed to be paid out of funds or to volunteer to reduce draw on how estate assets are distributed. A will can reduce the risk of irresponsible distribution and use of assets by naming a trustworthy, frugal person who would safeguard assets and distribute the way the deceased would desire. An executor can distribute assets according to the will to reduce draw on assets from paying the attorney to distribute. A will is needed for naming beneficiaries including charitable institutions, church, etc.. An allowance for a percentage or whatever to go to the work of God's kingdom can be arranged. Special collections, etc. can be listed to go to specific beneficiaries. Previous distributions noted on a list and passed among recipients can be done to lessen conflict and meet wishes of the deceased.

Estate planning needs to be done not only to reduce taxes and give peace of mind but to prevent/reduce the rivalry and ill feelings among recipients of inheritances. When everything is left up to an attorney, rather than naming an executor/executrix, treasured items may be sold and proceeds distributed and, in needy families, a huge percentage goes to the attorney rather than to needy beneficiaries.

Some people write in the will that the child beneficiary has to have the assistance of a financial planner (s) before proceeding with proceeds. The will thus protects the particular child and his or her whims in spending. Write or update by ensuring inclusion of these items:

____ Full names, ages, date of birth for spouses and children

____ Husband's executor or personal representative, an alternate

____ Wife's executor or personal representative, an alternate

____ Guardian of the person, children, and where residing; alternate

____ Separate guardian of the property

____ Single sum $_____ to guardian, if death occurs prior to _____

____ Relief provision for expenditures by guardian for any minor children

____ Special instructions for special needs children, disabled, or irresponsible recipient

____ Personal articles to spouse, named children, or exception_____

____ Residence to spouse, other items to spouse

____ Charitable Bequest $_____ or to _____
____ Special bequest $_____ or to _____
____ Close order to death, defer for statutory period, i.e. 60 days
____ Contingent provisions or ( ) contingent trust for minor children
____ Marital and Non-marital trust
____ Whether farm or family business will follow rules of succession or inheritance
____ If simultaneous death for spouses, which will will be honored first
____ Power of attorney document needed for husband, wife, durable, to each other, power
        extended to_____
____ Appointment of Health Care Agent or Health Care Power of Attorney/Living Will
        (Name of one or more persons as Health Care Agent.)

Tools for Charity in Estate Planning[235]

Gift Annuities. "A charitable gift annuity (CGA) is a contract between you and a charity through which the charity promises to make an annual payment to you (or someone else you select) for your lifetime or that of your beneficiary; in exchange, you contribute cash or other property. A portion of each payment won't be subject to federal income tax because it's treated as a return of your initial contribution; the balance will be taxed. You can take a charitable deduction on your 1040 for the year in which the CGA is established.

A CGA can make sense when you're looking for a guaranteed stream of payment for the remainder of your lifetime; you'd like the charity to keep the assets following your death; and you don't need control over the assets during your lifetime."

Pooled Income Funds

"A pooled income fund (PIF) is maintained by a charity to receive gifts from many donors. All the gifts are held in a single investment pool, and each year contributors receive a pro rata share of the fund's net income. For smaller gifts, the PIF can be an ideal way to donate today and receive, for yourself or your designated beneficiary, a stream of investment income each year.

A PIF can make sense when you're comfortable letting the charity invest the funds as part of its pool, you don't mind receiving (or having a beneficiary receive) a stream of payments equal to the charity's net investment income from the pool, and you'd like the assets to go to the charity following your (or your beneficiary's) death."

Charitable Remainder Trusts

"For greater flexibility or control, particularly with larger gifts, consider a charitable remainder trust (CRT). This irrevocable trust provides the initial interest to you or other beneficiaries through annual payments. Payments can continue for a set term of up to 20 years or for the lifetime of your non-charitable beneficiaries. At the end of this period or at the death of the last surviving beneficiary, the balance of the trust will go to a charity you select.

There are two basic types of CRTs: a charitable remainder annuity trust and a charitable remainder unitrust. They vary in how the annual payment is determined and can be created either

---

235   Staff. TIAA-CREF. *Chart.* Spring 2004.

during your lifetime or at your death." The CRT is useful for a tax deduction, using unproductive and/or highly appreciated assets, and for use during life or at death.

Net Worth Statement and Assessment for Adjusting

Estate planning continues with writing a Net Worth or Wealth Statement. (The Net Worth Statement is used for other purposes, also.) In making a net worth statement, items need to be analyzed to first see if person has an estate planning problem or if estate is excluded from taxes: estate, probate, inheritance. If total estate assets are over the limits (keep up to date), ownership may need to be changed, titles may need to be changed, contracts may need to be set up, and a will drawn to decrease attorney fees at distribution. New purchases or sale of properties and gifts to people may need to be done before person is deceased. The will also gives information needed by executor and recipients. The net worth statement needs to be reviewed periodically to increase assets, reduce debts, and makes changes because of changes in the law.

The net worth statement or wealth statement, which is a list of assets minus liabilities, is used for analyzing the need for estate planning, i.e. making a will. After each item, note how it is owned, how it is to be distributed upon person's death, how it is to be distributed after second person's (spouse, usually)death, taxes subject upon death *before* estate planning, taxes after each death *after* estate planning.

Net worth items are analyzed for diversification for protection in times of an uncertain economy. Assets are the items that are owned measured by their fair market value. Items are acquired for income production to combat inflation. Durable goods are chosen that last (1) even when income is reduced and (2) make one more productive. The net worth statement and assets are used when applying for a loan, in establishing the need for insurance protection, and assessing growth versus deterioration. Analyze items on the net worth statement to see if changes need to be made. These are the aspects to watch for changes:

Ownership
Maturity
Interest rate, dividends, return on investment
Specific goal for that asset – earmarked
Willingness to reposition or not, trade in for retirement home, liquidate
Check writing privileges or not
Appreciation prospects or depreciation trend
Wealth figure used to assess progress toward money goal
Percentage of liquid versus non-liquid
Put in trust, charitable trust
Individual item equity (market value minus liabilities).

Debts, loans, and credit need to be assessed whether secured or not, whether bankruptcy will help or not, how titled for distribution at death, action by creditors, date that debt was last paid, and ways to reduce debt more quickly.

Cash Flow

The **Cash Flow Statement** is calculated by listing the **Inflows,** the **Outflows** of 1) Church and charity, 2) Savings and investments, 3) Fixed outflows, 4) Variable outflows resulting in **Total Outflows,** and subtracting from total inflows to report **Net Inflow.** If net inflow is negative, new borrowing or asset liquidation has occurred.

The Cash Flow Statement with inflow and outflow yielding a net flow is analyzed by recording every penny spent, saved, and shared. Then a new cash flow can be developed. It needs to be done formally or casually when there is a decision about use of inheritances. It is analyzed for changes and to have better balance among increasing, reducing expenses, and changing dollar amounts, even after changes in lifestyle and renewed commitments.

Dr. Carlos changed offices, cut down on staff, cut out the water dispenser, reduced overhead, lived in an older house, and kept his used car in order to give more to his church. Dr. Carlos said many doctors are still feeding their egos. They borrow $500,000 or so to have everything new and expensive all at the same time rather than sequentially over the years. The interest paid could go toward more savings and sharing.

Both **cash flow and net worth analyses** can be used to calculate ratios for specific interpretative purposes:

- "Basic Liquity Ratio" – savings to months of expenses. Total savings ÷ monthly expenses for determining position of security if income should be reduced.
    - "Debts to Equity Ratio." Debts ÷ equity to determine solvency and eligibility requirement.
    - "Debts to Income Ratio." Debts ÷ income to determine possibilities for repaying and reducing debt for future security and eligibility requirements.
    - "Investment Assets to Net Worth Ratio" to assess achievement and capital accumulation.

Financial Report

This contains household composition (names, ages, makeup), income, net worth, goals, assumptions, risk tolerance (general outlook), decisions, and concerns. The "report" can be written for each area category with the outline: analysis, objectives, assumptions, recommendations, and implementation. The **areas are** Standard of living (cash flow, expenses, debts, charity and lifestyle changes), Savings (cash reserve, investments), Protection (insurance, employee benefits, government benefits), Accumulations (money, goods, business, real estate, education, retraining), Financial Independence (retirement), Estate Planning (wills, trusts, contracts and trustees on death), Taxation, and Security (job, business, miscellaneous).

Ages are very important to analyze the financial situation, objectives and suggest changes in investments. An overall picture with complete analysis is important. Included should be human assets, human capital for employing various skills and transferring jobs, history of chronic illnesses, and prospects for inheritances.

Illustrations to Educate the Shepherd to Assist Others

Analysis of Net Worth Statement of Julie and Jim Wilcox (November 2005)

Assets and Liabilities (how owned) and their Values

Cash, saving deposits (joint and single)	
Private home, market value (joint)	$366,000
Farm, 80 acres (joint)	100,000
Furnishings, collections, equipment, paintings, jewelry	100,000
Rental property	
Insurance, face value (Jim owns on himself)	35,000
Stocks (Jim owns)	70,000
Annuities (est. cash surrender value)	
Trust account	
Government securities of all kinds	
Tax-exempt state and local bonds	
Corporate bonds	
Mutual funds	
Money Market (Julie owns)	7,500
Other long-term assets	
Short-term business assets	
Vehicles, boat, trailer	
Other retirement assets	
TIAA and CREF (Julie's pension account)	840,000
Total	$1,518,500

Liabilities

Mortgages	
Private home (Owner occupied, owned joint)	60,000
Farm (owned joint)	15,000
Notes and loans payable	
Other unpaid bills	
Long-term business debts (farm)	
Short-term business debts	
Loans against life insurance	
Debts/credit obligations	14,500
Student Loans	
Taxes	
Insurance premiums	
Other liabilities	
Total	$75,000

Net Worth

$1,428,500

Recommendations by Financial Planner: They are under the limit of the exemption now $3,000,000 net taxable estate after certain deductions for transfer of income and gifts during his or her lifetime. (It is 0 in 2010 and then the "Sunset rule" in 2011 will go to $1,000,000.) Deductions include charitable bequests and property passing to a surviving spouse. Gifts and bequests in any amount and at any time made to recognized charitable and educational organizations escape the federal gift and estate tax. These gifts lower the taxable estate for gift and estate liability.

Recommendation #1 gift tax consequences: Change title of farm to children. The children would receive the income from rental of crop land. Design plan so that children are under the $100,000 exemption for inheritance tax. Do not prepay the mortgage because of the tax deductions and mortgage exemption.

Recommendation #2: Keep beneficiaries as they are: husband for pension. There is no state tax on life insurance at estate distribution unless it is paid to the insured's estate. The policy's face value is included in one's estate, however. That is why the husband should own the policy on the wife and vice versa. In earlier years, Jim's "cash value" life insurance bought for the children was a gift to the children. (The reason it was a gift was that the children could continue the insurance on themselves without a physical examination. The cash value was taken out for various purposes.)

Recommendation #3: Keep money market for cash flow even though return would be greater on a fixed, longer term certificate.

Recommendation #4: Reexamine beneficiaries of Jim's stocks. They were acquired by Jim's putting three percent of each paycheck over his working life into a supplemental retirement fund. Upon retirement, Jim bought a used vehicle, paid on repairing the roof, and distributed the remaining fund into five different stocks. His choices were bad in that the return on all of them has been poor.

Recommendation #5: Jim's options: First thought is to give the "first fruits" as told in the Scripture so Jim would give 10 percent to church and charities where he thought his money (given as a gift from God) would do the most good, not as legal act but because his heart wants to do this.

Recommendation #6: Options are: keep the house, sell the house, gift one pension fund to children, buy a much smaller home, use the pension for payment into retirement home with yearly escalating fees, put 10 percent of pension funds into a charitable remainder trust, or put 90 percent into a charitable remainder trust.

Julie and Jim Wilcox, when asked if the primary pension owner were to die tomorrow, checked the records held by the provider. The beneficiary was the husband who had the choices of taking as a lump sum, rolling it over into a qualified plan, or receiving monthly payments. The worst choice would be taking it as a lump sum because of the tax liability. The husband thought about signing the required paper of excluding him from the pension so that it would go to the contingent beneficiary – **the children**. But that would be the worst since they would be required to take it as a lump sum with all the tax liabilities.

The decision to give each child $200,000 would be a poor choice since the tax advantage of Jim rolling the pension fund to other funds would be lost and the children would have to pay over 50 percent taxes. They have no college debts since their mother worked at a university and so their tuition was half price, children had jobs, and some semesters they lived at home. Two of the three have other large credit debts. The other with no debt has a low paying job.

Ann Receives $30,000 Inheritance

Ann received $30,000 inheritance and wants the shepherd's opinion before she goes to a professional if that is needed. Together they decided to give ten percent first, pay off her debts, buy a better used car, and put the remainder in three savings and investment accounts. One would be an emergency fund with check writing privileges, one would be a medium risk investment (probably mutual funds,) and another into a longer term, high risk stock. This is appropriate since she is young and the amount in high risk is small in proportion to the other. (The riskier the investment, the potentially higher the return. Risk needs to be balanced against the "safe" savings which does not keep pace with inflation.) She was going to read the Wall Street Journal and Value Line to educate herself and then use a discount broker. She could also read Money Magazine, Business Week, Forbes, Barons, Fortune, Moody's publications or Standard and Poor's publications. There is risk with individual stocks.

Letter to Timothy

by Flora Williams, Ph.D, M.Div., RFC (Registered Financial Consultant) July 20, 2006

Timothy is making $16,000 per month in a dangerous occupation but he will probably have several months without pay between projects. How should he distribute his income? This question is similar for athletes and others making huge but temporary income. Timothy is not married and is currently renting out his house. His question is: "What should I do with $150,000?"

First in the financial report, credibility is established and homework documented. I did consult three other advisors, got current information off the Internet, and studied two books.

Following are short answers due to the urgency of the decision. Urgency is because every day you do not "reposition" assets, you are losing money known as the "opportunity cost" of money by remaining in a lower return account. Also, certain rates as "specials" are only available for the "window of opportunity." Formulas, more explanations, and other scenarios could be written if requested.

Six month's expenditures should be kept in the checking account or investments with check writing privileges to cover emergencies or unexpected real opportunities such as travel for an interview. An appropriate budget with specific goals would be useful. Limits can be established. Charity can be a discipline.

In response to the question, "Should I pay off my house?" No, because 1) In your income bracket, you need the interest from a loan for tax deduction; 2) You need the mortgage exemption; 3) It is possible to receive a higher return than the mortgage interest rate you are paying; 4) You retain more flexibility in use of your money for emergency fund or opportunities for education, another house, or job seeking, 5) You have dependable, reliable and clean renters currently; 6) The main principle is diversification against all types of risks; and 7) By keeping some money fluid or liquid, you can pay cash avoiding use of credit which is much higher than the mortgage interest.

In response to how to diversify? Generally, a wise plan is invest in three places or more for diversification. In your case, therefore, you could:

a) Reposition with $50,000 in short term liquid certificate of deposit (not just savings with low interest) of six-seven months, (penalty if taken out sooner). This is an emergency fund, a maintenance fund, a liquid fund.

b) Reposition $50,000 in moderate term certificate of deposit of 12-13 months (depending on the time period for the special, high rate) (penalty if taken out sooner). This is a moderate return but higher than just ordinary savings account.

c) Reposition $50,000 into long term18 months certificates of deposits (penalty if taken out sooner). This is a retirement fund deliberately held to reduce temptation. The delay of current pleasure results in future security and peace of mind over time. Time and interest result in growth and appreciation. The sooner a person starts such a fund the less he or she needs to deposit to obtain financial objectives. In other words, avoid the cost of procrastination.

How to get started? The most important action to do quickly is to comparison shop within the financial institution and between institutions. Generally, over the years credit unions have paid higher interest rates, for example. (It is true this time.)

Information was obtained from the Internet for a Savings Bank www.lsbank.com and for an Employees Credit Union www.purdueefcu.com.

An illustration to make the point and show the cost of delay in repositioning assets was the three scenarios:

a) six months with $50,000 at 4 percent interest would yield $2,000 per year and $170 per month, ($50,000 X .04 = $2,000).

b) 12-13 months with $50,000 at 5.15 percent interest would yield $2,575 per year and $216 per month.

c) 18 months at 7 percent interest would yield $3500 per year and $291.70 per month.

All together with this plan of diversification you would have $8,075 per year and $673 per month with the bank using your money. Assuming you are only getting 1.34 percent on $100,000 of your money and 4 percent on $50,000 (yielding together $3,350 per year and $278 per month), you would have an *increase* in yield (savings) by repositioning now of $4,735 per year and $395 per month. Therefore, every month you do not reposition, the "opportunity cost" or what you are losing by not changing is about $400.00. That is the urgency mentioned in the introduction above.

In reality, when I checked the rates currently being offered for July, the following results were found for over $15,000 in some offers and over $25,000 in others (You qualify in all scenarios):

Savings Bank: Checking Account   0.50 percent Annual Percentage Yield

(.0075 X $50,000 =		$ 375
Savings Account	0 .75 %	1,325
Access Plus	2.65	1,375
*7 months C.D.	2.75	2,250
*9 months C.D.	4.50	2,575
*13 months C.D.	5.15	2,575

*Hypothetical ANNUAL YIELD FROM THREE PLACES = $6,200.

Employees Credit Union:

Money Market	2.25	1,125
* 7 months C.D.	4.65	2,325
*11months C.D.	5.10	2,550
*52 months (4.3 yrs)	5.40	2,700

*Hypothetical ANNUAL YIELD FROM THREE PLACES = $7,575.

The income difference between the bank and the credit union is $1,375 which makes it worth the effort to reposition. (A motivation to study and change is this: Calculate hours it takes to change and divide by savings to see a hypothetical wage for your effort.) However, you may want to negotiate with the bank for an equal or higher rate.

To convince you to reposition and act quickly to see how much you would gain, I could calculate the difference between what you are now getting (which I am not sure exactly) from the income gained from repositioning and/or changing banks.

For more long range planning, D_____, an experienced, ethical planner, would like to consult with you. The first visit is free, to decide if you want riskier, and hence higher yield, investments in January. I can show you how much by saving $50,000 a year you would have in 15 or 30 years. It is amazing. My employer put 5 percent of my salary in addition to my salary for 30 years into 403 B nonprofit retirement plan. I had over one million dollars value at retirement. But I did lose over $200,000 value in just one year and 40 percent in the market in another year.

Answer to question about contributing to your company's 401 K plan:

This is immediate action for long-range savings to avoid loss of opportunity and growth. Contribute consistently and regularly before receiving income (wages weekly or monthly), bonuses, and raises into 401K and any company matching stock plans. These are withdrawn to start earning interest before income is taxed. Therefore, you have more capital to invest. Your 401K is not available to spend without penalty. (Have some money as shown above that is liquid or for a house.) This lack of availability is good because it reduces your temptation to spend on current pleasures. At the rate of interest, if you invest before taxes, you will have more capital to invest. If you are not taxed in any way, it is a moot point. Anyway, have a regular withdrawal going into a high rate return account. For people taxed at 28 percent, the withdrawal reduces taxable income and they will have more take home pay.

If your $50,000 is left in savings at 5 percent annual return (not adding to it), it will grow to $216,100 in 30 years. If you deposited about $4,000 per month in 30 years you would have $3,321,950. If you save $100 per week at 8 percent starting at age 39, at age 65 you would have $451,711. But if you start one year later, the dollar cost of delay is $39,000 because your final balance would be that much lower.

Mary's Response to the Inheritance Dilemma

I am on staff with a para-church organization. I intentionally live a sacrificial lifestyle. I have a one bedroom apartment, and a "seasoned" car. I take my laundry to a laundromat. I have three windows and two fans in the summertime. I could easily handle doing my own taxes.

In 2000 I received a surprise inheritance of $386,000. Suddenly, I needed an investment counselor and a tax preparer. I did not want to change my style of living. I prefer to be able to give more to others in ministry and to specific ministries. I sought the counsel of a Christian professional who understood my desires and shared my convictions. I added to my monthly TDA payments, was able to invest for dividends that enabled me to give more generously each month, and was able to establish a Roth IRA. The one initial purchase was my first laptop. This was essential for communications in ministry.

Still, giving/saving was/is a constant challenge. I am in personal contact with pastors in Africa and very aware of desperate needs. I wanted to fix those situations. However, they were never-ending. I was being taught to seek God's purposes daily, with each need. I also realized that I was not supposed to fix it "single-handedly" nor was I to "shut down" on the overwhelming needs. I was to share these needs with the rest of the Body of Christ and learn to trust God with each need. I wanted to be responsive to His leading.

This led me to using most of the inheritance for building the MacKeefer Building in Kenya where I work very closely with the pastors and periodically go there as missionary and director. The MacKeefer Building now houses the orphanage, provides the distribution center for food and medicine, has educational rooms, provides a recreational center for girls, and contains the chapel for worship. These all brought out the struggles in me that are in each person's heart: desiring control over circumstances, desiring a good reputation (approval), and desiring security. The principles of sharing and storing can seem contradictory. These "living tensions" exist so that we see the need to seek God's specific direction in each circumstance, not assuming we have sufficient information to sit in His position. As each call comes for help and supporting "my" orphanage, I share the needs with others on the Internet network family – the Body of Christ who share with those in Kenya.

◊◊◊ ⧗ ⧗ ◊◊◊

Chapter 13. **Sharing the Pasture**

The shepherd inspires, counsels, advises, teaches, and arranges for the Great Transformer to develop loving attitudes, behaviors, and practices. The goal here is increasing generosity and stewardship. The outcome leads to choosing to grow spiritually by giving time, talent, effort and money. These goals are described in Acts 10:2, "He and all his family were devout and God-fearing; he gave generously to those in need and prayed regularly." The shepherd leads in the spiritual journey from rejection of God to acceptance of Lord as Savior, to an attitude of gratitude, generosity and sharing as a disciple. The follower is disciplined and committed to expand talents, show mercy, stand against injustices and give all for work of the kingdom and other people as response to God's love.

Time and time again the Scriptures remind that "God is with us!" People relax and feel comforted, but their spiritual journey and response are lacking when they forget the next steps: Share God! Pass on the grace one has received. Share gifts received. Peter wrote, "Each one should use whatever gifts he or she has received to serve others, faithfully administrating God's grace in its various forms. If anyone speaks, he or she should do as one speaking the very words of God. If anyone serves, he or she should do it with the strength God provides, so that in all things God may be praised through Jesus Christ. To him be the glory and the power for ever and ever. Amen" (1 Peter 4:10-11).

Sharing is The Plan for People of the Pasture

Sharing is the plan for people to live together in families and communities. The first and foremost action is glorifying God, the Creator, by sharing. This fulfills God's love in designing the world, the purpose for life, and work in the kingdom of God. Sharing grows out of trusting God to meet our needs.

Sharing the pasture means loving and caring enough to give. People can give their money, time, energy, abilities, unique strengths, possessions and wealth in a variety of ways. Service and contributions are only two of the ways. Compassion, mercy, doing justice and encouragement are also God's ways. Stewardship is implicit. Sharing is unique to the individual and can be creative. Just a little sharing, like a little grain of faith, can do a lot of good. Sharing resources are investments in the growth and maintenance of God's kingdom on earth. The basic dilemma is that there is enough for everyone's need but not for everyone's greed, selfishness and self-centeredness. Conflict and deprivation result in the rejection of God's love.

The shepherd can help people grieve or rejoice as they give up old desires, possessions, and satisfactions for the new ones in a life renewed. The shepherd rejoices with those desiring changes. Although world citizens, God's people are different from others. God's people answer the call of the Creator to care for all. The Spirit indwelling in the generous heart and creative mind move the wheels of generosity. The Spirit nudges people to respond. Sharing is random as well as focused as needs are observed. Sharing or generosity becomes ingrained in individual nature, life-time habits, obligations, and felt responsibility for sharing the pasture. These lead to disciplined patterns of generosity.

"God has made us in his own image, to be like him in our creativity and work. But most of all in love and generosity".[236] Since most fall short, they need grace, rescuing, forgiveness, and restructuring. Salvation results in an openhearted response to gratefulness to God. They are generous in spite of failures to cooperate with God in sharing the good news, possessions, and wealth. *To live a life of love is to live a life of sharing.* Shepherds help others choose the Light that guides the path to sharing. Jesus said, "I have come that they may have life, and have it to the full [life abundant]" (John 10:10). Simon says, "God has great plans for you. But the plans call for giving, not getting; and serving, not being served." [237]

Giving is a response not only to God's love but to gratitude for God's gifts. Gratitude prompts sharing with others. The greatest blessing is that God would walk with people through their financial troubles, financial uncertainties, and decisions. Giving does not guarantee financial success, happiness, and selfish prosperity. It does confirm that God walks with people through the valleys of the financial shadows. The Great Shepherd leads to the blessings on the table.

With generous hearts people keep sharing with others, working, and caring for others even when they are hurting, fearful, and anxious for their own future security. Loving followers have a security not based on material wealth. Financial challenges can be a reminder that they are not God. They are driven by God's love which has been proven for generations and in many lives. They depend on God with an inner strength to follow and serve. They find new ways to reach out to those hurting and insecure.

Compassion is giving practical aid without expectation of remuneration, reciprocity, and gratitude. It is giving in spiritual ways as well as material ways.

Types of Sharing

Types of sharing include strengthening the ministry, expanding outreach, maintaining stability of the church as well as feeding the hungry and comforting the afflicted. The giving is for supporting ministers and missionaries for their needs or for their housing, building funds, and foundations. Sharing is done with self-help groups and starting new enterprises in the name of Jesus or otherwise. Sharing or giving can be efforts for fundraising, volunteering, and/or a budget line to adhere to religiously and allow for more giving.

Giving to others to use at their discretion or for work in the kingdom include general funds or special organized programs designed with different names by denominations, community groups, and organizations. Giving may be spontaneous as in generous tipping, buying something to support the seller or maker, or paying more than asked in garage sale items.

Sharing includes supporting missionaries or those with a worthwhile mission. In Luke 8:3 women were reported helping support Jesus and his disciples out of their own means. In I Timothy 5:9-10, a widow was considered worthy of support herself if she had shown hospitality, washed the feet of the saints, helped those in trouble, and performed good deeds.

---

236   Arthur Simon. *How Much is Enough? Hungering for God in an Affluent Culture.* Baker Books, Grand Rapids, Michigan 49516. 2003. P.64.

237   Ibid. P.134.

In Acts 4:34-37, the illustration of sharing is selling lands or houses and bringing the money from sales to put at the apostles' feet for their distribution to anyone in need. A reason for giving to church, outreach, or to the deacons' fund is for the minister's support. Today reduced giving and reduced volunteerism are resulting in deprived ministers, closing of church doors, and reduced programs.

Another form of sharing can be called hospitality. This is caring by use of money, time, energy, housing, sharing meals with those that cannot pay back, friendship, and smiling. It is to make the alien, the immigrant, the stranger, the disadvantaged, the disabled, and the ill feel welcome, valued, at home and to have hope.

Rev. Gates encourages giving by asking "what to Give Up for Lent?"[238] He included in this traditional practice of giving up one evening a week to visit a lonely or sick person. Also it is giving up a luxury to help meet someone's basic need. It is giving up a steak dinner to buy chickens for Heifer International. It is giving up a movie by getting a video at the library and to contribute to summer camp for an inner city child.

Unique ways to give or opportunities to share are abundant. There are service projects for young people. Giving time has a monetary value since the time could earn money if not used for sharing. Caring for elderly parents, caring for children so their parent can go shopping or to Bible study, and driving out of one's way to transport someone are a few examples. Cleaning house for a new parent or an elderly person are other examples. A person could give one half day to help someone or just sit with an ill person. A disabled person, now called God-abled, could sit with someone or baby sit, etc. for example. The best present to give is time and presence.

When making a Christmas list, include special offerings at church, funding drives, the sick, the widowed, and the poor along with family members. Giving to a special project in the name of children such as giving animals and chickens through Heifer International rather than another doll, for example, models and teaches generosity. One teenage girl rather than having a birthday party gave the money to the Save A Girl's Project.

Illustrations show unexpected ways to share, to "grab a moment to give." Only a tap on the arm by a homeless boy told Matthew to give him his sandwich. The booth owner then gave Matthew one free. The elderly man lacked just a few dollars to pay his grocery bill. The woman behind made up the difference. Little boys were sitting outside the church fence where the church was selling pumpkins and food for battered women. An after thought was to give the boys money to go in and buy something.

In a system with which one disagrees, some would argue about giving to just anyone. They would say one is supporting the system with which one disagrees. Some carry granola bars to give to beggars. In Matthew 5:42, however, Jesus said, "Give to everyone who begs from you, and do not refuse anyone who wants to borrow from you."

"Money gives power to good intentions."[239] Ramsey supports building wealth for God's purposes. One cannot say they love God and not give money to support God's reign and God's provision to others. This supports asking a professional advisor about transferring securities, giving real estate while retaining ability to live in home, naming church as beneficiary of life insurance, setting up charitable remainder trusts, naming church as beneficiary of qualified retirement plan, arranging retirement plan endowments, and updating wills.

---

238   Craig Gates. Jackson, Mississippi.

239   Dave Ramsey. *The Total Money Makeover: A Proven Plan for Financial Fitness.* Thomas Nelson, Inc. Nashville, Tennessee. 2003. P.213.

Sharing in the Economic Plan

The joy of giving is in the plan with the joy of spending and saving. The examples in the Scripture are clear that God wants people to enjoy and to share the good things of life. Since God delights in them (Zephaniah 3:17), he gives them delights to enjoy. The celebrations reported in Jesus' life and his parables suggest a few delights. There are delights in nature and social interactions. There are many worldly delights, some provided by culture and others by God. In the process of increased sharing, some delights have to be forsaken. Spiritual growth is revealed by finding more delights or joy in giving or pleasing God and less and less in previous passions (See James 4:3).

A balanced life is a blessed life. Balance is achieved by distributing income to spending, saving, and sharing. This balanced distribution contributes to security and to fulfilling economic obligations. Brokenness occurs if any of these parts are missing. Any part left undone causes anxieties and distracts from God's calling one to share. A blessed life contains generosity, spiritual wholeness, and security in God's everlasting love.

Difficulty and trouble result when any part - sharing, saving, or spending - are omitted. Omission or imbalance occurs because these are economic and spiritual realities. It is the balance not the amount that gives financial peace of mind. Focusing on only one or two parts not only brings disaster in living but also bring unhappiness and confusion.

Sharing is an integral part of one's life since it is part of God's plan, a personal plan with money set aside for it, since God is personal. Birthdays and emergencies come under sharing. An obvious need for sharing is reflected in "taking" and not giving back in some form which shows selfishness and immaturity. Sharing is necessary to act upon the Spirit's nudge to share, the continuation of worthwhile ministries, and the heart-felt desire to act upon compassion and mercy. By sharing, the need to a make a difference in the world or community is met. (Be careful that this is not an addiction. The danger is having pride in planning or in security in the planning rather than in God alone.) An obvious need for saving is for emergencies or increasing the yield from investments. Less obvious is that most people underestimate expenses or do not prorate yearly or semi-yearly the expenses. Saving covers the underestimated and the prorated.

Therefore, a sound financial plan or budget has a category for sharing whether it is setting aside a percent of any or all income as "first fruits" or a pot for sharing. When spiritual maturity has reached the mind in financial plans and arrangements, one is moved to be generous and share. Through the desire to respond to God's love, generosity and hospitality become automatic and compelling. When income or wealth is received and when money is saved from reduced spending and credit use, more is available for sharing. These are blessings to be shared, to be even more generous. The "cup over floweth" for others.

Challenges for the Shepherd

Although shepherds may not initially feel equipped, they can learn with practice and they learn from those they counsel. Shepherds can lead in the relationship of financial giving and spiritual development. This expertise needs to be developed.

The shepherd's obligation to inspire, teach, confront and counsel about sharing with courage is supported by teachings of Jesus. Jesus spoke about money, wealth, and possessions more than any other subject. He was both theological and practical in the illustrations and parables. Possessions and giving appear over 2,000 times and 17 of the 38 of the parables are about money and possessions. Reluctance to be bold and direct in discussing money and possessions is due to the shepherd's lack of training in the area, inexperience, complexity of the topic, and the willingness to include the subject in sermons, conversations and prayers. Yet the shepherd has a vested interest in that his economic well-being, wage increases for staff, and maintenance of physical facilities depend on the willingness of members to share. The Lord desires maturity in this on the part of all. In many cases, the shepherd transfers the responsibility to the stewardship committee or fund raisers.

Well equipped means having the ability and creativity of showing implications and applications of Scripture to financial matters, financial problems, sharing and financial renewal. Time is set aside to listen to how God would change one's sharing and stewardship. Support by the shepherd include encouragement to "just say no" to other things so that "yes" can be said to sharing, generosity, stewardship. Examination by the counselor helps individuals to decide where to say "no" to "keeping up with Jones." Keeping up with God in the path can lead to more sharing, with a bigger heart for generosity and more money to give.

The voice of God can be heard when wanting to follow more fully or to get out of financial despair. Too much despair causes someone not to care. The shepherd's role is to help those in despair out of the pits, to take the hand of God, to be filled with gratitude so they can reach out to others.

The purpose here is to confirm that a major responsibility of the shepherd is to lead people to share. It is in God's plan to share money, possessions, time, energy, and the gospel. The shepherd guides people to share, changes the heart and mind toward increased sharing, gives techniques and practical ideas to enable more sharing, and arranges mechanics for sharing. Sharing is put forth in every occasion. As in other predispositions and habits, "A person becomes what they think about." Continuous thinking on the part of the shepherd on how to increase sharing by himself or herself and how to put sharing in the minds of members is done through persistence.

"Holding one another accountable to a moral tradition is hard work, requiring both humility and stubbornness, both patience and daring".[240] God will show the way and creative thoughts will give possibilities. Possibilities and programs have been developed as models. For example see "12 Month Planning Guide for Churches" and "Fund Giving Ideas" by Brian Kluth: **www.kluth. org**, "practices to increase giving" on **http://www.kluth.org/solutions**, and newsletter "Ministry of Money" **www.ministryofmoney.org**, and Network for Charitable Giving on **tomnetgv@pacbell. net** among others.

The shepherd cannot lead others to where he/she has not been or struggled in the practicalities of life under commitment to God's plans. The shepherding task is arduous since it involves
- heart changes in teaching generosity,
- taking responsibility for caring and compassion,
- confrontation for drastic changes in economic activities,
- de-programming from the influences of consumerism and materialism,
- release from captivity of credit,
- internal transformation to outward generosity, and
- overcoming resistance to sharing.

---

240   Sondra Ely Wheeler. *Wealth as Peril and Obligation: The New Testament on Possessions.* William B. Eerdmans Publishing Co., Grand Rapids, Michigan. 1995. P.145.

The shepherd needs encouragement. "Let us not become weary in doing good, for at the proper time we will reap a harvest if we do not give up" (Galatians 6:9-10). Also "God is not unjust; he will not forget your work and the love you have shown him as you have helped his people and continue to help them" (Hebrews 6:10). Jesus did not stop healing although only one of ten healed returned to thank him (Luke 17:11-15).

Scripture gives the model of selling possessions and bringing profits to lay at the disciples' feet. The problem for shepherds is how to get people to sell, liquidate and, in proper timing, lay the assets at their feet. All ministries of the church depend on this kind of sharing and generosity. Missionary efforts and disaster relief are dependent on this. The efforts are successful through the promise, "I can do all things through Christ who strengthens me" (Philippians 4:13).

Durall[241] suggests, "If your congregation offers only a few giving opportunities to give throughout the year, you are perpetuating an element of scarcity and depriving people of ways they can live more fulfilling lives and accomplish the work of God."

The shepherd needs to show the vision and the mission of the larger purposes of God's kingdom. The focus on sharing, generosity, and stewardship are interwoven in all the activities with the God-given vision and the congregation's stated mission.

Expected services of the pastor are occasionally mentioned to remind congregants of the need to support the church. Many people underestimate the responsibilities of the pastor and shepherds. These include preaching, teaching, conducting funerals, grieving, conducting weddings, celebrating graduations, counseling, pastoral care, training, and attending meetings. An answer to any complaints about asking for money is to enumerate the accomplishments by church, and how fortunate they are to be a part of it!

Shepherding is relevant when understanding people's dilemmas and choices. Sermons cannot just talk about God's love, how people should be grateful, and pleading to contribute more to the church. Praying cannot just say the words about becoming more generous. Relevancy is increased by giving people an opportunity to be heard. People need a chance to express their fears about financial matters, their captivity to materialism, their bondage to commercialism and credit, their fixed commitments and bad past financial decisions. People need to discuss and cry about their ties to peer group pressures, security in wealth and insurance payments, predicaments when recently unemployed, financial devastation of divorce, overwhelming debts and mandatory expenses. People need to share the hopelessness with financial pressures, their ignorance of alternatives in changing lifestyles, and their meaning of money.

The shepherd needs to understand that for most people money is a more powerful influence on lifestyle than is Scripture. Different uses of money are power, security, self-worth, independence, getting approval, love, excitement, relief from boredom, guilt, making up for past deprivation, control, and ways to show acceptance by the group. Therefore, the challenge is to change the spiritual meaning of life and self-worth. The greatest excitement then becomes sharing with others, giving, and contributing.

The goal is to be more generous and faithful in following Scriptural teachings and to be more caring as encouraged in Deuteronomy 15:7-11 and Matthew 6:1-2. For many people, this necessitates the secondary goal of "getting out of debt" to be more free to see the problems of others, to reduce expenses paid by interest and late fees, to say no to temptations, denial or deferment, and discipline to practice changing lifestyle or desires of the flesh. It means adjusting downward

---

241   Michael Durall. *Creating Congregations of Generous People*. Alban Institute. 1999.

as costs for basics increase or deciding what is not basic in God's wisdom. It means analyzing whether expenditures are out of habit, convention, social pressure or "for the glory of God and our neighbor's good" (Martin Luther and Christopher Sauer).

The purpose of sharing is critical for spiritual wholeness of the individual, financial support of the church leadership, and facilities. The task is more difficult than ever based on current survival in the economic structure, increased prices, culture's lure for increased goods, fear of the future, and personal bent to greed and selfishness.

Shepherds are equipped to guide people to experience the wonders of God's love and the blessings of living, working in God's kingdom. However, many shepherds are not interested nor equipped for assisting others to live in the world. People need encouragement and practical advice for employment, family responsibilities, participating in a world of war, combating corrupt and greedy businesses and professionals, personal finance, credit process, and choosing between food and fuel. The call to shepherds is to help people in their human, physical, economic, financial, and the everyday living to be directed in a new way under the Lord. Pertinent to this discussion is how to choose daily bread so it can be shared with others. In the Lord's Prayer, the dependence on God for bread is a community sense of "us."

People who are citizens in God's kingdom are strangers on earth. Sometimes they are persecuted for their strangeness in this world. The discrimination or persecution is subtle and most try to avoid it. They would be persecuted if they did not fit in. They are "strangers." They would not fit in the worldly kingdom by what they talk about, think about, their purchases, their entertainment, their way of living, their appearance, their vacations, their use of money in general, i. e. their sharing. They are persecuted if they do not go with the flow of the majority. Since most do not want to be considered strange or persecuted, they serve society, mammon not God. They fear people and their rejection more than God.

The challenge is moving people from observing needs of others to commitment to share. As well as spiritual strength, it takes practical steps, change of habits, workable money mechanics, regular contributions, disciplines, and combating consumerism in its advertising. It takes realization of what God has given. In summary, commitment to God's plan is changing desire and discipline. It takes cooperation of everyone in the family. Saying "yes" to sharing is saying "no" to expensive gifts, to toys, to food as entertainment, to expensive recreation, services, or to what the particular item could be for the unique situation and family.

As Simon[242] says the challenge to clergy and members is, "The way of the cross involves sacrifice. We can rein in our spending and give willingly so that others might have reason to praise God for the gift of life. Far from denying us joy, however, such generosity brings more satisfaction than does the pursuit of things for ourselves." Simons says it is the "fear of letting go – that causes us to miss out on the freedom" that God would have for us.

Distractions from the Narrow Path

The shepherd's voice and the needs of the church are competing among many voices. These are Internet activities, movies, videos, recreational activities, gambling, participation in sports, travel, music, etc. Professional organizations compete. Prior commitments and business distract (Luke

---

242   Arthur Simon. *How Much is Enough? Hungering for God in an Affluent Culture.* Baker Books, Grand Rapids, Michigan 49516. 2003. P.134.

10:25-37). Billboards and television hold out signs that compete with sharing. The shepherd holds out verbal banners and signs to attract sharing by continuous mention in conversations, classes, prayers and sermons.

Competition was described by Jesus when he taught: "And the one who received the seed that fell was among the thorns, this was the man who hears the word, and the worry of the world and the deceitfulness of riches choke the word, and it becomes unfruitful" (Matthew 13:22).

The basic assumption is that when people are citizens of God's kingdom, they live on a different level in the world than they would otherwise. This competes with the dominant worldly theme of "Be all you can be." God's call is "Give all you can give." It is difficult for shepherds to feel generous when members of the congregation or group have more than they. It is difficult to confront conscientious people who are living in affluence due to their perceived own effort, own created abilities and who participate in leadership. The sin of allegiance to others and things rather than God is difficult to transform when it is a lifetime of thinking and comfortable living. Examples of small steps toward more sharing and generous living leading to a totally surrendered life are helpful. It is difficult to confront people who are conscientious in every way while there is just not enough money to provide the "cultural ideal" as parents, citizens, tax payers, home maintenance, and neighborhood appearance. Then there are expenses to participate in family reunions with travel and housing, wedding gifts, church functions, etc. Respectability and appearance compete with giving to the less fortunate. Challenging those suffering with huge medical bills or those of their children is difficult. Each must examine what the Lord requires. The pastor-counselor or shepherd is to "comfort the afflicted and afflict the comforted." The crunch of the changing economy at large and personal economy causes fear and severe discomfort. So the cry is "Lord help us!"

A popular motto currently is "live simply so that others may simply live." Personal gratification needs to be changed or modified in order to save and share. Some find there is an intrinsic reward from sharing that brings joy greater than spending or saving for oneself.

Commercialism and Materialism

Teaching may be required on how to think critically and to recognize the messages that conflict with kingdom perspectives. Commercialism and materialism are often cited as the enemies, competition to "seeking first the kingdom" and to sharing. The shepherd has to know the enemy to overcome it. Possessions are gods when so cherished that they cannot be given. This violates the commandment: "Have no other gods before me." People believe buying is necessary to obtain delights. For example, if someone is told to get a health plan to survive, automatically they think "join a health club" or buy with credit the advertised products. Many people think buying products and services is the solution to solving an emotional, psychological, spiritual, or social problem.

People are led to believe the meaning in life, their self-worth, and their purpose in living is to acquire possessions, and buy into the American dream for happiness and success. Their allegiance is to wares and words of those selling or providing services for their own benefit not the customer. Material possessions and wealth are an end in themselves, fulfillment to life, self-enhancement, rather than used as instruments or means to be more effective in service to God and others.

"Let us throw off everything that hinders and the sin that so easily entangles, and let us run with perseverance the race marked out for us" (Hebrews 12:1). Shepherds can help members run the race by throwing off distractions and addictions, praying to "lead us not into temptations," and using the power of God to have courage to counter them. Distractions engage selfishness, the basic instinct of self preservation, not sharing everything, destructive habits, greed, and world standards rather than God's.

There are crises in personal life that distract from wanting to protect and care for others, to be "our brother's keeper." A distraction which on surface would sound good is the need to fit into one's culture, to adhere to peer pressure, to belong to a group for support including family, church, and work groups. One way to combat peer pressures and demands of a group is to change groups. Individuals may be more content in a group with less income than they have. They can get into a group which supports one as worthwhile for inner qualities, not consumption and outward appearance AND supports sharing with others.

Distractions from God's will are the desires and needs based on self identity. The question of who one is and to whom one belongs have to be resolved before determining how much to share, contribute, and give. Identity is shown and clarified by actions, time, possessions, talk, goals, and expenditures. Purchases show whom one is trying to please, impress, go along with, and copy. Behavior is greatly, mostly, or somewhat influenced by one's reference group – education and occupation. Possessions and wealth define one. People define the "good life" as their reference group defines them. Associating with the reference group or watching television influenced by cultural groups at large not only identifies people but molds them. The shepherd assists in changing one's identity to encompass Christ's purposes rather than captivity to peers, a commercial world, and worldly leaders with questionable benefits.

If one wants to be a child of God, a believer, or a follower, the patterns will show the new identity. It will be enriched by associating with believers, reading materials with sound theological basis, studying Scripture, and serving/caring for those in Jesus' name. One gets more excitement from giving than watching a football game or working on a political issue. One participates in the work of God's kingdom, not war. Generosity is on one's mind all day rather than "What am I to get out of this?" "How am I winning?"

Advertisements are designed to make people feel inadequate or unworthy unless buying the product or service. They get the impression "Buy or die." The lure of wanting to be happy, successful, and not lonely are convincing distractions. The process of buying or acquiring which gives fulfillment is a distraction which promotes overbuying and addictions. Appearing "smart" to others is a detraction for using money rather than working "smarter" for the kingdom and sharing.

Decreased Real Income

Since about 1900, graphs vividly show the predicament. Gross income and wages have increased greatly. Net income or disposable income on the graph has also increased. But when adjusted for inflation, the real net income has decreased. Yet expectations have increased for what is acceptable. For example, standards of living for housing and tele-communications have greatly increased. However, the real net income has decreased for many people since 1950. Gross incomes have tripled over the years. After tax (federal and Social Security) income still showed increases but not as much. When the Consumer Price Index is used to adjust these figures, salaries have actually decreased in real purchasing power. This silent culprit is the competition to giving.

Fixed incomes have decreased purchasing power and many have to choose between food and fuel. Reports[243] are that "The purchasing power of most church benevolent funds has actually

---

243   Barna, a nonprofit research and program development organization (Call 800-774-3360.)

decreased by about 25 percent over the last 20 years. The actual dollars received by the church may have increased, but the purchasing power of those funds has decreased when inflation is taken into account." Actual contributions or decreased real income affect giving and hence church workers' purchasing power, morale and new ventures.

The documentation of effect of decreased real income is that it takes two earners in a family to buy what one earner did years ago. In other countries as well as America, families maintained level of living with the decreased real income by having nearly all the mothers working, using credit to the maximum, so the only alternative left is do services for oneself rather than hiring or buying them. This activity and doing work oneself is in direct competition to the sharing, hospitality, serving, and volunteering.

When CNN interviewed the author about the predicament of families and decreased real income, the conclusion reported on television was that families would have a "third job." Doing family services for themselves, producing goods, and frugality take time, energy, and skills - hence the "third job." But this competes with sharing time.

Many have lost value in investments and in their homes. Medical costs are prohibitive for many, and health insurance takes more than half of many people's income. Gas for vehicles and utilities for homes take a greater percentage of income than they did for generations. Patterns of consumption remain except for reduced generosity.

In persuading members to give, the shepherd competes with the phenomena of expanding wants of many goods and services. The shepherd can work with this concept by expanding wants to include increasing the desire to give.

In 1985 the Church of the Brethren[244] Annual Conference declared that "Sharing possessions is also a personal journey of discipline and maturity in faith. Jesus' teachings and life of total commitment and sharing are examples to us and challenge us to love our neighbors and serve their needs," ..."reach beyond ourselves, to simplify standards of living and keep materialism in perspective."

The splendor of many things and the glorious thrill of earthly passions lure people away from God's might. They are so busy with the earthly delights or stressed over money that they forget that God delights in them. They are so worried about their money use and the temptations and captivity of credit that they miss the blessings of serving God. Many of the earthly blessings and things are not bad in themselves but the full attention to them distract people from the call to share, to think of other's needs, and to tell others of the good news of God's kingdom, God's plans of generosity.

The problem with credit as a distraction is that easy credit causes over buying. The easy terms and the persuasion of business, acting not in the customer's best interest, bring creeping indebtedness. When "maxed out" it prevents flexibility and ability to move away from credit. Then the focus is on credit not Christ. Severe financial anxieties can cloud the plight of others who need us to share. The shepherd has to transfer happiness and hope from accumulating things to receiving the joy of sharing/giving. Obedience, pleasing God not self and others, produces the joy. It is a slow process of change unless the individual is in crisis and a rebirth/renewal is necessary for life instead of death.

---

244   Church of the Brethren Annual Conference Statement on Stewardship. 1985. P.4.

Self-reliance, self-sufficiency, and independence are prominent values in today's culture. Smith and Alcorn describe the "rich fool."[245] He is a person who "did not earn and spend his money in a God-centered but in a self-centered way. He hoarded and stockpiled money and possessions rather than freely releasing them to serve God and meet human needs. He was too self-sufficient to seek God in prayer, too independent to ask God's counsel on how much to keep and how much to give, too preoccupied with the business of 'success' to open his heart in love to meet the needs of those around him."

Addictions, Passions, and Money

Addictions and ungodly passions are strong distractions from God as Master, the Master of Money, the Master of Gratitude, and the Master of Generosity. By definition, addictions are things or substances of which more and more are required to satisfy. "They nourish a never-satisfied craving for more."[246] They are trying to fulfill the need for respect, love, acceptance, or fleshly passions. The needs are misdirected and unquenched by the addictions. More and more are needed and usually cost more and more. Addictions lead to inability to stop, even if it destroys relationships, family, or employment. Addictions are enemies of the purpose in giving more and more. As Scripture says only Christ can supply the living water that quenches the thirst. Gratitude is what drives the demons of addiction and depression away.

The love of money rather than perceiving money as an instrument to fulfill God's purposes is the root of evil. Simon[247] says "the problem is *preoccupation* with mammon more than the *amount of mammon*." He continues, "Preoccupied with keeping what we have or getting what we do not have, the needs of others fade from our thoughts. It is not so much that we wish them harm as that we have no wishes for them at all."[248] The rich young man was distracted from following the path of generosity by hanging onto his possessions rather than sharing.

Smith and Alcorn[249] state that "Money – whether by presence or absence must never rule one's life. Money is "not put to death" but is trained and handled with discipline. Saying "there's no money, so I cannot" is serving money. "How we use money is always of critical importance to our spiritual lives"…impacting this world and the next. They maintain that money is not automatically and always evil nor is it always good. Excesses, they say, "undermine rather than further kingdom purposes."

The dilemma continues about how much to give. Smith and Alcorn[250] note that Jesus did not say to give 10 percent to the poor or set up a trust fund and give interest to the poor but to give up everything. The willingness to give up everything reflects the spiritual maturity or place on the journey of full commitment. Smith and Alcorn[251] say "The first Christians' transformation was most clearly evidenced in their willingness to surrender their money and possessions to meet each

---

245   Brian Smith and Randy Alcorn. *The Treasure Principle Bible Study. Discovering the Secret of Joyful Giving.* Multanomah Publishers, Sisters, Oregon. 2003. P.57.

246   Simon. Ibid. P.74.

247   Ibid. P.62.

248   Ibid. P.63.

249   Smith and Alcorn. Ibid. Pp. 36-37.

250   Ibid. Pp. 18–19.

251   Ibid. Pp. 19.

other's needs (Acts 2:44-45; 4:32-35). "The joyful giving and sharing of this property became the new 'norm' of supernatural living."

Risk Involved

The shepherd or pastor helps people to expand their comfort zone and take risks based on increased commitment and action of sharing. A distraction from generosity is the fear of taking risks and the fear of changes, particularly the unknowns. People want a comfortable lifestyle. Hoarding resources seems safe and under one's control. Investing and expanding resources contain risk as other people and factors have control. Yet Jesus' parable infers hoarding shows irresponsibility and neglect.

There is risk in trusting God to provide, sharing or giving to others. Faith encourages to err on the risky side rather than conservative. The question of judging "real need" is beset with real problems. Who is to judge another's need? Are psychological, emotional needs as important as material needs?

A gift of God is learning from mistakes in the practice and risks of generosity. The risk and cost of doing nothing and giving nothing are even greater as warned in Matthew 25 and James 5. Education reduces the risk. Prayer reduces the **fear** of risk. A committed heart considers alternatives that reduce danger. A consoling promise is "The Lord did not promise life would be easy but he did promise to be with us each step of the way" (book marker based on Isaiah 61).

Quick Fix

A quick fix is sometimes used as the reward for giving. An appeal to giving by a television preacher was that by giving to his organization it would solve one's financial problems and help one get a job. Testimonies were by people who received help from God within the day or two. The appeal was enticing because people are anxious for a "quick fix" or prosperity and if giving brings that, they would be eager to give. The way of the cross, total sacrifice, has a cost. This contrasts with the notion that everything will be all right by giving a tithe. A careful reading of Scripture reveals the rewards of generosity is the ability to be more generous. Followers are not called to always be successful but to be faithful, to run the good race, not always to win it. God gives the energy to share in ways that they are called to share. God lifts people up so they can lift others.

When in extreme despair, most people do not care about others. They resist appeals for sharing or fixing their finances in a new way. They borrow more which brings even more anxiety.

Some people, when in despair or crisis, are more receptive to help, learning, change, and renewal. The step is helping the spiritual needs which resolve the despair. This moves to hope, trust, energy, and discipline to help self and others out of despair. Sharing continues - physically, socially, emotionally, mentally, and spiritually.

In times of crisis, downward economy, loss of employment, housing, etc., one is forced to re-prioritize and trust God. Never-the-less a crisis is a "wake up call." They may question the use of separate churches located close together which spend most all their budget to pay the pastor and maintain the building rather than sharing among them and with others.

Trust is having confidence in God, not money, that the Spirit will lead in the financial path of life. This takes prayer, practice, and perseverance. As confidence in God increases, courage to change worldly habits and passions increase. "As we grow in confidence in the Lord, we gain courage in the world."[252]

How to Share More

The spiritual approach starts with changing the heart and soul. The closer to God, the more content one becomes. The more content, the more grateful one becomes. The more grateful, the more the person wants to share. The shepherd guides people in their path to becoming closer to God. The ultimate source to change generosity and financial behavior is from the strength and indwelling of the Spirit. The shepherd assists spiritual renewal to motivate generosity, change priorities, and implement new management practices.

The financial management approach is using the mind to change expenditures. Analysis to change financial management is done by recording each expenditure and then shining a spotlight on each activity, the light of the Son. Financial problems, time problems, or the sincere desire to share more can be resolved by implementing alternatives. Restructuring, transformation, balance, and examination occur under New Management which is a new allegiance. The questions for each expenditure are: "Will it glorify God and be for my neighbor's good? Will it promote or support work in God's kingdom of which one is a citizen? How can one see differently through God's lenses, seeing Christ not money and becoming wiser?" Creative changes to give more are by increasing income, decreasing expenses and wants, increasing the desire to share, being more efficient by comparing prices, controlling addictions, and changing lifestyle.

The assumed and prescribed goal of many publications and talk shows in Christian finances is to get out of debt as the supreme good. In this chapter the goal is to be more generous, i.e. give more. Therefore, for many families this entails reducing expenses in order to give more, increasing income, and efficiency. Not using credit to reduce interest cost is an example of efficiency. For other families or at other times, use of credit meets the goal of "seeking first the kingdom" or sharing more. Surrendering to God and sharing God are difficult when the whole family is captive to credit and overwhelmed with the problems of not paying bills. The reality of captivity or bondage "to the company store" is detrimental to creative ways of thinking of other people's needs. Therefore, changes in financial management for paying bills, getting out of debt, and living simply are necessary.

Sharing with the Poor

Jesus said the poor widow gave all she had. Two copper coins in those days were less than the value of a penny. What can the poor without a penny share? By definition of sharing, they can share the "good news" of the blessings God has given them, their gratitude for God's love, and their ways for surviving under the trust in the Lord to provide. (Christians in countries where poverty is the stark reality of life are teaching this trust.) Percentage-wise, the lower income brackets of people contribute a higher percentage of income to charity than do middle and higher income.[253] The poor have the gifts to share of knowledge and experience in dealing with hard knocks of life,

---

252   Stephen Kirk, Covenant Presbyterian Church, Feb. 3, 2008.

253   Simon, Ibid. P.125.

first hand acquaintance of life and death, of crime and punishment, and of resource management. These experiences give to the poor an appreciation of resources, maximizing use of resources, a garner for them whereas middle income people think they can be wasteful and can afford careless decisions. The poor are forced to be stewards of their limited resources.

Although everyone has limited resources with expanding wants, the poor can share wisdom from a different perspective than middle income people. Middle income people generally expand wants for more frivolous spending. Some poor people share a higher percentage of their income more than other income levels.[254]

Gifts that are unique and useful to others can be shared as Paul said (Romans 12:6-8 (NRSV): "We have gifts that differ according to the grace given to us: prophecy, in proportion to faith; ministry, in ministering; the teacher, in teaching; the exhorter, in exhortation; the giver, in generosity; the leader, in diligence; the compassionate, in cheerfulness."

The guide in Deuteronomy 15:7-10 is: "If there is a poor man among your brothers in any of the towns of the land that the Lord your God is giving you, do not be hard-hearted or tightfisted toward your poor brother. Rather be openhanded and freely lend him whatever he needs....Give generously to him and do so without a grudging heart; then because of this the Lord your God will bless you in all your work and in everything you put your hand to. There will always be poor people in the land. Therefore, I command you to be openhanded toward your brothers and toward the poor and needy in your land."

Congregations and agencies have experienced "abuse, misuse, or unwise management of such special funds" and have grown indifferent and overly protective. Burkett says the answer is better planning, wiser management, and more realistic goals. Arrangements must be made for responding to requests when they are unexpected and the shepherd is preoccupied. At the minimum, a list of agencies and transportation to emergency resources can be given. Designated persons must be trained. A deacons' fund is sometimes called to contribute available funds. Classes can be set up for education as well as compassion.

The challenge to the shepherd is to open eyes and hearts to injustices. The challenge is to open minds to constructive ways to help the poor. New ways and education are needed as well as housing. "An amendment to end property tax exemptions for nonprofit groups was proposed for those who did not provide housing for prisoners, orphans, the elderly, the disabled, and the homeless."[255] The challenge is to do more than a band-aid approach. For those who have the abilities, their gift is to change public policies, entitlement policies, and/or provide education that help the poor.

The statement "Sell your possessions and give them to the poor," argues Wheeler[256] stands as a model of "seeking first God's kingdom." "It is a counterweight to every complacent self-assurance 'I have enough. It "calls into question many of the assumptions of middle-class existence" including that Christians are entitled to "economic security." "The response to human needs is a sign of the advent of God's kingdom and a test of the love that identifies Jesus' true followers." "There is also a canonical foundation for a universal duty to care for the needy. Beside the general admonition to 'give to every one who asks you' (Matthew. 5:42, Luke 6:30) and the instruction to invite the poor in to feast (Luke 14:12-14), there is the general command to love the neighbor (cited six times)"

---

254   Simon. Ibid. P.125.

255   Mark Vincent. *A Christian View of Money: Celebrating God's Generosity.* Herald Press, Scottsdale, Pa. 15683. 1997. P. 88.

256   Wheeler. Ibid. P.136.

including stranger and enemy, and to provide material needs as implied in the Good Samaritan story (Luke 10:25-37) and Paul's command "If your enemy is hungry, feed him" (Romans 12:20). Also, followers are to lend without expecting return (Luke 6:35). Intentions are clear in Isaiah 58:7: "Is it not to share your food with the hungry and to provide the poor wanderer with shelter – when you see the naked, to clothe him, and not to turn away from your own flesh and blood?" Relevant directions for today are in Leviticus 25:35: "If one of your countrymen becomes poor and unable to support himself among you, help him as you would an alien or a temporary resident, so he can continue to live among you." Religious leaders and shepherds should treat every member with respect and a person of value regardless of their possessions, appearances, and contributions to church or other causes. The shepherd is not bitter or resentful of his/her own status although others have more or less. The shepherd identifies genuinely with the poor and the rich, the educated and uneducated, who may have more street smarts. The attitude is that one can learn something from everyone. Therefore, ways for anyone to share and become more generous are possible. A promise is: "You will be made rich in every way so that you can be generous on every occasion, and through us your generosity will result in thanksgiving to God" (2 Corinthians 9:11).

Behind the Scenes of Generosity

Generosity and financial management are an external reflection of the inward spiritual response to God's love. However, structure and habits need to be changed to implement generosity. Attitudes can be developed from the Scripture, education, leadership of shepherds, and role models.

Attitudes behind stinginess are:
— - "What is yours is mine and I am going to take it."
— - "What is mine is mine and I am going to keep it."
— - "I choose who is my brother."
— - "I hold to the letter of the law and I do not need to love."
— - "I have given my tithe so I do not need to care about the homeless or fatherless."

Attitudes behind generosity are:
— - "I choose to respond to God's love by loving God."
— - "My actions toward others are my response to God's love."
— - "What beyond our needs can benefit others?"
— - "I can give without loving, but I cannot love without giving."
— - "What is mine is God's and I am going to share it."

As a criteria for giving, some would ask, "What would Jesus do?" Now-a-days this perspective has been watered down to minor changes rather than drastic changes to follow Jesus. More challenging questions to guide behavior are "What did Jesus do?" and "What does Jesus want me to do?"

People making new patterns seem like walking up a sand dune. They may go a few steps and slip back. Encouragement is necessary.

Trusting God

The shepherd can encourage people to trust in the security of God's provisions in order to reach out to others. Trusting God to provide sounds good but to put it into practice (obey) is another step in the generosity journey.

God was teaching the Israelites to trust and know that God was in charge (Exodus 6:11-27). They stored up manna in disobedience and God said any extra would perish, which it did. The danger is that money (wealth) as a storage facility causes "spoilage" as God continually provides for each day's needs.

Perspectives on trusting God are these:

1. Even if all wants are not supplied, one can learn, as Paul experienced, to be content whatever the circumstances (Philippians 4:11). Paul wrote, "And my God will meet all your needs according to his glorious riches in Christ Jesus" (Philippians 4:19).
2. Through prayer, one can have courage to seek resources and ways to meet needs available in the extended family, community, church, and government.
3. Joy can be experienced in other ways than consuming products or services in having needs met.
4. As Scripture reports for several people, angels may provide.
5. One is led by the shepherd to resources of extended family, community, church, and government; finding reduced cost or free medicine, for example.
6. In trusting God to provide one's needs, he or she can concentrate on meeting the needs of others.
7. Submission to God's way can release creative energy and ideas.

Trusting includes asking God for forgiveness for mistakes, stealing, guilt burdens, cheating, indifference to needs of others, and selfishness. One asks for healing. One participates in the grieving process of giving up the old and receiving joy in the new as a more generous person, displaying grace to those receiving assistance.

One trusts God to provide alternatives, the next step to take, and empowerment to carry on even if one becomes ill, loses job, income, spouse, or parent. The premise is that God created people, is creating a changed heart, and is providing in miraculous ways. Therefore, God expects people to use their creative minds in providing for those entrusted to their care. Creative ways may be cutting out or limiting some things to have more money to give or it may be giving or sharing in ways that do not cost money. The basic sins here are not trusting God to provide nor be with one in every step of the way even in negative financial circumstances.

Trusting God in action means not ignoring the poor but helping in little ways. It also means working in the economic and political systems to correct injustices that contribute to poverty. Therefore, one takes action in reshaping legislation, employment opportunities, education, and program policies. Decisions that one makes in employment, housing, church participation, and acquisition of possessions or wealth take into consideration how these decisions and actions could impact injustices, oppression of the poor, and ability to share.

Trusting God in action verifies one's allegiance and demonstrates: "You shall have no other gods before me." Trusting leads one to realize the promise in Psalm 37:4: "Delight yourself in the Lord and he will give you the desires of your heart."

Reasons for Giving or Not Giving

People give for varied reasons. Some reasons may be questionable and selfish but they do encourage giving. On the other hand, shepherds should question the reasons they are using to promote giving. Some are offered to congregants in subtle or blatant ways. Honesty rather than abuse is the guide to decide. Examples are prevalent in the literature and on television that are *not* scriptural, are deceptive, unethical, and misleading. Shepherds need to examine if they are using abusive language in speaking to congregants. Are the reasons for their own benefit and harming the givers? Are they scriptural? Are they truthful? Are they ethical? Abusive? Misleading? Manipulative?

Reasons for Giving:
- — - Fear of consequences including God's judgment and if one does not give God will not answer prayers
- — - False teaching that God requires payoffs in order to respond to human needs
- — - Guilt and giving covers up guilt, relieves guilt, and reduces shame
- — - Giving promises prosperity, job, and more wealth
- — - Complete a bargain such as God saved one or gave a promotion
- — - Gives control of the church, what the pastor says, and who else is allowed into the church
- — - Duty to give. One feels that "Now that I have given, I do not want to hear anymore about it."
- — - Recognition, attention, and love of which one feels deprived otherwise
- — - Continues habit and joy received from giving as a youth
- — - Meaningful ritual, part of worship service
- — - Follows custom of regular giving weekly, monthly, yearly, or on special occasions
- — - Convenience using technology to contribute rather than debating the issue
- — - Form of insurance to use services of the church, i.e. weddings, funerals, dinners, visitation, counseling, children's education and moral development
- — - Responsibility to the community with a social conscience
- — - Received benefit and so gives back in gratitude for what has been received
- — - Conscience with feeling or knowing it is the right thing to do; to do one's part
- — - Sensitive in remembering when oneself was in need
- — - Enjoyment experienced in "random acts of kindness" with a heart of love to the less fortunate
- — - Response to God's love and forgiveness with a heart that goes out to others
- — - One is eager to identify with a good cause
- — - Promise that in giving, one will be blessed spiritually and financially
- — - Biblical directive to give and so one will be able to give more
- — - Being "caught up in the moment" for special gifts appealing to the emotions
- — - Response to disaster relief mission, or special projects that tug at the emotions to give emergency assistance
- — - Realization that one's wealth came from luck or inheritance and want to pass it on
- — - Taking tax advantages in estate planning, charitable deductions, charitable bequest, tax planning, or gifts of stocks
- — - Financial advisor suggested it is a good thing to do.

Burkett[257] writes that some "may give for self-motivated reasons...[They] bribe God into blessing them... [or as in] Acts 8 is a spiritual prerequisite....[They] require and demand God's blessing because of what they consider their sacrifice..." "They are in subjection to God but are trying to exercise control over Him."

Pastor Herman counseled a woman to give less to care for herself more. Revealed in conversation, she had been giving out of guilt.

Some would argue that whether people give for self or unselfish reasons, it still does some good. Research reports that giving and sharing wherever makes people feel good and happier.

Some give because it "Feels so good: A team of economists and psychologists at the University of Oregon have discovered that giving money to charity activates parts of the brain that have to do with the experience of pleasure. The researchers see this as evidence that there is such a thing as pure altruism-people will take actions that help others when to do so is not in their own best interests."[258]

Resistance and Barriers

Reasons for resistance must be understood before the shepherd can help overcome barriers whether they are real or perceived. The question is why do some people have a giving-caring heart and others have a selfish-greedy heart? An examination of resistance to share infers some ways for the shepherd to help change behavior.

Reasons for Stinginess or Lack of Generosity:

a. Needs of others are not close at hand, not visible, not continuous
b. Illustrations and models of sharing have not been seen
c. Alternatives are not apparent such as giving to the "Save a Girl" project rather having an expensive birthday party
d. Individual is insecure, feels worthless, and not respected by others
e. Trapped in bills with insufficient income and captive to credit or debt
f. Barely surviving and not enough money for fuel and medicine
g. No one has shared the love of God and how to respond by sharing with others
h. Does not take care of self or in addictions, depressed and so lack purpose of caring for others
i. Does not worship in a church which teaches how to become more generous rather than entertained
j. Have not experienced the joy and fulfillment of giving, of sharing
k. Providing for one's own family takes precedence over helping others and "Keeping face to children" are most important
l. One is under the control of vehicle or hobby and are attached to their accumulation of possessions
m. Security is based on amount of money rather than trusting God as promised in Hebrews 13:5: "Never will I leave you; never will I forsake you."

---

257   Larry Burkett. *Using Your Money Wisely Biblical Principles Under Scrutiny*. Moody Press, Chicago. 1985. P.213.

258   Reported in *Christian Century*, July 10, 2007, page 6 from the Chicago Tribune, June 15.

376 | *Flora L. Williams, PhD, MDiv, RFC*

n. So stuck on self and the desire to be independent that one does not hear the whisper of God to see and feel another's need

o. Not having been poor enough or long enough to recognize a need

p. Too busy with own interests and prior commitments to share extemporaneously

q. Too fixed on other commitments to vary the schedule or vary the giving to meet an unexpected need

r. Not tuned to the situation quickly enough to see or to know how to give, share

s. Lack personal contacts or experiences with those less fortunate or in need

t. Overwhelmed by one's despair and having an "emotional shut-down"

u. Overwhelmed with people or agencies asking for contributions and having a compassion over-load resulting in resistance to all

v. Disappointment and anger with not meeting household expectations and desired lifestyle and, therefore, shut others out.

What is behind the statement? "I would really like to give more but…?"

Too lazy to find new ways

Do not know alternatives

Do not compare prices, quality, and services to reduce expenses and have more to give

Cannot let go of addictions, hobbies, expensive lifestyle

Perceive most expenses are fixed rather than providing possibilities

Do not want to make drastic changes

Afraid to change

Cannot take the risk of changing or trusting God

Giving all they can and are tired.

The shepherd's challenge is to overcome resistance to give by changing perspectives, giving alternatives, and increasing spiritual confidence for renewal. Story telling of how others changed in their maturity to give is useful. Opportunities increase awareness and inspire contributions.

Questioning the Rich Young Man

The dilemma for many is in the question, "What else must I do to achieve eternal life?" (Luke 12:16-21). The rich young man had achieved success and status. He was conscientious, having kept all the Jewish laws, and he wanted to be even better. He wanted to insure that he would have eternal life. This is the basis of conversions and contributions of many Christians today. Jesus' answer of "Go and sell everything and follow me" was rejected by the rich young man. The dilemma was the love of possessions more than of Jesus. Following Jesus would mean a change in priorities, lifestyle and allegiances. Not that possessions and keeping the law were bad but they got in the way of total surrender in following Jesus. Giving all to others and surrendering, unconditionally, was too risky, too difficult for the young man's attitude to change. Money was the master which he chose rather than surrender and having Jesus as the Master. Independence, self-reliance, and individualism were the rich young man's dominating directives, as they are in our current culture, rather than generosity, the group's benefit, sharing, and dependence on God's will.

The rich young man was asked to give all which was asking him to change priorities and redefine goals. His goals were similar to what many people have today: to be "good," following the law to be conscientious, to be comfortable, to rely on material security, and depend on outer strengths. People do not want the life of "basic minimum," just to survive. The new goals Jesus may have had in mind were: to follow Jesus in uncomfortable situations, work with demon possessed people, to be sacrificial, to take risks, and to be unselfish. The new goals are to rely on inner strengths and the strength of Jesus, to use the wisdom of God, and receive power from the Spirit. This causes progress toward genuine love for the work of God's reign, not earthly passions.

The message to the rich young man was to change priorities. It was to find satisfaction in Christ alone. Paul said, "All else is rubbish" (Philippians 3:8). The new goal is to be sacrificial, discomforted, to bear the cross of discipleship, to be devoted to the call, to take risks, and rely on the inner strengths. Security is in relationship with the Lord. It is dependence on God's ability, power, and provisions not one's own. Money is servant, rather than people serving money. Money is treated as a gift from God and valued as such. A person concentrates on following patterns of generous living rather than habits of bitterness about not "having enough" or having less than others.

The new purpose for the rich young man and for people today is to follow Christ rather than comforts.[259] Other purposes such as selfish goals, feeding fears, hoarding or squandering are not in keeping with Christ's purposes. "You ask and do not receive, because you ask with wrong motives, so that you may spend it on your pleasures" (James 4:3). By having firm rooting, one can resist the temptation when affliction or persecution arises to fall away, to drift, or to follow the crowd. (Matthew 13:21) in Burkett, 1985.[260]

Most followers are not asked to sell everything, but there are many times they are asked to sell or give up something to truly follow Jesus. It is holding things lightly and being ready to "hand them over" to the Lord. This is what it means to "seek first the kingdom" and then trust that God will continue to care for all. For example, Jackie Pullinger, totally surrendered to God, was led to go into the Forbidden City in Hong Kong leaving her family, orchestra, and comfortable life in London. She restored prostitutes and drug addicts to new life in Christ. She was led to sell her beloved oboe, her last possession, to rescue a woman from slavery in the walled drug dens and sinful city in Hong Kong.[261]

Changing Attitudes, Behavior and Management

Tactics to Increase Generosity

Tactics to increase giving do not need, nor should include verses or approaches to shame people into giving. Neither do they need to scare people into giving. Insurance for eternal life is not an appropriate approach either.

Positive tactics include honoring God through faithfulness and habits. In Proverbs 3:9, for example, it says, "Honor the Lord from your wealth, and from the first of all your produce." Then in I Corinthians 16:2, it says, "On the first day of every week let each one of you put aside and save, as he may prosper, that no collections be made when I come." We are reminded to pay debts

---

259   Larry Burkett. *Using Your Money Wisely: Biblical Principles Under Scrutiny*. Moody Press, Chicago. 1985. P.200.

260   Ibid. P.200.

261   Jackie Pullinger and Andrew Quicke. *Chasing the Dragon: One Woman's Struggle Against the Darkness of Hong Kong's Drug Dens*. Ventura, CA: Regal Books. 1980.

(Psalm 37:21) and provide for our family's needs (I Timothy 5:8). Other supporting verses are 1 Chronicles 29:14-18, 2 Chronicles 31:3-10, Psalm 112:4-5, Proverbs 11:24-25, Proverbs 22:9, Matthew 20:1-16, Acts 10:2-4, and Romans 12:4-8.

Faithfulness in finances means adjusting daily choices in light of the commitment to give. A commitment of a regular dollar amount or of a bonus causes people to adjust other spending to meet the commitment. The commitment discourages impulse spending, whims, or expensive food/entertainment because of the first commitment to be generous with a set amount.

"A secret to more joyful and generous giving and living" is to "count your blessings" inferred in 1 Cor. 16:2.[262] One can write down what income, unexpected gifts, people's hospitality, discount or sale items, or purchase of possession require an extra gift to "the Lord's work."[263] Anyone can start a "blessings fund" to help in becoming more joyful in giving and which is then used to support missions, special projects and need organizations (see www.kluth.org).

A motivation for helping people think and pray in thankfulness is that gratitude drives away depression. Categories for thankfulness everyday include daily necessities for life, gifts that enrich life and make it meaningful, a spiritual blessing.

Biblical Motivation

Biblical basis for use of wealth, money, generosity, and care of the earth's resources has been verified. Rather than proof texts, the important goal is to pray that the Spirit gives one the personal applications from reading Scripture.

Current popular appeals to giving are based on Bible verses emphasizing happiness, financial blessings and prosperity. Threats are given in some appeals about breaking the "laws of prosperity." In 2 Corinthians 9:6 a reminder is given about sowing generously so that one will reap generously. When it says sowing generously will reap generously, some interpret that as monetary and others interpret it as spiritual blessings. In 2 Corinthians 9:11 the message is receiving richness in every way so one can choose to be generous on every occasion. Generosity will result in thanksgiving. The return is righteousness and thankfulness for their generosity. The reward is not that one will prosper, have a quick fix for mistakes, or that finances will be easy. In Deuteronomy 8:18 a reminder is given that it is God who gives the ability to produce wealth, thereby confirming this covenant. Luke 6:38 is direct in saying "Give, and it will be given to you" using your measure. In Proverbs 3:9-10 the promise of giving first fruits is having barns "overflowing" and "honoring the Lord." In Malachi 3:8-10 withholding tithes and offerings are ways that God is robbed. But when one tithes God will "pour out so much blessing that you will not have room for it." There is no guarantee of prosperity and riches as the world defines them but blessings in other areas. Prosperity promises seem to be in contrast to the call of Jesus to give all, which he said is losing one's life, counting the cost, and bearing the cross. By giving one's life, Jesus said a person would find it (Matthew (16:25).

A strong motivator is in Deuteronomy 15:10-11: "Give generously to him and do so without a grudging heart; then because of this the Lord your God will bless you in all your work and in everything you put your hand to. There will always be poor in the land...be openhanded toward

---

262   Brian Kluth. *40 Day Spiritual Journey to a more Generous Life.* Biblical Generosity Resources. 2007. 5201 Pinon Valley, Colorado Springs, Co. 80919. 719-930-4000.

263   Brian Kluth. Ibid.

your brothers and toward the poor and needy in your land." The returns are grace, good work, and blessing in work.

Among motivators to "grow up generous"[264] are:

1. having symbols and reminders of giving and serving displayed prominently in the congregation;
2. emphasizing the habit of giving, not the amount;
3. having opportunities for youth to talk about and reflect on their financial giving;
4. having role models for young people who share and serve; and
5. providing for all generations to give and share together.

More Scriptures to Contemplate as Motivation

In Deuteronomy 16:10, it says, "Bring God a free-will offering proportionate in size to his blessing upon you as judged by the amount of your harvest." In 2 Corinthians 8:3, it says, "They gave as much as they were able, and even beyond their ability." In 2 Corinthians 8:12 it adds, "For if the willingness is there, the gift is acceptable according to what one has, not according to what he does not have." In Acts 11:29 help is inferred: "The disciples, each according to his ability, decided to provide help… ."

Particularly in the Old Testament, the tithe was the rule as well as the first of their crops, money, and everything. Rewards were attached. See Deuteronomy 14:22-23; Genesis 14:20, Malachi 3:8-11, 2 Chronicles 31:5, 12, and others. Going beyond the tithe is inferred as Jesus said in Luke 11:42 (TLB): "Though you are careful to tithe even the smallest part of your income, you completely forget about justice and the love of God. You should tithe, yes, but you should not leave these other things undone." The return is righteousness.

"Good will come to him who is generous and lends freely, who conducts his affairs with justice" (Psalm 112:5). "A generous man will himself be blessed, for he shares his food with the poor" (Proverbs 22:9). "Command them to do good, to be rich in good deeds, and to be generous and willing to share" (1 Timothy 6:18).

In the American system, sharing the pasture occurs through taxes which redistribute the wealth. "Render to all what is due them: tax to whom tax is due…" (Romans 13:7). Laws require the choice to follow just ways.

Sharing God's love is the most important gift. "Leave your gift in front of the altar. First go and be reconciled to your brother; then come and offer your gift" (Matthew 5:23-24). Giving from selfishness and pride, etc. is prohibited.

"If any of you lacks wisdom, he should ask God, who gives generously through Jesus Christ our Savior…" (James 1:5). Vincent has said, "God has given us much. We are made in the image of God and, therefore, our nature is to be generous."[265]

In Romans 12:8 people are reminded: "If it is encouraging, let him encourage; if it is contributing to the needs of others, let him give generously; if it is leadership, let him govern diligently; if it is showing mercy, let him do it cheerfully."

---

264   Eugene C. Ropehlkepartain, Elanah Dalyah Naftali, and Laura Musegades. *Growing Up Generous: Engaging Youth in Giving and Serving.* Alban Institute. 2000. Pp. 106-107.

265   Vincent. Ibid.

Other advice in Romans 12:10 is: "Be devoted to one another in brotherly love. Honor one another above yourselves. Never be lacking in zeal, but keep your spiritual fervor, serving the Lord. Be joyful in hope, patient in affliction, faithful in prayer. Share with God's people who are in need. Practice hospitality."

In 2 Corinthians 8:7, the argument is given that the church has excelled in faith, speakers, knowledge, enthusiasm and love. "See that you also excel in this grace of giving."

In the Scripture the concept of giving to the poor is supported by "duty" or what God desires. Justice and kindness are intertwined with care of the "oppressed."

A model way to live is expressed: "Because of the service by which you have proved yourselves, men will praise God for the obedience that accompanies your confession of the gospel of Christ, and for your generosity in sharing with them and everyone else" (2 Corinthians 9:13).

Making a Difference as Motivator for Sharing

The appeal "to make a difference" motivates people to make a practical difference with their time, money, and energy. A difference in the life of someone who is poor, lonely, imprisoned, widowed, orphaned, or confused is made by creative, unique, and organized ways. A selected day when everyone is encouraged to do this moves the community with a spirit of generosity to act and share.

Giving money gives hope and a better community. When one gives to those who have experienced devastation it is not just the shattered homes, destroyed crops and basic needs that are restored. "Rebuilding homes, schools, and hospitals bring a community's livelihood,… spirit, integrity and hope."[266]

Christ's Spirit teaches how to act out of love. "When God's grace meets us, we realize that salvation means peace and wholeness, and we cannot hoard anything. We cannot be selfish with income or possessions because of the generous God we serve."[267] Vincent says a sentimental view of Jesus as a Bethlehem baby, meeting as a church out of tradition, preaching the gospel, proclaiming mission, and teaching doctrine are insufficient for becoming "ministers of mercy." When "we meet Jesus as Creator, Provider, Redeemer, King, and Cause for our life we know what it means to share.…" Vincent says that since "our values are rooted in God's character"…we gladly dedicate all of life, including money, to God's purposes."[268]

Motivators for sharing and giving have been cited such as: "knowing that one has benefited richly, there is a need to put something back, to add to the stream from which we have dipped our vital nourishment."[269] A theme in many writings is to give because one has been given much. A statement on stewardship says, "The knowledge of what God has done and continues to do for us through Christ is a most precious gift."[270] Thus, returning to God a portion of what one has been given seems appropriate. It satisfies one's drive toward generosity, a basic spiritual principle, the "right thing to do," and a way to build stronger faith commitments.

---

266   One Great Hour of Sharing – Church of the Brethren, 2008.

267   Vincent. Ibid. P.61.

268   Vincent. Ibid. P.79.

269   Thomas C. Rieke. What's a Steward to Do? *The Clergy Journal.* 2001. P. 23.

270   Church of the Brethren Annual Conference Statement. Christian Stewardship: Responsible Freedom. Updated 2007.

The shepherd or family member can motivate others to share by using a technique for those not accustomed to sharing. One can ask: "What should we share and with whom should we share it?" Then name several places or people. Check off a list of things, money, time, wisdom, service. Know the purpose for giving, not just the name of the agency. This approach assumes sharing is the goal. There is no choice of "not sharing." This technique includes the giver in the process with his or her input for increasing implementation.

Getting cooperation can use new words or "sharing." These have more appeal than the tired used words of contributing, giving, stewardship, or tithing.

Habits for Motivating Generosity

When generosity is a goal, the shepherd will include prayers in worship service, somewhere in the service, every Sunday for increasing generosity. The shepherd will teach this personal prayer as a habitual activity when waking up each day: "What is one thing I can do today to show someone I care? To make life easier for someone? To share my gifts and talents?" This is also a powerful habit for helping a spouse or other family member.

The challenge to shepherds is to encourage good habits and sensible priorities. This involves de-programming the brain as well as the heart. A person may reprioritize to develop sacrificial living. One habit is to "pay God first" not because one has extra money or left-overs. Otherwise, the natural phenomena of expanding wants for passions of the flesh, worldly enticements, thousands of advertisements repeatedly and personally persuasive, identifying with a peer group, keeping up with the Jones, and meeting basic physical and safety needs squeeze out "extras."

Therefore, it is helpful to make a habit, ritual, or custom of putting money into three envelopes – real or abstract – for sharing, spending, and saving. This is done in planning for the week, month, or year. Regular giving is decided from regular income or from irregular income such as the tax refund or bonuses. The decision to share a set amount, made once and for all, is a habit rather than questioning each time what to do with left-overs. The attitude is the feeling that God deserves more than left-overs. One can recall Nehemiah 18:29 that God deserves more than left-overs. Jesus said, "But when you give to the needy, do not let your left hand know what your right hand is doing, so that your giving may be in secret. Then your Father, who sees what is done in secret, will reward you" (Matthew 6:3-4). This implies first hand response.

The shepherd gives alternatives for changing the structure and habits in giving. One may have to start with changing the structure, i.e. a set budget amount or a weekly practice. With the structural approach, the shepherd arranges for the mechanics of giving, a legal approach, and then works with the attitude to follow rather than starting with changing all the emotions to automatically feel like giving, giving, and giving some more. Balance not manipulation is the goal. Habits of giving continue even through rough times based on one's structure and faith rather than on fear.

The Shepherd's role through interviewing, scriptural referring, counseling, teaching, preaching and praying is exciting because of the multifaceted approaches available to increase generosity and improve stewardship. The areas intertwined to bear upon decisions include emotional makeup, greed, selfishness, fear, habits of behavior, knowledge of the financial world, practice in use of resources, and mathematics.

Decisions and behavior about spending, saving, and sharing are different in the various stages. A telescopic vision is needed to create a relevant mission at a particular time in life. Important also are celebrations, deeds of mercy, and feelings of compassion impacting one's sharing at various times of life. Celebrations for life passages, joys in serving God, earthly delights, new births, and victories in the Lord are supported by Scripture. Money spent on celebrations give glory to God depending on timing. A quiet presentation of award may glorify God.

A plan for generosity and stewardship is not designed to be "one shoe fits all." The ultimate decision of what and how to give is between the individual and God, not a legalized or customary route. Never-the-less, the shepherd is responsible, with the Great Shepherd's help, for encouraging examination of current practices, changes and growth in each person's life.

Reprioritizing in a group or family is to determine the necessities (essentials) versus the luxuries (non-essentials). The next decision is what part of nonessentials or money for them can be given to others for their essentials. A small part can provide a large part for others, especially for those starving physically and spiritually.

Simon says, "...we have an uncanny ability to rationalize our advantages, forget Parables about the rich (Luke 12:20 and Luke 16:19-31) describe the man after building bigger barns wanting to take it easy and enjoy his wealth and the man who lived in luxury who ignored the beggar Lazarus." Simon[271] declares, "This subversive teaching overturns the prevailing notion that those who prospered had God's favor and were the ones destined to join Abraham." Simon continues with: to confuse having with being is to worship the gift rather than the giver, fragments of creation instead of the Creator. It is also to forget that God alone determines our worth, not what we have or what others think of us. God has made us in his own image, to be like him in our creativity and work, but most of all in love and generosity. Though in our fallen state we do not do that very well, God has rescued us in Jesus Christ. Through the cross, God has declared us righteous in his eyes by virtue of forgiveness." Would we "exchange that status"..."measured by a pair of sneakers?"[272] The sufferings of others, skim lightly over the words of the prophets and of Jesus, and we become prisoners of our own interests."[273]

The shepherd is the spiritual advisor in an area in which people would just as soon be left unnoticed, probably more so than in other areas. Never-the-less, the shepherd assists people in examining their spending. In some cases it is replacing the joy from acquiring consumer goods to the joy of giving divine goods. Goods are made divine in their purpose for sharing for survival, restoration of lives, and the work of building the kingdom of God.

Disciples display discipline in God-breathed habits. They may start with a certain percent of the decision income (available after taxes, fees, payroll deductions). Or they may start with a percentage of gross income. The challenge is to increase percentages. They may set a modest amount such as $25 while they are just surviving. This trusts that God will provide daily needs and provide income or ways to meet the commitment.

Habits that are relatively expensive like smoking, drinking, gambling, certain forms of recreation, and entertainment foods are reduced or forbidden in choosing "God first, others second, and oneself last." Paul's statement that "the spirit is willing but the flesh is weak" applies to good intentions for generosity that are not implemented. One's spirit being weak can also be a function of bad habits or an excuse. What tempts one to spend money set aside for God varies with individuals. Some would say "everything" tempts one to turn from God toward selfish wants. Giving out of left-overs is rarely possible since wants are always expanding. Therefore, few people

---

271   Simon. Ibid. P.25.

272   Simon. Ibid. P.64.

273   Simon. Ibid. P.119.

see "left-overs." There are too many temptations to use the money occasionally set aside for God. Probably this is the reason Jesus included temptation in the Lord's Prayer.

Many of the "goodies," defined by culture, are not bad in themselves. The exclusive seeking after them sap the energy and distract from sharing with those in need. Creative energy is diverted from working for God's reign, the kingdom. The goodies become gods when the acquisition, maintenance, and enjoyment come before "seeking first God's kingdom." To change behavior for more sharing, one continually strives to seek first God's kingdom and righteousness in sharing, trusting all things will be given to us as well (Matthew 6:33).

Education

"Going the extra mile" is more than giving extra money. Giving advice begins with, "How can I help you? What other help do you really need? What questions do you have?" One can be committed with the mind and heart to insist on giving education with the money. Giving education displays giving is done out of real concern, not just to relieve guilt. Time along with money is given. Community, church, and spiritual resources are mobilized. This is investing in human capital, not hoarding our time and energy for ourselves. (See Matthew 25.) Education at time of baptism or confirmation could emphasize that under the concept of "priesthood of all believers," we are called to minister by sharing God's truths, love, and provisions.

Giving hope by selected words in addition to money is giving a bit of education and encouragement. The shepherd can simply relay, "There is a love and power wanting to propel you." This motivates giving and completeness in life.

Sharing education and hope are seen in the story about the beggar in Acts 3:6 and 16: "Then Peter said, 'Silver or gold I do not have, but what I have I give to you. In the name of Jesus Christ of Nazareth, walk. By faith in the name of Jesus, this man whom you see and know was made strong.' It is Jesus' name and the faith that comes through him that has given this complete healing to him, as you can all see." This education and hope are analogous to the disciples who told the beggar they had no money but something more important to share - healing to walk and encouragement of their faith.

Change comes about because of trusted relationships with the shepherd, principal leader, teacher, not just the education or service. Therefore, sharing is improved when the shepherd acknowledges personally not necessarily publically "parishioners of modest means who give in proportion to their income or assets" and to those who give generously feeling a sense of ownership in the church.[274]

Harmon[275] explains by telling stories of how people can be transformed. Stories pull "us out of our self-imposed, self-defined existence and open us up to the unknown. They make us vulnerable. We are no longer dealing with ideas or philosophies, but with people and with basic needs, such as survival and pride and relationships and mutual responsibilities."

Rather than continually using generalities about loving God, the shepherd can use the expression of "becoming generous people," or say "God's people are generous people. God's people are caring, sharing people." Focusing on sharing or generosity changes the shepherd's habit of speech. The shepherd gives specific opportunities to pray and to give. The shepherd plants the

---

274   Durall. Ibid. P.64.

275   Joseph Harmon. *Philanthropy in Short Fiction.* Essays on Philanthropy, No. 6. Indiana University, Indianapolis, Indiana. Pp. 1-2 in Durall. 1991. P.77.

seed that when people are in God's kingdom, they are generous, caring, and sharing people. This begins the transformation process.

Accountability Plus

The standard accounting model is having a line with a percent to give each month and then a neat and tidy record. In contrast, accounting is to God. The unexpected event or person occurs and sensitivity to the Spirit nudges action. God puts someone, something in the path that is unexpected, who needs monetary or other support. An accountability attitude expects God to put something or someone in the followers path for their care. "Accountability plus" is when the percentage or dollar amount is met as accountability to God and a **plus** when meeting an unexpected opportunity.

Never-the-less, accountability to God requires discipline and regular habits. That is where a percent is useful. A signed commitment promotes regular giving as a percent which is a goal to strive for and work around other obligations. In this approach, the amount to share is decided before subtracting expenses and saving from income.

Another method of accountability is to decide how much to share and then acquire income and earnings to cover that with commitments to live simply, controlling one's lifestyle, paying taxes which redistribute the wealth and provide services, and determination to *not* use credit if it costs more and enslaves one.

Some people are already socially responsible and have a social conscience. They are responsible and disciplined in other areas. They are unselfish in work, community and families. Others are undisciplined in many areas, socially incompetent, selfish, not responsible and disorganized. For some, their only problem is procrastination out of fear, lack of knowledge, or laziness. The shepherd is challenged to deal with these immaturities, leading to a more spiritually mature and socially sensitive individual who manages resources well. The shepherd arranges for some type of accountability and curtails procrastination so the individual can become a "giver" as well as a disciple.

Accountability begins now by stating what to share today, tomorrow, next week, next month, and next year. A person to whom to report is assigned. A commitment is made to pray every day for guidance, creativity, control, and wisdom. A commitment is made to contact the person assigned regularly at a particular time.

Burkett suggests that self-indulgence is wrong for those concerned about the physical and spiritual well-being of others.[276] Williams, the author, says it is wrong when self-indulgence is at the expense of others or causes another to stumble.

The shepherd cares for people who do not love themselves, cannot forgive themselves, and are dominated by guilt. The shepherd helps them to receive God's love so that they are free to extend it to others. On the other hand, if people love others as themselves (or their kin) as Jesus commanded, then they spend for the good of their health (Matthew 19:19), for the delights God would have them cherish, and to replenish the soul. If people provide living water to others, their well has to be replenished so a budget line for self is not selfish if it is for benefiting others and glorifying God.

In Matthew 6:31-34 the inference is that the Heavenly Father knows people's needs and by "seeking first God's kingdom and righteousness" these things will be added. *God in his love*

---

276   Larry Burkett. *Spiritual Fitness in Business.* No date.

is realistic and practical, as well as spiritual.   God is a personal God, so the percent contributed is personal and realistic in accordance with one's financial affairs.

Techniques

The goal is faithfulness to God in finances. Techniques are needed that enhance joy, that make giving an appealing event, convenient, a part of worship, and creative with today's technologies. Some have found giving by credit card useful. Some give monthly using a check when paying other bills. Addressed stamped envelopes, pledges with reminders of status to date, paychecks deposited electronically into bank accounts and electronic transactions, and website on-line payments are useful. Electronic giving has demonstrated larger donations and "a stream of steady contributions that can be used to advance a church's mission."[277]

Prayers to Motivate Generosity and Sharing

The shepherd leads in the path of gratitude. President Lincoln led the nation in prayer on April 30, 1863 when he proclaimed "a national day of fasting, humiliation, and prayer. We have been the recipients of the choicest bounties of heaven. We have been preserved, the many years in peace and prosperity. We have grown in numbers, wealth and power, as no other nation has grown. But we have forgotten God. We have forgotten the gracious hand which preserved in peace and multiplied and enriched and strengthened us. We have daily imagined, in the deceitfulness of our hearts that all these blessings were produced by some superior wisdom and virtue of our own. Intoxicated with unbroken successes, we have become too self-sufficient to feel the necessity of redeeming and preserving grace, too proud to pray to God whom made us. It behooves us to humble ourselves before the offended Power, to confess our national sins, and to pray for clemency and forgiveness."

The shepherd moves people toward habits and techniques such as beginning the day thanking God, asking God for "opportunity to serve", "opportunity and where to share." What is most important to God are the trust, spiritual development, and witness. God has the whole universe and so does not depend on us. People were created to depend on God. Generosity is based on that trust our Creator will provide in creative ways all our days.

Prayer can include any financial decisions and actions, about all the economic areas of life. Life under God's dominion includes all aspects of life. A reminder in Ephesians 6:18 is: "And pray in the Spirit on all occasions with all kinds of prayers and requests. With this in mind, be alert and always keep on praying for all the saints." People can ask their Generous God to lavish ideas and energy to implement them everyday. They can ask for a mind of generosity. They can ask to break the spirit of procrastination. They can ask for a heart of compassion. Realizing no one is perfect, people can ask for forgiveness for sins of commission, omission, and disposition. They can ask for help in making changes in lifestyle and the courage to say "yes" and to say "no." They can look for progress, not perfection by prayer, practice, and perseverance.

The shepherd can help people to ask at the end the day "Where have I seen God's hand at work?" Prayer includes asking the Spirit to help one to be more frugal not squander the wealth or goods one has, release possessions for the good of others, and to use them for the good of others.

---

277   Chelan David. "e-giving. Embrace the Future of Tithing." *Your Church: Trusted Solutions for Church Leaders.* 2006. Pp.12-20. www.yourchurch.net.

They can include in every prayer a petition for creativity in restructuring, and forgiveness for failure to not place God first in our lives.

Williams', the author's, prayer each morning is for life renewed, life disciplined: "Great God of the universe, Gracious God of the world, Creator God of everything good and beautiful, show me what I can share. Show me how I can make life easier for someone. Tell me how to encourage someone who is struggling or climbing. Give me strength to develop my gifts so that I can benefit others. I thank you for your love and blessings realized today. With gratitude, forgive me for my selfishness, greed, and laziness. Let my praise to You be my acts of kindness, the wise use of resources, and generosity from the heart and mind. Amen"

A constant prayer of any one with a new purpose is found in Psalm 119:36-37, "Turn my heart toward your statutes and not toward selfish gain. Turn my eyes away from worthless things …". One premise is that God blesses each so that each can be a blessing to others. The person is a gift which can be celebrated. Telling a person he or she is a gift from God when he or she has said, given, or done something is a powerful encouragement to them.

Each one has a "unique" blessing or gift that can be used for others or used for encouraging others. When someone is paying attention to God, he or she will be shown which gifts he or she has and where to use the gift or talent given or yet to be developed.

How Much Does the Lord Require?

The first record of giving the tithe was when Melchizedek, king of Salem, blessed Abram for winning the battle (Genesis 14:18-20). After the king blessed God, Creator of heaven and earth, "who delivered your enemies into your hand," Abram gave him a tenth of everything. Then in Leviticus 27:30, the writer proclaimed, "A tithe of everything from the land…belongs to the Lord; it is holy to the Lord." In Numbers 18:26 Moses says, "Speak to the Levites…When you receive from the Israelites the tithe I give you as your inheritance, you must present a tenth of that tithe as the Lord's offering." Deuteronomy 14:22 reads, "Be sure to set aside a tenth of all that your fields produce…eat the tithe…in the presence of the Lord your God…to revere your God always." (See 1 Chronicles 26:20, Malachi 3:7-12.) In contrast, Jesus was critical: "Woe to you, teachers of the law and Pharisees, you hypocrites! You give a tenth of your spices-mint, dill and cumin. But you have neglected the more important matters of the law – justice, mercy and faithfulness. You should have practiced the latter, without neglecting the former" (Matthew 23:23).

The question is "What does the Lord require?" In Micah 6:6-7 the questions are asked - with what shall we come before God, burnt offerings, rams, rivers of oil, and offerings of firstborn for transgressions? The answer in Micah 6:8 is: "He has showed you, O man, and what is good. And what does the Lord require of you? To act justly and to love mercy and to walk humbly with your God." To act could be changing policies and practices to reduce injustices. Mercy could be sharing and giving to others. Walking humbly could be a simple life style regardless of one's wealth. The answer infers that people cannot just give the tithe and ignore the oppressed, omit mercy ministries, or live proudly, lavishly and selfishly after they have met a tithing requirement. (See Matthew 23:23).

The shepherd leads people to realize that giving is a way of thanking God. It is a response to God's everlasting love. Giving is based on the idea that God owns all. Everything is a gift from

God. Then one can humbly accept a portion to sustain life and make one more effective in working for the kingdom of God and for benefit of people in the world.

Anderson[278] explains tithing combined with offering "first fruits" became a vehicle for the Israelites' loyalty to God and a symbol of a giving priority to the God who delivered them. It supported the priesthood and provided for the poor. But Jesus criticized those who measured their righteousness by the amount of contribution. Anderson continues, "The tithe, in itself, is no guarantee of the right relationship with God…It can be another idol, …false substitute for trust in God's mercy alone. Jesus challenged his followers to give everything, not just a tithe."

People receive "the gift of the kingdom" to use "whatever they have to serve others," "to receive grace"… "to show grace to others." Flowing "from the heart of God through Christ to them, and then from them to others"…"the grace of giving is dependent upon a grace received; but once received, it instinctively embraces others." [279]

The criteria for receiving eternal life is not how much we give as a formal ritual or monetary commitment to organized church and keeping the laws. Rather it should be caring for "the least of these," (marginalized, oppressed, immigrants, aliens), feeding the hungry, giving drink to the thirsty, inviting in strangers, clothing the naked, caring for the sick, visiting those in prison, or sharing with the lonely (widows and orphans) (Matthew 25:34-36, Luke 10:30-37, Isaiah 58:6-8). The warning is that people cannot say they love God and ignore their brothers and sisters, neighbors, and strangers. Jesus' followers are strange in many ways such as greeting strangers, not just their friends. They invite people to dinner who cannot invite them back in return. They give not expecting a return or a favor. They give all they have – their abilities, their talents, their possessions (the extra coat), their possessions, their home, their convenience, and their money. They are not so preoccupied with the work of the church or their employment that they do not notice another's need, someone lying in the gutters, someone with a broken heart, or someone abused by others.

Those that care give encouragement as well as money to help others on their way. They continue the work of Jesus using their resources or the money miraculously gathered. Simon[280] reminds us that

> "A faithful reading of the Bible leaves no doubt that God has called us to give
> ourselves to others… We are called to reach those who are spiritually starving
> and impoverished….We are not fully engaged in loving others if we tend to
> their physical needs but ignore their need for God." We are to point to the
> One "who has provided for us so generously with unmerited love and forgiveness.
> Otherwise we witness to our pride and self-righteousness rather than to
> God's goodness…." (Simon).

Responding to the Call to Give All

In the Old Testament, God's people were under the law of the tithe. In the New Testament, Jesus' followers are under grace. The commandment applied to money is to give all – losing one's life so one can find it, laying down one's life for brothers and sisters, and sharing as a response. This

---

278   H. George Anderson. 1990. "Entrust Your Heart to God." Evangelical Lutheran Church in America.

279   Simon. Ibid. P.125.

280   Simon. Ibid. P.44.

follows the two greatest commandments of loving God with heart, soul, mind and strength and your neighbor as one's self.

New guides and new priorities under grace rather than under the law of the Old Testament reflect new changes in the heart and reprioritizing in the mind. New choices as guides exist under the Lord as Master of Money, Creator of everything beautiful and bountiful, the Gracious God, Owner and Provider of all resources, Giver of All including opportunities to earn money. One is surrendering self, all wealth, and possessions to God. "Each one should use whatever gift he has received to serve others, faithfully administering God's grace in its various forms. If anyone speaks, he should do it as one speaking the very words of God. If anyone serves, he should do it with the strength God provides, so that in all things God may be praised through Jesus Christ. To him be the glory and the power for ever and ever. Amen" (Peter 4:10-11).

Under the concept of "giving all" and total surrender, a radical approach is starting with giving 100 percent to give to God in one way or another. Then the individual keeps 10 percent for self. This is for sustenance to maintain health as the "temple of God." The percent is increased for education to be equipped and skilled for serving God and others. The percentage is increased as older and younger dependents depend on the income. Giving God 100 percent at first promotes a mind set of responsibility to God's love in generosity.

Jesus said when he saw the poor widow drop two pennies in the collection, "The plain truth is that this widow has given by far the largest offering today. All these others made offerings that they'll never miss; she gave extravagantly what she couldn't afford-she gave her all!" (Luke 21:2 The Message).

Rather than the law of the tithe, the choice is based on informed dedication to seek first the kingdom with trusting other needs will be met. Percentages used or given recognize inflation's effect on purchasing power. Some people will have to adjust spending downward accordingly. The power of the Spirit is called upon everyday to make choices, change one's heart, and see new ways to serve or increase percentage given to God's control.

Some, under grace rather than law, will give their life but no money at particular times and places. Some, rather than saying "I have to give 10 percent until I do not feel guilty," say, "Ten percent is built in and therefore I have to reduce expenses to give beyond the call yielding to the call of surrender."

Giving a percentage of income or being disciplined to tithe regularly before any other expenses or savings are made gives an individual or family rewards and peace of mind. It is easy to calculate and some people live sacrificially to meet it and others, with higher incomes, meet it easily. They receive their rewards. More difficult, more challenging, and more scripturally faithful is applying "complete surrender" and "how one gives all." (Perhaps this is why the common approach is pushing the tithe rather than all.) Also, the question is the tithe, with offerings beyond that, as mandated in the Old Testament for supporting the kings and priests, the law and prescription for everyone? In contrast, if today's faithful followers perceive their giving is for the work of the kingdom, they arrive at different amounts of money, time, energy, and all resources.

Responding to the Call to Choose to Share

Commitment and habit-forming support the steps toward faithfulness, starting with one percent and moving up to 99 percent as the goal for those who are "able," or can become able. The goal is to set one percent immediately as the new habit, replacing the old habit of not giving any. Action, thus, becomes in line with heart's desire. The discipline of discipleship has begun if one percent consistently given and sacrificially felt is the first step in growing in faith. Then percentages are increased each year (or each month) with increased efficiency and reduced expenditures in other areas. Some refer this as "climbing the ladder a rung at a time."

Rather than thinking one has given 10 percent so now he or she is off the hook and, therefore, do not have to worry about sharing any more, one can say this is just the beginning. The tithe, 10 percent, is a convenient amount to remember. But Jesus asked the rich young man to give all. He could have thought "I have given enough by my 10 percent." So the story refutes the comfort of giving just the tithe.

Hawkins[281] says it this way:

"If you do not tithe, God will not love you less because through grace there is nothing you can do or not do that changes God's love for you. The devil cannot snatch you. God will pull you back. On the other hand, just because you tithe does not give license to break commandments. But in response to God's love, living for God and not oneself (2 Cor. 5:15) one has a new focus - to give and share which is now called obedient love based on trust. When God has your heart, He has your resource dollars. Scripture teaches that a cheerful giver is from the heart saying "I am thankful." Tithing is about trusting God to provide. *Tithing is a way to worship not a box to check off.* When we do not give when *we can*, we are left out of the blessing, not God. If one is afraid that if he stops tithing, God will do bad to him, he is tithing for the wrong reasons. But if you cannot pay bills or feed your family, there are still ways to worship without tithing for a season." (Hawkins).

The complexity of credit and many demands of the culture make determining a set amount difficult. The demands of work and family obscure the observation of others in need. Care for the immediate family and work group is a large task. The challenge is to not be blinded to needs of a larger family concept. So the task is to determine what to share, care, and give at this time, in this place with an expanded family of church and community.

Another perspective is that God has given them 90 percent to make choices with care for their families, pay taxes, and save. The questions are how can they spend and save for the "glory of God and their neighbor's good" with the 90 percent. How can they spend more money on themselves to become equipped, educated, to be more effective in God's work? How can they care for their bodies so they can share time and effort in helping others? How can they develop talents and abilities to share the gospel? How can they save to have more to share? How can they listen every hour to where God is leading them, taking others with them under the Great Shepherd's direction without fear? How can they get the equipment for the journey with less expense than first thought?

Sharing out of the daily living expenses can be counted. A few examples are tipping, giving food to the community pantry, cooking a dish for someone busy or ill, helping with studies, teaching grandchildren, and helping someone find a job. Time in service, an "opportunity cost" or wages foregone from a second job are forms of sacrificial sharing.

Stewardship or Care of the Pasture and God's Provisions

Shepherds assist in developing faithfulness to God's call to care for the garden. Love of God is shown in actions based on the heart of caring, the mind of knowing, and strength for everyday activities. It is based on the soul of responding to the Creator. God has been revealed through the

---

281   Ron Hawkins. Notes from presentation. New Focus. Lafayette, Indiana. 2006.

words of the Scripture which verify God cares for people in all ways and point to stewardship and caring for each other. People can choose to respond by revealing God to others, to re-present God. One way people do this is demonstrating responsible stewardship in the care of the garden and God's creations. This includes areas of physical, emotional, social, and spiritual care.

Stewardship is the first commandment as described in Genesis 2:15: "The Lord God took the man and put him in the Garden of Eden to work it and take care of it." The commandment continues in Romans 1:19-20: "Since what may be known about God is plain to them, because God has made it plain to them. For since the creation of the world, God's invisible qualities – his eternal power and divine nature – have been clearly seen, being understood from what has been made, so that men [and women] are without excuse." Since the beginning of time, God's nature has been revealed in nature. Human nature, since made in the image of God, is to respond to the power, order, beauty, and majesty of nature. God has been revealed in people's internal compass pointing to right and wrong responses to God and behavior. One's conscience is mindful that the air and water can be safer, that television and video games can be better for the mind, and that organizations can educate for positive change.

The shepherd's garden are those creations under his or her guidance and care. The shepherd helps people to support legislation that reaches beyond the immediate garden to protect and provide for all God's creation. Caring is reflected through day to day actions for both the physical environment and the social environment. Caring is shown by spreading the word that responsibility of stewards is for the material well-being and spiritual well-being of children in the world, young people, families, singles, and the elderly.

Stewardship Defined

"Stewardship is a total orientation of working for God and with God and others for peace, wholeness, and the glory of creation."[282] Stewardship is caring, protecting, and conserving the earth's resources, God's resources, human made goods, one's abilities, one's assets, the knowledge of God's love and plan. Earth's resources include humans, animals, fish, birds, land, water, vegetation, and atmosphere. Stewardship is using God's resources for God's purposes and design (Luke 10:23). This sharing provides for the continuation of sharing and for expansion.[283]

Stewardship is fulfilling entrusted responsibility in caring for what belongs to God which includes everything and humans based on the premise that everything belongs to God. Stewardship is feeling responsible, acting responsively, and giving witness that all resources belong to God. Behavior and choices are based on sound principles of managing God's property. Responsibilities are accepted in light that God has given individuals their things for a reason.

Problems begin when individuals think money is theirs and they do not have to depend on God for learning how to manage it or to give an account to the Master Owner about their behavior. In the current age of entitlements, individuals are unfaithful in thinking they have the right of ownership rather than the gift of use of God's resources. Problems begin when "Mammon" (riches) are people's master rather than their loyalty first to God. We are given the freedom to choose between the gifts of God versus the gifts of materialism. We are called to be faithful, not perfect (1 Corinthians 4:2). Generosity, sharing, and giving are purposefully designed to give

---

282   Church of the Brethren Annual Conference Statement.

283   Ibid.

witness to the revelation and power of God's world, God's work, for our good. Attention is given to the care of the environment to protect that good for all peoples.

Followers are called to give testimony to a just and merciful God who designed them to be in his image. The premise under arrangements for sharing includes justice for all people in their participation of resource use and fullness of life. Time, energy, health, and wealth through acts of stewardship are protected and cared for in order that justice can prevail and sharing can be utilized.

Stewardship recognizes the two parts: Accountability along with acceptance of God's gifts. A Church of the Brethren Statement[284] reads, "As the people of God, we look beyond our own salvation and security and deal with God's yearning that all peoples of the earth know and accept divine love. It is the call to mission beyond ourselves." Responsibility over resources by the servant or manager until time of accountability is described in parables: Matthew 25:14-30 (parable of the talents); Luke 19:11-28 (trustworthy in small matters increased responsibility in large matters); Luke 12:42-48 (faithful steward); and Luke 16:1-18 (shrewd manager).

In the General Assembly Presbyterian Statement[285] living as stewards is described as answering the call to "redemption" (Ephesians 2:4-9), for faithful living (Ephesians 2:10), as "stewards of God's mysteries" (1 Corinthians 4:1-2), and "stewards of the manifold grace of God" (1 Peter 4:10-11).

"Stewards do not give because they happen to have enough to give. Stewards have received what they have *for the very purpose of giving it away*....Gifts we possess have been bestowed by God and entrusted to us on the condition that they be distributed for our neighbor's benefit (John Calvin)."[286] "Stewards are to use and build on the gifts...that reflect the character and purposes of the owner [God]" bearing "witness to the love, mercy, and grace of the triune God [who] creates, redeems and sustains the world."[287]

Gifts Used in Caring for the World

People's gifts change throughout life so they constantly have to evaluate goals, experiences, and situations to know what being a good steward means for them for that day. Shepherds can help others think through what it means to them to be good stewards. Each situation is different and there is not one right answer. A person with three little children and barely earning above the poverty level has to take care of the family to be a good steward.

Expanding the role of steward is similar to expanding talents or investing assets. First identify assets which show the greatest potential. Capital assets are human and material, tangible and intangible, personal, family, and community, social, emotional, and environmental. Common sense as well as Spiritual guidance assume care of assets and resources in order to have more to share and give. Caring and protecting the pasture expands the yield for more sharing and generosity.

As mentioned in www.stewardship.com people are blessed with talents or gifts they may not readily identify. (Assets by definitions are attributes or possessions that can be expanded, used for the benefit of others, and can receive a return.) Assets or talents include, mentioned

---

284   Ibid.

285   Statement of the General Assembly of the Presbyterian Church (USA). "Living Grateful Lives: Stewardship Theology in Our Time." 2001. P.3.

286   Ibid. P.4.

287   Ibid. P.5.

on the website, personality, interests, skills, loving to interact with people, ability to express self, occupational and vocational experiences. Some talents mentioned on the website are: smiling, relief of suffering, encouragement, patience to just be with someone, telling of "signs and wonders," musical expressions, hospitality, pleasant disposition, charisma, sharing of mystical experiences, energy, physical strength, mental acuteness, shrewd insights, ability to manage, money, wealth, and possessions. The calling and the challenge are to care for, as a steward, any asset one has and "capitalize" on it. Good health would be an asset, but poor health or disability can also be an asset in that it can make someone more sensitive and understanding of others who are less than perfect. (All people are less than perfect.)

Economic principles are applicable in choices among competing uses for which people will be held accountable. One is "pareto optimality" in which a choice, program, or path of resource use is where/when at least "one person is better off and no one is worse off." "Efficiency" is getting the most return with the least resources, using resources in the right way. "Effectiveness" is using the right resources, doing the right thing under the Lordship of Christ for the benefit of people. But God sometimes directs in "inefficient" ways. Therefore, one must seek novel ways.

Invested money and possessions, and all God-given resources, are used to accomplish God-given ends (Matthew 25 and James 5). Hoarding wealth and denying needs of others are severely judged by God. (See the story of the Israelites who stored extra manna which perished. They disobeyed God and denied He was in charge.) The worse sin is using resources for ourselves that rightfully can be shared with others. This includes taking advantage of others, which would be the opposite of generosity.

Sharing God's love and accountability of use of the earth's resources provide the reward: "Well done, my good and faithful servant." This is taking on responsibility. The result of exercising wisdom and good judgment based on education and the Spirit's power. It results from seeking and being obedient to God in everyday use of resources.

Accountability must support financial and environmental education in community and church programs. Accountability supports sermons on mission and vision, use of money and the earth's resources. As stewards we are to call others to account.

Generosity and stewardship are vital in caring for God's gifts to us, the earth and its resources. In Romans 8:22, it states "The whole creation has been groaning in travail together until now." For now, this responsibility includes reducing smog, acid rain, pesticides in the food chain, depletion of the ozone layer.[288]

"Stewardship involves caring for both earthly, [financial] and spiritual needs."[289] Roop says it well: "Some who are homeless need shelter for their bodies and others need it for their souls." Responsibility as stewards of the "mysteries of God (1 Cor. 4:1), is reflected in "not being ashamed of the gospel, responding to suffering of the oppressed, and leading those who "wander aimlessly through life." Responsible stewards "soothe the pain of the world" and do justice.[290]

---

288   John Reumann. *Stewardship and the Economy of God*. William. B. Eerdmans Publishing Company. 1992. P. 96.

289   Eugene F. Roop. *Let the Rivers Run. Stewardship and the Biblical Story*. William B. Eerdmans Publishing Company, Grand Rapids, Michigan. 1991. P. 98.

290   Ibid. Pp.98-100.

Followers are called to invite and lead people into the Promised Land.[291] Roop reminds us that the Creator has started the movement and is at work[292] and followers are simply stewards of the creation.[293] A good steward acts in the image and spirit of God[294] enhancing "life for all those around" us.[295] This is done through "divine presence and power"[296] directing people's skill, wisdom, and energy .[297]

Responsible Response

Irresponsible morals and habits should be addressed by spiritual leaders and teachers of disciples. Roop[298] described these in the culture and individuals as rampant overconsumption, wastefulness, stealing, hoarding, and lack of covenant based on the "gift."

Some people have to be taught what responsibility is. Some say responsibility is not taught but rather caught. Some ask, "What can this church (versus another one) give me? How can it benefit me?" Rather they could ask in choosing how they can benefit the church, what they have to contribute, and what does this particular church need?

Others need to be taught what responsibility for the earth, the land, and the environment is under allegiance to God. Lifestyle, choice of products, recycling, and industrial production are questioned as to their effect on the environment and depletion of resources. Then practices are initiated that renew resources and promote healthy environments. People are witness to the larger effects of everyday choices, everyday in everyway.

Some young parents need to be taught what is responsibility for their family. A state wide program of the Cooperative Extension Education aimed at young fathers was titled "It is My Child Too" to teach skills leading to responsibility. Their responsibilities included developing their personal resources, family resources, and getting community resources. Some parents think of only the physical needs rather then the responsibility for social, security, emotional, mental, and spiritual needs in providing a balance among all these needs. On the other hand, some parents use Scripture to justify caring only for their immediate family rather than expanding family responsibilities to the church, the non-churched, the neighborhood, and those who are "fatherless" (Malachi 3:5). Provision does not need to be lavish or selfish to heed the warning in 1 Timothy 5:8: "But if anyone does not provide for his relatives, and especially for those of his immediate family, he has denied the faith and is worse than an unbeliever."

The challenge is taking responsibility for stewardship in lean times and in prosperity. Many people naturally feel overwhelmed with their responsibilities and the challenge to faithful stewardship. This is because their focus on God's power, purpose and sovereignty is limited. Teaching responsibility for others and stewardship is similar to teaching unselfishness, reduced pleasure from accumulating, reduced greed and less "me first" thinking. Helpful ways to teach responsibility are: Telling stories, giving alternatives, giving opportunity with trust to complete the

---

291   Roop. Ibid. P.99.

292   Ibid. P.76.

293   Ibid. P.92.

294   Ibid. P.81.

295   Ibid. P.79.

296   Ibid. P.74.

297   Ibid. P.73.

298   Ibid. P.58.

job, building in accountability during the job, discussing how someone felt when done, discussing what to do differently next time, and giving respect and trust (maybe more than deserved).

Sharing the pasture in today's world could be manifest as sharing earth's resources such as gas for vehicles. A policy could be to always take someone along when going shopping, to church, or on a sight-seeing short trip.

Responsibility implemented into resolve and then action glorifies God. Responsible people wonder what are the new responsibilities for faithful stewardship in today's environment. Shepherds can open people to new "signs and wonders." Hopefully, people can experience new gifts from God to expand and to share in a sometimes difficult and fragile world.

Answering the Call of the Great Shepherd as Stewards

The shepherd's special role is to assist people to answer the call to stewardship. Dunham[299] said justice is practiced for the common good "even when it may go against our own self-interest." This is accomplished through frugality, simplicity, satisfaction with material sufficiency, and spiritual discipline.[300] Simplicity "is about shedding things that do not bring deep satisfaction and an inner sense of peace and well-being."[301] The rich young man said he had kept all the laws. Micah in the Old Testament asks the question, "What does the Lord require of you?" and the answer in verse 6:8 was "To act justly and to love mercy and to walk humbly with your God."

In the name of care-giving, an annual conference promoted in one session to care first for oneself for wholeness and health. The practice advocated was to physically run as a family which was demonstrated in front of the large attendance. A criticism of this demonstration is that many families are thinking too much of themselves and stop there, rather than growing in generosity and stewardship. The shepherd can suggest alternative practices to show stewardship. Beyond the health practice of running for self-care would be how to help others in their health. This might be to have the family, children and all together, care for someone's yard/garden. Besides helping an elderly or ill person, the children choose to learn skills of how to care for things of the earth and how to get exercise in working for the common good. With limited resources of human time and energy, choosing to share in this way would be a priority.

Good stewardship is caring for oneself in order to care for others effectively and efficiently. This can include caring for others in the process. For example, when going to the exercise gym or the mall to walk, one could take another. In the winter when the elderly cannot walk their usual path, one could take them to the shopping center mall. When taking a walk, a lonely young person could be invited to go along. When going to the store, shop for someone else or take someone along. An exercise program can be useful and caring to others if it includes shoveling snow or trimming the shrubbery.

The vow of stewardship is to "make a difference" by helping others develop resources and improving the environment, social and material. Making a difference may be unique to each or may be a community movement in answering the call to faithfulness. Everyday the vow in prayer can be to do something different or differently. The change can be in areas of

---

299   Laura Dunham. *Graceful Living: Your Faith, Values, and Money in Changing Times.* Commissioned by the Ecumenical Stewardship Center. RCA Distribution Center, 4500 60th St., SE, Grand Rapids, MI 49512. 2001. P.12.

300   Ibid.

301   Ibid. P.9.

1. Caring for own money, resources, and talents.
2. Caring for people and God's creation in any form.
3. Caring for safe water, food, and the environment nearby and the global community by choices everyday.

The call to sharing and stewardship may be contrary to people's desired preferences. The answer to the call may be what is needed by those nearby, around the faithful steward. The answer everyday is choosing products that do not harm the environment. It is following practices that protect the environment. It is supporting agricultural methods that keep the land fertile for feeding God's creation.

The shepherd helps those under his or her education to be mindful and prayerful. Prayer can be about the use of precious time, limited energy, hard-earned money, and inheritances. Everyday the prayer includes, "Thank you Lord for entrusting me to care for your world and your people. Thank you, Lord for caring for me as I care for others."

The rewards and outcomes of stewardship are many. One reward is surviving when income is drastically reduced. Everyday with the Spirit's power, people of the pasture can use resources and talents for protecting and providing for all God's creation. The rewards are heard in the words, "Well-done, good and faithful servant!" (Matthew 25:21,23). Love, joy, and peace can fill life as faithfulness in stewardship is fulfilled. "To God be the glory and the power for ever and ever" (1 Peter 4:11b).

◇◇◇ ⧖ ⧖ ◇◇◇

Chapter 14. **Spirituality of Financial Management Rebirth**

The Call to Crisis Intervention and Financial Change

Financial management is a spiritual as well as an economic issue because trust in God and accountability from studying Scripture are involved. Decisions everyday about everyday things involve choice between allegiance to God before everyone and everything else. Financial behavior reflects acceptance or rejection of God's love. Faith is strong in planning and pursuing "first God's kingdom and righteousness" knowing "all these things will be *given* to you as well" (Matthew 6:33).

Financial rebirth in management is necessary to survive the earthquakes of financial disaster, insecurity, distress, despair, lack of control, and confusion. Financial security and management are the major concerns in most families. For over 20 years, various agencies and research have estimated from 66 to 70 percent of people live from paycheck to paycheck, at the brink of disaster if an unexpected change occurs. There are foreclosures, consumer bankruptcies, marriage failures because of finances, suicides over money and debt, loss of benefits for the poor, and loss of productivity due to financial mismanagement. The pull of worldly passions which control people's money is strong. The enticements of wasteful spending are prevalent. Addictions requiring large money outlays to overcome pain, rejection, and boredom are rampant. Financial habits blindly leading to destruction are uncontrolled. Capitulating to human nature, the focus has been on material possessions and the pursuit of ever-expanding wants at the expense of working with God and for his kingdom in sharing his gifts.

Need or desire to change can be inferred by statistics. The Barna survey found that Christians (27 percent) and non-Christians (28 percent) were similar in stating their personal financial situation was getting better.[302] Obviously, others may think it is getting worse. Christians (33 percent) and non-Christians (39 percent) said, "It's impossible to get ahead because of financial debt."[303]

Change is possible with *desire to change and openness to empowerment of the Spirit.* The shepherd's role is creating a desire to change and increasing spiritual awareness, inspiring spiritual development and providing practical resources in helping to resolve a financial crisis.

Resolving a financial crisis or adjusting to an economic downturn is through exploring new options and setting up a new budget plan as well as changing perspectives about the situation. Changes in expectations and lifestyle are helpful to many people.

As God touches the heart, mind, soul, and strength, God may reveal a crisis, a need to change one's journey, a deep yearning to be more faithful in finances, a need for reexamination,

---

302   James MacDonald. *I Really Want to Change…So, Help Me God.* Chicago: Moody Bible Institute. 2000.
303   Ibid. P.121.

transformation, and renewal.[304] Clearly, financial change is required because the event does not fit or conform "to their cognitive understanding or belief about themselves, about life, or about the way the world is supposed to work."[305] The individual in crisis is in a situation in which the structures have been broken and need to build them back. Some build in positive ways and others in destructive ways. A conversion of the heart, mind, soul and strength is necessary to find meaning in life, abundant living, joy and peace in other ways than money.

The shepherd can lead the way to financial wellness and help those out of the pits of financial despair because of *unique contributions*.[306] The shepherd or pastor is often the first to whom an individual looks for help and admits a crisis. A research study found that 42 percent of those receiving assistance for psychological difficulties sought help first from clergy.[307] Shepherds can go to the people, even unannounced. Pastors or shepherds are responsible for worship or religious rituals in which he/she can observe despair in people's eyes. In messages he/she can address the developmental tasks of life. Shepherds and pastors can mobilize external resources of a wider range than other professionals. The role as representative of God puts the shepherd in a larger context. Shepherds and pastors assist through worship and spiritual conversion which develops cognitive and emotional mastery over circumstances that most others cannot provide.

Economics and *difficulties in matters of financial management* are addressed in the teachings of Jesus, the wisdom literature, and the commandments. The Lord's Prayer includes a request to be kept from the power of evil or the evil one. Today this includes selfish money pursuits, greed, scams, bondage to credit, deceptive advertising, destructive and expensive lifestyles, financial ignorance, and spiritual warfare. These have been causes of crises in many ways. The Ten Commandments (Exodus 20), designed to guide community faithfulness, include the financial temptations of having other gods, stealing, and covetousness. "One must battle the enemy by fixing the ... mind and heart on Christ whom one loves, worshipping Him, learning from Him, and being with His people."[308]

Shepherd Counseling Process for Financial Rebirth

What Shepherd Counseling does in Financial Crisis
It sustains the individual or family by helping them cope in a situation that cannot be changed. Shepherds in counseling:
1) Suggest immediate actions, giving them hope that they will get through it, mobilizing all types of resources for sustenance,
2) Reconciles a belief system that is challenged about providing material, physical needs, and strength,
3) Guides with concrete "next" steps, and
4) Helps heal the hurts, the pains from financial mistakes, wrongdoings, accidents, abuse by others, the worries from financial insecurity, and the grieving of giving up a lifestyle.

---

304   Roy L. Horneyutt. *Crisis and Response*. Abingdon Press. 1965.

305   Ibid.

306   Karl A. Slaikeu. *Crisis Intervention*. Boston:Allyn and Bacon. 1990.

307   Ibid.

308   Ron Hawkins. Sermon. Covenant Presbyterian Church. West Lafayette, Indiana. May 2005.

Working with the initial crisis and trans-crisis points helps the person to not slip back into the pathology (or temptations) of previous life.[309]

In a crisis situation, the shepherd provides opportunity for people to open mind and heart. The shepherd prays for God to take *charge of the process* and helps identify procedures to move forward. Then the counselor directs the process and the person provides the content. The shepherd functions as the non-anxious person who looks at the situation objectively. The shepherd is clear about steps to take, thoughts to challenge, and making use of prayer as the mightiest force in the world. Therefore, the shepherd needs a counselor for directing ideas and strategies, specific and immediate steps to take on the journey. Jesus promised to send this Counselor – The Spirit of Christ. Therefore, "Christians affirm that counselor and counselee must face a third, unseen Person. The Spirit of Christ operates in moments of extremity and perplexity. Those who confess their limitations and daily wait (hope) upon God will find light rising up in the midst of darkness."[310]

Be aware of resistance to change because of anxieties, habit, or culture. Most people would rather die than change consumption, especially in food patterns or tastes. However, in severe crises, they change. The Spirit initiates and facilitates changes. The voice is small and gentle, compared to the many loud competing voices. The shepherd starts the first step in the office and helps the individual in crisis overcome procrastination, not knowing, not caring, or anxieties.

The shepherd can direct a *process for change*[311] by first making relational contact that establishes trust, identifying the precipitating event, assisting catharsis, and building hopeful expectation. With no time to waste, people are not allowed to talk about just anything that comes to mind.[312] The focus then, is on getting details of the present situation and identifying (and resolving) threats. Some share openly. Others cannot or will not share their pain as details open the wounds again. Pain is financial, emotional, social, and spiritual. The reality of accepting a different world or environment for which previous beliefs and rules have not worked is painful and anxiety-ridden. The counselor facilitates getting information while maintaining respect for an embarrassed, distraught individual about whom gossip has been spread, or observations have been made, by saying, "Yes, I have heard some things. How much or what do you want *me* to know?" Then, coping is getting an inventory of problem-solving resources, assisting in decision-making, emphasizing relationships with others, and summarizing new learnings. The counselor counteracts a decision if it would cause harm, if it is a running away from the situation, or if it is premature until other decisions are acted upon.[313] In the process, the individual grows less dependent upon the counselor or shepherd for decision-making and action. New learnings from the crisis move outcomes to be positive and give hope for renewal.[314]

Post Traumatic Stress Disorder is a spiritual disorder since it involves a loss of hope, trust, and relationships.[315] The Biblical story is of hope given, hope lost and hope regained. The

---

309   Burl E. Gilliland and Richard K. James. *Crisis Intervention Strategies.* Pacific Grove: Brooks/Cole Publishing Company. 1997.

310   Samuel Southard, "The Emotional Health of Pastoral Counselor," Wayne Oats, Ed., *An Introduction to Pastoral Counseling,* Nashville: Broadman Press, 1959. P.43.

311   David K. Switzer. *The Minister as Crisis Counselor.* Nashville: Abingdon Press. 1974, reporting on model of Warren Jones.

312   Ibid. P.72.

313   Ibid. P.82.

314   Switzer, Ibid.

315   N. Duncan Sinclair. *Horrific Traumata.* New York: The Haworth Press. 1993.

examples and the reality of lost hope and hope regained are affirmed over and over again.[316] Crisis interveners, counselors, and friends are told in the Scripture to be ready to give an answer for the hope that is within them (1 Peter 3:15).

Hope is strengthened by identifying some possible responses for developing patterns of financial behaviors designed for surviving the current crisis. The shepherd helps the individual cope. Hope is created from setting up new structures, especially financial, and following them with the hope that positive attitudes will follow. A deficit in significant material resources such as food, housing, medical needs, and transportation can turn a modest event into a crisis and, therefore, emergency relief must be found.[317] Hope which generates energy is increased by knowing there are community resources for food or children's education, buying food that will last, getting more income each month through Earned Income Credit or more tax withholdings, moving in with someone, controlling impulsive or miscellaneous spending, controlling the timing of paying bills, and actively reducing energy costs. Providing hope helps an individual face financial consequences with a plan, changing the meaning of money and its hold on people. An individual can change identity into being defined as a child of God. It may mean telling Satan to get out of the spending plan. It may mean asking the Spirit to help control the desires, the spending, and the plan or budget. It may mean to use talent and skills to make money for God's glory, not one's greed, being careful that it does not cause others to stumble. It may mean spending money to celebrate, to be educated as a sharper tool for God's work, or to acquire soul restoration objects such as flowers or music all to be used for the glory of God.

The shepherd *assesses how the crisis is affecting* people in all areas related to becoming new creations. Information is obtained about financial behavior before the crisis and since then. What was working well before and what is working well now. Emotional states and physical symptoms are assessed and ideas given for relieving them through counseling, medication, changes in spending/ saving/sharing, physical activity, and participation in a supportive or inspirational program. An assessment is made of possible changes in the interpersonal area and social behavior. Changes in expenditures or lifestyle can be made and still meet the needs for communication and relationships. In the cognitive area, assessment of the thinking patterns about themselves and the crisis includes how money use is wrapped up in their identity and resolution of crisis. Their attachment and control under a reference group is assessed. An individual can change his or her identity as well as behavior. For example, some husbands are so controlling, secretive, and "stingy" with the family money or their money that it hampers cooperation and positive growth in financial affairs. The area of spiritual growth is assessed for the presence of hope, feeling the strength of the Spirit, and being in Christ (Philippians 2:1-3) rather than in the material world for sustenance and nurturance.

"The primary task of the financial counselor [or shepherd counselor] is to assist clients in *changing inappropriate financial behaviors* by replacing them with more appropriate approaches."[318] The process of changing bad habits is replacing them with good habits. A crisis usually promotes dissatisfaction and discontent with the present state of things. Such a time can open a person to change in a way that good times cannot. The counselor can create dissatisfaction with "dissemination of correct information." A reality check can be done on information that was thought to be correct

---

316   Ibid.

317   Karl A. Slaikeu. *Crisis Intervention.* Boston: Allyn and Bacon. 1990.

318   Aimee D. Prawitz and Mary Elizabeth Garrison. "Application of a Change Equation in Financial Counseling." In *Proceedings of the Association for Financial Counseling and Planning Education.* Nov. 19-22, 2003. P.54.

but is *not*. For example, the counselor can show the disparity between take-home income and living expenses/debt payments.[319] Then, the counselor gives vision by describing differences in behaviors and beneficial outcomes. A "map of changing" shows the process designed partly by appropriate family members. The perceived costs of change are examined. The goal of the counselor and the effective way to move toward the next stage of change is to clearly show more "pros" than "cons" of changing.[320]

Changing financial behavior is a process beginning with pre-contemplation, contemplation, preparation and action.[321] Research has found effective change in financial behaviors ends with "maintenance," beginning about six months after the "action" stage. Struggle continues for those attempting permanent change. "Lapses and relapses are frequent, and vigilance is necessary. The counselor helps assess what conditions would cause relapse and suggests coping strategies. "Valuing the self that is changed and for having at least one significant other who also values the changed self" are necessary.[322] They may be only the counselor and God.

Spirituality and Financial Rebirth

Spiritual rebirth means a replacement of desires, even if they are not evil, by a new desire to serve the Lord. It means a cleansing of sins and restitution for those that have been hurt by the misuse of money. It means a *seeking of righteousness about finances* with God, family, businesses, and others.

"Religious coping" has been found to predict spiritual outcomes, changes in mental health, and improvements in physical health.[323] Research has documented the power and positive influences of prayer upon crisis resolution and healing.[324] Religious participation has been found to influence positive growth and self-image of low-income people.

Definitions of spirituality vary. One that is useful for counseling someone in crisis or change is: Spirituality is concerned with a life-giving force/animating principle such as God, Spirit, True Nature, Source with an attempt to remember through direct experience who one truly is.[325] Spirituality defines who one truly is in relation to "The Great I Am."

Transformation to higher levels of development tends to be gradual although in crisis may happen dramatically. The journey is at its highest when individuals or organizations focus their energies on the needs of others.[326] Stages of the spiritual journey begin with the basics which give temporary satisfaction such as physical needs, food, shelter, and clothes. Then there is the need for security with money and insurance as a source, followed by pleasure, companionship, and sex.

---

319   Ibid.

320   J.O. Prochaska, J.C. Norcross, and C.C. DiClemente. *Changing for Good.* New York: Avon Books. 1994.

321   Susan S. Shocket and Sharon B. Seiling. "Moving Into Action: Application of the Transtheoretical Model of Behavior Change to Financial Education." *Financial Counseling and Planning.* 2004. Pp.41-52.

322   Ibid.

323   Kenneth Pargament, Harold G. Koenig, Nalini Tarakeshwar, and June Hahn. "Religious Coping Methods as Predictors of Psychological, Physical, and Spiritual Outcomes..."*Journal of Health Psychology.* 9,6. Nov. 2004. Pp.713 -821.

324   Judith Acosta and Judith Simon Prager. *The Worst is Over – What to Say When Every Moment Counts.* San Diego: Jodere Group. 2002.

325   Reggie Marra. "What Do You Mean, 'Spirituality'?" *Journal of Pastoral Counseling.* Vol. 35, 2000. Pp.?

326   Ibid.

Stage 3 is "conformist" and operates from the expectations and judgments of significant others without reflection or examination. Next could be career and other experiences which give ground to critical reflection, individuality versus group identity and then self-actualization. Transforming vision and loyalties are acted out in radical actualization.[327] The journey continues when lower levels have been sufficiently satisfied. The ultimate is God-actualization (author unknown), serving and witnessing to others. Completion of lower levels has not been "able to quench the core thirst-satiate, the essential hunger that consists in our attempts to remember and return to Who We Are."[328]

Conversion in Economic Life

Conversion is changing financial *habits*, financial *actions* and then transforming the character, heart, and desire. The heart follows habits. Habits can follow heart changes also. Conversion is dying to self, sinful attitudes and actions in every economic corner and financial curve of life. In fact, Jesus said unless one dies, nothing new will come forth. "I tell you the truth, unless a kernel of wheat falls to the ground and dies, it remains only a single seed. But if it dies, it produces many seeds" (John 12:24).

Conversion in most cases is continuous for changing patterns of consumption. It may be instant in a crisis. Those with crises as a way of life or a response to treating everything equally (without priorities) need conversion in management and perspectives in priorities. People around them may resist the change in the converted individual. However, Jesus is walking with them on the journey of financial faithfulness and renewal. God calls people to walk, to work, be responsible, and be accountable. Accountability to someone for progress helps in the conversion of the pocketbook, the billfold, the credit cards, the saving, and the sharing.

The challenge in financial counseling is to *de-program* the individual's or family's patterns of measuring their worth based on accumulation of money or possessions. For rebirth to occur, de-programming is necessary in the method of paying for goods, the definition of what are goods, when to acquire goods, and the lure of advertisements of goods.

"Seeking first God's kingdom and righteousness" can be illustrated. Rather than having a plan and asking for blessings on it and help for fulfilling it, reprogramming is seeking first God's plan and asking how one can fulfill it. Reprogramming is to see and talk with Christ in the crisis not just the payments and financial pressures. Reprogramming is done so that the individual automatically goes first to God with financial questions in prayer, first to God with any windfall income, first to God with fruits of labor, and first to God seeking plans and purposes for life.

The shepherd tells stories of what others have done to motivate and inspire. The story is told of a little girl when given some money, first said, "I must take this to Jesus." Children sometimes lead the way in generosity. The story is told of a little boy cured by surgery. His family had no money. So he gave his only possession, his teddy bear, to the physician in gratitude.

The challenge in shepherd counseling for submission to God is to change communication with God, the business world, unscrupulous scam artists, and creditors by being assertive and following through on a plan to pay off debts even though harassed or tempted to run away. Being connected to God by talking before a crisis, during, and after the crisis keeps one afloat. Talking continually with God keeps one from drowning in temptations in shopping, addictions, and peer

---

327   Ibid.

328   Ibid.

pressures to consume. Talking with other people about financial plans and transaction helps one get more with less expense, consider alternatives, be shrewd, and be creative rather than culture-bound. Paul said in Romans 7:6, "But now, by dying to what once bound us, we have been released from the law so that we serve in the new way of the Spirit, and not in the old way of the written code."

Conversion is remembering the *premises for becoming a new creation in Christ*, not just the financial payments and the financial worries. Being in Christ is continual talking with Christ about one's allegiance to His control over financial desires and behavior. Being in Christ empowers one to make financial changes, gives comfort in crisis, and the courage and vision to change.

"Faith can move mountains (1 Corinthians 13:2)." The mountain may be a new way to manage money so that bills are paid on time thus saving over thousands of dollars a year. Courage to manage money in new ways can involve mountains of:

- Managing all bills, comparison shopping, and being shrewd - not "throwing pearls to the pigs that will turn and tear you to pieces" (Matthew 7:6),
- Having "strength for today and bright hope for tomorrow" (source: hymn Great is Thy Faithfulness) which can help one apply for a new job or develop a new role,
- Going to authorities for financial or consumer rights,
- Saying no to some people and saying yes to others,
- Explaining to children a different way of living or feeling important, giving up the dream of a new car, saying yes to creative spending and no to wasteful spending,
- Paying off debts or taking risks in going into debt for a good cause,
- Taking risk by paying a tithe or more and hoping to live on the rest by cutting utility bills by $50 a month, gasoline bills by $30, doubling up in living quarters, etc.,
- Struggling to know which bills to pay with insufficient income as a single parent (or grandparent) not knowing whether the crisis is temporary or forever,
- Keeping track of spending for reevaluating goals and setting up a new spending plan, making a spending plan and following it, eating different types of food, etc.,
- Taking in a foster child,
- Getting a different education, living with minimum TV and telephone services,
- Changing type of vacation,
- Correcting a financial abuse from an adult child, or
- Committing more than 10 percent of one's income to work of the kingdom and sharing with others.

Promises for Change on the Journey

Scripture provides a theology of personal financial management. It provides *promises and mottos* as anchors under the New Management. As advertisers know, repeating mottos and slogans changes behavior. Repeating Scripture as guides to behavior can deprogram patterns, replace bad habits, and spur to action. Reprogramming can be achieved with the constant repetition of "I can do everything through him who gives me strength" (Philippians 4:13, NIV). An example of a promise is, "All things are possible, only believe."[329] These words of a song can change the heart which can change financial behavior.

---

329   Paul Rader. "Only Believe." The Rodeheaver Co. 1949, 1972.

Promises burnt on the heart and mind go with people when shopping, at work, in the financial planning office, at household tasks, and with unruly and selfish children. "Trusting God" is doing finances differently than before. "Do not be anxious about anything, but in everything, by prayer and petition, with thanksgiving, present your requests to God" (Philippians 4:6 NIV). When we are anxious for nothing, the command with a promise is "the peace of God, which transcends all understanding, will guard your hearts and your minds in Christ Jesus" (Verse 7 NIV). "God gives us not only the action but the reaction."[330] "I am the Lord, your God, who takes hold of your right hand and says to you, Do not fear; I will help you" (Isaiah 41:13 NIV). "Cast all your anxiety on him because He cares for you" (I Peter 5:7). "Humble yourselves, therefore, under God's mighty hand, that he may lift you up in due time" (1 Peter 5:6 NIV). "Take care! Be on your guard against all kinds of greed; for one's life does not consist in the abundance of possessions" (Luke 12:15 NRSV).[331]

Spiritual Rebirth of Financial Behavior

The shepherd can guide by giving ideas how to respond to God's love with all one's heart, mind, soul and strength. Loving God with mind, heart, soul and strength is applied to personal financial affairs. The loving and personal God nudges and blesses changes. The mind starts first in deciding the changes and expectations, but there is a lag time until the heart changes. It takes awhile until what is given up does not continue to have the pull of the heart. Some things or services have more of a pull than others. The soul needs to be in a state of surrender to God to accept the changes required somewhat reluctantly. Strength to take action is required for renewal not just wishful thinking. Strength is required and so is grieving to change lifestyle, self expectations, and worldly pulls upon the heart and pocketbook. Here are suggestions for financial rebirth:

"**Change the Heart.** Sweep out the dust in every corner for inspection. Accept the transforming love and support in meeting financial challenges differently than before. Feel the everlasting love of God to replace spending money to be loved and respected. Learn as Paul said, "I have learned to be content whatever the circumstances. I know what it is to be in need; I know what it is to have plenty; I have learned the secret of being content in every situation, whether well-fed or hungry, whether living in plenty or in want" (Philippians 4:11-12). Focus on growing the fruit of the Spirit rather than spending all the time on growing material assets. However, there is a responsibility to make money for the Lord's work. "Allowing a love of money to rule prevents wholehearted commitment to Christ," regardless whether one has little or much.[332] "Loving riches will cause us to dismiss Scriptural teachings about money and to justify ungodly behavior." "Do not be misled. Remember that you cannot ignore God and get away with it. You will always reap what you sow! Those who live only to satisfy their own sinful desires will harvest the consequences of decay and death" (Galatians 6:7-8 NLT).

"**Change the Mind, the Structure.** Get in touch with the mind rather than only the feelings. Let the mind direct your actions. Set up disciplines such as whenever you spend money on a hobby, give the same amount to someone in need. Realize the ultimate in economic security is the "ability to adjust." Apply the fruits of the Spirit to how money is managed. Be diligent and informed about

---

330   Guy Baker, CLU, MSFS. "A Higher Call – The Next 10 Commandments." In *Financial Services Advisor*. November/December 1999. P.31

331   Other useful scripture is Psalm 32:5, Exodus 14:13, and John 15:4.

332   Devotional. *In Touch*. January 2005. P.27.

care of finances and household. Work "as unto the Lord." Choose to simplify lifestyle in order to serve the Lord and share with others. "And so, dear Christian friends, I plead with you to give your bodies to God. Let them be a living and holy sacrifice – the kind He will accept. When you think of what he has done for you, is this too much to ask? Do not copy the behavior and customs of the world, but let God transform you into a new person by changing the way you think" (Romans 12:1-2 NLT).

"Change the Soul. Change the source of security to The Almighty Father, not the almighty dollar. Be able to recognize the "sacred cow" in your allegiance to fine food, fortune, and self-glorification as gods. Pray at every spiritual bump on the journey. Jesus said, "I have come in order that you might have life – life in all its fullness" (John 10:10 TEV).

"Change the Strength, the Energy. Stop watching and buying poisons. Move each day toward a short term goal and toward a long term goal. Combat temptations and inertia. Follow Jesus' advice, "Watch and pray so that you will not fall into temptation. The spirit is willing, but the body is weak."

Realize that the journey is not smooth and costless. It is more like climbing a sand dune, slipping back at times. Get rid of excess baggage for easier climbing. "…Throw off everything that hinders and the sin that so easily entangles, and let us run with perseverance…" considering "him"… so that you will not grow weary and lose heart" Hebrews 12:1-3). Ask the Lord to help carry the burdens. Move because the Spirit of God moves in our midst. Be faithful in finances although not always successful.

"Repent (turn around). Repentance is necessary in all change. "God is always working to change us."[333] Turn away from the old way of doing things. Turn away from the love of money, addictions, or any sin that separates you from God's love and wholeness or thinking of other's needs. Choose a different path. Resolve no longer to live our lives for ourselves, as we see fit. Turn toward all God has for us. Jesus said, "Turn from your sins and turn to God, for the Kingdom of Heaven is near" (Matthew 4:17 NLT). Repentance is switching to different habits. For example, flip the switch from pornography to daily devotions on the internet. Money is not the only thing that will be saved.

Repentance is changing action. It is no longer watching or listening to certain programs or people that feed the mind with unhealthy messages put out on radio, television, on the Internet, or loud people talking a lot. It is avoiding the temptations, not going past something, not shopping for certain things, and not going certain places. Repentance is turning from all rationalization, purposing within the heart to be different, choosing to do what is right[334] for your situation, resources, goals, family and friends at the right time. It is refraining from surfing the Net or doing whatever time consuming passion in your life prevents you from faithfulness.

Repentance is choosing to thirst for righteousness designed by God's principles rather than self-righteousness, doing finances our own way or the usual way of the culture. It is healing brokenness by getting "right" with God, neighbors, family, and businesses by restitution. That means paying back loans, paying back where one has cheated someone, caring for the needs of family members rather than self-pleasures or ambitions, etc.

Become God-centered, not self-centered. Become more generous by feeling and knowing the struggles of others. How can anyone say they love God and ignore their brother's needs? "If

---

333   James MacDonald. *I Really Want to Change…So, Help Me God."* Chicago: Moody Press. 2000. P.80.
334   MacDonald. Ibid. P.123.

anyone has material possessions and sees his brother in need but has no pity on him, how can the love of God be in him?" (1 John 3:17 NIV).

Seek wisdom, seeing the world through God's eyes. Seek wisdom and counsel by studying the Scripture and being in the Word. ("If you have the capacity to worry, you have the capacity to meditate on the Scripture."[335]) Know the Godly principles and practice them with power, knowing that you will continually slip and need forgiveness and grace.

"**Confess.** Name the change(s) and be specific in identifying financial management, possession, actions, beliefs, and desires. Openly confess your financial sin: anything that separates you from God, keeps you from receiving God's gifts, or keeps others from receiving them. Be a "card-carrying" member of the body of Christ. As a tool, write on the card the personalized, financial confession, promises, rules for financial God-directed living, and specific changes you are striving to make. Ask each time an expense, purchase or saving is made how it contributes to the new mission in life, glorifies God, and is for the neighbor's good. Another card could list where changes are being made and what is not being changed. Tell others and show the card to them.

"**Commit Self to Changes.** Write a contract to God which he already signed in blood and you sign with your life when changing finances. Write down new love habits to replace the financially sick and uninformed ones. Commit to spending as much time in the Word as watching television.

"**Forgive and Seek Forgiveness.** To be reborn, one must receive God's forgiveness by forgiving others. This means to cease wasting energies on placing blame for financial mistakes and disappointments in your standard of living. It is turning to the "good" in the face of wrongdoing. It is merciful restraint from pursuing resentment or revenge. It can be shown in remembrances, generosity, and offering good things to others who have hurt. It does not demand compensation first, acknowledgment of wrong, or excuses. "Be kind to one another, tenderhearted, forgiving one another, as God in Christ has forgiven you" (Ephesians 4:32). Ask forgiveness where you have blocked others from receiving the gifts. (Some healthy boundaries may still need to be in place to prevent further abuse.)

"**Be Baptized with the Billfold, the Credit Cards.** Transformation implies new being in all our activities. In both Old and New Testaments there is evidence of God's "passionate interest in and concern for our human condition," our deepest healing, and that transformation comes from a living relationship with God rather than from laws and commands.[336]

"**Be Grateful.** Be thankful for the crisis or disaster that pushed you to the brink of decision for a new life in Christ. Accept the comfort that God loves you for what you are, not what you have. This is abundant life and a joyous circumstance. Be thankful that you can arise and go to the next place. Gratefulness turns you to pray: "What is the next thing you are asking me to do, God?" Trust and do not let the sense of failure corrupt the new action. God's gifts express that we are cared for, known completely, and loved uniquely. God wants financial wellness for us and allegiance in financial behavior. Gratitude takes us out of ourselves and brings us closer to God. The stronghold of materialism and selfish comfort are gone when gratitude is expressed more than complaint. Many find it easier to focus on what is not given, rather than on what is! Everyday, count on your fingers, if you have them, the gifts received from God. Help others to receive the gifts from God. Whenever you receive anything such as a job, a promotion, a profit, a piece of

---

335   Rick Warren. *The Purpose Driven Life*. Grand Rapids: Zondervan. 2002. P.90.

336   Flora Alosson Wuellner. "Transformation: Our Fear, Our Longing." *Weavings*. 6 March-April. 1991. Pp.6-14.

furniture, a friend, a kind act from a stranger, beauty in nature, a good night's sleep, say, "What can I do for you, Lord?" Begin each day being on the lookout for God's mercies that are new every morning (Lamentations 3:22-24). Look for the beautiful and the hand of God even in the midst of crises, sadness, and difficulties that happen every day. Do something for someone, secretly, in grateful response to God's gifts.

"**Share the Joy.** Give God the credit when good things come your way or you do good things. Consider you are blessed to be a blessing to others, to give more. Therefore, help the weak, reach out to others, empty self, and help others who seek your wisdom. Lift up the fallen as Christ has lifted you. Let someone be accountable to you as they journey on the road to financial faithfulness as new creations in Christ. Let your trust in the Spirit's guidance and power in financial crisis or change become a model and source of strength to others. Tell others of the good things God has given you, not the bad deck of cards dealt to you. On to victory with Christ, not crisis! Now journey with an eye for finding someone who needs love on his or her journey through crisis, or through change."

Lifestyle Defined and Evaluated for Making Changes

A lot of talk these days is about changing lifestyle. These are idle words unless the specifics of what, where, and how to change are written for sincere commitment. Otherwise, people will continue buying into the American Dream or the "standard package" which is prevalent and comfortable. The lifestyle or standard of living is the quantity, quality, and variety of goods/services desired, as well as the attitude toward them and the manner in using them. Standard of living is that which people feel deprived if they do not have - for which people are willing to work to obtain and protect.

The necessity to change rather than just modify is due to 1) changes in the economy such as job availability or loss of income, 2) divorce, 3) commitment to be a better faithful follower of Jesus Christ, 4) meeting obligations and desires to save and share more of income, and 5) adjusting during times of increased expectations and decreased real income. Change is difficult because of lifestyles constantly portrayed on television, pressure from peers and extended family, and habit or culture.

Definition of lifestyle is crucial for the establishment of a new family or anyone in new economic conditions. Much unhappiness in marriage or with parents is created by disagreement and fulfillment of the lifestyle expected. Discussions, including arguments, help clarify what is important to have and the manner in which goods and services are to be used. Observation has revealed the "standard package of goods and services" and the social use around these are carried with graciousness and ease in upper classes while lower classes struggle to meet these with effort and household work. Observation has revealed that the standard of living or expectation of what is a desirable way to live has increased over 100 years in all countries. Most Americans in the early 1900s performed household production, with larger families, in order to achieve the increase in standard of living. Later, wives were employed outside the home to acquire and maintain the standard of living. After everyone possible in the family was employed, credit was used to achieve and maintain the standards. When the credit was maxed and the credit was insufficient, the remaining options are additional household production or decreasing standards. These lead to the mandate that says, "Change lifestyle or be frustrated with financial failure."

Heart Examination

The heart needs an examination for determining the different goods and services obtained, desired, and the attitude in using them. A **hardened heart** has a certain mind set. It is not open to hearing the "Word." It is hardened against caring for others or changing lifestyle for any reason.

The **stubborn heart** would like to change but does not. It uses the excuse of "the spirit is willing but the flesh is not." It is a victim of the "moral gap" between what should change and the comfortableness of the familiar. A stubborn heart also is one that will not pay a bill because of a complaint or dispute. Instead of hurting the company, this hurts the customer in the long run.

The **proud heart** feels sufficient, independent, and powerful because of its achievements. Appearance is everything; therefore, goods and services are of the highest quality to impress others. The verse is ignored that says the world looks at the outside appearance but God judges the inside (John 7:24, 2 Corinthians 10:7).

The **anxious heart** has so many cares of the world on its shoulders that it cannot shrug them off. It does not take them to God in prayer. It does not simplify goods and services to have room for the Spirit to love and give peace.

The **trusting heart** asks God to help provide answers to life's dilemmas, to provide goods and services when in poverty, to provide answers when recently unemployed, and provide strength to change lifestyle.

The **servant heart** uses goods and services in the care of others. The **kind heart** is loving but firm in being different in lifestyle from another. The **Micah heart** does justice, loves mercy, and walks humbly before God (Micah 6:8).

The **obedient** heart is a surrendered heart putting into practice the teachings of Jesus. Jesus' said many people will say "Lord, Lord, I love you" but I will not know them because they do not obey, do not do the will of my Father or put into practice my teachings.

The **broken-heart** has two manifestations. One is that the brokenness prevents change, being overcome with grief. The other manifestation is that it becomes a healing balm to others. It reminds others of the promise that God is near to the brokenhearted. This nearness gives healing and power to change lifestyle.

The heart is compared to a house with several rooms which needs to be swept clean of goods and services unnecessary and cluttering. These result in a cumbersome and **inappropriate lifestyle**. There is not room for responding to God's love by loving and caring for others. The *Message* version of Matthew 3:11 explains lifestyle changes: "I'm baptizing you here in the river, turning your **old life** in for a kingdom life. The real action comes next: The main character in this drama - compared to him, I'm a mere stagehand – will ignite the **kingdom life** within you, a fire within you, the Holy Spirit within you, changing you from the inside out. He's going to clean house – make a clean sweep of your lives. He'll place everything true in its proper place before God; everything false he'll put out with the trash to be burned."

Jesus explained a lifestyle change for his followers in Luke 11:24-26, "When an evil spirit comes out of a man, it goes through arid places, seeking rest and does not find it. Then it says, 'I will return to the house I left.' When it arrives, it finds the house swept clean and put in order. Then it goes and takes seven other spirits more wicked than itself, and then they go in and live there. And the final condition is worse than the first." The **questions** for changing lifestyle are: What attitudes, way of life, contributions, manner of using goods, the actual goods and services, reading, and group participation should be (1) "trashed" and (2) be taken on as the new lifestyle. One cannot just trash old habits. One has to develop new habits and a better way of living.

Changes in Goods and Services in Lifestyle or Standard of Living

The shepherd helps people define the goods and services to support the heart changes for the unique individual regardless of other people's lifestyles. Ways to look at one's standard of living are described below which may prompt needed changes:

a. **"high"** – desire to have what the majority thinks is important but not relevant to one's current situation.

b. **"low"** – statistically low if less than median income of reference group.

c. **"too low"** – aspirations are too low, resources not used, unsatisfied, only material needs are met; may need encouragement to get more income.

d. **"too high"** – unrealistic, always feel dissatisfied, choosing too many wants.

e. **"too costly"** – too many other resources are sacrificed, such as health, in pursuit of goals.

f. **"too wasteful"** – more resources than necessary are being used, using less plentiful resources rather than more plentiful.

g. **"unbalanced"** - does not meet all types of needs of family members, present and future wants, or self and others' wants.

h. **"meeting basic needs"** - emotional, social, physical, spiritual - in new ways.

i. **"too rigid"** – cannot adapt or adjust to changing circumstances, or knowledge. May have to consider some investments of time, energy, or money as "sunk costs," those without realizing a return, because to continue as originally planned or performed would be more costly in the long run.

j. **"instantaneous"** – too impatient to have everything parents or others have or at same time. Think and plan sequentially. Prioritize by asking what can be done or purchased now and what could be done or purchased later. Prioritizing financial demands on a realistic income basis (net, not gross, decision income) is a necessity. Prioritizing has to be cognitively focused but with the awareness of all the emotions this engenders.

k. **"too haphazard"** – **"too whimsical"** – follow moods rather than rational thought, so outcomes and standard of living are "by default not design," not enough by objectives and too much by crises.

l. **"too influenced"** - by peers, social pressure, and convention rather than what is needed and appropriate. Need well stated goals that are individualized.

m. **"detrimental,"** - dead-end, harmful, mind pollution, noise pollution.

n. **"too stressful or harmful"** - because of fear, lack of food, financial problems, etc. so cannot concentrate on improvements or cannot use community resource such as school to advantage.

o. **"greedy"** – characterized by greed, envy, egotism, and damming everyone else.

p. **"Micah"** – characterized by doing justice, loving mercy, and walking humbly with God (Micah 6:8).

q. **"JOY"** - Jesus first, Others second, and Yourself last. Work of the kingdom comes first, thinking of others' needs before self, and caring for self also.

Assessment of lifestyle and standard of living demands value clarification, desired ownership, attitude, and manner in using goods. The business of the shepherd is assisting in reordering priorities which shape the standard of living. Some couples report that defining standard of living was the most important issue to resolve in their married life. Couples may disagree vehemently. Clarification of standard of living is done by asking: 1) what would they do with $30,000 inheritance money, 2) What would they cut out if they had to trim the monthly budget by $300.00 or by $3,000.

By definition, lifestyle or standard of living can include the desire to share and save as well as consume. Assessment uses cash flow analysis of actual level of living, which is always slightly below standard of living. Assuming the individual is the best judge of his/her own interests, the individual's standard of living can be only different from the counselor's. By definition, the standard of living is in the "eye of the beholder." The counselor assists in examining the individual's standard of living by listening to his or her assessment of one's own situation, suggesting the frame of reference, and then reorienting attitude and actions. Everyone makes different choices, given the situation.

Accepting others' standards can be done with full knowledge of their usefulness to a family rather than merely because neighbors have them. Thoughtless emulation of the consumption of other people involves an endless quest. Gratification of desires merely to be like others seems scarcely worth the struggle. The shepherd can give examples and stories of how individuals would consume when they are striving to be like Jesus – not watered down versions.

Some people are overly optimistic with too high standards or ideals for their income. They are conscientious about parenthood, citizenship, professional responsibilities, and contributing to charity, but they cannot provide for all of these. Some are caught in the squeeze of increasing expectations and standard of living while real income adjusted for inflation has decreased. Some do not know how to make adjustments or are scared to make them. Some need to combat the natural urge to expand wants or to fulfill wants leading to other wants. Let the natural response to God's love and blessing be creeping generosity or a creeping percentage of income given for work of the kingdom.

"The spirit is willing but the flesh is weak." (See Mark 14:37). However, some use this as an excuse for not planning, controlling, organizing and resisting temptations through financial management. When resources are limited, more planning, more management, and more value clarification are needed. However, by definition "resources are limited and wants are unlimited." Therefore, choices have to be made which are difficult because in a decision, something desirable or good is foregone.

Areas where changes are possible include child care, clothing, medical, gifts and celebrations, entertainment and recreation, transportation, housing, utilities, heating, cooling, communications, furnishings and supplies, food, property and income taxes, college and training. Examine every area and estimate reductions or where increases in spending would benefit "working for the kingdom" under God's reign. Subtotals for each area show a few dollars here and magna dollars there. Total the sub areas for savings and find thousands of dollars. An illustration of how the Rowe family estimated change in lifestyle and reduced thousands "yearly":

	Conservative estimate versus Liberal	
Change food plan from moderate to low cost	$ 2,400	$3,600
Eating out from 4 times to 2 times per month	600	900
Reduce Christmas gifts from $1,000 to $600	400	600
Change store for buying clothes ($100 to $50)	600	700
Postpone buying a used or new car	1,200	2,400
Do own painting, yard-work, cleaning, repairs hair cutting, manicure	300	400

Change style of vacation and travel from $1000 or $2000 to $500	1,000	1,500
Reduce utilities, gas & electricity ($50/ month)	600	800
Change phone system, TV cable, etc	600	1,200
Not consolidating debt	600	2,000
Total savings from changes	$8,300	$14,100

An Economic Model of Wholeness – Guiding Framework I

An economic model of wholeness addresses money ills, cure and commitment in the framework of renewal. In rebuilding financial structures, the shepherd addresses the meaning of money. The shepherd observes money illnesses and with the help of the Great Physician helps with cures to restore wholeness. The shepherd addresses addictions to various things or the desires for the new whatever or another. The shepherd guides others, not in crisis, who sincerely seek to increase faithfulness in finances in their small steps on their journey to spiritual growth. Usually this is long-term change.

According to Haughey,[337] there are two different kinds of money ills: moral, including avarice, covetousness, and greed; and preoccupation with distraction from "attention needed to hear the Word of God, receive it, and have it unfold in the soil of their souls" (Luke 8:14). The pervasive illness that Jesus perceived was "mammon illness" (systems created by humans that one trusts) which was not simply money.[338] It was a disorder, where or in what people put their trust that only God could claim. Jesus added "the image of the purse (Luke 12:33)" and of living in the reign of God where moths cannot get and treasures stolen. The culturally mediated mammon illness is caught by numbness, happening slowly "without one being aware of what was happening or fully choosing the condition".[339] The allegiance to material resources induces numbness which operates in less and less compassion – a sick relationship to others. Another effect is a split consciousness of trying to serve two masters, each claiming a total loyalty (Luke 16:13). Since mammon means "that in which one trusts," Jesus uncovered more than an illness – a way of life in attempting the best of both material security and religion. The cure is impossible due to absence of need, blindness to condition, dullness, and doubt about Jesus.[340]

Evidence of salvation (and curing money ills) is "sharing of one's belongings and the proper use of money now." In the Zacchaeus case, he did not sell all but disposed of his wealth as a disciple by "his largesse toward the poor, cleaned from exoneration of fraud and extortion of the abuses of the misuse of money."[341]

Taking concerns to God is superficial unless people solve their financial problems, have faith that directs their behavior, heart and mind, and have a *new orientation*.[342] Paul begged to not model behavior on the contemporary world, but to let the renewing of one's mind transform, so that people

---

337   John C. Haughey, S.J. *The Holy Use of Money*. New York: Doubleday & Company. 1986. Pp.10-21.

338   Ibid.

339   Ibid.

340   Ibid

341   Ibid. Pp.38-39.

342   Ibid. Pp.70 – 82.

discern for themselves what is the will of God – what is good, acceptable and mature (Romans 12:1-2). The everyday secular life of material needs is transformed into glorification of divine will.[343] The transformation shows a willingness to release financial anxieties and interests.[344]

Jesus said people will say, "Lord, Lord" but I will turn and say, "I did not know you – only those who obey." This obedience to God's will in things needed and in the way they are procured under the new covenant is a source of appropriate power, new order, and commitment.[345] "To love God is shown by willingness to forgo life, one's most intimate possession, and the possessions, material resources, assets, and capital which are all instruments for God's will but kept in subordinate position.[346] Those who have their stomach as god and their mind on earthly things (Philippians 3:19) operate "from a posture of acquisition rather than a self-emptying one."[347] Rather than see Christ as one's wealth, they "add Christ to their acquisitions and appendices with their wealth still in and of the world."[348]

The Economic and Psychological Meaning of Money – Guiding Framework II

The *meaning of money*, as well as the meaning of life, have to be reexamined in times of crisis. The shepherd's challenge is to help people identify its meaning and change it to be more appropriate, especially in light of what they assumed worked before, while not working now. Confusion and change have reigned over time and culture, rather than God's reign. Money, as a medium of exchange, is the supreme value for many because of what money can seemingly buy – prestige, worth, acceptance, respectability, relief from boredom, friends, food, medicine, shelter, and provision for the household.

The shepherd needs to understand that money for most people is a more powerful influence on lifestyle than Scripture. Different meanings are: power, security, self-worth, independence, getting approval, love, excitement, relief from boredom, guilt, making up for past deprivation, control, and ways to show acceptance by the group. Therefore, the challenge is to change the spiritual meaning of life. The central purpose and meaning of life becomes serving, adoring, and glorifying God. The greatest excitement becomes sharing with others, giving, and contributing.

The goal is to be more generous and faithful in following Scriptural teachings and to be more caring as encouraged in Deuteronomy 15:7-11 and Matthew 6:1-2. For many people this necessitates the secondary goal of getting out of debt to be free to see and help with the problems of others, to reduce expenses paid by interest and late fees, to say no to temptations, denial or deferment, and discipline to practice changing lifestyle or desires of the flesh. It means adjusting downward as costs for basics increase or deciding what is not basic in God's wisdom. It means analyzing whether expenditures are out of habit, convention, social pressure or "for the glory of God and our neighbor's good" (Martin Luther and Christopher Sauer).

---

343   Ibid. P.72.

344   Ibid. Pp.88-89.

345   Ibid. P.110.

346   Ibid. Pp.112-113.

347   Ibid. Pp.243-244.

348   Ibid.

"Among these many themes, Christian theology and medieval practice have emphasized the moral risks and short-sightedness of the pursuit of money."[349] "... one finds Biblical endorsements of this – worldly prudence and even avarice, as well."[350]

"Money as a token in the pursuit of God's approval is not so far from money as a token in the pursuit of the approval of mankind, which was Adam Smith's view of the basic motive underlying the pursuit of wealth. In neither case does the value of money lie in the commodities that money buys."[351] "The idea that work both should be and can be enjoyable enters analysis largely through the social sciences but not yet through economics, where the older tradition of work as pain or disutility prevails." "The shift from serving God to serving mankind permits the high value of work in the Protestant ethic to enter the *morally neutral* area of descriptive market analysis by way of the hidden hand: what is good for self is good for society. Both Protestant ministers and the market economists have been successful in persuading parishioners that in enriching themselves they were serving a nobler purpose, either through identifying work as service to God or a service to mankind through the 'hidden hand.'" Greek philosophers and the medieval church placed work and money more lowly because they distracted from contemplation of the good and worshipping God.[352] "The lower ranking of money is due to its connection with consumption, which implies indulgence, perhaps lack of prudence, and the failure of those restraints...associated with...character." In contrast, wealth is regarded as moral merit, respectability, and up-right citizens whereas "the poor are treated as if they were guilty."[353]

In the consumer-driven market economy, money is central to economic life. Price signals to all factors what to do, coordinates the economy, and controls money.[354] This is the invisible hand that guides supply and demand.

Thomas Edison approached *money* as raw material to be plowed back into something else. John Wesley's approach was "Earn all you can, save all you can, give all you can."[355] A growing group of Americans see God as the ultimate financial advisor and buying stocks is one more way to put His words into action.[356] Another message is that if one is financially faithful, prosperity is sure to follow. Observation reveals that some Godly people live sacrificially. Others warn to beware of false prophets who preach the "prosperity gospel" in which wealth, health, and prosperity rather than the cost of the cross with financial faithfulness are emphasized. (The prosperity gospel is based on Old Testament promises and curses; but it ignores the Sermon on the Mount.)

The *character of money* and the *power of money* create the culture but these change over time and conditions.[357] Hull explains:

"Money has literally become the God of our culture and has the traditional attitudes that people used to feel and express toward God.".....'Money, a human artifact, now

---

349   Robert E. Lane. "Work as 'Disutility' and Money as 'Happiness': Cultural origins of a Basic Market Error." *Journal of Socio-Economics* ; Spring 92, Vol. 21, Issue 1.

350   Lane, Ibid.

351   Ibid.

352   Ibid.

353   C. Simmel. *The Philosophy of Money*, translated by T. Bottomore and D. Frishby. London: Routledge & Kegan Paul. 1978.1907.

354   Lane, Ibid.

355   Andrea Neal. "Time Spent Agonizing Over Money." *Saturday Evening Post.* Jan/Feb. 1998. 270,1. P.16.

356   Susan Scherreik. "Investing on Faith." *Money.* November 1998. 27,11. P.168.

357   John M. Hull. "Money, Modernity, and Morality." *Religious Education.* 95,1. Winter 2000. Pp.4-23.

hangs over our culture as an almost irresistible power."[358] ..... "Jesus said if anyone tries to serve both God and money, he or she will 'hate the one and love the other or be devoted to the one or despise the other'" (Luke 16:13). We now see that there is another possibility: he or she will confuse one with the other, cleave to one thinking it is the other.'... "The modern person... will tend to read [and think] in the light of his or her own immersion in modernity, including contamination by the money-culture."[359]

One's culture is defined by what people are immersed in and in their response. People can change their culture which also changes the meaning of money. If the reference group continually buys and uses credit and spends for certain activities, people become hooked to that way of life. If people watch television for hours and continually drive past a certain billboard, eventually the salient, repetitive and internal programming will lead one to become what is seen and buy what is shown, enticed and drawn to it. These define who he or she is.

Spiritual rebirth means a total makeover in finances. It starts with the change in the love of money - or a change from the pursuit of happiness based only on what money can buy to the pursuit of God's purposes for an abundant life. In Hebrews 13:5-6, people are reminded to "keep your lives free from the love of money and be content with what you have, because God has said, 'Never will I leave you; never will I forsake you.' "So we say with confidence, 'The Lord is my helper; I will not be afraid." And in verse 16 it says, "And do not forget to do good and to share with others, for with such sacrifices God is pleased."

The love of money as the *root of all evil* (1 Timothy 6:10) is clearly seen when the desire for it causes stealing, killing, wars, employment at expense of family relationships, cheating, lying, dishonesty with family members or the church, money fights in marriage, cheating on income tax, taking advantage of other people, not contributing to a church which contributes to you, lack of generosity, snubbing the poor, etc. Anxieties over money, when not resolved, affect work and school performance, choice of jobs, marital/family relationships, and not accepting God's love, peace, and provisions.

The pursuit of money rather than the kingdom of God and his righteousness blinds people to where expenses could be reduced out of necessity to resolve a crisis or out of love to share. "Some people, eager for money, have wandered away from the faith and pierced themselves with much grief. But you, man [woman] of God, flee from all of this and pursue righteousness, godliness, faith, love, endurance, and gentleness" (1 Timothy 6:10-11 NIV).

Financial Freedom

Freedom in Renewal, as opposed to financial freedom in financial planning literature, means not to be under the control of money, possession, or the culture's whims and ways. Freedom is ability to be creative in sometimes searching for money and sometimes in searching how to give it away, and sometimes in getting along without money. It is trusting in God's provisions, mobilizing community resources, starting programs, and exchanging services with others, bypassing the need for money.

The shepherd analyzes why money is spent and how it is controlling people. With the Spirit, the counselor releases captivity from spending as a way of dealing with guilt, making up for

---

358   Ibid.
359   Ibid.

past deprivation, restoring respectability, feeding an addiction, overcoming boredom by spending, controlling others, maintaining possessions that absorb time at the expense of reading the Word, or getting away from the wolves that are betraying individuals and families, especially the trusting elderly and the uneducated. The shepherd assists those who are young in America, many of whom have never known scarcity. Some are "nomadic" or have unique concerns and issues. To make changes, the counselor may have to induce real fear or appropriate fear based in reality (scare enough to motivate to action), point out consequences, and then give hope for changing, thus injecting energy. Following through for financial freedom involves new ways and wisdom to communicate with family members and creditors and to implement plans.

Orientation to life, for many people, is based on income alone. Changes in the stock market determine their security and happiness as the daily report determines their income. Their lives are dominated and controlled exclusively by material values. The orientation of others, who have gone through spiritual transformation, looks for opportunities to serve God with their income. They see in the dollar sign "$" - a cross - the $uffering $avior and the dollar sign $ as "$timulation to $hare" with others and spend for them.

The shepherd assists in obtaining financial freedom and financial peace of mind, not based on wealth surplus. As used by the spiritual financial counselor, it is based on

- trusting God to direct one's path,
- being content in want or plenty,
- trusting that God provides for needs when seeking first the kingdom,
- having assurance that God directs one to alternatives in times of trouble,
- forgiving and learning from financial mistakes,
- adjusting in little and large ways,
- using one's mind to handle financial predicaments and manage better by new strategies and control of details,
- using one's spirit empowered by the Spirit to have courage to change, and
- knowing in one's heart that nothing such as an economic downturn can separate one from the love of God (Romans 15:30).

Balanced Activities as Response to God's Gifts – Guiding Framework III

Economic activities in another theoretical model are a function of, and response to God's gifts. All of life, earth's resources, income, possessions, businesses and ourselves are gifts from God for which gratitude is felt and which therefore are managed carefully, responsibly. Spiritual and good gifts from God can be received when one's hands are not full of so many possessions and having to care for them.

Sharing includes giving gifts to others and contributing based on generosity. The more one is given, the more one can give, not as a guarantee for success, but as a desire. The more blessings received, the more one can bless others. If someone is sent as a gift to someone or an organization, thanks for them is given. People can enjoy and are thankful for the gifts seen in others. Ability to touch someone in kindness is a gift.

Whereas, as a result of God's gifts, people can *Spend, Save,* and *Share* generously. All the economic activities in reality have to be balanced. All parts have to be managed and supplied.

Otherwise, dysfunction and brokenness result. Therefore, these activities can be summarized in an economic model: **EAs = ($p, $a, $h) $AL** where

"**EAs**" is a *summary of economic activities* for wholeness and security,

$p is *spending* for life sustenance, delights, celebrations for self, family, community,

$a is *saving* for emergency, opportunity, college, retirement, down payment of goods or services, seasonal or yearly purchases or taxes, unexpected events, and investing

$h is *sharing*, giving, contributing, and

$AL (the error term) is salvation based on spiritual rebirth in financial behavior, learning from mistakes, grace, and rescue from financial disaster.

Salvation is spiritual rebirth lived out in financial behavior. Salvation is repairing the brokenness in economic activities and finances. Brokenness can be repaired by the Financial Counselor or the Great Manager which are names for God. Salvation ($AL) results in looking to the Suffering Savior who gives ways to adjust in times of plenty and in times of want. Salvation is learning from the Word and from financial mistakes and wrongdoing. Salvation is forgiveness for misguided priorities and technical mistakes. It is a result of education, struggling, forgiveness, and grace for a more balanced financial plan and activity. It is response to God's love in spite of failure, seeking to cooperate with the work of God within and outside of us. Healing can occur for brokenness from the Wounded Servant, the Suffering Savior, who knows one's every need. There is salvation or forgiveness for failing each other and failure in finances. Salvation gives freedom to do, buy, or invest under Gods wisdom, rather than be captive to commercialism, credit, and costly addictions. Salvation includes rescue from evils such as scams, deceptions, greed, abuses, covetousness, and selfishness. Salvation results in moving with faith in the midst of complicated market interactions, incomplete information, and an unforeseen future.

Economic Model of Security – Guiding Framework IV

The Shepherd assists in decision-making and creative solutions to financial problems in any of the foundations for security. Renewed security is connected to the reality of the Spirit's guidance and sensible financial management. This security is summarized in the formula (model): **E$ = f ($, ATT$, FA, PA, MGNT, CR, DG, V, I) "a"** where E$ is *Economic Security*. Economic Security is a function (result) of

$ = *money* income,

ATT$ = *attitude* towards income adequacy,

FA = *financial assets,*

PA = *personal assets* including creativity, spiritual resources, determination, fruits of the spirit

MGNT = personal *management* including planning, comparison, and control of habits,

CR = *community resources and government programs,*

DG = *durable goods and equipment* for producing non-money income and sustaining existence,

V = value of *simplicity,* since it may be easier to reduce expenses than increase income, and

I = *insurance.*

"a" is the term, here explaining the ability to adjust.

Economic security is a function (result) of money income, attitude towards income adequacy, financial assets, personal assets, personal and household management, community resources, durable goods and equipment for sustaining life activities, value of simplicity, and insurance. Insurance, in the broad sense, is both a means of financial protection and the promises of God's protection, financial peace. (The "a," as used in other economic formulas, stands as the error term, variables uncounted for or controlled.) It is the "ability to adjust" spending/sharing, attitude, methods, and source of security.

Attitude toward income adequacy can be a result of comparing one's income with those who have more and those who have less. A way to increase attitude toward income is to compare with those who have less. Another way is to associate with those who have less. Some say income adequacy depends on one's number of children and size of one's mortgage. Attitude toward adequacy is improved by loving God alone, recognizing other things as idols. It is finding peace in the rest of God alone. It is a life perspective.

The call to financial faithfulness is to manage resources. By definition, financial management is planning, controlling the plan and money flow, in following through under God's control, and evaluating the plan periodically to see if it is appropriate for the situation and changing economy. Management means maximizing the use of resources, developing talents and wealth, and meeting responsibilities. It includes paying bills to prevent repossession of goods, cut in services, having to pay all owed before reconnecting, court action, and garnishment of wages. Resource management under financial rebirth is reprioritizing, planning, practicing, and persevering under power from the Spirit who directs the paths and the steps. Reevaluation of the plan and procedures continue on the journey to faithfulness. Plans, seeking the mind of Christ, are how to walk through the valley of crisis or manage crises as a way of life. Other ways for new management are to have a career working for God, manage household tasks and money in a timely manner, save for education and retirement, and release culture's hold in spending in order to share with others.

Adjusting Family Cooperation to Changes

The crash landing will be smoother if everyone involved in carrying out the plan is also involved in planning and where to make adjustments. The shepherd is prepared that people will resist changes and family members may not be in agreement as to where to make changes. In expecting resistance, one must be persistent. A tactic is to wear them out by persistence. Some may try to sabotage the plan. A tactic is to have each member write on a card what he/she can do to contribute to the change in financial behavior, sharing, expenditures, and savings. Each individual's miscellaneous category or allowances must be realistic to get cooperation. Change is accepted more readily if it is presented as a trial for a given time and then reevaluated later. This can help prevent barriers to cooperation and resentment because of labeling as the controlling person. An amount for persons to be responsible for are given. Explain how other families have found similar satisfactions with less expense and that, frequently, less spending in certain areas may be healthier. The natural urge to expand wants by spending more can be replaced with expanding wants in behavior such as being nicer, more talented or more spiritual.

The shepherd helps them embrace change, not to fear change. Ned said after the counselor suggested changes, "My family will never go along with this." Todd said, "We cannot talk about finances." But both were surprised how cooperative their families were after becoming sympathetic to the need to make changes.

Ability to Adjust in Changing Household Management

The ultimate in economic security is the ability to adjust consumption, lifestyle, attitude, methods, and source of security. Otherwise, people are captive to their past which may not move them forward and upward. The ultimate is ability to adjust if any of the steps to financial independence are lost. These steps are developing diversified skills, providing home services and self-care, having employment, having a variety of income sources, acquiring durable goods, having insurance to protect goods and health, acquiring savings, and holding investments. Maybe these steps to financial independence are not necessarily lost but are a call from God to give more time, energy to other people or institutions. Complete surrender to God is based on the trust that God will provide.

Adjustments are made in new budgets, new wants and desires, new food, overcoming addictions, and wise stewardship of financial affairs. Many changes in life require an ability to change financial plans. Change begins with re-evaluating the desires of one's heart. Then one uses one's mind with information and developing new strategies. Application is using one's strength for action. All this is possible with prayer.

Some young and middle age adults who have consistently lived 10-30 percent above their income consume with the assumption that their parents will continue to supplement their income, as they have for years. Many depend on grandparents to fill the gaps. Many have simply not been willing to look at the superficiality of their life and financial situation. The shepherd helps them analyze financial habits and patterns.

Shepherds need to pray for insight into the resistance to make adjustments. Individuals need to talk through deep emotional habits and assumptions, and face reality when financial surgery becomes a necessity. Counseling involves listening and helping individuals to grieve through the small changes or large lifestyle changes that are needed when living within a realistic budget. Counseling involves addressing the solutions to other problems of spending. Counseling provides alternatives for those blind to new possibilities. Shepherds can rejoice with changed prospects for greater happiness. Celebrations can involve using resources other than money for the changes they have made.

Weekend Vows for Renewal

Different management strategies can be implemented to free the Spirit to work in us and to glorify God. Different management techniques can be applied to free up time and stress so that concentration on God's work is easier without distractions and the burdens of other responsibilities. Different or improved management can free the time for mission or helping others. Just saying, "We need to do a better job of managing" usually does not bring about creative renewal, desired change to improve spiritual growth and personal relationships quickly enough. Specific changes have to be identified with accompanying plans for implementation. Accountability helps one to change.

A gift to God every weekend can be analyzing and changing one step of the organization of finances, space use, storage, and facilities to help the household be a smoother operating, peaceful, and efficient home. One main manager assures organization and giving responsibilities to different members for different areas. The family needs to switch who pays the bills periodically so that everyone understands financial pressures. Otherwise, an individual may say to the counselor, "I had no idea we were in trouble." Spiritual commandments and joy can permeate finances, food, and fun.

The game on each weekend, beside a football game, is to find and create a different way of managing. It can be a simple or complex change. It can be in household work, eliminating activities or things, rearranging or rescheduling, combining activities or space, and simplifying. It can be in communicating. It can be in financial management.

An example is the change in getting ready for work. Jim got up one hour before Faye. To dress he had to turn on the light, sit on the bed and pull out the drawers thereby waking Faye. The revised management included placing a dresser for his clothes in a nearby closet outside their bedroom. A light was installed for dressing with ample light. This change affected sleep, relationships, and getting to work on time.

Another example of change in communication was Faye's counting to ten before she answered or responded to her daughter. On another weekend the change was using "I" statements (versus the accusatory "you") when communicating with family members.

A different strategy in financial management was deciding one weekend to change the time and day of the month for discussing finances as the bills were paid then.

Rather than always arguing about which bills to pay and continually having them on the desk, a specific time was for family business. On another weekend the game of changing was to set up a notebook system for filing bills, receipts, and planning with the pages as dividers for monthly (or semi-monthly) paying, recording with notes for action or discussion.

New Organization under New Management

The purpose is to have focus and time, uncluttered, in order for the Spirit to be free to work in one's life. Organization results in having more joy and peace from controlling all spheres of life under God's control. "A place for everything and everything in its place" arose from frustrations of hunt time. There are enough frustrations and worries in life without wasting time and becoming annoyed trying to find something.

Some people, maybe 50 percent, have money problems not because of values, other gods, commercial/peer pressures, math ability or insufficient income, but because they are unorganized. They cannot find bills, do not have stamps/envelopes handy, do not know when bills are due, and do not have a regular place and time to do business. Time spent hunting and sorting could have been spent on creative ways to save and share. Worse yet, because of disorganization many individuals use credit for food at a fast food restaurant because they have not planned ahead to buy food for a week at a time or do not have a system for getting cash such as getting it every time they go to the grocery store.

Some people use the computer programs to organize, record, summarize, automatically pay whatever when due, and have utility bills and the mortgage automatically withdrawn from checking. Savings accounts for various purposes and a tithing account can have amounts withdrawn from paycheck before other bills are paid.

The only "budget" some people use to save hundreds of dollars each month is a calendar with not the due dates but when to send a check or transfer funds. Fixed or regular items that have prearranged automatic withdrawal must be noted on the calendar or in the check register. Another method is to have a regular time every two weeks to pay bills and then late payments are avoided. Entire salaries of bank employees are paid just from recording late payments. Credit card companies make more from their late fees than the credit. By having a designated time to work on financial obligations every week or two, individuals can concentrate on other aspects of life rather than worrying all the time or being unable to sleep.

An organizational system using a notebook is useful since it actually shows bills paid and bills yet to be paid, filed by pay times every two weeks or so. In front are the goals to remind individuals. As bills are paid, the date, check number and amount are written and retained in the page of pay date or bill paying. Bills that cannot be paid this time or due later, even semiannually, can be put ahead in page file. Charity and birthday reminders can be filed in future page files. There are plenty of lines to do the mathematics or write reminders. There are lines to focus and figure one particular category, the miscellaneous, or one particular individual's spending for changes that are needed. The notebook system provides proof that a bill was paid. (Anita caught $500 in mistakes one year by proving she did pay when accused of not paying.) Anyone in the family, by using this system, can check and take charge if the main manager is sick or absent.

A constable or sheriff's order catches organization and procrastination. For example, a $21 bad check (written with non-sufficient funds) can end up costing $147 or more if time in jail with $45 of fine for one day in jail. This includes $20 fee from merchant, $25 bank fee, nonsufficient funds fee, price for sending in a money order, court fee (constable or sheriff's order.) A check of $10 plus merchant's fee plus bank fee plus handling fee can cost $63.00 just because of disorganization. Disorganization costs money when people pay $45 for a $20 payment with late fees and overdraft fees.

For some individuals, someone needs to be assigned to coach or mentor over a period of time. Others need someone to be accountable to. Otherwise, they think if they talk about doing or buying something, it is the same as done.

Problems occur because individuals believe someone who says. "Do not worry. I will take care of it." They have to follow through, checking to see if something was done, calling again, or speaking to a higher authority.

People, even if not in trouble, need to take time to reorganize all of financial life. They can begin with organizing the important papers, documents, decrees, certificates, degrees, titles, professional advisors' names, credit card numbers and who to contact if lost, tax returns, banking records, what God has done in one's life, and updated wills. One or more individual in the household or extended family should know where these are. The shepherd should note "controlling" behavior which may be observed in not willing to have others see the records.

The shepherd whether it is the pastor, compassion minister, educator, mentor, financial counselor, social worker, money coach or others responsible for financial change can now be called "resource adjustment consultants." Resources are gifts from God, spiritual assets, words in prayer, opportunities to acquire possessions, and divine intervention. These can be subjected to the Creator God for shedding Eternal Light on decisions of buying and maintaining. The ultimate security, the consistent security, is to recognize and connect with God. The Spirit increases power to provide for the necessities, creativity to make changes, means to share with others, and build wealth (Deuteronomy 8:18).

Personal Management of the "Financial Commandments"

People carry cards with statements for daily references in billfolds or purses to remind and change behavior. Various organizations have provided such lists. Here is another list for financial management developed for the "card carrying" person who is committed. These are the "**Financial Commandments:**"

1. Seek first the kingdom of God (his reign) and these other things will be added to you. (Matthew 6:33).
2. Treat everything, everybody, and yourself as gifts from God.
3. Share with others and so give to greater purposes than selfish interests.

4. Be prepared to give all to follow Christ, in complete surrender, in whatever direction and financial steps he leads.

5. Manage and watch well the daily expenses, monthly bills paid on time, and investments growing over time in constant communication with the President of one's company - "God."

6. Celebrate life's joys, life passages, life's milestones, and another's victory with simplicity.

7. Yield not to the temptation of destructive impulsive spending and addictions.

8. Do not covet, do not cheat, do not be greedy, do not deceive, and do not take advantage of the poor, ignorant, young, or elderly.

9. Be aware of the "wolves," those taking advantage of you, and the "pigs" who would devour you and your pearls. (Wolves – Matthew 7:15, Luke 10:2-4, Ezekiel 22:27) (swine or pigs – Matthew 7:6).

10. Do not try to impress others with lavish appearance. Work to impress God as an offering in humble service and grateful glorification.

11. Do not be overcome with possessions but hunger after "righteousness."

An Economic and Financial Management Model – Guiding Framework V

Power, courage, and joy with desire to renew life give the framework to make changes in the economic journey. Financial management changes are necessary to resolve a crisis, turn from past ways, sustain life in economic downturns, and give more generously. The options for change are:

/\ - **Increasing Income** by taking a different job or a different shift, repositioning assets, liquidating assets, getting cash accumulated through life insurance, selling possessions, getting money owed, taking early inheritance, working an extra job, having a higher-paying job or promotion from more education or training, using talents or skills in miscellaneous ways, exchanging goods and services with others rather than buying them, having a day-care in one's home, renting garage or barn or equipment, making decisions for increased tax benefits such as more withholdings, taking bigger tax reductions thereby increasing income (See chapter 8), taking a reverse annuity mortgage, making and selling crafts or other items, growing or hunting food, consulting or tutoring.

() - **Decreasing expenses, wants** by avoiding credit, avoiding debt consolidation, performing family services such as hair or grass cutting, cooking, changing level of food spending, not being entertained by food to reduce costs, not buying sodas or beer, comparison shopping, being frugal, setting limits, eliminating wants or items, buying used car, sharing apartment, moving to smaller house, removing features on phones and cable TV that are not used enough, choosing housing so that at least one earner can use the bus.

E - **Achieving Greater Efficiency** by avoiding waste, planning, getting more with less, avoiding scams and deceptive practices, preventing frauds, combining uses, rearranging, simplifying, reducing impulsive use of money and miscellaneous items, controlling expenses, reducing energy use, avoiding late fees and overdrafts, gaining more output with less input, and not refinancing or borrowing to solve a problem. Choosing items to use in dedication to more efficiently do God's work. Avoiding captivity to commercialism and culture's pull. As Haggai 1:5 implies: "Give careful thought to your ways" by listing every expenditure and analyzing why you are spending for it or if the purpose could be met in some other way. Always keep in mind that "Wasting money is as much an act of violence against the poor as refusing to feed the hungry" (George Sweeting, President of Moody Bible Institute. Date?).

C - Changing lifestyle. This includes changing expectations of how to live, what to eat, and what to wear. It includes changing financial habits, addictions, sources of satisfaction and security, and control of finances for new goals. It means dependency on Christ rather than credit. It is not solving emotional problems with more spending. Therefore, priorities are changed in sharing, giving, and caring. One makes drastic changes or takes simple steps.

F - Frustration, failure results by continuing the same patterns of production and consumption, being blindfolded to new possibilities, continuing feelings of powerlessness and depression rather than hope and energy, and being overcome by anxiety rather than infilling of the Spirit.

In examining where and how to make changes to be more in line with God's dominion, seeking first the kingdom, we are expected to use our brain as well as our heart. Examination is being conscientious and watching where the money and investments go. The reminder is in Proverbs 27:23-24 (NIV) : "Be sure you know the condition of your flocks, give careful attention to your herds; for riches do not endure forever, and a crown is not secure for all generations." Then another method of analysis to make changes is to ask of each item **what** is the purpose, **who** is doing it or would someone else increase income and decrease expenses, **when** is a better time for transactions or performing activities, **where** could be a better place for transitions or returns, **when** is a better time for managing money or talking with family members, and **how** could money be handled to increase income, reduce expenses and be more efficient.

The "ideal" in the culture is promoted by industry, commerce, advertising, and friends. Rising expectations are a result. This leads to emphasis on consumption for the few, rather than fair distribution and sharing. The "good life" consists of a lot of goodies rather than a lot of giving. The antidote for rising expectations and continually striving for the ideal is to include in the rising expectations and ideals increased giving, increased percentage of income, and increased sharing of talents and possessions. In helping people plan and reprioritize, changing from "ideal" to "adequate" includes helping them be realistic, face reality, lower costs in one area so they can have other areas. A balance in spending, saving, and sharing is the goal. Seeking first the kingdom of God is the worthwhile purpose.

"Sunk Costs"

Resistance to change may be based on the investment of time and money in learning or acquiring a pattern of living, a career, a way of life. People want the return on that investment. However, the cost of continuing in that pattern would be greater than changing and "sinking the cost." This economic term can be applied to any type of change. Expectations have to change from the initial investment in exchange for greater rewards and reduced costs for the now and future. Initial plans are "sunk" in exchange for better plans relevant to the new situation and new life.

Financial Renewal after Death

After a financial conversion, people slip back to old ways and habits. Some have observed that the Bible is a history of human's fall and redemption again and again showing the need for renewal. Paul asked, "Since you died with Christ to the basic principles of this world, why, as though you still belonged to it, do you submit to its rules?" (Colossians 2:20). Although people now can operate under grace from forgiveness of financial mistakes, mismanagement, and misguided efforts, they need to set up new rules for themselves. New rules or policies are established for seeking "first God's kingdom and righteousness" (Matthew 6:33).

The shepherd can assist in the grieving process of material and financial loss. Time, perhaps a day, is set aside to have a "funeral" for the old life, lifestyle, obsolete management techniques, and things given up. These are perceived loses as one moves from an old life to one surrendered with new gains. On the time set aside, one can reflect on the good things missed. Memories are collected and shared. Paper written with what is released can be burned in a fire. This is how financial aspects of life die with Christ and rise with Christ. The old has passed away and life is renewed with peace, freedom, joy, and hope. The shepherd can rejoice with the individual or family in their new lifestyle.

An Economic Downturn Necessitates Financial Rebirth – Guiding Framework VI

Shepherds observe people who have done "everything right," have worked diligently, and have been faithful in finances. Suddenly they lose their jobs, their wealth, or their health. Shepherds know people including themselves who "seek after righteousness," live simply, are frugal in everything, spend just the minimum, manage carefully by comparing prices and never paying late fees, avoid frills and frivolous entertainment, and give a regular percentage of income to the church. Some cannot afford all the medicine, dentist, or medical tests suggested. Others reduce their energy bill by being too cold in the winter and too hot in the summer. One woman has just been informed her pension is reduced by eight percent. Another couple has been informed they no longer have any savings which was their income for living. One couple is getting $400 less per month from their annuity. Another couple was told the husband is no longer employed. In another situation the five days of work has been reduced to two days one week and three on the next. A pastor is now earning $10,000 less per year.

The economic downturn is national, global, and for many, as described above, personal. Yet it causes everyone to stop in their tracks and examine where they are going financially. Everyone is taking stock of their situation and examining what needs to be changed. (Use guiding frameworks above.) Even the comfortable are affected as they too examine how they spend, save, and share. Many are sensitive to the plight of others and do not flaunt their wealth or brag of travels before them. People have been "called" to be faithful in finances, to share the gifts God has given, to be good stewards of resources material and human, and to enjoy the abundance. Now is the time to "call" on God as people have done through the ages.

Response from calling on God in Psalm 91:14-15 was: "Because he loves me, I will rescue him; I will protect him, for he acknowledges my name. He will call upon me, and I will answer him; I will be with him in trouble, I will deliver him." The psalmist called upon God and reported "I love the Lord, for he heard my voice; he heard my cry for mercy. Because he turned his ear to me, I will call on him as long as I live. The cords of death entangled me, the anguish of the grave came upon me; I was overcome by trouble and sorrow. Then I called on the name of the Lord: 'O Lord, save me!'...The Lord protects the simple-hearted; when I was in great need, he saved me....For you, O Lord, have delivered my soul from death, my eyes from tears, my feet from stumbling, that I may walk before the Lord in the land of the living" (Psalm 116:1-9). Again the psalmist reported,

"Sacrifice thank offerings to God, fulfill your vows to the Most High, and call upon me in the day of trouble; I will deliver you, and you will honor me." Then Jeremiah in 29:11-14a heard God declaring, "For I know the plans I have for you, plans to prosper you and not to harm you, plans to give you hope and a future. Then you will call upon me and come and pray to me, and I will listen to you. You will seek me and find me when you seek me with all your heart. I will be found by you and will bring you back from captivity."

Through prayer and counseling with the shepherd, people can listen to ways to reexamine their financial issues without fears immobilizing them. They can listen for options or alternatives for changing expectations in standard of living, lifestyle, and budgets. They can pay their housing or mortgage first before other bills, trusting their needs will be met. They may need to contact the consumer credit counseling service. They can hear choices where they thought before they had no choice. New wisdom and abilities to manage can come to them where previously they were unaware. They can have the strength to contact creditors and explain. Perhaps their balance may be reduced, their interest lowered, or their payments extended.

People can listen through prayer but they need to filter what they think they hear, advised Landry.[360] The heart can be deceptive and people in distress are eager to do anything. Landry suggested several questions that filter: Does the decision reflect that God owns everything? Will the decision make progress toward God's purposes? Will it benefit others as well as self and do no harm to anyone? Does it camouflage real emotions? Does it help connect to Jesus Christ with a stronger relationship? Would one want others to follow the example? Will one have a clear conscience after the decision? Does it reflect greater love for God or for things? An individual can identify other filters.

Mobilizing resources is for creating happiness and economic well-being. In response to listening to God, people can mobilize resources within themselves, in their family, and in the community. They can participate in government programs and volunteer to help others. They can exchange goods and services bypassing the need for cash. This is the promise in Romans 8:28 where it reads, "And we know that in all things God works for the good of those who love him who have been called according to his purpose." Some manuscripts translate this as "And we know that all things work together for good to those who love God" or "... works together with those who love him to bring about what is good..."

Everyday people can praise God when in trouble and be thankful before petitions and requests are made. This opens the heart to receive God's gifts and delights when the economic situation is grim. Every day the 23rd Psalm can be recited with financial fears and troubles in mind. Since the Lord is the Shepherd, the individual will not be in want; he will be led to green pastures (daily mana for nourishment); his soul will be uplifted in hope; even in the valley of debt he will not fear the evil of foreclosure or repossession; God will provide a table of blessings and basic needs in spite of the enemies that brought on the corruption through their selfishness and greed; and goodness and love (God pursuing) will follow along with the assurance of eternal life.

Unexpected events on the journey such as loss of income and wealth can be met with disaster or opportunity (the two Chinese symbols for crisis). People can respond by falling off the cliff or by feeling God's hand that keeps them from falling (Jude 1:24). People can respond by the CCCC method – **C**ontact God with renewed **C**ommitment for receiving instructions in **C**hanging with

---

360   Mike Landry. "A Biblical Guide to Decision Making." Archived Sermons. www.sarasotabaptist.org. Sarasota, Florida. February 8, 2009.

Courage. Slight modifications in lifestyle will not work. New resources and resources used in new ways have to be discovered and developed.

Financial freedom and peace are obtained by following the instructions "In his heart a man [woman] plans his [her] course, but the Lord determines his [her] steps" (Proverbs 16:9-10). An economic downturn or loss of job and wealth necessitates reading the instructions. Just as in other enterprises the instructions are "If at first you do not succeed, read the instructions." Scripture readings have new meaning when one is facing the need to change. The spiritual is now combined with the material if they had separated them before.[361] Churches are forced to discuss money whether they want to or not.[362]

Loss of job, income, or wealth brings naturally the Scripture instructions in Micah 6:8b: "To act justly and to love mercy and to walk humbly with your God!" No longer can individuals depend on their own understanding. No longer can they be arrogant, independent, and relying on themselves. They are no longer in control but praise God that he is in control ultimately. They have to confess their inadequacies. They have to depend on God and accept God's love, peace, and provisions. They now can learn trusting with heart, soul, and mind in a life changing mode. They remember, "Trust in the Lord with all your heart and lean not on your own understanding; in all your ways acknowledge him, and he will make your paths straight (will direct your paths)" (Proverbs 3:5-6). They now can accept that being made in the image of God is being able to financially manage in new ways. They can accept their ability *to manage* in a difficult time as a gift from God who helps them visualize, think, process, plan, strategize, organize, say "yes" as well as "no," be disciplined, be patient, and get started. They can enjoy the little things since they do not have the big things. But expectations, source of satisfactions, and everyday choices have to change. They can accept new foodstyles, new places of buying, and new recreation as well as new lifestyle in general. After experimenting with new ways, people can say, "I sought the Lord, and he answered me; he delivered me from my fears...The Lord is close to the brokenhearted and saves those who are crushed in spirit. A righteous man [woman] may have many troubles, but the Lord delivers him [her] from them all" (Psalm 34:4, 18-19a).

For renewal to take place, most people will have to change their purpose in life. They can have new goals and new roles. Of necessity, they change their mode of operation. No longer can they have the supreme value of individualism. They pull together rather than pulling alone. They have "pitch-in dinners" while their children have their "play date." They may have to double-up in housing, share vehicles, share jobs, and exchange goods and services. Their attitude toward accepting food from food banks or pantries, free lunches/breakfasts, and sources of medicines may have to change and they can say, "When we are back on track we will contribute and volunteer." Otherwise, those who sneered at the poor and were proud because of their wealth (Ezekiel 28:6) will have difficulty changing to live like the poor.

People can use the CCCC method to find new jobs and income in uncommon ways and at unusual places. Pulling together includes networking. Renewal includes looking up and not down even if the economy turns down. Renewal in spirit and in financial management comes from believing the "signs and wonders" one sees. (Deuteronomy 4:34, 6:22; Daniel 4:2, 6:27; John 4:48; Acts 2:19, 22, 14:3; 2 Corinthians 12:12; Hebrews 2:4).

---

361   Landry, Ibid.

362   "Talking about Money, Like it or Not." Alban Institute advertising Alban Webinars on webmail. June 2009.

The shepherd can organize a support group, be a listening ear on a one-to-one basis, and review resumes and letters for interviews. Prayers for those in transition and renewal can be audible. (See chapters 3 and 9 for more details.)

The shepherd can assist people in accepting death of the old days, the old ways. The shepherd can remind them to hang on to the strengths that pulled them through the valley of the shadows. Then, they can arise with new visions, new goals, new roles, and new ways to manage their resources both human and material. They can remember that nothing – loss of job, income, corruption of executives, greed of business people, injustices, calamity, family, computer crashes, or financial insecurity – can separate them from the love of God. (Romans 8:38-39). They can remember that nothing can keep them from sharing the love of God and serving people in the work of the kingdom.

Renewal comes from victory in changing times by changing almost everything but one's faith to adjust. So, "to him who is able to keep you from falling and to present you before his glorious presence without fault and with great joy – to the only God our Savior be glory, majesty, power and authority, through Jesus Christ our Lord, before all ages, now and forevermore! Amen." (Jude 1:24-25).

New Goals and New Roles in Life Renewed

New financial management with new goals are *defined by individuals and families*. They are implemented in everyday decisions about spending, saving, and sharing. Possible goals as stated or adapted for individuals as their guides for financial decisions, spending, saving, and sharing are:

- Having abundant life with thankfulness for the many riches in God's love, peace, and provisions.
- Glorifying God with doing good, justice, and compassion shown in financial behavior.
- Seeking first the kingdom of God, trusting needs will be met.
- Feeling deep joy in fulfilling God's purposes unique to each, not worldly passions.
- Protecting, conserving, and providing for all God's creation.
- Gaining financial peace of mind in being faithful.
- Financial managing with efficiency so that one's heart and pocketbook increase in generosity and sharing.
- Accepting God's love and responding by feeling secure now and with assurance of eternal life no matter what the financial circumstances.